.NET 2.0 for Delphi Programmers

Jon Shemitz

Apress®

.NET 2.0 for Delphi Programmers

Copyright © 2006 by Jon Shemitz

Softcover re-print of the Hardcover 1st edition 2006

ISBN-13: 978-1-4842-2010-8

ISBN-10: 1-4842-2010-2

DOI 10.1007/978-1-4302-0174-8

Lead Editor: Jim Sumser
Technical Reviewer: Hallvard Vassbotn
Editorial Board: Steve Anglin, Ewan Buckingham, Gary Cornell, Jason Gilmore, Jonathan Gennick, Jonathan Hassell, James Huddleston, Chris Mills, Matthew Moodie, Dominic Shakeshaft, Jim Sumser, Keir Thomas, Matt Wade
Project Manager: Sofia Marchant
Copy Edit Manager: Nicole LeClerc
Copy Editor: Ami Knox
Assistant Production Director: Kari Brooks-Copony
Production Editor: Lori Bring
Compositor: Susan Glinert
Proofreader: Liz Welch
Indexer: Rebecca Plunkett
Artist: April Milne
Cover Designer: Kurt Krames
Manufacturing Director: Tom Debolski

Distributed to the book trade worldwide by Springer-Verlag New York, Inc., 233 Spring Street, 6th Floor, New York, NY 10013. Phone 1-800-SPRINGER, fax 201-348-4505, e-mail orders-ny@springer-sbm.com, or visit http://www.springeronline.com.

For information on translations, please contact Apress directly at 2560 Ninth Street, Suite 219, Berkeley, CA 94710. Phone 510-549-5930, fax 510-549-5939, e-mail info@apress.com, or visit http://www.apress.com.

The source code for this book is available to readers at www.apress.com in the Source Code section.

To Anders Hejlsberg, for Turbo Pascal, Delphi, and now C#;

And to the vegetable garden that I didn't grow in 2005
so that I'd have time to finish this book;

And, most of all, to Tané, Sam, and Arthur, with thanks
for all your patience and encouragement.

Contents at a Glance

PART 1 ▪▪▪ Common Language Runtime

PART 2 ▪▪▪ C# and Delphi

PART 3 ▪▪▪ The Framework Class Library

PART 4 ▪▪▪ Appendixes

Contents

PART 1 ▪▪▪ Common Language Runtime

PART 2 ▪▪▪ C# and Delphi

PART 3 ▪▪▪ The Framework Class Library

PART 4 ▪▪▪ Appendixes

Table Cross-Reference

About the Author

JON SHEMITZ has been programming since he was 12, when he learned Focal on a PDP-8. He's been programming professionally since he graduated from Yale in 1981, and has done everything from shrink-wrap programming to consulting. Jon has used Borland Pascals since Turbo Pascal 1, and has been doing .NET programming in C# since 2002. This is Jon's second book: he's written dozens of programming articles; contributed to four other books; and has given programming talks on two continents.

Jon does contract programming, consulting, and training—you can contact him at www.midnightbeach.com.

About the Technical Reviewer

 **HALLVARD VASSBOTN** is a senior systems developer at and partial owner of Infront AS (www.infront.no), developing state-of-the-art real-time financial information and trading systems (www.theonlinetrader.com). Hallvard has been a professional programmer since 1985, and has written numerous articles for *The Delphi Magazine* and tech edited several popular Delphi books.

You can read his technical blog at hallvards.blogspot.com/.

Hallvard lives in Oslo, Norway, with the three diamonds of his heart, Nina, Ida, and Thea. You can reach him at hallvardvassbotn@c2i.net.

Acknowledgments

This book represents a lot of effort over several years. It wouldn't have been possible without the help of many talented people—most of whom I've never met.

Dan Appleman and the editorial board at Apress had the good taste to agree that a book about .NET for Delphi programmers would sell better than the Delphi for .NET reference that they originally agreed to publish. More importantly, they've been willing to wait for a book that's longer and later than they originally expected. Sofia Marchant, my project manager, has been answering my questions for nearly three-and-a-half years, and she put together a production team that smoothly and painlessly turned my 4 meg of Word and TIF files into a printed book. Ami Knox, the copy editor, made my punctuation and capitalization consistent, and caught awkward phrases that made it past all my rewrites; I'd especially like to thank Ami for the extra effort involved in dealing with my 'scare quotes.' Liz Welch, the proofreader, did a great job transferring the syntax highlighting from my manuscript to the printed page, and she also caught several mistakes that made it past both Ami and me.

Google made it much easier for me to answer various questions. Without Google, the research would have taken much longer, and I might never even have found some of the more interesting details. VMWare generously supplied me with a free "authors copy" of *VMware Workstation*, which made it much easier (and safer) to install and uninstall beta software. My orthopedist, Dr. Howard Schwartz, was very patient with my impatience when a bike accident tore shoulder ligaments and disabled me for three months near the end of the first draft.

I have the good fortune to live with three fine writers—my partner, Tané Tachyon, and our sons, Sam and Arthur Shemitz. All three of them have had to put up with innumerable problem paragraphs, and inevitably made good suggestions that helped move things along.

Weyert de Boer, Mark Boler, Marcel van Brakel, Alessandro Federici, Marc Hoffman, Chuck Jazdzewski, Ian Marteens, Jon Skeet, and Danny Thorpe all read drafts of various chapters. Their comments helped improve the book, and their positive feedback helped keep me working.

I'd particularly like to thank Jon Skeet and Marcel van Brakel. Jon helped me understand the .NET *memory model* (Chapter 17) and how it affects interprocessor synchronization. Marcel read every chapter at least once, and made detailed comments on most of them. I've benefited greatly from his deep knowledge, his helpful suggestions, and his uncanny ability to find every point where I waved my hands vaguely and hoped no one would notice.

Finally, I can't say enough about Hallvard Vassbotn, my technical reviewer. This project was much more work (and took much longer) than he could possibly have anticipated when he signed on, yet he read every chapter two or three times—and caught errors and made suggestions, each time. Hallvard also wrote the Delphi syntax chapter when I was considering dropping it after my bike accident. I've enjoyed working with him, and have been thoroughly impressed by his intelligence, energy, and diligence. Naturally, any mistakes that remain are entirely my fault.

April 2006
Santa Cruz, California

Preface

It's rough being a Delphi programmer. We know we have a wonderful, productive environment—but jobs are few and far between. We know that we can write any sort of application with Delphi—yet Delphi is seen as a GUI builder and a database front-end. We've all seen (or at least heard of) systems where the 'interesting parts' are written in C or C++, in DLLs, and Delphi is just used for the GUI interface. We may know C++ and have significant Win32 experience—and yet not been considered for C++ jobs because we didn't know MFC or ATL.

.NET changes that. All .NET languages use the same Framework Class Library (FCL). Learn the FCL—in any language—and you're a .NET programmer. "Learn once, work anywhere."

What split the Windows programming world into mutually incompatible Delphi shops, VB shops, and C++ shops was never the languages themselves. Picking up any particular language has always been easy. The barriers to entry have always been the different libraries. Using a different language meant learning a new library. Learning a new library meant that every little thing required a documentation search; your productivity was near zero for weeks on end. But with .NET, once you learn the Framework Classes, you can easily move from project to project and from job to job.

What's more, in this bigger, broader job market, Delphi skills are a big advantage. .NET is not a knock-off or successor to Delphi, and there are significant differences between Delphi and .NET—but .NET **is** a lot like Delphi. .NET has components, events, exceptions, interfaces, properties, and objects that descend via single inheritance from a common ancestor. All just like Delphi. .NET has more in common with Delphi than it does with either MFC, ATL, or VB, and so Delphi programmers will find .NET easier to learn than VB or C++ programmers will.

This book presents .NET from a Delphi programmer's viewpoint. It doesn't ask you to plow through things you already know in the hopes of picking up a few choice bits of new information; it presents the core concepts of the .NET world in terms of the Delphi concepts you're familiar with. The examples are in either C# or Delphi, not both—unless I'm trying to highlight a syntax difference.

From your employer's point of view, .NET offers managed code plus most of Delphi's traditional productivity advantages, without Delphi's traditional drawback of being a niche product that few programmers know. From your point of view, .NET offers something like a hundred times as many possible jobs—and it puts the fun back in programming. Garbage collection frees us from the tyranny of Free What You Create and all the petty discipline of avoiding memory leaks. We can write functions that return objects; we never have to worry about a "tombstoned pointer" to a prematurely freed object leading to memory corruption.

.NET is fun. .NET is productive. .NET offers what you've always loved about Delphi, without locking you into a narrow ghetto. This book will help you transfer your Delphi skills to the broader, brighter world outside the ghetto walls.

Organization

As I wrote this book, I tried to write the book I wish I'd had when I was learning .NET. I tried to remember what I found confusing, and what key points made for Aha! moments. At the same time, I imagined the reactions of people I've worked with, or met online, and went into more detail on the points where they would be confused or argumentative. Hopefully, the result will spare you a lot of trial and error.

I assume you know Delphi well enough to get paid to write it, but I've tried very hard to avoid ambiguity and unexplained jargon. You should be able to read this book straight through, and understand it all well enough to go out and get yourself in trouble—you should not have to reread any section two or three times before it makes sense. (I also know that many people will **not** read the book straight through, and have provided plenty of parenthetical cross-references for the reader who wants to skip around, or who will only open the book on an "as needed" basis.)

The first part of the book is for a native code programmer (i.e., Win32 or Linux) with no *managed code* experience. Chapter 1 explains what managed code is, and how it makes you even more productive than you are with Delphi. Chapter 2 introduces the .NET programming model, and how it differs from the familiar Delphi programming model. Chapter 3 has garbage collection details, while Chapter 4 goes into more detail about how Just In Time (JIT) compilation works, and why .NET uses JIT compilation. Most of the examples in the first four chapters are in Delphi, except where I use a little C# to introduce generics in Chapter 2.

The second part of the book is (mostly) a Delphi programmer's introduction to C#. While you can probably decipher C# examples on your own, I think you'll find that Part 2 makes it easier—and that reading the C# chapters will make it **much** easier to actually write C#.

The third part of the book covers the .NET Framework Class Library, or FCL. This part is nearly as long as the first two parts put together, and is very much the heart of the book. The Microsoft documentation is a fine reference when you know what class to use, but it's not a particularly good introduction. I've tried to provide the conceptual overview that you need to make sense of the documentation and/or to ask questions that Google can answer. After reading Chapters 11 through 18, you should understand the FCL design philosophy well enough that you'll find it easy to learn new parts of the library. There are Delphi examples in every chapter, but most of the FCL examples are in C#.

Note This is not a Delphi book—this is a book about .NET, for Delphi programmers.

Typography

Inline code looks like this, and I use bold for **emphasis** and italics as a sort of quote, to introduce *new terms*.

I also distinguish single quotes from double quotes. A double quote is a 'strong' or 'true' quote, while a single quote is a *scare quote*—a 'weak' or 'sort of' quote. (Other former philosophy majors will find this convention familiar; my copy editor suggested that I may need to explain it to everyone else.)

That is, if I say that Benjamin Franklin said "Thank you," I'm saying that I am 100% sure that Benjamin Franklin said "Thank you" on at least one occasion. I use double quotes when I'm actually quoting something I've read or heard. By contrast, if I say that Benjamin Franklin said 'Those who will sacrifice Freedom for the sake of Security will soon find they have Neither,' I'm saying that Benjamin Franklin said something like that. I use single quotes when I'm paraphrasing, or when I'm using slang or a neologism.

The Sample Code

There are over 150 sample projects mentioned in this book. For the most part, I only print the few most interesting lines of each. In some cases, I don't even do that—I describe a technique, and refer you to a sample project for the details. To run the projects and/or read the code that I don't print, you'll have to download the appropriate zip file from the Apress web site, and install it on a machine with a .NET development environment.

You can get the code by going to the Source Code section of the Apress web site, www.apress.com, where you'll find complete download and installation instructions. I urge you to download the sample code. Reading the code and pressing F1 on various identifiers is a great way to dip into the .NET documentation. More importantly, while I've made every effort to keep the book self-contained so that you can read it away from a computer, some techniques are best grasped by experimentation. Using my working code as a starting point can be very helpful here. (Most of the projects are just snippets that demonstrate a single point, but there **are** a few that contain code you may want to borrow.) All the sample code—from the code that demonstrates various useful techniques to the utility units in my common directory—is distributed under a license that lets you use my code in any way you like, so long as you leave my copyright notice in the source code.

PART 1

■ ■ ■

Common Language Runtime

The Common Language Runtime (the CLR) is the foundation for all of .NET. These first four chapters cover key concepts like managed code, the Common Type System, garbage collection, Just In Time compilation, and intermediate languages. You should definitely read Chapters 1 and 2; Chapters 3 and 4 are optional, for readers who like details.

Chapter 1 is a high-level introduction to the .NET architecture: it describes managed code, and explains how and why managed code differs from native code. Chapter 2 details the similarities and differences between the Delphi object model and the .NET object model: while the single biggest difference is that .NET offers generics, the .NET object model is cleaner and more integrated than Delphi's in that an object can hold *any* value.

Chapter 3 covers garbage collection in more detail than Chapter 1, with sections on performance, resource protection, and the complications that cause some algorithms to perform worse with automatic memory management than with manual memory management. Similarly, Chapter 4 covers intermediate code and jitting in more detail than Chapter 1, with emphasis on the way IL offers type safety at a comparatively low run-time cost.

CHAPTER 1

Managed Code

Managed code is the foundation for all of .NET. Managed code combines type-safe, compiled code with fast garbage collection. This combination enhances programmer productivity and eliminates common security flaws. Garbage collection prevents dangling pointers and reduces memory leaks, and garbage collection encourages you to treat objects as simple values. Type safety blocks common program failure modes like buffer overruns and miscasting. What is special about .NET is that it delivers these benefits in a language-neutral way.

Beyond Delphi

You're more productive on .NET

Do you remember when you first used Delphi? Suddenly, everything became much easier. Reams of boilerplate code were swept aside, dramatically increasing your productivity. Concepts that were once hidden in Windows APIs were exposed in object hierarchies, making it easy to do things like hide and unhide groups of controls.

That productivity increase made it worth unlearning old habits and learning a new library.

Much the same experience is in store for you when you move to .NET. You have to give up native code, you have to come to grips with garbage collection, and you have to learn a big new object-oriented run-time library—but the payoff is a big productivity increase.

When you use a native code compiler (like Delphi 7, Kylix 3, or Delphi 2006's Win32 personality), your source code is translated directly to native Intel *object code*, which can run directly on a Windows or Linux machine. By contrast, Delphi for .NET and all other .NET languages compile to CIL, or Common Intermediate Language. CIL is the .NET version of Java's *byte codes*, and must be compiled at run time by a Just In Time (JIT) compiler. Though this may seem like an obviously foolish thing to do, you'll see in this chapter and in Chapter 4 that JIT compilation isn't particularly expensive and actually offers significant advantages.

Versions of Delphi that compile to native code use manual *heap-based* memory management. Your code calls library routines that allocate memory from a linked list of free memory blocks, and your code should free all memory when it is done with it. .NET uses *garbage collection*, which means the system automatically frees memory when it is no longer being used. This chapter discusses how garbage collection makes your code more reliable. Garbage collection also makes your code much smaller and clearer, which in turn makes it easier to write and to read. Chapter 3 has the details of the garbage collection mechanism and costs.

In a native code system, ongoing projects often can't use a new library until someone translates the headers (the library's contract with the outside world) into the language that the project is written in. Also, it's very hard to pass objects between languages. Cross-language programming is slow and painful, and rarely conducted much above the level of machine primitives, like simple numbers and arrays of characters. .NET, however, built language-neutrality into the very lowest levels of the system, and all .NET languages can easily share high-level object methods and instances—and a single run-time library. Part 3 covers the Framework Class Library, or FCL, the object-oriented run-time library that all .NET languages use.

Managed code systems like .NET (and Java) **are** different from unmanaged code systems like 'raw' Win32 or Linux. You have habits to unlearn, and new patterns to master. But the payoff is smaller, clearer code that's easier to write and to read.

Intermediate Code

.NET code is compiled to an intermediate code, not to native assembly language

The single biggest difference between .NET programming and native code programming is managed code. This difference is visible from the moment your application starts to run.

When you start up a native code Delphi application, the OS calls the main procedure, the Delphi-generated stub that calls each unit's init code, and then calls the project's main code block. The main procedure and all your code have been compiled to a stream of *x*86 instructions that the OS loads memory page by memory page, as needed. When you allocate memory by creating an object or building a string value, you call library routines that do suballocation of a chunk of memory that the OS gave your application. You have to be sure to release the memory when you're done, or else the system will run out of room. You also have to be sure not to free your dynamic data too soon, or you can get nasty memory corruption bugs that can be very hard to track down.

When you start up a .NET application, Windows (or other host OS) doesn't call the main procedure. For one thing, it can't. Neither the main procedure nor your code has been compiled to object code that can run directly on the current machine. Your code has been compiled into an intermediate language.

INTERMEDIATE LANGUAGES

Intermediate languages are a step between human-readable code and machine-executable code. The .NET intermediate language is a sort of idealized assembler language for an imaginary machine that has a typed stack instead of registers. Intermediate language is not as easy for humans to read or write as code written in high-level languages like Delphi (Object Pascal), C#, Java, and the like—but it's easier than reading and writing real assembler.

However, human readability is just a sort of epiphenomenon, not a reason to have intermediate languages. When you compile to an intermediate language, you don't have to worry about register allocations—you just push, pop, and use typed values on the stack. So it's easier for a compiler to generate intermediate language code than to generate actual CPU instructions.

Note An epiphenomenon (ep·i·phe·nom·e·non) is a side effect, not a cause or a purpose. Natural history has many charming tales of epiphenomenal takeover, such as the sort of mammalian self-monitoring system that became humans' abstract reasoning abilities and competitive advantage.

In turn, because a stack machine isn't a difficult abstraction to implement, it's not particularly hard for a compiler to turn the intermediate language code into machine-executable code. Installing the .NET run time on a machine installs a Just In Time (JIT) compiler designed for the machine's CPU. The *jitter* turns intermediate code into machine-specific code, on an as-needed basis.

Because the same jitter produces all of each application's object code, the system can ensure that **all** managed code does run-time checks. Just as Delphi has always done, .NET checks stack and numeric overflows, as well as making sure that every cast and every array access is valid. This run-time checking prevents many common security flaws.

Finally, a typed intermediate language is *verifiable* and type safe in a way that native machine language is not. You can't read native code and see that it's storing a reference to a Font object in a spot that is supposed to hold only references to Hashtable objects—but you can do that with typed intermediate code as easily as with Delphi or C#.

Note I'm getting ahead of myself, here—I cover verification later in this chapter, and again in Chapter 4.

Platform designers like intermediate language because it's easier to compile to intermediate language than to native code. This makes it more likely that compiler writers will support their platform. Platform designers also like intermediate language because it's much easier to run compiled intermediate code on a variety of CPU architectures than it is to run compiled native code. This makes it easier to run your platform on multiple processors and under multiple operating systems.

.NET uses an intermediate language both because an intermediate language can be type safe, and because intermediate languages support language and hardware neutrality.

.NET uses an intermediate language called CIL, or Common Intermediate Language. (CIL began life as Microsoft Intermediate Language [MSIL] and was renamed to encourage its acceptance by standards bodies like ECMA.) CIL code is easy to write, easy to read, and easy to compile to object code for several processor families. When your .NET application starts, the host OS can't run the main procedure until it compiles the CIL code to native code. To do this compilation, the native code main procedure of your .NET executable assembly calls .NET run-time libraries to initialize the Common Language Runtime, or CLR.

The CLR has a clever, efficient sort of coroutine interlace with your program. As soon as the CLR loads, it compiles the application's top-level code. Then the CLR calls the newly compiled main procedure.

Before JIT

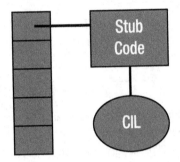

Figure 1-1. *Method tables initially point to stub code that jits the CIL.*

After JIT

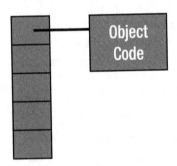

Figure 1-2. *After a method has been jitted, the method table points to object code.*

At this point, the main procedure is running as native code—there is no run-time loop that interprets every intermediate language instruction. Instead, the first time the main procedure makes a method call, the method address table actually points to a special CLR subroutine (as shown in Figure 1-1) that pages in the method's CIL code as necessary, and then compiles the method's CIL to native object code. The CLR then patches the method address table (as illustrated in Figure 1-2) to point directly to the newly compiled code, so that next time the same method is called it is executed directly, not compiled again.

Jitting done, the CLR jumps[1] into the newly compiled method, with all the method's parameters still on the CPU stack. When the newly compiled method returns, it returns to the native code of the method that first called the newly compiled method, just as if the JIT interlude had never happened. This same process is followed every time a method is called for the first time, whether the method comes from your application's code, from a third-party library, or from Microsoft's language-neutral Framework Class Library, or FCL.

■**Note** It is possible to precompile your .NET applications to native code. I talk about *NGen* in Chapter 4.

---

1. Yes, jump as opposed to call.

Garbage Collection

Garbage collection makes your life easier

The CLR calls your application's main procedure via the Just In Time compilation mechanism, and regains control briefly to jit each method as it's first called. Over time, the CLR is called upon to jit code less and less, as the program's working set is loaded and compiled. However, the CLR also regains control whenever your application requests memory.

When your .NET code allocates memory by creating an object or building a string value, you call CLR routines that carve off another chunk from the front of a big block of memory that the OS gave your application. When you've allocated "enough" memory, the CLR will decide to do *garbage collection* on the most recent allocations. The garbage collection algorithm takes advantage of the way that after "enough" allocations, "most" blocks are no longer being used. Since there isn't much live data, it doesn't cost all that much to find all the places that refer to live data. And, while it's not cheap to slide each block of live data down to the bottom of the memory partition, and then change each reference to the moved data to point to the block's new location, at least you don't have to do this for too many live data blocks. After the CLR has packed the live data, all the free memory in the partition is again in one contiguous block. This contiguity means that the overwhelming majority of allocations, the ones that don't trigger a garbage collection, are very cheap.

You'll find more details on how garbage collection works in Chapter 3.[2] What's important here is the way garbage collection frees you from a lot of memory management overhead. The system scavenges memory once it is no longer being used, so you never have to explicitly free the memory that you allocate. In turn, you no longer have to worry that the system will run out of room if you don't release every byte you allocate as soon as you're done with it. What's more, you never again have to deal with the nasty, hard to track down memory corruption bugs that spring from using some data that's already been freed and reallocated.

This is the sort of problem you get with *dangling* or *tombstone* pointers. Dangling pointers and tombstone pointers are two different names for the same thing: a dangling pointer is one that no longer connects to anything; a tombstone pointer is a pointer to a dead data structure, one that has already been freed. This is an easy state to find yourself in with heap-based, unmanaged code—all it takes is freeing an object in one place while you still have a live reference to it somewhere else.

Asking a dead object to do something is a common cause of memory corruption. You may get lucky and get an access violation, but the odds are that the old address is still within your program's address space. That is, you are essentially treating a random value as a pointer. The **very best** result you can get is for your program to crash right away, perhaps because you are not pointing to the start of an object, and the memory your code 'thinks' is a virtual method table is pointing to data, not code. However, it's entirely possible that you will scramble the internal state of some data structure. Sometime later, when you use the scrambled component, you will get garbage results or the program will crash. This is a bad outcome, because there is no obvious connection between the symptom and the real cause: a bad cast *here* results in mysterious behavior *there*, some indeterminate time later. These "Mandelbugs" can be very

---

2. Along with discussion of the (rare but not nonexistent) type of code that turns the garbage collector's design decisions against itself, and forces the system to spend all its time garbage collecting.

difficult to track down. Finding them—and trying to not make them in the first place—can take a lot of your time.

Garbage collection frees you from the productivity tax of the heap programmer's Free What You Create mantra. You don't have to write the destructors that do nothing but Free various fields. You don't have to place try/finally blocks around allocations that are freed within the method that creates them. You don't have to spend time making sure that under all circumstances you free data whose lifetime spans several events. Conversely, you don't have to worry about freeing memory too soon. Finally, you don't have to debug code that makes some memory management mistake.

You're more productive once you've been freed from the heap management productivity tax. You also start to program differently.

When you don't have to worry about freeing every object you create, objects become simple values, the way numbers and strings are. It doesn't matter if you never have more than one reference to an object or if an object accumulates one hundred and one different references in the course of the object's lifetime—it will last as long as there is at least one reference to it, and will go away at some point after there are no longer any references to it.

This means that you can write methods that create and return objects. This is something that is often discouraged with heap-based programming, since hiding the act of object creation does increase the chance that one will forget to free the object. With garbage collection, a returned object is just another value to be copied from one reference variable to another, or passed to various methods, without having to track references by hand or via some sort of reference counting mechanism.

You can even write methods that create complex object structures but return only indirect references to the new structure, like an interface reference or a *delegate* to one of the object's methods. ("Delegate" is the .NET term for a Delphi function of object or procedure of object— a pointer to the object paired with a pointer to one of the object's methods. I talk more about delegates in Chapters 2 and 8, and I have an example that uses delegates in Chapter 4.) You can create an arbitrarily complex object structure while you are calling a method that takes one of these indirect references as a parameter: the indirect references are sufficient to keep the structure alive until the method call returns.

Run-time Checking

Many common errors are no longer possible

So far, I've talked about how the CLR is called indirectly whenever you execute a managed code method for the first time, and I've talked about how the CLR is called directly whenever managed code does a memory allocation. The CLR is also called directly to do various run-time tests, much like the ones that Delphi has always done.

Because the CLR produces every byte of a managed application's object code, it can insert run-time library (i.e., CLR) calls to check that numeric operations didn't overflow or that every memory access is indeed a valid one. You can turn off numeric overflow checking for code that only cares about the low bits of your results (like some hashing algorithms), but you can never turn off the memory access checks. On .NET, you can never destabilize your application by miscasting or making mistakes with pointer arithmetic. The CLR will raise an exception if your program does miscast, and the CLR will raise an exception if your program does miscalculate an array index.

Note This is actually a slight overstatement. .NET does allow you to write "unsafe" code, which may do pointer arithmetic and which is not subject to run-time tests, but unsafe code is intended primarily as an interface to unmanaged, legacy code. (I talk about unsafe code later in this chapter.) Almost all .NET code is safe code, and safe code is subject to run-time checks.

Checked Casts

You can't change memory unless you're type safe

In a native code Delphi, there is a big difference between a 'blind' cast,[3] like TEdit(Sender), and a 'checked' cast, like Sender as TEdit. The blind version represents a sort of promise to the compiler—'Yes, I really know what I'm doing, so go ahead and treat this bit of memory as if it contains the structure that I think it does.' The checked version is a bit more cautious—'Please treat this bit of memory as if it contains the structure that I think it does, but please do raise an exception if I'm wrong.'

The blind cast is very fast, as all the action happens at compile time. At run time, all that happens is that the value is used as if it were a different type than it's declared to be. This is fine—if you really are using it the right way. However, if you have made a mistake like attaching the wrong handler to an event, the blind cast can have disastrous consequences. (Yes, there are plenty of other ways you might miscast—they're just less common.) If you treat a TFont as if it were a TEdit, you will get nonsense values back from the methods you call and the properties you read. Worse, if you change what you think is a TEdit in any way, you will actually be changing a TFont in ways it was not designed for. As with a dangling pointer, the very best thing that can happen is an immediate crash. Also as with a dangling pointer, it's much more likely that you will scramble some data structure—so that later you get seemingly unrelated garbage results or crashes.

Under .NET, all casts are checked casts. You can use the castclass instruction to do a checked cast that raises an exception on an invalid cast, or you can use the isinst instruction to do a checked cast that returns Nil on an invalid cast, but you can't do a blind cast that will let you scramble memory. You can still *write* code like TEdit(Sender), but under Delphi for .NET this uses the isinst instruction, and returns Nil on an invalid cast. Code like TEdit(Sender).Text will work just fine—if the Sender really is a TEdit—and will raise a NullReferenceException if the Sender is not a TEdit. The castclass and isinst instructions are the **only** ways you can do a cast in .NET—there is no way for a .NET application to do an unchecked cast.

---

3. Blind casts are also known as "hard casts," or "unchecked casts." It's largely a matter of taste—but I don't think that "hard" really implies "unchecked," and I prefer to use the positive "blind cast" to the negative "unchecked cast."

That is, a .NET application can never scramble its memory by treating This type of object as if it were That unrelated type of object.[4] One whole large class of difficult bugs has been wiped out, simply by disallowing blind casts. As with Delphi's as cast, the cost of doing the check is relatively modest—calling a subroutine that reads the 32-bit class type from the object, and compares that type (and, perhaps, ancestral types) to a constant—and the cost of raising an exception is basically irrelevant next to the value of having execution stop **before** you do any damage.

Pointer Arithmetic

Pointer arithmetic is strongly disparaged because it is error prone

Blind casts are risky, because there is always the possibility that you may be miscasting, and thus potentially scrambling memory. Pointers and pointer arithmetic expose you to similar risks. If you somehow give a pointer a bad value, you have in effect cast that address to some type that it probably is not.

One way to give a pointer a bad value is to simply load a bad address. It is in this sense that pointers are *unsafe* and error prone. Alternatively, you may try to write the 303rd element of a 256-element array. It doesn't matter if you have a valid pointer to the first byte of the array—this "buffer overrun" error has scrambled memory. Similarly, if you have a mistake in your pointer arithmetic code, even the right parameters may end up pointing outside the bounds of your data structure.

Any time you write to a random or miscalculated address, you have exactly the same chance of scrambling memory (in a way that will cause your program to fail some random time later) as you do when you miscast. Pointers and pointer arithmetic are dangerous in just the same way that blind casts are: while a competent craftsman will get it right **almost** every time, the cost of the rare mistake is high, and code that uses any of these techniques cannot be programmatically verified.

Accordingly, .NET all but bans pointer arithmetic. A pointer that you can't do arithmetic on is a *reference*. References are strongly typed, and all casts between reference types are checked. You can be confident that a non-Nil reference to an object of This type always points to an instance of a This object (or to an instance of a type that inherits from This type) and never to an instance of an unrelated type.

Without pointer arithmetic, you cannot allocate a chunk of memory for a buffer, and calculate addresses within the buffer. Instead, buffers of every sort are normally implemented as Array objects, much like Delphi's dynamic arrays. You can only read and write array elements via array subscripting, and all array subscripting is range checked. You can still cause problems for yourself by specifying the wrong array element, but you cannot access memory outside the array. Specifying the wrong array element is still a bug, but it's a much less serious bug, as it quickly gives wrong answers and is comparatively easy to track. Reading or writing the wrong array element is not a type violation, like a miscast or accessing memory outside of a buffer; it doesn't carry the same risk of scrambling memory and causing bugs that only surface later, in unrelated circumstances.

---

4. Strictly speaking, this is not true. Delphi for .NET **will** allow you to define and use variant records that overlay one type with another (which is precisely how one does blind casting in Standard Pascal) with nothing more than a warning about an unsafe type. C# does not support variant records.

Unsafe Code

Interfacing with legacy code may need pointers

.NET **will** let you use pointers and pointer arithmetic, but code that does so is considered *unsafe code*. Safe code is code that always follows *type-safety rules*—no unchecked casts, and no pointer arithmetic. Safe code may be buggy code, but bugs in safe code are comparatively easy to detect. Bugs in safe code give wrong answers, not scrambled memory.

Because all .NET programs are compiled to strongly typed CIL instead of untyped native machine language, it's possible to *verify* that a program contains only safe code. Verification is the process of reading an assembly's code, and programmatically proving that it doesn't break type-safety rules. (This is much like the way a Delphi compiler bans things like assigning a TForm value to an integer variable.) You can do this with peverify, a tool that comes with the .NET SDK that will verify a whole assembly, and will either assure you that it is safe or will let you know which methods contain unsafe code. .NET can also verify code each time it is JIT compiled from CIL to native code, and can be set to refuse to run any unverifiable code.

That is, whether or not your code is actually verified at run time is a matter of which *permission set* is in place. A permission set is a collection of privileges—things an assembly is allowed to do. Minimally trusted assemblies have no access to the registry and can't use *reflection* to read *metadata* (metadata is .NET's version of Delphi's RTTI, and I talk about it both later in this chapter and again in Chapters 4 and 13); fully trusted assemblies have full access to the registry, metadata, and the local file system. Fully trusted assemblies can even run code that fails verification. When an assembly is loaded, .NET decides which of the system's permission sets apply to it, based on various bits of "evidence" like where the assembly 'lives,' who wrote it, and so on. (Configuring permission sets is an administrative issue that's beyond the scope of this book.)

So, programs like Chapter1\PtrTest.dpr

```
program PtrTest;

{$APPTYPE CONSOLE}
{$UNSAFECODE ON} // DfN will not generate unsafe code without this switch

const
  A: array[0..2] of integer = (1223, 1224, 1226);

procedure Unsafe; unsafe;
// DfN will not generate unsafe code outside an "unsafe" routine
var
  P: ^ integer; // pointers are unsafe
begin
  P := @ A[0];   // this line generates a warning
  Inc(P);        // this line cannot be verified
  WriteLn(P^);   // this line generates a warning
end;
```

```
begin
  Unsafe;
end.
```

can be compiled even though they contain unsafe code that will not pass verification. Unsafe code can run on some systems but not on others. By default, all code on the local machine is given full trust, so you can compile and run this PtrTest program, and find that it does indeed print 1224. However, if you change your local policies so that even local code must be verified, you will get a System.Security.VerificationException—"Operation could destabilize the run time"—when you try to run the PtrTest program.

■ **Note** Most "permission sets" will not let you run code that fails verification.

Why would you **want** to write unsafe code when doing so exposes you to the possibility of Mandelbugs that will take forever to track down? Normally, you don't—almost all of your .NET code will be normal, safe code. The only really valid reason to write unsafe code is when you must use the P/Invoke (Platform Invoke) interface to call unmanaged, legacy code.[5] Much legacy code is not strongly typed, and requires the use of pointer arithmetic either to populate buffers before a call or to read out results after a call.

Since almost all your code should be safe code, both Delphi for .NET and C# make you go through a two-step process to write unsafe code. First, you have to use a pragma or a compiler switch to put the compiler in a state where it will even **think** of generating unsafe code. Second, you have to explicitly mark all unsafe code (see Chapter 10 and Appendix 0 for details).

If you have to write unsafe code to interface with legacy code, your managed code is no safer than the legacy code you interface with. If you are quite sure that the legacy code is safe, you can put your reputation on the line by *strong signing* your code. Strong signing uses the .NET cryptography libraries to attach a signature, or *strong name*, to a piece of code in a way that cannot be faked. Users can build permission sets that allow them to run code with particular signatures.

Microsoft does this with their WinForms code, which provides a managed interface to unmanaged Win32 UI code. By default, the "Full Trust" permission set lets a system run Microsoft-signed code, even though a WinForms application is not 100% managed code. When your development team is trusted, users can add your strong name to a list of trusted code sources, so that code you have signed can be run, even though it may contain unsafe code and so fail verification. This is a simple, flexible scheme that allows you to reuse legacy code in a safe, controlled way. Different departments can choose to trust different strong names, so that most users only run fully tested code while QA can run less-trusted code, or so that Accounting can't run the Order Entry code and vice versa.

---

5. P/Invoke is beyond the scope of this book. Not only is it a specialized operation that most will never touch, it is a specialized operation that will present unique challenges with every new piece of legacy code.

Language Independence

How .NET is better than Java

So far, much of what I have said of managed code applies to Java about as much as it does to .NET. Java is a high-level language, somewhere between C++ and Delphi. Java code is compiled to an intermediate language, and the Java run-time JIT compiles each method to native code on an as-needed basis. The Java run time enforces type safety and does garbage collection, just as .NET's CLR does.

This is no coincidence—.NET was conceived as a Java killer. Microsoft concluded that managed code has two compelling advantages in ease of development and freedom from some common security holes, but that Java still had a fatal flaw. Java's fatal flaw, according to the Redmond Doctrine, is Java itself.

There are two parts to this argument. The first (which is the one that Borland especially likes) is that it is easier to justify a *port* to a managed code system—especially when you can put managed wrappers around unmanaged pieces—than to justify a *rewrite* of an existing system. Many companies have decades' worth of unmanaged code, written in a variety of languages. They're simply not going to rewrite all this in Java to get the benefits of managed code. But they might well want to port their legacy code to a managed code system to eliminate some security flaws, or they might well want to run their legacy code from within a managed code system so that new development can sprint ahead without the productivity tax of unmanaged code. The way to let people port their code rather than rewrite it is to support as many languages as possible on the same managed code platform.

The second (and probably larger) part of the argument against Java is that less-skillful programmers can get very set in their ways, and resist learning new languages. The differences between Delphi and Java or between Delphi and C# are pretty minor—the average Delphi programmer will have much more trouble learning a new class library than learning Java or C#. The same is probably **not** true of the average Visual Basic programmer. The "typical" Visual Basic shop would never switch to managed code if it meant switching all their programmers to Visual Java! The way to get programmers to switch to managed code without giving up the languages that they know and love ... is to support as many languages as possible on the same managed code platform.

Accordingly, .NET language independence is built into .NET, from CIL on up to the language-independent metadata that allows code written in any .NET language to use code written in any other *first-class* .NET language.[6] CIL was designed to support a range of languages, from imperative languages like C# and Delphi to the various LISP-like declarative languages that use a lot of tail recursion. By contrast, the Java intermediate language is pretty strongly tied to Java syntax. While you **can** compile other languages to Java byte codes, it was certainly never designed with this in mind.

---

6. A "first-class" language is one that can both consume and extend objects. Thus, Visual Basic, Delphi, and C# are all first-class languages, even though both Delphi and C# support language features that Visual Basic does not.

Common Type System

All .NET languages can share data and code

The *Common Type System* (CTS) allows code written in one language to freely interact with code written in another language. I talk about the CTS in more detail in Chapter 2. What's important here is that the CTS allows .NET library assemblies to act like cross-language versions of native code Delphi packages.

Delphi packages contain type information, so that when you create an object defined in a package, your code knows many things about the object. For example, your code knows the offsets of the object's various public fields, so it can read and write the object's fields. When your code calls one of the object's methods, it calls code located in the package that defined the object. When your code calls a virtual method, it uses the virtual method table located in the package. And, code like

```
procedure TMyForm.EventHandler(Sender: TObject);
begin
  if Sender is TEdit then
    {do something};
end;
```

works, because the is operator is comparing the Sender's virtual method table pointer to the address of the TEdit virtual method table, in the package that defined TEdit.

Similarly, .NET assemblies all include metadata: information about the name and type of every field in every data structure, as well as prototype information for every method.

The run-time system needs all this type information so that it can enforce type safety across assembly boundaries, and so that it can garbage collect. Garbage collection needs to know the type of every field, so it can track live references. But, since every .NET language uses the same metadata formats and services, every .NET language can create and call methods of objects created in any other .NET language. What's more, any first-class .NET language can extend an object defined in any other .NET language.

It's worth stopping a moment and thinking about what a change this represents from unmanaged, native code programming on Win32 and Linux. Unmanaged program libraries are not self-describing. If a C++ program wants to use a C++ library, it has to include the header files that define the contract the library code follows. If a Delphi program wants to use a C++ library, it has to use a unit that contains a translation of the C++ header files. If you want to use a new library, you have to either translate the header files yourself, pay someone else to translate the header files, or wait for someone to translate the header files as a community service.

That is, the need for header translations is a significant productivity tax on everyone who is not working in the language the library was written in. Worse, header translation is error prone. For example, many Delphi programmers have run into cases in Windows.pas where an optional pointer is translated to a required pointer (a var parameter) or where a required pointer is translated as optional.

When you don't need header translations, you can use each and every release of another group's module as soon as it's released, no matter what language it is written in.

Beyond the header translation tax, in unmanaged environments like Win32 and Linux, every object-oriented language uses its own object layouts and calling conventions. Calling methods or passing objects from language to language is difficult,[7] or even impossible. This is why the Win32 API has never moved beyond a lowest common denominator approach, a series of 'flat' C functions that every different language can call, and upon which every different language can layer its own incompatible set of objects. When native Delphi code manipulates a TFont, not only does just about every action have to get translated to something that passes a HFont to a Win32 API function, it's also doing something very Delphi-specific: Delphi code can't pass a TFont to a Win32 API function or to VB or MFC code, nor can Delphi code expose a TFont to a plug-in written in VB or MFC.

In .NET, objects are primitives, at nearly the same level as an integer, double, or string. Every .NET language uses the same layout for fields and object description tables as every other .NET language. Every .NET language uses the same calling conventions as every other .NET language. Every .NET language can use any object created in any other .NET language.[8]

This means that the run-time library can be object oriented from the ground up; objects and exceptions aren't layered on top of a flat run-time library. Delphi code can call C# methods directly, without translation. Delphi code can create C# objects directly—both the API and the application use the same memory management code—and can embed the C# objects in Delphi data structures or pass them as parameters to Framework Class Library (FCL) methods. Delphi code can use the objects that various FCL methods return, without any wrapper code or header translations. Delphi code can create specialized descendants of C# library classes. Exceptions raised by a FCL method written in C# can be handled in the Delphi code that made the FCL call.

A Font instance (the FCL version of a TFont) **can** be passed between code written in Delphi and code written in VB or C#. Your code can serve or be served, or even both.

---

7. You may need to manually insert pad fields to compensate for different field alignment strategies. This is often hard to get right even when you know exactly which compiler generated the "alien" code—and is virtually impossible to do in a way that will work with multiple compilers or compiler versions.

8. This is actually a bit of an overstatement. Some .NET languages have primitive types that other .NET languages do not. For example, Visual Basic does not have unsigned integers, and very few (if any) other languages understand Pascal's bitmapped sets. Chapter 2 discusses the Common Language Specification (CLS), which details the primitive types that a first-class .NET language must understand. Also, some .NET languages (like JScript) can "consume" objects but not create them. The proper, if nitpicky, thing to say is "Every .NET language can use any **CLS-compliant** object created in any other **first-class** .NET language."

    Do note, however, that CLS compliance is a matter of field types and member names, not a matter of object layout or metadata creation. All .NET objects have the same internal structure, and all .NET objects are described in the metadata. The distinction between objects that are CLS compliant and objects that are not CLS compliant is nowhere near as strong and sharp as the distinction between a Delphi class and a Delphi object (let alone the distinction between a Borland Delphi class and a Microsoft C++ class), which are laid out differently and which act differently. An object that is not CLS compliant is a perfectly normal object that happens to have some members that some languages can't understand, not an object constructed according to different rules.

For example, just as a Delphi application running on top of the FCL run-time library (which was written mostly in C#) uses the same data structures as the run-time library, so do any plug-ins your application might load. VB or C# plug-ins will understand a Font object (or an IPluginServices interface that you might create) in a way that their native code equivalents will never understand a D7 TFont—because all .NET languages use the same object layouts, and because all .NET languages produce and consume type information metadata.

More Jobs

Learn once, work anywhere

Because all .NET languages use the same object layouts and can share data and code, all .NET languages can—and do—use the same object-oriented run-time library, the FCL. This is a major departure from traditional programming environments, where each language had its own run-time library.

All those different libraries are what locked you into a language, and made years of language experience a reasonable proxy for programmer productivity. Most modern languages are pretty similar, and when you know one, you can pick up another in a matter of hours, or maybe days. But nobody builds an entire system from language primitives anymore: Any real work involves extensive use of library code, whether the comparatively low-level routines in a vendor's run-time library, or the more specialized routines in a third-party toolkit.

Moving from language to language often means you have to learn how to do even the simplest things all over again. For example, creating a window and writing some text to it is totally different in Delphi than in MFC. It may come down to the same Win32 API calls—but each library has abstracted the API in different ways.

Thus, Delphi experience is Delphi experience, not "Win32 experience." Knowing Delphi well and knowing C++ syntax will usually **not** get you a job in an MFC shop—they'll be looking for MFC experience. They don't want to hire someone who'll spend his first weeks paging through a library reference all the time.

With .NET, once you learn the FCL, you are a .NET programmer. It doesn't matter all that much if your FCL experience is in Delphi or C# or even VB—your skills will transfer.

Key Points

Managed code is safer and easier to write than unmanaged code

- Garbage collection eliminates tombstone pointers, and sharply reduces memory leaks.

- Safe code—checked casts and a ban on pointer arithmetic—prevents a large class of memory-scrambling Mandelbugs.

- Garbage-collected safe code—managed code—is easier to write and more secure than traditional heap-based, unsafe code.

- You can write unsafe code to interface with legacy code.

- .NET provides the benefits of managed code in a very language-neutral way.

CHAPTER 2

The Object Model

The .NET object model can be described as "like Delphi's, with generics," though there are a number of subtle differences and a handful of striking ones. On .NET, everything is, or can be, an object. Flat routines and global variables are banned; all names are object oriented. Strings and arrays are objects, not discrete data types, and .NET doesn't have anything quite like Delphi's metaclasses. This is an instance of a general problem—no one language supports every language feature that can be implemented in safe, verifiable code—so the Common Language Specification is a set of rules that allow for cross-language programming.

Farther Beyond Delphi

Everything is (or can be) an object

Chapter 1 talked about how the **Common** part of the CTS (Common Type System—the formal name for .NET's object model) enabled cross-language programming. The CTS is implemented by the CLR, and all languages' output goes through the same JIT compiler. So: all languages use the same garbage collector; all languages use the same object layouts; all languages use the same exception handling machinery; and all languages use the same conventions for passing parameters to methods and for getting results back. Application code written in Delphi can understand objects created in C# library code and vice versa. Similarly, application code written in Visual Basic can create classes that inherit from Delphi classes and vice versa.

This chapter looks at CTS details. While Delphi doesn't have generics, you'll find that other key features of the .NET object model are quite similar to Delphi's. Both feature single inheritance, interfaces, events, properties, and exceptions. However, Delphi's object model was grafted onto a procedural language, and it does show. The .NET designers not only had the benefit of hindsight, they also had the luxury of not having to maintain backward compatibility: they created a system that is clean, elegant, and object oriented from the ground up.

In Delphi, objects and 'just plain values' are categorically different. Where objects have methods, values are loosely associated with a vast array of subroutines to convert numbers to and from strings, to get and set the lengths of strings and dynamic array, and so on. More subtly, Delphi has many such walled-off categories. Fixed-length arrays are totally distinct from dynamic arrays, which are totally distinct from strings, which are totally distinct from objects, which are totally distinct from numbers—and every enum is totally distinct from every other enum. You can't write a routine that can take any enum; you can't have a data structure that can hold any value. (Even the Variant type can't hold structured types or pointers.)

.NET does distinguish between *value types* and *reference types*, but this is an optimization, not a category difference. A value type can be allocated on the stack, while a reference type is always allocated on the garbage collected heap; but a value type can have methods, and a value type can be *boxed* and treated as an Object, which is the single ancestor of all reference types in the system.

■**Note** An Object can hold **any** .NET value.

In .NET, both strings and arrays are different types of objects. We still have strong typing—a string is not assignment compatible with an array, any more than it is assignment compatible with a Regex object—but strings, arrays, and Regex objects all have a common ancestor, System.Object.[1] Common ancestry means that the same *universal* data structure can hold strings, arrays, objects, and value types—or any combination.

There are more useful new features (like nested classes; class variables; sealed classes that can't be inherited from, and sealed methods that can't be overridden; and generics, iterators, and anonymous methods, in 2.0), and I talk about them in this chapter, but the most important new feature is the ability to write universal code that can handle all types **and** is still type safe. In 1.0 universal collections involve objects and boxing, while in 2.0 they use generics and open types, but the FCL collection classes (Chapter 12) are much better than the Delphi collection classes, and they make real-world programming tasks easier. Similarly, the ability to write universal methods that can take or return **any** value keeps the Reflection API (Chapter 13) clean and easy to learn.

Overall, though, generics and the single object model and all the other new features are innovations more akin to interfaces than to objects in general—useful new tools that may take you a while to fully appreciate, but nothing that's going to turn your ideas of programming inside out. .NET's objects **are** a lot like Delphi's objects. Object (the root of the .NET object hierarchy) has methods that TObject (the root of the Delphi object hierarchy) does not, and TObject has methods that Object does not, but the two are similar enough that in Delphi for .NET, a TObject **is** an Object, with the addition of a few TObject methods via a new class helper mechanism (see Chapter 10).

Accordingly, there's nothing in this chapter about basic object-oriented concepts like encapsulation, polymorphism, inheritance, and information hiding. Instead, I talk about the .NET object model and how it differs from the Delphi object model: what's new, what's different, and what's missing.

---

1. I've referred to both Object and System.Object, and it may not be obvious that these refer to the same type. System is the namespace (I'll talk about namespaces later in this chapter), and Object is the type name. Most C# code will declare that it is using System; so that it can refer simply to Object, instead of always having to refer to System.Object. (Similarly, most code that uses regular expressions will declare that it is using System.Text.RegularExpressions; so that it can refer to the Regex type, instead of always having to refer to the System.Text.RegularExpressions.Regex type.) In the interests of simplicity, I talk about type names like Object and Type, not System.Object and System.Type, except where keyword collisions make the longer names necessary in Delphi for .NET snippets.

What's New

Relatively little is really new

While the FCL is quite large and will take time to learn, the .NET object model itself doesn't contain all that much besides 2.0's generics that's genuinely new to a Delphi programmer:

- **Every** bit of data descends from Object, and this does make some things easy that were complicated before, but many people find that this only affects their day-to-day coding by making the .NET collection classes much more universal than their Delphi equivalents—because a single .NET collection class can hold any value, .NET doesn't need anything like Delphi's constellation of specialized TList descendants.

- Object orientation is taken to a new level, with the abolition of stand-alone procedures and functions, but you'll find that this doesn't really change all that much, besides adding a lot of dots in method names.[2]

- Static methods are not quite like Delphi's class methods, and static members (class variables) are something Delphi should have had ages ago, but these are not the sort of major innovations that take pages and pages to explain and months to master.

- Nested classes can make your code simpler and more modular but, as with most data hiding syntax, their benefit is a subtle matter of bugs prevented, not a radical matter of a new abstraction that tames previously insoluble problems.

- Sealed classes and sealed methods will probably take you a while to learn to use appropriately (the temptation is to seal too much, just as it's easy to make too much private), but the concept is pretty simple.

In fact, some people dismissively say that there's nothing new in .NET, that it's just a repackaging of existing technology. To some extent, they're actually right—but they're still missing the point. .NET may contain little that hasn't been seen before—but it does it all so well. The CLR works well; the language independence is really good; and the library design is clean and comprehensive. The .NET designers took all the best ideas they could find, and learned all the lessons that they could from other people's implementations.

Generics

CIL that supports generics that look like C++

Chapter 1 describes how and why .NET programs are compiled to CIL, an intermediate language, instead of to native code. CIL 1.0 is a strongly typed machine language that supports interfaces, exceptions, single inheritance, and boxing. CIL 2.0 adds intermediate language representations

---

2. Delphi for .NET (DfN) supports "flat" functions by creating special classes, one per unit, that define flat function and global variables as static members. Within DfN, you can refer to these unit class members with undotted names, just as in native code; from other languages, you must use qualified (dotted) names to refer to the public members of a unit class.

of *open classes* and *open methods*. C# 2.0 uses the new, generic CIL to support a generic syntax that looks like C++ templates. Generic intermediate language was such a big undertaking that even the mighty .NET design team decided to put it off to version 2.

The "Single Object Model" subsection, later in this chapter, talks about the way that every reference type descends from Object, and every value type can be boxed to an Object. This means that an Object can hold any .NET value, and a collection of objects can hold any .NET values. However, such a *universal collection* suffers from a couple of problems. First, the methods that add values take object parameters. This means that you can add any reference type (without any static checking). You can write type-safe wrappers, but these do have to be written and verified, and each method has to be jitted at run time. It also means that adding a value type is a *boxing* operation. As per the upcoming "Boxing" topic, boxing is not incredibly expensive, but it's not free, either.

The second problem is that the methods that return values from a universal collection return a universal Object type. They have to be cast back to the type that was actually put in the collection. This is checked and type safe, of course, and it's fairly cheap (though not free) for reference types, but it's an *unboxing* operation for value types. Unboxing isn't very expensive, either, but it is usually more expensive than a checked cast.

So, while .NET 1.0 featured universal collections, collection classes that can store any type, there is a certain run-time overhead involved in all the casting, and especially in any boxing and unboxing. .NET 2.0 uses generics to make universal collections much more efficient. Open classes (and open methods) use generic code. Members can use type parameters for field and property types, or for method parameter and return types. When you *construct* a closed class by applying an open class to an existing closed class, every type parameter is replaced by the specified closed class.

For example, Chapter 12's List<T> class maintains an array of T; can only Add values that are assignment compatible with T; and the get methods always return a T. The same open List<T> class generates a new closed, constructed class for each type you 'pass' it—List<int> only holds 32-bit integers, a List<string> only holds strings, and so on.

You don't need to write type-safe wrappers; adding a value type doesn't box it; you don't have to cast the values you read. This makes for smaller source code that doesn't incur the cost of a checked cast (with reference types) or an unboxing operation (with value types).

Open Classes

In C# 2.0, a class can be either an open class or a closed class. A closed class is a class just like in Delphi and C# 1.0. At compile time, the compiler knows the type of every variable, every parameter, every intermediate result. An open class can have one or more *type parameters*. For example, this Unique<T> class (from the Common\Shemitz.Utility C# project) has a single type parameter, T:

```
public static class Unique<T> where T : class, new()
{
    private static T cache = default(T);
    private static object cacheLock = new object();
    // can't lock cache field (which may be null) -
    // mustn't lock typeof(T) or typeof(Unique<T>)
```

```
public static T Instance
{
  get
  {
    lock (cacheLock)
      if (cache == null)
        return cache = new T();
      else
        return cache;
  }
}
}
```

I'll explain the new features more or less in parse order: a static class may contain only static members, and you cannot create instances of a static class. This is a C# 2.0 language feature, not something that took new CIL.

The class name, Unique, has something that looks a little like a method prototype, a single identifier in angle brackets—<T>. This list of type parameters marks the Unique class as an open class. The type parameter list can have multiple, comma-separated names, as in Chapter 12's Dictionary<K, V>, which takes a key type, K, and a value type, V.

The Unique class has a where clause that says that you can only use it with reference types that have a public, parameterless constructor. The where clause tells the compiler what a generic type parameter can do—Chapter 7 has the details.

All members of the open Unique class can use the type parameter T. For example, the class has a private static field named cache, of type T. Each class *constructed* from this open class will have its own cache field, each of a different type: a Unique<Printer> will have a Printer cache field, while a Unique<Clipboard> will have a Clipboard cache field. Setting the cache field to default(T) means that the field is initially set to null.

Static fields aren't created until you first refer to their class. When you first refer to a class, the CLR allocates space for its static fields, and runs any static initialization code. After that, any reference to the class's static fields refers to the existing static fields. Which is all way too far ahead of the "Type Initializers" subsection of this chapter, but is by way of saying that this is how a closed type such as you could have defined in 1.x gets constructed—and this is also how a closed type like a Unique<Printer> type gets constructed.[3] Space is allocated and initialized, and every Unique<Printer> is the same as any other Unique<Printer>. Every time you refer to Unique<Printer>.Instance, you get the same singleton object, the private Unique<T>.cache field.

Tip Notice how this class locks a private static field, Unique<T>.cacheLock, instead of a global value like typeof(T) or typeof(Unique<T>). Locking a global value runs the risk of deadlock. Chapter 17 covers .NET threading.

---

3. A closed type may be a *closed type* or a *closed constructed type*. A simple closed type is a type that's not open, a type like in 1.0. A closed constructed type is one that fuses an open type with a closed type, or types. Note that you can apply a template to a closed constructed type—Foo<Bar<int>> and the like.

Be sure to understand that an open type is a template. Every static field in an open class is replicated every time you construct a new type from the template. Every instance field in the template is replicated in every instance. For example, Unique<T>'s private cacheLock field is declared as an static object field.[4] The declaration private static object cacheLock = new object(); doesn't use the type parameter, T, but there is still a unique cacheLock static field for every closed class constructed from the open class, Unique—classes like Unique<Printer> and Unique<Clipboard>.

Template **code** works a little differently than template fields. There's a new set of static fields for every constructed type. There's a new set of instance fields for every instance of a constructed type. But there's only one constructed and jitted set of code for every type constructed around a reference type. Each constructed type has its own name for the method, but they all point to the same code. Since code is not normally unloaded once it's jitted, this can save memory at run time and improve performance by increasing cache reuse.

Value types work a bit differently with generic code. When you construct a class around a new value type, you might have already constructed a class for a native-code compatible value type—i.e., the field types and offsets match—and so the CLR may be able to reuse generated code. There may not be a compatible type, though, and then constructing a type generates new code (that gets jitted in the normal way, when it's first called). So constructed value types sometimes share code and sometimes do not.

■**Note** At least logically, constructing a class for the first time acts a lot like referring to a closed class for the first time. The CLR loads the CIL for each method, and builds JIT stubs, just like in Chapter 1. When a method is first executed, it's jitted and the method table is patched so that it points straight to the jitted code.

Open Methods

Normal methods, whether in an open class or in a closed class, are closed methods. The types they return, or the types they take as parameters, or the types they create as locals are fixed when the class is constructed, when you first execute code that refers to Unique<Printer> or Unique<Clipboard>.

Additionally, any class—whether open or closed—can have open methods. Open methods take a type parameter list in angle brackets between the method name and the method prototype:

```
public static class Concat
{
  public static List<T> ToList<T>(params IEnumerable<T>[] Data)
  {
    List<T> Result = new List<T>();
    foreach (IEnumerable<T> E in Data)
      foreach (T Datum in E)
        Result.Add(Datum);
```

---

4. The C# object keyword is an exact synonym for the System.Object class. Similarly, the int, float, and double keywords are synonyms for System.Int32, System.Float (the IEEE 4-byte float point number, like Delphi's single), and System.Double (see Chapter 5).

```
    return Result;
  }

  public static T[] ToArray<T>( params IEnumerable<T>[] Data)
  {
    return ToList<T>(Data).ToArray();
  }
}
```

This class, from the Common\Shemitz.Utility C# project, is a closed, static class. The class has no type parameters. But both methods are open methods that take type parameters. You might use it as

```
int[] Concatenated = Concat.ToArray<int>(
  new int[] { 1, 2, 3 },
  new int[] { 4 },
  new int[] { 5 }
);
```

Nullable Types

As you'll see, C# has the endearing habit of baking system conventions into its syntax, and enforcing patterns with its grammar. For example, 2.0's new System.Nullable<T> structure is exactly equivalent to a T?. The two forms are interchangeable, and either form turns a value type into a *nullable type*. A bool? is exactly the same as Nullable<bool>: a nullable bool that can be true, false—or null.

That is, a nullable value acts much like a normal (nonnullable) value of its base type, except that you can set it and compare it to null (null is C#'s equivalent of Delphi's Nil).[5] Thus, every possible base type value is a possible nullable type value, but not vice versa: you can set a nullable type to a base type value, but you cannot set a base type to a nullable value—you have to cast it, first. For example,

```
bool? NullableBool;
bool NormalBool = true;
NullableBool = null;
NullableBool = NormalBool;
NormalBool = (bool) NullableBool; // raises an exception, if NullableBool == null
```

■**Tip** Nullable types let you have unset values without having to reserve special flag values. For example, you can make any enum into a nullable enum. And you can make any integer or float into a nullable number. And you can have tristate booleans—true, false, and unset.

---

5. You can't declare a nullable reference type like a string?—a reference type can already be set to null.

Internally, a nullable type is just a `struct` type with a public `T Value` property and a public `bool HasValue` property. Casting a nullable value to its base type is just like reading the `Value` property: when a nullable value equals null, its `HasValue` property is `false`, and casting it to its base type (or reading its `Value` property) raises an exception.

C# operators support mixing nullable types with their base type—Chapter 5 has the details. Additionally, `Value ?? Default` is C# 2.0's new *null coalescing* (or "default") operator. If the left `Value` is non-null, the `??` operator returns the left `Value`. Otherwise the `??` operator returns the right `Default`. You can use the new `??` operator with any type that may be null—not just nullable types. For example, `stringParameter ?? ""` turns a null `stringParameter` into an empty string, while passing through any non-null `stringParameter`.

Single Object Model

Everything descends from `Object`

The way that a .NET `Object` can hold any value has big effects on .NET programming. For example, in Delphi, each enumerated type is a distinct type, and there's no way to write a function that can return any enumerated value. On .NET, too, each enum is a distinct type—but (as per the "Enums" subsection, later in this chapter) a method like `Enum.Parse` can return **any** enum, because each distinct type can be boxed to an `Object`. You have to cast each result back to the type you expect, but you can have a single method that can return any enum.

Similarly, Chapter 13's Reflection API has methods that can read or set any field or property. The setters take an `Object` parameter, and know what type to cast to; the getters return an `Object`. You have to cast each result back to the type you expect, but a single method can return any field.

.NET 1.*x* used this universal type ability a lot more than 2.0 does. In 2.0, the Reflection API still uses the `Object` type for a universal value, but the open classes in the `System.Collections.Generic` namespace have largely obsoleted the `Object` collections in the older `System.Collections` namespace.

■Note I cover collections in Chapter 12: the next three topics are meant more as a taste of FCL programming than as an introduction to the .NET collection classes.

Lists

An `ArrayList` is something like Delphi's `TList`—a variable-length list, with a `Capacity` that enables it to grow efficiently. The difference is that an `ArrayList` can hold **any** type of value, not just generic, untyped pointers. You can set values with Delphi code like `List[9] :=` `TObject(99.9)` or `List[10] := 'string'` and read it back with code like `double(List[9])` or `string(List[10])`. You don't need to do any explicit heap allocation to store an 8-byte double or a 37-byte record and, because every cast is checked, you never have to track down the bugs you can get where you **think** that `List[Index]` is This type when it's really That type.

You can copy all or part of an list to a typed array (as in the preceding `Concat.ToArray` open method). For example, you might add integers one by one, then copy the list to an array of integers.

Since you can enumerate or index an array much faster than you can enumerate or index a collection class, you will often read and write code that creates and populates a variable length ArrayList, then copies it to a faster array once it knows how many entries to allocate.

In 2.0, you use a List<T> where you would have used an ArrayList in 1.x. The functionality is almost exactly equivalent, and the open List<T> is often faster than the closed ArrayList, and certainly is never slower. In fact, even when you do want a heterogeneous, self-identifying list, you should use List<Object> instead of ArrayList—using List<Object> makes it clear you know what you want, while using ArrayList looks like unmaintained, legacy code.

Dictionaries

An *associative array* maps arbitrary keys to arbitrary values. Delphi has had something like this with the TStringList class's Key and Value properties, which allow you to map strings to strings, using a newline-delimited string of Key=Value pairs as a database. (TStringList associative arrays are pretty slow.)

Languages and libraries that implement an associative array as a *hash table* offer good performance. Older libraries (like Perl's) often required that the hash key be a string. The .NET Hashtable class can use any Object for a key, and can associate that key with any Object value. This is incredibly useful: You can have a collection of strings, indexed by string; or a collection of observations, indexed by timestamp; or a collection of objects, indexed by integers, that acts like a sparse array and only uses space for the key/value pairs that you've actually set. .NET can use an Object for a key because all objects can compute a hash value, and all objects can test themselves for equality against another object. (I talk a bit more about equality testing in the "Reference Equality vs. Value Equality" topic, later in this chapter.)

In 2.0, the open Dictionary<K, V> type replaces the original Hashtable, in just the same way that List<T> replaces ArrayList. (Again, new code should use Dictionary<Object, Object> when that's what you need—not Hashtable.)

Enumerations

Doing something to each item in a collection is one of the most common programming tasks, and the C# foreach loop (Chapter 6) and the similar Delphi for {...} in loop (Chapter 10) eliminate all the boilerplate code associated with iterating through a wide variety of collections, making your code smaller, clearer, and more reliable. The foreach loop relies on the collection supporting an interface (IEnumerable) that, indirectly, exposes one Object at a time, then does a checked cast to the type you specify. (.NET 2.0 is similar, but the IEnumerable<T> interface eliminates the need for a cast.)

For example, the C# code

```
public static int Sum(IEnumerable Collection)
{
  int Accumulator = 0;
  foreach (int Item in Collection)
    Accumulator += Item;
  return Accumulator;
}
```

will sum any collection of integers—however that collection is implemented, from a simple array to a network client that gets a packet every other second.

I cover IEnumerable in more detail in Chapter 12. What you need to know for now is that a foreach block's implementation does two things. First, it calls the IEumerable.GetEnumerator method to get an object that honors the IEnumerator 'contract'—a boolean function MoveNext and an Object property, Current.[6] Second, while the MoveNext function returns true, the foreach implementation casts the Current object to the type specified in the foreach clause and assigns the cast value to the loop control variable (that is, in the preceding example, it executes code like Item = (int) Enumerator.Current), and then executes the loop statement.

Thus, you can manually enumerate a collection in Delphi (see the Chapter2\Foreach project) as

```
function Sum(Collection: IEnumerable): integer;
var
  Enumerator: IEnumerator;
begin
  Result := 0;
  Enumerator := Collection.GetEnumerator;
  while Enumerator.MoveNext do
    Inc(Result, integer(Enumerator.Current));
end;
```

■**Caution** If you ever need to manually enumerate a collection, be sure to only call GetEnumerator **once**. If you call it as while Collection.GetEnumerator.MoveNext, each iteration will do a Reset on the collection, and you will loop indefinitely on the first item in the collection.

Of course, 2.0's IEnumerable<T> replaces IEnumerable just as Dictionary<K, V> replaces Hashtable. In IEnumerable<T>, the Current property is a T, not an Object. Value types aren't boxed, and a foreach loop doesn't have to do a cast on every pass through the loop body. So, IEnumerable is less important than it once was, and you may never need to manually enumerate a collection—but I do have two positive reasons to cover foreach internals in such detail in a chapter on the object model.

1. IEnumerable and foreach loops are absolutely ubiquitous. (Even in 2.0, you'll find that lots of older code still only supports IEnumerable.) The Microsoft FCL 1.1 documentation lists **126** FCL classes that implement IEnumerable, while the Chapter2\Enumerables C# project finds **298** types that implement IEnumerable in the FCL 2.0 System namespaces— and you will often implement it yourself, if only by returning a member that already implements it.

2. This ubiquitous foreach pattern relies strongly on System.Object being a universal data type that can hold **any** value.

---

6. I say "honors the IEnumerator 'contract'" instead of "implements IEnumerator" because, when C# code calls C# code, the object does not have to explicitly implement IEnumerator—it suffices to have a Current property and a MoveNext method.

Finally, you will often have to implement IEnumerable and/or IEnumerable<T>. In many cases, you will just pass on an existing implementation. (For example, an ArrayList can be enumerated via IEnumerable, while a List<T> can be enumerated via IEnumerable<T>.) In other cases, you have to actually implement IEnumerable by hand. C# 2's new *iterator* functions mean that manually enumerating a collection is easier in 2.0 than in 1.0—once again, Chapter 12 has the details.

No More Globals

Most names are qualified, with dots in them

The universal typing of the .NET Object class comes into play in low-level code that you will often use without really noticing. Probably the most **noticeable** change that .NET makes to your programming style is that everything belongs to a (class, record, or enumerated) type. Global constants and variables become *static fields*, so that, e.g., a global constant like Delphi's PathDelim becomes the DirectorySeparatorChar member of the Path class, or Path. DirectorySeparatorChar. Similarly, 'flat' functions like Delphi's Trim and Copy become the *instance methods* String.Trim and String.Substring, and code like Trim(ThisString) becomes ThisString.Trim().

Simple examples may make this move seem distinctly retrograde. Short, simple names have become much longer. However, you can't have all that many short, simple names. Before long, you end up with long, concatenated names, and DateTimeToString or DeleteFile aren't all that much shorter than DateTime.ToString and File.Delete.

If anything, the dotted names are a bit easier to read, as the dot provides a visual break in the middle of the long name. What's more, making all code into methods encourages unity in naming: instead of sometimes calling TrimString and other times calling StringTrim, every method is called as noun.verb.

Static Fields

"Static" has not been a Delphi keyword, but in the Delphi world "static" has been contrasted with "virtual" or "dynamic." That is, we have spoken of a "plain," or *early-bound*, method as a "static method." An early-bound method is one whose address can be determined at compile time, based on the declared type of the variable that you use to call the method. Early-bound methods have been contrasted with virtual, or *late-bound*, methods, which are looked up at run time in a method table.

The CTS uses a somewhat different nomenclature. .NET conventions reserve "late bound" for talking about Reflection, .NET's version of Delphi's RTTI (Chapter 13), and an early-bound method is usually referred to as an instance method. Following C usage, "static" applies to duration and scope, not to method address determination.

In C, a local static variable is like a local "typed constant" in Delphi—a statically allocated variable that's private to a function. A local static variable is a local variable that retains its value from call to call, rather than being allocated on the stack and automatically going away when the function returns. A global static variable is only visible within the declaring file.

By analogy, in C++ a static field is a variable associated with a class, not with any particular instance. That is, it's a variable allocated at compile time: a static field exists before any instances of the class have been created; there's only one copy of the field, no matter how many instances of the class exist; and a static field persists even after all instances of the class have gone away.

The CTS follows C++ usage: *static* is contrasted with *instance*. A static field is a class variable. There is always one and only copy of a static field[7] (or a static property—see the "Static Properties" topic, later in this chapter): static members exist before any class instances are created, and static members are shared by all instances that are created (if any). By contrast, instance members are regular object members, associated with individual instances of their class.

Because a static member **is** a member of a class, the class's author can decide whether the static member is public, private, or protected. Public static fields are the CTS equivalent of global variables.

Static Methods

By analogy with static fields, a static method is a method of the class, one called without reference to any particular instance of the class. As in Delphi, a static method can be called from within its class via the unqualified name, while it must be called from outside its class via its qualified name, e.g., ClassName.MethodName.

I used the rather cumbersome phrase "method of the class" rather than the more natural "class method" because a CTS static method is not **quite** like a Delphi class method. In Delphi, a class method always gets an implicit Self parameter set to the class of the type that was used to call the method. That is, if you call a class method as ClassName.MethodName, the *metaclass reference* is to ClassName. However, if you call a class method via an instance reference, as Instance.MethodName, the metaclass reference is to the actual type of the instance, which may be a descendant of ClassName.

Tip In C#, you cannot call a static method via an instance reference the way you can in Delphi.

.NET does not use metaclasses: neither C# or Visual Basic uses metaclasses. While Delphi for .NET does have a type-safe implementation of Delphi's metaclasses, this is implemented on top of the CTS: .NET static methods do **not** get an implicit Self metaclass reference parameter the way that Delphi class methods do. In Delphi for .NET, class procedure Foo; declares a Delphi class method with an implicit metaclass type reference parameter, while class procedure Foo; static; declares a regular .NET static method without an implicit metaclass reference parameter.

Delphi Note Unless your class methods really use their Self parameter (and most do not), your .NET library code should use static methods instead of class methods. Other languages **can** explicitly supply the metaclass reference (see the "Metaclasses" subsection of this chapter) but your library's users will find it cumbersome and error prone.

---

7. Technically, there is one and only one copy of a static field per AppDomain (Chapter 14), but this is a detail that won't affect most programs.

Static Properties

CTS supports static properties in much the same way that it supports static fields and static methods. A static property is a property whose getter and setter methods are static methods.

Attributes

Code annotations, retrievable at run time

Chapter 1 talked about how .NET maintains extensive metadata that describes every class and every member of every class. The CLR uses what might be called *standard metadata,* which includes the type of information that compilers maintain in a symbol table: the name and type of every field, as well as the name and signature of every method. Standard metadata also includes a set of *intrinsic attributes* (like public and private, and the BeforeFieldInit attribute that I talk about in the upcoming "Type Initializers" subsection) that are normally set by compilers.

The CLR also supports *custom metadata.* The CLR doesn't use custom metadata much; for the most part, custom metadata is a service the CLR provides for managed code. Custom metadata takes the form of symbolic *attributes,* which get compiled into your assemblies and which you can access at run time in pretty much the same way that you access standard metadata. Some attributes are defined by (and used in) the FCL, and you can easily create and use your own attributes.

An attribute can be as simple as a name that is either present or not. For example,

```
type
  [Flags] Bits = (One = 1, Two = 2, Four = 4, Eight = 8);
```

attaches the standard Flags attribute to the Bits enum.[8] More generally, attributes are objects with properties that you can set at compile time and read at run time.

For example, the CustomAttribute class of the Chapter2\Attributes Delphi project

```
type
  [AttributeUsage(AttributeTargets.Class)]
  CustomAttribute = class(Attribute)
  strict private
    fColor:  string;
    fFlavor: string;
  public
    constructor Create(); overload;
    constructor Create(Color: string); overload;
    constructor Create(Color, Flavor: string); overload;

    property Color:  string read fColor  write fColor;
    property Flavor: string read fFlavor write fFlavor;
  end;
```

---

8. The Flags attribute just controls how the ToString method behaves when a Bits variable has an unnamed value, like Bits(3). With the Flags attribute, you get 'One, Two', while without the Flags attribute you get '3'.

can be applied to a class as [Custom], [CustomAttribute], [Custom('Red')], or [Custom('Green', 'Salty')], and so on. An attribute can have read-only properties that must be set via a constructor, and it can also have optional read-write properties that can be specified after any constructor arguments via a Name=value syntax, like [Custom(Flavor='Salty')].

Note By convention, attribute classes descend from the Attribute base class, and have a name ending with Attribute. (Attribute classes don't **have to** descend from Attribute, but this is a violation of the CLS rules [see the "Common Language Specification" section of this chapter], and some languages may not accept attributes that don't descend from Attribute.) Thus, the Custom attribute is declared, as shown earlier, as CustomAttribute, and you can use it as either [Custom] or [CustomAttribute]. This is a .NET convention, not a Delphi or a C# convention—the Flags attribute, for example, is actually declared and documented as the FlagsAttribute class, and both Delphi and C# will accept either [Flags] or [FlagsAttribute].

At run time, you can use Reflection (Chapter 13) to get all attributes that apply to any particular code element. Reflection gives you actual instances of the attribute classes, and you can read the instance properties as appropriate.

Attributes can be attached to assemblies and modules; to classes, records, and interfaces; and to the method, field, and property members of classes or records or interfaces. Attributes can also be attached to a method's return value or to individual parameters. By default, an attribute can be attached to all of these elements, but a custom attribute type can be declared with an AttributeUsage attribute that specifies what sort of code element the attribute can be applied to. By default, you can only apply an attribute once per code element, and attributes are inherited by descendant types; you can use the AttributeUsage attribute to override both these defaults.

You can use custom attributes simply as a filter—you can enumerate all the classes in an assembly (or all the methods in a class with a particular signature) and extract (or reject) the ones with a particular attribute. You can also use them in more complex ways, such as the way WinForms components use custom attributes to control a property's behavior in Delphi's Object Inspector and Visual Studio's Properties window. Overall, custom attributes are a flexible, powerful mechanism that allow you to add object-oriented annotations to a wide range of code elements; their use is limited only by your needs.

Nested Classes

Particularly useful for implementing interfaces

Nested classes are classes declared inside of another class, and you refer to them just like you refer to other members of the outer class. For example, if an Outer class declares an Inner class that declares a static field named Field, outside of Outer you would refer to the nested class as the type Outer.Inner, and the Field field would be Outer.Inner.Field. Inside one of Outer's methods, of course, you would refer to the nested class as the type Inner and the Field field would be Inner.Field.

Do not confuse nesting with inheritance! Like any other class, nested classes inherit directly from Object by default, but can explicitly descend from any class that is visible at the point the inner class is declared. (Yes, this includes another inner class.) A nested class has only those members that it explicitly declares or explicitly inherits—a nested class does not automatically inherit anything from its outer class.

What a nested class does get from its outer class is privileged access. Methods of an inner class have the same access to members of its outer class as the outer class's members do. That is, an inner class's methods can access any of its outer class's **static** private members and, given a reference to an instance of its outer class, an inner class's methods can access any of its outer class's private instance members.

It is very common for instances of inner classes to contain a private reference to an instance of their outer class, so as to provide a specific 'view' of their 'owner.' An inner class's reference to its 'owner' is usually set in its constructor, as in the Chapter2\NestedClasses Delphi project:

```
constructor Outer.Inner.Create(Owner: Outer);
begin
  inherited Create;
  Self.Owner := Owner;
  Reset;
end;
```

Syntactically, an inner class type is just another element of the class definition, on a par with fields, properties, and methods. Thus, an inner class can be declared as public, private, protected, or (in C#) internal—just like any other class member. When an inner class is declared as private (strict private, in Delphi) or protected, no code outside of the outer class ("outside code") can create the inner class or call any of the inner class's methods. Conversely, when an inner class is declared as public, any code can create and refer to an instance of the inner class. This is relatively uncommon, but it can make sense for a class to declare a collection as a public inner class, so that you would refer to, say, a collection of widgets as a Widget.Collection instead of a WidgetCollection.

Within an inner class, member visibility controls access to the inner class's members in the normal way. The visibility of an inner class has nothing to do with the visibility of its members! Thus, though private members of the outer class are visible to all of the inner class's methods, (strict) private members of an inner class are **not** visible to its outer class's members.

Note Even a private inner class must have either a constructor that is visible to the outer class, or a static method (that is visible to the outer class) that calls a private constructor.

When a nested class is (strict) private or protected, it can only be created by a method of its outer class (or by a method of a 'peer' class nested within the same outer class), and outside code cannot directly call any of the inner class's methods. However, when a public method of the outer class returns an interface, the result can actually be an instance of a private inner class that implements that interface. Outside code can then call methods and read and write properties of the **interface**, even though they can't directly use the private inner object that's implementing the interface.[9]

Returning a private inner class as an interface implementation is actually a very common pattern. Consider, for example, the IEnumerator and IEnumerator<T> interfaces that foreach uses. There are at least three good reasons why you wouldn't want to put the 'current position' state variable(s) in the actual collection object. First, this would be a waste of space when the collection was not being enumerated. Second, any 'global' data in the object always runs the risk of being corrupted by some unrelated action, perhaps as a result of careless maintenance programming. Third, it's by no means impossible that one would need to support two or more simultaneous enumerations—think multiple threads, or perhaps an outer loop and an inner loop.

Thus, the usual way to implement IEnumerator is via a nested object that holds a reference to the outer collection object and some current position index. The Chapter2\NestedClasses Delphi project contains this implementation of IEnumerator:

```
function Outer.Inner.get_Current: TObject;
begin
  Result := TObject(Owner.Data[Index]);
end;

function Outer.Inner.MoveNext: boolean;
begin
  Inc(Index);
  Result := Index <= High(Owner.Data);
end;

procedure Outer.Inner.Reset;
begin
  Index := Low(Owner.Data) - 1;
end;
```

■**Note** This is a rather contrived example, in that Owner.Data is an array of integer, which is a System.Array and thus already supports IEnumerator. However, this example does illustrate the basic pattern of a tiny inner object containing just enough state to support an enumeration.

Type Initializers

An opportunity to set class static members

The CLR supports a special method called a *type initializer*. In Delphi, the type initializer is known as a *class constructor*, because you declare a type initializer as class constructor Create. In C#,

---

9. A related pattern is a class with methods that return instances of private nested classes that override the public, outer class's virtual methods. For example, Chapter 12's ArrayList has methods that return read-only and synchronized lists. These are prototyped as returning a standard ArrayList, and calling code has no idea that what it actually gets are instances of private classes that inherit from ArrayList.

the type initializer is known as a *static constructor* because you declare a type initializer as `static Classname()`. Whatever the name, a type initializer is primarily a place to set class static members. It is a static method called—once and only once—before you use the class.

There are no restrictions on what the class constructor can do except that, as a static method, a class constructor can't call instance methods or refer to instance fields. Thus, a class constructor can set static fields to simple constants, or it can call arbitrarily complex code to load resources from disk or off the network.

Unlike unit initialization code, type initializers are not all called at program load time. Type initializers are called by the CLR—you don't explicitly call them, nor does a compiler normally emit CIL to call a type initializer.[10]

The presence or absence of the `BeforeFieldInit` class attribute governs when the CLR will call a class's type initializer. `BeforeFieldInit` is a special, compiler-level attribute that you cannot set or clear in Delphi or C# code. All Delphi classes have the `BeforeFieldInit` attribute; C# classes are marked `BeforeFieldInit` **unless** they have a static constructor.

If a class does not have the `BeforeFieldInit` attribute, the type initializer is called just before you use the class. Thus, a C# static constructor will be called just before you first create an instance of its class, or call one of the class's static methods, or refer to one of the class's static variables. If a given program run never uses the class, the static constructor will never be called (see the Chapter2\ClassConstructors C# project).

In general, the `BeforeFieldInit` attribute loosens the semantics of type initializers in ways that are supposed to be less expensive for the CLR to implement. In particular, it is said to get quite expensive to guarantee that the type initializer has been called before any static methods are called, especially when code may run in multiple application domains.[11] Accordingly, in classes that do have the `BeforeFieldInit` attribute, there is no guarantee that the type initializer will have run before any particular static methods. Conversely, there is no guarantee that a type initializer constructor will **not** run before the first static method call—if the CLR can easily call the type initializer, it will. Thus, in the Chapter2\ClassConstructors Delphi project,

```
Randomize;
if Random(100) < 50
  then A.I := 1
  else B.C := 2;
C.Foo;
```

the class constructor `C.Create` does run before the static method `C.Foo`—but this might not be the case in more taxing environments like an ASP.NET Web application.

---

10. Delphi for .NET implements unit initialization code as a class constructor, and does use (System.Runtime.CompilerServices) `RuntimeHelpers.RunClassConstructor` to guarantee that the initialization code is always run before any code that might depend on its side effects, but this is a special case. Neither Delphi nor C# emits calls to `RunClassConstructor` to force the execution of a normal, user-defined class's type initializers. Even when you use `RunClassConstructor`, a type initializer is only run once—calling `RunClassConstructor` on a type initializer that has already run will **not** rerun the type initializer.

11. Application domains are an advanced feature (Chapter 14) that allow code to be loaded and unloaded, and that allow a single instance of the CLR to keep multiple executables isolated from each other. The ASP.NET server uses application domains.

In addition to removing the guarantee that the type initializer will be called before any static method, the BeforeFieldInit attribute also changes the time the type initializer is called from first use to at **or before** first use. For example, in the Chapter2\ClassConstructors Delphi project, the class constructors A.Create and B.Create are both always run, even though only one class's static field is set in any given program run.

What "at or before" means (in the 1.1 run time that Delphi 2006 still uses) appears to be "when a method that refers to me is jitted." Thus, if you change the preceding code to

```
if Random(100) < 50
   then AShell.TouchA
   else BShell.TouchB;
```

where

```
class procedure AShell.TouchA; // static;
begin
  A.I := 1;
end;
```

```
class procedure BShell.TouchB; // static;
begin
  B.C := 2;
end;
```

the class constructor A.Create is only called on program runs where A is touched, and the class constructor B.Create is only called when B is touched. (In the actual, downloadable Chapter2\ClassConstructors Delphi project, this behavior is ifdefed so you can experiment with it yourself.)

Sealed Classes and Sealed Methods

An optimization you should use very sparingly

Virtual methods and polymorphic behavior give us great power, but they are not free. When a compiler knows that a given method cannot be overridden, it can generate slightly more efficient code than if it has to look up method addresses at run time in the method table. Thus, the CLR supports the concept of *sealing* classes and virtual methods, so that the jitter can generate optimized code for frequently used, low-level types.

You should use sealing very sparingly, if at all, especially in library code. When you seal a class, you are preventing anyone from descending from your class. While a sealed class will sometimes be a part of a proper model of the problem domain—or a sealed method may let you take shortcuts safely, knowing that you will never get unexpected behavior from an overridden method—allowing people to use your code in ways that you don't expect is generally a sign of good library design. As a rule of thumb, if you are using sealing "for performance reasons," you should definitely benchmark your code to be sure that sealing is actually providing any benefit.

What's Different

.NET contains a lot of new twists on familiar concepts

It's been over 30 years since Brooks told us to "plan to throw one away; you will, anyhow."[12] Few of us ever have that luxury—hence the rise of refactoring, or evolving a bad and/or limited design into a good design—but we can all recognize the appeal of a *second system*. A second system can avoid the mistakes of the first; a second system has cleaner, more capable entities than the first, because the designers could see how things were really used.

.NET, with its *all the best ideas* eclecticism, is a shining example of this second system effect, and you'll find that lots of familiar concepts are slightly different under .NET.

Reference Types vs. Value Types

Value types are a bit cheaper than reference types

Although the terminology is new, and the concepts are slightly different, the distinction between reference types and value types is not new to Delphi programmers. In native code Delphi, objects live on the heap, while records and primitive data types live either in registers, or on the stack, or inside of larger data types. However, while .NET reference types are basically the same as native code Delphi class types, .NET value types differ from their native code Delphi cognates in three key ways. First, in native code Delphi, primitive data types can't have methods, the way .NET value types can. Second, in native code Delphi, you can allocate space for a 'value type' on the heap and then refer to it via a pointer, which is **not** possible on .NET. Third, native code Delphi has nothing like boxing a value type into an object.

A reference type is a class type. An instance of a reference type is an object on the heap. Reference types get their name from the fact that a reference type variable actually contains only the address of the object on the heap—a reference to the actual object. As per Chapter 1, a reference is a pointer that you can't do pointer arithmetic on: the only three operations allowed on a reference are setting it, to point to an object or to Nil (or null, in C#); dereferencing it, or doing something with the object the reference points to; and comparing it to another reference or Nil, or seeing whether or not two references are the same.

Value types are familiar, old-fashioned data types: characters, numbers, and records. Numbers and characters are machine primitives, and records have been features of programming languages for decades. .NET is more object oriented than Delphi, though, and even a simple value like a character or a number can have methods. For example, instead of a loose constellation of functions like IntToStr or IntToHex, the various .NET numeric types simply, and consistently, override Object.ToString.

As you can imagine, all that value type methods really mean at the object code level is that flat procedures with explicit parameters have been turned into methods with implicit Self (or this, in C#) parameters. At the same time, eliminating flat routines makes documentation searches easier—instead of hunting for a function that takes a 32-bit integer parameter and returns a string, you simply look at the methods that an Int32 supports.

---

12. Frederick Brooks, *The Mythical Man Month*, 1975

One key restriction is that, while value types can override the virtual methods that they inherit from Object, value types cannot declare virtual methods of their own—all new methods must be instance methods, resolvable at compile time. As with the obsolete Turbo Pascal object type, this means that value types don't have a virtual method table[13] or other hidden fields, and thus it is safe for the jitter to optimize code by storing a value type in a register.

In fact, optimization is precisely the point of value types. A value type can spend its entire life on the stack or in a register. A value on the stack cannot trigger a garbage collection and never needs to be moved (Chapter 3), and a value in a register is always faster than a value in even cached memory.

More generally, value types are always allocated 'inline,' unlike reference types, which are always allocated on the heap. This is just like in Delphi, where records are allocated inline, while class instances always live on the heap. Thus, an array of reference types is an array of pointers to heap blocks, while an array of value types is a single chunk of memory. Similarly, a reference member of a record or object is a pointer to a separate object, while a value member of a record or object is contained within the 'outer' record or object. Since every heap block has a 12-byte overhead (see Chapter 3), using small value types can represent a considerable percentage saving over small reference types. For example, a record X, Y: integer; end takes only 8 bytes, while a class X, Y: integer; end takes 20 bytes, or 150% more—and a single reference to the class pushes the total memory consumption to 24 bytes, or three times the amount of space that the equivalent record uses.

One final aspect of this focus on optimization is that while records can have methods and can implement interfaces, they can't inherit from other records. All records are implicitly sealed and secured against tampering. The point of sealing records is that the jitter may be able to generate more efficient code if it knows that any record of ThisType is bound to **be** a record of ThisType and can never be a (larger) descendant type.

Reference Equality vs. Value Equality

.NET distinguishes *reference equality* from *value equality*. Reference equality means that two reference variables both point to the same address. Value equality means that both values are equal, regardless of their address. For example, 11 = 10 + 1, even though the constant 11 and the result of the addition may be in different registers or memory addresses. Similarly, the boxed values TObject(11) and TObject(10 + 1) (see the "Boxing" topic, later in this chapter) have the same value, even though the two different expressions yield two different objects that reside in discrete heap blocks.

Reference equality is the more fundamental of the two. CIL supports direct equality comparison of two references, and the C# == and != operators are implemented via these comparison instructions.[14] Value equality is supported via the Equals method: you can call either the static method Object.Equals(This, That) or the instance method This.Equals(That).

---

13. The old object type only had a VMT if it had virtual methods. An object without virtual methods was basically just a record with methods, something like a C++ struct.

14. As in Delphi, you can't use the *equals* and *not equals* operators with user-defined value types unless you explicitly supply an implementation by overloading the operators.

Delphi Note When you use = and <> to compare reference types, Delphi for .NET uses Object.Equals—i.e., value equality. To test reference equality in DfN, you need to explicitly call Object.ReferenceEquals.

You have to override Object.Equals if you want your type to support value equality. Conversely, you don't have to do any extra work if two distinct instances of a type should never be considered equal (even when all fields and properties are the same), as System.Object has no fields or properties, and the standard Equals method that your classes inherit from System.Object only supports reference equality.

In most cases, reference equality **is** what you care about for reference types, and value equality **is** what you care about for value types. (As discussed earlier, 11 = 10 + 1, and one Point is the same as another Point if their X and Y values are the same.) The system provides efficient value-oriented implementations of Equals for primitive data types like numbers, and both Delphi and C# implement numeric comparisons via CIL primitives. Probably the most common reason to override Equals is to improve the performance of record comparison, as the default implementation uses Reflection (Chapter 13) to enumerate and compare each field of both records: a hard-coded comparison like (This.X = That.X) and (This.Y = That.Y) is much faster.

The standard Microsoft documentation (which comes with the free SDK and bundled with Delphi for .NET) is pretty clear on how your override of Object.Equals must act, and on which other methods must also be overridden when you override Object.Equals. Failing to abide by these "must" statements means that your classes may not work properly with various FCL classes.

Caution The C# compiler will warn you when you break the system patterns. The Delphi compiler will **not**.

Boxing

Although the Object type is the common ancestor of all objects, which are reference types, an Object variable can hold any value, including value types. This is done by a mechanism called *boxing*, which allows you to cast any value type to an Object, treat it as an object as long as you need to, and then cast it back to the original value when you need the value again.

For example, the following excerpt from the Chapter2\BoxingDemo project

```
var
  Sparse: Hashtable;

begin
  Sparse := Hashtable.Create();
  Sparse[ TObject(11)  ] := '11';
  Sparse[ TObject(11.1) ] := TObject(11.1);
  WriteLn(Sparse[TObject(11)], ^I, Sparse[TObject(11.1)]);
  WriteLn(string(Sparse[TObject(11)]), ^I, double(Sparse[TObject(11.1)]):4:1);
end.
```

prints out 11 11.1 twice (see Figure 2-1).

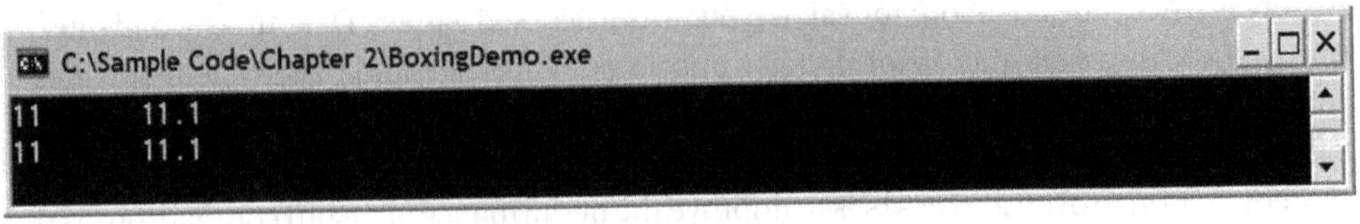

Figure 2-1. *A Hashtable uses value equality to look up keys.*

The expression TObject(11) creates a new object (on the heap) that contains both the information that it's wrapping a value of type System.Byte, and the actual value 11. Similarly, the expression TObject(11.1) creates an object that knows it contains a System.Double type, with a value of 11.1. To the Hashtable, which can save an object value for any object key (see Chapter 12), the boxed values are just ordinary objects, which is why you can use a Hashtable to build an 'array' indexed by any value you like, including strings, timestamps, and floating point numbers.

■**Tip** When you call Equals on boxed values, the underlying type matters. That is, TObject(byte(11)) does not equal TObject(integer(11)), even though byte(11) does equal integer(11).

Boxing is a great feature, and it gives you a lot of flexibility. You should be aware, however, that boxing is not free. For one thing, boxing copies data to the heap object, while unboxing copies data from the heap. For another, every time you box a value type, you create a new heap object. While heap allocation is cheaper on a garbage-collected system than on a manually maintained heap, it is still not free: Every allocation pushes you that much closer to the next garbage collection, and may have to be relocated (see Chapter 3). Feel free to create lots of little objects without fear of memory leaks, but always remember to use value types where you can, and not to box if you can avoid it.

Strings

Object-oriented, immutable, 16-bit Unicode

.NET strings are very like an object-oriented version of native code Delphi strings. That is, where native code Delphi strings are a fundamental data type that are treated specially by the compiler, the .NET String type descends directly from Object and is treated specially by the CLR. (Every string is a String, not a String descendant. Strings are the only variable-length objects the CLR supports.) Many of the flat string routines in the Delphi System and SysUtils units correspond to methods or properties of the String class—and, in fact, on .NET the Delphi string type is a System.String (just as TObject is a System.Object), and many familiar Delphi string routines are implemented on .NET as String method calls.

Tip You can continue to use the old, "portable" Delphi string routines in your Delphi for .NET code—but remember that learning the FCL is what will make you a ".NET programmer" with access to more jobs.

I cover String methods in Chapter 11, so this subsection just touches on the three major differences between a Delphi AnsiString and .NET's String type.

First, there is only one string type, and it uses the 16-bit System.Char data type, which contains Unicode characters in UTF-16 format. (Chapter 11 covers some of the issues that Unicode strings raise with regard to reading and writing ASCII text files.) While most Unicode characters fit into a 16-bit representation, not all do: just as on a native code system that uses a MBCS (Multi-Byte Character Set) language, some Unicode *code points*[15] might actually take two 16-bit characters. A string's Length property is a count of the number of elements in the string's Char array, which is **not** always the same as the number of Unicode code points. Similarly, string indexing is by Char, not by code point.

Second, strings are not reference counted on .NET. This may seem obvious, but I think it bears emphasizing, chiefly because of the way Delphi programmers use const parameters as a optimization technique, to avoid reference count manipulation. There aren't any reference counts on .NET, and (except, perhaps, in portable code) you should use Delphi's const parameters only for their semantics—that is, when you want the compiler to forbid you to change the parameter's value.

Third, and most significant, .NET strings are *immutable*. Once created, they cannot be changed, and any methods that appear to change a string's value actually create a new string. Immutable strings have three benefits. The first benefit is that immutable strings eliminate buffer overflow problems (where you change a string in place, but don't notice that the new string doesn't fit in the space allocated for it), which are very common with C-style string libraries. The second benefit is that immutable strings are inherently thread safe, as there is no way for one thread to change a string while another thread is reading it. The third benefit is that immutable strings prevent situations such as one method passing a string—by value—to another method,

---

15. A Unicode code point is a sort of abstract character—code point 32, for example, is the same Unicode character whether it's encoded as an 8-bit character (an ASCII space), a 16-bit character, or a 32-bit character.

which then makes some changes to its string parameter ... and finding that the method call changed the caller's copy of the string, because both string variables pointed to the same object. One way to prevent this *aliasing* problem is to force each string assignment (including 'assignment' to formal parameters) to make a unique copy of the string, but this wastes time and space. It's much more efficient to allow multiple string variables to all point to a single string object. Another way to prevent the aliasing problem is Delphi's "copy on write" semantics, where a change to a shared string creates a new, unique copy that can be changed safely. However, this requires that the run time maintain a reference count, and so doesn't work on .NET. Accordingly, the .NET string class simply doesn't provide any methods that let you change its internal Char array.

Now, while immutable strings are quite a change from a C-style string library, they're not really all that different from the way the Delphi AnsiString type works. An expression like Tag := '<' + Tag + '>' is not changing the Tag **buffer**, it's changing the contents of the Tag **pointer**. This is true of both native code Delphi and Delphi for .NET. What **is** different is an expression like Tag[2] := UpCase(Tag[2]).

On a native code Delphi, copy on write semantics may or may not create a new unique copy of the Tag value, but assigning to Tag[2] ultimately does change the string value 'in place.' Since this is forbidden on .NET, the Delphi compiler gets the same effect by generating code like

```
Tag := Copy(Tag, 1, 1) + UpCase(Tag[2]) + Copy(Tag, 3, MaxInt);
```

which is a considerably more expensive operation than its native code equivalent. If you're only changing a single character, you may find this a reasonable emulation; if you are changing multiple characters, you should use the StringBuilder class I talk about in Chapter 11.

Arrays

All arrays are instances of descendants of System.Array

On .NET, all arrays are actually objects, instances of classes that descend from System.Array. However, not only is Array an abstract class, one you never directly create, you never explicitly declare or create a class that descends from Array, either. (For that matter, there are static Array methods to create arrays, but you won't usually use them directly.) Rather, Array is a sort of system class, and you normally create arrays using the standard language syntax. For example, both var StaticArray: array[0..9] of double and var DynamicArray: array of double; SetLength(DynamicArray, 10) create the same ten-element array of doubles as the C# double[] CSharpArray = new double[10].

In native code Delphi, a static array is, in effect, a value type. A local static array is allocated on the stack; a static array embedded in a class or record is allocated inline. .NET arrays, being objects, are reference types and live on the heap. Thus, all array variables and fields are actually pointers to array objects. However, each array object **is** a single heap block, containing the array headers (number of total elements and the like) followed directly by the array data in a single contiguous block. Thus, an array of 10 integers takes up 40 bytes plus the header, while an array of 10 records each containing two integers takes up 80 bytes plus the header, and so on.[16]

Unlike Delphi's dynamic arrays, arrays are not resizable. Once created, the only way to change the array size is to create a new array and copy elements of the old array to it. (Of course, resizing a Delphi dynamic array does work just the same in Delphi for .NET as in native code Delphis.)

As per Chapter 1, **all** array indexing is range checked, as in Delphi native code in the {$R+} state. Array indexing and range checking is done inline: raising an out-of-range exception takes a subroutine call, but normal array access does not.

I cover Array properties and methods (like Length, Sort, Copy, etc.) in Chapter 12. I'd like to finish out this subsection by mentioning a couple of the more striking consequences of the implementation of arrays as objects. First, you can have arrays of arrays, just as with Delphi's dynamic arrays. However, since arrays are themselves objects, an array of TObject can be a LISP-like, general-purpose recursive list: any element of an array of TObject can itself be an array of TObject.

Second, because both Delphi's static arrays and Delphi's dynamic arrays are implemented via System.Array, you can copy a static array to a dynamic array by first casting the static array to a System.Array and then casting the System.Array to a dynamic array as in this code from the Chapter2\Arrays Delphi project:

```
DynamicArray := TDynamic(System.Array(StaticArray));
```

Delegates

Sophisticated method pointers

.NET has an event model that's a lot like Delphi's. (I cover the event model in Chapters 8 and 15.) One key difference is that in Delphi an event can have zero or one handlers, while a .NET event handler can have any number of handlers.

That is, a Delphi event property is a procedure of object method pointer that is either Assigned or set to Nil; event raising procedures execute code like if Assigned(Handler) then Handler(Control) that calls the handler if it has been set to a valid method pointer. If you need or want to call more than one method on a particular event, you have to handle the multiplexing yourself.

By contrast, a .NET event property is a *delegate*, which is basically a list of method pointers. When an event fires, each method on the chain is called and passed the same event arguments. If the methods return a value, the result of the delegate call is the result of the last method in the chain. You can add or remove individual methods from the *invocation list* as your application's state changes (see Chapters 8 and 10).

---

16. If you're interested in the details, the Chapter2\ArrayDump C# project contains an unsafe method that does a hex dump of an array's header and data.

DELEGATE PERFORMANCE

Multicast delegates are a nice event architecture, but note that delegates are the **only** method pointers that the CLR supports, and **all** delegates are inherently multiplexed. Somewhat as with arrays, all delegates—Delphi of object types and C# delegate types—are instances of compiler-generated descendants of the system class MulticastDelegate, which you cannot create directly. For example, in Delphi for .NET, you create delegates using the old method pointer syntax; if you port code that uses method pointers, it will be implemented via delegates. Even when you use the method pointer syntax to create a delegate that only calls a single method (as in this extract from the Chapter2\Delegates Delphi project)

```
type
  Delegate = procedure of object;

  Test = class
    procedure EmptyCall;
  end;

var
  TestObject:    Test;
  TestDelegate:  Delegate;

begin
  TestObject := Test.Create;
  TestDelegate  := TestObject.EmptyCall;
end.
```

the resulting procedure of object is implemented as a multicast delegate. When you actually call a 'method pointer' like TestDelegate, you are not calling the method directly, as in native code implementations; you are calling the delegate's Invoke() method, which has to walk the list of method pointers. This means that delegate invocation is rather slow in .NET 1.x—on the order of two-and-a-half times as slow as calling a method through an interface reference.

This 2.5x number comes from the Chapter2\Delegates project, which times delegate and interface calls. I have implemented this project in both Delphi and C# so that you can see for yourself that the timing differences between delegates and interfaces are not significantly different between Delphi and C#, and so you can experiment with the effects of various prototypes.

Note Delegates have been extensively reworked in 2.0, and calling a delegate is now actually very slightly **faster** than calling an interface method. In 2.0, you can choose between delegates and interfaces solely on the basis of their behavior, and you can disregard any 1.x tips like "Where performance matters, you should implement callbacks via interfaces, not delegates."

In .NET 1.*x*, delegates are always pointers to normal, named methods. Even when the method is only a single line and/or is only called via a delegate, the delegate creation code must refer to a separate method. In C# 2.0, you can create delegates as *anonymous methods*, which are simply special blocks within a larger method. When the delegate is very short, this can make your code much easier to read—you no longer have to jump around to see what your new Thread (say) is doing. Additionally, anonymous methods can *capture* any parameters or in-scope local variables, which can simplify calling sequences. See Chapter 8 for the details.

Finally, while you normally call a delegate exactly as if it were a normal method, all delegates support *asynchronous execution*. If the delegate has only a single method on its invocation list (i.e., it's not a multicast delegate), you can call BeginInvoke to execute it in the background, on a thread from the system ThreadPool (see Chapters 8 and 17 for details). You can then do some other work, and later call EndInvoke to release the background thread and collect the delegate's result, if any. Asynchronous execution can be a convenient alternative to either creating a thread or to explicitly manipulating the thread pool.

■**Caution** When you use asynchronous execution, you must always pair a call to BeginInvoke with a call to EndInvoke.

Namespaces

Hierarchical organization reduces naming conflicts

Namespaces are a familiar concept: if all the names in a program fall into a single pool, you're very likely to have naming conflicts, especially when you use libraries from multiple vendors. By allowing the creation of multiple, named pools of names, you greatly reduce the risk of naming conflicts. Namespaces also make it possible to resolve ambiguities when you do have name conflicts. For example, you might have a Colors enum for both computer case colors and monitor colors. With namespaces, you can refer to Case.Colors.Gray and Monitor.Colors.Black.[17]

Delphi's unit syntax is, in effect, a namespace scheme, but the .NET namespace model is a bit more general than Delphi's. The most obvious difference is that .NET namespaces are hierarchical—they can have dots in them. Less obviously, but equally importantly, .NET namespaces are not tied to source code files the way Delphi's are.

There are at least two advantages to hierarchical namespaces. First, hierarchical namespaces are "self-documenting" in much the same way that hierarchical method names are. For example, the similarities and differences between System.Web.UI.Design and System.Windows.Forms. Design are quite clear. Similarly, hierarchical namespaces force related namespaces together, making it easier to find what you want. System.Windows.Forms and System.Windows.Forms. Design are clearly related in a way that, say, WinForms and ComponentDesign would not be.

The second advantage to hierarchical namespaces is that they support a convention that nonsystem namespaces should be rooted in a trademarked company name. Hypothetical names like Microsoft.Sql.Adapters and Borland.Sql.Adapters don't conflict in the way that

---

17. This is an example of the .NET enum syntax, which I cover in the next subsection.

`Sql.Adapters` and `Sql.Adapters` would. Similarly, I can name this book's utilities namespace `Shemitz.Utilities` without interfering with **your** `Utilities` namespace.

Delphi for .NET lets you use hierarchical names, and it lets you create hierarchical names by putting dots in your unit names: in Delphi 2005 and later, everything up to the last dot is the namespace. (For example, both `Borland.Vcl.SysUtils` and `Borland.Vcl.Classes` are units in the `Borland.Vcl` namespace.) When you venture beyond Delphi, you will find that namespaces are a bit broader than this: not only may every assembly contain multiple namespaces, every C# source file may contribute to multiple namespaces and every namespace may span multiple source files and even multiple assemblies.

That is, most C# code is contained within a

```
namespace Name
{
}
```

block, and any given C# source file may contain multiple `namespace` blocks. More usefully, several different source files can contribute to the same namespace. This is useful in team situations, where multiple programmers can have bits of the same namespace checked out at once. It's also useful when it comes to partitioning an application into multiple versions: to remove functionality from a namespace, you simply don't compile that particular source file into the assembly.

Enums

.NET enums are always qualified

In Delphi, each element of an enumerated type is an element of the namespace. That is, type `Colors = (Red, Green, Blue)` defines four names: `Colors`, `Red`, `Green`, and `Blue`. This is very convenient in small programs, but in larger programs most people end up using some sort of qualified name like type `Colors = (clrRed, clrGreen, clrBlue)` or even type `Colors = (colorRed, colorGreen, colorBlue)`. Qualifying enum names like this reduces the potential for conflicts.

Adapting this reasoning to the general .NET hierarchical naming scheme, .NET enums are referred to as `TypeName.ValueName`. For example, given type `Colors = (Red, Green, Blue)`, individual elements are `Colors.Red`, `Colors.Green`, and `Colors.Blue`. This scheme minimizes name conflicts because each enum, no matter how large, contributes only its type name to the namespace. At the same time, because each enum is, in effect, its own namespace, individual element names can be simple and clear, without fear of conflicts.

When you use enums from the FCL or any other non-Delphi assembly, you must use this new (e.g., `Colors.Green`) syntax. Within 'pure' Delphi code, you can use either the old syntax or the new syntax, as in this extract from the Chapter2\Enums Delphi project:

```
type
    Colors = (Red, Green, Blue);

var
    Color: Colors = Colors.Green;
```

```
begin
  Color := Red;
end.
```

The Chapter2\Enums project also illustrates the formatting and parsing features of enums in the .NET environment. All enums descend from System.Enum and thus have a ToString method[18] that returns the enum's name, without any dots or type names. For example,

```
Color := Colors.Red;
WriteLn(System.Enum(Color).ToString);
```

prints Red, not Colors.Red. Note that the Delphi for .NET compiler will **not** let you simply say Color.ToString any more than a native code Delphi compiler will: you have to cast the enum to System.Enum, much as you have to cast a static array to System.Array before you can cast it to a dynamic array.

.NET enums can also work the other way, from strings to enums. Enum.Parse(typeof(Colors), 'Blue') returns Colors.Blue, boxed to a generic Object. (Again, boxing allows a method to return an instance of any object type.) The first parameter to Enum.Parse is the Type of the enum, while the second parameter is obviously the string to parse. Enum.Parse also has an optional third parameter that allows you to override the default case sensitivity.

Note I talk about Type in the "Metaclasses" subsection of this chapter, and again in Chapter 13, which covers Reflection. The typeof() operator (in both Delphi and C#) gives the Type for a type name. Additionally, in Delphi, applying the typeof() operator to a variable calls GetType on the variable's contents. The GetType method will return the **actual type** of a value; as with Delphi's ClassType, the actual type may be a descendant of the variable's declared type.

What's Missing

Delphi concepts you won't find in other .NET languages

Borland has done an amazing job of bringing the Delphi object model to .NET, so you can get away with not paying much attention to what's in Delphi that's not in the C# or VB object models—until you need to write C#, or until you need to write Delphi code that can be called from other languages. Code written in other languages will find it difficult or impossible to access Delphi code that relies on Delphi language features like subranges, array types, sets, class of types, and so on.

---

18. As a matter of fact, **all** types have a ToString method. You will occasionally call ToString directly, but you will most often call it indirectly, by passing an object to String.Format (or to a method like Console.WriteLine, which calls String.Format), which calls ToString to display each object it is passed. (I cover String.Format in Chapter 11.) Most value types have a reasonable default implementation of ToString, but reference types' default implementation simply returns the instance's fully qualified class name.

Subranges

Represented as an enum, which loses some semantics

When you declare a subrange like type Subrange = 1..10, the Delphi compiler both chooses an integer type that can hold a Subrange value and creates compile-time constants for High(Subrange) and Low(Subrange). This means you can declare variables of the Subrange type, like var Index: Subrange, and can write code that knows the variable's range, like for Index := Low(Index) to High(Index). It also means that the compiler can detect illegal assignments both at compile time and at run time: Index := 11 will not compile, and Index := IntVar will cause a run-time check if Index is out of range and {$R+} is on.

The CLR and the CTS have a much weaker notion of ranges and subranges than Delphi does. Array indexing is checked at run time, and arithmetic operations can be checked for numeric overflow, but there's no support for static checking of array indexes or of subranges in general. That is, array variables are declared in terms of their base type and rank (number of indices, or dimensions), but not in terms of low and high indices. Similarly, there's no way to declare, say, a 32-bit integer that can only hold values between -10 and 10.

Of course, Delphi can still support the full subrange semantics, within Delphi code. var Subrange: 1..10 = 99 will not compile under Delphi for .NET any more than under Delphi 7, and code like

```
{$R+}

var
  Limited: 1..10;

begin
  Limited := 6;
  Limited := Limited + Limited;
  WriteLn(Limited);
end.
```

will still range check on Limited := Limited + Limited. **But** you can't export these semantics. A Delphi assembly that exports a subrange actually exports a .NET enum with a static MaxValue and a static MinValue. When other assemblies use this assembly, they can create variables that can hold values between MinValue and MaxValue, and they can even step loops from MinValue and MaxValue, but MinValue and MaxValue are just names—there's nothing in the enum definition that says that a value smaller than MinValue or greater than MaxValue should raise a run-time exception.

Array Types

Not even visible to other languages

The situation with array types is somewhat similar to that with subranges, but even more extreme. In Delphi, you can say type Vector = array[0..2] of double to declare a new type— a Vector is not assignment compatible with any other array[0..2] of double. Also, as with subranges, Delphi can detect illegal indexing at compile time—you can't compile code that refers to the seventh element of a Vector.

However, CTS has absolutely no way to declare this sort of array type. That is, while all arrays are instances of compiler-generated descendants of the Array class, CTS array types only know about rank (number of dimensions) and element type: for example, a one-dimensional C# int[] is not assignment compatible with a two-dimensional int[,] or a double[], but it **is** assignment compatible with any other int[], regardless of the number of elements. C# has no way to define a type like the preceding Vector that is walled off from other one dimensional arrays of double elements: every C# double[] is assignment compatible with every other double[].

Note Just to be clear, array instances **are** range checked, and you can't access the fifth element of a three-element array. However, upper and lower bounds are properties of the **instance**, not the **type.**

While a Delphi subrange gets exported as an Enum, a Delphi array type doesn't get exported at all: a Delphi assembly contains no metadata for an exported array type, and other languages won't even see the type name. If you export an instance of this type, it will be exported as an array of the right base type and rank (number of indices, or dimensions), but without any information about the low and high indices. Those are set at run time, when the array object is actually created, and other languages don't do the sort of static index checking that Delphi does.

Sets

No other language supports Delphi-style sets

Many objects have a collection of Boolean features that sometimes you want to read or write independently, while other times you want to deal with a group of them at once. For example, sometimes you want to toggle a font's Bold property, while other times you care if the font is both Bold and Italic. A bitmap is an efficient way to represent these Boolean collections: it costs little (if anything) more to set, clear, or test several bits than to set, clear, or test a single bit.

Accordingly, Pascal has always contained bitmap support, in the form of sets. The low order byte of the set [0, 1, 6, 7] is $C3, or 11000011. Sets map ordinal values to bit positions, and replace low-level operations like Bitmap and Mask <> 0 with high-level operations like Value in Set. This is very legible, and reduces the chance of error—but other languages just don't do it that way.

The way you build bitmaps in C# is like the way you do it in C++. You build an enum with values that are powers of two, like enum Colors {Red = 1, Blue = 2, Green = 4}, and you use logical operations to access individual bits (see Table 2-1). It's no use grumbling that this is error prone (it's easy to miss a typo in a enum declaration) and burdens the programmer with tasks that are better suited to a compiler—this is how most of the world programs.

■**Note** The [Flags] attribute supports this C# bitmap model. If the preceding Colors enum is declared with the [Flags] attribute, calling ToString on Colors(7) will give you Red, Green, Blue. Similarly, Enum.Parse can handle a string like Red, Blue and will return a boxed Colors(5).

Table 2-1. *Set Operators and Their Bitmapped Equivalents*

Set Operation	Bitmapped Delphi Equivalent	Bitmapped C# Equivalent
A + B	A or B	A | B
A – B	A and not B	A & !B
A * B;	A and B	A & B
A = B	A = B	A == B
A <> B	A <> B	A != B
A <= B	A and B = A	(A & B) == A
A >= B	A and B = B	(A & B) == B

Since other languages don't support Delphi-style sets, you should never expose a Delphi set to the outside world, even though it's technically possible. To begin with, you'd have to carefully document whether your users would see a byte, an unsigned 16-bit integer, an unsigned 32-bit integer, or an array of bytes. Beyond that, your users would have to handle all the bit-shifting operations that Delphi does for you. They **can** do all the bit shifting, but they won't want to.

If you need to expose a bitmapped property, the best approach is to use C#-style bitmaps: define an enum whose values are powers of 2, and manipulate the bitmap with bitwise logic operators. If you're not willing to do that, document the Delphi set as an *opaque type* that your users can copy but not manipulate, and provide methods that manipulate it.

Metaclasses

.NET's Type *is not strongly typed like Delphi's metaclasses*

This chapter has shown the .NET object model to be pretty similar to Delphi's. However, there **is** one big difference besides generics: .NET has no metaclasses.

■**Delphi Note** Just to be clear: Delphi for .NET **does** have metaclasses, just as native code Delphis do. However, no other .NET language does, and you need to remember this when designing cross-language assemblies.

Metaclasses are Delphi's class of types. Metaclasses support virtual class methods, but metaclasses are most commonly used for polymorphic object creation. For example, you may have used code like

```
type
  MetaException = class of Exception;

function AnyException(Meta: MetaException; const Msg: string): Exception;
begin
  Result := Meta.Create(Msg);
end;
```

to write a routine that could log and throw any exception. Other common uses of metaclasses include object streaming and container forms. Delphi's form loading depends on metaclasses, and many applications include custom object streamers that likewise rely on some sort of mapping of object name to metaclass (this lets you create an object, based on a string containing its name). A container form may define an abstract type named something like HostedFrame, which would be an abstract TFrame descendant with specific behaviors, and have a class of HostedFrame property that allows you to switch from one hosted frame to another. Other examples of container forms include Wizards and Property dialog boxes that include the same frames in either a linear order or on a tabbed dialog box.

One key feature of metaclasses is that they are strongly typed. Metaclass references follow much the same assignment-compatibility rules as normal class references. That is, you can set a class of TObject variable to any metaclass value, like Exception or TForm. (Class names act much like metaclass constants.) However, while you can set a class of Exception variable to EConvertError because EConvertError descends from Exception, you can't set a class of Exception variable to TForm, because TForm does not descend from Exception.

Strong typing also applies to method and constructor calls. That is, method binding for class methods and for constructors depends on the declared type of the variable that holds the reference, just as with instance methods. If you call AnyException(EConvertError, Msg), you get a value that is an EConvertError, but the only constructor that gets executed is Exception.Create. This is OK because, for the most part, specific types of exceptions are defined only so that exception handlers can distinguish between them: they don't add new fields, and they use the inherited constructor, Exception.Create, anyhow. However, when you are working with a very generic metaclass like class of TFrame or class of TComponent, you want the appropriate descendant constructor called, so that the descendant's fields get initialized properly.

This is why Delphi supports *virtual constructors*. If you Create a class from a metaclass reference, and that metaclass (or its ancestor) has a virtual constructor, you will get a correctly initialized object, not just an object that is the right type. That is, calling the virtual constructor acts just like calling a virtual method, and looks in the class's method table for the constructor that is most appropriate for the type you are actually constructing.

Note Delphi only needs virtual constructors because it has strongly typed metaclasses.

.NET does not have metaclasses. That does **not** mean that you cannot do polymorphic object creation. The Chapter2\Polymorphic Delphi project contains the .NET equivalent of the AnyException function:

```
function AnyException(Meta: System.Type; const Msg: string): Exception;
begin
  Result := Exception( Activator.CreateInstance(Meta, [Msg]) );
end;

var
  E: Exception;

begin
  E := AnyException(typeof(System.ApplicationException), 'Indirect create');
  WriteLn(E is System.ApplicationException);
  raise E;
end.
```

The project prints True and then raises an ApplicationException—this AnyException function works just as well as its metaclass equivalent.

The static method Activator.CreateInstance takes a Type, finds and calls its constructor, and returns the newly created Object. (Activator.CreateInstance has several overloads; the AnyException function uses the overload that allows you to pass the constructor arguments via an array of objects.)

As per the "Enums" subsection of this chapter, the typeof(TypeName) operator gives you the Type that corresponds to the type name. That is, a typeof(TypeName) expression is a Type 'constant' in much the same way that a type name is a metaclass constant.[19] Deepening the analogy between Type and metaclasses, the Object method GetType[20] returns the actual run-time type of a variable, just as the Delphi method ClassType returns the actual run-time type—in both cases, the run-time type may be a descendant of the declared type.

However, while the FCL Type class and Delphi metaclasses are similar in these ways, they also differ in three key ways. The first and biggest difference is that Type is untyped. That is, while Type is itself a type, and not assignment compatible with an integer or a string or whatever, Type is the typeof() of **all** types. You can't declare a type of Exception or a type of UserControl that will only hold the Type of Exception or UserControl descendants in the same way that you can declare a class of Exception that can't be set to TFrame.

This lack of strong typing removes a powerful guard against careless errors. The strongly typed metaclass version of AnyException won't compile if you mistakenly pass it a nonexception class; the Type version **will** compile if you mistakenly pass it the typeof() for a nonexception class. While the Type version will raise a run-time exception if you pass it, say, typeof(UserControl) instead of typeof(Exception), this only helps if you do actually exercise this branch in testing—

---

19. I put 'constant' in scare quotes, because a typeof(TypeName) expression actually involves a subroutine call that maps a metadata token to a run-time Type—see Chapter 13 for details.

20. Note that you can apply typeof() to a type name in both Delphi and C#. Additionally, Delphi (but not C#) will let you apply typeof() to a variable as an alternative way to call GetType on the variable. It is thus an error to apply typeof() to an uninitialized variable.

and you won't even get a run-time exception if you pass in the Type of a class that has a constructor that takes a single string argument.

It's a bit hard to understand why the .NET design team—which included Anders Hejlsberg, who was also the lead designer for Delphi 1—chose to discard the protection of strong typing on Type. My best guess is that they decided that strong typing for instances prevents common mistakes and so is worth the implementation effort, but metainstances are used much less often (and usually by the most sophisticated users), so strong typing for metainstances prevents many fewer mistakes and is just not worth the effort.

The other two differences between Type and metaclasses flow from this lack of strong typing. That is, the second difference is that polymorphic object creation via Type does not require virtual constructors the way polymorphic object creation via metaclasses does. Remember that the real reason for virtual constructors is that method binding for a strongly typed metaclass depends on the declared type of the metaclass, with, e.g., a call to Create from a MetaException variable calling Exception.Create, not the constructor for the actual type that the MetaException variable points to. Since Type values are not strongly typed, they don't support this sort of static typing, and the weakly typed Type has to get the correct constructor from the metadata in pretty much the same way that a virtual constructor gets the correct constructor from the method tables in a native code Delphi. Thus, eliminating strongly typed metaclasses eliminates the need for virtual constructors.

Similarly, the third difference between System.Type and metaclasses is that .NET doesn't support virtual class methods the way Delphi does. After all, without a metaclass for every class, and a virtual method table for every metaclass in case the class has a virtual constructor, how **could** there be virtual class methods?

The lack of virtual class methods will probably not affect many designs. I'm not sure I've **ever** used a virtual class method. Some people use virtual class methods in class factories as ways to represent the capabilities of various candidate types in a way that doesn't require them to actually instantiate any of the candidates, which is the sort of task that attributes and Reflection (Chapter 13) can handle very nicely.

Let me conclude this lengthy discussion of metaclasses by repeating that Delphi for .NET **does** have metaclasses, just as native code Delphis do. However, languages that don't have virtual constructors can't be expected to call them properly if you expose metaclass values.

Similarly, Delphi class (as opposed to static) methods appear to other languages as static methods that take an explicit parameter of type @MetaClassname. (That is, a class named Foo has a nested class named @MetaFoo.) While each Delphi class implements its metaclass as a nested type named @MetaClassname, and each @MetaClassname has an @Instance static field that contains the appropriate metaclass constant, other languages can only access names that start with @ by using Reflection.[21] While it is possible that future versions of Delphi for .NET will change this naming convention, this looks rather unlikely after three versions.

---

21. C# can't access the nested metaclass because it uses @ as an escape character for symbols imported from other languages that clash with C# keywords. That is, when C# code refers to, say, Foo.@ClassFoo.@Instance, it gets turned into Foo.ClassFoo.Instance, and C# reports that your Delphi assembly does not export a symbol named Foo.ClassFoo.Instance.

VB can't access the nested metaclass because @ is not a legitimate character in VB identifiers, any more than it is in Delphi (or C#) identifiers. When VB code refers to either Foo.@ClassFoo.@Instance or Foo.[@ClassFoo].[@Instance] (square brackets are the VB equivalent of C#'s @ and Delphi's & escape for imports that clash with keywords), it gets an "Identifier expected." error.

If you must expose class methods to other languages, each class that does so should either include a static method like

```
// prototyped as "class function Exporter.MetaExporter: ClassOfExporter; static;"
class function Exporter.MetaExporter: ClassOfExporter; // static
begin
  Result := Exporter;
end;
```

that returns the appropriate class of metaclass constant, or the equivalent static property (see the Chapter10\ClassMethods Delphi project).

Common Language Specification

The rules for cross-language programming

If your goals for .NET don't include cross-language programming—if you intend to write or port only all-Delphi applications with no plug-in architecture—then you can ignore this section. If, however, you do plan to write applications that support plug-ins, or you want to write libraries that will (or may) be used from other languages, then you do need to understand the restrictions that the Common Language Specification (CLS) places on your code.

As you've seen in this chapter, the Common Type System (CTS) includes a set of standard types and operations that can be combined in a wide variety of ways. Again, it's the fact that these standard types and operations are defined by the CLR, not by individual languages, that lets code written in any .NET language use the FCL, which is written in C#. But the CTS is low-level and broad, and allows languages like Delphi to create safe, verifiable code that languages like C# and Visual Basic don't know what to do with.

The CLS is a set of rules that define a subset of the CTS: code written in a *first-class language* (one that define and extend classes, and that supports all CLS features) can interact with any CLS-compliant code. When you restrict yourself to CLS compliance, your code can be used or extended by programmers working in any language that supports all CLS features.

ECMA-335, the standards document that describes the CLR,[22] lists 41 CLS rules. I **could** list all 41, with commentary, but this wouldn't be very practical as some of the CLS rules apply more to languages than to applications. Accordingly, I've divided this section into two parts: the first summarizes the CLS rules that apply to authors of cross-language programs, while the second contains a **very** simple demonstration of Delphi code using a C# class, which inherits from a Delphi class, which inherits from a VB base class.

---

22. If you want to be really pedantic, ECMA-335 describes the Common Language Infrastructure (CLI). The CLI is a *specification*; the CLR is an *implementation* of the CLI.

CLS Rules

What it takes to be CLS compliant

While CLS compliance is prima facie a sort of lowest common denominator affair, it's not as bad as it may sound. CLS-compliant code can use inheritance, interfaces, exceptions, and attributes. In fact, it's even OK for a CLS-compliant assembly to include noncompliant features— it just has to explicitly label them as noncompliant with the [CLSCompliant(false)] attribute. Naturally, if you do expose noncompliant features, like sets or unsigned integers, you should also expose compliant methods that manipulate them for the benefit of programmers using languages that can't access these features, but this is a practical requirement, not a CLS rule.

What's more, compliance isn't incredibly hard to achieve, as many of the CLS rules apply more to compilers than to applications, and neither Delphi nor C# will generate code that violates some of these rules. In fact, 90% of CLS compliance for a Delphi or C# assembly comes down to declaring noncompliance for public or protected features that use generics; or signed 8-bit integers; or unsigned 16, 32, or 64-bit integers; or boxed value types. In addition, Delphi programmers should label as noncompliant subranges (a Delphi-only feature that can't even be represented in CTS metadata), sets (which may be implemented on top of unsigned integers), metaclasses (whose names are not CLS-compliant), and arrays that aren't based at 0.

Naturally, there's a **bit** more to it than that, but not really all that much.

Before going into the details, I want to emphasize that CLS compliance is a matter of the public and protected features of your code, the 'contract' your code makes with the outside world. You can fulfill your compliant contract using any noncompliant language features that seem appropriate. Your Delphi code doesn't have to give up metaclasses or sets to be CLS compliant; it just shouldn't expose them to the outside world without warning. Similarly, your C# code doesn't have to give up generics, or avoid the convention of using a private field with a lowercased name (like name) to back a public property with a proper-cased name (like Name).

By default, all assemblies are noncompliant. You have to explicitly add an [assembly: CLSCompliant(true)] attribute to your code to mark the assembly as CLS compliant. In Delphi, this can be in the .dpr file or in any unit file; in C#, it's usually in the AssemblyInfo.cs file. The CLS compliance attribute is 'inherited' by every class in the assembly, and by every member of every class in the assembly. That is, when you've marked the assembly as CLS compliant, you don't have to subsequently mark each class and each member. Conversely, if you mark a class within a CLS-compliant assembly as [CLSCompliant(false)], every member of that class will also be marked as noncompliant.

Note If you mark an assembly as CLS compliant, C# will enforce it. Using noncompliant features in a compliant assembly is an error unless you explicitly label these features [CLSCompliant(false)]. Unfortunately, Delphi does **not** enforce CLS compliance in this way.

Once again, noncompliant features include signed 8-bit integers; unsigned 16, 32, or 64-bit integers; boxed value types; and C# 2.0 generics. If you use these in a CLS-compliant assembly's `public` or `protected` contract, you **must** explicitly mark them noncompliant, and you **should** provide compliant workarounds. There are also four more arcane restrictions:

1. Except for overloading, names must be unique within a type. This means that class members can't have the same name as their type: a property or method named `Foo` in a class named `Foo` is not CLS compliant. (Note that this rule does not prohibit, e.g., the `Regex.Match` method from returning a `Match` class.) Also, CLS is case **in**sensitive.[23] Thus, in C# (which is case sensitive), a class cannot have members that differ only in case (e.g., `Name` and `name`) unless one of them is private.

2. Although you can raise an exception with any object, as in Delphi, CLS-compliant exceptions must descend from `System.Exception`. Similarly, though the CLR supports custom attributes that don't descend from `System.Attribute`, CLS-compliant attributes must descend from `System.Attribute`.

3. All types in a CLS-compliant signature must be visible. This rule has little effect on Delphi code, as all (unnested) types in the interface sections of all units in an assembly are public, but C# allows `public`, `private`, and `internal` access modifiers on classes. (An `internal` type is visible as the assembly is being built, but is **not** visible to code that uses the assembly. Thus, using an `internal` type for a public or protected member is not CLS compliant.)

4. All types in a CLS-compliant signature must also be CLS compliant. That is, you can't mark an assembly as CLS compliant if it has methods that take parameters or return results whose types come from a noncompliant assembly: You have to either mark the exporting assembly as CLS compliant, or mark just the types you use as CLS compliant.

Finally, the CLS specification includes a couple of suggestions that you should know about. You can break these and still be compliant, but breaking these suggestions will make your libraries less appealing to users:

1. You should try to avoid using identifiers that are keywords in other languages, especially VB and C#. All CLS-compliant languages have an escape mechanism to allow you to use 'imported' classes with names that conflict with the language's keywords, but the less your users have to use these words, the clearer their code will be.

2. While nested types are CLS compliant, and all CLS-compliant languages can **use** nested types, CLS compliance doesn't require that a language be able to **create** nested types. Avoid designs that require users to create nested types.

---

23. Specifically, "two identifiers are the same if their lowercase mappings … are the same." [CLS Rule 4].

Cross Language Programming

Or "An example of why I don't use Delphi for .NET"

You already know cross-language programming is possible, because both Delphi and VB can use and extend the FCL, which is written in C#. However, there's nothing quite like having all the code in your hands, so I'll conclude this chapter with an example of a trivial Delphi application creating and inspecting an object with layers written in three different languages, the Chapter2\CrossLanguage BDS 2006 project group.

The first layer, or base class, is written in Visual Basic:

```
imports System

namespace vbLayer
  public class BaseClass
    sub New()
      Console.WriteLine("Here we are in the Visual Basic constructor")
    end sub
    public VB as integer = -1
  end class
end namespace
```

This code defines a constructor (the Sub New) and a public field. The middle layer, which is written in Delphi for .NET, builds on the VB layer:

```
unit delphiLayer;

interface

uses vbLayer;

type
  MiddleClass = class (BaseClass)
    Delphi: integer;
    constructor Create();
  end;

implementation

constructor MiddleClass.Create;
begin
  inherited Create;
  Console.WriteLine('Here we are in the Delphi layer');
  Delphi := 0;
end;

end.
```

This unit is compiled into the **package** delphiLayerPackage.dll. When you build a Delphi for .NET library that will only be used by C# or VB, you can build a library project. When you build a Delphi for .NET library that will also be used by Delphi for .NET, you should build it as a package, not a library. The package compiles to a normal library assembly that other languages can use directly, plus a special Delphi symbol file, the .dcpil file, that Delphi can't seem to do without. The second reason to use a package is that packages automatically get their Borland library code (the System unit, Borland.Delphi.System—not to be confused with Microsoft's System namespace) from Borland.Delphi.dll. It's important to do this—you don't want each Delphi assembly using its own copy of the System unit—and packages make this easy. You **can** configure a 'raw' library to reference Borland.Delphi.dll, but packages do this automatically.

This unit uses vbLayer; it can see the vbLayer namespace because it requires (contains a *reference* to) vbLayer.dll (see Figure 2-2).

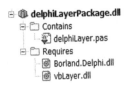

Figure 2-2. *The* delphiLayerPackage *package refers to* vbLayer.dll.

Libraries and assemblies use namespaces that come from library assemblies, or DLLs; a single assembly will often contain several namespaces. Since there can be many assemblies, compilers may have to be told where to find the namespaces you refer to. Standard namespaces like the System namespace live in the Mscorlib assembly, which compilers look in automatically. When you use a assembly **besides** Mscorlib.dll (even System.dll), you have to explicitly *add a reference* to the assembly. When a compiler tries to find a namespace, it will look in the Mscorlib assembly and in all assemblies on the list of referenced assemblies.

■**Tip** To add a reference to a project, right-click the project in BDS's Project Manager, or Visual Studio's Solution Explorer, and select Add Reference from the context menu.

The top layer, which builds on both the Visual Basic and Delphi layers, is written in C#:

```
using System;
using delphiLayer;

namespace csharpLayer
{
  public class TopClass: MiddleClass
  {
```

```
    public TopClass()
    {
      Console.WriteLine("Here we are in the C# layer");
    }

    public int CSharp = 1;
  }
}
```

This code (like the VB and Delphi layer code 'below' it) declares a constructor and a single public field.

Note that even though the C# code does not directly reference the VB layer, it still needs a reference to vbLayer.dll (see Figure 2-3), because it creates objects that descend from delphiLayerPackage.dll. Similarly, the Delphi consumer application has to reference all three DLLs. The application also has to reference Borland.Delphi.dll, so that both the application and delphiLayerPackage.dll are using the same copy of the System unit (see Figure 2-4).

Figure 2-3. *The C# layer needs to reference both the Delphi **and** the VB layers.*

□ 🗊 **CrossLanguageConsumer.exe**
   □ 🖏 References
       🖾 csharpLayer.dll
       🖾 delphiLayerPackage.dll
       🖾 vbLayer.dll

Figure 2-4. *The "consumer" needs to reference all three layers.*

The consumer code itself is pretty trivial, and only tries to show that the top-level object has access to its ancestors' public fields.

```
uses
  csharpLayer;

var
  Instance: TopClass;

begin
  Instance := TopClass.Create;
  WriteLn;
  WriteLn('Instance.VB =', Instance.VB);
  WriteLn('Instance.Delphi =', Instance.Delphi);
  WriteLn('Instance.CSharp =', Instance.CSharp);
  ReadLn;
end.
```

When you run the resulting EXE file, you get output

```
Here we are in the Visual Basic constructor
Here we are in the Delphi layer
Here we are in the C# layer

LayeredObject.VB =-1
LayeredObject.Delphi =0
LayeredObject.CSharp =1
```

that shows that all three constructors are being called, and that the top-level object does indeed have access to its ancestors' public fields. Nothing very exceptional—except that the definition of the csharpLayer object is spread over three separate DLLs, and is written in three separate languages.

This was definitely easier to describe than to do! I originally wrote this project in Delphi 8, and the VB and C# projects were in a separate Visual Studio solution. It was not particularly easy to get Delphi 8 to consume Visual Studio output. By final revision time in December 2005 (when I checked each chapter against the .NET 2.0 release libraries), I was able to compile all three languages within BDS 2006. It was still a painful process, actually. I eventually found that the Delphi consumer application didn't like a namespace that spanned three DLLs, and it could only import the Delphi library when that was built as a package.

Key Points

The .NET object model is like Delphi's, with generics but without procedural baggage

- An Object can hold **any** value—objects, strings, arrays, records, numbers, characters, and enums.

- There are no 'flat' names in .NET—every identifier is a class or a class member.

- Value types are an optimization that may make a big difference to performance.

- Delegates are sophisticated method pointers—capable of either multicasting or asynchronous execution.

- Delegate sophistication is not free—for indirect single-cast method calls, calling an interface method is faster than calling a delegate.

- .NET strings are immutable, but this isn't all **that** different from the way reference-counted Delphi strings work.

- The Common Language Specification is a set of rules that let you write code that can be called or extended by any "first-class" language.

CHAPTER 3

■ ■ ■

Garbage Collection

Garbage collection's benefits are worth garbage collection's costs. Garbage collection works well on transaction-oriented programs like network servers and desktop applications: it does not work as well when a long-running process continually burns temps as it builds its working set. Garbage collection largely obsoletes destructors, but there are some finalization details.

This chapter is for two types of reader. One type likes to know details. They'll find them, starting three paragraphs down. The second type may not yet be convinced that .NET is a good idea. If you're the second type of reader, you probably like what you've heard so far. Garbage collection increases programmer productivity. Language neutrality makes Delphi and Visual Basic programmers into first-class programmers, instead of members of the trailing tier who depend on header translations. The .NET object model is even simpler and more powerful than Delphi's, which makes for code that's simultaneously type safe and universal. And, though I really haven't done more than hint at it yet, you may have heard that the FCL (Framework Class Library) is both extensive and well designed.

But you probably still have at least two doubts, one bigger than the other. I'll address the little doubt, about JIT overhead, in Chapter 4. The short answer is that JIT compilation isn't a very substantial cost on top of demand loading, and that it is a price worth paying to bring type safety to deployed code.

This chapter addresses the big concern, "Isn't garbage collection awfully slow?" The short answer is No.

The long answer is that garbage collection offers some substantial benefits both in terms of programmer time and in terms of run time: **in most cases** garbage collection actually costs less than manually freeing heap blocks.

1. Garbage collection offers very fast allocation. The system is usually just advancing a pointer, not searching and manipulating a linked list.

2. Consecutive allocations are adjacent, not scattered all over the heap. It helps cache performance when all of an instance's fields and all of a method's locals are right next to each other.

3. Your code is smaller and simpler because you never have to worry about who owns a block, and because you never have to free the memory you allocate.

4. Your code is faster because it doesn't have to call system routines (that manipulate a linked list) to free the memory it's done with.

5. Your code is more reliable, because you reduce memory leaks and because you never have data structures that refer to memory that's already been freed.

These are five rather impressive advantages. Reference counting (which native code Delphis use for strings, dynamic arrays, and interfaces) offers the same no-need-to-free simplicity and safety—but you pay for it with the overhead of maintaining the reference counts, and reference counting can't handle circular references.

Incrementing a counter every time you pass a value to a method and decrementing it when the method returns isn't particularly expensive, but it does bloat your code, and it does add up when method A passes the same value to methods B and C, each of which may in turn pass it on two or three times. (Many Delphi programmers make a point of passing reference counted parameters as const parameters, because const parameters don't touch the reference count.) Reference counting incurs execution costs.

A circular reference is an object referring to another object that ultimately refers back to the first object. If A refers to B, and B refers to C, and C refers to A, none of the reference counts will ever go to 0, and neither A, B, nor C will ever be freed. That is, reference counting can lead to memory leaks. By contrast, garbage collection can handle circular references because it doesn't do reference counting. Instead, it keeps the memory that's in use, and trashes the rest, no matter what its inner relationships.

With a conventional heap system, you pay a price for every block you allocate and you pay a somewhat higher price for every block you free. With a garbage collection system, allocation is almost free and deallocation is cheap: for the most part, you pay only for the data that you have to relocate.

Performance

More on generations

The first garbage collection systems,[1] in the '60s and '70s, only garbage collected when an allocation failed. This meant that they were prone to locking up your program for several seconds, at random intervals. This gave garbage collection a bad reputation.

On .NET, most garbage collections take less time than a page fault, which you typically don't even notice. (Some programs are less "garbage collection friendly" than others. I talk about this in the "Pathological Cases" subsection, later in this chapter.) Partly, of course, this is just that machines are so much faster than they were 30 or 40 years ago—but mostly this reflects decades of experience.

Garbage collecting **some** memory takes less time than garbage collecting **all** memory. This should be obvious.

What may not be so obvious is that memory life spans are distributed according to a power law. Most memory is freed quite soon after it's allocated. Most of what's left is freed within seconds or minutes. And most of what lasts longer than **that** lasts until the program shuts down.

---

1. Garbage collection was invented by John McCarthy in 1958.

Think about the typical desktop app. Most code executes in response to event handlers. An event handler might run to tens and hundreds of thousands of native instructions, but that's only a fraction of a second to the CPU. The event handler might have used the merest handful of local values or it may have allocated hundreds and hundreds of temporary objects—but once the event handler returns, none of the transient values are needed any more. None of them lasted more than a fraction of a second. Some events allocate objects that last a little longer—examples include modal dialogs, IO transactions, and multi-event protocols like drag and drop—but even that is typically just seconds or minutes.

Think also of stateless server apps. Servers get a request, handle it, and move on. They answer each request as fast as they can and, once the socket has transferred the result, they have no further need for any of the temps or results.

The way this distribution of memory life spans helps the garbage collector is elegantly simple, in a probabilistic way. When most allocations are ephemeral, a garbage collector that only looks at the most recent allocations will not only scavenge **most** of the free space, it will also find that **most** of the recent allocations are no longer in use and don't need to be moved. At the same time, it doesn't have to move every bit of older data that finds itself above a hole in memory. 90% of the benefit with 10% of the work, or something like that.

So, the CLR has a three-generation garbage collector. When the system has allocated 'enough' memory (by default, this is tied to the size of the processor's cache), it does a generation 0 garbage collection (see Figure 3-1). This looks at all data allocated since the last garbage collection, and finds the data that are still in use. For the most part, the system only has to do real work on memory blocks that **aren't** garbage. (The "Finalization" section, later in this chapter, talks about the exceptions.) These get moved down to the bottom of the partition,[2] and promoted to generation 1, which means that the next generation 0 collection won't look at them. Once all the current data has been moved to the bottom of the partition, what's left is free memory.

The heap, before a generation 0 garbage collection.

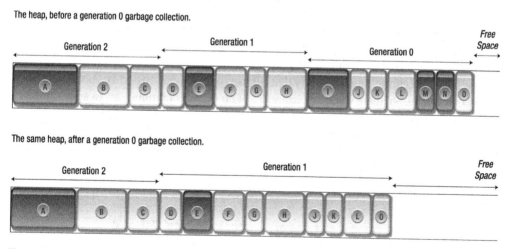

Figure 3-1. *Most memory has gone stale since the last garbage collection.*

---

2. Actually, the system will scan the chain of allocated blocks, and will only overwrite a block of free space if it's 'large enough'—it may decide to leave a small amount of free space alone, on the grounds that the cost of overwriting it is greater than the benefit of reclaiming it.

Each time an allocation triggers garbage collection, the system also checks the generation 1 and 2 partitions. If you have done 'enough' allocation since the last generation 1 collection, the system will find any surviving generation 0 blocks and promote them to generation 1, as usual, but it will also scan the existing generation 1 blocks, to scavenge the blocks that have become garbage since being promoted to generation 1 (see Figure 3-2). All survivors are moved and marked as generation 2, and won't be touched again until after generation 2 reaches its threshold and the system does a full generation 2 garbage collection. A generation 2 garbage collection just moves the surviving blocks down; it does not promote them to generation 3.

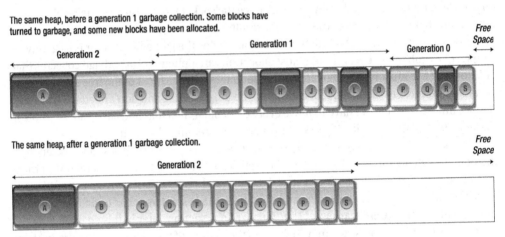

Figure 3-2. *Generation 1 collection scavenges most of the survivors of generation 0.*

As you can see, this three-generation garbage collection minimizes the time the system spends repeatedly noticing that a long-lived object is still alive. This in turn decimates the number of times a long-lived block gets moved. Since finding and moving live data is what drives garbage collection costs, generations keep the garbage collection cost down.

Conversely, higher generation garbage collections are more expensive than lower generation garbage collections. Much memory that survives past generation 0 will be permanent, but not all of it will be. So, there will be typically lots of holes in generation 1, and a generation 1 garbage collection will have to relocate most of the still-living generation 1 heap blocks. Similarly, most allocations that make it to generation 2 are going to last forever, but some will die. So there will be holes in generation 2, and a full garbage collection may have to relocate most of the live data in the system.

■**Note** Relocations are expensive because they run at bus speed, not at CPU speed.

Detecting Live Data

What happens on each sweep

The idea of generations also saves time in a more subtle way. The way the system detects that an object is still live is to walk every reference from a set of "roots" on down. (Again: it can do this because it has type data for every structure in the system. It knows every field of every structure.) This walk can stop as soon as it reaches a 'clean' object that is a higher generation than the garbage collection: e.g., every reference in a generation 1 object may be to a generation 1 or 2 object, which a generation 0 sweep doesn't care about.

The "roots" are what tie various object structures to the earth, the references that keep them alive. Roots include local variables (in CPU registers and on the CPU stack) and global variables. The garbage collector examines each root. If a particular root contains a reference[3] to an object that is already known to be live, the garbage collector checks whether the object is in the set of generations being collected—whether it may need to be moved during this garbage collection. If the known-live object **is** one that the current garbage collection might move, the garbage collector adds the root's reference to the list of references that will need to be changed if the object is moved. If the known-live object is in a higher generation, the garbage collector can just move on to the next root, because objects that have survived one or more garbage collections are only moved during the relatively rare high-generation garbage collections.

However, the garbage collector has to do a bit more work when a root contains a reference to an object that's not already on the list of live objects. If this newly discovered live object is young enough to be moved in the current sweep, the garbage collector must initialize the list of references that will need to be changed if the object is moved. Additionally, it also may have to treat every reference in the newfound object as another root: the root reference to the new object keeps the object alive, and it also keeps alive every object that the new object directly or indirectly refers to.

If the new object is in a generation that's being collected, then the garbage collector will have to recursively check every reference it contains. However, with older objects, there may be no need to walk the reference tree. If none of the reference fields in a generation 1 object have been changed since the last garbage collection, the object can only be referring to objects that also survived the last garbage collection and thus will not be moved in a generation 0 garbage collection. The garbage collector saves time by not walking the reference chains from clean old objects.

Of course, if an old object is **not** clean, if any of the references it contains have changed since the last garbage collection, then it may well be pointing to young objects that do need to be moved and promoted to the next generation. The garbage collector has to walk the reference chains from dirty old objects, just as if they were young, collectible objects.

---

3. The root may be a simple reference variable, or it may be a value type (like a record) that contains reference fields.

Accordingly, the jitter automatically emits code to set an object's *dirty bit* every time it sets a reference field to something besides Nil.[4] When the sweep encounters a dirty object, no matter how old, it will recursively scan the dirty object's references. When the garbage collector has thus scanned a dirty object's references, it will reset the dirty bit, marking the object as clean until the next time you change a reference field.

Pathological Cases

When garbage collection still hurts

Garbage-collected code is always more reliable than heap-based code, because memory is never prematurely freed. Garbage-collected code is usually faster than heap-based code, because "just forgetting" data is cheaper than threading it back into a free list. Long-lived data does still have to be found and relocated, but most server and desktop code is transactional, and little state is maintained from transaction to transaction. Thus, most garbage collections have very few pieces of data to move, and very few references to update. Similarly, a long-running, nontransactional process with a working set that rarely changes size is also garbage collector friendly.

I think it's important to emphasize that garbage collection does actually speed up most programs. However, programs that gradually build data structures (symbol tables and the like) will see less improvement and may actually be slowed a bit, simply because less of their allocations become garbage: the long-lived knowledge they build does have to be relocated. More generally, **any** program can include code that burns large quantities of temporary variables, which raises the rate of garbage collections and hence the proportion of "wall clock" time that garbage collection takes up.

String Concatenation

The garbage collector relies on the assumption that most allocations don't last very long and so will not need to be relocated. This assumption is usually true—but it's not **always** true, and the consequences of violating the assumption can be severe. For example, it's easy to bring even the fastest computer to its knees with a loop like

```
for Index := 1 to 10000 do
    StringVar := StringVar + SmallString;
```

Now, of course, this sort of repeated concatenation is not cheap even in native code. Each concatenation has to allocate room for a result string, copy each character of the old StringVar to the result string, and then copy each character of the SmallString to the result string, and

---

4. Dirty bits are a CLR implementation detail, not part of the semantics of the CIL virtual machine. The jitter emits code to set the dirty bit as part of its implementation of the stfld opcode: you'll never see any CIL that explicitly sets the dirty bit. Similarly, the dirty bit is only cleared by the garbage collector, and you'll never see any CIL that explicitly clears the dirty bit.

Maintaining a bit for every allocated byte would obviously be rather expensive. Accordingly, the dirty bits are maintained in a structure called the *card table*, which maps heap blocks to bit numbers by discarding the low bits of each heap block's address. Thus, a change to one heap block can actually cause several blocks to be marked as dirty. Conversely, a change to one field in a large object may only dirty the fields that share its dirty bit.

finally free the old value of StringVar. Do this in a loop with a string containing a megabyte text file, and you're talking some serious performance issues.[5]

But, while repeated concatenation is inherently expensive, with native code it does take megabyte strings, or tens of thousands of repetitions, to take a noticeable amount of time on a modern machine. Table 3-1, which is based on the Chapter3\MakingTrouble Delphi project,[6] shows that under .NET repeated concatenation causes performance problems much more quickly than with native, heap managed strings: a mere 6400 repetitions of adding a 16-character string to an initially empty accumulator takes **one and half seconds** on a 2GHz P4, running XP with a gig and half of RAM!

Table 3-1. *Results from the Chapter3\MakingTrouble Project*

Repetitions	Concat micro Seconds, with Precollect	Concat microSeconds, without Precollect	StringBuilder microSeconds, with Precollect	StringBuilder microSeconds, without Precollect	StringBuilder Advantage
100	888	405	35	31	25.4
200	880	532	65	49	13.5
400	2103	2203	104	99	20.2
800	9689	10,636	206	206	47
1600	58,272	60,351	432	421	134.9
3200	385,350	342,189	769	847	501.1
6400	1,644,412	1,543,448	1485	1540	1107.3

Why is this relatively common operation so much more expensive on .NET than in native code? It doesn't really have anything to do with *immutable strings*, which are often blamed for this behavior—the strings are also immutable when native Delphi code does repeated concatenation. Rather, what we are seeing is a high rate of memory consumption triggering frequent garbage collection. Each garbage collection incurs the overhead of checking all dirty references,

---

5. Repeated concatenation has a cost proportional to the square of the number of repetitions, or $O(N^2)$. The cost of each concatenation is the cost of copying both strings to the new string, plus some relatively fixed memory management overhead. If the left string has length L and the right string has length R, the copying cost of the first concatenation is proportional to L+R. The copying cost of the second concatenation is proportional to (L+R)+R, or L+2R. The copying cost of the third concatenation is proportional to L+3R, and so on. The total copying cost is thus L×N + R×(N^2+N)÷2—a quadratic equation, even when you add in the memory allocation overhead

6. The project benchmarks repeated string concatenation in four different ways. The first column of run times is ThisString + ThatString, with an explicit GC.Collect() before every benchmarked pass, to minimize the number of garbage collections within each pass. The second column does not do an explicit GC.Collect() before every benchmarked pass, and so is a bit noisier—and more reflective of real conditions. The third and fourth columns uses a StringBuilder class instead of concatenation; this class preallocates a large buffer (expanding it as necessary) and concatenates by copying the new tail string to the end of the buffer, thus eliminating many allocations and avoiding the need to copy the whole buffer on each concatenation. As with the first two columns, the difference is in whether there's a forced garbage collection before the benchmark begins. The last column is the ratio between times in the first and third columns.

and often has to move the current value of the accumulator down to the top of the generation 1 partition.

■**Note** Large objects normally are long-lived objects. The memory manager puts all allocations larger than 85,000 bytes on a special *Large Object Heap*, which is collected but not compacted (see the upcoming "Complications" section) **and** marks them as generation 2. This increases the total size of generation 2 data, and makes it more likely that the next collection will do a full, three-generation sweep. Thus, repeated concatenation with longish strings not only causes a large number of garbage collections, it causes a large number of **expensive** garbage collections.

The longer the strings, the more frequent the collections. The trigger points vary, but let's look at what happens when you keep adding the same 16-character string to an accumulator, and the system triggers a generation 0 garbage collection after every 256K bytes of allocation.[7] That first 16-character string is 50 bytes long—32 bytes of text plus 16 bytes of string class header and a 2-byte null terminator char. (I talk a bit about string internals in the "Large Object Heap" subsection of this chapter.) A 32-character string takes 82 bytes, a 48-character string takes 114 bytes, and so on. Assume that the accumulator is initialized to an empty string, so that the first concatenation creates a copy of the 16-character constant string. The first concatenation allocates a new 50-byte block. The second concatenation allocates a new 82-byte block, and the loop has allocated 132 bytes. That is, the first N concatenations take $N\times18 + 1\times32 + 2\times32 + \ldots + N\times32$ bytes and it takes only 127 concatenations to total more than 256K in new allocations, and so trigger a generation 0 garbage collection. Then it takes only another 53 concatenations to trigger the next generation 0 garbage collection, and so on. After a thousand iterations, the accumulator is 16,000 characters long, or 32,018 bytes, and we are doing a garbage collection every nine iterations. By the time the accumulator is bigger than the cache (at iteration 8192), we're doing a garbage collection every iteration.

Basically, "heap churning" is much more expensive on .NET than under native code. Each garbage collection is more expensive than manually adding a freed block to a free list; the key to making garbage collection work for you is to keep collections far apart and to limit the amount of data they have to relocate.

You can and should feel free to adopt a more object-oriented style, creating little objects for every bit of state, but you should also keep an eye on the number and size of the objects you create. When you're writing a UI event handler that runs straight through, you don't need to pay attention to how your object creation might affect the heap. However, in any loop that executes more than a handful of times, you should try to avoid creating objects—especially large objects—that are only used briefly.

In general, when an algorithm calls for appending a series of items to an array, you should separate the array Capacity from the array Length (or item Count), so that you can do several appends without having to reallocate. This is true with native code and manual heap management, which is why Delphi's list classes separate capacity from length. It is even more true with

---

7. The garbage collector may move its trigger points as it watches the way an application uses memory, and the defaults will depend on your actual hardware and .NET release. In 1.1, the default trigger point for a generation 0 collection is the size of the L2 cache, which is 256K bytes on the P4 of Table 3-1.

managed code and automatic heap management, which is why the FCL ArrayList and List<T> classes (Chapter 12) also separate capacity from length.

In the specific case of string concatenation, the FCL includes the StringBuilder class (Chapter 11), which limits heap churning by preallocating a large character buffer and appending each new string to the end, reallocating as needed. As you can see from the final column of Table 3-1, the result is quite a lot faster than building up a string via successive concatenations.

Tip If you know how big your final string will be, you can pass the buffer Capacity to the StringBuilder constructor, and the whole process will only do two large allocations: creating the StringBuilder instance creates the initial buffer, and calling the ToString() method at the end creates a new string.

More narrowly, many string concatenations actually just put a few pieces of variable data into a standard "picture." Accordingly, the FCL also includes the String.Format (Chapter 11 again) function, which acts much like Delphi's familiar Format function[8] or C libraries' sprintf function. Since the Format function can precalculate the length of its result string, it can be more efficient than a series of string concatenations.

Should you conclude from this that string concatenation is bad, and that you should always use Format or a StringBuilder? No. There is some overhead involved in interpreting a Format pattern string, or in creating the StringBuilder and in converting the buffer into a string, so that the alternatives usually aren't faster than a concatenation or three. But, even if concatenation was always the slowest approach, I'm sure you'll agree that

```
Result := '</' + Tag + '>';
```

is clearer than

```
Result := String.Format('</{0}>', Tag);
```

and that both are clearer than

```
Builder := StringBuilder.Create('</');
Builder.Append(Tag);
Builder.Append('>');
Result := Builder.ToString();
```

Use inline concatenation in moderation to keep your code clear; use the Format function or a StringBuilder for large strings or big loops.

Other Pathologies

Repeated string concatenation is certainly the most common way to run afoul of the garbage collector. However, a process that runs for a long time, continually building a working set while temps come and go, is also hard on the garbage collector. When you have a lot of data that

---

8. In fact, Delphi for .NET's Format function is actually just a wrapper around the FCL function.

sticks around for a long time, you have a lot of data that needs to be shuffled down as data below it goes out of use.

Most programs don't continually build their working set, but many heavily used utility programs do naturally consume memory as they work. For example, a compiler has to add a symbol table entry every time it encounters a new symbol. Similarly, a Bayesian spam filtering program breaks messages into a stream of words, and continually updates the word lists for each bucket that it assigns a message to.

If you have to write such a program, you can't really do much about the fact that most garbage collections will find new data to promote and relocate. What you can do is to minimize the volume of data that needs to be relocated, minimize the number of references that need to be fixed up, and maximize the amount of time between relocations.

While you may not be able to do much about the number of data points that your algorithm accumulates, you typically do have some control over the size and internal structure of each datum. Tradeoffs between saving derived values (spending memory to save CPU cycles) and rederiving them later (spending CPU cycles to save memory) are very common. Programs that build their working sets are generally rather heavily biased towards saving memory, as they always run a risk of running out of room, even in an era of machines with gigabytes of RAM. All that garbage collection really changes, here, is that saving memory may actually end up saving time, by minimizing the amount of work that the garbage collector has to do.

■**Tip** One particularly well-supported trick is to use string subranges instead of copying pieces out of a larger string. Many of the FCL routines that take string parameters have overloads that allow you to specify a base string plus a starting index and character count.

Fields that contain shortcuts into a larger data structure are a special case of derived value. Every reference to a piece of long-lived data has to be changed when the data moves. If you can replace a shortcut reference with a method that does a little lookup, you may find yourself saving both time and space.

These tradeoffs affect the cost of relocation. You can also decrease the frequency of garbage collection. The fewer allocations you do and the smaller their average size, the less often the system will do garbage collection.

One rule of thumb here is that using *value types* (a Delphi record or a C# struct) can reduce the need for garbage collections. A local value type is allocated on the stack, not on the heap. This helps in two ways. First, every use of the data is very slightly faster than using a similar reference type. Second, and more substantially, data on the stack is invisible to the garbage collector, except as a source of roots. That is, allocating stack space can't trigger a garbage collection, and local value types never need to be moved by the garbage collector.

Similarly, value type members of classes (or other value types) are allocated 'inline,' as part of the larger data structure, instead of as a separate heap block that the 'outer' data structure points to. This again results in a slight speedup—and, more importantly, reduces total memory consumption (if only by the size of the heap block header, and the size of one reference) and reduces the number of heap blocks that may need to be moved.

A second rule of thumb is to pay attention to the **size** of your temporary reference variables. Remember, every byte you allocate brings the next garbage collection that much closer. Pay particular attention to large strings. .NET uses Unicode, so that every character takes 2 bytes, and thus every string is twice as big as its AnsiString equivalent in a native-code Delphi. It's not at all hard to have a string that's just shy of the 85K Large Object cutoff—appending to such a string allocates room for the result, and a single operation thus brings you a third of the way to another generation 0 garbage collection.

Finalization

Destructors are very different than in unmanaged code

In unmanaged code, we **have to** obey the Free What You Create rule. Disobeying this key rule leads to memory leaks. Managed code, of course, is quite different, as the only way to have a memory leak is to keep a reference to an object that you no longer use.

In turn, this radically reduces the use of destructors. In unmanaged code, every object that creates other objects needs to be sure to free them, and many (most?) Delphi destructors consist of little more than a list of Free statements. In managed code, we don't need to free the objects that we create. All that a destructor needs to do in managed code is to free resources— things like file handles, device contexts (aka DCs)—that the object has open.

However, it's still important that this cleanup code gets called, that the garbage collector never discards an object that's keeping a resource open. Accordingly, the Object root class defines a Finalize method that any reference type can override. An overridden Finalize method is a *finalizer*, which is a special method called by the garbage collector when the object is discarded.

There are four special rules regarding finalizers. One is that a finalizer should return as soon as possible—finalizers are run on a background thread that may not get much time in a compute-intensive application.

The second special rule is that a finalizer should always call its base class's finalizer, all the way up to Object.Finalize(). Now, finalizers are run within an exception handler, so that no exception can stop the finalizer. But the CLR doesn't make any clever attempts to call the base finalizer of the type that raised an exception—any exception will abort ancestral finalization. The proper pattern is to execute any finalization code in a try/finally block that always calls the base finalizer.

■ **C# Note** You do not override the Finalize method. Instead, you write something that looks like a C++ destructor. For example, a class named MyClass has a destructor ~MyClass(). The compiler generates a Finalize method that wraps your destructor code in a try/finally block that always calls the base class's Finalize method.

■ **Delphi Note** Finalizers must manually code a try/finally block that always calls inherited Finalize.

The third special rule is that the fewer references to managed memory a finalizable class has, the better. Having all fields be value types is ideal. This is because of the way finalization works.

Whenever you create an instance of a class that has a custom finalizer, the CLR adds the instance to a list of objects that will need to be finalized at some point. When the garbage collector sees that a stale object is on this list of finalization candidates, it brings the stale object—and every object reachable from the stale object—back to a sort of half life, by placing it on a list of objects that need to be finalized, the *freachable queue*. A dedicated thread finalizes each object on the freachable queue—hijacking an application thread would run the risk of inadvertent deadlock. Meanwhile, the freachable queue is one of the roots that the live object detector examines, so placing an object on the freachable queue also revives every object reachable from it.

That is, this memory that was dead is alive after all, and so it (and everything it refers to, directly or indirectly) has to be relocated and possibly promoted to generation 1 or 2. Thus, reviving an object is a comparatively expensive operation, involving both relocation and memory that's not available for reuse until the next (relatively rare) high-generation collection. It's cheap enough to do this for a single handle, but you sure don't want to revive megabyte data structures with hundreds of thousands of parts!

The fourth special rule is that the finalization thread provides *nondeterministic finalization*. You don't have any idea when the finalization will happen, just that it will happen sometime between the object going out of scope and the end of your program. This can leave a file or database handle open for a long time, with all the potential for sharing issues and unflushed buffers that open handles imply. Less obviously, any objects you refer to may have already been finalized, so that calling their methods might have unpredictable results. That is, a finalizer should only call methods of objects in global data structures, or static methods, or unmanaged primitives that do things like close handles.

Between nondeterministic finalization and revival cost, you should avoid finalization as much as possible. You should implement a finalizer if your class opens an unmanaged resource that must be closed, but you should also implement a way for your code's users to explicitly free resources when they know they are done with them.

The way you do this is to implement the IDisposable interface, which is sometimes called *the Dispose pattern* because IDisposable contains only one method, Dispose. You will implement Dispose differently in a class with a finalizer than you will implement Dispose in a class that doesn't have a finalizer.

Disposing and Finalizing

Disposing suppresses finalization

A class that implements IDisposable in addition to a finalizer provides a normal method, not the finalizer, that does all the cleanup that the finalizer does. In addition, the IDisposable method should call GC.SuppressFinalize(Self) to remove the object from the list of finalization candidates, thus avoiding the resurrection cost. While the IDisposable method is free to call instance methods on any instances that the object contains references to (because it is called from normal code, not the finalization thread), the **usual** implementation is for both the IDisposable method and the finalizer to call a third method, which contains the actual cleanup code. For example, Listing 3-1 is an extract from the Chapter3\FinalizerDemo C# project that turns this pattern into a base class.

Listing 3-1. *A Finalizable and Disposable Base Class*

```
public abstract class Finalizable: IDisposable
{
    protected virtual void DisposeManaged() {}
    protected abstract void ReleaseUnmanaged();

    public void Dispose()
    {
        Dispose(true); // Safe to Dispose of reference fields
    }

    ~Finalizable()
    {
        Dispose(false); // only release unmanaged resources
    }

    private void Dispose(bool Managed)
    {
        if (!disposed)
        {
            if (Managed)
            {
                DisposeManaged(); // may be no-op
                GC.SuppressFinalize(this); // DON'T call the finalizer!
            }
            ReleaseUnmanaged(); // the whole point of all this
        }
        disposed = true;
    }

    private bool disposed = false;
}
```

■ **Note** When a class implements both IDisposable and a finalizer, you should call Dispose as soon as you're done with the object. (In C#, the using statement [Chapter 7] makes this easy and automatic.) The finalizer is a fail-safe mechanism that keeps an unmanaged resource from leaking. Explicitly calling Dispose is almost always cheaper than waiting for finalization, and it frees resources sooner. Calling SuppressFinalize is not very expensive, and using the Dispose pattern means that the object's memory gets reclaimed at the next garbage collection.

Disposing and Not Finalizing

Many classes dispose, few classes finalize

You don't need a finalizer just because you use classes that have finalizers. Those classes are already fail-safe, and your class's finalizer couldn't call any methods on those objects, anyhow. However, if you Dispose of (or Close) those objects in your Dispose method, they won't need to be finalized.

That is, many classes support IDisposable without also supporting finalizers.[9] In general, if you use a class that implements IDisposable, you should call its Dispose method, even if you don't know that it uses finalized objects and even if not calling Dispose doesn't cause any obvious misbehavior. Calling Dispose may suppress finalization, and finalization is expensive.

For example, the Graphics class (Chapter 16) wraps a standard Windows GDI+ drawing surface, which is a **very** limited resource, and you should always Dispose of any Graphics object that you explicitly create. The Brush, Pen, and Font drawing objects wrap less limited resources, and it's not a bug to not Dispose of them—but overall your program will run a bit faster and use a bit less memory if you Dispose of any drawing objects that you create.

■**Note** I talk more about the Dispose pattern in Chapter 7, which discusses the C# using construct, and in Chapter 10, which discusses the way Delphi for .NET automatically implements IDisposable whenever you override the standard Destroy destructor.

Complications

Optimizations add a bit of complexity

What I've presented so far is the general architecture of the garbage collector. As you've seen, the basic three-generation design was chosen with an eye to the typical program, so that **most** programs will run faster with an automatic, garbage-collected heap than with a traditional, manually maintained heap. In addition, there are a few complications that were added to broaden the range of programs that benefit from garbage collection.

This section covers those optimizations that are most worth knowing a little about: the Large Object Heap; self-tuning; and the way the garbage collector responds to threads and multiple processors, on both workstations and servers.

---

9. Some disposable classes, in fact, don't even use any classes with finalizers—they support IDispose just so that a C# using block can automatically run Dispose at the bottom of the block. Examples include Chapter 6's benchmark code, or GUI code that 'pushes' and 'pops' a cursor.

Large Object Heap

It's expensive to relocate large objects

The same studies of program behavior that laid the empirical basis for the garbage collector's three-generation design also found that large allocations **tend to be** long-lived objects—IO buffers, application-level caches, and the like. This means that a large object is more likely than a smaller object to need to be relocated. At the same time, relocating a large object is a comparatively expensive operation, both because it runs at memory speed, not CPU speed, and because it pushes other, smaller bits of data out of the cache.

That is, in a unified heap, moving a comparatively few large, long-lived objects will tend to represent a disproportionately large part of the total relocation cost budget. Conversely, moving large objects into a separate heap both reduces relocation costs and minimizes garbage collection's effect on the cache.

This is why any object that takes at least 85,000 bytes[10] (on a 32-bit Intel platform, in both CLR 1.1 and 2.0) is allocated from a separate, Large Object Heap. Because relocation of large objects is expensive, the Large Object Heap is **collected, not compacted**. That is, garbage collection finds live data, just as in the main heap, but it's cheaper to thread garbage into a free list than to relocate live data. One consequence of this is that allocation of large objects is not quite as simple and fast as allocation of small objects—instead of simply taking the first N bytes of a large contiguous chunk of free space, the allocation operation may have to walk the free list, looking for a big enough chunk, in exactly the same way as a traditional, manual heap manager in unmanaged, native code.

■ **Note** Even though the Large Object Heap maintains a free list like a traditional, manual heap, it's still automatically managed, and the free list and separation from the main heap are implementation details that are invisible to applications. You create a large object in exactly the same way that you create a small object; there are no special instructions in CIL for allocating large objects. More importantly, you don't manually free large objects any more than you manually free small objects; this is done automatically, by the garbage collector.

Finally, because finding dead blocks and threading them into a free list **is** comparatively expensive, and because large blocks are assumed to be long-lived blocks, all data on the Large Object Heap is created as generation 2, not generation 0. This means that the Large Object Heap is usually collected relatively infrequently. It also means that (as in the "String Concatenation" topic, earlier) any code that breaks the garbage collector's design assumptions about the longevity of large data pays a heavy performance price, triggering full garbage collections much more often than usual.

---

10. Yes, though the precise number is not particularly important—and is, of course, subject to change—that **is** a decimal eighty-five thousand, not 85K.

You can use this assignment of large objects to generation 2 to find the exact cutoff point between regular objects and large objects. The Chapter3\LargeObjectHeap Delphi and C# projects use a binary search to find that strings up to 42,490 characters are created as generation 0, while longer strings are created as generation 2. The Rotor source (basically a published version of an early draft of CLR 1.0) and the Chapter3\StringDump C# project shows that on 32-bit platforms strings consist of a 16-byte header[11] followed by a null terminated stream of 16-bit Unicode code points. Thus, a string with 42,490 characters takes $16 + 42490\times2 + 2$, or 84,998 bytes, while a string with 42,491 characters takes 85,000 bytes.

Self-Tuning

The garbage collector adjusts its trigger points

I've said a couple of times that **by default** the garbage collector does a generation 0 garbage collection when the running total of your recent allocations exceeds the size of the processor's L2 cache. This does not mean that you can programmatically control this trigger point, or the trigger points for generation 1 and 2 collections. Rather, the garbage collector pays attention to the number of live blocks that are relocated during each garbage collection and, over time, adjusts the trigger points for all three generations so as to optimize the tradeoff between memory consumption and the proportion of run time spent in the garbage collector.

As a rule of thumb, if the garbage collector sees that a given generation shows a pattern of lots of live blocks that need to be relocated, it will raise the allocation limits for that generation. This means that it waits longer before collecting, and so gives each allocation more time to go stale. Conversely, if the garbage collector rarely has to move blocks, it will lower the limits. While this means that it has to scan the roots more often, it's found that this isn't turning up many live blocks, and a smaller heap means a smaller set of dead blocks to check against the finalization candidate list.

While this self-tuning obviously isn't proof against the sort of heap churning I discussed in the "String Concatenation" topic, overall the garbage collector probably gets it right. The developers have been able to see how a wide variety of real .NET programs use memory, and the garbage collector does see how your program acts in real time. While you can use the System.GC class to force garbage collection, this is usually a case of premature optimization. Garbage collection doesn't cause your program to lock up at unpredictable intervals, so there's not a lot of point to second guessing the trigger algorithm.

About the only time you might want to force a collection is when you create a lot of pieces of long-lived, heavily referenced data. It's comparatively expensive to update each reference as the long-lived data gets promoted from generation 0 to generation 1, and again as it gets promoted from generation 1 to generation 2. It may make sense to force a collection with GC.Collect(GC.MaxGeneration), so that each piece of your newly created data set gets promoted to

---

11. Every object on the heap has three system fields, and takes at least 12 bytes (24, on 64-bit architectures): the pointer to the method table [MT] for its class; the SyncBlockIndex used in thread synchronization (see Chapter 17); and a size field. The garbage collector uses the size field (and a couple of constants "reachable from the MethodTable") to calculate block size as MT.BaseSize + this.SizeField * MT.ComponentSize. Strings are null terminated (just like in native code Delphis) and the size field contains the actual length of the variable length portion of the string; strings also have a string length field, which **usually** is one less than the array length field.

generation 2 in a single collection, thus minimizing the number of times that it will be moved and all references to it updated.

Multithreading

Garbage collection suspends secondary threads

In any heap system, whether manual or automatic, multithreaded programs have to synchronize access to the free list, in exactly the same way that they have to synchronize access to any other global data structure. For example, in a native code Delphi, when `IsMultiThread` is `True` (because you set it manually or you created a `TThread`), the memory management functions use a critical section to assure exclusive access to the free list. Using a critical section means that no matter what thread changes the free list, the changes are *atomic*—the changes are whole and indivisible. No other thread ever sees the free list in a partially updated state.

Automatic heap management adds another level of complication: a garbage collection triggered by one thread may move an object being used by any other thread! Thus, garbage collection has to be as atomic as allocation. There can never be a gap between moving an object and updating a reference that would allow another thread to dereference a tombstoned pointer. The jitter could probably maintain this atomicity by using a critical section to synchronize every object reference, but that would be painfully slow.

Instead, garbage collection in one thread suspends all other threads. A suspended thread may be using an object that's being relocated, but the thread's reference to the relocated object will be changed before the thread has a chance to use it again.

There are actually a couple of complications lurking behind the four words "suspends all other threads." The first complication is that "all" doesn't really mean all threads, it means all threads running managed code. Threads running unmanaged code are allowed to run, as they are expected to avoid managed memory unless it has been *pinned* down so that the garbage collector won't move it. The CLR can suspend a thread when it switches from unmanaged to managed code.

The second complication has to do with suspending the thread. It turns out that there are points in optimized jitted code where it is not possible to find all object references. Thus, there are some points where it is safe to run a garbage collection, and other points where it is not safe. One of the things the jitter does is to build lists that let the CLR detect whether a given thread is at a *safe point* or not. When a thread is suspended, the CLR checks the thread's instruction pointer against these lists, to decide if the thread is at a safe point. If it **is** at a safe point, the CLR goes on to any other threads and thence to the garbage collection.

If a suspended thread is **not** at a safe point, the CLR *hijacks* the thread, by changing the CPU stack so that the current method "returns" to a CLR routine. This special routine is known to be a safe point and the CLR suspends the thread once it gets control. When garbage collection finishes and the hijacked thread resumes, it returns from the hijack routine to the same point that it would normally have returned to.

Since some methods run for a very long time, it's possible that hijacking the return address won't take effect for quite a while. Thus, the CLR sets a timer, and when a hijacked thread hasn't "returned" to the CLR suspension routine after "enough" time, it resuspends the thread, and checks to see whether the thread is still running the same method. If it is not—if it has called another method—the CLR puts the old return address back and hijacks the current method.

The CLR repeats this process of waiting, resuspending, and rehijacking until the thread is finally at a safe point.

■**Note** A long-running loop that makes no method calls can affect other threads.

When all threads are suspended at a safe point, the thread whose allocation triggered the process can actually do the garbage collection.

Multiprocessors

Optimizations for true concurrency

Waiting for garbage collection is more expensive on a multiprocessor system than on a uniprocessor system. On a uniprocessor system, the CPU is kept busy running the unblocked thread(s). On a multiprocessor system, blocked threads can mean idle hardware.

Accordingly, on multiprocessor machines, each thread gets its own generation 0 heap partition, each with its own free list.[12] This means two or more threads can do allocations simultaneously, without any danger of corrupting "the" free list.

■**Note** This partitioning is done **within** the process's address space, and each thread has the same access to data allocated by other threads that it does on a uniprocessor system. The only data that's hidden from other threads is the free list, which is never visible at the application level, anyway.

Maintaining multiple generation 0 heaps is the sort of optimization that can benefit any program running on a multiprocessor system. Beyond this, though, servers and workstations have different requirements. What matters most to a server is the number of transactions per second, and threads are likely to be running independent transactions using the same code. On a server, the most meaningful measurement of garbage collection speed is total CPU time. However, what matters most to a workstation is the time it takes to respond to each user interface event, and threads are likely to be background tasks created to allow the main thread to respond quickly to user events like mouse movement and keyboard or mouse button presses. On a workstation, the most meaningful measurement of garbage collection speed is how long the main thread is suspended and not responding to user input.

---

12. This is only true for the "workstation" build of the CLR, which is what normal .NET executables use. The "server" build (ASP.NET) has one memory partition per CPU. (Advanced applications can contain a native component that hosts the run time manually, and thus allows the application to choose the CLR build and other parameters. This topic is far beyond the scope of this book.)

These different requirements suggest different collection strategies on multiprocessor machines—parallel collection for servers, and background collection for workstations. These strategies are different enough that there are actually two different builds of the CLR— `mscorsvr.dll` for servers and `mscorwks.dll` for workstations. Uniprocessor machines always use the workstation build, while multiprocessor machines **can** use the server build. Loading the CLR is done by the unmanaged stub code in a .NET executable file, and it is this code that can try to load the server build if it is appropriate. GUI and console applications normally use the workstation build; ASP.NET applications are loaded by the ASP.NET server, which uses the server build on multiprocessor systems.

Garbage collection is a highly parallelizable task. While updating the list of live objects (and the lists of references to each live object) needs to be kept atomic, there's no reason why one processor can't be checking *this* root while another processor checks *that* root. Similarly, once all live blocks have been detected, the job of relocating each live object can be shared out, one to a processor, until the whole job is done. Accordingly, the server's garbage collector uses one thread per processor, and garbage collection takes roughly $1/_N$th the time on an N processor system as on a one-processor system. (Obviously there is **some** synchronization overhead.)

This strategy works well on servers, minimizing the time each processor is unavailable for transactions. On a workstation, though, it suffers from the disadvantage that the user interface is not responding while the garbage collector is detecting live data **and** while the garbage collector is relocating the live data. Accordingly, when the workstation build does a full generation 2 garbage collection on a multiprocessor machine, it does not suspend all threads while detecting live data. Rather, it creates a background thread that detects live data, while application threads keep on running. When the background thread is done, the garbage collector suspends all the application threads, and compacts memory as normal.

In most cases, this maximizes application responsiveness, as a multiprocessor system can pretty much dedicate a processor to detecting live data while the other processor(s) are handling UI events and any application-level background tasks. However, you may find that this background collection can actually slow down compute-intensive applications that are already using every cycle of each processor. You can use the .NET Framework Configuration tool of the Control Panel's Administrative Tools applet to experiment with background vs. foreground collection. This tool creates and/or edits the application configuration file (see Appendix 3). If you want to distribute your application with background collection disabled, you can use the configuration file it produces as a model.

Weak References

Support for "optional" caching

One final nice point about garbage collection is that it lets you have *weak references*, just like Java does. A weak reference is a reference that does not protect the object from garbage collection. Any object referenced only by a weak reference will disappear at the next garbage collection, even one of the relatively frequent generation 0 collections.

Weak references are thus useful for objects that you can regenerate, if you have to, but that you'd like to keep around, "if it's no trouble," because regeneration is comparatively expensive. Good candidates for weak references are singleton objects like the system Printer or Clipboard that you may not use very often—but where using them once suggests that you may use them again pretty soon.

■ **Tip** A "lazy create" property is a good place to use a weak reference.

When you need the data again, you can examine the weak reference's Target and/or IsAlive properties. The Target property will either contain a valid reference or Nil/null; the IsAlive property is true whenever Target is non-Nil. If the Target is Nil, that means the weakly referenced object has been garbage collected and you need to re-create it. If the Target is not Nil, you now have a normal (strong) reference that you can cast to the appropriate type, and that will keep the data from being garbage collected just like any other normal reference does.

For example, the Chapter3\WeakReferenceDemo Delphi project creates and sets a weak reference as

```
var
  Weak: WeakReference;

begin
  Weak := WeakReference.Create(Nil);
  WriteLn('Weak.IsAlive = ', Weak.IsAlive, ' before assignment');

  Weak.Target := System.String.Create('*', 32); // a small string
end.
```

The weak reference constructor's first parameter is the initial Target object. (As you can see, you can change a weak reference's Target after creation.) The weak reference constructor's optional parameter is a boolean that allows you to specify either the default *short* weak reference or the optional *long* weak reference. A short weak reference is only tracked until the Target is found to be dead; a long weak reference is tracked until the Target is actually finalized.

Code like

```
if Weak.IsAlive then
  WriteLn(&String(Weak.Target));
```

can examine the IsAlive property, and cast the Target to a String. However, after the demo project exerts a little memory pressure by allocating a few thousand strings, the weak reference no longer points to live data: IsAlive is false, and Target is Nil.

Key Points

Garbage collection speeds development and can speed applications

- Garbage collection makes your life as a developer much easier.

- Most applications are faster with garbage collection than with manual heap management.

- Finalization prevents resource leaks, but is expensive. You should use the Dispose pattern whenever possible.

- There **are** situations, mostly involving large quantities of large, short-lived objects, that can cause garbage collection performance issues.

CHAPTER 4

■■■

JIT and CIL

.NET is not interpreted. Your code is delivered as CIL (Common Intermediate Language), not native machine code. Yet, your code is always compiled to native code before being run. This compilation can happen at install time, but is usually done on a Just In Time basis. Managed code is good for both users and developers, and delivering your code as CIL is key to delivering the benefits of managed code to users: intermediate code can be verified before it's run, and running all code through a single compiler means all code does the same run-time checks. CIL is a high-level, strongly typed, stack-oriented assembler language that's easier to read (and write) than any real, native assembler.

.NET Is Not Interpreted

Managed code is not expensive

Chapter 1 covered a number of important advantages of managed code:

- No memory corruption from unchecked casts; from unchecked array indexing; from dangling references, aka tombstoned pointers; or from pointer arithmetic.

- Many fewer memory leaks.

- Managed code is easier to write than unmanaged code, because it doesn't need to be cluttered with memory management boilerplate, and because eliminating certain common types of errors means that you get your code working sooner.

- Managed code is easier to read than unmanaged code, because it's not full of boiler-plate. And, of course, code that is easier to read is easier to debug.

Managed code is clearly good for programmers, who can deliver code faster and cheaper. Naturally, customers like faster and cheaper, too. Customers also like the way managed code closes many of the holes that can give an intruder control of their computer.

Some people conclude from these important advantages that .NET must be interpreted. This is an understandable mistake, as .NET offers benefits that, historically, only interpreted systems offered. But, it **is** still a mistake.

.NET is not interpreted. Yes, there is some table lookup, for things like virtual method calls and for operations like is and as—but those lookups are compiled in, in exactly the same way that code for similar lookups is compiled in when you work with a native code Delphi. .NET does not have any sort of control loop that reads each intermediate language instruction from an assembly and decides how to implement it.

When your .NET methods execute on a Wintel machine, they execute as native *x*86 machine code, exactly as they do with a native code Delphi. Your safe source code uses references, a high-level abstraction that can be type checked and that cannot do pointer arithmetic—but the native code that is jitted from the CIL for your high-level source code uses real pointers, just as with a native code Delphi.

Real Pointers

Object references jit to small, fast machine code pointers

Some older garbage collectors required that all user code use handles (values you pass to an API method to get an actual address) to memory, or perhaps pointers to entries in a table of pointers to memory blocks. This made life easier for the garbage collector, which never had to update more than a single pointer when it moved a piece of allocated memory. The price was bloated object code, and an across-the-board slowdown of all user code.

The tradeoff was probably worth it on the small, slow machines of that obsolete era. When memory's so tight that you have to GC every few allocations, you spend a high proportion of your clock time in garbage collection. Updating multiple references would only have increased an already barely tolerable burden.

But, Moore's Law Happened, as I'm told they say in Redmond. .NET doesn't use handles, or pointers to pointers, because nice things happen to garbage collection costs when you've got lots of memory.

You can just keep allocating merrily, and when you do have to seek out live references, you find (as per Chapter 3) that there aren't all that many. Most transactions have completed, leaving no references to trace. Since garbage collection cost is directly proportional to the number of live references that have to be detected and updated, this means that the total garbage collection cost is fairly low, even if the garbage collector does spend time finding and updating every live reference.

.NET code is smaller and faster than old-style garbage-collected code because the references in our Delphi or C# code compile directly to machine-level pointers. Dereferencing a reference takes a single instruction, not two (as with pointers to pointers) or more (as with calls to API methods).

References in .NET source (whether VB, Delphi, or C#) compile to pretty much the same object code as they do in Win32 native compilers like D7.

Demand Loading

Jitting is a modest tax on demand loading

You'll remember that Win32 and Linux applications are not loaded in a single huge chunk when the application begins. The executable address space is virtual, marked in CPU-level page tables so as to cause a fault when a page is first referenced. The page fault handler loads the whole page from disk, then it resets the page tables so that the next reference won't page fault. Finally, it jumps back to the instruction that caused the page fault, on the newly loaded page, just as if nothing had happened except that the clock jumped ahead.

In strikingly similar fashion, loading an assembly lays out tables with entries for every type in the assembly, but it doesn't actually load a type until the type is first referenced. First reference creates any static fields, and first reference builds the type's method table. As per Chapter 1, each pointer in a new method table is to CLR code that loads the appropriate CIL and compiles it. Everything is delayed as long as possible, so that types that aren't used aren't loaded and so that code that's not used is not jitted.

When a method is called for the first time, the jitter compiles the CIL and changes the type's method table to point to the new native code. Then the jitter jumps into the newly compiled code just as if it were being called normally, right down to the parameters and return address on the stack that the jitter left untouched. Subsequent calls to the method go straight to the new native code. That is, the first call to any method is through the CLR and the jitter; subsequent calls are direct. Almost like a page fault.

While JIT compilation is not free, it's not very expensive, either. According to Danny Thorpe (at the time, Delphi's main compiler guy), the 1.*x* jitter is about as fast as Delphi's native compiler. Given that Delphi can compile and link large programs in 'next to no time'—and that linkage is usually the slower of the two operations—JIT times are not a particularly noticeable addition to demand load times. While it **is** true that page faults and demand loading are particularly expensive operations from the CPU's point of view, it is also true that from a human perspective page faults and demand loading can be hard to notice once an application's core code is loaded and page faults drop below a few dozen a second.

Some will take this as yet more testimony to the superior skills of the .NET design team—Delphi compilation speeds in a production jitter. There probably is some truth here, but it's also true that the jitter has a much easier job than the Delphi compiler does. For one thing, CIL is a lot lower-level than Object Pascal and, for another, assemblies contain preparsed, tokenized CIL. Since parsing is one of the slowest operations for most compilers, preparsing is actually quite a significant speedup.

■**Tip** Those interested in reading more about the binary CIL and 32-bit tokens in a compiled .NET assembly will find these details later in this chapter.

Code Quality

The jitter's object code is pretty similar to Delphi's

The .NET jitter and the Delphi native compiler represent similar decisions on optimization tradeoffs. Compiler designers have to come down somewhere between two extremes. One extreme is to optimize each subroutine as a whole, spending a lot of time compiling and producing code that's hard to distinguish from the finest handcrafted code. The other extreme is to do no optimization at all, mechanically spitting out the exact same code every time you encounter a given construct, regardless of the context.

The very first Turbo Pascal compilers were deep into this latter, No Optimization territory. They compiled incredibly quickly, but generated the sort of code that even the greenest human assembly language programmer would sneer at, like copying expression results from a register to a memory location, and then—even in the next instruction—from that memory location back to the same register. Over time, the compiler got smarter, but always in modest, local ways that were consistent with fast compilation—the cheap and easy optimizations that probably generate most of the possible benefits.

So, while even now it only takes a moderately skilled assembly language programmer to see differences between Delphi 7–generated code and human-generated code, the Delphi 7 compiler is really pretty good about register usage, factors out some common subexpressions, and can do some modest algebraic simplification. The code's not perfect, but these days it's really rare that a routine can be sped up more than a few percent by replacing it with hand-written assembler. Since running time usually depends far more on your algorithm than on the optimizer—e.g., the best optimizer in the world can't save a algorithm with $O(N^2)$ run time, a run time that's proportional to the square of the number of items—most Delphi programmers happily trade a fast compile-link cycle for object code that could be fractionally better.

The same sort of tradeoffs are visible in the .NET jitter. You could probably improve upon it at the level of a whole method, but it's hard to fault it either line by line or line to line. (That is, it generates decent code for each line, and it makes good use of the registers for local variables and/or temporary results.) What's more, the .NET jitter can do automatic function inlining. That is, it decides on its own when it makes sense to treat a short function as a macro, and insert the code inline rather than calling a subroutine. The tradeoff is that inlined code is generally faster but consumes more memory. (Code size can have an effect on code speed if, for example, an inner loop is too big to fit in cache, or if bigger code means fewer methods are cached, or if your code is competing with your data for cache space.)

There are a couple of key restrictions on inlining. One is that the system will normally only inline intra-assembly calls. Inlining across assembly boundaries raises security issues.

The other key restriction is that the system can only inline sealed or nonvirtual methods. If the system can't know at compile time which method to call, it can't inline the call! In particular, this means that the system won't inline calls to a class that descends from MarshalByRefObject, which includes most WinForms (Chapter 15) types. (Chapter 14 describes how instances of MarshalByRefObject descendants may actually be system-generated proxies that use serialization to communicate across various boundaries with 'true' instances of MarshalByRefObject descendants.) Every method of a MarshalByRefObject descendant is effectively virtual, called through the type's method table.

Inlining and Properties

.NET may be able to optimize property access

One place that inlining can make a big difference is with object properties. While .NET includes the notion of object properties, just as Delphi always has, one of the differences between .NET and Delphi is that you can only read or write .NET properties via methods, not via direct field access as in Delphi. That is, in Delphi one might write

```
type
  Foo = class
  private
    fBar: integer;
  public
    property Bar: integer read fBar write fBar;
  end;
```

The native Delphi code uses the field directly as a property: reading and writing a Foo's Bar property compiles to code that reads and writes the Foo's fBar field. The CTS only supports property access through explicit methods, and the C# equivalent of the preceding class would be

```
public class Foo
{
  private int fBar;
  public int Bar
  {
    get {return fBar;}
    set {fBar = value;}
  }
}
```

which is very like the code that a Delphi for .NET compiler generates when it supports fields in property read and write terms. However, if the jitter opts to inline property getter and setter methods, your CIL code with explicit property access methods will compile to native code that's quite like a native Delphi's field access code.

Note Remember, inlining is usually only done within an assembly, and can't be done on methods of MarshalByRefObject descendants. The WinForm's Form class descends from MarshalByRefObject, so all Form classes (the FCL version of Delphi's TForm descendant classes—see Chapter 15) are also MarshalByRefObject descendants, and so their property access methods will never be inlined.

Precompilation

CIL is generally compiled every time it's run

Whatever machine you're running on,[1] your .NET methods have to be compiled to native code before they can be executed. For the most part, this means your code is recompiled every time it's run—jitted as I've been describing. But the benefits of using intermediate code come from using intermediate code, not from jitting. Why not just compile the CIL to native code once, when you install the application, or perhaps when you run it the first time?

---

1. While obviously a machine **could** be built that runs CIL as its native object code, as of February 2006 there doesn't seem to be any such machine. Even the embedded CLR solutions like the .netcpu are built on top of general-purpose processor chips.

Well, CPUs are a lot faster than hard disks, so jitting just doesn't take very long, at least not compared to hard disk transaction times. So, you can run a CIL assembly (or application, in 2.0) through the NGEN utility at install time, and generate a native code executable that does load a little faster than the jitted version. But it doesn't really load all **that** much faster, and you've just made install and uninstall that much more complicated.

In 2.0, precompilation may be a reasonable choice for large applications that you install on users' workstations or servers. In 1.*x*, NGEN is much less appealing, as it compiles a single assembly at a time, and calls out of a compiled assembly are slightly slower than calls within a compiled assembly, or between jitted assemblies. (This isn't a huge slowdown, but then neither is jitting.) Since most programs make many calls in and out of library modules, the extra cost of intermodule calls can swamp the load time advantage in a long-running program.

Under CLR 1 and 1.1, it doesn't really make sense to NGEN an assembly unless it does not make many library calls. The .NET Framework only precompiles a few large 'terminal' assemblies, like System and System.Windows.Forms.[2] A terminal assembly makes few if any calls out; a terminal assembly provides services for higher level code.

JIT Benefits

Productivity and portability

This chapter has focused on jit costs so far, because pretty much every programmer's first reaction to jitting is along the lines of "How can it possibly make sense to recompile my code every time it runs?" My answer has two parts. First, Just In Time compilation isn't very expensive. Second, using intermediate code that must be compiled on every user's system has benefits that do justify the costs.

I hope you agree with me that the cost of jitting is not particularly high. However, even if you don't agree that jitting is pretty cheap, I'd like you to remember the two main benefits of using intermediate code—productivity and portability.

Productivity

CIL can be verified

Delivering intermediate code lets you deploy your code to the same type-safe environment you develop it in. It wouldn't do you all that much good to eschew pointer arithmetic and to check every typecast in your code if any of the code you call is not so scrupulous. Using a single system compiler for all intermediate code lets you be sure that all code plays by the rules. In particular, compiling intermediate code on the target system lets you be sure that each and every method will raise an exception rather than miscast (which might corrupt memory).

---

2. You can see for yourself what's been precompiled with NGEN /show.

Conversely, delivering intermediate code means users don't have to trust your programming discipline and testing regimen. Each users' jitter can verify your code and assure them that it follows type-safety rules.[3]

Programmers are more productive in a type-safe, managed code environment (especially one with a really good run-time library, like .NET's Framework Class Library [FCL]). Deploying CIL is key to running your code in the same managed code environment on field machines as on your development machines.

Portability

Intermediate languages are hardware independent

Portability is the most cited reason for Java using its "byte code" intermediate language. Java can run on servers as on telephones, because the intermediate language ignores processor-specific details like the size and orthogonality of the register set. Compiling intermediate code to processor-specific native code is much more efficient than running nonnative code on an emulator.

.NET gets the same benefits from CIL. CIL can be as easily compiled 'up' to a 64-bit server as 'down' to a PDA or telephone.

CIL

Details you don't need but might like

You can program in a high-level language without knowing assembly language. However, those who take the trouble to learn assembler invariably report that it was worth it. You gain a deeper understanding of your high-level language, and that biases you towards simplicity and efficiency.

Common Intermediate Language (CIL) is .NET's machine language, and learning CIL will help you understand .NET high-level programming in exactly the same way that learning Intel assembler helps you understand Delphi programming. Learning CIL will give you a deeper understanding of managed code. Learning CIL will also shed some light on the differences between *reference types* and *value types* that I talked about in Chapter 2.

If you've got a boss who wanted results last month, you may want to skip the rest of this chapter. That's fine—you can get by in the .NET world without knowing CIL just as well as you can get by in the unmanaged code world without knowing assembler. However, if you do skip

---

3. Imagine that you compiled all the CIL in your application to native code, on your development machine (or on your team's build machine). You'd have a native code executable, something like a native Delphi executable. Your type-safe CIL would compile to type-safe native object code. The object code would check every cast at run time, and the object code wouldn't use any pointer arithmetic. But, even though this object code **would be** 100% type safe, you could never **prove** that. There could have been a high-level blind cast in the code—it wouldn't leave any trace in the object code. Verification is a compile-time operation: there's no way an after-compilation verifier can know that compiled object code includes a cast that's not being checked. Similarly, there is no way an automatic verifier can tell after compilation whether a bit of `pointer + offset` object code is type safe or whether it is actually referring to memory outside the object. Conversely, delivering CIL means final compilation and verification can be done on the users' machine.

this section, I urge you to come back later to read it. This section has the sort of type safety and verification details that are rather 'nice to know' even if they aren't exactly 'need to know.' You'll find these details easy to grasp, because CIL is easier to read and write than ordinary assembler. While you will rarely need to either write CIL or tweak generated code, reading CIL brings the same benefits to the author of high-level managed code that reading native assembler does to the author of high-level unmanaged code—you gain a deeper understanding of the whole system, and you write better code when you have a feel for how each high-level construct is implemented in CIL, and how that CIL in turn will typically be implemented on various target machines.

■Tip This section is not a comprehensive guide to CIL. I've tried to cover only the key concepts that an experienced programmer needs to make sense of CIL—just enough of the CIL programming model to understand disassemblies of your code in browsers like ILDASM or Reflector. (I show both of these code browsers, later in this chapter.)

Type-safe Assembler

Real machine languages aren't type safe

CIL is a high-level assembly language. It enforces type safety in a way that no real machine language does.[4] Real machines don't know what type of data is in their registers. A given value may be used arithmetically in one instruction and as a pointer in the next. In CIL, you cannot put a reference on the stack top and then add 5 to it. That is, you **can** write the code, but it will not compile to native code. You'll get a type safety exception at jit time.

When a high-level language like Delphi is compiled to native code, type safety exists only at compile time. The compiler is a bridge between symbolic code that refers to code and data by name, and real machines that know only about streams of bytes in registers or in numbered addresses. The compiler has a symbol table; for every symbol it knows both type and address. This is how it can know that, say, the expression Foo + 5 actually is trying to add a number to a string, and either disallow the operation or perform the appropriate conversions.

But the type information is lost along with the symbolic information when the compiler converts your high-level code to a sequence of low-level load/operate/store instructions. Once again, you can't verify native code.

What makes CIL a type-safe assembler is that it has 'machine sized' instructions like "Read a named member, and push the value to the stack top" or "Push a constant to the stack top." These abstract instructions are close to real machine instructions, so it is easy to compile CIL to native code. But all these instructions come in typed variants: there are different instructions to load an 8-bit signed constant than to load a 32-bit unsigned constant. There are different instructions to load a 32-bit signed integer value than to load a 32-bit object reference.

This is how type safety is deployed to every machine that runs your code. Verification can detect unsafe combinations of instructions like adding five to a reference.

---

4. Unless the machine language **is** a type-safe intermediate language, as with a Java chip or a (still hypothetical in early 2006) CIL chip.

CIL and the CLR

CIL is tightly linked to the CLR

CIL is similar to Java "byte codes," the binary representation of the typed assembly language that Java compiles to. Java byte codes are usually JIT compiled, just as CIL is, though Java byte codes may be interpreted in environments that can't spare the memory for jitted code. However, while there **are** compilers that translate various languages to Java byte codes, the JVM and Java byte codes were originally designed to run one language—Java—on multiple platforms. For example, since Java doesn't support reference parameters like var/ref and out parameters, it's hard to compile high-level code to Java byte codes if the high-level code does use reference parameters.

CIL, by contrast, was designed to run multiple languages on multiple platforms. So, CIL does support reference parameters, which can change the caller's value of a parameter. For that matter, CIL supports "tail recursion," which isn't needed in "imperative" languages like C# or Pascal.

All assembly languages reflect the machine they run on. Just as Java byte codes run on the Java Virtual Machine (JVM), so CIL runs on the Common Language Runtime (CLR). Thus, CIL is not just a type-safe assembler that's easy to translate to real object code. CIL is an object-oriented assembler with deep hooks into the CLR. While CIL instructions like *load*, *store*, or *add* will translate to a single instruction on most machines, CIL also contains high-level instructions that are typically implemented as calls to CLR subroutines. For example, CIL includes high-level instructions to create objects and to cast references from one type to another. Similarly, CIL also includes instructions to box and unbox values.

The important point here is that CIL is the interface between code that runs on .NET (library and application code) and the CLR machinery that runs it. It is not just shared metadata that allows C# library code to return objects to Delphi or Visual Basic application code; it is the fact that both use the same object layouts, and so can read and extend each other's objects. All languages use the same object layouts because all languages use the same newobj instruction to create objects.

Actual CIL

CIL has a stack architecture

CIL codes come in mnemonic form and in binary form, just like any other machine language. You see the mnemonic form when you use a tool like ILDASM, but that's just a representation, a transformation of the binary format CIL that is stored in a compiled assembly. There is an ILASM utility that will let you compile handwritten CIL,[5] but almost all CIL is written by compilers. High-level compilers compile to preparsed, binary form CIL, not to human-readable mnemonics.

---

5. I suspect few people will ever ILASM truly handwritten code. There are so many assertions to learn that it's foolhardy, really, not to get a "roundtrip" dump from a tool like ILDASM, tweak it, then ILASM the tweaks.

   Portable compilers, too, may use ILASM. A compiler back-end that writes assembly language to a text stream, and uses an existing assembler to produce the actual object file, only has to understand the CPU instruction set—it doesn't have to worry about hardware bit patterns and OS object file formats. Some compilers do use ILASM to generate their .NET assemblies.

Small compilers can take shortcuts like using the Emit namespace (Chapter 13) to build binary .NET assemblies, while production compilers like Delphi build binary assembly images by hand.

■**Note** I cite ILDASM because it comes with the .NET SDK, and so is thus authoritative and already installed on your machine. However, I highly recommend Lutz Roeder's *Reflector*, available at www.aisto.com/ roeder/dotnet. Reflector is a much more sophisticated browser than ILDASM—Reflector is wonderfully easy to use, and can show you a lot about your code. Reflector can decompile CIL into something that looks almost like the original C# or Delphi source, and you can easily jump from a method call to the method's code (and decompiled source).

High-level languages have a symbol table that includes type information. When you say Foo + 5, the compiler looks up "Foo" in the symbol table to know that Foo is (say) a string. A lot of symbolic information has been stripped from CIL. You create objects and call methods by name, but local variables and method parameters are referred to by a slot number, not by name. The declarations of parameters and of local variables specify only types, no names.[6]

When an instruction like ldloc 0 loads the contents of the first local variable onto the stack, you have loaded a value of a known type onto the top of stack. It might be a reference; it might be an integer or a floating point number; it might be an arbitrary size record. The jitter keeps track of the types of the values on the stack, and will not let you store, say, a reference value to an I4 location, nor will it let you add a number to a reference.

In Delphi native code, the compile-time symbol table includes entries for object and record fields. Each field entry includes name, type, and offset within the structure. When you refer to a field of an object, the compiler reads or writes the field with machine-friendly code that refers to the value of a pointer register plus an offset.

■**Tip** You can see this by setting a breakpoint and using the Ctrl+Alt+C (View ➤ Debug Windows ➤ CPU) window.

CIL does not let you refer to a structure's fields as offsets from the start of a data block. Not only would the pointer arithmetic be unverifiable, this would mean layout decisions were being made at the time of compilation to CIL, not at the time of jitting to native code. Late layout (at jit time) is superior to early layout (at compile time) because the jitter can use whatever padding strategy is best for its target architecture, and conversely because the jitter may be able to save space by packing byte fields together without losing speed.

So, how **does** CIL handle field access? By pushing symbol table information into the metadata, so that the ldfld and the stfld instructions consist of a 1-byte command token followed by a 4-byte metadata token. The high byte of a 32-bit metadata token specifies which table it's

---

6. You can add parameter name information, but this is strictly for the benefit of debuggers: CIL does not use parameter names.

an index into; the low 3 bytes specifies which of the 16 million possible entries it is. The field table contains an entry for every field of every object. When an assembly is loaded, each field entry just contains type information; the loading process assigns every field an actual, physical offset within its type, using whatever alignment strategy it thinks best. The jitter uses the actual offset to generate pretty much the same pointer register plus offset code as native Delphi compilers.

ILDASM shows a `ldfld` instruction as

```
ldfld int32 [MyAssembly] MyNamespace.MyClass::MyField
```

Obviously this is not a high-level language, but it should be pretty easy to see that this is specifying a particular member of a particular class in a particular namespace in a particular assembly. The type information (the `int32` in this example) is supplied by ILDASM as a courtesy; you don't need to specify it when you write CIL. The member's metadata includes the type information.

The `ldfld` and `stfld` instructions include field information, but not instance information. They pop an object reference off the top of the stack and read or write the specified field from that object. The `ldfld` instruction pushes the value it reads onto the stack, while the `stfld` instruction pops first the new value and then the object reference. This is asymmetric with `ldfld` (in that they are not each entered with an object reference on the stack top), but it means that field assignments are written as *push reference, push value, set field*. It seems to me that it's easier to interpret this sequence as *reference.field := value* than it would be to interpret *push value, push reference, set field* as *reference.field := value*.

■**Note** This is the general pattern of CIL instructions. There are no registers for instructions to specify as a source or destination. Instead, instructions operate in a defined way on the stack top. The jitter analyzes each method, and assigns available registers to local variables and intermediate results, much like the Delphi 7 compiler does.

Every instance method has a `Self` (this, in C#) reference as the implicit first parameter, argument number 0. Any explicit parameters start at argument number 1. Remember that static methods are not quite the same as Delphi's class methods. Delphi class methods get a meta-reference as their `Self` parameter, the class of the class used to call this method. Static methods do not get a meta-reference; their explicit parameters, if any, start at argument 0.

Thus, in an instance method, the `ldarg 0` instruction loads the instance reference, parameter number 0, onto the top of the stack. Now, many CIL instructions have short and long binary forms, just like many other machine languages. Short forms of CIL instructions save storage space, transfer time, and cache space. They may even jit faster. Thus, you won't often see `ldarg 0` in real code, as this is a 4-byte instruction. You're more likely to see the 1-byte form `ldarg.0` (note how this is dot 0, not space 0), or perhaps the 2-byte form, `ldarg.s 0` (dot s, space 0).

One way to think of the different instruction forms is as overloads. Some overloads supply default parameters for other, bulkier forms of the instruction. As previously, the `ldarg.0` (dot 0) overload takes only 1 byte, while the general form `ldarg 0` (space 0) takes 4 bytes. The two are equivalent in the sense that they both JIT to the same code, but compilers use the short form because it saves space and time.

Note Instruction size affects only CIL code size and jit speed. It should have no effect on the native code the jitter produces.

Expressions

No implicit type conversions

Local variables, method parameters, and object fields all have types. Constants and arithmetic or logical expressions have types, too. This is like Delphi and C#, so far. Of course, unlike Delphi and C#, CIL **is** a machine language, so a high-level expression like Foo + 5 becomes a sequence of simple instructions—load, load, add. However, the differences are substantial beyond even this structural difference. CIL has no notion of 'implicit type' and CIL does not support 'implicit conversion.' All constants must have a declared type, and you can only do arithmetic when both operands are the same type.

That is, in a native code Delphi, when you say thisInt32 := thatInt32 + 5, the compiler will *implicitly type* the constant 5 to match the variable thatInt32. It will automatically emit code to first load thatInt32 and then add the 32-bit constant 5. Conversely, when you say thisInt64 := thatInt64 + 5, the compiler will automatically emit code to load thatInt64 and then add the 64-bit constant 5.

CIL doesn't work that way. You can't code

```
ldarg.0                          // push Self parameter
ldfld int32 thisClass::thatField // Self.thatField replaces Self on stack
ldc 5                            // push 5 on top of thatField
add                              // replace stack top with sum of stack tops
```

You have to include the data type in the ldc instruction—in this case, either ldc.i4 5 or the shorthand ldc.i4.5.

Similarly, in Delphi you can write thisDouble := thisInt32. In Delphi you can do this *implicit conversion* because Delphi will automatically emit code to do the type conversions, to convert the thisInt32 32-bit integer value to a floating point double. Similarly, you can say thisInt64 := thisInt64 + thatInt32, because Delphi emits the code to convert the thatInt32 32-bit integer value to a 64-bit integer.

CIL doesn't do any implicit conversion. Yet, all binary operations require two values of the same type. You get an error if you try to add an int32 to an int64. You can convert the int32 to an int64, or the int64 to an int32, but you must be quite explicit about your conversions. You can convert to and from long and short values, signed and unsigned values, integer or floating point values, and with or without overflow—but, again, you must make all conversions explicitly.

For example, code like

```
ldc.i4.1    // push a 32-bit signed 1
ldc.i8.2    // push a 64-bit signed 1
add         // pop 2, push (cross-typed) sum
```

will generate an error, not the 64-bit value 3. To make this snippet work, you'd need to change it to

```
ldc.i4.1    // push a 32-bit signed 1
conv.i8     // convert to 64-bit signed
ldc.i8.2    // push a 64-bit signed 1
add         // pop 2, push 64-bit signed sum
```

The conv.i8 takes any value on the stack top and changes it to a 64-bit signed integer, if possible. Once the two values on the top of the stack are both 64-bit integers, the add operator can pop them both and push their 64-bit integer sum.

In safe code, the general rule is that all arithmetic operands must have the same type, and that will be the result type. (Note that this general rule also covers operations that have only one operand, like arithmetic negation: neg pops one value, and pushes a new value of the same type as its one argument.)

Note In unsafe code, you can also add and subtract 32-bit integers to and from pointers, and you can do arithmetic between "native" integers and 32-bit integers.

By default, arithmetic operations do not do overflow checking, and simply return the low order bits of their result. There are overloads, like add.ovf and mul.ovf, that will check the results and raise an exception on any overflow.

OPERATORS AND TYPES

You have perhaps noticed that the load and store instructions are all very explicitly typed, while we use the same add instruction for adding 1-byte integers as for adding 8-byte floats. Is it fair to say that CIL operators are untyped? Is there any possible loss of type safety here?

No. CIL operators don't carry explicit type tags the way, say, the ldc instructions do, because every value on the stack has a known type. The way the operator is implemented depends on the type of the value(s) on the stack top, and on whether they match.

This is heavily typed behavior. In fact, you can describe operators like add and or as if they were methods of the various types that can be on the stack. If a 4-byte single is on the top of the stack, the single.add 'method' looks at the next value on the stack. If the next value is not a single, single.add raises an exception; if the next value is a single, it knows how to add the two values.

Please do not think this metaphor is an interpretive system! To the extent that 'methods' like single.add or i8.or exist at all, they exist only in the jitter. (I am describing behavior, not describing an implementation.) When an add 'method' executes, it doesn't add a pair of numbers; it emits code that can add a pair of numbers of some particular format. All type checking is done at jit time, not at run time; type mismatch exceptions are raised at jit time, not at run time. (The native code the jitter builds is just as impossible to verify as the native code that a native code Delphi builds.)

Remember also that the whole CIL stack is a high-level construct. The jitter turns CIL stack code into the native code of registers and stack variables. Types leave no trace in CIL jitted to native code, just as types leave no trace in native compiled code.

Logical Operations

Simple branching instructions

Like other machine languages, CIL implements control structures in terms of branch-to-a-label, not in structured terms like if statements or for loops. However, the branch instructions are clean and high level compared to, say, the Intel architecture, which has arithmetic and logic instructions that may or may not set various flags, and branch instructions that rely on various combinations of flags.

CIL contains instructions like brfalse and brtrue, which branch or fall through depending on whether the value at the top of the stack is True or False, 1 or 0. As with the arithmetic and bitwise operators like add and or, the branch operators 'do the right thing' whether the value on the stack top is a 1-byte bool, any of several sizes of integer, or a reference. (For that matter, they do the right thing if the value on the stack top is of none of these types—they raise an exception at jit time.) False is zero or Nil; True is nonzero or non-Nil.

Since any nonzero integer is True, the brfalse and brtrue instructions can consume the result of an arithmetic sequence. This is branching based on a single value. When you need to branch based on two or more values, you have two options. You can use the *branch operators*, or you can use the *logical operators*. Branch operators pop two values off the stack, and branch if the first one pushed bears the right relationship to the second one pushed. Logical operators pop (one or) two values off the stack, and push a boolean result.

That is, a binary comparison pops two values off the stack, and compares the first value (the value that was put on the stack first, the value that is popped second) to the second value (the value that was put on the stack second, the value that is popped first). For example, the beq instruction branches if the first value is equal to the second value, while the blt instruction branches if the first value is less than the second value. There are also ble (branch less than or equal to), bge (branch greater than or equal to), and bgt (branch greater than) instructions, as well as unsigned versions of all these instructions. Interestingly, you can only bne.un (unsigned branch not equal)— there is no signed bne instruction.

Most boolean expressions are composed of terms linked with and and or (&& and ||) that can be *short-circuited* by branching straight to the equivalent of the else clause (or the next statement) after every term. However, some boolean expressions, like (Value = RadioMatch1) xor (Value = RadioMatch2) can't be short-circuited: you want to compute a true or false result for each explicit comparison clause, and then xor the two values. The ceq, clt, and cgt instructions are binary operators that pop two numbers and push a True or False result, an Int32 1 or an Int32 0 result. (You would also use these three instructions when you need to set a boolean variable.) The ceq instruction is an equality test; clt tests whether the first value is less than the second value, while cgt tests whether the first value is greater than the second.

■**Note** There are no <> (!=, in C#), <=, or >= instructions.

You can always be sure that a ceq, clt, or cgt instruction will generate 0 or 1, so that—just as in Delphi—a bitwise and, or, or xor is also a logical and, or, or xor.

Methods and Results

A new CIL stack for every call

Native Delphi compilers place each method's parameters and locals on the stack, at positive and negative offsets from a base pointer. While that's also pretty much what the jitter does on an Intel machine, CIL uses a higher-level, type-safe model.

To call a method, you push a reference to the object (if this is a normal, instance method, not a static method) followed by any parameters. You call the method, and on return the parameters you pushed are gone and the result (if any) is left on the top of the stack. From the standpoint of the calling method, a call looks a lot like any operator that consumes stack values and may push a result.

But the called method doesn't see the calling routine's stack, because each method gets its own stack. Methods don't access their parameters at some offset on the CIL stack from a base pointer.[7] CIL methods don't use the same instructions to access parameters as they use to access local variables, even though a jitter will probably implement a ldarg (load argument) in pretty much the same way as it implements a ldloc (load local).

Note The CIL stack is an abstraction. Stack underflow errors (e.g., calling add on an empty stack) cause a jitter exception; they can't affect the return address or the calling environment.

All methods terminate by calling the ret instruction. (The ret instruction may occur in more than one place within a routine.) A Delphi procedure returns nothing (like a C# void method) and should have no values on the stack when it calls ret. A Delphi function (or a C# method with a nonvoid return type) should have exactly one value on the stack—of the right type—whenever it calls ret. You can imagine the ret instruction popping the result from the bottom of the called method's stack (if the method returns a result); raising an exception if the stack isn't now empty; and pushing any result to the top of the calling method's stack.

ILDASM

See for yourself

The CIL programming model should be clear by now. The key abstraction is a strongly typed stack. This stack gets compiled to registers and stack locals at jit time, but CIL code pushes values on a stack and calls operators or methods, which leave any result on the stack. However, while the model is simple enough, most real CIL programming will need to use instructions that I haven't shown here.

---

7. In general, CIL contains no instructions that let you edit the stack. You can push and pop values, and you can dup the stack top, but you can't exchange the two values on the top of the stack. Nor is there any indexed access—you can't reach down and change the value 2 (or N) spaces below the top without saving and restoring all values on top of it.

When you run into a gap, a How Do I Do It? moment, your first impulse should be to write some code in Delphi for .NET or in C#, and use ILDASM (or, really, Reflector) to see what each line compiles to. If you see a CIL instruction you don't recognize, the .NET SDK includes ... adequate ... documentation on the CIL instruction set.[8] Like much Microsoft API documentation, it's a reference, not a tutorial: it's clear enough once you've read a lot of different pages several times each, but it can be slow going at first.

■**Tip** Each field of the OpCodes type corresponds to an instruction overload. So, the page for, say, OpCodes.Br_S contains both the ECMA description of the br.s instruction plus some clues as to how to supply the branch target when using the classes in the System.Reflection.Emit namespace.

There are a few things you might find puzzling about ILDASM, so I'll walk you through the unassembly of a couple of methods. Those of you wanting more background on more instructions will find some of that in these two walkthroughs.

The sample code in this section is in C#. I do this for several reasons. First, the C# code is considerably shorter than the equivalent Delphi code, and each page of each copy of this book has an economic and environmental cost. Beyond printing costs, I think you'll agree that this C# code is just as type-safe (and as clear about the author's intentions for each field and each method) as the equivalent Delphi source would be. What's more, I think you'll find the methods of the C# are just as easy to read as the equivalent Delphi source would be. (Part 2 has a Delphi programmer's high-speed introduction to C#.)

The code here interleaved with the text (Chapter4\testClass.cs) is rather pointless and contrived, but it does show basic structure and a few key constructs.

```
using System;
```

The C# using clause lists namespaces, not units, but this isn't too different from Delphi's uses statement. One difference is that C# using statements do not take a comma-separated list of namespaces. Another difference is that C# doesn't implicitly use the System **namespace** the way that Delphi code implicitly uses the System **unit**.

```
namespace testLibrary
{
  public class testClass
  {
```

As per Chapter 2, the namespace testLibrary declaration is a lot like unit testLibrary, except that more than one file can go to make up a namespace. Also, a single file may contain code for more than one namespace. The namespace syntax is just like that for a class; everything within the matching braces after the namespace name is in the namespace. In this case, so far the testLibrary namespace contains only the still incomplete testClass.

---

8. In addition, Reflector shows a quick summary of each CIL instruction in a mouseover tool-tip box.

```
private int aField = 0;

public void Set(int Value)
{
    aField = Value;
}
```

aField is an integer field, initialized to 0, accessible only to methods of the testClass.[9] The public Set method sets aField to Value, as a property setter would. The Set method returns nothing, or void—in Delphi, it would be called a procedure.

The Conditional method is a bit more complicated:

```
public int Conditional(object O)
{
    Array asArray = O as Array;
```

The Conditional method takes an object parameter and returns an integer. In Delphi, it would be called a function. Array asArray = O as Array declares a local variable, asArray, of the Array type, and initializes it to the result of the conditional cast O as Array. The conditional cast returns a non-Nil reference only if O is an Array object: it returns a Nil (null, in C#) reference if O is Nil or not an Array.

```
    if (asArray != null)
        aField = asArray.Length;
    return aField;
    } // Conditional
  } // testClass
} // testLibrary
```

If the object parameter O really is an Array, set aField to the array length. Finally, always return the current value of aField, which may or may not have just been changed.

ILDASM of the Set Method

The Set method—public void Set(int Value) { aField = Value; }—simply changes one field. This takes three CIL instructions, plus the method ret instruction.

If you view Chapter4\testLibrary.dll with the ILDASM utility in the .NET SDK Bin directory, you'll get something that looks like Figure 4-1. If you double-click the Set method, you'll get a disassembly window, as in Figure 4-2.

---

9. No, it's **not** also available to every method of every other class in the same file. That has always been a mistake in Delphi.

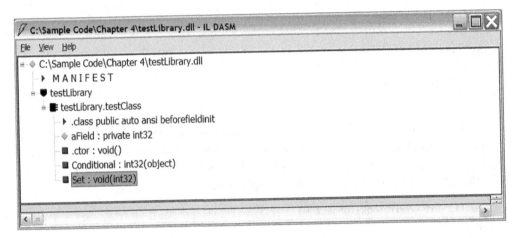

Figure 4-1. *ILDASM view of testLibrary.dll*

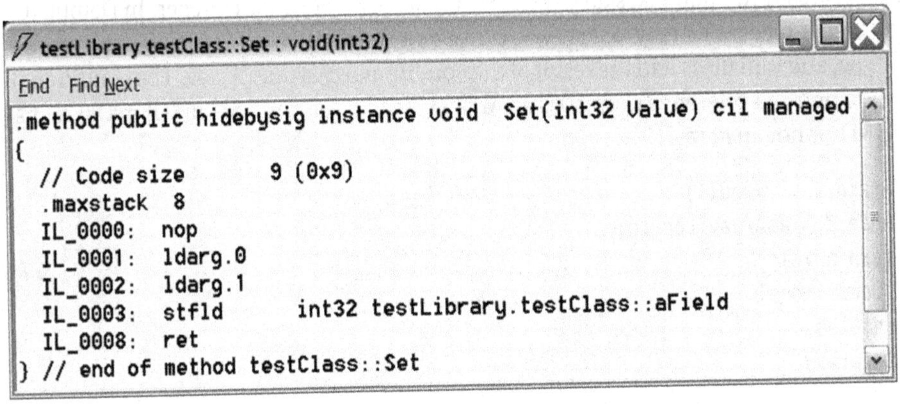

```
 testLibrary.testClass::Set : void(int32)                          _ □ X
Find   Find Next
.method public hidebysig instance void  Set(int32 Value) cil managed
{
  // Code size       9 (0x9)
  .maxstack  8
  IL_0000:  nop
  IL_0001:  ldarg.0
  IL_0002:  ldarg.1
  IL_0003:  stfld       int32 testLibrary.testClass::aField
  IL_0008:  ret
} // end of method testClass::Set
```

Figure 4-2. *Disassembly of testClass.Set*

Taking this line by line,

```
.method public hidebysig instance void  Set(int32 Value) cil managed
```

This is a public method named Set. It is a normal, instance method, that gets a this (Self, in Delphi) reference as the first, implicit parameter, and so can read and write instance fields. It has an explicit int32 parameter named Value,[10] and returns no result. hidebysig means that this method should shadow any ancestral method named Set with the same prototype, just like in Delphi or C#. cil managed means just what it says: managed code, written in CIL; don't worry about what the alternatives might be. (You'd pretty much only see something besides cil managed if looking at Managed C++ assemblies, which mix managed and unmanaged code, CIL code and native code.)

---

10. The actual prototype for this method has no parameter name information; ILDASM gets the parameter name from the debug metadata.

{

CIL has a syntax modeled loosely on C#: methods within brackets, comments from // to the end of the line.

```
// Code size       8 (0x8)
```

This is just a comment that ILDASM puts in, saying the CIL takes 8 bytes. You wouldn't need to supply a correct value, here, if you were writing CIL for the ILASM assembler.

```
.maxstack  2
```

Every method must have a `.maxstack` declaration. If any path through the method ever uses more stack 'slots,' the jitter raises an exception. Compilers track stack use as they generate code, as do the classes in the `Emit` namespace: you only need to calculate `.maxstack` by hand when you use ILASM.

```
IL_0000:  ldarg.0
```

The `this` (`Self`) reference. It's up to you to remember that this is the instance reference; ILDASM doesn't do anything sensible like show this as `ldarg.0 // this`.

■Note Remember, when you set a field of an object instance, you always put the instance reference on the stack first, before the field value.

```
IL_0001:  ldarg.1
```

The first formal parameter, the `int Value`. Again, you have to keep track of which parameter has which number; ILDASM misses its chance to annotate this as `ldarg.1 // Value`.

```
IL_0002:  stfld       int32 testLibrary.testClass::aField
```

The first value on the stack is a reference (`ldarg.0`); set the object's `aField` field to the second value (`ldarg.1`). These three instructions implement `this.aField = Value`.

```
IL_0007:  ret
```

Return, with an empty stack.

```
} // end of method testClass::Set
```

The closing `}`. Remember, the `ret` instruction can occur in more than one place. The comment here is another ILDASM flourish; you do not need to supply it to ILASM.

ILDASM of the Conditional Method

The `Set` method was pretty simple, the sort of code that Delphi for .NET generates for a `write fieldVar` property setter. Its one line of code compiled to three CIL instructions, plus the `ret` instruction. The four lines of the `Conditional` method are a bit more complicated, but they still only compile to eleven CIL instructions, plus the `ret` instruction (see Figures 4-3 and 4-4 and Listing 4-1).

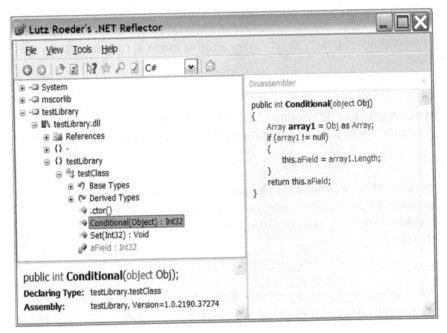

Figure 4-3. *Reflector, showing the* Conditional *method in C# view*

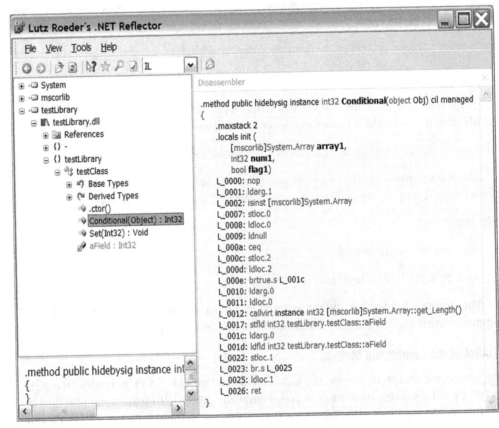

Figure 4-4. *Reflector, showing the* Conditional *method in CIL view*

Listing 4-1. *The C# Source to the* Conditional *Method*

```
public int Conditional(object Obj)
{
  Array asArray = Obj as Array;
  if (asArray != null)
    aField = asArray.Length;
  return aField;
}
```

The code is pretty pointless, but it does illustrate both casting and branching, as well as how the difference between a Delphi-style procedure and function maps to CIL. In what follows, I skip boilerplate and focus on content.[11]

```
method public hidebysig instance int32  Conditional(object 0) cil managed
```

Where the Set method returned void (i.e., no result), the Conditional method returns an int32. In Delphi terms, Set is a *procedure* while Conditional is a *function*, but they're both just methods to C# and CIL.

```
.locals init (class [mscorlib]System.Array V_0)
```

This declares a single local variable, a System.Array from the mscorlib assembly. You'll notice that the name this had in Listing 4-1 (asArray) has been lost. That V_0 isn't really a name, it's just ILDASM's way of showing you that this is local 0. In typical ILDASM fashion, it never uses the V_0 'name' again.

```
IL_0000:  ldarg.1
```

This loads the first explicit parameter (the this reference is parameter 0), the object 0 reference.

```
IL_0001:  isinst     [mscorlib]System.Array
```

The isinst instruction pops the reference on the stack top, and replaces it with either null/Nil or a valid reference to a System.Array.

```
IL_0006:  stloc.0
```

Whatever the value, store it in the local variable.

```
IL_0007:  ldloc.0
```

Reload the local variable, asArray. **Don't worry** about a store followed by a load of the same data—the jitter will optimize this away.

```
IL_0008:  brfalse.s  IL_0016
```

---

11. The CIL code I show is what a particularly old VS .NET (v 7.0.9466) generated in "Release" mode. (As you can see, it's not identical with the 2.0 libraries in Figures 4-3 and 4-4, but the differences are trivial.) The "Debug" mode is longer and harder to read.

Remember, a null/Nil reference is a False value. brfalse.s is a short, 2-byte branch instruction, which can add a 1-byte signed offset (-128 to 127) to the 'instruction pointer' if the stack top is False. CIL instructions are variable length; all branches are in terms of CIL bytes, not instructions.

```
IL_000a:  ldarg.0
IL_000b:  ldloc.0
IL_000c:  callvirt   instance int32 [mscorlib]System.Array::get_Length()
IL_0011:  stfld      int32 testLibrary.testClass::aField
```

This is the code that gets executed if (asArray != null). First, load the this reference. Second, load the asArray reference. Then, callvirt Array.get_Length() to replace the second value (the asArray reference) with asArray.Length. Finally, set the instance field.

■**Note** CIL distinguishes between call and callvirt. As it happens, Array.get_Length is **not** virtual. Why, then, does C# use callvirt to call the nonvirtual Array.get_Length? Using callvirt touches the this parameter in the calling code, raising an exception at the point of call on an unassigned this parameter, rather than at some time later when an instance method refers to an instance field. (When an instance method does an in-class call to another nonvirtual instance, it will use call, not callvirt, as the this parameter is already known to be non-null.) Obviously enough, if Array.get_Length **was** virtual, callvirt would do a normal, polymorphic call to get_Length. Then if the parameter 0 were actually an Array descendant with its own virtual implementation of get_Length, callvirt would call the descendant method. By contrast, the call instruction allows you to specify a particular class's implementation of get_Length.

```
IL_0016:  ldarg.0
IL_0017:  ldfld      int32 testLibrary.testClass::aField
IL_001c:  ret
```

Whether asArray is set or not, return aField.

You should now know enough to pose and answer your own questions about how CIL works. Writing snippets of Delphi or C# code and examining them with ILDASM or Reflector can tell you more than hours spent pouring through the Microsoft documentation.

Key Points

Managed code isn't much slower than unmanaged code

- .NET is not interpreted; it uses Just In Time (JIT) compilation.

- JIT compilation is relatively cheap.

- .NET's JIT compilation actually produces somewhat better object code than native code Delphi.

- JIT compilation is a low price to pay for the productivity and portability benefits of managed code.

- Learning CIL adds to your understanding of managed code.

- CIL is easier to read than real assembler, because the branching instructions refer to values on a stack, not to arcane combinations of flag bits.

- CIL is easier to write than real assembler, because CIL describes a high-level, strongly typed, stack machine with no registers.

PART 2

■■■

C# and Delphi

Like Delphi, C# is an object-oriented language that avoids some of the more esoteric complexities of C++. That is, C# is more like Delphi than C++ is, and it's even easier to move between Delphi and C# than it is to move between Delphi and C++. The C# chapters are more a cross-reference than a tutorial: when a C# feature is exactly like its Delphi counterpart, I say so and move on; when a C# feature differs in important ways from its Delphi counterpart, I detail the differences; and when a C# feature is new to Delphi programmers (as with various 2.0 features), I cover both the purpose and the details.

Chapter 5 explains the differences between C# and Delphi expression syntax, and goes into some detail about 2.0's *nullable types* and the C# operators like ++, --, ?:, and ?? that Delphi doesn't have. Chapter 6 briefly surveys the structured programming constructs that are basically identical in Delphi and C#; gives more space to the differences between the Delphi case statement and the C# switch statement; and goes into some detail on the using and lock statements. Chapter 7 skims basic object syntax, while giving some space to the various field modifiers—and detailing the syntax and semantics of both generics and operator overloading. Chapter 8 covers the syntax of delegates and interfaces, but the bulk of the chapter is concerned with event semantics, anonymous methods, and asynchronous delegate invocation. Chapter 9 is where I cover everything that didn't fit anywhere else: namespaces and the using directive; attributes; the @ escape; preprocessor directives; and partial classes. Chapter 10 is a quick summary of changes to Delphi syntax since Delphi 7.

I urge you to read Chapters 5 through 9. While Delphi and C# are similar enough that you can pick up basic C# from IDE help files and compiler error messages, there *are* subtleties that will take you a while to pick up that way. If you only need a reading knowledge of C# (because you plan to program in Delphi for .NET), you should read at least the event and asynchronous sections of Chapter 8, and the attributes section of Chapter 9—they are not repeated in Chapter 10.

CHAPTER 5

■ ■ ■

C# Primitive Types

*C# uses type-first declaration (with an optional initializer) for fields and variables. C#
supports all CLR System types; the built-in primitive types are aliases for CLR types. C# has
more operators than Delphi, as well as different operator precedence and different
expression typing rules. Arrays and enums have different syntax and semantics than in
Delphi. In 2.0, nullable types add an optional "unset" state to any value type.*

Types and Expressions

Strikingly different syntax than Delphi

Perhaps the most fundamental difference between a Pascal-based language like Delphi and a
C-based language like C# is that Pascal uses **French** adjective order and C uses **English** adjective
order. That is, where Delphi code declares an integer field or integer variable as `ThisInt: integer`,
C# declares the same integer field or integer variable as `int ThisInt`. This difference between
type-first and type-last can be jarring when you first start reading or writing C# after years of
Delphi, and it can be jarring every time you switch from one language to the other, but I find
that keeping the French/English analogy in mind helps minimize the pain: neither order is
logically superior, nor is either order intrinsically better fitted to human cognition.

■**Tip** It's worth learning to love C# like you love Delphi. C# is like Delphi in all the ways that matter. There's
more C# work than Delphi work. And the C# compiler will always be several large steps ahead of the Delphi
compiler.

You can declare a number of fields or variables of the same type in a single statement, by
separating the names with commas. This is much like Delphi. Thus,

```
int This, That; // Possible to lose track of what's going on with long lists
```

is functionally equivalent to

```
int This; // Bulky but clear
int That;
```

but the latter, bulkier, form is probably a bit easier to read, especially with long lists of variables.

Unlike in Delphi, you can initialize both local and global variable declarations. Thus you can say either

```
int Query, Response;
Query = 1226; // C# uses = for assignment
Response = 1958;
```

or just

```
int Query = 1226, Response = 1958;
```

Note C# uses = for assignment, not : =.

You get a compile-time error if you use an unitialized variable. While the compiler doesn't demand it, in practice most C# variable declarations **do** include an initialization.

Aliases for System Types

CLR types are C# native types

In some sense, C# doesn't have any primitive types of its own: while it has keywords for primitive data types, these are simply *aliases* for CLR types like System.Int32. Unlike both Delphi and Visual Basic, C# has keyword aliases for **all** CLR numeric types (see Table 5-1).

Note that while keywords like int and long **are** keywords—you cannot have types or members named int or long, and the IDE's syntax highlighting colors them just like any other keyword— they are also syntactically identical to their System aliases like System.Int32 and System.Int64. For example, System.Decimal.MaxValue is absolutely equivalent to decimal.MaxValue.

Table 5-1. *System Types*

C# Type	CLR Type	Description	Sample Value	CLS Compliant	Native Delphi Equivalent
bool	System.Boolean	8-bit boolean	true	Yes	boolean
byte	System.Byte	Unsigned 8-bit	222	Yes	byte
char	System.Char	16-bit character	'x'	Yes	WideChar
decimal	System.Decimal	128-bit software float	12.99m	Yes	None
double	System.Double	64-bit hardware float	13.45	Yes	double
float	System.Single	32-bit hardware float	12.26f	Yes	single
int	System.Int32	32-bit signed integer	-1234	Yes	integer

Table 5-1. *System Types*

C# Type	CLR Type	Description	Sample Value	CLS Compliant	Native Delphi Equivalent
long	System.Int64	64-bit signed integer	-1234L	No	Int64
sbyte	System.SByte	Signed 8-bit	-10	No	ShortInt
short	System.Int16	16-bit signed integer	32767	Yes	SmallInt
uint	System.UInt32	32-bit unsigned integer	1234U	No	cardinal
ulong	System.UInt64	64-bit unsigned integer	123UL	No	UInt64
ushort	System.UInt16	32-bit unsigned integer	32768	No	word

Numeric Literals

Hexadecimal prefix, and type suffixes

Hexadecimal literals are prefixed with 0x, not $ as in Delphi. Though C# is case sensitive, hex literals may use uppercase or lowercase letters A through F. Thus, 0xDeadBeef, 0xCafeBabe, and 0x12261958 are all valid 32-bit values.

By default, any integral literal between int.MinValue and int.MaxValue is typed as an int. Constants out of the 32-bit signed integer range are typed as uint if they fit, then long, and then ulong. This does not cause problems with code like byte B = 5 because integer literals (but not integer **expressions**) are implicitly narrowed on assignment.

There are times when this default numeric typing is not what you want. For example, you might want to add a long literal 5 to an int value to force the calculation to be done as a 64-bit operation instead of a 32-bit operation. You could do this by casting the 5 to a long (see "Numeric Expressions," the next subsection), but C# also supports a set of numeric suffixes that allow you to specify the type of a numeric literal.

- Adding u or U (without any white space between the last digit and the suffix) to a value in the int range turns it into an uint. For example, 32767u.

- The suffix u or U turns a long into a ulong. For example, 3000000000u.

- The suffix l or L turns an int into a long. For example, 1L. Note that using the l suffix will generate a warning that l and 1 are easily confused; that you should use L instead of l.

- The suffix ul or LU (or any of the case permutations like uL and Lu) will generate a ulong. For example, 123ul.

While Delphi will compile a literal like "1." and C# will make you say "1.0", for the most part the two compilers treat floating point literals pretty much the same. Just about all Delphi floating point literals are valid C# floating point literals, and (except for suffixes) just about all C# floating point literals are also valid Delphi floating point literals.

By default, **all** floating point literals are typed as double. Thus, float F = 123.45 will not compile; you have to force the literal to be a 32-bit float with float F = 123.45f.[1] The m or M ("money") specifies a decimal literal, while the d or D suffix specifies a double literal.

You might use the d suffix in code like ThisDouble = ThatInt * 10d. While ThisDouble = ThatInt * 10 will compile, this does integer multiplication and then converts the result on assignment (see "Operators," the next section of this chapter) while ThatInt * 10d converts ThatInt to a double and then does floating point multiplication.

Numeric Expressions

Subtly different from Delphi

In Delphi, the type of a numerical expression like A + B is the type of the "wider" of A or B; the "narrower" of the two operands will be implicitly widened. Similarly, when you assign a wide result to a narrow variable (e.g., IntVar := ThisInt64 + ThatInt64), the result will be automatically narrowed, and optionally checked for overflow.

C# also automatically widens operands, but does not do any implicit narrowing of expression results on assignment. You can say ThisInt = ThatInt + ThisByte but not ThisByte = ThisInt + ThatByte.

To assign a wide result to a narrow destination, you have to explicitly narrow the result, by *casting* it to the desired type. In C#, casting numeric types is done as (type) value, not type(value), as in Delphi.[2] Casting has higher precedence than most operators (see the "Operator Precedence" subsection, later in this chapter) so ThisByte = (byte) ThisInt + ThatByte evaluates as ThisByte = ((byte) ThisInt) + ThatByte. To narrow an expression result, you have to put the expression in parentheses, like ThisByte = (byte) (ThisInt + ThatByte).

■**Caution** Arithmetic expressions have a type of int unless one of the operands forces a **wider** width. For example, the result of an operation on a pair of bytes is an int, not a byte as in Delphi. Thus, ByteA = ByteB + ByteC will not compile; you have to use ByteA = (byte) (ByteB + ByteC).

Note that casts from float types to integer types round towards 0. (For example, (int) 1.9 == 1 and (int) -1.9 == -1.) You can use static functions of the System.Math class to do other conversions.

Whether or not a narrowing cast can raise an overflow exception depends on whether the code is in the *checked* or *unchecked* state. The default state is unchecked but, as in Delphi, this can be overridden globally via the /checked compiler switch (or, more typically, an IDE check box). Within a code file, the checked and unchecked keywords allow you to tell the compiler that certain parts of the code should always be checked or should always be unchecked. A checked

---

1. You could also use (float) 123.45, but this is—at least in principle—casting a double to a float. It's at least theoretically possible that casting a double constant could give a (very!) slightly different value than using the f suffix.

2. There is also an expression as type cast (which returns null on miscast, instead of raising an exception), but this is only valid for reference types. Numbers are value types.

arithmetic or cast operation raises an exception when the result won't fit into the result's type, while the result of an unchecked operation returning an out-of-band value depends on the type:

- Unchecked integer operations yield the low bits of the result. For example, unchecked(uint.MaxValue + 1) equals the 32-bit unsigned integer, 0.

- Unchecked floating point overflow gives positive or negative infinity. This includes casts to the 4-byte float type from a double with an absolute value greater than float.MaxValue.

- Unchecked floating point underflow gives 0. This includes casts to the 4-byte float type of very small double values.

- Unchecked casts from float types to integer types gives "unspecified" values when the float value is out of the integer range. Note that an assignment **does** take place—but you can't count on the value, and should think of the result as an uninitialized variable.

The checked and unchecked keywords can be applied to either an *expression*, as checked (expression), or a whole *block*, as checked {statements}. The expression form gives you fine-tuned control over just what checking is done:

```
ThisInt = (int) checked (ThisLong + ThatLong);   // checked +, unchecked cast
ThisInt = checked ((int) (ThisLong + ThatLong)); // both + and cast are checked
```

The block form can be used anywhere within a method body that you can use a compound statement. That is, you can write code like if (test) unchecked {actions;} (Chapter 6), but you cannot put checked or unchecked between a method's prototype and its body.

Operators

More punctuation than Delphi

C# has all the operators that Delphi does, but it **is** a different language, and there are several major differences. First, C# treats assignment as an operator that has a value. Second, C# supports operators that Delphi does not: the ?: *conditional* (or *ternary*) operator; the ++ and -- *increment* and *decrement* operators; and the new ?? *null coalescing* (or *default*) operator. And third, precedence is more complex in C# than in Delphi.

Most basically, some things are just plain **different**: C# uses a lot of punctuation where Delphi uses English words like and and or. Plus, C# separates some operators that Delphi merges and vice versa: where Delphi uses div for integer division and / for floating point division, C# uses / for both; where C# uses & for bitwise *and* and && for logical (short-circuit) *and*, Delphi uses and for both. Table 5-2 summarizes the **differences** in appearance or semantics: it doesn't list operators like + and – that are the same in both languages, nor does it list the operators that C# introduces to Delphi programmers.

Table 5-2. *C# Operators That Are Different Than Delphi Operators*

Operator	C#	Delphi	Comments
Assignment	=	:=	In C#, assignment **is** an operator, and it has a value.
Bitwise *and*	&	and	Bitwise *and* is distinct from logical (short-circuit) *and*.
Bitwise complement	~	not	~ is actually used in formal (academic) logic.
Bitwise *or*	|	or	Bitwise *or* is distinct from logical (short-circuit) *or*.
Bitwise *xor*	^	xor	This is just plain weird, but you get used to it.
Conditional *and*	&&	and	There is no pragma to disable short-circuit behavior.
Conditional *or*	||	or	There is no pragma to disable short-circuit behavior.
Equals	==	=	Easy to type = where you mean == and vice versa, but the compiler will warn you about most mistakes.
Integer division	/	div	C# uses / for both integer and floating point division.
Left cast	`(Type) value`	`Type(value)`	Raises exception on invalid cast. Looks more like a Delphi left cast; acts like a Delphi right cast.
Logical negation	!	not	Logical negation is distinct from bitwise complement.
Not equals	!=	<>	Makes at least as much sense as <> ...
Remainder	%	mod	% is obviously related to /.
Right cast	`value as Type`	`value as Type`	Returns null on invalid cast—does **not** raise an exception. Looks just like a Delphi right cast, but acts like a Delphi (for .NET) left cast.
Shift left	<<	shl	Bits shifted out are discarded; << never overflows.
Shift right	>>	shr	Unlike Delphi, does an arithmetic shift on signed values.

"Left cast" and "right cast" are not standard notation, but I think it's clear enough what they mean—a left cast has the type to the left of the value, while a right cast has the type to the right of the value, after an as keyword.

Assignment Operators

Assignment has a value

Aside from the obvious fact that Delphi uses := for assignment where C# uses = for assignment, there are two key differences between assignment in Delphi and C#. First, in C#, assignment is an operator like any other, and you can write code like

```
TopLeft.Left = LeftSide.Left = BottomRight.Left = ClipRect.Left + Inset;
```

that sets three properties to the same value in a single statement. This is very simple and clean; the single statement *communicates intent* better than the equivalent code split into three or four statements.

Note Where most operators are *left associative*, meaning they are evaluated left to right, the assignment operators are *right associative*, and are evaluated right to left. That is, where A + B + C is evaluated as (A + B) + C, an inline assignment statement like A = B = C + D is evaluated as A = (B = (C + D)).

You can also write code like A = (B = C + D) + E—but clearly this can get very confusing, very quickly. As a rule of thumb, avoid any use of inline assignment more complicated than setting several variables to the same value.

The second key difference between assignment in Delphi and C# is that C# supports C's op= operators, where op can be any binary operator like + or - or /. A statement like Left op= Right is almost equivalent to Left = Left op Right. The left side can be a local variable, a record or object field, an array element, or a property. For example, Flag ^= true toggles a Boolean Flag, and Counts[Row, Column] += ThisCount adds ThisCount to a particular position in the two-dimensional Counts array.

Note that I say "almost equivalent" because the op= operators are **not** macros. Any calculations on the left side (like method calls or array indexing) are only done **once**. Code like Complex.Reference.Expression.Property += SomeValue will

1. Evaluate the complex reference expression.

2. Save the final reference in a temporary location (typically using the CIL dup instruction).

3. Call the get_Property method.

4. Do the addition.

5. Call the set_Property method.

The Conditional Operator

Adds clarity, when used carefully

The conditional (or *ternary*) operator has three operands: `first ? second : third`. If the `first` expression is `true`, the conditional operator evaluates and returns the `second` expression; otherwise it evaluates and returns the `third` expression. This is something like an `if` statement that can return a value.

■**Tip** The conditional operator has very low precedence, so you only **have** to put parentheses around any of the three operands if they include an inline assignment, like `A < B ? (C = D) : E`—but it certainly won't hurt if you do. For example, `(A < B) ? C : D` executes exactly the same as `A < B ? C : D`.

In some cases, the conditional operator can make your code smaller and clearer. Code like `Complex.Reference.Expression.Property = A < B ? A : B` evaluates the complex reference expression and sets the final reference's `Property` to the lesser of A or B. By contrast,

```
if (A < B)
    Complex.Reference.Expression.Property = A;
else
    Complex.Reference.Expression.Property = B;
```

is equivalent, but you have to read both branches to see that—and if you should ever need to change the `Complex.Reference.Expression`, you have to be sure to change both copies. Using the conditional operator communicates the intent to—and makes it easier to—always change `Complex.Reference.Expression.Property`.

In general, the longer the expression between the `?` and the `:`, the harder it is to read the code. You can maximize readability by formatting your code like

```
LeftSide = Test
    ? long.expression.evaluated.if.Test.succeeds
    : alternate.long.expression.evaluated.if.Test.fails;
```

but, as a rule of thumb, you should only use the conditional operator when you are choosing between two simple values.

The Null Coalescing Operator

Supplies a default value for unset values

As in Chapter 2, C# 2.0 adds a new `??`, or null coalescing operator. The `??` operator has a right-side default expression, which is only evaluated if the left side evaluates to `null`. You can think of `Value ?? Default` as a shortcut for `Value != null ? Value : Default`. That is, `Value ?? Default` equals `Value` (and `Default` is not evaluated) if `Value != null`, while `Default` is evaluated and `Value ?? Default` equals `Default` if `Value` does equal `null`.

The null coalescing operator is right associative, like assignment. That is, One ?? Two ?? Three is evaluated as One ?? (Two ?? Three).

The Increment and Decrement Operators

Convenient, but can be hard to read

You may recognize the assignment and ternary operators from C. C# also supports C's ++ and -- operators. These can appear to the right or left of a variable, field, or property—which I'll refer to as a *location*.

When ++ or -- appears to the right of a location, as in Location++ and Location--, they are referred to as *postincrement* and *postdecrement* operators. Location is incremented or decremented, but the value of the operation is the initial value of Location—the location is changed **after** the operator is evaluated.

When ++ or -- appears to the left of a location, as in ++Location and --Location, they are referred to as *preincrement* and *predecrement* operators. Location is incremented or decremented, and the value of the operation is the new value of Location—the location is changed **before** the operator is evaluated.

For example, in a stack class, we have the *push* operation

```
Data[Top++] = Value; // push
```

and the *pop* operation

```
return Data[--Top]; // pop (Chapter 7 covers the "return" keyword)
```

■**Tip** Notice how carefully you have to read these two snippets to see that Top is the next-write pointer, not the last-write (or next-read) pointer. (Conversely, note how the mirroring [that is, Top++ and --Top] gives you a quick visual indication that these are complementary actions.)

You can use the ++ and -- operators to increment and decrement any number (including floating point numbers) by 1. When used with pointers, in unsafe code, they increment and decrement the pointer by one element; that is, if a pointer was pointing to the first element in an array, after incrementing it with ++ it would point to the second element in the array.

Postincrement and postdecrement operators are particularly useful in loops, where they may be able to turn a block containing two or three statements into a single statement—but use them sparingly: while code like for (int I = 0; I < 10; I++) {} (Chapter 6) that just uses ++ to change the loop control variable is pretty innocuous, any code that actually **uses** the value of a ++ or -- operator (that is, where it matters what side the ++ or -- is on) has to be read very carefully.

Operator Precedence

15 levels of precedence!

As in C and C++, operator precedence is very complicated in C#. There are 15 levels of precedence (see Table 5-3) in C# 2.0! This strikes me as unnecessarily complicated—why, for example, don't & and | and ^ all have the same precedence? and how many people will remember that & (bitwise *and*) takes precedence over ^ (bitwise *xor*), which takes precedence over | (bitwise *or*)?—but you can, as always, just use parentheses when in any doubt.

Also, do note that despite the proliferation of precedence levels, overall the precedence scheme is pretty simple: expressions have higher precedence than comparisons, which have higher precedence than shortcut ops (like &&, ||, ?:, and ??), which in turn have higher precedence than assignment. The precedence rules work, and you rarely **have** to use parens to make your code do what you expect it to. For example, because C# separates conditional && from bitwise &, you can write code like

```
bool InRange = Value >= LowLimit && Value <= HighLimit;
```

You don't have to use extra parens, the way you do in Pascal, to make code like
`InRange := (Value >= LowLimit) and (Value <= HighLimit)` compile.

Table 5-3. *Operator Precedence*

Category	Operators	Notes
Primary	x.y f(x) a[x] x++ x-- new typeof checked unchecked	
Unary	+ - ! ~ ++x --x (Type)x	Unary minus is -A, not A - B
Multiplicative	* / %	
Additive	+ -	
Shift	<< >>	
Relational and type testing	< <= >= > is as	Tests are lower precedence than arithmetic
Equality	== !=	
Bitwise *and*	&	
Bitwise *xor*	^	
Bitwise *or*	|	
Conditional *and*	&&	All tests have higher precedence than && and ||
Conditional *or*	||	
Null coalescing / default	??	(2.0 and up) No need to put parens around a ?? in a ?:
Conditional	?:	Very low precedence— almost never needs parens
Assignment	= *= /= %= += -= <<= >>= &= ^= |=	

C# supports operator overloading (Chapter 7); user-defined operators have the same precedence as the operators they overload.

Note C# also supports C's * operator for declaring and using pointers, as well as the & address operator. These are only valid within unsafe code, which I talk about in Appendix 0.

Strings and Characters

Different quotes for strings and characters

Where Delphi uses single quotes for both strings and characters, so that a single element string looks just the same as a single character, C# uses single quotes for characters and double quotes for strings.

Both string and character literals use the same four slightly different escape mechanisms for characters that you can't see on the screen and for characters that may not be on your keyboard. The first (*symbolic*) escape mechanism (see Table 5-4) supports a small set of traditional ASCII control characters plus the \\, \', and \" sequences you need to specify actual \, ', and " characters in string and character constants.

Table 5-4. *Symbolic Character Escapes*

Escape Sequence	Character Name	ASCII Control Character	Unicode Equivalent
\'	Single quote		0x0027
\"	Double quote		0x0022
\\	Backslash		0x005C
\0	Null	^@	0x0000
\a	Alert	^G	0x0007
\b	Backspace	^H	0x0008
\f	Form feed	^L	0x000C
\n	New line (line feed)	^J	0x000A
\r	Carriage return	^M	0x000D
\t	Horizontal tab	^I	0x0009
\v	Vertical tab	^K	0x000B

You can also use one of three hexadecimal escape mechanisms (listed in Table 5-5) to specify any of the preceding characters, as well as any characters that are not on your keyboard.

Table 5-5. *Hexadecimal Character Escapes*

Description	Encoding	Notes
Hexadecimal	\x1234	\x followed by 1 to 4 hex digits
16-bit Unicode	\u1234	\u followed by 4 hex digits
32-bit Unicode	\U00001234	\U followed by 8 hex digits

Although there is a 32-bit Unicode escape, \U, code points above 0x10FFFF are not supported, and code points from 0x10000 to 0x10FFFF must be manually encoded in UTF-16 (i.e., a pair of 16-bit characters).

Character literals include keyboard characters in single quotes, or any of the preceding escape mechanisms, also in single quotes. Thus, 'a', '\n', '\xA', and '\u000A' are all single characters.

There are two types of string literals. The first consists of a stream of characters and escape sequences between double quotes—like "This is a \"quoted\" string". This sort of string literal cannot include newline characters—that is, it must begin and end on the same line.

The second type of string literal consists of a stream of characters between an opening @" and a closing ". The character stream can include line breaks, but does not include any escape sequences except the double quote. That is, to include a " character within an @" string, you double it (much as you do with single quotes in Delphi strings) like @"This is a ""quoted"" string". However, since there are no escape sequences in @" strings, you don't have to double backslashes the way you do in normal strings, and so @" strings are particularly useful for filename literals and Regex patterns (Chapter 11). In addition, since an @" string **can** include line breaks, they are commonly used for long, structured strings such as String.Format (Chapter 11) patterns.

For example,

```
string Literal = @"this string
contains a CR-LF pair.";
```

produces the same string literal as string Literal2 = "this string\r\n contains a CR-LF pair."[3]

As in Delphi, you can concatenate two strings with the + operator, and can access individual characters via array indexing. Note, however, that (unlike Delphi) the first character of string S is S[0], while the last is S[S.Length - 1].

Strings overload the == and != operators to do case-sensitive comparisons of the strings' **value**. For example, given string A = "test", B = "te", and C = "st", the test A == B + C evaluates to true, even though obviously A is not pointing to the same string object as B + C.

Finally, remember that strings are reference types, and that there is a difference between an empty string ("", with length 0) and a null string reference that does not point to a string object ("" != null). Some methods act differently when you pass an empty string than when you pass null; others may signal different result states by returning null than by returning "".

---

3. Chapter 11's Console.WriteLine, the FCL equivalent of Delphi's WriteLn, gives you a line break with just a \n; you don't need to write "\r\n".

At the very least, your code needs to be aware that some methods that return a string will occasionally return null. Similarly, you should not write public library code that assumes that every string value is non-null.

Arrays

Syntax is quite different than Delphi's

Arrays are declared as a type name followed by square brackets, as in int[] or object[]. C# arrays are **always** indexed by numbers, starting at 0. Multidimensional arrays are declared by adding commas between the square brackets, as in int[,] for a two-dimensional array of integers or int[,,] for a three-dimensional array of integers.

Unlike Delphi, there is **no** static sizing in array declarations, and there is no way to declare a particular sort of array as a new, named type. That is, you declare fields and variables as, say, int[] Field, and you also declare method parameters as, say, int[] Parameter. Any *N*-dimensional array of the same *base type* is assignment-compatible with any other *N*-dimensional array of the same base type: you can't (as you can in Delphi) say that This field is a ten-element int array, which is not assignment-compatible with That twelve-element int array parameter.

Expressions like new Type[size] create an array of the specified size, where each element contains the base type's default value (0 for numbers, null for references, etc.). For example, double[] Vector = new double[3] or double[,] = new double[4,4].

You can also specify the array values by enclosing them in curly braces, as in

```
int[] Vector = new int[] {1, 2, 3, 4};
int[,] Matrix = new int[2,3] {{1, 2, 3}, {4, 5, 6}};
int[,,] Cube = new int[,,] {{{1, 2}, {3, 4}}, {{5, 6}, {7, 8}}};
```

When you specify array values, you do not need to (and usually do not) include size information in the new Type[]—that is, new string[] {"this", "that"} is more common than new string[2] {"this", "that"}. When you do include size information, it **must** match the number of terms in brackets. As in the Matrix and Cube examples earlier, you can initialize multidimensional arrays as an array of arrays: each plane an array of rows, each hyperplane an array of planes, and so on.

Note that multidimensional arrays must be 'regular' or 'rectangular'—each row must contain the same number of columns, each plane the same number of rows, and so on. A multidimensional array is a single object: the first element on the second row follows immediately after the last element on the first row. You can also have 'irregular' or *jagged* arrays, which are arrays of arrays. Each element of an array of arrays is a reference to another array object.

You declare and initialize jagged arrays as arrays of arrays, like

```
int[][] Jagged = new int[10][]; // a ten-element array of integer arrays
```

or

```
int[][] Jagged = new int[][]
  {new int[] {1, 2}, new int[] {3, 4, 5}}; // two-element array of integer arrays
```

Arrays declared using C# syntax **are** instances of System.Array descendant types, and you can call any System.Array methods (Chapter 12). For example,

```
Console.WriteLine("{0}: {1}, {2}",
  Jagged.Length, Jagged[0].Length, Jagged[1].Length);
```

prints 2: 2, 3—the Jagged array has two rows, the first row has two elements while the second row has three elements. (Chapter 11 covers the {0} string format 'pattern language.')

Note As with strings, arrays are reference types: there **is** a difference between an empty array (with length 0) and a null array reference that does not point to an array object.

Enums

Hierarchically named constants, not a Pascal-style ordinal type

A C# enum like enum Color {Red, Green, Blue} looks somewhat like a Delphi enum, but this superficial similarity conceals important differences. To start with, as per Chapter 2, you have to refer to the members of this enum as Color.Red, Color.Green, or Color.Blue, not Red, Green, or Blue. More broadly, C# enums are not *ordinal types* as in Delphi: there is nothing that corresponds to Succ(Green) or Pred(Blue), nor is there anything like High(Color) or Low(Color). You can get functionality like High/Low by defining MaxValue and MinValue aliases, like

```
enum MinMax {Red, Green, Blue, MinValue = Red, MaxValue = Blue};
```

but you have to do this manually; C# won't do it for you.

C# enums are always implemented as specialized integer types. By default, the underlying type is int, but you can specify any integer type from sbyte to ulong using syntax somewhat like Chapter 7's object inheritance. For example,

```
enum Sign: sbyte {Negative = -1, Zero, Positive};
```

declares an enum with the sbyte underlying type, and values -1, 0, and 1.

Note Although enums 'inherit' from integer types, they are themselves sealed: you can't inherit from an enum.

Enums are often used to implement bitmapped sets, where each value is defined as a power of two:

```
[Flags] enum Beatles {John = 1, Paul = 2, George = 4, Ringo = 8};
```

You can combine enum values with arithmetic and bitmapped operators to build a bitmap like Beatles Living = Beatles.Paul | Beatles.Ringo. The [Flags] attribute marks the enum as a collection of bit values, so that Living.ToString() will return "Paul, Ringo", not "10". ([Flags] also works the other way, allowing Enum.Parse to parse "Paul, Ringo".) However, the [Flags] attribute will **not** prevent you from misdeclaring a bitmapped enum like

```
[Flags] enum Typo {John = 1, Paul = 2, George = 4, Ringo = 7};
```

The Typo enum will compile just fine, and you'll have to discover the mistake when the code doesn't work quite right.

Although enums are best thought of as collections of named constants, you cannot implicitly convert an enum to an integer. That is, you cannot say int ThisColor = Color.Red; you have to say int ThisColor = (int) Color.Red. However, this cast **is** just a compile-time construct: int ThisColor = (int) Color.Red generates the exact same code as int ThisColor = 1.

XML DOC

VS .NET (but not Borland's C#Builder, even in BDS 2006) has very good XML Doc support. If you declare an enum like

```
enum Sample
{
  /// <summary>
  /// This text will appear in VS.NET code completion dropdowns
  /// </summary>
  Value
};
```

the <summary> text will automatically appear in the tip window when you hover the mouse over Sample.Value, as well as in *IntelliSense* (code completion) drop-down lists.

VS .NET also makes it easy to build this documentation: if you position the cursor on a blank line above any of the enum's members, when you type ///, VS .NET will supply a blank

```
/// <summary>
///
/// </summary>
```

template for you to fill in.

Similarly, typing /// on a blank line above any enum, class, or struct declaration generates a <summary> template; filling in the template supplies text for tool tips and IntelliSense.

Boxing

Implicit boxing, explicit unboxing

As per Chapter 2, any value type can be *boxed* into an object (i.e., a class reference) and then *unboxed* by casting it back to the proper value type. You can explicitly cast a value type to object:

```
object O = (object) 99L;
```

but you can also implicitly box a value type simply by assigning the value to an object, like so:

```
object O = 99L;
```

or passing it to a method that expects an object parameter, like String.Format:

```
string S = String.Format("{0}", 77L);
```

You can test the boxed object with O is long &c, and you can unbox the value type by casting it back:

```
long L = (long) O;
```

Nullable Types

Arithmetic and logical operations with a "none of the above" value

C# 2.0 adds *nullable types*. A nullable type is a normal value type with a question mark after it. Where a normal bool enum value can be true or false, a bool? nullable bool can be true, false, or null. Similarly, an int? can hold any int value or null, while a Color? can hold Color.Red, Color.Green, Color.Blue, or null. This adds a not-set value to every number, enum, and struct.

■**Note** The point of a nullable type is that it adds null to the range of values. Thus, it doesn't make sense to make a nullable reference type—a string or array value can already be null, so there's no point to a string? or array? type. The compiler will not accept a ? after a reference type's name.

Do not confuse nullable types with a compiler detecting reads of potentially uninitialized variables! First, nullables are runtime types, not compile-time abstractions. Second, nullables can repeatedly change state from set to unset, null or non-null, at runtime, while once an unassigned variable is assigned, it stays assigned until it goes out of scope. (The value may change—even to null—but it's still assigned. It's no longer random garbage.)

You can assign normal values to nullable variables. You can cast a nullable value to its base type. You can also use nullable values in comparison and operations either with other nullable values or with normal, base type values.

```
int? LastYear = 46;              // A nullable integer, != null
int? Almost50 = LastYear + 1;    // A nullable int + a literal int
int MyAge = (int) LastYear + 1;  // 47, iow
bool NotNull = Almost50 != null; // Almost50 is set, != null
bool? Tristate = null;           // true, false, null
bool IsNull = Tristate == null;  // Tristate is unset, == null.
// bool GoBoom = (bool) Tristate; // a null value cannot fit in the base type
```

System and user-defined operators are automatically *lifted* to support nullable values, chiefly by the expedient of only calling them if both operands have a value, and by applying a few simple rules to determine the value of operations on null values.[4] Thus, lifted operators act just like normal operators when both operands are non-null, while following a few new rules when faced with null values. As per the Chapter5\LiftedOperators C# project:

- A null value always equals another null value, and never equals a non-null value.

- No number is greater than a null value, nor is any number less than a null value. That is, comparing any number to a null returns false—it does **not** return null.

- Both arithmetic and *xor* (the ^ operator) with a null value returns a null value.

- The & (bitwise *and*) operator and the | (bitwise *or*) operator act specially with nulls. true & null == null, but false & null == false. true | null == true, but false | null == null.

■**Note** For the most part this is what you'd expect. The strange special casing with & and | is meant to make bool? act the same as SQL Booleans.

Boxing a non-null nullable type returns a boxed copy of the value (that is, a boxed T, not a boxed T?), while boxing a null nullable type returns null, not a boxed T? structure. You can think of this as a semantics-preserving optimization: in particular, unboxing a nullable value and comparing it to null is much more expensive than comparing a reference (to a boxed nullable value) to null.

You can unbox a boxed T to either a T or a T?. For example,

```
object Boxed = 47;
int? Nullable = (int?)Boxed; // Nullable == 47 && Nullable != null
int Normal = (int)Boxed;     // Normal == 47
```

However, (T) Boxed will throw an exception if Boxed == null. You can only unbox null to a nullable type:

```
object Null = null;
int? NoValue = (int?)Null; // NoValue == null
```

---

4. See comments in the Chapter5\LiftedOverloadedOperators C# project.

Internally, nullable types are closed constructed value types (Chapter 7). A bool? is an alias for a Nullable<bool> in much the same way that an int is an alias for a System.Int32. A T? is the **exact same type** as a Nullable<T>, even though they don't look it, and even though the compiler makes a T? act so much like a T.

Each nullable value has a public T Value property and a public bool HasValue property. You can read and write these properties directly, but the real point is that the compiler implements operations on nullable types via references to the Value and HasValue properties (and related methods). Specifically, setting a nullable type to a normal, base type value sets the HasValue property to true, while setting a nullable type to null resets the HasValue property to false. Comparing a nullable type to null reads the HasValue property. When a nullable type's HasValue property is false, reading its Value property or casting the nullable type to its base type raises an exception. And boxing a nullable returns a boxed Value or null.

Key Points

C# is so similar to Delphi that the small differences can trip you up

- Variable declarations can include initialization.

- Expression typing rules are not what you're used to.

- Assignment is an operator, and can be done 'inline.'

- Strings and characters use C-style escapes for non-typewriter characters.

- Array declarations are not as strongly typed as in Delphi.

- Enums are not ordinals.

- C# 2.0 does a lot of work to make nullable types interoperate with their base types.

CHAPTER 6

∎ ∎ ∎

C# Control Structures

With operators and expressions, you have to contend with different rules for operator precedence and expression typing as you move between Delphi and C#. By contrast, you'll find that control structures and exception handling are pretty similar between Delphi and C#. The syntax is different, but the semantics are about the same—although C# does offer language-level support for the Monitor and the Dispose patterns. Most syntax differences are familiar C vs. Pascal issues: C# has variables local to a block; C# has mandatory parens around all boolean control statements; C# treats a semicolon as a statement terminator, not a statement separator, and so requires semicolons in places where they're optional or illegal in Delphi.

Blocks and Statements

Unlike Delphi, variables can be local to a block

As in Delphi, when a control structure expects a *statement*, this can be either a *simple statement* or a *compound statement*, which is a *block* of simple statements. A statement block consists of 0 or more simple statements between a pair of *curly braces*. That is, { is the same as Delphi's begin, and } is the same as Delphi's end.

In Delphi, the semicolon is a statement *separator*, which means that it is optional at the end of a compound statement, and illegal between a simple (noncompound) then clause and an else clause. In C#, as in C and C++, the semicolon is a statement *terminator*, which means it's required after every statement, even the last statement in a compound statement, and even between a simple if statement and an else clause. For example:

```
if (Test)
  Some.Method(); // C# has no "then" keyword
else
  Some.OtherMethod();
```

Unlike Delphi, each statement block can include local variable definitions, anywhere in the block—C# does not require you to declare all of a method's local variables in a special block at the beginning of a method. For example,

```
if (test)
{
  int BlockLocal = 1;
}
```

You will find that moving variable declaration to the point of first use aids readability by eliminating the need to constantly jump back to the top of the method.[1] It also helps reduce bugs in that a variable declared at the top of the method is global to the whole method, and reusing such 'local globals' is a common source of bugs: while the compiler can detect the use of a possibly uninitialized variable, the compiler **cannot** ensure that variable has always been reset before being reused.

A variable defined in a block is *in scope* (is visible) to all blocks contained within the block. You can reuse generic identifiers like Index in 'parallel' blocks, but you **cannot** redefine an identifier that is already defined in the current block or in an outer block. That is,

```
for (int I = 0; I < 10; I++) ;
for (int I = 0; I < 10; I++) ;
```

is legal (for loops can declare variables in their *initialization* section—see the upcoming "The for Statement" subsection) while

```
for (int Index = 0; I < 10; I++)
{
  int Index = 9; // Can't redefine Index, even if
                 // you have no need to refer to the loop control variable
}
```

is a syntax error. The loop body can't overload the loop control variable—which is a variable defined in a parent scope—even if you don't need to refer to the loop control variable within the loop body.

As in Delphi, // starts a comment that runs to the end of the line. Any text between /* and */ is a *comment block*—a comment block can appear within a line of code, just as Delphi's {} and (* *) comment blocks can. Nested comment blocks are not legal—as in Delphi, in a sequence like /* /* */ */, the first */ matches the first /*, and the second */ is a syntax error.

Conditionals

Different syntax, very similar semantics

C# conditional statements include the if and switch statements. In Delphi, these are the if and case statements. The syntax is a bit different, but the behavior is **almost** the same: Delphi's case statement can include ranges, which C#'s switch statement cannot; while C#'s switch statement can match strings, which Delphi's case statement cannot.

---

1. Some ex-Delphi people like to declare all of a block's locals at the beginning of the block, **not** at the point of first use. They say that this gives them fewer places to look for a declaration. For my part, I use F12 (in VS) or Ctrl+Click (in BDS) to go to a variable's definition when I need to, and I just find a declarations block to be a distraction. Most C# code you will read declares variables at the point of first use.

The if Statement

Quite like Delphi's

An if statement consists of the if keyword, followed by a boolean expression which must be enclosed in parentheses, followed by a statement which is executed if the boolean expression evaluates to true, optionally followed by the else keyword and a statement which is executed if the boolean expression evaluates to false. Thus, either

```
if (expression)
    statement;
```

or

```
if (expression)
    statement1;
else
    statement2;
```

▪ **Note** All C# control statements put the control expression in parens.

Unlike Delphi, there is no then keyword: the then clause follows directly after the parenthesized test, though usually on a new line, and indented. Remember, each simple (noncompound) statement ends with a semicolon, so C# requires a semicolon between a single-statement if clause and the optional else clause. Standard formatting conventions place the optional else keyword on a line of its own, lined up with its if keyword; VS .NET contains an automatic formatter that will (usually) do this for you.

The switch Statement

Awkward syntax, but can switch on strings

A switch statement consists of the switch keyword, followed by an integer or string expression in parentheses, followed by a series of *case statements* within a pair of curly braces. Each case statement consists of a *case clause*, followed by a list of statements. Each statement list must end in a *jump statement* (or an infinite loop)—control may not pass out of the statement list.

A case clause is one or more *regular* or *default* case clauses. A regular case clause consists of the keyword case, followed by a constant expression of the same type as the switch expression, followed by a colon, :. For example, case 1: or case "href":. A default case clause consists of the keyword default followed by a colon, :. You can have any number of case statements in a switch, and any number of clauses within a case statement, but each constant expression may appear only once per switch statement. There can be no more than one default clause.

Case statement lists are usually zero or more normal statements, followed by a jump statement. In turn, the jump statement is usually a break statement, which transfers control out of the switch statement; but it can also be a return statement (Chapter 7), which exits the method;

a goto case Expression statement, which will jump to the appropriate case statement; or a throw statement, which raises an exception (see the "Exception Handling" section, later in this chapter). However, the jump statement is not required: the statement list **can** end with an endless loop, like do {} while (true)—the real key is that control may not pass through the statement list to the next statement.

For example,

```
switch (IntegerExpression)
{
  case 1:
  case 2:
    Some.Code();
    break; // exit the switch statement
  case 3:
    Some.Other.Code();
    goto case 4; // this is how you implement C-style fall-through
  case 4:
    More.Code();
    return; // exit the method, not just the switch statement
  default:
    Default.Code();
    throw new Exception("Out of range"); // this counts as a jump
  case 5: // Yes, it's valid to have more case statements after a default
    break; // not even the last case statement can fall-through
}
```

Note that, unlike Delphi, switch statements **can** switch on string values. Switch statements are heavily optimized, but (at least logically) the test is done via the same case-sensitive call to String.Equals as the string == operator overload.

Also, unlike Delphi, each case clause can contain only one expression: a case clause can't contain a comma-separated list or a range. This is bulky and inconvenient, and I suspect deliberately so: it encourages you to limit yourself to small switch statements that can be implemented via a jump table.

Loops

Three standard types of loop, plus foreach

C# looping constructs are a bit more powerful than Delphi's. The test-at-top while is pretty identical to Delphi's while loop, and the test-at-bottom do is almost the same as Delphi's repeat {...} until loop, but the for loop is much more flexible: as in C, both while and do are just syntactic sugar that **could** be written as for loops.

Within a loop, break and continue function exactly as in Delphi. C#'s return acts much like Delphi's Exit, except that within a function (a method that doesn't return void) return must be followed by a value to return.

The for Statement

Standard C syntax

The C-style for loop can look pretty daunting to a Delphi user. It consists of the for keyword, followed by an open parenthesis, zero or more *initializers*, a semicolon, an optional *test* clause,[2] another semicolon, zero or more *iterators*, a close parenthesis, and finally a statement to repeat. That is, for (initializers; test; iterators) body. A for loop first executes the initializers and then, while the test returns true, executes the loop body followed by the iterators.

The **loop initializers** consist of either zero or more comma-separated statements, or a normal variable declaration and initialization phrase like int Index = 0, Count = 0. The scope of variables declared in an initializer is the for loop: that is, they are visible only within the test, the iterators, and the loop body. To initialize variables of different types, you must declare them outside of the initializer, as either

```
int Index;
long Count;
for (Index = 0, Count = 0; Index < SomeLimit; Index++) ;
```

or

```
int Index = 0;
long Count = 0;
for ( ; Index < SomeLimit; Index++) ; // note the empty initializer
```

Of course, both of these examples are a bit contrived, and usually you'd use code more like

```
long Count = 0;
for (int Index = 0; Index < SomeLimit; Index++) ;
```

The **loop test** can be any boolean expression; it will always execute at least once. The test can access any variable in scope: it's not an error to test a variable that's not local to the for loop and (unlike recent Delphis) it's perfectly legal for the loop body to modify a variable that the loop test reads. Conversely (and also unlike recent Delphis), a **for** loop control variable is valid outside of the loop body—subsequent code can read the last value, the value that first failed the test.

```
{
  int Index; // unassigned
  for (Index = 0; Index < Limit; Index++)
    ; // It's perfectly OK for loop body code to change Index
  bool TestFailed = Index >= Limit; // Index is now assigned, and is >= Limit
}
```

The **loop iterators** consist of zero or more comma-separated statements. They are executed after the loop body and before the next test; they will execute as many times as the test returns true. (In other words, they may not be executed.)

---

2. An empty test clause implies true—e.g., for (;;) ; is an endless loop. You should eventually break or continue out of an endless loop.

Tip You **can** fold the iterator into the test—e.g., Index++ < Limit—but this is a bad practice for two reasons: you have to pay attention to the difference between Index++ and ++Index, and the loop body never 'sees' the initial value of Index.

The most standard for loop has an initializer that declares a loop control variable and an iterator that increments it with ++. For example

```
for (int I = 0; I < 10; I++)
  Loop.Body();
```

will call the Loop.Body method ten times. More complicated forms are possible, of course:

```
for (int Index = 0; Index < 10; Index += 2)
  Loop.Body(Index);
```

will call the Loop.Body method **five** times, passing it 0, 2, 4, 6, and 8.

The foreach Statement

A concept that may be familiar from scripting languages

The foreach loop is both like and unlike the for loop. The for loop is a low-level, almost macro-like construct that can actually implement all three of the other loop types.[3] The for loop imposes few restrictions on its three clauses, or on the loop body: you can read every other entry, if you need to, and you can change the loop control variable. By contrast, in some ways the C# foreach loop actually acts more like Delphi's for loop than the C# for loop does: you have to declare an iteration variable that's local to the loop body, and the loop body can't change the iteration variable. While you can break out of an enumeration in various ways, the foreach loop doesn't let you supply a test that can stop the enumeration: by default, you will visit every element in the collection.

The syntax of the foreach loop is much simpler than the syntax of the for loop, because the foreach loop doesn't offer as many options as the for loop:

```
foreach (Type Identifier in Collection) Body;
```

Just a declaration of a typed *iteration variable*, a collection, and a loop body: no init clause, no test clause, and no loop iterators. Note that you always have to supply a type and a local identifier: you cannot use an existing variable as the iteration variable.

The loop Body executes once for each item in the Collection, unless you either throw an exception, or break out of or return from the loop. The iteration variable is local to—and read-only within—the loop body. The iteration variable is set to a different member of the collection on each pass through the loop Body.

For example,

---

3. See, for example, the Chapter6\ForeachAsFor C# project.

```
long Accumulator = 0;
foreach (int Item in IntArray)
  Accumulator += Item;
```

sums up each item in the `int[]` `IntArray`.

The `foreach` loop makes your code simpler and more maintainable by abstracting away details like loop control variables and the internal structure of the collection (e.g., the collection could be a simple array, a linked list, a tree, the contents of a directory, or whatever). As a lot of code consists of processing some sort of collection or another, `foreach` is very common in C# code.

As per Chapter 2, the collection is normally an object that supports `IEnumerable` or `IEnumerable<T>`.[4] When you do `foreach` on an `IEnumerable`, the generated code calls `IEnumerable.GetEnumerator()`, which returns an `IEnumerator` interface. Then, while the enumerator's `MoveNext()` method returns `true`, the generated code sets the iteration variable to the enumerator's `Current` property cast to the type of the iteration variable, and runs the loop body code. That is, `foreach (T Identifier in Collection) Body` expands to something like

```
IEnumerator E = Collection.GetEnumerator();
while (E.MoveNext())
{
    T IterationVariable = (T) E.Current;
    Body;
}
```

In 2.0 and up, when you do `foreach` on an `IEnumerable<T>`, the generated code calls `IEnumerable<T>.GetEnumerator()`, which returns an `IEnumerator<T>` interface. Then, while the enumerator's `MoveNext()` method returns `true`, the generated code sets the iteration variable to the enumerator's `Current` property and runs the loop body code. That is, `foreach (Type Identifier in Collection) Body` expands to something like

```
IEnumerator<T> E = Collection.GetEnumerator();
while (E.MoveNext())
{
    T IterationVariable = E.Current; // no cast on each loop!
    Body;
}
```

In other words, `foreach` on an `IEnumerable<T>` is almost identical to `foreach` on an `IEnumerable`, except that setting the iteration variable doesn't involve a cast because `IEumerable<T>.Current` is a `T`, not an `object`. As per Chapters 2 and 12, this provides a modest performance boost with reference types because it avoids an `is` test on every pass through the loop, and provides a rather heftier performance boost with value types, which don't have to be unboxed.

---

4. Normally, you will use `foreach` on objects that explicitly implement `IEnumerable` (or `IEnumerable<T>`). However, as a special case that you may find useful in bootstrapping a custom collection, when a C# type doesn't explicitly implement `IEnumerable` but **does** have a `GetEnumerator` method that returns an object that has a `MoveNext()` method and a `Current` property, the compiler will call those methods directly, instead of via the interfaces. This special case is related to Chapter 7's way in which C# will accept inherited methods as filling an interface contract.

You may have performance concerns about using foreach. After all, calling GetEnumerator, and calling MoveNext, and reading the Current property is not free.

Except that sometimes it is: when you foreach an array, the compiler generates the same sort of inline array-indexing for loop that you might generate by hand. A for (int Index=0;Index<ThisArray.Length;Index++) loop is no faster than a foreach (Type Element in ThisArray) loop.

Beyond that, in linked data structures, using foreach is faster than using collection indexing, even with the IEnumerable overhead. With array-based types like Chapter 12's ArrayList and List<T>, calling MoveNext and getting Current **is** a bit slower than indexing with a for loop, but the foreach equivalent is easier to read and write. It's generally worth the cost for all but the very most frequently executed code, especially in 2.0 where the costs are even lower.

1.1 PERFORMANCE NOTE

Unless the iteration variable is simply an object, enumerating an IEnumerable means that each assignment to the iteration variable involves a cast. This means that foreach can raise miscast exceptions, and it also has performance implications for (nonarray) collections of value types.

As per Chapter 2, a universal collection **can** contain items that can't be cast to the type of the iteration variable. The compiler does static checks where it can—you can't compile code like foreach (string S in new int[99])—but this is pretty much limited to cases where the collection is an array. When the collection is **not** an array, but some other object that implements IEnumerable, the compiler can't know at compile time whether each item in the collection is really of the right type. Thus, foreach code that tries to miscast a collection's items will compile. The error will be detected at test time only if you actually exercise the code.

In 1.1, using foreach with collections of value types **is** significantly more expensive than using foreach with arrays of value types. Storing a value type as an object is a boxing operation; assigning it to the iteration variable is an unboxing operation.

The while Statement

A standard test-at-top loop

The C# while loop—while (Test) Body—is almost identical to the Delphi while Test do Body loop. Syntactically, C# requires parens around the test, and there is no do keyword between the test and the body. Semantically, the two are identical. The Test is evaluated; if it returns true, the Body is executed, and then the code jumps back to evaluate the test again. The Body may not execute at all; the Test will be evaluated one time more than the Body is executed.

The do Statement

A standard test-at-bottom loop

Similarly, the C# do loop—do Body while (Test)—is almost identical to the Delphi repeat Body until Test. Note, though, that the sense of the test is reversed between

Delphi and C#: C# executes the do loop while the test returns true; Delphi executes the repeat loop while the test returns False. Beyond that, the two are basically identical: the loop body is executed, the test is evaluated, and if the test returns true, the code jumps back to the top of the loop. The Body will always execute at least once; the Test will be evaluated once for every time that the Body is executed.

Exception Handling

Semantics identical to Delphi's

Although C# uses different keywords and slightly different syntax, exception handling acts exactly the same as in Delphi. You catch and throw exceptions, and you can use try {} finally {} to write cleanup code that will execute even if the *try block* throws an exception.

Note You can combine catch and finally in a single C# try statement.

Unlike the if statement and the various looping constructs, exception syntax **requires** the use of blocks. The try block **must** be enclosed in curly braces

```
try
{
}
```

even if it consists only of a single statement; similarly each *catch block* and each *finally block* **must** be enclosed in curly braces:

```
catch (OverflowException) // Catch any OverflowException or descendant
{
  // this block can't 'see' the exception object
  Console.WriteLine("OverflowException");
}
catch (Exception E)  // Catch any Exception or descendant
{
  // This block 'sees' the Exception as E
  Console.WriteLine("Overflow: {0}", E.Message);
}
catch // Catch any non-CLS exception
{
  Console.WriteLine("General exception handler");
}
finally // finally block comes after any catch blocks
{
  Console.WriteLine("finally block");
}
```

As the example suggests, a try statement consists of the try keyword, followed by a block in curly braces, followed by **either** one or more catch blocks **or** a finally block **or** both, with the finally block after any catch blocks.

A catch block consists of one of three forms:

1. catch (T Identifier) {}: This form will catch any exception that is T—that is, any exception of the specified type T or one of its descendants. Within the block, the caught exception object is bound to Identifier for the block's exception handling code to examine.

2. catch (T) {}: This form will also catch any exception that is T. When you don't specify an Identifier, the block's exception handling code has no access to the caught exception.

3. catch {}: This **general** form will catch any exception, even a non-CLS exception that doesn't descend from System.Exception. (C# will not let you throw an object that doesn't descend from Exception, but other languages aren't so scrupulous.) A try block may have no more than one general form catch clause, and if present it must be the last catch clause.[5]

As in Delphi, you always throw an Exception object—an instance of the Exception class or one of its descendants:

```
throw new Exception("Something's wrong!");
```

Special Blocks

Some wonderful syntactic sugar

Aside from the C-style for loop—which I promise you'll get used to—I think you'll agree that C# has a cleaner, more maintainable syntax than Delphi. Block-scoped locals improve clarity and reduce bugs. The foreach loop eliminates lots of really common boilerplate code. Eliminating boilerplate makes your code easier to write and easier to read, and makes it less error prone by eliminating the 'idiomatic' code that you don't necessarily pay full attention to.

The using and lock statements similarly eliminate boilerplate. They're not as ubiquitous as foreach, but they're equally convenient.

The using Statement

Automates the Dispose pattern

Chapter 3's "Finalization" section talked about the IDisposable interface, which is also called the Dispose pattern. You'll recall that the point of the Dispose pattern is that it's expensive to rely on a finalizer to release any resources (like file or GDI handles) that an object has open: the garbage collector has to notice that an object can be collected, then it has to revive it (and any

---

5. Any specialized catch clauses following a general catch clause would never be triggered.

objects it directly and indirectly refers to) so that a special finalization thread can call the finalizer. If you can explicitly call Dispose when you're done with a resource, you can avoid the cost of finalization.

You **could** do this with code like

```
ResourceUsingType Resourceful = new ResourceUsingType();
try
{
  // Code that uses the Resourceful instance
}
finally
{
  if (Resourceful != null)
    Resourceful.Dispose();
}
```

but that's a fair amount of boilerplate, and it's probably fair to assume that many people would 'forget' to use the try/finally block. Accordingly, C# supplies the using statement,[6] which automates the preceding code.

The using statement consists of the using keyword, followed by a parenthesized initialization expression, followed by a simple or compound statement. The initialization expression can consist of either an expression that evaluates to an object that supports IDisposable or a variable declaration of the form T Identifier = InitCode. As with normal variable declaration, the latter form can contain more than one Identifier = InitCode clause, so long as all the identifiers are of the same type.

For example, the preceding example would become

```
using (ResourceUsingType Resourceful = new ResourceUsingType())
{
  // Code that uses the Resourceful instance
}
```

When control leaves the using statement, the compiler-generated finally block will call Dispose() on any objects listed in the parenthesized initializer.

Note that the IDisposable and the using statement aren't only about resources: you can use them whenever you have some code that you want to run at the end of a block. For example, the Benchmark class in Common\Utilities.cs uses IDisposable so that you can run simple benchmarks as

```
using (new Benchmark("Describe the code"))
{
  // Code to benchmark
}
```

The Benchmark class's constructor saves the time it was created and the message string, and the Dispose method reports on the elapsed time. Similarly, I've used IDisposable in XML

---

6. That's a "using **statement**" as opposed to a "using **directive**" like the ubiquitous using System;. Chapter 9 talks about namespaces and the using directive.

generation[7] code: the constructor writes a <block_tag>, and the Dispose method writes the </block_tag>. By using using, you can reduce clutter **and** your chances of not cleaning up properly.

The lock Statement

Automatically acquires and releases a mutex

.NET has broad and deep support for threading. (I cover threading in detail in Chapter 17.) You can lock and unlock **any** object O via System.Threading.Monitor.Enter(O) and System.Threading.Monitor.Exit(O)—you don't have to create a special mutex object.[8] As with using, however, this is a lot of boilerplate, and many people will fail to use a try/finally block, so C# supports the lock statement:

```
lock (ObjectExpression) LockedStatement;
```

This is exactly equivalent to the much bulkier

```
{
  object O = ObjectExpression;
  System.Threading.Monitor.Enter(O);
  try
  {
    LockedStatement; // may of course be a compound statement
  }
  finally
  {
    System.Threading.Monitor.Exit(O);
  }
}
```

The following excerpt from the Chapter6\LockDemo project shows a simple use of the lock statement:

```
private void threadProc()
{
  object Current;
  do
  {
    lock (Enumerator)
      Current = Enumerator.MoveNext() ? Enumerator.Current : null;
    if (Current != null)
      List.Add(Current);
  } while (Current != null);
}
```

---

7. The FCL includes very good XML support—I only wrote my own XML generation code so that the results would look exactly like Visual Studio project files.

8. The Monitor class locks reference types using the SyncBlockIndex field in every object's header; Chapter 17 has the details.

The locked `Enumerator` is a private field (of type `IEnumerator`) of the same object as the `threadProc` method. By locking the `IEnumerator`, this routine is effectively sharing a `foreach` between threads. This is a very trivial multithreading demo, but you might use code like this on a multiprocessor machine when you had some expensive processing to do on each item of a list.

I assume you can read the code without a line-by-line gloss, and so will only talk about how simple and clear the code is. It's not all that different from the single-threaded

```
while Enumerator.MoveNext do
  Inc(Result, integer(Enumerator.Current));
```

of the Chapter2\Foreach Delphi project. Think about what the Win32 alternative would be like! Not only would there be all the `try`/`finally` and `Enter`/`Exit` boilerplate, but also you'd have to create and free a separate mutex. By letting us lock the object that we need multithreaded access to, the CLR reduces our code volume and aids clarity—no matter how carefully you name and comment it, a separate mutex is a separate object, not necessarily connected with the object it's protecting.

Key Points

Lots of parens in C#!

- Statement syntax is slightly different from Delphi's—in particular, all statement blocks can define local variables.

- The `if` statement is quite like Delphi's, except that the test must be parenthesized, and that there is no `then` keyword.

- The `switch` statement is a lot like Delphi's `case` statement, just a bit clunkier—and it can switch on strings.

- The `for` loop is a bit cryptic but very flexible.

- The `foreach` loop is very useful.

- The `while` and `do` loops are almost identical to their Delphi equivalents.

- Exception handling is much like Delphi's. The biggest difference is that you can write `try`/`catch`/`finally` blocks.

- The `using` and `lock` statements spare you a lot of boilerplate.

CHAPTER 7

C# Objects

In C#, a type is either an enum, a struct, a class, a delegate, or an interface. Chapter 5 covered enums, which are more like constants than like Delphi enumerated types. This chapter covers the creation and direct manipulation of the object types—classes and structs. Chapter 8 covers delegates and interfaces, which are ways to slice object behavior. C# objects are much like Delphi objects, though the syntax is more like C++ (including generics, in C# 2.0, which may be new to Delphi programmers).

No Headers

No forward declarations in C#

One of the major differences between C and Pascal has always been that, in C you can use an identifier before you declare it, while in Pascal you have to declare every identifier before you use it. This has been somewhat obscured by the way that C and C++ have relied on a header file convention for module linkage. In C and C++, an .h or .hpp file is a public interface; it contains the declarations that the module contracts to implement. In Delphi, a unit's interface section contains the declarations that the unit contracts to implement.

One of the reasons I used Delphi through the years was that I thought then, as I do now, that Delphi's unit syntax is better than a C-style header file convention. Annoying as it can be to keep Delphi's interface section in synch with its implementation section,[1] it sure beats keeping two separate files in synch.

But, a .NET module's public contract can be read from the metadata. Public members of public classes are visible to outside code, while private classes and private members of public classes are not visible to outside code.

So, why bother manually building and maintaining a public contract? It **is** nice to be able to browse an object's interface to see what it can do—but does it matter whether you browse an object's interface by reading a manually maintained interface section or with an active object browser? Both are hyperlinked (when source code is available) to the actual code. The Visual Studio IDE **does** include your /// comments on each type (and on each method, and on each parameter of each method) in the object browser just as in *IntelliSense* tool tips and code completion drop-downs.

---

1. The Delphi IDE's Shift+Ctrl+C command does a good job of propagating new method prototypes from the interface section to the implementation section and vice versa, but it doesn't even try to keep the two in synch when you change a method's prototype.

Some people really love the interface section, but I've come to think that this is something like the way some people (including me) really love stick shift cars. While a stick **is** great on hills, the real appeal is the hands-on-the-hardware feel of waggling a live drive shaft. But there's no equivalent of "great on hills" for the interface section: you don't get anything from an interface section that you don't get from an active object browser. However, the converse is not true: in an object browser, you can order and group members any way you like, which you can't do with a static text interface section.

C# doesn't have header files. C# doesn't have a Delphi-style interface section. Each assembly consists of a collection of public and internal types. A *public type* is visible to code in other assemblies; an *internal type* is only visible within its own assembly. A type without an explicit access modifier is internal, but you can also mark a type as internal, if you prefer that all access be explicitly specified.

This is very liberating. You don't have to clone declarations and keep them in synch. An empty C# class type looks like

```
class Empty
{
}
```

This Empty object has internal visibility, because it wasn't declared as public. Changing that and adding a method,

```
public class Empty
{
  public int Answer()
  {
    return 42;
  }
}
```

gives us a public class, Empty, with one public method, Empty.Answer(), which always returns 42.

That's all it took to add Empty.Answer to the assembly's public contract: implementing it. If I change the Answer method's prototype, the assembly's public contract changes with it.

This *single declaration model*, where the implementation **is** the declaration, is just as type safe as the *double declaration model* of Delphi's unit syntax. At the same time, it's a great time saver. As you implement a public method, you may need to add private methods that implement parts of the public method's functionality. In C#, you just call these private methods from the public method and define them (typically) below the public method; you don't ever need to clone headers. As the code evolves and the private method's prototypes change, you don't have to change the private parts of the interface section.

Not having to maintain an interface section adds up to a significant productivity boost for Delphi programmers moving to C#. At the same time, between a dynamic object browser and code folding, your code is at least as easy to read as Delphi code.

When a public method has its own private machinery, I create a folding #region (Chapter 9) where the public method comes first, followed by all the private fields, properties, and methods that the public method refers to, in the folding region underneath the public code. When you fold the method's region, all the code that implements it is hidden. When you expand only one region, you can page about within that region almost as if it were a whole file that was only a few screens tall. It's easy to read code written this way, because methods are implemented top-down, with the public methods serving as the documentation on what the private methods do. When you have a complex private method, you can even use a recursive organization, where each complex private method is in its own folding region, containing the code that implements **it**.

Generics

May be new to Delphi programmers

To briefly recapitulate Chapter 2, .NET 2.0's generics let you write open classes that can be constructed around existing closed class(es), creating a new closed constructed class. Where the open class may be a Stack of T, a closed constructed class will be a Stack of integers, or a Stack of strings, or maybe a Stack of InterruptedTask structures. Each closed constructed class jits down to native code as if it were handwritten for a 4-byte type or a 16-byte type. Each closed constructed class is a unique type, with its own rules about what types it takes as arguments and returns as results. However, in some cases, two or more strongly typed methods can actually share the same native code. For example, classes constructed around reference types can share code, because all member access is by metadata index tokens, not offsets into a data structure. Also, high-level code that does only assignment on its parameterized types compiles to code that just copies data of a certain size from one location to another, and types like Stack<char> and Stack<short> and Stack<ushort> can probably all share method code.

Generics are a productivity boost: you have less code to write, and fewer opportunities to make mistakes. Generic collections are also an efficiency boost—generic collections store specific types, not an all-encompassing object. There is no need to write wrapper classes to ensure that **this** collection can only hold integers and **that** collection can only hold strings. Nor is there any need to box a value type to store it in an object slot, and there's no need to cast (and possibly unbox) an object value to an int value or a string value.

Any class or struct can be made into an open type by placing a list of comma-separated type parameters in angle brackets between the type name and the curly brackets:

```
public class OpenClass<T> {}
public struct OpenStruct<K, V> {}
```

Also, any method—even a method of a normal, closed class—can be made into an open method by placing a list of comma-separated type parameters in angle brackets between the method name and the left parenthesis. See the "Methods" section for details.

Type parameter names can be any legal C# identifier. Obviously, if a type has multiple type parameters, each must be unique—you can't declare class NoWay<T, T>{}. You can have open and closed types with the same name in the same scope: class Overloaded {} can coexist with class Overloaded<T> {} and class Overloaded<T, U> {}. What you **can't** have is class Collision<T> {} and class Collision<U> {}—the type parameter names don't really matter, except as placeholders, and what matters for type identity is the number of type parameters.[2] (This is somewhat similar to the way that overloads have to have different lists of parameter types, while the parameter names don't matter.)

---

2. The number of type parameters really is all that matters for type identity. Constraints (or where clauses) don't matter—class Collision<T> where T: struct {} collides with class Collision<U> where U: class {}, too. I cover where clauses later in this section.

An open class or an open struct can use a type parameter in any member declaration, either directly or via a type constructed from one of the type parameters. For example,

```
class Sample<T>
{
    private Stack<T> Pending = new Stack<T>();    // Stack<T> is constructed from T
    public void Process(T Datum) {}               // a parameter of type T
    private void Method() {T Local = default(T);} // a local variable of type T
}
```

The preceding code uses the new default keyword, which solves a potential problem with generics. As you know, an uninitialized field declaration like T Field; declares a field that will be filled with 0x00 bytes. However, an uninitialized local variable declaration like T Local; declares ... an uninitialized variable, which is an error to read. In C# 1.0, while we can set a reference to null, a number to 0, a boolean to false, or a struct to new StructName(), there is no way that we can write code that will fill **any** local variable with 0x00 bytes, nor is there a way to write code that can test if any variable has its default value.

The default keyword allows you to do this. For any type T, default(T) will return the default value, whether that's null, 0, false, or new T(). Thus, in the preceding Sample<T>.Method method, T Local = default(T); creates an initialized local variable, no matter what type T may be.

Inline Types

No type aliases

C# does not have anything like Delphi's type statement: you can't declare an alias for a complex constructed type like type DataArray = Dictionary<DateTime, SampleData> and then pass parameters of type DataArray, or declare variables of type DataArray and populate them with a new DataArray(). Rather, somewhat as with array types, you have to include the whole type definition every time you refer to it. For example, you declare a parameter with a closed constructed type as, say,

```
public void Function(Dictionary<DateTime, SampleData> Data) {}
```

and you declare and initialize a field as, say,

```
private Dictionary<DateTime, SampleData> Data =
    new Dictionary<DateTime, SampleData>();
```

This **can** get bulky and hard to read, and one might be tempted to characterize it unkindly as the typical C tradeoff: fewer lines ... of harder to read code. However, my experience so far has been that the angle brackets tend to cluster around relatively low-level code, and that generics make for smaller, faster application code that more than justifies a bit of ugliness at the bottom.

Also, though looking ahead a little bit, C# 3.0[3] is slated to do a bit more type inference than 2.0 does. If you declare the type of an initialized local variable as var, the compiler will infer the

---

3. In alpha before 2.0 RTM-ed!

type of the variable from the initializer expression. That is, coding var AutoType = 2 + 2 would be just the same as coding int AutoType = 2 + 2, because 2 + 2 is an int expression as per Chapter 5.

Of course, that's a bad example, because you have to know that the type of the expression 2 + 2 is int to know what type AutoType is. A better example is var Data = new List<DataType>, which is just the same as coding List<DataType> Data = new List<DataType>, though the 3.0 var form is easier to type and, to me, easier to read.

Similarly, imagine that you have a list of collections of named values— List< Dictionary<string, MyData> >. Right now, you have to enumerate it as

```
foreach (Dictionary<string, MyData> Collection in ListOfCollections) ;
```

while the current 3.0 syntax would let you code simply

```
foreach (var Collection in ListOfCollections) ;
```

and the compiler would automatically infer that Collection is a Dictionary<string, MyData>.

Constraints

Tell the compiler what a parameterized type can do

Any open type (or open method) can include *constraints* on what sort of types can actually be passed as type parameters. Syntactically, constraints are a where clause before the curly brackets in an object or method (or, as per Chapter 8, before the semicolon in an open delegate or an open interface method):

```
class OpenClass<T> where T: class
{
  delegate R OpenDelegate<R, P>(P Parameter) where R: struct where P : List<int>;
  void OpenMethod<U>() where U: class, new() {}
}
```

When you need to declare multiple constraints on a single type parameter, you declare them as a comma-separated list of constraints following the where keyword, as in the preceding OpenMethod. When you need to declare constraints on multiple type parameters, you use multiple where clauses, separated by whitespace, as in the preceding OpenDelegate. When you have multiple where clauses that declare constraints on separate type parameters, the constraints do not have to appear in the same order as the type parameters appear in the angle brackets.

There are four different types of constraint:

1. where T: struct declares that T can only be bound to a value type. Note that this value type does **not** have to be a struct: a system primitive like int or double is compatible with a struct constraint. However, nullable types (Chapter 5) like a float? or a Nullable<bool> are not compatible with a struct constraint.

2. where T: class declares that T can only be bound to a reference type. Note that this reference type does not have to be an explicit class instance: interfaces, delegates, strings, and arrays are all compatible with a class constraint.

3. where T: *TypeName* declares that T must be assignment compatible with the class or interface *TypeName*. Note that *TypeName* cannot be a type that you can't inherit from, like a struct or a sealed class: declaring that a type parameter must be assignment compatible with a type that you can't inherit from would be the same as declaring that the type parameter may only be that type. Note also that this restriction does **not** mean that you cannot pass a struct or a sealed class as a type parameter! It only means that you can't use a struct or sealed class name in a where clause.

4. where T: new() declares that T must have a public, parameterless constructor. A new() constraint must always be the last constraint in the list.

Now, "constraints" is actually rather a bad name, as it focuses attention on type construction. While constraints certainly do limit what you can pass as a type parameter, the point of constraints is really that they make a positive statement to the compiler about the sorts of operations that your generic code can do with the type parameter. For example, an unconstrained method like

```
public static void Process<T>(T List)
{
    foreach (object O in List)
        ;
}
```

can't be compiled, because the compiler can't be sure that the List parameter will have a GetEnumerator method—after all, you can't enumerate an int or a float. However, the compiler **can** compile

```
public static void Process<L, E>(L List) where L: IEnumerable<E>
{
    foreach (E Element in List)
        ;
}
```

because now you can't construct a method like Process<int, string> that will take a parameter that can't be enumerated.

In general, you do not need constraints on collection types that simply store elements but never call any element methods. However, you generally do need constraints on any type parameter that you actually use—the constraints tell the compiler what type members your generic code can use.

C# Object Types

Lightweight struct types vs. full-function class types

C# has two slightly different object-oriented types. The class keyword defines a reference type: instances live on the heap, and a class variable or parameter is really just a pointer to the object on the heap. The struct keyword creates a value type: instances live on the stack or even in registers, and a struct variable or parameter is an actual data structure. As a value type, no struct can descend from a parent struct—and without posterity, a struct can't include any virtual methods. A class **can** have descendants, and so does support polymorphism. Value types have limited functionality and lower cost: they're lightweight objects, for special cases. Reference types have full functionality and incur garbage collection costs: they're regular objects, for normal use. (For more information, see the "Which Object Type?" section, later in this chapter.)

Inheritance aside, the two types of object are very similar. The struct syntax is a subset of the class syntax, and a struct can be made into a class just by changing one keyword.[4] Both can have tangible members like fields, properties, and methods. Both can implement interfaces. Both can contain nested types like objects, interfaces, and enums. In 2.0, both can be open types.

Similar syntax means it would be wasteful and boring to talk about struct syntax in a value types chapter, only to then repeat the same syntax (with optional elaborations) in a reference types chapter. Seeking to avoid repetition has led me to talk about **both** object-oriented types simply as *objects*, referring to class and struct only when I need to emphasize a difference. Talking about objects is a lot cleaner than always saying something like "class and/or struct types" and is familiar terminology being used correctly, instead of rather obtrusive repetition of a couple of keywords. At the same time, I do know that my talking about objects and object types can be confused with the C# keyword object, which denotes a reference type, the root of the class hierarchy. As dilemmas go, this one is pretty lopsided, so I've opted for simplicity and tried to avoid ambiguity. There probably **are** places where you'll have to read closely, but overall I think you'll find the object terminology pretty clear.

So, objects are reference or value objects, instances of a class type or instances of a struct type. The two are very similar, and while I point out the difference as I go along, and cover them thoroughly in the "Inheritance" section, the most important differences can be summarized as

1. Only class members can have protected access.

2. Only class constructors and methods can refer to the base class.

3. Only class methods can be virtual or abstract. Only class objects can be abstract.

Access

Every member has its own access—no public or private groups

In C#, member visibility is the same for both reference objects and value objects, aside from protected being reserved for class objects (because struct objects can't have descendants). C# member visibility **is** somewhat different than Delphi's. In Delphi as in C++, access keywords like public and private create *regions* within the declaration: all members declared in a public region are public; all members declared in a private region are private; and so on. C# doesn't have visibility regions: in C#, every member is private unless an explicit *access modifier* gives it a different visibility.

---

4. You can do the converse transformation, if your class doesn't use any of the superset syntax.

In the example in the earlier "No Headers" section, the `Empty.Answer()` method

```
public int Answer()
{
   return 42;
}
```

is public because the `public` keyword comes before the method's prototype. In the same way, each member can be preceded by an access modifier: either `public`, `private`, or `internal` for struct members, and either `public`, `protected`, `private`, `internal`, or `protected internal` for class members.

For example, where `Empty.Answer()` is a public method, count

```
private int count = 0; // Private field
```

is a private field, and Count

```
protected int Count // protected property
{
   get { return count; }  // the get method
   set { count = value; } // the set method
}
```

is a protected property that provides access to the private count field. (I cover properties later, in the "Properties" section of this chapter, but this sort of public property with a Proper name, backed by a private field with a common [lowercase] name, is actually a common C# convention.)[5]

Access modifiers can also be applied to nested types like objects, interfaces, delegates, and enums. Like tangible members, nested types default to `private` but can be declared more visible simply by prepending an access modifier. As a nested type, this Colors enum

```
enum Colors {Brown, Yellow, Green}
```

would only be visible within the object it's nested in. However,

---

5. Coming from a case-insensitive language, this can seem like the rankest of heresies—two identifiers that differ only in case! But, after you use a case-sensitive language like C# long enough, it starts to seem a bit more sensible. You start to wonder, is differing only in the case of one letter **that** much smaller a difference than differing only by one letter? You start to see a Proper Noun as being as different from a common noun in code as it is in English, and it starts to seem natural that Proper Nouns and Pascal-Cased identifiers are public while common nouns and camelCased identifiers are private or protected.

Still, no one will revoke your "programming license" if you stick to a convention of backing a public Property with a private _Property or a private fProperty. For what it's worth, all my recent code uses an underscore for the field behind a property—i.e., public Property and private _Property.

In the end, you might even come to think that while case insensitivity is good because you don't have to follow every addled capitalization scheme adopted by the crank who wrote one of the libraries you use, case sensitivity is not so horrible if it encourages a sensible capitalization convention ... like C#'s.

```
public enum Colors {Brown, Yellow, Green}
```

would be visible from methods of other objects. Code outside the enclosing type always uses fully qualified names to refer to a public nested type. For example, if the preceding `Colors` enum were nested in a `Spring` object, code outside the `Spring` class would refer to the `Spring.Colors` enum.

Public means exactly the same thing in C# as in Delphi. Protected and private mean **almost** exactly the same thing in C# as in Delphi—C# has none of Delphi's "in the same file" wiggle. Protected in C# means what `strict protected` does in Delphi for .NET: visible only to methods of this class and any descendants. Private in C# means what `strict private` does in Delphi for .NET: visible to methods of this class.

Internal visibility means the same thing for object members as for namespace-level types: public within its own assembly, private outside of it.

■**Note** Internal visibility is broader than Delphi's {almost} `private`: internally visible members are visible to all types in the whole assembly, regardless of namespace. Delphi almost private members are visible only to code in the same source file.

The special hybrid visibility, `protected internal`, means the member is both protected and internal. In its own assembly, the member is visible to both peer and descendant objects, as an internal member is. In other assemblies, the member is visible only to descendant objects, as a protected member is.

■**Tip** The C# compiler will not let you write a library that declares a `public` method that takes a parameter with an `internal` type.

Modifiers

The syntax category that includes access modifiers

I've covered the *access modifiers* like `public` and `private` and so on, but their optional position before a member's type is actually just a special case of the more general group of *modifiers*. There are other modifiers, like `static` and `virtual`, `new` and `override`.

Modifiers come between any attributes and the member's type:

```
[Member] private static int Field = 0;
```

There are rules that govern when a modifier is present, so I will discuss each modifier as it applies to particular members. But, as a syntax category, all modifiers are created equal and when a member has more than one modifier, they can appear in any order. For example, a `public virtual` method is exactly the same as a `virtual public` method.

There doesn't seem to be any official convention on modifier ordering, but 99% of everybody comes from "access region" languages like Delphi and C++, and they're accustomed to seeing a single declaration appear as, say, public int field = -1. They put the access modifier before other modifiers, so public virtual and not virtual public, protected static not static protected.

Fields

Like Delphi, but with cleaner scope options

So far, a field declaration has been pretty much the same sort of T Name or T Name = Value syntax that you've seen in Chapters 5 and 6, with an optional access modifier. A basic field definition like this, unadorned with scope modifiers, is an instance field like an instance field in Delphi. The only real differences between C# instance fields and native code Delphi instance fields are that on .NET there's metadata on even private and protected members, and not just on specially published members—and that, in 2.0, a field can be of an open, or parameterized, type.

Static Fields

Static fields are like Delphi's writeable typed constants

A static field is a field of the class or struct type. There is only one copy of each static field per running application, and it exists from the time the class is first referred to until the application unloads.[6] Static variables will exist and be properly initialized even when no instance variables have been created; the static constructor (Chapter 2, and "Constructors," later in this chapter) will ensure that static fields are initialized before any code reads a static field or calls a static method.

A static field is declared with the static modifier:

```
static int count = 0; // a (default) private static field
public static int Count = 0; // a public static field
```

Constant Fields

A constant with object scope

The static modifier can never go with the const modifier: a static field is not a constant, and a constant is not a static field. However, an object-scoped constant does **look** like a field with the const modifier:

---

6. While this is a rather advanced detail, technically there is one copy of a static field per *application domain*, and the field lasts until the application domain unloads. While a single .NET process can support multiple application domains, in most .NET processes "application domain" **is** synonymous with "application." See Chapter 14 for details.

```
const int empty = 0; // a private constant
public const int NoValues = -1; // a public constant
```

You can't ever change a constant 'field,' even in a class or instance constructor. As in Delphi, a constant value is a compile-time construct, and doesn't really exist as a field the way static and instance fields do. However, constant fields are not exactly like either Delphi's constants or Delphi's typed constants. Unlike Delphi's constants, constant fields **do** always have a type. That is, a constant can be a long 3 or a float 3, but never just an untyped 3. Unlike Delphi's typed constants, constant fields aren't static fields, read at run time—they are true compile-time constants, which end up inlined into code like Delphi's untyped constants.

■**Tip** You can also declare const local variables (see the "Methods" section, later in this chapter), which are constants scoped to a single block of a method.

Read-only Fields

True fields, with immutable values

Unlike a const 'field,' a readonly field is a true field, either a static field or a normal instance field. What is special about a readonly field is that it can only be set at compile time (via an initializer, like any other field) or in a constructor. Unlike normal static and instance fields, a readonly field cannot be set by any method except a constructor;[7] unlike a const 'field,' a readonly field is a true field. When you read its value at run time, you are reading an actual field; the value is not compiled into the code, as with a constant.

With one major exception, you would not normally use a readonly field where you could use a const field—the point of a readonly field is both that it is immutable and that it is a true field. Because it is a true field, each instance can have a unique value. For example, if you have the two fields

```
static long objectCount = 0;
public readonly long ObjectSerialNumber;
```

a constructor line that says

```
ObjectSerialNumber = objectCount++;
```

will maintain a static count of how many objects have been given a serial number, and each object you 'brand' this way will have an immutable[8] serial number. (The first serial number will be 0. Using ++objectCount [instead of objectCount ++] would make the first serial number be 1.)

---

7. While a field's readonly status is recorded in the metadata, this is a matter of compiler-enforced convention. The CLR **will** let you change a readonly field via either Reflection or handwritten CIL.

8. While in principle this is not a **unique** serial number, 2^{64} is a very large number, and a server creating a million objects a second would take over half a million years to wrap a long. Hence, a 64-bit serial number is **effectively** unique, and there's no real need to explicitly code unchecked(objectCount++).

The exception to the preceding rule of thumb is that in a public class you might want to use a readonly field instead of a public constant. If a public constant changes during development, every dependent assembly needs to be recompiled before it will inline the new value. If this is a realistic possibility, you might be better off using a readonly static field instead of a true constant, as downstream code will then automatically get the correct value, without recompilation.

Volatile Fields

Useful in some threading scenarios

In a single-threaded program, the program's behavior doesn't change if a memory read actually comes from memory or if a memory read comes from cache or a register. Registers are faster than cache, which in turn is faster than memory, but the program will still follow the same path and give the same results. However, in a multithreaded program, a field value that the optimizer has kept in a register (instead of writing to memory) is not visible to other threads. Similarly, in a multiprocessor machine, a value written to one processor's cache may be shadowing a more recent value written to memory by another processor. And, some architectures may have memory-mapped hardware where writes shouldn't be shadowed by the cache, and that may give different results with every read.

CIL includes a volatile modifier that allows the compiler to specify that a memory access really needs to go to or come from physical memory. The static methods Thread.VolatileRead and Thread.VolatileWrite allow application writers to do volatile reads and writes on an as as-needed basis; the volatile field modifier allows you to guarantee that **all** access to a field is done as a volatile access.

Caution Volatile access does have performance implications, and is only necessary in certain very specialized cases. In most cases, normal locking is sufficient to guarantee synchronization across threads and processors. See Chapter 17 for details.

The new Modifier

Acknowledges reintroduction

The new modifier is only appropriate in derived classes, ones that explicitly inherit from a base class. (As a special case, you can use new to reintroduce Object methods, instead of overriding them, even in value types or classes that don't explicitly inherit from Object.) The new modifier, like Delphi's reintroduce, is for cases where a class needs to shadow an ancestral member. If you have a Base class

```
class Base
{
  protected int Field = 1;
}
```

and a Derived class that inherits from Base

```
class Derived: Base
{
  double Field = -1d; // will give a warning
}
```

the redefinition of Field will compile, with a warning (not an error) that "it hides [the] inherited member." If you change the redefinition in Derived to

```
new double Field = -1d; // no warning
```

the warning will go away.

Conversely, the new modifier is **only** for cases where a class wants to shadow an ancestral member. Code like

```
class Base
{
  new protected int Field = 1; // will generate a warning about misuse of new
}
```

will generate a warning about misuse of new.

■**Note** The new modifier can be used with properties and methods as well as with fields.

Whether or not you use new to cancel the warning about hiding an inherited member, you can access a hidden member with the base pseudo-reference. For example, methods of the preceding Derived class could refer to base.Field in much the same way that they can refer to this.Field. If you are mixing references to a new member and a shadowed member, like

```
this.Field = base.Field;
```

it's a good practice to explicitly use the this reference—even if you don't need to—to minimize any confusion.

Methods

No distinction between a procedure and a function

As with other members, method declarations can be preceded by attributes in square brackets, [], which can optionally be followed by an access modifier and one of the scope modifiers static, virtual, override, and new. I discuss instance and static methods in this section; I cover the virtual, override, and new modifiers in the upcoming "Polymorphism" section; I cover attributes in Chapter 8.

After the optional attributes and modifiers, a method has a mandatory return type, the method's name, an optional type parameter list (in 2.0), the method's parameters in parentheses, and the method body block in curly braces.

```
public void Procedure() {} //  does nothing, returns nothing
public static bool KnowAirspeedOf (Swallow Unladen)
{
  return Unladen is AfricanSwallow;
}
```

All methods have a return type: methods that do not return a result (Delphi procedures) have a return type of void. All methods have a parenthesized prototype: unlike Delphi, even methods that don't take any arguments are always declared and called with an empty pair of parens, (). (Delphi methods that take no parameters **can** be called with empty parens, even though this is so uncommon that the first time I saw this usage [on a whiteboard, at a job interview] I said "that's C, not Delphi—that won't compile.")

Methods can overload one another, provided the parameter lists are different. Note that this is "different" as in "different types"—the parameter names do not matter, nor does the return type. There is no overload modifier; you simply declare multiple methods with the same name and different parameter lists. Overloaded methods can differ in access and in return type.

Note Overloading refers to methods with the same name and different parameter lists. The "Polymorphism" section, later in this chapter, discusses the ways a descendant can *shadow* (hide) an inherited method with the same name and the same prototype (i.e., the same parameter list and return type).

Method parameters are declared within the prototype's paren pair, (), as uninitialized Type Name declarations. Multiple parameters are separated by a comma; unlike Delphi, each parameter has its own type definition. That is, in Delphi one can write both

```
procedure Foo(A, B: integer);
```

and

```
procedure Foo(A: integer; B: integer);
```

but in C# only

```
void Foo(int A, int B)
```

is valid.

METHOD PROTOTYPES AND /// COMMENTS

In Visual Studio, if you insert a blank line before a method prototype like

```
public static bool KnowAirspeedOf (Swallow Unladen)
```

and type /// on the blank line, you will automatically get an XML Doc template like

```
/// <summary>
///
/// </summary>
/// <param name="Unladen"></param>
/// <returns></returns>
public static bool KnowAirspeedOf (Swallow Unladen)
```

If you fill this in as

```
/// <summary>
/// What is the airspeed of an unladen swallow?
/// </summary>
/// <param name="Unladen">Is that an African, or a European swallow?</param>
/// <returns>Whether 'I' know the answer</returns>
public static bool KnowAirspeedOf(Swallow Unladen)
```

the <summary> text will show up in the Alt+RightCursor code completion drop-down and in mouse-hover tool tips, while the <param> text will show up in the Shift+Ctrl+Space parameter hints. (The <summary> text will also show up in the Shift+Ctrl+Space parameter hints, if you cursor back to the method name.) *IntelliSense* doesn't show the <returns> text, but the Visual Studio Object Browser window shows all three. If you use the /doc switch (from the command line, or via the project property's Build/XML Documentation File textbox), your help text will be available to anyone who uses your assembly.

Visual Studio automatically treats each block of /// lines as a folding region. When the XML Doc block is folded, it shows as a boxed, gray /**/ comment block—like /**/. When you hover the mouse over the boxed comment block, you get the text of the XML doc block in a tool tip, as in Figure 7-1.

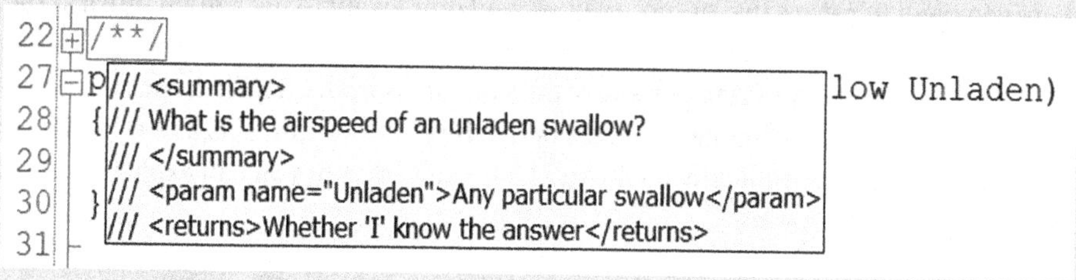

```
22  /**/
27  p /// <summary>                                           low Unladen)
28  { /// What is the airspeed of an unladen swallow?
29    /// </summary>
30  } /// <param name="Unladen">Any particular swallow</param>
31    /// <returns>Whether 'I' know the answer</returns>
```

Figure 7-1. *The XML doc as a tool tip for a folded /// block*

You can also type /// on a blank line above other members, and will get a similar XML doc template.

If a method's final parameter is an array parameter, you can mark it with the `params` keyword, like

```
public int Sum(params int[] Values)
{
  int Result = 0;
  foreach (int Value in Values)
    Result += Value;
  return Result;
}
```

When you call a method with a `params` parameter, you can pass it any number of arguments (of the right type). That is, you can call `Sum(1, 2, 3, 4, 5)` instead of `Sum(new int[] {1, 2, 3, 4, 5})`—the 'variadic' version generates exactly the same CIL as the explicit array creation version, but is significantly smaller and easier to read.

Note that C# does not support default parameters. The proffered rationale is that a default parameter gets replicated as a constant in every bit of code that uses the default. Using an explicit overload with fewer parameters to supply the default means that the default parameter only exists in one place, not every call, and so all the code that uses the default form is a little smaller. More importantly, a replicated constant presents the same versioning issues that a public constant does: if you change the default parameter, dependent code will continue using the old default value until it's recompiled.

Method parameters can optionally be marked as `ref` or `out` parameters:

```
void IncrementsParam(ref int Param)  { Param++; }
void ZeroesParam(out int Param)       { Param = 0; }
```

As with Delphi var and out parameters, `ref` and `out` parameters specify a *pass by reference*—a change to the parameter changes the calling environment. Inside the method, you use `ref` and `out` parameters just like you use other parameters, but (unlike Delphi) you must explicitly **pass** parameters as `ref` or `out` when calling the method, as in `IncrementsParam(ref Variable)` or `ZeroesParam(out Variable)`. It is an error to pass an uninitialized variable as a `ref` parameter, but you can pass both initialized and uninitialized variables as out parameters. It is OK to not change a `ref` parameter, but it is an error to not set an `out` parameter. (Out parameters are often used where you need to `return` two or more values, and don't want to pack them into a `struct`, perhaps because you want to return a `bool` for use in various conditional statements.)

The method body consists of zero or more of the statements from Chapter 6, each terminated with a semicolon. Within an instance method's body, the `this` keyword acts as a reference to the object instance: you can implicitly refer to an instance `Member` or you can explicitly refer to `this.Member`.[9]

---

9. The this keyword acts a bit differently in constructor prototypes, as does the syntactically similar base.

Tip Both `struct` and `class` objects can have `static` methods, which cannot refer to instance members either implicitly via an unqualified name or explicitly via the `this` reference (which they don't have). While static methods **are** methods of the object, and **can** refer to private instance members, they can only do so via an explicit instance of their type—either a static field or a method parameter.

The method body and any block statements it contains may declare local variables with the standard `T Name` or `T Name = Value` syntax. The only modifier that can be applied to a local variable is `const`—local variables can't be static, and access modifiers don't apply to local variables. A `const T Name = value` local 'variable' is actually a local constant.

Local variables and local constants are visible from the point they're declared to the end of their block, including any enclosed blocks, but disappear when control passes to an outer block. Locals can shadow instance members and static members, but cannot shadow method parameters or other in-scope locals. (There is no `..` syntax that gives access to an outer scope.)

As in Delphi, within a method the meaning of an unqualified identifier depends on the current scope (see Figure 7-2). Any local variables and local constants shadow any instance members, which shadow any static members. In case of ambiguity, you can use explicit instance references like `this.Identifier` to specify an instance member, or explicit class values like `ClassName.Identifer` to specify a static member.

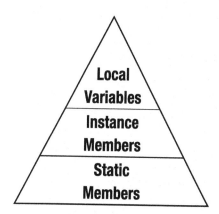

Figure 7-2. *Local variables shadow instance members, which shadow static members.*

C# does not have any statement like Delphi's `with`, though `foreach` is somewhat similar (in that you create and initialize a local variable outside a statement block, and the variable goes away when control passes out of the statement block), and you can always have a block like

```
{
  Item ThisItem = Some.ComplicatedExpression.ThatReturns.AnItem;
  // do something with ThisItem
}
```

that saves some complicated expression to an explicit temporary variable, and then works with that temporary variable as a shortcut.

A void method can simply execute to the end of its method body, or it can explicitly return (without specifying a value) at any point. A method can return from more than one point. A method that does not return void **must** explicitly return a value of the right type; it cannot simply execute to the end of its method body. The compiler generates an error (not a warning) if a method that should return a value has any code path that does **not** either return a value or raise an exception.

In 2.0, any object or interface—whether open or closed—can declare an *open method* that takes type parameter(s) between the method's name and the prototype, just as with open delegates. For example, this method from the Chapter7\FirstThat project is an open method in a closed class:

```
public static int FirstThat<T>(Predicate<T> Test, params T[] Data)
{
    for (int I = 0; I < Data.Length; I++)
        if (Test(Data[I]))
            return I;
    // else
    return -1;
}
```

■**Note** Although it doesn't make much sense for an open method to not use its type parameters in its prototype or its body, this is not required: void Dumb<T>() {} may be dumb, but it's perfectly legal.

When you call an open method, you can supply types in brackets between the name and the prototype, much like when you declare or create a closed constructed type. For example, FirstThat<int>(IntPredicate, 1, 2, 3, 4, 5) or FirstThat<string>(StringPredicate, "this", "that", "the other").

In many cases, you can omit the types in brackets when calling an open method. For example, given FirstThat(IntPredicate, 1, 2, 3, 4, 5), the compiler can **infer** that you really mean FirstThat<int>(IntPredicate, 1, 2, 3, 4, 5). You only need to use the type parameter list when type inference fails.

An open delegate (Chapter 8) instance can be created around any method with the right signature: it doesn't matter whether that method is a closed method that 'naturally' has the right signature, or whether that method is a closed constructed method, created by supplying the right type to an open method. For example, in the Chapter7\FirstThat project, given the bool Positive(int Value) and the bool NeverTrue<T>(T Value) methods, the int FirstPositive(params int[] Data) method can call FirstThat<int>(NeverTrue<int>, Data) or FirstThat<int>(Positive, Data)—but not FirstThat<int>(NeverTrue<string>, Data).

Inheritance

Note Structs have encapsulation—they can have public and private methods and members. As light-weight, optimization-oriented objects, they don't have inheritance and polymorphism. Thus, this section and the subsequent "Polymorphism" section apply only to C# `class` types.

Very like Delphi

In Delphi, all classes inherit from a single ancestor, `TObject`. In C#, all classes inherit from a single ancestor, `object`, the keyword alias for `System.Object`.

A class that does not explicitly descend from any class,

```
class Parent
{
  protected int member = 0;
}
```

implicitly descends from `object`. A class can explicitly descend from `object`

```
class Parent: object
{
  protected int member = 0;
}
```

or from any other object by putting a colon, `:`, after the new class's name, and then following that with the base type's name. Thus, adding

```
class Child: Parent
{
}
```

gives us a `Child` class, which descends from the `Parent` class, which descends directly from `object`.

Within a child class, the `base` keyword acts something like the `this` reference—you can refer to `base.Member` as you would refer to `this.Member` or call `base.Method()` as you would call `this.Method()`. While the `base` reference is a reference to the same object as the `this` reference, the `base` reference can only be used to qualify names inherited from the parent class. When the current class shadows `Member`, `base.Member` refers to the inherited, shadowed member, while `this.Member` refers to the new, shadowing member. That is, you **can** use `base` just to show that you are referring to an inherited member, but the real point of `base` is that it gives you access to shadowed members, like the parent's implementation of a virtual method.

Note The `base` keyword has semantics like ("acts like") Delphi's `inherited` keyword, though the syntax is slightly different.

Polymorphism

■**Note** Structs are lightweight objects that don't support inheritance and polymorphism. Thus, this section and the previous "Inheritance" section apply only to C# class objects.

Reference types support polymorphic behavior

An object can have more than one method with the same name, so long as each has a different parameter list. A descendant type can add a new method to the overloaded set simply by defining another method with the same name and different prototype. That is, a descendant type can overload ancestral methods. If you have a reference to the parent type, you will only 'see' the overloads available to the parent type. If you have a reference to the descendant type, you will see both the parent class overloads and the descendant class overloads.

However, if a descendant defines a new method with the same name and parameter list as an ancestral type, the descendant is shadowing that particular overload. This will generate a compiler warning unless you mark the descendant's method with the new modifier. If you call the shadowed method through a reference to the parent type, you will get the shadowed method. If you call the shadowed method through a reference to the descendant type, you will get the new method.

This is instance method binding, and it acts in C# much as in Delphi, despite the way that C# uses the new keyword where Delphi uses the reintroduce keyword. C# is also similar to Delphi when it comes to virtual method binding.

The virtual modifier lets you define a method that you expect descendant types will shadow with override methods. You can only use the override modifier when both the return type and the parameter types match. It is a syntax error to use the override modifier when you are not shadowing a virtual (or abstract) method with the same name and prototype.

Whether you call the method from a reference to the type that defines the virtual method or from a reference to a descendant type, the system will use a hierarchy of *method tables* to call the method the from the type 'closest' to the type of the actual instance. Thus, given

```
class Parent
{
  public  virtual int Function(int N)
  {
    return N + 1;
  }
}
class Child: Parent
{
  public override int Function(int N)
  {
    return base.Function(N) + 1;
  }
}
```

```
class GrandChild: Child
{
}
Parent ParentInstance = new Parent();
Parent ChildInstance = new Child();
Parent GrandChildInstance = new GrandChild();
```

ParentInstance.Function(0) returns 1, while both ChildInstance.Function(0) and GrandChildInstance.Function(0) return 2.

A method can also be marked abstract, which means that it is a virtual method that **must** be overridden by a descendant type. An abstract method has no method body; only a semicolon.

```
public abstract class abstractParent
{
  public abstract int Function(int N);
}

internal class Child: abstractParent
{
  public override int Function(int N)
  {
    return N + 1;
  }
}
```

Only abstract classes can have abstract methods, but abstract classes do not **have** to have abstract methods. You mark a class abstract by applying the abstract modifier to the class name, usually after the public or internal access modifier, if any.

You cannot create instances of abstract classes. (You can, however, call static methods of abstract classes.) Any descendant of an abstract class must either be itself an abstract class or must override **all** abstract methods that it inherits, regardless of whether these abstract methods were declared directly in the parent class or higher up the inheritance chain.

■**Note** In C# 1.0, the only ways to prevent users from creating instances of a class are to mark it as abstract, or to explicitly declare a private, parameterless constructor without declaring any public constructors. These techniques work, but do some violence to the semantics if the real reason that you want to prevent instantiation is that the class has only static members. In 2.0, classes can be marked as static. Static classes can't have instance members, and you can't create an instance of a static class.

Properties

More novel syntax for familiar semantics

A property declaration is something of a cross between a field declaration and a method declaration. This is appropriate enough, given that a C# property is something that looks like a field but is actually a pair of get and set methods. A property has optional access modifiers, then an optional virtual, abstract, or static modifier, then a type, a name, and a set of curly braces, {}. Within the curlies, you can have a get and/or a set method, in either order. (That is, you don't have to have **both** the get and the set methods, and you can't have more than one get method or more than one set method, but you do have to have either a get or a set method.)

Both get and set methods have a special syntax, simpler than normal instance methods. They look like a get or set keyword followed by a block in curly braces. The get block must return a value of the same type as the property; the set block has a special, implicit parameter named value, of the same type as the property itself.

Thus, a read-only property

```csharp
int count = 0;
public int Count
{
    get { return count; }  // a read-only property
}
```

a property that keeps track of how many times it's been 'set'

```csharp
int count = 0;
public int Count
{
    get { return count; }
    set { count++; }
}
```

and a property that only redraws when the value changes

```csharp
string caption = "";
public string Caption
{
    get { return caption; } // standard public Caption / private caption
    set
    {
        if (caption != value)
        {
            caption = value;
            Redraw();
        }
    }
}
```

This Caption property uses the standard format—with the curlies on separate lines, lined up with the set or get keyword and the code indented within that—for the set method. That's awfully bulky for a single statement method, and most people do run single statement methods onto a single line like the preceding get { return count; } and get { return caption; } methods.

Note Though the block-after-a-keyword syntax is unusual, `get` and `set` methods **are** separate methods. An `int` property named `Example` with both get and set methods actually defines two methods, `int get_Example()` and `void set_Example(int value)`. The method body for each of these methods is the contents of the code block after the `get` or `set` keyword. You can find these `get_` and `set_` methods with Reflection (Chapter 14), and you may very occasionally need to access a cross-language property via these CLS-compatible `get_` and `set_` methods.

Like methods, properties can be `static` properties or instance properties, and reference types can have `virtual` properties or `abstract` properties. A `static`, `virtual`, `abstract`, or `override` modifier before the property type applies to **both** get and set methods, if both are defined: you can't have, say, a `virtual` get and an instance set.

As with abstract methods, abstract properties can only appear in abstract classes. Also as with abstract methods, abstract properties

```
public abstract int Count
{
  get ;
  set ;
}
```

have no method body, just a semicolon.

Indexers

Specialized version of property syntax

C# indexers are a lot like Delphi's default array properties. The syntax is something like a standard property, except that the property name is always the keyword `this`, and it is followed by a parameter list in **square brackets**, [ ], not the parens of a method's parameter list. Also, unlike a normal method, the parameter list cannot be empty—while indexers can have multiple parameters, indexers **must** have at least one parameter.

```
public object this[string S]
{
  get  {  return null;  } // yeah, yeah ...
}
public object this[object O]
{
  get  {  return this[O.ToString()];  }
}
```

As with normal methods, you can overload indexers, as long as the parameter list is unique. Unlike normal methods, you call the indexer's **get** and **set** methods by using what looks like normal array syntax—you read or write `ObjectVar[Parameters]` just as you read or write array elements.

An indexer's set method has an implicit `value` parameter, just like any other set method.

Note Delphi classes can have any number of index properties, so it's always a bit of a shock for Delphi programmers to find that C# classes can only have a single indexed property, `this`. However, you can always write code like `ThisInstance.IndexedProperty[ThisIndex]` if each `IndexedProperty` is an instance of a class that has an indexer of its own.

Mixed Access

Different access for get and set methods

In C# 1.0, a property's access applied to both the set and the get methods. A public property with set and get methods (as opposed to a set method or a get method but not both) had public set and get methods; a private property with set and get methods had private set and get methods; and so on. In C# 2.0, the get and set methods can have different access: you can have, say, a public get method and a private or protected set method.

The access declared before the property type still applies to both methods, by default, but a property with both set and get methods can impose lower visibility on either of the two access methods. That is, you can have an access modifier before either the set or the get, but not both, and this secondary access modifier must be more restrictive than the primary access.

For example,

```
public int Count
{
            get { return _Count;  } // public get
   protected set { _Count = value; } // protected set
}
```

Parameterized Properties

Parameterized types, but no open access methods

Open types can have properties with parameterized types:

```
public class OpenClass<T>
{
   public T OpenProperty
   {
       get { return _OpenProperty; }
   }
   private T _OpenProperty = default(T);
}
```

However, while procedure get/set methods are true methods, they cannot be open methods. That is, you **cannot** write code like

```
public int OpenProperty<T>
{
  get { return SomeMethod<T>(); }      // not allowed
}
```

or

```
public int OpenProperty
{
  get <T> { return SomeMethod<T>(); } // not allowed
}
```

Constructors

Surprisingly complex

A simple class or struct constructor looks a little like an anonymous method—optional access modifiers, and maybe static; a return type, **no name**, a param list in parens, an optional *initializer*, and a method body (see Table 7-1).

Table 7-1. *Constructor Syntax*

Syntactic Element	Notes
Optional access modifiers	public, private, protected, internal, or protected internal.
Optional static	A static constructor is a class constructor; C# does not support (or need) virtual constructors.
Mandatory return type	The type the constructor initializes, as a matter of fact.
No name	Ever since BCB, we've been urged to not use any name but Create in Delphi, so it's hard to mourn the 'lack' of named constructors, especially when named static factory methods can always return new instances.
Parameter list, in parens	1) Value type parameters must have at least one parameter; parameters are optional for reference types. 2) Constructor overloading acts differently than method overloading.
Optional *initializer*	It looks something like inheritance, with a : after the parens, and a base() or this() call.
Constructor body	In {} curly braces.

By convention, constructor parameters that initialize fields have the same name as the field that they're initializing, and the constructor uses the this reference to copy the parameter to the field.

```
public class Tree
{
  protected Tree Left, Right;
  public Tree(Tree Left, Tree Right)
  {
    this.Left = Left;
    this.Right = Right;
  }
}
```

You can overload constructors just as you overload methods, simply by defining multiple constructors with different parameter lists. When you create a class instance, or when you initialize a struct, you call a constructor by using the new operator, followed by the name of the type, and a parameter list inside a pair of parens. (Parameters are optional for reference types; value type constructors always have at least one parameter.) The type and order of the parameters select a constructor overload exactly as the type and order of parameters selects a method overload.

For example, new ArrayList() calls the no-parameter constructor to initialize a new ArrayList (Chapter 12) to a default Capacity, while new ArrayList(1000) calls the constructor that takes an int capacity parameter to initialize a new ArrayList to a Capacity of 1000.

■**Note** The new operator works a bit differently with reference types than with value types. With reference types, new creates a new heap block, calls the constructor to initialize this, and returns the new reference. With value types, new *constructs in place*, passing a reference to an existing struct as the constructor's this parameter. Declaring a value type local like Rectangle Unset; allocates space on the stack, but does not initialize the Unset variable. Declaring a value type local like Point Origin = new Point(0, 0); allocates space for Origin on the stack, then passes a reference to Origin to the Point constructor that can accept a pair of integers. (Value type fields in class types are not unset; they are filled with 0x00 bytes when the class is instantiated. Using the new operator to initialize value type fields in class instances also constructs in place.)

Because of constructors' optional initializer, constructor overloading acts a bit differently than method overloading. For example, the following code will not compile:

```
public class ExpressionTree: Tree
{
  protected Expression thisExpression;
  // These constructors will not actually compile -
  // "No overload for method 'Tree' takes '0' arguments"
  public ExpressionTree()
  {
    this.Left = null;
    this.Right = null;
  }
```

```
public ExpressionTree(ExpressionTree Left, ExpressionTree Right)
{
    this.Left = Left;
    this.Right = Right;
}
}
```

If these two constructors were methods, they would compile, aside from the lack of a method name. As constructors, they don't compile, even though they're syntactically well-formed constructors.

You get a compiler error message about how *No overload ... takes '0' arguments* and the sheer, old-fashioned "true, but not helpful" of that message can take your breath away. After all, C# error messages **are** pretty helpful for the most part, and they catch a fair number of bad practices. That this one is so retro hostile is a clue that it's going to take a while to explain why the preceding two constructors won't compile.

There are two issues interacting here, which makes for a tangled web that's not particularly amenable to being summarized in a single message ... or even a single page.

Optional Initializer

'Inherit construction' all the way up to object

The optional initializer syntax—which the preceding constructors did not use—allows each constructor to 'inherit construction' from a peer or from a base class constructor. Not using the optional syntax to explicitly inherit construction acts just like explicitly inheriting construction from base(), the base class constructor with no parameters.

Thus (assuming no mutual recursion) no matter which constructor overloads you call, ultimately **some** base constructor will get called, and so ultimately constructors will be called all the way up to the root object. (Value objects have no parent struct and so no base() constructors.) This in turn assures that the compiler-generated part of each constructor (the part which initializes all the instance fields) will always be run.[10]

The initializer syntax looks somewhat like class inheritance, which is why I speak of inheriting construction. A constructor like

```
public Empty() {}
```

that doesn't explicitly inherit construction is "exactly equivalent"[11] to

```
public Empty(): base() {}
```

which does explicitly inherit construction, from base().

---

10. Instance fields are only initialized once, no matter how many this() constructors are called. The compiler **could** do this by calling the generated field constructor before any user constructor, not calling it again on this() calls, and calling the base class's generated constructor when calling a base() constructor.

11. *C# Language Specification*, section 10.10.1, "Constructor initializers."

That is, the optional initializer syntax is signaled by a colon after the constructor prototype, followed by either this or base, followed by parameters whose type and order selects an appropriate constructor overload. (Again, a struct has no base or base() constructors.)

Thus, the ExpressionTree example should actually read

```
public class ExpressionTree: Tree
{
  protected Expression thisExpression;
  public ExpressionTree(): this(null, null) {}
  public ExpressionTree(ExpressionTree Left, ExpressionTree Right)
    : base(Left, Right) {}
}
```

which compiles **and** has a lot less duplicated code.

This second ExpressionTree example shows a constructor overload that calls this() to set all fields to default values. It's also common to have 'trees' of constructors,[12] each 'descendant' constructor adding another parameter to an existing overload. For a very simple example, a constructor for the Identified structure (following this paragraph) always takes an explicit string Identity but can default both the int Value, and the DateTime TimeStamp. The overload that takes only a string passes this Identity and a default Value on to its ad hoc parent, the overload that takes a string and an int, which in turn passes both parameters and a default TimeStamp to the overload that takes all three parameters:

```
struct Identified
{
  private const int DefaultValue = 0;
  private int Value;
  private string Identity;
  private DateTime TimeStamp;

  public Identified(string Identity):
    this(Identity, DefaultValue)
  {}
  public Identified(string Identity, int Value):
    this(DateTime.Now, Identity, Value)
  {}
  public Identified(DateTime TimeStamp, string Identity):
    this(TimeStamp, Identity, DefaultValue)
  {}
  public Identified(DateTime TimeStamp, string Identity, int Value)
  {
    this.Value = Value;
    this.Identity = Identity;
    this.TimeStamp = TimeStamp;
  }
}
```

---

12. And, yes, trees of method overloads.

There are four constructors here, but only the last one actually sets fields. The two in the middle call that last one directly, and the first, (`string Identity`), constructor calls the last constructor via the second, (`string Identity`, `int Value`), constructor. Note the way that each field gets either set or defaulted, but never both set and defaulted.[13]

The overloads that don't start with `DateTime TimeStamp` pass `DateTime.Now` to an overload that takes an explicit timestamp. There is only one read of this static property, while the constant `DefaultValue` is inlined twice.

Initializer calls do not have access to the `this` (or `base`) reference, and cannot refer to instance members in any way. They can pass on parameter values; they can create objects and call static methods; and they can involve constant expressions that refer to parameters and/or to primitive literals like numbers and strings.

Note Most Delphi programmers find initializers rather strange at first, and indeed it is rather hard to construct a better rationale than that it makes it easier for the compiler to guarantee that every class calls a base class constructor, and that field initialization is always done (once and only once) before explicit construction—which is a pretty strange rationale, when you think of all the hard work that the C# compiler does that the Delphi compiler does not. About all I can say is that after three years of C#, the initializers don't seem at all strange any more.

Also, please note that while the C# compiler will not let a constructor inherit construction from itself,

```
public class Forbidden
{
  public Forbidden(int I):  this(1) {} // "Constructor ... cannot call itself"
}
```

it does **not** detect mutually recursive constructor calls like

```
public class Recurse
{
  public Recurse(int I):  this(1L) {}
  public Recurse(long L): this(1)  {}
}
```

You can compile this class, but when you call either constructor (via either `new Recurse(1)` or `new Recurse(1L)`) you get a stack overflow.

---

13. A struct can't have field initializers. This makes it useful for illustrating set-once discipline.

Default Constructors

Declare one, declare them all

The first ExpressionTree example generated the *No overload ... takes '0' arguments* message because it didn't use explicit construction inheritance, and so implicitly inherited construction from base()—and the Tree class doesn't have a no-parameter constructor.

The reason the Tree class doesn't have a no-parameter constructor is that it declared a constructor with explicit parameters. This may sound strange.

When you **don't** explicitly declare any constructors, C# will implicitly define a

```
public ClassName(): base() {}
```

constructor that does nothing but call base(). This implicit constructor is a perfect match for a descendant's implicit base() call.

However, if you declare **any** constructors, you have to declare **all** constructors: C# will only supply the default, no-parameter constructor if you don't declare any constructors.

■**Note** The reasoning appears to be that an object that sometimes needs some initialization beyond field init may actually **always** (or, at least, often) need some initialization beyond field init. Supplying a no-parameter constructor that does no extra init would hide the fact that you hadn't supplied a no-parameter constructor that does the extra initialization, and would allow a user to accidentally bypass some required initialization.

If you don't declare a public, no-parameter constructor, your descendant classes' constructors have to explicitly inherit construction from a constructor that does take parameters.

Which lets me finally lay the *No overload ... takes '0' arguments* message to rest. The Tree class didn't define a no-parameter constructor, because it wanted to always set both links in the constructor. When the first ExpressionTree example didn't explicitly call a base constructor it implicitly called base()—even though it absolutely doesn't look that way. This was violating the Tree semantics that don't include a no-parameter constructor, because both links should always be set in the constructor—which is part of why there was so much duplicated code in the first ExpressionTree example and why the second ExpressionTree example is so much smaller.

The semantics violation led to the error message: the first ExpressionTree example doesn't compile because there are no no-parameter constructors. There are no no-parameter constructors because Tree 'wants' to always set both links in the constructor.

In young, rapidly evolving code, the *No overload ... takes '0' arguments* message **may** be a signal that you haven't thought through your base class thoroughly; that you need to add a no-parameter constructor. However, library code has generally been both thought through and tested, and if you get this message descending from library code, it's more likely to be the case that you don't understand the library classes than it is to be the case that a library class fails to include a constructor that it should.

Value Types

A constructor for a struct *is a special method that must set all fields*

A struct object can have constructors just like class objects can, and can use the : this() syntax to 'inherit construction' from a peer constructor.

A struct cannot use field initializers, and cannot have an explicit parameterless constructor. Calling new StructName() will initialize all fields to 0 or null. Note that this **is** different than declaring a struct field or variable without calling new, which allocates space but leaves it uninitialized.

A struct constructor must set all fields before returning, directly or by 'inheritance,' but the compiler won't 'see' settings in normal methods that the constructor calls—e.g., you have to inline Reset(), not call it.

Note that in Delphi for .NET, when you Create() a record variable like

```
var R: MyRecord;
R := MyRecord.Create(X, Y, Z);
```

you are getting a copy operation: since Delphi doesn't require that a record constructor set every field, the MyRecord.Create(X, Y, Z) compiles to a newobj CIL instruction, which creates a new record on the stack; initializes all fields to 0/Nil; calls the constructor; and then copies it to R.

The equivalent C# syntax

```
MyStruct S = new MyStruct(X, Y, Z);
```

constructs in place—it does not do a copy the way DfN does. The constructor receives a pointer to the new struct as its implicit this reference in pretty much the same way as any other method.

Finalizers

Finalizers look like C++ destructors

Most objects don't have finalizers. No struct ever has a finalizer, and the only reference types that should have finalizers are those that must release operating system resources—files, timers, sockets, graphics tools, and the like (see the "Finalization" section of Chapter 3).

In C#, you don't override the Finalize method and you don't explicitly call the base finalizer. Rather, you write a destructor using C++ syntax: optional attributes, a ~ (tilde) character, the type name, a paren pair, and the method body in curlies:

```
class Finalizer
{
  ~Finalizer()
  {
  }
}
```

Destructors take no parameters, and so cannot be overloaded. That is, there is never more than one destructor per class.

Somewhat as with uses and lock, C# uses the destructor's method body to create a Finalize method with an implicit try/finally block: the destructor's method body is the body of the try block, and the finally block calls base.Finalize(). This assures that all finalizers get called (most derived gets called first, object gets called last) even if one (or more) raises an exception.

As per Chapter 3, classes that have finalizers should also implement IDisposable. Typically, both the finalizer and the Dispose method call a third method that actually closes the operating system resource; the Dispose method also calls GC.SuppressFinalize():

```
public class Finalizer: IDisposable
{
  ~ Finalizer()
  {
    FinalizeInstance();
  }
  public void Dispose()
  {
    FinalizeInstance();
    GC.SuppressFinalize(this);
  }
  private void FinalizeInstance()
  {}
}
```

Operator Overloading

Can clarify and cut bloat; can confuse and waste time

C# supports operator overloading for both class and struct object types. All overload methods must be explicitly declared as public static methods—you can't declare an operator method that's not public and static, but the operator keyword does not make a method public and static. You can use the operator keyword to overload both arithmetic operators like + and - and relational operators like < and !=. You can also use the operator keyword to control various aspects of type conversion by overloading keywords like true and false, and implicit and explicit.

The syntax of infix operators and type conversion differs enough that I discuss each in separate subsections, following the "Background and Warning" subsection. I briefly discuss the special case of type conversion to bool in the final subsection, "Truth."

> ■**Note** "Operator Overloading" is a long section because it's a **complex** subject—not because it's an **important** subject that you must master. Very few libraries and almost no applications will overload operators.

Background and Warning

Since you may have no direct experience with operator overloading

C# has many numeric types and is well suited to algebraic calculations. However, some more sophisticated maths require numeric types that are not supported. Common examples include complex numbers (with a real and imaginary component), vectors, matrices, and big numbers (integers with thousands of digits, each of which is significant). It doesn't make sense for a compiler to support these numerical types, because there are too many of these types to support them all, and even the most common are only used by a small subset of those who use the compiler. Operator overloading is desirable for specialized numbers, because code like `(A + B) / (C - D)` **is** easier to read and write than either `A.Add(B).Divide(C.Subtract(D))` or `Complex.Divide( Complex.Add(A, B), Complex.Subtract(C, D) )`.

When you're not coding an actual numeric type, though, operator overloading gets hard to justify. Appending to a collection is somewhat like addition, but deletion isn't quite like subtraction (do you mean delete first, or delete all?), and replacement is nothing like multiplication. In most cases, it doesn't make a lot of sense to overload one common operation while leaving others symbolic, and while `List.Append(Item)` and `List.Prepend(Item)` are longer than `List + Item` and `Item + List`, they're clearer and easier to trace. (You may find `List + Item` clearer than `List.Append(Item)`, but I believe that's mostly a matter of habit. In reality, concatenation is a bad metaphorical fit with addition, which is *commutative* [3 + 5 = 5 + 3] where concatenation is not ["this" + "that" != "that" + "this"].)[14]

You may be tempted to write code like if (`Assets > Obligations`) (where both `Assets` and `Obligations` are collections of accounting line items) or if (`Queue`) `Queue.ProcessFirst()` (where `Queue` is `true` when not empty). You shouldn't. I do use examples like if (`Queue`) `{}` because they are very short and—in the context of a discussion about type conversion— very clear. But in the wild you really should use a explicit method or property, like if (`Queue.Populated`) `{}`, because it's much clearer what's going on than code like if (`Queue`) `{}`.[15]

Operator overloading is almost entirely for types that act like simple values. Objects with state should stick to explicit method calls except in the very few cases where you have a common operation that is often done iteratively and the order of execution with the *infix* notation of `A + B + C` **is** easier to read than with the *prefix* notation of `A.Concatenate(B.Concatenate(C))` or `List.Concatenate(A, List.Concatenate(B, C))`.

---

14. This is why native code Delphi's didn't have operator overloading until Delphi 2006: it's invaluable in a small set of technical programs, but of limited use and potentially much harm in most others.

15. You can make a *two-tier argument*, that it's really obvious that a collection is `true` when not empty, that it is very analogous to null vs. assigned, zero vs. nonzero, &c. There's even something to say for it, in the case of collections. But it seems such a thin tier compared with all the other object types that clearly shouldn't overload truth, that it does seem to me best to not make truth any more metaphorical than it already is.

Infix Operators

Almost always return a value type

You can overload the *unary* (one argument) operators +, -, !, ~, ++, and --, as well as the *binary* (two argument) arithmetic operators +, -, *, /, %, &, |, and ^, and the relational operators <<, >>, <=, <, ==, !=, >, and >=. For example,

```
public static CustomNumber operator - (double Operand)
public static CustomNumber operator +(CustomNumber Left, CustomNumber Right)
```

Note that you can have multiple overloads for an operator just like you can have multiple overloads for a method or constructor: `public static List operator + (List L, object O)` is **not** the same as `public static List operator + (object O, List L)`.

A type cannot define operators that do not involve itself: at least one of the input or output types must be the type that's defining the operator, the *enclosing type*. Arithmetic operators like + and % usually return the enclosing type; relational operators like < and != **usually** return bool.[16]

Except for the relatively rare cases where you want your class to overload + with something like string concatenation, most objects that overload arithmetic operators will be value types (or struct objects). This is because any arithmetic expression with more than one operator involves intermediate results. It's usually more efficient to keep intermediate results in registers or on the stack than to keep creating objects on the heap.

Note that it's not **always** more efficient to do operator overloading with value objects than with reference objects. There's the same sort of stack vs. heap and copy vs. reference tradeoffs as in native code: while heap management is never free,[17] doing a byte-wise copy every time you assign one struct to another can be more expensive than simply copying a pointer. Because this tradeoff depends on how often you copy values—how often you assign a result instead of using it as input to another operator—it's not possible to give a single size above which a numeric type should be a reference type and below which a numeric type should be a value type. (In fact, the exact same type may be faster as a struct in one application but faster as a class in another application.) The best rule of thumb is to try it both ways: use a struct unless a class is significantly faster in real situations.

---

16. For some reason, the relational operators are **not** constrained to return a bool. I find it hard to imagine a valid reason for this: I **might** want to overload == to return an Eta object, and then give the Eta object an implicit conversion to bool so that `if (A == B)` works as expected—but why wouldn't I just explicitly create an Eta object and then call methods like `Equals()` or `Equals(double Tolerance)`?

17. Operator overloading with garbage-collected types is in fact more efficient than operator overloading with manually freed types—you just overwrite the garbage, you don't have to thread it into a free list— but you do still have to allocate memory, and each allocation does put you that much closer to the next garbage collection.

Type Conversion

Caution Budget lots of time before overloading cast operators. There is new jargon, some special casing, and complex interactions. This section is introductory, not encyclopedic—be sure to read and reread all of sections 6 (and especially 6.4.*) and 10.9.3 of the *C# Language Specification*.

Overloading cast operators can be tricky

The type conversion operators are intended to be used much as the built-in type conversions like float to double are used: converting to and from different representations of the same value. The implicit and explicit type conversion operators

```
public static implicit operator OutType(InType Operand)
public static explicit operator OutType(InType Operand)
```

allow you to overload casting to or from the type that's defining the operator. Every cast operator must be declared either implicit or explicit, but the signature includes only the OutType and the InType: you can't overload an implicit cast with an explicit cast or vice versa.

One key rule is that you cannot "redefine a pre-defined conversion."[18] Specifically, it's an error if OutType is InType because you can already do an explicit conversion with DescendantVar = (DescendantType) BaseVar. Conversely, it's also an error if InType is OutType because there's already an implicit conversion—a descendant (in) type is always assignment compatible with a base (out) type.

An explicit cast operator overloads ... explicit casts. If a List type has a

```
public static explicit operator object[](List Operand)
```

operator, you can write code like String.Format(PatternString, (object[]) L) to convert a List L to an object[] and pass the object[] to Chapter 11's String.Format() method. (You could also explicitly invoke an implicit cast operator via a cast operator—the difference is that explicit casts can **only** be invoked explicitly.)

One thing to note is that the compiler is willing to do built-in conversions from an actual type to an operator's InType, and from the operator's OutType to the actual desired type. Thus, a single explicit cast operator may actually support a whole family of not-obviously-related casts. For example, given

```
class Parent
{
  public static explicit operator float (Parent Instance)
  {
    return 1f; // just to return something
  }
}
```

---

18. *C# Language Specification*, section 10.9.3, "Conversion Operators."

```
class Child: Parent
{}
```

you might not expect to find that

```
Child Instance = new Child();
double D = (double) Instance;
```

will compile and run, but it will—the compiler invokes the built-in implicit Child-to-Parent compile-time conversion, the user-defined Parent.float operator, and then the built-in implicit float-to-double run-time conversion.

An implicit cast operator like

```
public static implicit operator object[](List Operand)
```

reduces the need for explicit casts, by performing the cast automatically when you code, say, object[] Objects = L, or when you try to pass a List to a method that expects an object[] parameter.

An implicit type conversion operator should never lose information or throw an exception. Think of the built-in implicit conversion from int to long: there is no int that can't be converted to a long. Going the other way, though, most long values can't be stored as int values. An operation that may lose information (as from double to float) and/or throw an exception (as from long to int) should be coded as an explicit type conversion (or even a named method) that the user must call explicitly.

An implicit operator can be invoked in just the same way an explicit operator is, by doing an explicit cast. This is no different from long L = (long) IntVar—you don't **need** to do the cast, because the compiler will do an implicit conversion, but you still **can**.

The compiler will also automatically do implicit casts in several different cases, including

- An otherwise illegal assignment—when you assign an object to a variable or parameter, and the object is not of the variable or parameter's type.

- Returning an object that is not the declared result type.

- In the boolean context of a conditional or looping expression, like
  while (Queue) Queue.ProcessFirst().

The compiler will **not** do an implicit cast in the middle of an expression. For example, the compiler will not perform the implicit conversion

```
public static implicit operator CustomNumber(double Operand)
```

to add a double number to a CustomNumber; that would require explicit CustomNumber operators

```
public static CustomNumber operator + (CustomNumber Left, double Right)
public static CustomNumber operator + (double Left, CustomNumber Right)
```

that add a double to a CustomNumber and return a new CustomNumber.

Somewhat similarly, the compiler will not invoke an implicit conversion when it can use an overload that avoids the conversion. For example, String.Format has (string, object) and (string, object[]) overloads—even when there is an implicit conversion from List L to object[], String.Format(PatternString, L) calls the first overload because a List object is an object type.

Also, while the compiler will do a built-in conversion before and after an implicit conversion, **implicit casts do not 'chain'**: if there is not an implicit (or explicit) conversion from type A to type C, the compiler will not let you assign an A to a C, even if there is an user-defined implicit conversion from A to B, and from B to C.

Finally, some languages do not support calling implicit or explicit conversions. CLS compliance requires that you provide normal methods like FromInt or ToString so that users of such languages can call your conversion code.

Truth

Two ways to convert to bool

The bool datatype is privileged, in that the loop and conditional statements of Chapter 6 expect a bool value. In simple situations like a collection that is always either true or false, populated or empty, you would overload public static implicit operator bool. However, there are more complex situations, such as a SqlBoolean (or a bool?, in 2.0), that can be true, false, or null (not set), or perhaps a fuzzy logic type where a value from 0.4 to 0.6 might be a "maybe"— neither true nor false. In these rare, more complex situations, you can use the infix syntax to overload the true and false operators.[19]

```
public static bool operator true(EnclosingType T)
public static bool operator false(EnclosingType T)
```

Implicit and explicit casts—like bool B = Queue or bool B = (bool) Queue—require a cast operator that returns a bool. Conversion in a boolean context—like if (Queue) {}—can use either a cast operator or a true operator; if you define both a cast operator and a true operator, a boolean context will use the cast operator.

In addition, if you define & and | operators, the compiler will use the true and false operators to evaluate expressions like if (Queue && ThreadPool) {}. This is a very specialized subject— if you really need to create a new ambiguous boolean type, play with the Chapter7\TrueFalse project, and see for yourself how commenting out the cast, &, and | operators affects the evaluation of various boolean expressions.

Nested Types

Simpler syntax than in Delphi

Since C# does not separate declaration from implementation the way Delphi does, nested types have a simpler syntax than in Delphi. Syntactically, a nested type is just another member of the class, enclosed in curlies like a method body. For example,

---

19. If you define one, you must define both.

```
class Outer
{
  public enum Inner {First, Second};
  private class InnerClass
  {
    public static void Method()
    {}
  }
}
```

Note For a longer example, see the Chapter7\NestedClasses C# port of the Chapter2\NestedClasses Delphi example.

Do remember that a nested type is a **type**, not a field. A nested class (or a nested interface or a nested enum) is a member of its enclosing class in the sense that it's not visible where its enclosing class is not visible, and in the sense that code outside of its enclosing class has to use a dot notation, like Outer.Inner, to refer to it. Creating an instance of an outer class does not automatically create an instance of any inner classes!

The point of nested classes is fine-grained control over visibility: as in Chapter 2, a nested class is a member of the class that declares it, and all methods of an inner class have full access to all private and protected members of their outer class.

All nested types are scoped like the nested classes of Chapter 2. That is, within methods of the preceding Outer class, you can declare Inner variables and refer to Inner.First and Inner.Second static fields. Outside of the Outer class, you have to declare Outer.Inner variables, and refer to Outer.Inner.First and Outer.Inner.Second static fields.

Nested types are **usually** private to their outer type; public types are normally defined as part of a namespace (Chapter 9).

Which Object Type?

When to use a struct instead of a class

As value types, structs 'live' on the stack (or in classes that declare struct fields) and so allocating them never triggers a garbage collection and they are never relocated by the garbage collector. This is an important optimization, but you need to balance it against the way that copying a value type—as when you do a pass-by-value to a method, or when you assign one value type to another—does a byte-wise copy of the whole structure. That is, the cost of passing or assigning a struct is related to the size of the struct, while passing or assigning a class is always a single machine-language instruction, no matter how large the class is. Don't forget, though, that even an expensive copy operation is only expensive when you actually perform it; if you never copy a large structure, its copy cost is irrelevant while its nonimpact on garbage collection is always relevant.

Thus, be wary of any rules of thumb about when to make a type a struct and when to make it a class. In particular, the Microsoft "Struct Usage Guidelines" that recommend "that you use a struct for types that ... [have] an instance size under 16 bytes" are often misinterpreted. They are saying that small types should be structs; they are **not** saying that no struct should be >= 16 bytes.

In 1.1, if you want to be able to use `null` to signal 'no value,' then you should probably use a class, not a struct. (In 2.0, you can use a nullable type, as in Chapter 5.)You **can** use special values, somewhat like `double.NaN`, but then you need to call a static method like `double.IsNaN(Value)` instead of just doing an inline `!= null` test. While calling a method is generally more self-documenting than inline syntax, a `!= null` test is pretty clearly a 'do we have a real value' test.

When a type could be either a struct or a class, look at how you (will) use it. If it's very small **or** you rarely if ever make copies, and if it's used primarily (or only) as a strictly local variable, then you should probably make it a struct. (Remember that adding a `struct` to a collection makes a copy—and will often box it, in 1.1.) If you aren't sure, try running some benchmarks to see if a `struct` is faster than a `class` or vice versa.

Thus, a complex number type is a classic example of a type that makes sense to implement as a struct. Many copies come and go in the course of evaluating expressions, so keeping them on the stack can reduce garbage collection pressure a lot, yet at a mere two floating point numbers, it's small and cheap to copy.

A more nuanced example is a program that parses a large string, extracting substrings of the large string, and substrings of the substrings. As per Chapter 3, this program will benefit from working with subranges—an index into the larger string, coupled with a length—rather than extracting each substring as an actual string. These subrange types come and go like the string values they replace, and at two integers and a string reference, they're smaller than a pair of doubles—yet, like the string values they replace, they tend to get passed from method to method. A Bayesian filter program of mine actually runs about 8.5% **slower** using substring structs instead of substring classes.

Key Points

Different object syntax than Delphi, but the semantics are quite similar to Delphi

- No headers.

- C# 2.0 supports generics—open types and open methods.

- Modifiers apply to every member.

- You can use a member before it's defined.

- Structs are much more object oriented than traditional native-code Delphi records. (Delphi 2006 does lets Win32 records have methods.)

- Constructor syntax is surprisingly complex, but in practice it's pretty straightforward.

- Operator overloading is syntactically simple, but a semantic minefield.

CHAPTER 8

C# Interfaces and Delegates

Interfaces are much the same in C# as in Delphi, except that (in 2.0) interfaces can have type parameters; also, 2.0 adds support for iterators, which are an easy way to implement IEnumerable. *Delegates provide the same functionality as a Delphi method pointer— plus delegates are inherently multicast (can contain several instance/method pointer pairs), and delegates can be called asynchronously. In 2.0, anonymous methods provide a way to pass a method block to another method as a delegate; the constructed delegate can capture the parent method's parameters and local variables.*

Interfaces

Not reference counted, but otherwise only differ from Delphi in minor details

Interfaces are types (as are enums, classes, structs, and delegates) and can be declared either as members of a namespace (Chapter 9) or nested in a class. Interfaces can contain both method and property declarations. Like abstract method declarations, interface declarations have a ; (semicolon) instead of a method body.

Classes can only inherit from a single base class in both C# and Delphi (Chapter 7). However, in native code Delphis, interfaces can only inherit from a single interface, while C# interfaces can inherit from multiple interfaces, as in the Chapter8\InterfaceInheritance project:

```
public interface IMommy
{
  int Fn(int Param) ;
}
public interface IDaddy
{
  double Fn(double Param) ;
}
public interface IBaby: IMommy, IDaddy
{
  int RPM { get ; }
}
```

Implementing a child interface means implementing all methods and properties declared in the child interface and in any of its ancestral interfaces. In this project, for example, IBaby includes the read-only RPM property and two inherited overloads of the Fn method.

In native code Delphis, any interface that doesn't explicitly extend another interface implicitly extends IInterface (aka IUnknown), which supports reference counting and as casting. IInterface adds three methods that an object must support before it can implement any explicit interface. This is often done by inheriting from TInterfacedObject instead of from TObject.

.NET doesn't use reference counting, and the CLR handles all the cast checking, so .NET interfaces don't need any of the three IInterface methods. A C# interface has no hidden methods that come from an implicit parent like IInterface. An empty interface like interface IEmpty {} contains no methods, and class Empty: IEmpty {} will compile.

■**Note** Unlike Delphi, C# doesn't make you explicitly inherit from a base type to implement an interface.

Both class and struct objects can implement interfaces. As in Delphi, the syntax that you use to declare that an object supports an interface is very similar to the syntax that you use for inheritance. More precisely, the optional colon after an object's name is followed by a comma-separated list of identifiers. In a class type, the first identifier in the list can be a base type; all the other identifiers are interfaces that this object implements.

An object implements an interface by implementing all of the methods and/or properties in the interface, in one of two ways. The first way is a public method or property with the right name and prototype. The second way is a method or property that has no access modifier (and is thus private) and has a name qualified with the interface name. In both cases, parameter type and order matters, but parameter names do not.

```
class Implementor: IBaby
{
  public int Fn(int Param)
  {
    return Param;
  }
  // could be "public double Fn(double)" but NOT "double IBaby.Fn(double)"
  double IDaddy.Fn(double Param)
  {
    return Param;
  }
  int IBaby.RPM { get { return 45; } }
}
```

Note the way that the qualified implementation of double IDaddy.Fn(double) needs to be qualified with the interface that actually declares it—IDaddy—not the descendant interface that the type is implementing.

When you implement an interface method as a public method, you can call that method normally, through an instance reference. By contrast, when you implement an interface method as a private method with an interface-qualified name, you can **only** call that method through the interface. There are two common reasons to accept this limitation and use an interface-qualified name. The first is that you actually want the limitation: that you are willing to expose the functionality through the interface, but there are good reasons for it to not be part of the class's set of public methods. For example, sometimes you want a class to have no public members, only interfaces that it implements. The second is to resolve conflicts: a class must support a method with a particular name and prototype, because it inherits a virtual or abstract method from an ancestral class, but this is not the method that it wants to use to implement the interface. In this second case, the method and/or class's tool tips should definitely emphasize that calling the public method is not the same as calling the interface's method.

A class can implement an interface with an **inherited** public method or property of the right name and prototype. However, you cannot cast an object to an interface that it doesn't explicitly support—it's not enough that the object **could** support the interface because it implements all the interface members.[1] You can compile code that explicitly casts an object to an interface that it does not support, but the cast will throw an InvalidCastException at run time.

Following the parallel with inheritance, an instance of an object that implements an interface is assignment compatible with a variable or field of the interface type. For example, you can write IBaby myBaby = new Implementor(), and the compiler will implicitly cast the instance reference to an interface reference. An interface reference is also a reference to an instance of the object that implements the interface, and can be cast back with InterfaceReference as InstanceType or (InstanceType) InterfaceReference. In fact, you can explicitly cast any InterfaceReference to any other interface or object reference type—like any other cast, this is subject to run-time checks, and will only succeed if the object behind the InterfaceReference really is the right type or supports the right interface.

■**Note** C# does not support anything like native code Delphis' implements keyword,[2] which delegates interface implementation to a specific property. However, you can get much the same effect by declaring a property or method that explicitly returns an interface reference—the method can change which implementation it returns, at run time, based on the object or system state.

In 2.0, any interface can contain open methods, as in this excerpt from the Chapter8\ OpenInterface project:

```
public interface IClosed
{
  T OpenFn<T>(T Param); // New in 2.0
}
```

---

1. Internally, each interface an object supports has its own method table.
2. For that matter, neither does Delphi for .NET.

An *open interface* has a type parameter list in angle brackets, between the name and curly brackets:

```
public interface IOpen<T> // New in 2.0
{
  T Fn(T Param) ;
}
```

An open class can implement an open interface:

```
public class Open<T> : IOpen<T> // New in 2.0
{
  public T Fn(T Param) { throw new NotImplementedException(); }
}
```

When you construct a class from an open class that supports an open interface, the constructed class supports the corresponding closed interface. For example, Open<int> supports IOpen<int>, while Open<string> supports IOpen<string>.

A closed class can implement an interface constructed from an open interface:

```
public class Closed : IOpen<int> // New in 2.0
{
  public int Fn(int Param) { throw new NotImplementedException(); }
}
```

Iterators

Vastly simplify enumeration

Chapter 2 and 6 discussed IEnumerable and IEnumerator, which support the C# foreach enumeration. Using foreach both hides the details of how a collection is implemented and also makes your code smaller and clearer, by giving the compiler the responsibility for generating a lot of boilerplate code. Supporting IEnumerable makes your users' lives easier and isn't very hard—if your collection is simple and linear, like an array or a linked list. However, it's much harder to navigate nested data like all the files and subdirectories in a directory, or all the controls on a form. You have to build a state machine by hand,[3] which is one of those time-consuming tasks where it's very easy to make subtle errors that take lots of debugging to track down.

C# 2.0's *iterators* make enumeration much simpler, without adding a lot of overhead. An iterator is a method that 1) either returns an interface constructed from IEnumerator<T> or IEnumerable<T>, or returns the closed interfaces IEnumerator or IEnumerable; and 2) uses the special keyword pairs yield return and/or yield break.[4] The iterator steps through a collection in whatever way is easiest—for example, iterators can be recursive—and calls yield return on each value in turn. The enumeration runs until the iterator returns, or until it calls yield break.

---

3. See, for example, my article, "Object-Oriented State Machines," at www.devsource.ziffdavis.com/article2/0,1759,1550549,00.asp.

4. You can **only** use yield return and yield break in methods that return either IEnumerator or IEnumerable or an interface constructed from IEnumerator<T> or IEnumerable<T>.

When the compiler sees a yield return (and/or a yield break), it turns your method into a state machine where the first MoveNext advances to the first yield return and then stops; the second MoveNext advances to the second yield return and then stops; and so on.

Four interfaces may seem daunting, but in practice it's really pretty simple: enumerables can be enumerated; enumerators are implementation details.

- If you want to be able to enumerate an object instance, like an array or one of Chapter 12's collection classes, the object should support IEnumerable or (preferably) IEnumerable<T>. This means providing a GetEumerator method that returns IEnumerator or IEnumerator<T>. The GetEumerator method may return a small object that implements IEnumerator or IEnumerator<T>, or it may use yield return and yield break.

- If you want to be able to enumerate a method result or a property value (perhaps the iterator should only return some of the elements in the collection, or the iterator will apply some sort of transformation to each element), you should return IEnumerable or (preferably) IEnumerable<T>. This IEnumerable **can** be an object with a GetEnumerator method but (in 2.0, at least) it's usually a method that calls yield return and yield break.

In general, your iterators should return an IEnumerable<T> instead of the older IEnumerable, and GetEnumerator should return a new-style IEnumerator<T> instead of the older IEnumerator. The new, open interfaces inherit from their older, closed counterparts, so interfaces constructed from them will work with code that still works in terms of IEnumerable and IEnumerator—but the open interfaces are more efficient. When you return one of the open interfaces and the foreach loop's iteration variable is assignment compatible with the type that the enumerator returns, the foreach loop doesn't have to do a cast on every iteration.

OPEN ENUMERATORS ARE MORE EFFICIENT

When you do foreach (int I in Collection) on a Collection that supports IEnumerable, the foreach loop expands to something like

```
IEnumerator Enumerator = Collection.GetEnumerator();
while (Enumerator.MoveNext())
{
  int I = (int) Enumerator.Current;
        // IEnumerator.Current is an object - the cast unboxes
  /* loop body */
}
```

However, when Collection supports IEnumerable<int>, the foreach loop expands to

```
IEnumerator<int> Enumerator = Collection.GetEnumerator();
while (Enumerator.MoveNext())
{
  int I = Enumerator.Current;  // no cast = no unboxing
  /* loop body */
}
```

That is, when you foreach through an IEnumerable, unless the iteration variable's type is object, each pass through the loop has to cast the Current property from an object to the iteration variable's type. A cast is never a free operation, and when the iteration variable is a value type, a cast unboxes a value ... which may just have been boxed into an object to 'fit' in the Current property.

By contrast, when you foreach through an IEnumerable<T> and the iteration variable is assignment compatible with type T, each pass through the loop can do a simple assignment from the Current property to the iteration variable, with no casting. This saves at least the cost of checking the cast, and can eliminate the need for a pair of back-to-back boxing and unboxing operations.

Some examples of actual iterators may help clarify this rather abstract discussion a bit. This simple method from the Chapter8\FileIterators project enumerates a collection of FileSystemInfo objects (see Chapter 11) and returns the file/directory names:

```csharp
private static IEnumerable<string> Name(IEnumerable<FileSystemInfo> Files)
{
  foreach (FileSystemInfo File in Files)
    yield return File.Name;
}
```

The Name method is a filter that enumerates the FileSystemInfo collection it's passed; extracts the FileSystemInfo.Name property; and passes the Name on out, via the yield return. As you can see, there's nothing at all preventing an iterator (like this Name method) from using a foreach loop to enumerate some lower-level enumeration. Since the Name method returns an IEnumerable<T>, you can use it in a foreach loop, as the Chapter8\FileIterators project does in statements like

```csharp
foreach (string Filename in Name(ProjectDirectory))
  // The ProjectDirectory object supports IEnumerable<FileSystemInfo>
  Console.WriteLine(Filename);
```

For a somewhat more complex example, this pair of methods from the same Chapter8\FileIterators project does a depth-first traversal of a directory, with each directory sorted according to an arbitrary Comparison<FileSystemInfo> predicate:

```csharp
public IEnumerable<FileSystemInfo> Sorted(Comparison<FileSystemInfo> Sorter)
{
  return Sorted(Root, Sorter);
}

private IEnumerable<FileSystemInfo> Sorted(DirectoryInfo Root,
  Comparison<FileSystemInfo> Sorter)
{
  FileSystemInfo[] Elements = Root.GetFileSystemInfos();
  Array.Sort(Elements, Sorter);
```

```
    foreach (FileSystemInfo Info in Elements)
    {
      yield return Info;
      DirectoryInfo Directory = Info as DirectoryInfo;
      if (Directory != null)
        foreach (FileSystemInfo Child in Sorted(Directory, Sorter))
          yield return Child;
    }
}
```

The public method simply passes the private this.Root to the recursive private function, which does all the work. The private method gets the directory contents and sorts them. Then it enumerates the sorted array, first passing each directory entry on out via yield return, and then checking whether or not it is a subdirectory. If a directory entry is a subdirectory, the Sorted method recursively enumerates the subdirectory, again passing each result on out via yield return. As you can see, iterators can support an indefinite chain of nested iterators: when the Chapter8\FileIterators project is enumerating the .\bin\debug directory, the top-level iterator does a yield return of the files it gets from the iterator enumerating the bin directory, which does a yield return of the files it gets from the iterator enumerating the debug directory, which does a yield return of the files it gets from enumerating a (sorted) array.

Finally, the most complex example in the Chapter8\FileIterators project is a primary enumerator—a collection's recursive GetEnumerator method:

```
public IEnumerator<FileSystemInfo> GetEnumerator()
{
  foreach (FileSystemInfo Info in Unsorted(Root))
    yield return Info;
}

private IEnumerable<FileSystemInfo> Unsorted(DirectoryInfo Root)
{
  foreach (FileSystemInfo Info in Root.GetFileSystemInfos())
  {
    yield return Info;
    DirectoryInfo Directory = Info as DirectoryInfo;
    if (Directory != null)
      foreach (FileSystemInfo Child in Unsorted(Directory))
        yield return Child;
  }
}
```

The Unsorted private method here is actually just a simpler version of the preceding Sorted private method: it enumerates a directory in unsorted order, passing on each entry via yield return and recursing on subdirectories. The extra complexity in this example is in the public GetEnumerator method.

The Unsorted method has to return an IEnumerable<T>, or else it can't call itself in a foreach statement. Conversely, the GetEnumerator method has to return an IEnumerator<T> (because that's what an IEnumerable<T>.GetEnumerator method returns). Consequently, the GetEnumerator method has to itself be an iterator, which does nothing more than enumerate the top-level call to the Unsorted iterator.

Delegates

Superficially like Delphi method-of-object types

Delegate types are compiler-generated types that descend from System.MulticastDelegate, which in turn descends from System.Delegate. Delegate instances pair an object instance with a method that has the right prototype, much like Delphi procedure of object or function of object types. (Delegates can refer to either instance or static methods. With a static method, the delegate's instance pointer is null.) As in Delphi, you call a non-null delegate just as if it were a method—e.g., double Result = F(8d).

The key difference between a delegate and the method pointers in a native code Delphi is that a method pointer is a single pair of pointers—a pointer to an instance and a pointer to a method's entry point. A delegate is an object that manages an *invocation list* of method pointers—a non-null delegate always points to one or more instance/method pairs. Calling a delegate's Invoke method calls all the instance/method pairs in the invocation list; a delegate that returns a value returns the result of calling the last method in the list. If one of the methods in the list throws an exception, subsequent methods are not called, and the exception propagates out of the call to Invoke to the code that called the delegate.

Delegate types (like other types—i.e., enums, object types, and interfaces) can be declared as members of a namespace (Chapter 9) or nested in a class. A delegate declaration consists of optional attributes, optional new and/or access modifiers, the keyword delegate, a return type or void, the delegate name, an optional type parameter list in angle brackets (in 2.0), and a method prototype in parens. For example, from the Chapter8\Delegates project,

```
public delegate void Callback();
internal delegate double Fn(double D);
```

In 2.0, an *open delegate* has a type parameter in angle brackets, between the name and prototype:

```
internal delegate T Function<T>(T Parameter);
public delegate double Score<T>(T State);
```

You create an instance of a delegate by calling the delegate constructor via new. To create a delegate to an instance method, you pass the delegate constructor a method name qualified by an instance name as the constructor's arguments:

```
Class1 C = new Class1();
Fn F = new Fn(C.Function);
Score<ThisState> S = new Score<ThisState>(C.ScoringFunction);
```

To create a delegate to a static method, you pass the delegate constructor a method name qualified by the type name, like Fn F = new Fn(Class1.StaticFunction). When you are creating a delegate to a static method of the current type, you can omit the type name, and simply code something like Fn F = new Fn(StaticFunction), just as you can omit the this when creating a delegate to an instance method of the current object.

C# 2 supports a new syntax that lets you omit the new DelegateName(), and simply pass the method name, as in Delphi:

```
Class1 C = new Class1();
Fn F = C.Function; // new Fn(C.Function) still works, too
Fn S = Class1.StaticFunction;
```

Note that this new *method group*[5] syntax is purely a convenience: it generates exactly the same CIL as the older new DelegateName() syntax.

As in Chapter 7, you can create a delegate to **any** method with a compatible prototype. It doesn't matter whether this method comes from a normal type or a constructed type, nor does it matter if the method is itself a constructed version of an open method. For example, the Chapter8\DelegateTests project declares a delegate int IntFn(int N) and an open type:

```
public static class Test<T>
{
  public static int Closed(int N) { return N; }
  public static T Constructed(T N) { return N; }
  public static X Open<X>(X N) { return N; }
}
```

Given these declarations, the following are all valid delegate creation expressions:

```
IntFn A = Test<int>.Closed;
IntFn B = Test<string>.Closed; // Closed doesn't depend on the type parameter T
IntFn C = Test<int>.Constructed; // Constructed types are OK
IntFn D = Test<string>.Open<int>; // Constructed methods are OK, too
```

■**Note** In many cases, one can use either an interface or a delegate for, say, a callback function. They both have their advantages and disadvantages: Table 8-1 summarizes the tradeoffs, and should help you choose the right approach in each case.

---

5. When the compiler encounters a method name, it may have to choose one of several overloads. The candidates—which may include methods from the instance type and any of its ancestors—are known as a *method group*. Delegate creation is legal only if the method group contains one and only one method compatible with the delegate's method prototype.

Table 8-1. *Interface and Delegate Tradeoffs*

Interface Advantages	Delegate Advantages
In 1.*x*, calling a method through an interface reference is significantly faster than calling a method through a delegate. In 2.0, there's no real speed difference.	Creating a delegate can take less code than supporting an interface, especially if supporting an interface involves creating a nested class.
An interface reference can give you access to multiple callback methods.	You can create a delegate to any compatible method; you can only pass an interface reference to a class that explicitly supports the interface.
You can control which methods implement the interface.	A single class may have several methods that are compatible with a particular delegate.
An interface implementation that returns an interface can return different implementations at different times, depending on the system state.	You can create a delegate to a static or *anonymous* method. (See the "Anonymous Methods" subsection, later in this chapter.) Interfaces are always implemented by named instance methods.

Events

The .NET event model is based on delegates

Once again, all delegates are compiler-generated classes that descend from MulticastDelegate, which descends from Delegate, which descends straight from object. So, delegates are either assigned (i.e., a Delegate instance) or unassigned (null or Nil). Unassigned delegates are 0-length delegates: you will never see an assigned delegate with zero handlers when you use the system Delegate methods to manipulate the invocation list. All assigned delegates contain at least one method pointer.

C# allows you to add delegates to each other with + and +=, or with the static method Delegate.Combine:

```
DelegateValue = DelegateValue + OtherDelegateValue; // or
DelegateValue +=  OtherDelegateValue; // or
DelegateValue = (DelegateType) Delegate.Combine(DelegateValue, OtherDelegateValue);
```

You can also subtract delegates with -, -=, and Delegate.Remove.

The CLR supports the notion of an *event*, which uses delegate types to create something like a property. Just as a property is a value of a user-specified type that can be read and/or written using special methods, so an event is a value of a user-specified delegate type that you can add to or remove from. When you += a delegate to an event, or -= a delegate from an event, C# uses the event's property-like add and remove methods. The add and remove methods are an event's only public interface. Outside code can only subscribe and unsubscribe delegates with += and -=.

But inside methods in an event's class, an event looks like a delegate. An event can only be triggered by a method of the event's class—not even a method of a descendant class can see an event field as a delegate. Events allow you to create a public face that offers subscription services to the outside world, without letting outside code trigger the event at the wrong time.

■**Note** Events are used heavily in the .NET component model. See Chapter 15 for examples.

Simple Event Syntax

In C#, you declare an event as a named instance of a specific type of delegate, using one of two syntaxes. The simple syntax event `DelegateType ThisEvent` creates an event that looks a lot like a simple `DelegateType` delegate. However, the simple event has two key differences from a delegate. The minor difference is that a simple event is always an object member—never a local variable— while a delegate may be either a member or a local. The major difference between a delegate and a simple event is that C# automatically creates public `add` and `remove` methods for the event, and these public `add` and `remove` methods are all that outside code can see. The automatically generated public `add` and `remove` methods `+=` and `-=` their `value` argument from the event's private delegate.

Inside an event's object, it can appear anywhere a delegate can: in 'arithmetic' expressions with + and - operators; in logical expressions with `==` and `!=` operators; or on the left side of an assignment. So an automatically generated `add` method acts a lot like

```
public void add (DelegateType value)
{
  ThisEvent += value;
}
```

and both simple events and delegates can be on the left side of a parenthesized parameter list, as if they were normal method calls. For example,

```
private void Fire()
{
  if (ThisEvent != null)
    ThisEvent();
}
```

checks to see if there are any handlers for `ThisEvent`, and fires the event if there are. However, outside of the event's object, you can only write code that subscribes

```
ThisComponent.ThisEvent += ThisHandler; // subscribe
```

or code that unsubscribes

```
ThisComponent.ThisEvent -= new DelegateType(ThisHandler); // unsubscribe
// Something look funny here? See "Delegate Value Equality" subsection, below
```

Explicit Event Syntax

The second type of event declaration uses a more complex event syntax, with explicit `add` and `remove` methods:

```
event DelegateType EventName { add {/*add value*/} remove {/*remove value*/} }
```

declares an event that—even within its own object—can only be accessed through the add and remove methods. (That is, subscribe with += or unsubscribe with -=.) Typically, this second type of event will be pretty straightforwardly mapped to a private delegate field:

```
public event EventType EventName // EventType must be a delegate type
{
  add    { _EventName += value; }
  remove { _EventName -= value; }
}
private EventType _EventName;
```

EventName is an event that allows anyone to add to (or remove from) the private _EventName delegate, while only the object that owns _EventName can actually trigger the event.

Of course, an event's add and remove methods are real methods, which can do as much as you need them to do. For example, the NoDups event in the Chapter8\EventLists C# project

```
private event Method NoDups
{
  add    { _NoDups = (Method) NoDuplicates.Combine(_NoDups, value);  }
  remove { _NoDups = (Method) NoDuplicates.Remove(_NoDups, value);   }
}
private Method _NoDups;
```

calls static methods of the project's NoDuplicates class to ensure that the private delegate field _NoDups only ever has a single copy of any method pointer, using the delegate value equality that I describe next.

Delegate Value Equality

Delegates use value equality, not reference equality

Delegate.Combine and Delegate.Remove use value equality, **not** reference equality. You can say EventList += new Method(MethodName) to add a handler, and you can later remove the handler with EventList -= new Method(MethodName). It doesn't matter that the new Method(MethodName) you are removing is not the same delegate instance that you added.[6]

Combine appends any right method pointers to any left method pointers. For each method pointer in the right delegate, Remove will remove the first matching method pointer in the left delegate. That's why Remove doesn't care which delegate instance contained a method pointer: it just removes the first match(es).

For example, the Chapter8\EventLists C# project defines a delegate void Method(object sender), an event Method EventList, and the void Dummy(object sender) {} method. Given

```
Method This = new Method(Dummy); // C# 1.0 - explicit delegate creation
Method That = Dummy;             // C# 2.0 - new "method group" syntax
```

---

6. This is still true with the new C# 2.0 *method group* syntax that allows you to say
   EventList += MethodName and EventList -= MethodName instead of EventList +=
   new DelegateType(MethodName), as the new syntax does generate the same CIL as the old syntax.

you can say either `Method Two = (Method) Delegate.Combine(This, That)` or `Method Two = This + That`, and `Two` will have two calls to the `Dummy` method. You can check this with `Two.GetInvocationList().Length`, or by running the delegate.

If you do either `Two -= new Method(Dummy)` or `Two -= This`, you'll end up with a single method pointer. If you do `Two -= This` again, you'll end up with `Two == null`.

On the other hand, imagine you have

```
Method AnotherTwo = This + That;
Method Four = AnotherTwo + AnotherTwo;
```

Would you expect `AnotherTwo - Four` to be an error, an empty event list, or no change?

What you get is no change: `Delegate.Remove` checks that each method pointer in the right-hand delegate matches at least one method pointer in the left-hand delegate. If they do, then the first matching method pointers are removed, and a new delegate is returned; if not, the left-hand delegate is returned, unchanged. (The left-hand set did not contain the right-hand set, and so the right-hand set could not be removed from the left-hand set.)

The `Delegate.RemoveAll` static method removes **all** method pointers from the left-hand delegate that match any method pointer in the right-hand delegate. As previously mentioned, any "empty" result is `null`—all actual delegate instances are a list with at least one method pointer.

Anonymous Methods

Create a delegate to a statement block

In C# 1.0, delegates always refer to normal, named methods. As a Delphi programmer, you have ample experience of the utility of method pointers in event handling and callbacks, but you are probably also aware that there are some drawbacks to referring to a stand-alone method:

- A stand-alone method creates clutter and bloat. A stand-alone method take five lines (a blank line between methods, a prototype, a { line, the actual code, and a } line) for a single line of code. If you have a convention that **every** method should be documented, the count goes to eight lines (assuming at least three lines of /// comment) or more.

- There is no obvious connection between a stand-alone method and a method that passes it as a callback. Reading code involves a lot of jumping around. While this is true to some extent with **any** method call, it's easier to justify with code that is used in several places, or with methods that give a name to a chunk of code. When the delegate is to a tiny method used only in one place as a callback, the jumping around represents pain without gain.

- Especially with a callback, the method may need access to the current method's parameters and/or local variables. Giving the method this access requires creating an instance of a nested object, copying the parameters and/or locals to this object, and then creating a delegate to a method of the nested object. Not only does this add yet more clutter, but also defining this nested object is tedious and prone to maintenance errors: it has disproportionately high development and maintenance costs.

That is, defining a method just so that you can create a delegate to it can make your code harder to write and harder to read. Accordingly, C# 2.0 supports *anonymous methods*, which allow you to create a delegate to a special statement block within a method.

An anonymous method consists of the keyword `delegate`, followed by an optional parameter list, followed by a compound statement in curly braces. An anonymous method is only valid in an expression that returns a delegate—that is, 1) on the right side of an assignment like

`DelegateType DelegateInstance = delegate {}; // note the ; after the }`

or 2) as a parameter to a method that expects a delegate, like `Fn(delegate {})`, or 3) in an event list editing statement like `SomeEvent += delegate {};`.

An anonymous method without a parameter block is assignment compatible with a delegate only if the type(s) it returns are assignment compatible with the delegate's return type. An anonymous method without a parameter block can be assignment compatible with a delegate that takes parameters, but (obviously, I hope) cannot refer to those parameters.

An anonymous method with a parameter block is assignment compatible with a delegate only if the type(s) it returns are assignment compatible with the delegate's return type **and** each of the anonymous method's explicit parameters is assignment compatible with the corresponding delegate parameter's type.[7] For example, given a delegate `long LongFn(long N)`, one can write `LongFn L1 = delegate { return 1; }` because the returned int is assignment compatible with a `long`, but one cannot write `LongFn L2 = delegate(int N) { return 1L; };` because a `LongFn` might receive a parameter that can't be converted to an `int`.

■ **Note** Trying to pass an anonymous method without a parameter block to an overloaded method that can take delegates with different parameter lists (like the `Thread` constructor in Chapter 17) generates ambiguity that the compiler can't resolve. You can resolve the ambiguity either by explicitly supplying a parameter block (e.g., `new Thread( delegate () {} )`) or by explicitly casting the anonymous method, like `new Thread( (ThreadStart) delegate {} )`.

An anonymous method's parameter list can include the `ref` and `out` modifiers, but not the `params` modifier—although an anonymous method **can** match a delegate with a `params` modifier on the last parameter.

An anonymous method body may read or write any local variables that are in scope, and it can read or write its 'parent' method's value parameters: anonymous methods cannot access its parent method's `ref` or `out` parameters. An anonymous method that accesses value parameters or local variables is said to *capture* these variables. Internally, the anonymous method is a normal public method of a special, compiler-generated class (CGC) that has these captured variables as public fields. The parent method creates an instance of this CGC as a local variable, copying any captured parameters to CGC fields, and thenceforth referring to these CGC fields instead of the actual parameters. Similarly, captured locals don't reside on the stack, as local variables usually do: captured locals are CGC fields.

---

7. Reference parameter type matching is looser in 2.0 than in 1.x—see the "Covariance and Contravariance" subsection, later in this chapter.

A delegate to an anonymous method that captures variables counts as a reference to the CGC instance, just like every other delegate counts as a reference to each class instance on its invocation list. So captured locals are not subject to garbage collection until the locals go out of scope **and** there are no longer any references to the capturing anonymous method. Using an anonymous method with captured locals as an event handler can be a sort of memory leak.

Finally, it's not easy to come up with small examples of anonymous methods, so I'll just list a few places where I've found them useful:

- As I've mentioned a few times, anonymous methods are great for callbacks, like a single line that updates a progress bar to show download status.

- In GUI apps (Chapter 15), anonymous methods can be useful as event handlers for controls created manually, at run time, as opposed to controls laid out at design time and then created automatically. When, say, a click handler takes only one statement, it can be both clearer and smaller to use an anonymous method than to use a normal, independent, named method.

- I've found anonymous methods to be particularly useful in benchmarking code fragments. I can call the anonymous methods before benchmarking them, and thus be sure that I've jitted **all** code before timing it.

- Because anonymous methods can capture parameters and local variables, they can be used to replace Delphi's local procedures.

- .NET threads (Chapter 17) take a delegate parameter and execute it in a thread. If the thread's top-level code takes only one or two statements, using an anonymous method is smaller and clearer than using a stand-alone method. It also eliminates the 'moral hazard' that you might call the thread proc in the wrong thread.

Covariance and Contravariance

Looser rules for prototype matching in 2.0

Consider the following extract from the Chapter8\NoCovariance[8] project:

```
class Base
{
  public static Derived BaseFn(Base B) { return new Derived(); }
}

class Derived : Base {}

delegate Base BaseFunction(Base B);
```

---

8. Both Chapter8\NoCovariance and Chapter8\NoContravariance are C# 1.0 projects, built in VS 2003. Chapter8\Covariance and Chapter8\Contravariance are C# 2.0 projects, built in VS 2005.

In 1.*x*, you can't say BaseFunction F = new BaseFunction(Base.BaseFn). A BaseFunction returns a Base instance, and Base.BaseFn returns a Derived instance.

However, it is true that every Derived instance is also a Base instance, and Base.BaseFn can't return anything that can't be assigned to a Base variable. In 2.0, *covariance* means that you can create a delegate to a method that returns a type that's assignment compatible with the type that the delegate returns. For example, you **can** say BaseFunction F1 = new BaseFunction(Base.BaseFn) or BaseFunction F2 = Base.BaseFn.

Consider also the following extract from the Chapter8\NoContravariance project:

```
class ContraVariance
{
  class Base
  {
    public static void BaseProc(Base B) { }
  }

  class Derived : Base
  {
    public static void DerivedProc(Derived D) { }

  }

  delegate void BaseMethod(Base B);
  delegate void DerivedMethod(Derived D);
}
```

You can never write code like BaseMethod DerivedP = new BaseMethod(Derived.DerivedProc) because Derived.DerivedProc expects a Derived argument. Since you can have Base instances that are not Derived instances, you cannot create a BaseMethod delegate to Derived.DerivedProc—you could pass the BaseMethod delegate a Base instance that can't be passed to Derived.DerivedProc.

However, since every Derived is also a Base, you can't pass any parameters to a DerivedMethod that a method that takes Base parameters can't handle. (A method like Base.BaseProc will only deal with a Derived instance as a Base instance, but that's OK.) In 1.1, methods are only compatible with a delegate type if the parameter types match exactly. 2.0 adds *contravariant* matching, where a method that takes a base type is compatible with a delegate that takes a derived type: in 2.0, you **can** say DerivedMethod BaseD = new DerivedMethod(Base.BaseProc).

Note Contravariance only works with reference types. You still can't create a delegate void IntProc(int N) delegate to a void Proc(long N) { }: the IntProc delegate will not widen its integer argument to fit Proc's long parameter.

Asynchronous Execution

Delegates can be called asynchronously

When you call a delegate as if it were a method of the current class—e.g., double Result = Fn(46D) or Callback(PercentComplete)—you are making a *synchronous* call. The compiler turns what looks like a method call into a call to the delegate instance's CLR-generated Invoke method, which takes the same parameters as the delegate. The Invoke method executes each method on the delegate's invocation list in the current thread, and control doesn't return to the delegate's caller until Invoke has executed each method on the invocation list.[9]

If a delegate only has a single method on the invocation list (normally this means that you got the delegate from a new delegate operation, not from Delegate.Combine, as in the earlier "Events" subsection), you can also execute the delegate *asynchronously*. That is, in addition to the synchronous Invoke, every delegate has two asynchronous methods: BeginInvoke and EndInvoke. (All these invoke methods are *run-time methods*, which are generated by the CLR on first call, instead of being jitted from CIL.) You can call BeginInvoke to run the delegate in a ThreadPool thread (Chapter 17), do some other work in the current thread, and then call EndInvoke to collect the delegate's results.

Asynchronous invocation is a rather advanced technique, but you might use it any time an IO-bound method is just one of the inputs that you need before you can perform some task. For example, you might need to read a file and initialize some complex data structures before you can call some method. Rather than read the file and then do the computations, you can BeginInvoke a delegate to the method that reads the file, and do some (or all) of your other setup during the milliseconds that file IO spends waiting for interrupts from the disk controller. Similarly, if you need to read two (or more) files, you could BeginInvoke delegates that read each file to a string, and then call each delegate's EndInvoke to collect the file contents. At least conceivably, the operating system can optimize disk access so that reading files in parallel is faster than reading them sequentially.

A delegate's BeginInvoke method has the same parameters as the delegate's Invoke method, plus two extra parameters that are used for an optional callback when the method terminates—I cover these in the upcoming "Callback on Completion" topic, but it's always perfectly safe to just pass null to each. BeginInvoke returns an IAsynchResult that you must save and pass to the delegate's EndInvoke method.

The EndInvoke method takes a single IAsynchResult parameter; waits for the call to complete; and returns the delegate result, if any. Note that EndInvoke does not return an object that you have to cast to the right type. Rather, EndInvoke has the same result type as the delegate itself: a delegate that 'returns' void has an EndInvoke method that 'returns' void; a delegate that returns int has an EndInvoke method that returns int; and so on.

---

9. In 1.*x*, Invoke is a 'magic' method that you can't actually call from application code. In 2.0, you **can** explicitly call Invoke—e.g., Fn.Invoke(46D) instead of Fn(46D)—although there's not really any point to doing so.

There are several different ways to detect that an asynchronous call has completed, but you **must** pass the IAsyncResult that you get from ThisDelegate.BeginInvoke to ThisDelegate.EndInvoke. Yes, even if you already know the delegate has returned, and even if EndInvoke does not return a result.[10]

Thus, the simplest asynchronous scenario is something like

```
IAsynchResult Asynch = ReadFileDelegate.BeginInvoke(Filename, null, null);
//
// Do as much as you can until you need the file contents: EndInvoke() blocks.
//
string FileContents = ReadFileDelegate.EndInvoke(Asynch);
```

Calling EndInvoke like this is not unlike calling Join on a thread (Chapter 17): you don't need to know the current state of the operation, you just block until it's completed.

Polling for Completion

It's not always a good idea to block the application's main thread. It's OK in a command-line utility that simply runs to completion with no user intervention, and it's OK in a web server where each incoming request runs in its own thread, but it's generally not OK in a GUI app, where blocking the main thread means that the app is not responding to mouse clicks and key presses. If you initiate a lengthy asynchronous call from the main GUI thread, you might poll the IAsyncResult.IsCompleted property and call Application.DoEvents (Chapter 15) until the delegate returns:

```
IAsynchResult Asynch = ReadBigFileDelegate.BeginInvoke(Filename, null, null);
//
// Do something while waiting for file IO
//
while (! Asynch.IsCompleted) // we need the file contents now
  Application.DoEvents(); // handle events until delegate returns
string FileContents = ReadBigFileDelegate.EndInvoke(Asynch);
```

---

10. I wish I could explain the need to always call EndInvoke. Microsoft has been quite emphatic since version 1.1, using different strong language to insist that you always EndInvoke every IAsyncResult that you get from a delegate's BeginInvoke call. But they don't say why, and BeginInvoke and EndInvoke are run-time methods, supplied by the CLR on an as-needed basis. The debugger won't step into run-time methods, making them harder to reverse engineer.

The most probable explanation seems to me to be that some or all calls to BeginInvoke add their IAsyncResult result to one or more lists before they return. So that their IAsyncResult can't be finalized —until EndInvoke cancels all subscriptions, disposes of all resources ... and calls GC.SuppressFinalize.

Do note that asynchronous execution of delegates in a thread pool thread is not the same thing as sending a control a message asking it to execute a delegate in the control's thread. A (System.Windows.Forms) Control has a BeginInvoke method that takes a delegate, and an EndInvoke method that takes the IAsyncResult that BeginInvoke returned. These Control methods act differently than the delegate's own BeginInvoke and EndInvoke methods. The Control methods don't take callback parameters, and it **is** safe to not EndInvoke an IAsyncResult that you get from a Control.BeginInvoke call. See Chapter 15 for details.

A better design is usually for the ReadBigFileDelegate to run to completion, unmonitored. The last line of the ReadBigFileDelegate would use Control.BeginInvoke (Chapter 15) to have the GUI thread run a delegate that will do ReadBigFileDelegate.EndInvoke and display the fetched data.

■**Tip** While file IO is slow, it's not all that slow, and you can usually get away with reading a small (1 or 2 kilobyte) file during an event handler. As a rule of thumb, if you can do something synchronously without impacting GUI responsiveness, the asynchronous version can certainly block on EndInvoke without impacting GUI responsiveness.

Waiting for Completion

If the asynchronous delegate has any side effects, other threads may want to wait for it to complete before doing anything that depends on those side effects. These threads can use WaitHandle methods (Chapter 17) like the IAsyncResult.AsyncWaitHandle.WaitOne instance method or the static WaitHandle methods WaitAll and WaitAny to wait until the IAsyncResult.AsyncWaitHandle event is signaled.

While you can call BeginInvoke in one thread and call EndInvoke in a different thread, this still allows only one thread to wait for the delegate. The AsyncWaitHandle property returns a ManualResetEvent (Chapter 17, again) that blocks all waiting threads until the event is signaled, and then lets all threads through after the event is signaled. That is, the AsyncWaitHandle property allows any number of threads to wait for the delegate. (However, you should only call EndInvoke once.)

Callback on Completion

Every delegate's BeginInvoke method has two extra parameters after any Invoke parameters: the first is an AsyncCallback delegate and the second is an arbitrary object. If the AsyncCallback delegate is non-null, the asynchronous mechanism will Invoke it synchronously (in the same ThreadPool thread[11] that runs the delegate—see the Chapter8\AsynchTest project) once the asynchronously invoked delegate returns. An AsyncCallback delegate takes a single parameter, which is the same IAsyncResult that BeginInvoke returns and that you must pass to EndInvoke. The AsyncState property of the IAsyncResult that's passed to your AsyncCallback delegate contains the object parameter that you passed to BeginInvoke.

I have to confess, I'm not quite sure what the point of this callback facility is. While I suppose you might sometimes run a delegate synchronously and sometimes run the same delegate asynchronously—and you have to do some special handling after you run this primary delegate asynchronously—why wouldn't you just create a compound delegate that calls the primary delegate and then calls the special handling delegate?

---

11. ThreadPool threads are "background" threads that are aborted when the last "foreground" thread terminates. See Chapter 17 for the details.

About the only real use I can imagine for this callback mechanism is a 'fire-and-forget' scenario, where you want to run a delegate (that takes several parameters) in a background thread, but don't want to have to store the IAsyncResult and eventually EndInvoke it. While it would be far simpler (and more efficient) to just use Chapter 17's ThreadPool.QueueUserWorkItem, that method does only support zero or one parameters. In 2.0, with anonymous methods, you can just write something like this snippet from the Chapter7\FireAndForget project to asynchronously call a method that takes several parameters:

```
System.Threading.ThreadPool.QueueUserWorkItem(
    delegate { Quartet("Fred", "George", "Ron", "Ginny"); }
    );
```

but, of course, anonymous methods were not available in .NET 1.0, which is where the asynchronous call mechanism was introduced.

You can write the equivalent code in .NET 1.*x*, but this **does** require you to pass the parameters to a wrapper object that can then pass them on to the asynchronous delegate—much like the compiler does for you automatically, with the anonymous method. This is a fair amount of error-prone boilerplate, and it's probably easier to use a callback routine, like this one from the Common\Shemitz.Utilities project that uses Reflection (Chapter 13) to call EndInvoke on the passed IAsyncResult:

```
public static void EndInvoke(IAsyncResult Async)
{
#if DEBUG
  Delegate D = (Delegate)Async.AsyncState;
    // raise an exception if AsyncState is not a delegate
#else
  object D = Async.AsyncState;
#endif
  Type TypeofDelegate = D.GetType();
  System.Reflection.MethodInfo EndInvoke =
    TypeofDelegate.GetMethod("EndInvoke", new Type[] { typeof(IAsyncResult) });
  EndInvoke.Invoke(D, new object[] { Async });
}
```

As in the Chapter8\FireAndForget project, you'd pass a delegate to this late-bound EndInvoke routine as the penultimate argument to BeginInvoke (the AsyncCallback delegate) and you'd pass the asynchronous delegate itself as the final argument:

```
FourStrings Background = new FourStrings(Quartet); // FourStrings is a delegate type
Background.BeginInvoke("John", "Paul", "George", "Ringo",
    FireAndForget.EndInvokeDelegate, Background);
```

Is this fire-and-forget scenario the whole point of the callback mechanism? A way to pass parameters to a background thread without resource leaks? Seems like overkill, to me, so I suspect I'm missing something here.

Key Points

Interfaces are familiar, but delegates are more complex than Delphi method pointers

- Interfaces act much like Delphi's interfaces, except that there is nothing like Delphi's implements keyword.

- It's much easier to write an iterator to enumerate a collection than it is to write an IEnumerable class.

- Delegates are multicast versions of Delphi's method pointers. You can edit a delegate's list of instance/method pairs.

- An event is a special sort of delegate field: inside its class, an event is a delegate; outside its class, an event is just a pair of add/remove methods.

- 2.0's anonymous methods allow you to treat a statement block as a delegate.

- Covariance and contravariance mean that 2.0 can create delegates to methods that would not have been compatible in 1.*x*.

- You can easily execute any delegate asynchronously, in a background thread.

CHAPTER 9

■ ■ ■

C# Topics

Six small sections that didn't really fit in the other four C# chapters, and that don't really fit together well as a chapter: the Main method; namespaces, the using directive, and 2.0's :: operator; attributes; the @ escape that lets you use imported identifiers that conflict with C# keywords; preprocessor directives; and 2.0's partial classes.

The Main Method

A program's top-level code

All C# executables (as opposed to libraries) must have at least one object (either a class or a struct) with a static Main method. The Main method, like a Delphi program file's begin {...} end. block, is the program entry point.

The Main method must return either int—the application's result code—or void. That is, either static void Main() or static int Main(). Whether void or int, Main can have a string[] args parameter, which allows easy access to any command-line parameters. You do not have to declare a string[] parameter to read the command line, nor do you **have** to pass the Main method's string[] on to other code; you can always use the System.Environment class to get the command line as either a string[] (the Environment.GetCommandLineArgs() method) or a raw string (the Environment.CommandLine property).

If a program has only one object with a static void Main method, that Main method is automatically the program's entry point. You **can** have more than one object with a Main method, but in that case you have to specify (on the compiler command line or from an IDE property window) which object's method to use. The designated *startup object* can't overload Main— you can't have both a parameter-less static Main and a static Main that takes a string[].

Usually, you just edit a Main method generated by a wizard.

Namespaces

Hierarchical organization, not tied to assemblies

As per Chapter 2, a C# namespace looks something like a class declaration:

```
namespace Name
{
}
```

Namespaces can contain any of the five types—classes, structs, delegates, interfaces, and enums—within the curly braces.

The sole effect of a namespace is to prepend the namespace's name to any types defined within it. Thus, given

```
namespace a
{
  public class b
  {}
}
```

the full name of public class b is a.b. Namespaces can contain dots, and namespaces can be nested. Thus both

```
namespace a.b
{
  public class c
  {}
}
```

and

```
namespace a
{
  namespace b
  {
    public class c
    {}
  }
}
```

define a class a.b.c. Note that these are not two different classes with the same name, but two different ways to define the same class c, in the a.b namespace. If you tried to compile both snippets together, you'd get a *namespace 'a.b' already contains a definition for 'c'* error.

Thus, a name with dots in it describes a *hierarchy* of nested namespaces. a.b says that b is nested in a. It says little about what b is—b is a namespace, but could also be any type. Similarly, a.b.c says that c is nested in b, which is a namespace nested in the a namespace.

While 'bare' types are very rare, types do not **have** to be declared within a namespace. A bare type acts just like a type in a namespace; the only difference is that the declared name **is** the full name; it doesn't have any namespace part. That is, where the full name of class Type in namespace Normal is Normal.Type, the full name of the bare class BareType is just plain BareType. This behavior continues in 2.0, but explicit namespaces and bare types are now said to be part of the global namespace—see "Namespace Versioning" (later in this section) for details.

There is no syntactic connection between namespaces and either code files or assemblies: a single code file can contain several different namespaces, and a single namespace can span multiple code files and even multiple assemblies. This means that the actual contents of the namespace depend on compile-time configuration: if you build an assembly without a particular code file, the types defined in that file will not be part of the namespace in that assembly. Similarly, if a namespace spans multiple assemblies and you only have a compile-time reference[1] to some of those assemblies, you will 'see' only the namespace members in the assemblies that you refer to.

Name Resolution

Name resolution in C# is quite unlike name resolution in Delphi

While namespaces reduce naming conflicts and make it easier to organize large libraries, they can make for very long names. A Regex object is a lot easier to deal with than a System.Text.RegularExpressions.Regex object! Accordingly, the using directive[2] allows for shorthand references. You can always refer to a type by a fully qualified name like System.Text.RegularExpressions.Regex, but if you declare that you are

```
using System.Text.RegularExpressions;
```

you can just refer to the Regex type. Whenever the compiler encounters an unqualified type name that's not in the current namespace (i.e., the one you're defining), it checks all the namespaces that you're using to see if the *unresolved identifier* is defined in one of the namespaces that you're using. If the identifier is found in exactly one of those namespaces, your code will compile. Zero or multiple matches is an error.

This is quite unlike what you're used to with Delphi.

In Delphi, you cannot refer to any unit that's not in the uses clause, and the uses clause takes a comma-separated, ordered list of unit names. The uses list is ordered in that the compiler looks for unresolved identifiers last to first, stopping on the first match. If the same identifier appears in two or more units, the last occurrence is the one the using unit will see by default. You can use unitName.identifier notation to refer to shadowed types.

In C#, you can use any code in any assembly that you have a compile-time reference to; the using directive is just a way to abbreviate names. The using directive does not take a list of names, and does not define an ordered list of namespaces: it's ambiguous and a compile-time error if an unqualified identifier is found in more than one namespace.

using directives can appear at the file level, before any namespaces or bare type declarations and after any #define pragmas (see "Preprocessor Directives," later in this chapter). using directives can also appear within a namespace, before any type declarations. File-level directives affect namespaces and code that follow them within the file. Namespace-level directives affect namespaces and code that follow them within their namespace. But using directives are never visible to other directives at their own level.

---

1. As per Chapter 2, you have to "add a reference" to an assembly—either on the compiler command line, or via VS's Solution Explorer or BDS's Project Manager—to be able to compile code that refers to code in the assembly.

2. As distinct from Chapter 6's using **statement**, which automates the Dispose pattern.

For example, using the next subsection's *alias* syntax:

```
namespace Outer
{
    using Regexen = System.Text.RegularExpressions;
    //using Regex = Regexen.Regex; // can't see Regexen, here
    namespace Inner
    {
        using Regex = Regexen.Regex;
    }
}
```

The using directive in the Outer namespace declares Regexen as an alias for the System.Text.RegularExpressions namespace. The subsequent //using Regex = Regexen.Regex is commented out, because using directives in the Outer namespace don't see using directives in the Outer namespace. But, using directives in the Inner namespace **do** see using directives in the Outer namespace, and Inner **can** say using Regex = Regexen.Regex to declare an alias to a particular type in the System.Text.RegularExpressions namespace.

Aliases

Compile-time aliases for namespaces and types

The using *namespace* syntax of the using directive adds all the public names in a namespace to the set of simple, unqualified names available to code in the using file. The alternate form

```
using Alias = NamespaceOrType;
```

allows you to define an alias for a namespace or for a type. This aliasing form of the using directive can appear anywhere the namespace form can appear—i.e., before any namespaces or type declarations at the file level, and before any type declarations within a namespace.

■**Note** Aliases are compile-time constructs, not public members of a namespace. Code outside of the preceding Outer/Inner fragment can never refer to Outer.Regexen or Outer.Inner.Regex.

Namespace Aliases

You might use a namespace alias like

```
using My = MyCompany.MyLibrary.MyCollections;
```

so you can refer to MyCompany.MyLibrary.MyCollections.List as My.List. This can be handy when two different namespaces both use the same name for a type; using a namespace alias means you don't have to use an ambiguous type's full name to refer to it.

Note that where using Dotted.Name allows you to refer to types from the Dotted.Name namespace by their unqualified names, creating a namespace alias via using Alias = Dotted.Name does **not**; you have to refer to them as Alias.SomeType, not just SomeType. However, you **can** list the same namespace in both a 'normal' using directive and an alias using directive

```
using System.Collections.Generic; // home of List<T> and the like
using MyCompany.MyLibrary.MyCollections; // home of List and the like

using My = MyCompany.MyLibrary.MyCollections; // My.List
using Std = System.Collections.Generic; // Std.List<T>
```

and you might do so whenever you need to use a full name to resolve an ambiguity. A short alias is often better than a long full name.

Type Aliases

A type alias like

```
using MyInt = System.Int32;
```

defines MyInt as an alias for System.Int32 in nearly exactly the same way that int is—the only difference being that MyInt is a normal, shadowable name, not a keyword like int. That is,

```
typeof(int) == typeof(System.Int32) && typeof(int) == typeof(MyInt)
```

Now, aliasing int makes for a short example, but it's not exactly useful. In fact, it really just obscures things without adding anything. A longer, but more realistic, example is that instead of

```
using My = MyCompany.MyLibrary.MyCollections; // My.List
using Std = System.Collections.Generic; // Std.List<T>
```

and then referring to My.List and Std.List, you can say something like

```
using My = MyCompany.MyLibrary.MyCollections; // namespace alias
using System.Collections.Generic.List; // normal using directive

namespace Application
{
    // alias directives in a namespace see file-level namespace directives
    using MyList = My.List; // sees My alias
    using StdList = List<MyList.Element>; // sees System.Collections.Generic.List
}
```

and then refer to MyList and StdList in type declarations.

As in the previous My/Std example, the MyList alias is defined using the My alias. What's new here is the way that StdList is an alias for a closed constructed type. Within a file or namespace, you can use aliases for closed constructed types to replace boilerplate code. That is, you can get rid of lots of angle brackets and turn code like

```
List<MyList.Element> Elements = new List<MyList.Element>();
```

into much more legible code like

```
StdList Elements = new StdList();
```

More, as your code evolves and you want to change the collection type from `MyList.Element` to `MyElement`, you only have to change the alias directive to change all code that uses the `StdList` alias.

Note   Just remember it all happens at compile time, on a per-file basis. A type alias is a C# construct, not a CTS construct. A type alias is never a public member of a namespace. A type alias is local to a file, or to a namespace section within a file. `Application.StdList` is not visible to other files in the same project, or to code that refers to the assembly.

Namespace Versioning

Support for multiple versions of the same library

C# 1.0's name resolution easily handles the case where you use two different libraries, each of which uses the same name to mean two different things—provided that they put that name in unique namespaces like `MyTrademark.Whatever`. It doesn't work, though, when you want to load multiple versions of the same library. A `Junky.Ported.VbControl` is a `Junky.Ported.VbControl`, and you can't use an ambiguous full name.

2.0 handles this by adding parallel, named namespaces. The default namespace, the namespace that contains every explicit namespace, as well as every type defined outside of a explicit namespace, is now known as the `global` namespace.[3] By default, every assembly you refer to is part of this global namespace, but it doesn't have to be. Every reference to another assembly can have a list of *aliases*. (You can set a reference's aliases with a compiler switch, or through the IDE—in VS 2005, each assembly reference's Properties include an `Alias` property.)

For example, imagine you have three versions of the assembly that implements the `MyTrademark.Reports` namespace. You might have

- The 1.4 library aliased to `Legacy`,

- The 2.6 library aliased to both `global` and `Current`,

- And the 2.6.4.7 library aliased to `Beta`.

By default, you see the types in the current library, 2.6, because you have a normal, `global` reference to it. If you create a `MyTrademark.Reports.RoiByDept` object, you will get the `RoiByDept` object from the 2.6 library. Similarly, if you are using `MyTrademark.Reports`, you are using the 2.6 library, and the unqualified name `RoiByDept` refers to the 2.6 object.

If you declare the three aliases with the new `extern alias` syntax

```
extern alias Legacy;
extern alias Current;
extern alias Beta;
```

---

3. Using this new notation, file-level using statements are in the global namespace, and so only affect namespaces within global, not global itself.

the same application can use all three versions, with the new :: operator. If you are using MyTrademark.Reports, then new RoiByDept() gives you the 2.6 object, as before. But you can also use the Legacy::MyTrademark.Reports.RoiByDept and the Beta::MyTrademark.Reports.RoiByDept, as needed.

Basically, the :: operator—the *namespace alias qualifier*—lets you specify an alternate root namespace. The name to the left of a :: operator must be either global or a name declared as an extern alias. The name to the right of a :: operator starts at the root of the namespace—full names like global::System.Text.StringBuilder, and never unqualified names like global::StringBuilder—but you can use the :: in using statements like

```
using Current::MyTrademark.Reports;
using OldReports = Legacy::MyTrademark.Reports;
using NewReports = Beta::MyTrademark.Reports;
```

so that you can just refer to RoiByDept, OldReports.RoiByDept, and NewReports.RoiByDept instead of always having to read and write Legacy::MyTrademark.Reports.RoiByDept or Beta::MyTrademark.Reports.RoiByDept.

■**Note** The extern alias statement must appear at the file level, before any using statements. At least one assembly must use an alias before you can use the alias in an extern alias statement.

Strangely, you can use aliases without the :: operator, too. Using the preceding examples, Beta.MyTrademark is exactly the same namespace as Beta::MyTrademark. You can refer to either Beta.MyTrademark.Reports.RoiByDept or Beta::MyTrademark.Reports.RoiByDept. What's strange about this is the asymmetry: Beta.MyTrademark but not global::Beta.MyTrademark and not global.System.String. Probably the best way to think of this is that the extern alias directive creates an assembly alias that can be used with the :: operator ... as well as anywhere that a using namespace alias can be used.

Attributes

Code annotations, with and without parameters

Attributes are annotation objects attached to bits of program code like classes or methods, individual enum elements, or individual parameters. An attribute may be, in effect, just a name attached to a code element, but attributes can also have various properties, set at compile time and readable at run time. Most attributes apply to a single program element, but there are also global attributes that apply to whole assemblies and modules.

As in Chapter 2,[4] attributes appear in square brackets. You can place multiple attributes within a pair of square brackets by separating them with commas:

---

4. Chapter 2 used Delphi syntax, but Delphi's attribute syntax is modeled on C#'s.

`[John, Jacob, Jingleheimer, Schmidt]`

More formally, each such set of attributes within square brackets is an *attribute section*. An attribute section consists of a [(a left square bracket); an optional *target* (see the "Attribute Targets" subsection, later in this chapter); one or more attributes, separated by commas; and a] (a right square bracket). Attributes are standard C# names (which refer to `System.Attribute` descendant classes), with an optional set of parameters in parentheses. You can have comments at any point (except within a string parameter) within an attribute section.

There are very specific points in C# syntax where an attribute section can appear, such as before modifiers (like `public` or `virtual`), and before each method parameter. Wherever you can have one attribute section, you can have several attribute sections. The order of attributes within an attribute section—and between sections that have the same target—doesn't matter at all. That is, `[John, Jacob, Jingleheimer, Schmidt]` is exactly equivalent to both `[Schmidt, Jingleheimer, Jacob, John]` and `[John] [Jacob] [Jingleheimer] [Schmidt]`.

Attribute syntax is relatively complex, with three mutually compatible pairs of syntax options, which makes for a total of eight different acceptable ways to specify a simple attribute like `[Flags]`. Presumably this complexity is meant to keep common uses simple while still allowing for more complex uses.

Attribute option 1—the `Attribute` suffix: As in Chapter 2, attributes are classes that descend from `System.Attribute`. By convention, attribute class names end in `Attribute`, like `FlagsAttribute` and `ObsoleteAttribute`. You can use an attribute by its full name, but you usually drop the `Attribute` suffix, and say simply `[Flags]`. The compiler will match `Flags` to `FlagsAttribute`. If you have `class My: Attribute {}` and `class MyAttribute: Attribute {}`, as in the Chapter9\AttributeParsing project, then `[My]` is ambiguous and will abort compilation, but `[MyAttribute]` is not ambiguous. You should change your types' names to avoid ambiguity; if there is some reason that you can't, you can use the @-escape mechanism (that I discuss later in this chapter) to specify `[@My]`.

Attribute option 2—qualified names: Attribute objects are members of namespaces like any other object, and you can use a fully qualified name like `[System.Flags]` in case of a name collision, or if the attribute's namespace is not in scope via a `using` directive.

Attribute option 3—attribute parameters: When an attribute class has a constructor that takes parameters, the attribute can be followed by the parameters in parentheses. For example, the `CLSCompliantAttribute` object has a constructor that takes a `bool` parameter, so you write `[CLSCompliant(false)]` to mark a non-CLS-compliant part of an otherwise compliant assembly.

Attribute classes can have overloaded constructors, just like any other class, and an attribute's parameters will be mapped to the available constructor prototypes, just as when you invoke the constructor with the `new` operator. You get a syntax error[5] if there is no constructor that matches the prototype implied by your attribute use. For example, you can't compile `[Flags(1)]` or `[CLSCompliant]`.

When an attribute class has a constructor that takes no parameters, you don't have to put an empty pair of parens after the attribute name. That is, while you can write `[Flags()]`, you don't have to, and usually write `[Flags]`.

---

5. Somewhat confusingly, the error message talks about method overloads, not **constructor** overloads.

Note that attribute constructors are the **only** place in C# syntax where you can call a no-parameter method the way you do in Delphi, with the empty pair of parens optional and not mandatory. This is one of two ways in which attributes have a complex syntax quite unlike any other C# language element. The other is that attributes can have two sorts of parameters: *positional* parameters and *named* parameters.

Positional parameters look and act like normal method or constructor parameters. Their type and order has to match (or be implicitly convertible to) a constructor overload, and positional parameters get passed to the constructor in a perfectly ordinary way when you create an attribute instance at run time. Positional parameters are mandatory parameters: while you may have a choice of overloaded constructors, and thus a choice of attribute syntax, you do have to supply parameters that match one of the available constructors.

Named parameters are optional parameters, specified as Name=Value items in the parameter list, following any positional parameters.

For example,

```
[AttributeUsage(AttributeTargets.Class, Inherited=false)]
class LifetimeAttribute: Attribute { }
```

declares a [Lifetime] attribute that can only be applied to classes, and that only applies to classes that are expressly decorated with the [Lifetime] attribute, and not to any descendant classes. I talk about the AttributeUsage attribute later in this section: the way it is used here, it mixes positional and optional parameters. When the CLR retrieves this [AttributeUsage] attribute for the LifetimeAttribute type, it calls the constructor that takes a single AttributeTargets enum parameter, then sets the public property (or public field) named Lifetime to true.[6]

■**Tip** Parameters can be both named **and** positional. For example, the Chapter9\Attributes project has a JonAttribute class with both a no-parameter constructor and an int age constructor, as well as a writable property int Age. You can thus apply the attribute as [Jon], accepting the default age, or you can explicitly supply the Age as either [Jon(45)] or [Jon(Age = 47)].

At run time, you can retrieve attributes for any program element in the current assembly. (The Chapter9\Attributes project has an example, and Chapter 13 has the details.) If your code has ReflectionPermission, it can also get attributes for (and other information about) any member—public **or** private—of any assembly it uses or loads. If your code does not have ReflectionPermission, it can only retrieve information about the public members of other assemblies. By default, code that resides on a local hard disk has "full trust," and "full trust" includes ReflectionPermission.

---

6. C# will not let you use a named parameter unless the attribute class defines a public field or a public writable property. Delphi doesn't check: if you use the named parameter to 'set' a read-only property, Delphi will blithely generate invalid metadata, and the CLR will throw an exception when you try to retrieve the malformed metadata.

When you retrieve attributes at run time, you get a list of actual attribute instances. C# will not let you use an attribute that breaks the CLS mandate that all attributes descend from System.Attribute, but other languages may not be so scrupulous.[7] That is, when you retrieve attributes of C# code, you get an object[], each of whose elements is a System.Attribute instance; when you retrieve attributes of non-C# code, some of the elements of the object[] may not be Attribute descendants.

Like other objects, an attribute object that you retrieve at run time may have properties (and/or fields) that you can read. The run time state reflects the compile-time positional and named parameters. Attributes are stored in the metadata as a metadata token that refers to the attribute class, along with all the attribute's parameters. When you retrieve an attribute at run time, the library code basically does a normal new of the constructor that matches the positional parameters (which calls any field initializers, then calls the constructor with the appropriate positional parameters) and then applies any named parameters. That is, named, optional parameters can override positional, mandatory parameters, which can override default field values. For example, if you apply the JonAttribute of the Chapter9\Attributes project as [Jon(25, Age = 47)], the Age of the retrieved attribute is 47, not 25 or 45.

Note Optional parameters require public, writable properties or fields. But while you can retrieve an attribute object and change its fields or properties, this doesn't affect the stored metadata. The next time you retrieve that attribute, you will get a new object, with the original values. See the Chapter9\Attributes project for an example.

Attribute Targets

Optional targets make it clear what the attribute applies to

C# syntax has only six places where attribute sections are valid. While some of these are quite unambiguous—an attribute before a parameter declaration can only apply to that parameter—others are not. For example, an attribute before a method declaration can apply to either the method as a whole or to the method's result type.

The optional target syntax allows you to specify exactly what each attribute section applies to. An attribute target consists of one of the nine attribute location specifiers—assembly, field, event, method, module, param, property, return, and type—followed by a : (colon), between the [and the attribute list. For example, [assembly: CLSCompliant(true)] applies to the whole assembly, while [CLSCompliant(true)] applies to an individual element of an assembly.

The following topics cover each of the six syntactic groups. Each topic includes an attribute section's default target, and lists the valid optional targets.

Type Declarations

Any of the five types of type declaration can include attribute sections, before any access modifiers like public or internal. For example,

---

7. After all, look at how cavalier Delphi is about CLS compliance.

```
[type:Serializable] public class Foo {}
[Obsolete] public delegate void Deprecated ();
[Flags] public enum Colors {Red, Green, Blue}
```

Except for delegate declarations, an attribute that is part of a type declaration always applies to the type declaration, whether or not you explicitly specify the type: target.

With a delegate declaration, the attribute could apply to either the delegate as a whole or the attribute could apply to the delegate's return value. By default, or if there is an explicit type: target, the attribute applies to the delegate; if there is an explicit return: target, the attribute applies to the return value.

For example,

```
[Obsolete] public delegate void Deprecated ();
```

applies the Obsolete attribute to the whole delegate, while

```
[return: ResultCode] public delegate int OptionalResult ();
```

applies the hypothetical ResultCode attribute to the int result.

Member Declarations

Any member of a class or struct can include attribute sections, before any modifiers like public or private, static or virtual, and so on. For example,

```
[NonSerialized] private readonly DateTime creationTime;
[Obsolete] public void Deprecated() {}
```

By default, an attribute that is part of a member declaration applies to the member as a whole. You can make this explicit by using the field, property, method or type targets. As you might expect, a field: target must precede a field; a property: target must precede a property; and so on.

Much as with delegate declarations, an attribute applied to a method (or an operator) could apply either to the method as a whole or to the return value. By default, or if there is an explicit method: target, the attribute applies to the method (or operator); if there is an explicit return: target, the attribute applies to the return value.

Parameter Declarations

Any parameter declaration can include attribute sections, before the parameter type. For example,

```
public void Procedure() {}
public void Procedure([Optional] int Defaultable) {}
public void Procedure([param: Optional] string Defaultable) {}
```

Attributes that are part of a parameter declaration apply only to that individual parameter, not to the whole parameter list, even if you don't explicitly include the param: target.

Properties and Events

Attributes before a property or event type apply to the property or event as a whole, whether or not they use the property: or event: target.

Any property or event declaration can include attribute sections, before the get or set, and add or remove keywords. With a get method, as with normal methods, an attribute could apply either to the method or result. As with methods, the default is to a method: target, but you can override that by explicitly targeting the return: value.

The set, add, and remove methods all have an implicit value parameter. Since the value parameter is never explicitly declared, there's no place to apply an attribute to it, and an attribute on the method could thus apply to either the set, add, and remove method or to the value parameter. By default, any attributes apply to the method as a whole; you can make that explicit with the method: target, or you can apply the attribute to the parameter with the param: target.

```csharp
private DelegateType eventField;

[event: Example] // event: target is optional here
public event DelegateType PublicEvent
{
    [method: Example] // method: target is optional here
    [param: Example] // applies to the value parameter
    add { eventField += value; }

    [param: Example]
    remove { eventField -= value; }
}
```

Indexed properties have explicit parameters (in addition to the implicit value) and these parameters can have attributes in a perfectly normal way:

```csharp
string this[ [Ignored] int Index]
{
  set {} // do nothing
}
```

Enum Elements

An enum can include attribute sections within an enum, before each enum member. These attributes have an implicit field: target, and always apply to the following enum member. For example,

```csharp
public enum Evaluate
{
  [Description("Compiled scripts execute faster than interpreted scripts " +
    "but do incur setup costs and cannot be unloaded.")]
  Compiled,

  [field: Description(@"Interpreted scripts don't incur compilation cost, and do not
    remain in memory once done, but do execute slower than compiled scripts.")]
  Interpreted
}
```

The difference between the preceding (System.ComponentModel) Description attribute and /// XML Doc comments is that Description attribute strings are compiled into the assembly's metadata, while /// comments **are** comments that aren't compiled into the assembly. Thus, any development environment that knows about the Description attribute could show you the Description attributes when you use identifiers from a compiled assembly. By contrast, XML Doc is compiled into .XML files that IntelliSense can read (and into human-readable HTML documentation pages) but is not available to a development environment that doesn't have the source and doesn't understand (or doesn't have) the separate IntelliSense files.

Compilation Units

Attributes can also appear in any code file, between any using directives and the first namespace declaration. These attributes do not apply to the subsequent namespace; they can only apply to the code file's module or assembly. These *global* attributes **must** have either an explicit module: target or an explicit assembly: target.

My standard example, here, is

```
[assembly: CLSCompliant(true)]
```

but there are also several assembly attributes that specify version info (like AssemblyTitle and AssemblyDescription), which usually appear in a separate AssemblyInfo.cs file.

Compile-time Attributes

Attributes that affect compiler behavior

Most attributes are essentially transparent at compile time. They are custom metadata, meant to be read at run time. All that the compiler does with these run-time attributes is syntax check the declarations, and add them to the metadata; run-time attributes don't affect the compiler's symbol table the way that types and type members do. There are, however, five special attributes that do have compile-time effects: CLSCompliant, DllImport, AttributeUsage, Conditional, and Obsolete.

As per Chapter 2, assemblies default to CLS noncompliant, but if you declare [assembly: CLSCompliant(true)], you will get a compile error on any noncompliant program element that's not flagged as [CLSCompliant(false)].

You use the DllImport attribute in conjunction with the extern modifier to use a static method from a DLL. See the online help for more information.

I cover the Conditional and Obsolete attributes in the "Conditional Compilation" and "Warnings and Errors" subsections of the "Preprocessor Directives" section, later in this chapter. Because the AttributeUsage attribute changes an attribute's default behavior, I talk about it here, in the "Attributes" section.

Attributes have three default behaviors that you can override with the AttributeUsage attribute:

1. By default, any attribute can be applied to any program element that can have attributes. (Namespaces, for example, can never have attributes.)

2. By default, an attribute can only be applied once per program element.

3. By default, descendant classes inherit attributes from their parent class, and override methods inherit attributes from their base method.

The `AttributeUsage` attribute—which C# will only let you apply to classes that derive from the `Attribute` class—has one mandatory (positional) parameter, an `AttributeTargets` bitmap that specifies what program element(s) the attribute can be applied to. The optional (named) `AllowMultiple` parameter lets you declare an attribute as a *multiuse* attribute, which (like the `Conditional` attribute) can be applied more than once to the same program element. The optional (named) `Inherited` parameter allows you to keep an attribute from propagating to the descendants of the type or method that the attribute is declared on.

When an attribute class has an `AttributeUsage` attribute like

```
[AttributeUsage(AttributeTargets.Class | AttributeTargets.Struct)]
class MyObjectAttribute: Attribute { }
```

the compiler will only let you apply the attribute to program elements in the `AttributeTargets` bitmap. For example, `MyObjectAttribute` is marked for `AttributeTargets.Class | AttributeTargets.Struct`, and so `[MyObject]` can only be applied to class or struct types— no enums, interface, delegates, methods, results, parameters, or other `AttributeTargets`.

Note The compiler will enforce `AttributeUsage` for an attribute class declared in (and compiled along with) the current module just as it will for an attribute class in a library module. This is also true for the `Obsolete` and `Conditional` attributes: they 'take effect immediately' and can be used within executable assemblies; they are in no way reserved for library code.

The @ Escape

When code written in other languages uses keywords as identifiers

One problem with cross-language programming is that different languages use different keywords. A VB library might declare a `long` type, and a Delphi library might declare a `new` type. These are both keywords in C#, not in VB or Delphi.

If you are going to use cross-language libraries, you have to be able to handle the cases where they use the current language's keywords as identifiers.[8]

In C#, the @ character before an identifier allows it to be treated as an identifier, not a keyword. For example, normally you can't have a class named `new`, or a constant named `const`, because both `new` and `const` are keywords. But, if you qualify both names with the @ sign, you **can** compile

```
class @new
{
  public const int @const = 1;
}
```

and can subsequently refer to `@new.@const`, as in `int N = @new.@const`.

---

8. It's not just a good idea, it's the law—the CLS requires that compliant languages offer an escape mechanism.

Obviously enough, you had better have an especially good reason to use a keyword as an identifier in C# code. The escape facility is intended primarily so that you can use, say, a VB class that actually has a @new.@const identifier.

Preprocessor Directives

C# has no macros

C# doesn't really have a preprocessor the way C and C++ does. In particular, there are **no macros**. However, C# does retain C's preprocessor syntax for #define, #if, and the like: a # command must be the only statement on a line, and any parameters run to the end of the line. Block comments, /* */, are not allowed within preprocessor directives, but preprocessor directives may end with a // comment. That is, you can't say

```
#if /* enable the extra features for the Gold SKU */ GOLD
```

but you can say

```
#if GOLD // enable the extra features for the Gold SKU
```

I break the preprocessor directives into three groups, and cover them in the "Conditional Compilation," "Warnings and Errors," and "Folding Regions" subsections.

Conditional Compilation

Traditional conditional compilation, plus conditional methods

Conditional compilation in C# depends only on the presence or absence of *conditional symbols*— you can't test the value of compile-time expressions the way you can in newer Delphis with {$if}. You can define conditional symbols on the compiler command line, or in IDE dialog boxes, or in source code.

#define FOO defines the FOO symbol (whether or not it already exists) within the file that it occurs in. That is, as in Delphi, the command line and IDE dialog boxes define global symbols, while #define defines file-local symbols. Conversely, #undef FOO deletes the FOO symbol within the file that contains the #undef; if FOO was defined globally (it is not an error to #undef a symbol that does not exist), FOO will still be defined in other files compiled at the same time.

Note Any #define and #undef directives must be the first tokens in a file—they can follow comments, but they cannot follow using directives.

The #if directive controls conditional compilation. At its simplest—#if FOO—subsequent code will compile iff FOO is defined. An #if directive **must** be matched with an #endif directive; there are also #else and #elif directives, which may appear between an #if and its #endif.

You can also use #if (and #elif) with expressions involving !, &&, ||, ==, !=, true, false, and parentheses. Within an #if expression, a symbol is true if it is defined, and false if it is not defined. Thus, code following #if SILVER && !GOLD will compile only if the SILVER features are enabled but not the GOLD features.

This is a flexible form of traditional conditional compilation, but it **is** traditional conditional compilation, and thus is subject to *bit rot*. When the compiler totally skips over some code, it can no longer stop on code that uses a type or method that's been deleted, renamed, or modified. When you do 'throw the switch,' you may find that you've been skipping over code that is long out of date. C# also supports *conditional methods*, which are not subject to bit rot because they are syntax checked every time you compile, regardless of whether they are generating code or not.

A conditional method is a method that has the Conditional attribute, which allows you to say that a call to this method should only generate code when a specific conditional symbol (like DEBUG or PREMIUM) is defined. For example, given a declaration like

```
[Conditional("SILVER"), Conditional("GOLD")] public void Method(int I) {}
```

a statement like

```
Method(ThisInt * ThatInt);
```

is always compiled and syntax checked—but will not generate code to multiply ThisInt * ThatInt, or to push the result and call Method, unless either SILVER **or** GOLD are defined.[9]

Do note, though, that conditional methods **are** compiled into your assemblies. They may not be called, but the code's still there. That is, conditional methods can bloat your executables in a way that conditional compilation doesn't. This is not a problem if you put your conditional methods in assemblies. (The Conditional attribute is stored in the metadata just like any other attribute, and works just fine across assembly boundaries.) If you want to have multiple versions of a program, each different version only has to distribute the assemblies it actually calls into.

■**Tip** Your EXEs only need the assemblies that they actually call into. A compile-time reference to an assembly (in, say, the VS Solution Explorer) does not automatically create a dependence on that assembly. See the Chapter9\Conditional project.

You cannot create a delegate with a conditional method, and there are a few restrictions as to which methods can be marked conditional:

---

9. Do note that the preceding example calls Method if either SILVER **or** GOLD are defined. To get **and** behavior, you need to have one conditional method call another:

```
[Conditional("GOLD")] public void GoldMethod(int I) {}
[Conditional("SILVER") public void SilverMethod(int I) { GoldMethod(I); }
// ...
SilverMethod(ThisInt * ThatInt);
```

- Conditional methods must return void. That is, conditional methods must be the C# equivalent of a Delphi procedure.

- Conditional methods can be virtual (in which case any overrides inherit the conditionality) but not override. That is, either all members of a virtual 'tree' are conditional or none are; you can't have some branches be conditional while other branches are unconditional.[10]

- Conditional methods can't be interface methods, or implementations of an interface method.

Note The ConditionalAttribute class is defined in System.Diagnostics, and you cannot use the Conditional attribute unless you are using System.Diagnostics or unless you explicitly qualify the attribute use, like [System.Diagnostics.Conditional("DEBUG")]. System.Diagnostics also contains the Debug class, which supports assertions and various sorts of tracing via conditional methods that depend on the DEBUG symbol.

In C# 2.0, you can also have *conditional attributes*. You can apply the ConditionalAttribute to an attribute definition, just as you apply the AttributeUsageAttribute. You then use these conditional attributes exactly as you use normal attributes, except that they are only actually applied (i.e., stored in the metadata) if their conditional symbol is defined at the point the attribute is compiled. Just as with conditional methods, a given attribute definition can have multiple [Conditional("SYMBOL")] attributes, each with its own symbol: a conditional attribute will be applied to its target if any of its conditional symbols are defined. The Chapter9\ConditionalAttribute project has an example.

Warnings and Errors

Traditional directives, plus [Obsolete] methods

The #warning directive allows you to insert a custom compiler warning. Any text between the #warning and the end of the line is the warning text: you don't need to quote the warning text as in Delphi. A warning appears in the compiler output, and generates a wavy red underline in Visual Studio, but does not abort compilation. A common use of #warning is to flag incomplete or poorly tested code with something stronger than a mere //TODO: comment.

The #error directive is like #warning but stronger: an error halts compilation. You might use #error to flag an unsupported combination of conditional symbols. (For example, SILVER or GOLD, but not both SILVER and GOLD.)

Both #warning and #error generate messages every time they are compiled: the Obsolete attribute allows you to mark a type or method as obsolete, with an optional workaround message.

---

10. Note that in an overridden conditional method, a call to the base method is also a conditional method, and will not be called unless the conditional symbol is defined for the overridden conditional method as well as the original caller. See the Chapter9\ConditionalInheritance project, which does **not** call the base method because the conditional symbol is commented out in Derived.cs.

Compiling an obsolete type or method doesn't generate any messages, but actually **using** the obsolete type or method does generate a warning or an error. The default behavior is weak obsolescence, which generates a compiler warning when someone uses an obsolete type or method. The IsError positional parameter lets you optionally specify strong obsolescence, where using an obsolete type or method is an error that aborts compilation.

The #line directive can be used to hide lines from the debugger and/or modify the line counter and filename so that errors in generated source correspond to lines in the source script; see the Microsoft documentation for details.

Folding Regions

Create a folding region manually

Visual Studio (and, to a lesser extent, BDS) does a pretty good job of generating folding regions automatically: you can automatically fold methods, classes, /// blocks, and so on. When you want to combine several methods and fields into a folding region of their own—or when you want to divide a long method into multiple folding regions—you use the #region and #endregion directives.

Any text between a #region directive and the end of the line will appear in gray, in a gray box, when the region is folded. Any text after the #endregion directive is optional, but I always copy the #region text, to make it clear what this #endregion directive matches:

```
#region Complex public method implementation
#endregion Complex public method implementation
```

Folding regions can be nested, but every #region directive must be matched with an #endregion directive; unmatched #region directives generate compiler errors that can be hard to track down.

Partial Classes

Spread a class over several files

As you've seen, a class ClassName {} or struct StructName {} declaration is very flexible—you can refer to members before they're defined, so long as they are ultimately defined. However, in C# 1.0, the whole object must be defined in a single file, within a single pair of curly brackets. For the most part, this is not a major restriction—many C# programmers even adopt a One Public Object To A File strategy.

However, when an object contains a mix of manually and automatically generated code, as with Chapter 15's Form classes, things can get messy. The WinForms code editor keeps most of its generated code in a folding #region of its own, but Form files can get awfully long, and adding controls to an existing form does tend to mingle manually generated fields with the automatically generated fields that refer to on-form controls. Accordingly, 2.0 adds the new partial modifier that allows a class, struct, or interface to be defined in two or more places.

For example,

```
namespace a.b
{
  public class Whole { }

  public partial class Partial
  {
    private const float OneIota = float.MinValue;
  }
}
```

defines a normal class, Whole, that is completely defined. It also defines a partial class, Partial, that will be assembled at compile time from all of the public partial class a.b.Partial that the compiler sees. If you also compile

```
namespace a
{
  namespace b
  {
    // this is part of existing namespace a.b

    // won't compile - conflicts
    //public class Whole { }

    public partial class Partial
    {
      protected readonly float TwoIotas = OneIota + OneIota;
    }
  }
}
```

the Partial class will gain a protected field, TwoIotas, that's defined in terms of the private constant, OneIota.

When defining a partial object, only one definition needs to have an access modifier like public or internal—but if more than one definition has an access modifier, then all must agree. You can't have public partial class Partial {} and internal partial class Partial! Similarly, only one partial definition needs to specify a base class, but if more than one definition specifies a base class, then all must agree.

Partial types open up all sorts of possibilities for new errors: a partial type's members—and even whether the type compiles or not—depends on the configuration of the project files, not just on the contents of .cs files. At the same time, partial types provide new possibilities for team programming and supporting multiple versions.

For example, Joe may be working on one tab of an app's main form while Jane is working on a different tab. If Joe's code is in MainForm.Joe.cs and Jane's is in MainForm.Jane.cs, both Joe and Jane can have their parts of the main form checked out simultaneously.

Or you can use partial classes so that your *Standard* or *Professional* versions contain functionality that the *Trial* version does not. Any method defined in a partial class that the Trial version doesn't compile won't end up in the Trial assembly. That is, the code is not just not called, it's not even present. This may protect your intellectual property, and it sure minimizes the chances that a hacker can throw some switches and un-cripple your Trial version. You can get the same effect with conditional compilation, but then your code is cluttered with lots of #if statements: partial classes can be a cleaner solution.

Key Points

Program structure is generally more flexible than Delphi equivalents

- Every executable must have a Main() method , which contains the top-level code.

- All types are part of a namespace, which gives them a hierarchical name.

- The using directive allows you to omit namespace prefixes and create aliases.

- Attribute syntax is surprisingly complex, but most attributes use only the simplest options.

- C# supports both conditional compilation and conditional methods; conditional methods are not subject to bit rot.

- Folding regions let you impose a hierarchical organization on your code.

- 2.0's partial types let you spread a class, struct, or interface definition across multiple files.

CHAPTER 10

Delphi for .NET

by Hallvard Vassbotn

Note from Jon This chapter is the only one I didn't write. I firmly believe that a single-author book is a better book than an anthology, because it has a single style and a consistent level of detail. But, despite being a devoted user of Turbo Pascal/Delphi ever since Turbo Pascal 1.0, I don't use Delphi for .NET: I find C# to be a much better language for .NET development. So I put off this chapter until the very end and then, just as I was starting this chapter, I had a mountain bike accident that tore ligaments in my shoulder and left me unable to work for months. I was willing to cancel this chapter rather than further delay an already late book by researching and writing it on short days with a sore shoulder. Fortunately, Hallvard volunteered to write this chapter, which provides much better coverage of Delphi for .NET syntax than the online documentation in Delphi 2006. Thanks, Hallvard!

The Delphi language has been adapted and evolved to match the managed .NET environment. Along the way, it has stayed as compatible as possible with native code Delphis, even while pushing constructs like raw pointers into the "unsafe method" sandbox. Unlike C#, Delphi has a long history and a large installed code base to take into consideration when adapting its language to a new platform like .NET.

Adapting to Change

New features for a new platform

This chapter provides an overview of the Delphi language on the .NET platform. It assumes you already know the base language from Delphi 7, the last native code version before the first .NET version. There have been three versions of the Delphi for .NET language so far: Delphi 8, Delphi 2005, and Delphi 2006. The latter two also include new versions of the Win32 compiler and language support: except where noted, all the new features discussed here are supported both in .NET and Win32.

Delphi language syntax and how it differs from C# has been covered throughout the book (but specifically in Chapter 2 and Chapters 5 through 9). This chapter summarizes the Delphi for .NET language and what is new and different compared to native Delphi. The Chapter10 folder contains numerous projects that demonstrate the new language features.

The end of this chapter contains two conversion tables that should help you port C# code or samples to Delphi, and to port native Delphi code to C#.

The Object Model

Becoming a first-class .NET citizen

The native Delphi 7 language already had mature support for modern object-oriented concepts such as inheritance, encapsulation, polymorphism, interfaces, methods, events, properties, and so on. Still, to match the richer and cross-language model in .NET, the language was updated with many new features.

Many of these extensions were needed to allow Delphi to become a full first-class .NET citizen, one that can be both a framework consumer and a framework extender. Most existing, high-level, object-oriented code should just work as-is, but with these new features you can write code that is clearer, more efficient, and easier to use for other .NET languages, and you can access code in CLS-compliant assemblies (such as the .NET Framework library itself).

Getting Classy

The object model has been extended with static members; `class static` methods, `class` constructors, `class var` fields, and `class` properties. For example, the Chapter10\ClassStatic project shows this:

```
type
  TFoo = class
  strict private
    class constructor Create;
  private
    class var FYank: integer;
    class procedure SetYank(const Value: integer); static;
  protected
    class procedure OldVirtualClassProcedure; virtual;
  public
    class procedure OldClassProcedure;
    class function ClassStaticMethod: integer; static;
    class property Yank: integer read FYank write SetYank;
  end;
```

Note that CLS-compliant static methods must be declared as `class procedure` or `class function` with a `static` directive, after the argument list. Borland chose this syntax instead of the more natural `static procedure` or `static function`, because that would have made `static` a keyword, which might have broken some existing code.

Note Old-style class procedures still get an implicit Self parameter, the class of the type that was used to actually call the method. Code that may be called from other languages should include a CLS-compliant way to call any public class procedures, like a static function (or a static property) that returns the appropriate metaclass. See the Chapter10\ClassMethods Delphi project and the Chapter10\CallClassMethods C# project for an example.

A class var declaration introduces a block of global-lifetime, class-scoped fields, the Delphi equivalent of C# static fields. Traditionally, Delphi programmers have used global variables in the implementation section of the unit for this purpose, but declaring class var fields directly in the class is cleaner and clearer—and class var fields can be declared public or protected. Note that to be consistent, normal (instance) fields can now also optionally be declared in a var block.

The availability of class fields and static methods also opened the path for class properties.[1] These are declared like normal instance properties, but use a class property prefix. The read and write accessors can be class fields or class static methods (but not the older class methods).

Finally, a class's single class constructor is guaranteed to run exactly once before any members of the class are referenced. It should be declared strict private[2] and cannot be referenced directly from user code[3]—the CLR calls the class constructor as necessary (see Chapters 2 and 7). Often, code in the initialization section of the unit would benefit from being moved to a class constructor—then you would not incur the overhead unless you actually use the class.

Tip Class constructors are not supported in Win32. You can partially emulate a class constructor in Win32 by putting the code in a private class static method and calling the method from the initialization section of the unit. Note that this technique preserves the "before first use" semantics while losing the "not called until actually used" semantics.

---

1. In Delphi 7 and earlier, you could actually *declare* instance properties that referenced class methods as the read and write accessors, but this was a compiler quirk and didn't actually work correctly at run time (using the implicit Self: TClass parameter such as calling a virtual class method would crash, for instance). Also while Delphi 8 allowed you to declare class properties, there was no intuitive way of accessing them (you had to access them via an instance reference, not a class reference). This issue has been fixed in Delphi 2006.

2. While Delphi 2006 does allow declaring nonprivate class constructors, it is cleaner and clearer to declare them private since you can never call a class constructor directly and since the compiler will always generate a private CIL .cctor (regardless of the class constructor source visibility).

3. Hackers and compilers can ensure that the class constructor has been called by using the RuntimeHelpers. RunClassConstructor method from the System.Runtime.CompilerServices namespace. Note that this method is not available on the Compact Framework.

Protecting Your Privates

Native Delphi already had four class member visibility levels: private, protected, public, and published. (There is also Delphi 2's automated visibility—but that is obsolete and not supported in .NET.) One quirk with these is that private and protected members are fully visible to all the code in the unit they are declared in,[4] not just the class they are part of (almost like an implicit version of the C++ *friend* concept). To match .NET's concept of truly private and protected, two new access levels named strict private and strict protected were introduced. The Chapter10\PrivateParts project demonstrates this:

```
type
  TFoo = class
  strict private
    FCantTouchMe: integer;
    FAnyOneAndDelphiRTTI: integer;
  private
    FClassAndUnit: integer;
  strict protected
    FClassAndDescendants: integer;
  protected
    FClassDescendantsAndUnit: integer;
  public
    FAnyOne: integer;
    constructor Create(Report: boolean = True);
  published
    property AnyOneAndDelphiRTTI: integer
      read FAnyOneAndDelphiRTTI write FAnyOneAndDelphiRTTI;
  end;
```

Delphi classes can now be explicitly sealed and abstract. The syntax here has the mildly surprising order class sealed and class abstract. This **is** consistent with Pascal's use of the French noun-adjective word ordering instead of the English adjective-noun order, but the main reason for this syntax is to avoid reserving more language keywords than absolutely necessary—sealed and abstract are directives that only have special meaning after the class reserved word. This means that existing code that already uses these identifiers will not break. As in C#, a sealed class cannot be inherited from and an abstract class cannot be instantiated (even if it does not contain any abstract methods).

Finally, a virtual method that you override can now be marked final, preventing derived classes from overriding that method.

---

4. One native Delphi trick is to declare a local descendant of a class in the current unit. Then you hard-cast an object instance into this local class. Now you have access to all the protected members of the object. This hack is so common that the .NET compiler has special logic to handle it too. It does work as long as the original class code is in the same assembly as the hacking code. This is because Delphi's protected access maps to the .NET family or assembly access level. Similarly, Delphi's private access maps to the .NET assembly access level, but the Delphi compiler itself enforces the cross-unit privateness.

```
  TAbstractClass = class abstract
  public
    procedure Bar; virtual;
  end;

  TSealedClass = class sealed(TAbstractClass)
  public
    procedure Bar; override;
  end;

  TFinalMethodClass = class(TAbstractClass)
  public
    procedure Bar; override; final;
  end;
```

Nesting Habits

The compiler now allows you to declare nested types (including classes) and constants inside another class or record declaration. The implementation of a nested class method must have its name preceded by both the outer and inner class names, like this:

```
type
  TOuter = class
  public
    const
      MeaningOfLife = 42;
    type
      TResult = integer;
      TInner = class
      public
        function  Method: TResult;
      end;
  end;

implementation

function TOuter.TInner.Method;
begin
  Result := TOuter.MeaningOfLife;
end;

procedure Test;
var
  Inner: TOuter.TInner;
  Result: TOuter.TResult;
begin
  Inner := TOuter.TInner.Create;
  Result := Inner.Method;
end;
```

Note that a nested class can reference all types and constants nested within its parent class—the TOuter prefix in the preceding example is optional. Any code outside of a class must use an explicit type prefix—for example, the external test code in the Chapter10\NestingHabits project must use the TOuter prefix to get at the types and constants declared in the TOuter class.

As per Chapter 2, the nested class gets privileged access to the private members of its outer class.[5] This makes it possible for the inner class to implement an enumerator of its outer class, for instance. The reverse is not true; the outer class does not have access to the private members of their inner types.

The main purpose of nested classes is to reduce namespace clutter by keeping (often private) helper classes within the public classes that use them. This also makes it easier to hide implementation details. (See Chapter 2's "Nested Classes" subsection.)

▪ **Tip** Delphi's global-level constants are not CLS compliant (or rather, the name of the class they end up in is an implementation detail generated by the compiler, and should not be relied upon), so you should declare constants you want to export to other languages inside a class or record declaration. The same advice goes for global routines and variables—declare them as static methods and fields.

Setting New Records

Records have now been upgraded to proper object-oriented citizens.[6] Instead of being just a collection of passive fields, a record declaration can now contain most of the features of a full-fledged class. This includes visibility specifiers (private, strict private, and public), instance methods, constructors (as long as they have at least one parameter), static class methods, class fields, class properties, class constructors (only in .NET), and nested types and constants.

Records do not support inheritance, virtual methods, protected sections, destructors or constructors with no parameters. In .NET, a record can implement one or more interfaces, and it is also possible to forward-declare a record (just like you can with classes). From the Chapter10\OORecords project,

```
type
  TFoo = record;  // forward record declaration
  IRecordInterface = interface
    procedure Method(Foo: TFoo);
  end;
  TFoo = record(IRecordInterface)
  strict private
```

---

5. Don't be fooled by the Code Completion issue that fails to list these members as available from an outer class reference inside a nested class method.

6. Old-time Delphi and Turbo/Borland Pascal programmers may remember the old object-style classes that could also be used as a kind of object-oriented record. Borland chose to extend the record concept instead of reviving the deprecated object syntax, mostly to avoid breaking old code. The old object model supported inheritance and a number of other features that the new OOP records don't (and cannot in .NET).

```
    class constructor ClassCreate;
    procedure Method(Foo: TFoo);
    class var FCount: integer;
    var FBar: integer;
  public
    procedure SetBar(const Value: integer);
    class procedure SetCount(const Value: integer); static;
  public
    constructor Create(ABar: integer);
    property Bar: integer read FBar write SetBar;
    class procedure ReportCount; static;
    class property Count: integer read FCount write SetCount;
  end;
```

It is useful to be able to declare methods as part of a lightweight record object[7] instead of encoding them in separate global routines (as has been customary in native Delphi). This couples data and behavior in a way that is object oriented, easy to understand, and easy to share with other languages. Records with methods are also requisite for supporting operator overloading, which brings us to our next topic.

Redefining the Operators

Long-time Delphi programmers have looked at the operator overloading features of other languages (such as C++) with both fear and envy. Operator overloading lets application code use infix operators with user-defined types. When used properly, this is a powerful and elegant technique that can make code smaller and clearer; however, when used improperly, operator overloading can make your code much harder to read and maintain.

■ **Note** This subsection only outlines Delphi operator overloading syntax. See Chapter 7's "Operator Overloading" section for background discussion, including coverage of type conversion semantics.

Delphi now supports operator overloading. This is an advanced concept where a class or (more commonly) a record[8] can have a special method called when a standard operator (like +, -, /, *, div, mod, and so on) is applied to an instance of the class or record. To define operator overloads, you must define class operator functions with specific names for each operator. In addition to normal operators, implicit and explicit casts (or conversions) can be implemented; see the Delphi language documentation for the full list of class operator names.

The Chapter10\OperatorOverloading project demonstrates the potentially confusing aspects of operator overloading. It defines a TStrangeInt record where the operator semantics have been reversed. That is, - adds and + subtracts, * divides and / multiplies, and so on:

---

7. See Chapter 5 for more details of value types vs. reference types.
8. Win32 only supports operator overloading for records.

```
type
  TStrangeInt = record
  public
    Value: Integer;
    class operator Add(const Left, Right: TStrangeInt): TStrangeInt; inline;
    // [snip]
    class operator Implicit(const AValue: Integer): TStrangeInt; inline;
    class operator Implicit(const AValue: TStrangeInt): Integer; inline;
    class operator Implicit(const AValue: TStrangeInt): string; inline;
    class operator Explicit(const AValue: Double): TStrangeInt; inline;
  end;

class operator TStrangeInt.Add(const Left, Right: TStrangeInt): TStrangeInt;
begin
  Result.Value := Left.Value - Right.Value;
end;
```

The implementation of a class operator method should create and return a new record or class instance and not modify any of the parameters. Often operator methods are very short and simple, and thus perfect inline candidates[9] (see the "Inlined Routines" subsection, later in this chapter).

Invoking the overloaded operators is just a matter of declaring/creating an instance of the type and using the standard Delphi operators:

```
var
  Strange: TStrangeInt;
  StrangeResult: TStrangeInt;
begin
  Strange := 42;
  StrangeResult := Strange + Strange * 3;
end;
```

Because of the reversed TStrangeInt implementation, StrangeResult will be 28 (42-42÷3) instead of the expected 168.

■**Tip** For a more complete example of operator overloading in Delphi, see the Borland.Vcl.Complex .NET unit (or the Vassbotn.Vcl.Complex unit in the Demos\DelphiWin32\VCLWin32\ComplexNumbers\ folder for the corresponding Win32 unit).

---

9. Marking overloaded operators with inline is purely optional, of course. Currently (Delphi 2006) it seems like the compiler manages to inline all simple operators except the Implicit and Explicit conversion operators. In .NET, it may be better to rely on the jitter to inline the operator calls for you.

Other Language Changes

Applying the sugar coating

In addition to the object model enhancements I have discussed earlier, the Delphi language has been extended with even more convenient features. These are also supported on both the .NET and Win32 platforms.

Enumerating Collections

To make it easier and more convenient to enumerate over the contents of collections, the traditional for statement has been extended into a for in statement. In general, the for in syntax is

```
var
  Element: ElementType;
begin
  for Element in Collection do
    Writeln(Element.Member);
end;
```

ElementType must be assignment compatible with the type of the actual elements stored inside the collection. The collection must either explicitly implement the enumerator pattern (discussed later) or be an array, string or set. You cannot change the iteration variable, Element, but you can change any properties and fields that Element references.[10]

All .NET collections and most VCL container classes like TList and TStrings implement the required pattern, so now you can transform old code like

```
var
  S: string;
  i: integer;
begin
  for i := 0 to MyStrings.Count-1 do
  begin
    S := MyStrings[i];
    writeln(S);
  end;
end;
```

into the simpler, less error prone, but equivalent

```
var
  S: string;
begin
  for S in MyStrings do
    writeln(S);
end;
```

---

10. But be careful that you do **not** change properties of the element that could affect the element's order in the collection.

To enable for in for your own collection classes, you need to implement the enumerator pattern. This involves writing a GetEnumerator function that returns an instance (class, record or interface)[11] that implements a boolean MoveNext function and a Current property. In .NET, you can also achieve this by implementing the IEnumerable interface.[12] In Win32, these methods must be public.

```
type
  TMyObjectsEnumerator = class
  public
    function GetCurrent: integer;
    function MoveNext: Boolean;
    property Current: integer read GetCurrent;
  end;
  TMyObjects = class
  public
    function GetEnumerator: TMyObjectsEnumerator;
  end;
```

The Chapter10\EnumeratingCollections project demonstrates the differences between the old manual enumeration loops and the new for in loops. It also includes an example of how to write your own classes that support for in enumeration.

Inlined Routines

The .NET Just In Time (JIT) compiler will automatically perform many optimizations, including inlining small and simple methods at call sites (see Chapter 4). In addition to this JIT inlining, Delphi now supports explicit inlining of nonvirtual routines, both in .NET and Win32.

```
function InlineMeToo(const Value: integer): integer; inline;
begin
  Result := Value * 200 div 300;
end;
```

The inline directive is just a **hint** to the Delphi compiler that it should **try** to expand the code inline whenever the routine is called, at compile time. The exact rules of what and when it **can** be inlined differ slightly between the two platforms.

In .NET, Delphi inlining occurs at the CIL level; the Delphi compiler injects the CIL code corresponding to the inlined routine at the call site. The CIL code generated at the call site must obey CLR limitations and rules regarding member visibility, preventing CIL inlining of routines that access private members, for instance. This limitation is mitigated by the less-constrained JIT inlining that occurs at run time; the jitter will generate inlined machine code for small methods regardless of private member access or assembly boundaries.

---

11. Implementing the enumerator as a record allows the compiler to inline the code, generating more efficient for in loops than is possible with an IEnumerable-based enumerator.

12. This is exactly analogous to the way that C# allows you to use foreach with types that implement a GetEnumerator method without explicitly supporting IEnumerable. As in C#, any type that may be used from another language should explicitly support IEnumerable: calling GetEnumerator directly is a strictly intralanguage feature in both languages.

Win32 inlining was first made available in Delphi 2005, but it has been improved in Delphi 2006—now even methods that access private members can be inlined. Assembly (BASM) code cannot be inlined.

The rest of the inlining restrictions are common for both platforms, and the most important ones are

- No inlining across package boundaries.

- The inlined routine cannot access implementation section identifiers.

- The call site must have access to all identifiers used in the inlined routine.

Note The last point means that a routine cannot be inlined unless the call site is in a unit that uses all units that the routine requires. If the compiler can't 'see' an inlined identifier, it emits a hint like

```
[Pascal Hint] InlinedRoutinesU.pas(14): H2443 Inline function 'InlineMe' has not
been expanded because unit 'RequiredUnit' is not specified in USES list
```

To resolve the issue, add the missing unit name to the call site's uses clause.

The {$INLINE ON/AUTO/OFF} compiler directive can be used both at the definition and the call site. The OFF mode turns off all inlining. The default ON setting tries to inline routines explicitly marked inline. AUTO additionally tries to inline all small routines (consisting of less than 32 bytes of machine or CIL code).

Caution Be careful with inlining too much code; the potential code size increase may actually reduce performance by reducing the number of methods that fit in cache.

Unicode Identifiers

Traditional Pascal and Delphi has restricted identifier names to be lower- and uppercase ASCII letters (a–z), underscore, and digits. In .NET, all strings are Unicode and identifiers can use Unicode characters, including national characters such as the Norwegian Æ, Ø, and Å.

Delphi now supports Unicode characters in identifiers, as long as the source file is encoded in a Unicode format (UTF-8 or UCS2). Identifiers that end up in RTTI data (unit names, class names, and published members) must still be pure ASCII—the main reason is to avoid breaking code that read RTTI strings.

```
type
  TUnicodeClass = class
  private
    FAntallÅr: integer;
```

```
public
    procedure SetAntallÅr(const Value: integer);
    property AntallÅr: integer read FAntallÅr write SetAntallÅr;
end;

procedure TestÆØÅ;
var
  Unicode: TUnicodeClass;
begin
  Unicode := UnicodeClass.Create;
  Unicode.AntallÅr := 42;
end;
```

Tip To change the encoding of a source file to UTF-8, right-click in the Delphi editor and select File Format ➤ UTF-8, then save it.

Escaping Keywords

All programming languages have certain keywords reserved—meaning they cannot be used as user-defined identifiers. However, since .NET is inherently a multiprogramming language platform, each language needs to have a mechanism to import and use any identifier.

In Delphi, you can prefix an identifier with an ampersand (&) to have it interpreted as an identifier and not a language keyword. All Delphi keywords (or reserved words) are listed in the online documentation.

If the keyword identifier is the name of a type, you can often avoid using the escape character by fully qualifying the type name with its namespace. From the Chapter10\EscapingKeywords project,

```
var
  T1: &Type;
  T2: System.Type;
  A1: &Array;
  A2: System.Array;
```

If the keyword identifier is a member of an instance, you must use the escape character. For instance,

```
var
  HR: HttpResponse;
begin
  ...
    HR.&End;
```

You can even abuse the ampersand escape to use Delphi keywords for your own type or member identifiers, although this is obviously a very bad idea. For example,

```
type
  &resourcestring = string;
  &Begin = class
    &for: &resourcestring;
    procedure &Goto(&if: &resourcestring; &is: &resourcestring);
    function &End: &resourcestring;
  end;
```

■**Tip** The ampersand (&) escape can also be used to turn off Delphi's special mapping of the Create identifier to a constructor. To call a *method* named Create, you must use &Create.

With a Little Help from Your Friends

When Borland looked at porting the Delphi compiler, RTL, and VCL to the .NET platform, they saw they had a problem. The object model and naming conventions of the FCL classes and methods are strikingly similar to native Delphi, but the .NET classes don't have such common methods as Free and ClassName. Basically, Borland had three options:

- Create a shadow class hierarchy (where TObject inherits from System.Object).

- Alias FCL classes, ignore missing methods, break lots of existing code.

- Invent something to close the gap.

The shadowing option was just as unappealing as breaking code, because they also wanted, e.g., a Delphi TComponent, to be a System.ComponentModel.Component. So, they invented the class helper, a compiler trick that can inject new members into an existing class and all its descendants.

With this solution, TObject is defined as a type alias for System.Object, and it has an accompanying class helper, TObjectHelper, which injects the missing methods into TObject and all its descendants.[13] The effect is that the Free and ClassName methods are now available for *all* Delphi and .NET classes. Similar tricks have been done to implement VCL for .NET classes such as TPersistent, TComponent, and Variant.

To define a class helper, you use the syntax

```
type
  TMyClassHelper = class helper(TBaseClassHelper) for TExternalClass
    procedure NewInjectedMethod;
  end;
```

where TBaseClassHelper is the name of an optional class helper that you inherit from. This is useful when you want to help an already helped class or if you want to override a virtual method of a base helper class.

---

13. For all the gory details, read Marcel van Brakel's in-depth article "Delphi for .NET Class Helpers Inside Out" in *The Delphi Magazine*, issue 208 (August 2004).

A class helper can contain instance methods, class methods, and class fields, but you cannot add instance fields. (You can emulate instance fields with a class var HashTable keyed by the helper method's implicit Self parameter.) In some cases you can reuse the helped object's general storage mechanism. For instance, the TComponentHelper uses the Site property of Component to store the per-component properties Tag, Components, and Owner. Note that VCL for .NET's TControl class is *not* an alias for the WinForms Control class; instead, TControl inherits from TComponent, including the injected methods and properties from TComponentHelper.

Here is an excerpt from the Chapter10\ClassHelpers project that shows all the different kind of members that can be injected.

```
type
  TMyClassHelper = class helper(TObjectHelper) for TExternalClass
  private
    class constructor Create; overload;
    class var
      FNewClassVar: string;
  public
    constructor NewConstructor(const AName: string);
    procedure NewInjectedMethod;
    procedure NewVirtualMethod; virtual;
    procedure NewDynamicMethod; dynamic;
    class procedure NewClassMethod;
    class procedure NewVirtualClassMethod; virtual;
    class procedure NewClassStaticMethod; static;
    property NewProperty: integer
      read GetNewProperty write SetNewProperty;
    class property NewClassProperty: string
      read FNewClassVar write SetNewClassProperty;
  end;
```

In general, it's a good idea to heed Borland's suggestion that while class helpers can be useful to close the gap between different platforms or component sets, they should normally not be used as a design element. If you have full control of a class, you should not inject methods into it by using a class helper; you should change the class itself (or derive from or aggregate it). Why? Well, while class helpers may sound temptingly like multiple inheritance, they're really a good deal more limited. Each class helper is tightly bound to a single class, and you can't have a set of classes that, e.g., 'descend' from ThisClass and ThisHelper, ThatClass and ThisHelper, ThisClass and ThatHelper, and ThatClass and ThatHelper. Also, class helpers **are** a bit fragile. They work well enough to implement the VCL for .NET, but it doesn't seem like they've really been through a full, general-purpose QA cycle.

The Free Pattern

The Borland.Delphi.System unit declares the TObjectHelper class helper that injects methods like Free and ClassName into all classes (including FCL classes). The Free method is special and implements deterministic disposing of unmanaged resources by calling IDispose.Disposable (if it is implemented by the class).

```
procedure TObjectHelper.Free;
begin
  if (Self <> nil) and (Self is IDisposable) then
  begin
    // ...
    (Self as IDisposable).Dispose;
  end;
end;
```

To complete the cycle, the compiler effectively transforms an overridden Destroy destructor into an implementation of the IDisposable interface. For example,

```
type
  TFoo = class
  public
    destructor Destroy; override;
  end;
```

is transformed by the compiler into the equivalent of

```
type
  TFoo = class(TObject, IDisposable)
  public
    procedure IDisposable.Dispose = Destroy;
    procedure Destroy;
  end;
```

This means that the traditional Delphi pattern of calling Free to clean up and writing a destructor to implement the cleanup will have the same semantics in .NET. The difference is that actually deallocating the memory allocated by objects is deferred to the garbage collector. It can be argued that if all your destructors do is free the memory of other nested objects, calling Free and implementing destructors in .NET is pure overhead. The counterargument is that if any of the subobjects implements a resource releasing IDisposable.Dispose (now or in the future), this is the correct way of doing things.

Record Helpers

Just as you can have class helpers to inject methods for a specific class (and its descendants), you can now also declare record helpers for a specific record type (or any value type defined in a .NET assembly). The syntax and capability is basically the same as for class helpers, but with class replaced with record.

```
type
  TMyRecord = record
    Field: string;
    procedure Foo;
  end;

  TMyRecordHelper = record helper for TMyRecord
    procedure Bar;
  end;
```

Note The `record helper` feature is mostly undocumented in Delphi 2006. It is currently used in the `Borland.Delphi.System` unit to inject methods into the `System` types `Decimal`, `DateTime`, and `Double` that would otherwise not be available on the Compact Framework platform.

Overloaded Default Array Properties

A class or component can have an array property that is declared as `default`. This mechanism has now been extended to allow multiple overloaded default array properties—as long as the number or types of indexer parameters are different.

```
type
  TMyObject = class
  public
    property Items[Index: integer]: string read GetItems write SetItems; default;
    property Items[const Name: string]: string
      read GetNamedItems write SetNamedItems; default;
  end;
```

This means that you can use the array indexing syntax on the object instance—effectively overloading the array subscript operator [ ].

```
procedure Test;
var
  MyObject: TMyObject;
begin
  MyObject := TMyObject.Create;
  MyObject[42] := 'The Answer';
  MyObject['Bar'] := 'Yes';
end;
```

.NET Platform Support

Custom features for a managed environment

Most of the language extensions so far have been general in nature, and applicable to both managed and native code. In addition, Borland has added new language features that map directly to intrinsics of the .NET platform. These make it easier for you to integrate with the FCL, external assemblies, the CLR, and so on.

Boxing

Boxing is the process of converting a value type instance into a `System.Object`-compatible reference, copying the value to the garbage-collected heap (see Chapter 2). By default in Delphi, boxing is an explicit operation involving a cast expression from the value type to `System.Object` (or to its alias, `TObject`).

While explicit boxing helps you identify spots where potentially expensive copy operations are going on, it can become bothersome in the long run. To enable implicit boxing operations (just like in C#), you can use the {$AUTOBOX ON} compiler directive.

The syntax to perform unboxing is the same as in C#—just cast the boxed value to the required value type. You can use the is operator to verify the actual value type held by the object reference.

```
procedure Test;
var
  Collection: ArrayList;
  O: TObject;
begin
  Collection := ArrayList.Create;
{$AUTOBOX OFF}
  Collection.Add(TObject(42));
{$AUTOBOX ON}
  Collection.Add(84);
  for O in Collection do
    WriteLn(Byte(O));
end;
```

Note When boxing an integral constant, the compiler will use the smallest integral type that can hold the constant. If you want to box a constant as a specific type, you need to cast it or store it in a correctly typed variable first, like this Collection.Add(Integer(84)). This is in contrast with C#, which boxes all integral constants as int. Consequently, some .NET code may only expect to find boxed integers, raising exceptions if it finds a boxed Byte or a boxed Word.

Attributes Support

Any proper .NET language must support associating attributes to classes and members, and Delphi is no exception. The attribute syntax closely resembles the C# syntax in Chapter 9. The attribute class name (with or without the Attribute suffix) is placed inside square brackets before the element it applies to. The attribute name may be followed by parens with constructor parameters and property assignments. Normally, the compiler will figure out what element the attribute belongs to by its context, but you can prefix the attribute name with a target indicator and colon, such as assembly:.

```
type
  [MyCustom(Age=42, Name='Frank Borland')]
  TMyObject = class
    [MyCustomAttribute('Ida Emilie', 10)]
    procedure Foo;
  end;
[assembly:MyCustomAttribute('Thea Ulrikke', 3)]
```

Note One major difference between attributes in Delphi and attributes in C# is that Delphi does not enforce the CLSCompliant attribute the way that C# does. That is, Delphi will allow you to declare [assembly: CLSCompliant(True)] even when the library contains noncompliant members like class methods or sets.

Floating Point Semantics

Native Delphi signals invalid floating point operations by raising exceptions such as EZeroDivide and EOverflow. By default, these semantics are preserved in Delphi for .NET. However, while the native code floating point exceptions come straight from the processor hardware and so are quite efficient, getting floating point exceptions under .NET means that the compiler must explicitly emit the ckfinite CIL instruction.

For example, a division statement generates CIL code like

```
FloatingPointSemanticsU.pas.51: Three := Two / One;
IL_0063:              ldloc.1
IL_0064:              ldloc.0
IL_0065:              div
IL_0066:              ckfinite
IL_0067:              stloc.2
```

At run time the ckfinite CIL instruction actually expands into seven x86 instructions, including a subroutine CALL—doing this for every floating point operation slows things down noticeably. If you have time-critical code that does not depend on exceptions being raised, you can speed it up a little by using the {$FINITEFLOAT OFF} compiler directive, as in Listing 10-1. In this mode, invalid operations will return special floating point values like NaN (Not a Number), +Inf, and -Inf (Infinity) instead of raising exceptions.[14] To get the same semantics in native code, you use the SetExceptionMask function from the Math unit.

Listing 10-1. *An Example of the FINITEFLOAT Pragma*

```
{$IFDEF CLR}
  // .NET
  {$FINITEFLOAT OFF}
{$ELSE}
  // Native code
  Math.SetExceptionMask( [exInvalidOp, exDenormalized, exZeroDivide,
    exOverflow, exUnderflow, exPrecision] );
{$ENDIF}
```

---

14. The System.Single and System.Double structs define methods like IsNaN and IsInfinity that you must use to test for out-of-range results: you **cannot** use = and <> to compare values directly to constants like Single.NaN and Double.PositiveInfinity. (The Borland Math unit provides platform-neutral wrappers for IsNan and IsInfinity, but does not have a single overload for IsInfinity, nor does it have methods like IsPositiveInfinity and IsNegativeInfinity.)

```
Zero  := 0;
Two   := 42;
Three := Two / Zero; // Returns +Inf (PositiveInfinity), no exception raised
```

Tip Unless you absolutely need floating point exceptions, turn them off with {$FINITEFLOAT OFF}.

Multiunit Namespaces

With the trinity of a logical unit concept, physical unit source .pas files, and compiled .dcu files, Delphi has always had a very efficient and useful module concept. To address the hierarchal namespace support required in .NET while still being backwards compatible, Delphi 8 introduced the concept of dotted unit names, such as Borland.Vcl.SysUtils and Borland.Vcl.Classes—these unit names were mapped directly to .NET namespaces.

    This was a step in the right direction, but Delphi 2005 extended this concept to allow multiple Delphi units to contribute to the same logical namespace. Now the namespace of a dotted unit name is everything up to the last dot. For example, a library with units MultiUnit.Namespaces. Unit1 and MultiUnit.Namespaces.Unit2 exports a single namespace, MultiUnit.Namespaces, which contains both units. Similarly, both Borland.Vcl.SysUtils and Borland.Vcl.Classes now reside in a single Borland.Vcl namespace. This allows the programmer to split his code into multiple physical units, while exposing the contained classes in a single logical namespace. This makes it easier and more convenient to write assemblies that can be used by other languages (such as C#).

```
unit MultiUnit.Namespaces.Unit2;
// ...
class procedure TBar2.Foo;
begin
  Writeln(TBar2.ClassInfo.ToString, '.Foo');
end;
```

    The preceding code writes the fully qualified name of the TBar2 type, and the output is MultiUnit.Namespaces.TBar2.Foo in this case. (Note the way the Unit2 unit name is not part of the fully qualified name.)

New Array Syntax

While native Delphi supports both static and dynamic arrays, Delphi for .NET now also supports multidimensional, rectangular dynamic arrays. These differ from jagged array of arrays in that there is only a single, continuous block of memory allocated for the items in it, and the size of all dimensions can be set dynamically at run time. This is mostly a performance and memory usage optimization, but it is also required to be able to interface with external code that uses multidimensional arrays.

    The syntax to declare a multidimensional dynamic array is array[,] with one comma for each extra dimension. To allocate a new array, use the New(array [dim1, dim2 ..] of TElement) syntax. To change the size of an existing array, use SetLength with one or more dimension parameters—this will preserve the contents of the array.

```
var
  MyArray: array of integer;
  JaggedArray: array of array of integer;
  MyMatrix: array[,] of integer;
  MyCube: array[,,] of integer;
begin
  MyArray := New(array [4] of integer);
  JaggedArray := New(array [3] of array of integer);
  MyMatrix := New(array [3,3] of integer);
  MyCube := New(array [2,2,2] of integer);
  //...
  SetLength(MyMatrix, 10, 20);
  SetLength(MyCube, 10, 20, 30);
end;
```

Note While it is possible to create new arrays using SetLength, the New syntax generates slightly smaller and more efficient code. And SetLength cannot (as of Delphi 2006) be used to create a new multi-dimensional [,] array.

There are two new ways to create a new initialized dynamic array from a list of elements. You can use the New statement and follow the array type with a parenthesized list of elements, or you can use a new TArrayType.Create constructor syntax with the elements as parameters. (Both forms are also supported in Win32.)

```
begin
  MyArray := New(array[] of integer, (1, 2, 3));
  JaggedArray := New(array[] of array[] of integer,
    (New(array[] of integer, (1, 2, 3)),
    New(array[] of integer, (1, 2)),
    New(array[] of integer, (1))));
  MyMatrix := New(array[,] of integer, ((1,2,3), (4,5,6)));
  MyCube   := New(array[,,] of integer, (((1,2), (5,6)), ((3,4), (7,8))));
  // ...
  MyArray := TIntegerArray.Create(1, 2, 3);
  JaggedArray := TJaggedArray.Create(
    TIntegerArray.Create(1, 2, 3),
    TIntegerArray.Create(1, 3),
    TIntegerArray.Create(1));
end;
```

This way of initializing dynamic arrays inline is a great improvement over the old way of first allocating the array using SetLength and then explicitly setting the value of each indexed element. This is particularly useful when calling one of the many FCL methods that have array parameters.

Unsafe Code

Delphi for .NET now supports unsafe code. As in C# (Appendix 0), you have to first enable unsafe code with the {$UNSAFECODE ON} compiler directive, and then you have to mark the method with the unsafe directive. Unlike C#, you cannot have unsafe classes with pointer fields, and you cannot have unsafe blocks within safe methods.

```
{$UNSAFECODE ON}
function Foo(const A: array of char): integer; unsafe;
var
  P: PChar;
  Fixed: GCHandle;
begin
  Fixed := GCHandle.Alloc(A, GCHandleType.Pinned);
  try
    P := Pointer(Fixed.AddrOfPinnedObject);
    Result := 0;
    while P^ <> #0 do
    begin
      Result := Result + Ord(P^);
      Inc(P);
    end;
  finally
    Fixed.&Free;
  end;
end;
```

■**Tip** Delphi for .NET does not currently have a fixed keyword to pin managed objects in memory. Use GCHandle.Alloc from the System.Runtime.InteropServices namespace instead.

Multicast Events

Delphi for .NET has full support for both old-style single-cast events and .NET-style multicast events.

To write a traditional Delphi event, you first declare a delegate type using the procedure of object syntax, then declare an event property that references a delegate field in the read and write specifiers.

```
type
  TLevelChangedEvent = procedure (Sender: TObject; NewLevel: integer) of object;
  TMyComponent = class
  strict private
    FOnLevelChanged: TLevelChangedEvent;
  public
    property OnLevelChanged: TLevelChangedEvent
      read FOnLevelChanged write FOnLevelChanged;
  end;
```

This is a single-cast event that will compile both in .NET and Win32.[15] It supports direct assignment of a method reference or nil to the event property, and it supports directly invoking the event property. For instance, most VCL events are single cast and support assignments like this:

```
MyComponent.OnLevelChanged := MyTest.FirstTarget;
MyComponent.OnLevelChanged(nil, 1);
```

However, many .NET consumers will expect multicast events in your classes. To enable this in a Delphi for .NET class, you simply use add and remove specifiers instead of read and write, like this:

```
TMyComponent = class
strict private
  FOnMultiChanged: TLevelChangedEvent;
public
  property OnMultiChanged: TLevelChangedEvent
    add FOnMultiChanged remove FOnMultiChanged;
end;
```

The simplest way to support multicast events is to simply reference a delegate field in an add or remove clause—the compiler will then implement proper add_*EventName* and remove_*EventName* methods for you, just as in Chapter 8. In some special cases, you may want to implement your own logic in these routines—to do that you simply write and reference your own add and remove methods, like this:

```
TMyComponent = class
strict private
  FOnCustomChanged: TLevelChangedEvent;
public
  procedure add_OnCustomChanged(Value: TLevelChangedEvent);
  procedure remove_OnCustomChanged(Value: TLevelChangedEvent);
  property OnCustomChanged: TLevelChangedEvent
    add add_OnCustomChanged remove remove_OnCustomChanged;
end;

procedure TMyComponent.add_OnCustomChanged(Value: TLevelChangedEvent);
var
  Inlist: Delegate;
begin
  if Assigned(FOnCustomChanged) then
    for Inlist in Delegate(@FOnCustomChanged).GetInvocationList do
      if InList.Equals(Delegate(@Value)) then
        Exit;
```

---

15. On .NET, it creates event add and remove handlers that enforce single-cast semantics. For example, adding a delegate will replace the existing handler, not append the new handler to the invocation list.

```
    FOnCustomChanged :=
      TLevelChangedEvent(Delegate.Combine(
        Delegate(@FOnCustomChanged),
        Delegate(@Value)));
  end;


  procedure TMyComponent.remove_OnCustomChanged(Value: TLevelChangedEvent);
  begin
    FOnCustomChanged :=
      TLevelChangedEvent(Delegate.Remove(
        Delegate(@FOnCustomChanged),
        Delegate(@Value)));
  end;
```

This example add handler only allows unique delegate targets (as in the NoDups event in the Chapter8\EventLists C# project), ignoring any attempt to add the same object's method more than once. Note the tricky-looking code with casts to Delegate and use of the @ operator. The Delegate casts are required to force the compiler to treat the procedure of object as a System.Delegate instance (which is an implementation detail from the compiler's point of view). The @ operator is required to prevent the compiler from trying to *call* the event instead of evaluating its value.

Most WinForms events are multicast events—they support multiple methods as targets. To add or remove a method from a multicast event, you use the Include and Exclude intrinsic procedures:

```
  Include(MyComponent.OnMultiChanged, MyTest.FirstTarget);
  Include(MyComponent.OnMultiChanged, MyTest.SecondTarget);
  MyComponent.TriggerMulti(6);
  Exclude(MyComponent.OnMultiChanged, MyTest.FirstTarget);
```

This corresponds directly to the += and -= operators that C# supports on events.

■**Tip** Use multicast add/remove events for WinForms code and components. Use single-cast read/write events for VCL for .NET code and components, unless you really need multicast behavior.

Undocumented Corner

I have already mentioned the new semi-undocumented record helper feature in Delphi for .NET. Another undocumented and more subtle extension is the ability to initialize global variables and typed constants with simple casting and constructor calls using constant parameters.[16]

---

16. The existence of this new syntax was first published by Chee Whee Chua (Borland Singapore) at http://blogs.borland.com/chewy/archive/2005/11/23/22210.aspx.

```
type
  TFoo = class
    constructor Create(A, B, C: integer);
  end;
  TBar = record
  public
    class operator Explicit(Value: Integer): TBar;
    class operator Implicit(Value: Double): TBar;
  end;

var
  Foo: TFoo = TFoo.Create(1, 2, 3);
  Bar1: TBar = TBar(42);
const
  Bar2: TBar = 3.14;
```

In native Delphi, you can initialize global variables with constant expressions such as integers, floating point values, and strings. In .NET, this has been extended to allow initialization of object references and records using a `constructor` call or an implicit or explicit cast operator. This feature can't be used for instance fields or `class vars`, only for global variables and typed constants, so its usefulness is a little limited. The Chapter10\InitializeGlobals project demonstrates this new syntax.

Note While this is currently an undocumented feature, it is fairly safe to assume it will continue to be available in the future. For instance, the `Currency` type in the `Borland.Delphi.System` unit is implemented as a `record` with operator overloading, and it has implicit conversion operators from `Double` and `Integer`. Without this feature, there would be no way to initialize a global `Currency` variable (breaking existing Win32 code). Also, in .NET, all initialized variables have to be compiled as executable assignments in the startup code, so allowing constructor calls there is a nice bonus.

P/Invoke Magic

Moving into the slightly more esoteric topics, Delphi for .NET supports two Platform Invoke (P/Invoke) technologies called Reverse P/Invoke (or Unmanaged Exports) and Dynamic P/Invoke (or Virtual Library Interfaces).

Reverse P/Invoke lets you write a .NET DLL that can be used like any other DLL from Win32 code. It is a quick way of introducing .NET functionality into a Win32 application without performing a complete porting process or hosting the CLR explicitly.

Unmanaged exports must reside within a `library` project and generate thunks of unmanaged code, so you must turn {$UNSAFECODE ON}. The syntax is the same exports declaration as is used in Win32 Delphi. Only global-level routines can be exported, not class methods.

```
library ReversePInvoke;
procedure Foo(const S: string);
function Bar: integer;
function Greeting(Name: string): string;
//...
{$UNSAFECODE ON}
exports
  Foo,
  Bar,
  Greeting;
```

On the Win32 side, you import these routines just like you would import any other DLL, using external declarations.

```
const
  LibName = 'ReversePInvoke.DLL';

procedure Foo(const S: string); stdcall; external LibName;
function Bar: integer; stdcall; external LibName;
function Greeting(Name: string): PChar; stdcall; external LibName;
```

Caution Not all managed types can be used as parameters in exported routines. Generally you can use simple types and strings. String input parameters map to Win32 AnsiString, string results and output parameters map to PChar.

Virtual Library Interfaces use Dynamic P/Invoke to load a Win32 DLL at run time by using an interface to specify what routines to import. The DLL can be seen as a singleton object that implements the interface. The advantage is that you can use the Supports function from the Borland.Delphi.Win32 unit to check if the DLL and all the methods are available.

```
uses
  Win32;
type
  IMyInterface = interface
    procedure Foo(const S: string);
    function Bar: integer;
    function Greeting(const Name: string): string;
  end;

procedure Test;
var
  MyInterface: IMyInterface;
begin
  if Supports('Win32NativeDLL.DLL', TypeOf(IMyInterface), MyInterface) then
```

```
begin
  Writeln('.NET App dynamically calling into Win32 DLL');
  Writeln('The Answer is ', MyInterface.Bar);
  MyInterface.Foo('.NET client');
  Writeln(MyInterface.Greeting('Ida'));
end
else
  Writeln('Cannot find Win32NativeDLL.DLL!');
end;
```

In effect you are dynamically loading the DLL if and only if it is available. If not, the application can continue running, but with reduced functionality. It also allows the application to control the folder the native DLL is loaded from—this can be tricky to do otherwise.

Tip Use the LibraryInterface attribute to control calling convention and the wideness of string parameters. The defaults are CharSet.Auto (PChar on Win9x and PWideChar on WinNT) and CallingConvention.Winapi (or stdcall).

Obsolete Features

Some things are not possible in managed code

Due to the managed and garbage-collected nature of the .NET environment, a number of features specific to native code had to be left out of the Delphi for .NET dialect of the language (see Table 10-1). Most of these are already warned against when you compile with the Win32 compiler, easing the porting process.

Table 10-1. *Obsolete Features*

Feature	Comment
Pointers	Including PChar, @ operator, GetMem, etc. See "Unsafe Code" earlier.
absolute	Variable overlaying not supported.
Real48	This is a relic from the Turbo Pascal days.
File of <type>	Size of records are not fixed in .NET.
BlockRead / BlockWrite	Size of records are not fixed in .NET.
Old-style objects	Another TP relic—deprecated since Delphi 1.
BASM	Built-in Assembler—is specific to x86 and native code.
IUnknown	No longer has AddRef, Release, and QueryInterface.
implements	Interface delegation, not implemented (yet?).
automated, dispid	OLE Automation not supported.

Win32 and .NET Differences

Minor differences can cause trouble

While Delphi for .NET is as compatible as possible with native code Delphis, there are some implementation details that are different between the native and .NET versions of the Delphi language. These differences are generally minor, but it is useful to know about them.

Untyped var and out Parameters

It is interesting to note that Delphi supports typeless var and out parameters in a strictly typed and managed environment like .NET.

```
var
  GlobalInt: integer;

procedure FooVar(var Bar);
var
  BarValue: integer;
begin
  BarValue := Integer(Bar);
  Inc(BarValue);
  Bar := BarValue;
end;

procedure TestFooVar;
begin
  GlobalInt := 1;
  FooVar(GlobalInt);
end;
```

The implementation relies on boxing the actual argument to and from System.Object before and after the method call. The compiler compiles the preceding code like this:

```
procedure FooVarImpl(var Bar: TObject);
var
  BarValue: integer;
begin
  BarValue := Integer(Bar);    // Unbox
  Inc(BarValue);
  Bar := TObject(BarValue);    // Autobox
end;

procedure TestFooVarImpl;
var
  Temp: TObject;
```

```
begin
  GlobalInt := 1;
  Temp := TObject(GlobalInt); // Autobox
  FooVarImpl(Temp);
  GlobalInt := Integer(Temp); // Unbox - after the routine returns
end;
```

Because of this implementation, you will not see intermediate modifications of the actual argument until the call returns.[17] The compiler allows direct assignments to the untyped parameter in .NET (as if $AUTOBOX is turned ON just for that TObject parameter)—this is not allowed in Win32. In addition, left-hand-side casts of an untyped parameter are not allowed in .NET—only in Win32. This can make it hard to write single-source routines using var and out parameters without resorting to ifdefs. The Chapter10\UntypedParameters project demonstrates these differences.

Casting

There are also some casting differences between the two platforms.[18] In native code, hard-casts are unsafe, because the compiler will not complain if you perform obviously illegal casts. Hard-casts are a way of telling the native code compiler, "Relax, I know what I'm doing. Just close your eyes and reinterpret these bits as the type I'm telling you it is." So there are no checks and no conversions going on—it is just looking at the bits in a different way.

In .NET, even hard-casts are safe, in the sense that the compiler and run time will check that the cast is valid (see Chapter 1). The CLR will check that the source is compatible with the target type—if not, nil is returned instead. Conceptually, .NET hard-casts like

```
Target := TTargetClass(Source);
```

work like

```
if Source is TTargetClass then
  Target := Source
else
  Target := nil;
```

This means that a typical native Win32 pattern of

```
if O is TMyObject then
  TMyObject(O).Foo;
```

has the same semantics in .NET, but a slightly more efficient .NET-only alternative is

```
MyObject := TMyObject(O);
if Assigned(MyObject) then
  MyObject.Foo;
```

---

17. Because of this implementation and the fact that .NET unboxing is a safe operation, old Win32 code that would silently assign the 'wrong' type of data to an untyped out or var parameter will cause an exception at the call site, after the call returns in .NET.

18. For more details about how casting works in Win32 and .NET, see my blog posts at http://hallvards.blogspot.com/.

As you know, casting between TObject and value types in .NET performs boxing and unboxing operations (see Chapter 5 for the details). Win32 does not support boxing; hard-casting value types to and from TObject is only allowed if the size of the value type is 4 bytes or less. As always, a Win32 hard-cast is just a binary reinterpretation, not an actual conversion.

Initialization and Finalization

In native code, the Delphi unit initialization and finalization sections have exact (static) execution order and execution time semantics. On the .NET platform, the Delphi compiler implements a unit's initialization section in terms of the UnitName[19] class constructor. This guarantees that it will run before any global routines in that unit executes. In addition, all classes and records get an implicit class constructor that calls RuntimeHelpers.RunClassConstructor to ensure that the UnitName class constructor will be run. Finally, the UnitName class constructor has calls to RunClassConstructor to invoke all the class constructors of all used units. This arrangement ensures that a unit's initialization section is run before any other code in that unit. For stand-alone executables and for Delphi package assemblies loaded by a Delphi application, the initialization order will be the same as in Win32. .NET does not have the equivalent of LibMain for DLL assemblies, so for an assembly loaded by a non-Delphi application, the unit initialization order may be dependent on the order the client application uses the types from the assembly.

Likewise, running of an assembly's unit finalization sections is triggered by a global object's Finalize method—this implies that the code runs at an unspecified time on the CLR's finalizer thread (and it is not always guaranteed to occur).

While most simple initialization and finalization code should work as is, you should be careful with code that relies on the execution order of these sections, code that touches types from other units, and code that closes physical resources such as files. Old code that only frees memory in the finalization section can typically be ifdefed out in .NET code.

Abstract Classes

The concept of abstract classes is strictly enforced by the CLR—it will not allow you to instantiate instances of abstract classes or classes containing abstract methods. In native code, you *can* create instances of classes containing abstract methods. Normally you will get a compiler warning, though—this warning has been turned into a compiler error in .NET.

When creating instances through a class of reference, the compiler's static checking cannot prevent you from compiling code that could potentially instantiate abstract classes. In native code, this will go undetected at run time, unless you actually call an abstract method—then you will get an EAbstractError exception. In .NET, the run time will raise an exception if you try to call the constructor of an abstract class. The Chapter10\AbstractClasses project demonstrates these differences.

---

19. The compiler places global declarations (global variables, constants, functions, and procedures) inside a class named after the containing unit, for instance, UnitName. This class is then placed inside a namespace called UnitName.Units, making the fully qualified name UnitName.Units.UnitName. This is an implementation detail invisible to Delphi code, but you'll notice it if you try to use global Delphi routines from other languages.

Class References

For the most part, the semantics of using class of references to create late-bound types of classes is unchanged in .NET. The only noticeable difference is that in .NET the constructor you call through the class reference **must** be declared virtual. In Win32, it doesn't strictly have to be, but normally it should be declared virtual.

Constructors

While it is a good rule in native code to have all constructors call an inherited or peer constructor, the compiler does not enforce it. In .NET, the run time refuses to load types that break this rule. In addition, you cannot access inherited fields or call any methods until you have called an inherited constructor.

```
type
  TBar = class
  protected
    FInheritedField: integer;
  end;
  TFoo = class(TBar)
  private
    FField: integer;
    procedure Method;
  public
    constructor Create;
  end;

constructor TFoo.Create;
begin
  FField := 42;
{$IFNDEF CLR}
  Method;
  FInheritedField := 13;
{$ENDIF}
  inherited Create;
  FInheritedField := 13;
  Method;
end;
```

Note that (unlike C#) in Delphi you can still modify the fields of the current instance before calling the inherited constructor.

Delphi vs. C#

Very similar, but different in the details

It is useful to know the unique strengths and features of each language if you need to port code from native Delphi to C#, or to convert C# code snippets to Delphi, or to make informed decisions about which language to use. This section quickly iterates over the highlights of each language, and includes some tips on porting between them.

Note that the comparison is between Delphi for .NET and C# version 1.0, not version 2.0—Delphi 2006 runs on .NET 1.1, and doesn't support 2.0 features like generics, nullable types, and iterators.

Delphi Language Highlights

C# doesn't support some minor Delphi features

Class helpers, unmanaged exports, and virtual library interfaces are unique Delphi language features. In one sense, class helpers are very similar to the extension methods of the upcoming C# 3.0 standard to support the LINQ (Language Integrated Query) technology. The main difference is that class helpers cannot help interfaces (at least not yet), and class helpers are more structured.

Table 10-2 lists the most important Delphi language features that C# does not have and what their alternative is when porting code.

Table 10-2. *Delphi Language Features*

Delphi Feature	Comment	C# Alternatives
class helpers	Platform-leveling compiler magic	Explicit static methods C# 3.0 extension methods
Unmanaged exports	aka Reverse P/Invoke	Use C++, hacks
Virtual Library Interfaces	aka dynamic P/Invoke	Use unmanaged C++, hacks
sets	Limited to ordinal types with <= 256 elements	enum flags, BitArray, int bit-fiddling
class of references	Metaclasses	System.Type
virtual class methods	Metaclass polymorphism	System.Type, reflection
virtual constructors	Class factories	Activator, reflection
Typeless var and out parameters	Poor-man's generics	C# 2.0 Generics, System.Object function
type aliases, typed types	Logical vs. actual types	Explicit typing
Default parameters	Simpler than overloading	Overloading
resourcestrings	Simplified internationalization	Resources and ResourceManager.GetString
Named constructors	Simulated using overloading	Overloading
message methods	Dispatching windows messages	switch statement in an overridden WndProc method, or attributes as in the Chapter15\WndProc C# project
Variants	One type fits all	System.Object boxing

Table 10-2. *Delphi Language Features (Continued)*

Delphi Feature	Comment	C# Alternatives
Global routines	Non-OOP code	Static methods of a class
Global variables	Non-OOP data	Static fields of a class
Named array properties	Multiple array properties	Overloaded this indexer Nested class with this indexer
Local (nested) procedures	Implementation hiding, automatic access to outer variables	Private method, anonymous method (C# 2.0)
variant records (case)	Structure overlaying (union)	[StructLayout(LayoutKind.Explicit)] [FieldOffset()]
Text files, WriteLn, etc.	Easy input/output	Console and Stream classes
Supports Win32, Linux	Cross-platform capabilities	Use C/C++, Mono for Linux

One difference that is important to be aware of is that hard-casts and safe-casts have opposite syntax in Delphi and C#. The safe exception–raising cast is (O as TargetType) in Delphi and (TargetType)O in C#. The Nil/null-returning cast is TargetType(O) in Delphi and (O as TargetType) in C#.

C# Language Highlights

Delphi doesn't support several high-level C# features

The C# 1.0 features listed in Table 10-3 are not directly available in Delphi, but there are alternative ways of achieving the same goal.

Table 10-3. *C# Language Features*

C# Feature	Comment	Delphi Alternatives
lock	Thread synchronization	Monitor.Enter(O); try .. finally Monitor.Exit(O); end;

fixed	Garbage collection object pinning	H := GCHandle.Alloc(..)
		try
		   P := H.AddrOfPinnedObject;
		finally
		   H.&Free;
		end;

using	Deterministic releasing of unmanaged resources	O := TO.Create; try .. finally O.Free; end;
C# destructor ~ClassName	Garbage collection deallocate notification	override Finalize method

Table 10-3. *C# Language Features*

C# Feature	Comment	Delphi Alternatives
stackalloc	Unsafe code temporary allocations	GCHandle.Alloc, dynamic array
checked/ unchecked	Integer arithmetic overflow checking	{$OVERFLOWCHECKS ON/OFF}, {$Q+/-}
readonly field	Read-only fields initialized in a constructor	const, read-only property, normal field
return	Set function result and return to caller	Result := 0; Exit;
volatile field	May be modified outside current thread	Explicit locks, Thread.VolatileRead/ Thread.VolatileWrite
internal access	Per-assembly cross-class implementation details	public protected with cracker-cast
ternary ? : operator	Inline test and return result	if .. then .. else, IfThen routines
switch (string)	Multicase testing of strings	Nested if..then..else, TStringList.IndexOf, AnsiIndexStr

In Delphi, an overridden Destroy *destructor maps to an implementation of* IDisposable, *while in C# you must implement* IDisposable *explicitly. In C#, a* ~ClassName *destructor maps to an overridden* Object.Finalize *method, while in Delphi* Finalize *must be overridden manually. In most cases, application-level code needs to implement* IDisposable, *but should not override* Finalize—*that should be left to low-level leaf classes in the FCL.*

Key Points

More new syntax than Delphi has seen in some time

- Delphi for .NET strives to be backward compatible. This makes ports easier, and may make component vendors' lives easier.

- Most of the new syntax is now available in Win32 native code Delphis.

- This chapter was written by Hallvard Vassbotn.

PART 3

■■■

The Framework Class Library

This is the most important part of the book: learning the cross-language FCL is what makes you a .NET programmer. By all means, use Borland's VCL for .NET compatibility layer for ports—but use the FCL for new code. The FCL has many functions that aren't part of the VCL, and programs that use only the FCL are smaller than programs that include VCL for .NET. And, of course, learning the FCL is your ticket to *learn once, work anywhere* freedom.

These last eight chapters describe the main ideas that shape key libraries. Chapter 11 covers basic old-fashioned programming the .NET way, though you may be surprised to find regexs considered as fundamental as strings and streams. Chapter 12 explores .NET's collections libraries—and how they've changed from 1.1 to 2.0—in quite a bit more depth than Chapter 2. Chapter 13 compares Reflection to Delphi's RTTI. Chapter 14 covers both the CLR serialization machinery and serialization's major customers, the remoting and application domain systems. Chapter 15 mentions the deep similarities between WinForms and traditional VCL forms, and discusses the most important differences. Chapter 16 compares the GDI+ the FCL uses to the GDI that we're used to from the VCL, having a bit more fun than you'll need for the average departmental app, but nowhere near enough for consumer software or component vendors. Chapter 17 covers the excellent thread and synchronization primitives. Finally, Chapter 18 is an impressionistic tour of the .NET XML libraries, which are much too good to not know about.

Strings and Files

The FCL has its own style, and you'll find it easy to learn new parts of the library once you get a feel for the style. Strings are a good place to start—the String *class offers a lot of standard functionality. Many classes offer methods that wrap core* String *methods, and so the core method's prototypes tend to propagate up the chain of wrappers. For example, the* Console *class has* Write *methods that look like* String.Format *because they wrap text file IO, which wrap* String.Format. *I speed over functionality that's familiar from Delphi, and lavish more attention on functionality that may be strange or new to Delphi programmers, such as the entirely new pattern language that* String.Format *uses, and the excellent regular expression implementation.*

Learning the FCL

".NET programmers" know the FCL—learn once, work anywhere

The FCL documentation can be baffling at first. It's often more precise than clear, and new technical terms are often used without links to their definitions. The more of it you read, the clearer it all becomes.

Context-sensitive help on a class name will generally take you to the class's "Members" page. The Members page links to the class overview page and lists every member—all public constructors, all public properties, all public methods, &c. For all but the smallest, simplest classes, the class Members page is too long to be really useful as anything besides an entry point.

The class overview pages are generally worth reading, but often the best thing to do at a class Members page is to use the Help ➤ Sync Contents menu command (in 1.1—there is a tool button in both 1.1 and 2.0: see Figure 11-1) to show the class's entries in the Class Library reference section. In the table of contents, a class Members page is under the overview page, followed by pages that list all constructors on a single page, all properties on a single page, and so on. When the Members page goes on for several screens, the Methods page or the Properties page may be more manageable. Even so, some classes have so many methods that it takes several screen pages to list them all, which not only can make it easy to miss a method that might do what you want, but can also make it hard to get an idea of the sorts of things that the class can do.

Figure 11-1. *The Sync Contents button in 1.1 and 2.0*

The String class is one of these potentially overwhelming classes with a large number of methods. The next section of this chapter, "Strings," breaks the String methods into functional groups. The intent is not to specify syntax—the Microsoft documentation is perfectly adequate for that—but to give you a feel for the sort of functionality that's available.

In general, these FCL chapters aim to explain enough of how various key FCL modules work that you can start using them and understand the documentation on edge conditions, &c. Easing into the documentation this way will hopefully help you understand it better when you start exploring aspects of the FCL that I don't cover.

Delphi Note I do describe a few 2.0 methods, but my focus on key methods means that **most** of the methods I describe here are available in 1.1, and hence in Delphi 2006 (which can only use FCL 2.0 via the --ClrVersion switch to the command-line compiler).

You'll find that many FCL methods are heavily overloaded. For example, the String class's Concat method has nine public overloads. After a while you'll find that different methods are often overloaded in similar ways. They tend to follow a few common *models*. ("Model" is shorter than "pattern" and is not as heavily overloaded in developer talk. You know what I mean when I talk about following a model, but you aren't distracted by thoughts of *Design Patterns*.)

Learning to see these models in action is part of learning the FCL: when you see that a new type follows a familiar model, you know something about how the new type works.

Now, it's pretty clear that the FCL developers built these models into their code. They're much too ubiquitous not to be intentional. But the developers didn't give these models any public names, so I use short, made up names, like *Defaults* and *Smaller*, which I print italic and proper cased, so they stand out. I do this to make it easier for me to talk about these models, and to make it easier for you to think about them: giving a complicated subject a simple name can act as a sort of magnet to pull together disparate facts as you learn them.

Overall, *Defaults* is perhaps the most common overload model. Since C# doesn't support optional parameters, many overloads are just single statements that add various default parameters to their parameters, and pass the resulting expanded parameter list to the overload with real code. You'll see examples of the *Defaults* model throughout all these FCL chapters.

Strings

Look like Delphi, but (because of garbage collection) don't act like Delphi

As a Delphi programmer, you will find .NET strings look very familiar. A string variable is actually a reference to a string object (a reference type, on the heap) with a length field and an array of characters.

Because the string values have an explicit length field, operations like concatenation or right trimming do not need to calculate the string length by scanning for a null character, as in C-style string libraries.

Because strings are reference types, not value types, assigning a string value to a string variable is just a matter of changing the address in the string variable. Similarly, passing a string value to a method simply passes the address, not the actual string contents.

Delphi strings are in a syntactic class of their own and, in their own way, so are .NET strings. On .NET, strings are objects, but string objects **are** treated specially by the system. With every other type, every instance of the type is the same size as every other instance of the type. String objects are sized to fit their character buffer, but every string value is a string instance, not a string descendant:

```
/* if */ string AnyString = "The value doesn't matter";
/* then */ AnyString.GetType() == typeof(System.String)
```

There are larger differences between .NET strings and a native code Delphi's AnsiString. While sequences of operations are always relatively slow with long strings—so **many** cache-hostile character operations—creating lots of longish temporary strings is particularly expensive in a garbage-collected environment. This is because the frequent heap allocation triggers frequent garbage collection, and also because even modest-size strings end up on the Large Object Heap (and thus in generation 2), which makes the garbage collections more expensive. Chapter 3 has the details.

Also, .NET strings are not reference counted, the way that a native code Delphi's strings are. No reference counting means that passing string values from method to method doesn't add setup and teardown costs to method calls. No reference counting is also a reason that .NET strings are *immutable* in a way that native Delphi strings are not.

That is, Delphi's reference-counted strings make it easy to check at run time whether a given string value is unique or whether there are multiple references to the same value. If you change characters within a string value, the compiler emits calls to the run-time library that ensure the string value is unique, so when you change a character you only affect a single string value.

Doing a similar test on .NET would require a full sweep of the whole reference forest, from each root to every leaf, which is obviously impractical.[1] Thus, .NET strings have no methods that can change the actual character array. You can read a string character by character, but you can't change characters, nor can you insert or delete either characters or substrings.

---

1. The garbage collector sweeps from roots much less often than a unique string check might get called, and optimizes that as much as possible. You simply do not want application code doing this sweep— and especially not in a loop!

With immutable strings, it doesn't matter how unique your reference is, you can't change the string itself. Calling a method can't change a string parameter's value, unless it's explicitly passed as a ref or out parameter. Threads can't cause problems for each other by changing a shared string's contents. Certain types of buffer overflow bugs are simply not possible. Similarly, immutable strings eliminate security attacks that rely on changing a string buffer after it has passed various tests, but before some actual resource is accessed.

Instead of changing a character buffer, you create a new string. Code like ThisString.Insert(4, AnotherString) returns a new string, it doesn't change ThisString.

■ **Note** It takes an explicit assignment to change a string value. Forgetting to do the assignment is a common mistake.

DfN (Delphi for .NET) users should note that while indexed assignment **appears** to allow you to change characters within a string, this actually creates a new string by a three-way concatenation of a left substring, the replacement character, and the right substring. This concatenation is OK in extreme moderation, but is a very expensive operation within even comparatively short loops.

The String Class

Many standard operations are System.String methods

A Delphi string and a C# string are both a System.String. C# programmers need to—and Delphi programmers ought to—learn the various classes and methods of .NET's FCL (Framework Class Library) string code. The string code in the System namespace alone pretty much exceeds VCL units like SysUtils and StrUtils, and then there's the regex code in the System.Text.RegularExpressions namespace and the hash table code in the System.Collections and System.Collections.Generic namespaces. (I cover collections in the next chapter.)

Delphi programmers **can** mix Turbo Pascal procedures like Str and Val with VCL functions like Trim and Format and with FCL methods like String.Split, but you will probably find that the more you use the new FCL methods, the more you use FCL methods in place of their Delphi equivalents. Calls to ThisString.Trim go better with ThisString.Split than Trim(ThisString) does.

Concatenation Methods

In which we meet some common overload models

The String.Concat overloads set a pattern that you'll find repeated throughout this chapter. There are overloads that take one, two, three, or four object parameters, and there is an overload that takes a params object[] parameter. There are overloads that take two, three, or four string parameters, and there is an overload that takes a params string[] parameter. All Concat overloads return a single string.

Now, as per Chapter 9, the params array overloads mean that the overloads that take one, two, three, or four object parameters or two, three, or four string parameters are redundant. If they are not defined, the params array overload will be used. However, these overloads make for *Smaller* code, as it takes fewer bytes of CIL to push a handful of parameters than it does to create and populate an array. (String.Concat is heavily optimized, so that *Smaller* code is also faster; less widely used code will often just chain to the params array overload.)

The params array overloads also mean that you can concatenate any number of string or object parameters. As per Chapter 7, the C# compiler will automatically gather any extra type-compatible parameters into a temporary array, and pass that as the last params array parameter. Thus, in C# you can Concat any number of strings or any number of objects. Delphi does not support params parameters—a params array just looks like any other array to Delphi, and you have to use open array syntax to explicitly create an array once you have more than four parameters to concatenate. This makes String.Concat (and the other methods that overload like it) seem stranger and more discontinuous in Delphi than in C#—Delphi programmers see a syntax change at five parameters that C# programmers do not.

Note For the most part, the String.Concat overloads that add strings together are for compilers to use, in generating code for expressions like ThisString + ThatString. You may occasionally have an array of strings that you want to concatenate, but otherwise you will have little direct use for the string forms of String.Concat. The String.Join method (discussed later in this chapter) also concatenates its array of strings parameter, adding a separator string between each string in the array parameter.

The String.Concat overload that takes an object and returns a string simply calls the object's ToString method, returning an empty string on a null parameter. The overloads that take multiple objects and return a string all call each parameter's ToString method and concatenate the results.

For example, in C#, which boxes automatically, String.Concat(12, 34) returns "1234". Similarly, a string is an object—a string's ToString() method simply returns the string[2]—and String.Concat("(", 12, 34, ")") returns "(1234)".

Accepting object parameters instead of strings cuts boilerplate, making your code both smaller and *Simpler*. It's a lot easier to read code like String.Concat(This, That) than it is to read code like String.Concat(This.ToString(), That.ToString()). It's easier to write it, too.

Note that cutting boilerplate is not always the same thing as generating smaller CIL. In particular, C# code that takes advantage of params parameters is usually clearer—but not smaller—than code that explicitly creates an array. For example, String.Concat(0, 1, 2, 3, 4) is undoubtedly easier to read than String.Concat(new object[] {0, 1, 2, 3, 4})—but it compiles to the exact same CIL.

---

2. That is, Object.ReferenceEquals(ThisString, ThisString.ToString()).

The Format Method

Much like the SysUtils Format function, but with a different pattern language

The String.Format methods follow some of the same models as the String.Concat methods. Accepting object parameters instead of strings keeps calls to ToString() out of application code, and makes for *Simpler* code. String.Format accepts object parameters, calls ToString on each, and interpolates the results into a pattern string. This in turn becomes the *Format* model of passing parameters on to String.Format and doing various things with the results, which is followed by code from text streams on up to Console IO.

Accepting some small fixed number of parameters on the stack generates *Smaller* code, because calling CIL doesn't always have to construct a temporary array inline. String.Format also follows this model, adding a format string before the one, two, or three objects to be formatted. Again, because C# supports params arrays, these overloads are more noticeable in Delphi than in C#.

The format string is usually the first parameter to String.Format.[3] The result is the format string with any {} escape sequences replaced in various ways with one of the parameters. (Within a format string, use {{ and }} where you want the result to have { and } characters.) The simplest {} escapes are like {0} and {1}—just a single nonnegative integer between {} curly braces. Obviously enough, {0} is the first parameter in the main params array overload, and also in the overloads that take individual object parameters, while {1} is the second parameter and so on.

For example, String.Format("{0}{1}", 12, 34) returns "1234", while String.Format("{0} and {1}", "This", "That") returns "This and That" and String.Format("{2} and {0}", 1, 2, 3) returns "3 and 1". The format string does not have to include any escape sequences, but String.Format will raise an exception if any escape sequence in the format string refers to a nonexistent parameter.

You've probably got years of experience with variants of the C-style printf format language (like Delphi's Format function), and you may wonder what makes a format like "{0}{1}" enough better than "%d%d" that you should learn a new format language. There are two main reasons. First, an indexed escape like {0} handles repeats (and rearrangements) more clearly than a sequential language where each subsequent % escape refers to a subsequent parameter. (Think of the weird way that Delphi's Format('%d %d %d %0:d %d', [1, 2, 3, 4, 5]) returns '1 2 3 1 2', not '1 2 3 1 4'.) This can be particularly helpful when it comes to localization, as different languages may call for different term orders.

The second main reason is that the {} language is more extensible than the % language, because it has a start and a stop character. This means that it can have a sort of params parameter, an optional subsequence that runs to the end of the escape sequence and which can be fed to a parameter's ToString method to control the parameter's formatting. This makes extensibility much simpler (with many fewer reserved characters) than when everything must be shoehorned in between the % escape and the closing type code[4] character.

---

3. The one exception is the overload that takes an IFormatProvider parameter before the pattern string. Explicitly passing a format provider lets you control the locale, or *culture*, without changing the current thread's culture settings. You may need to juggle several different locales; you may only need to format a few values in a particular locale; or you may not have permission to change a thread's culture.

4. Type codes like %s for strings and %d for decimals.

Extensibility is important to String.Format because, unlike printf and Delphi's Format function, String.Format does not actually format any of its parameters. That is, when a printf-like function evaluates an escape sequence like %5.3d, it rips that into a width of 5 and a precision of 3, and passes the width and precision to internal integer formatting code. Getting a bit ahead of myself, when String.Format evaluates an escape sequence like {0,5:z3}, it rips that into parameter 0 with a width of 5. String.Format will use the field width to align the formatted parameter—but String.Format doesn't know anything about precision, or long and short formats, or the like. If parameter 0 supports custom formatting, String.Format will pass the z3 string to the appropriate ToString overload; otherwise, String.Format will just use the basic, no-parameter ToString overload.

Note The String.Format pattern language is untyped. Every parameter is a System.Object, responsible for formatting itself with a ToString overload. The good side of this is that when your escape sequences just specify a parameter, with no format string—like {0} or {7}—you can change the type you're formatting without having to change the Format pattern string (which sure isn't true of printf-like methods). The bad side of relegating formatting to the type itself is that passing the wrong format string can give you spectacularly wrong results, or even an exception.

Escape Sequence Specifics

One mandatory component, and two optional components

Every {} escape sequence has an *index component.* The index component is a sequence of digits— that is, it is always an integer >= 0. The index component may be followed by an optional *alignment component* (a comma followed by an integer), which may be followed by an optional *formatting component* (everything between a : [colon] and the closing } character). For example,

```
{0}
{1, 5}
{3:g7}
{0, -5:z3}
```

The alignment component **must** precede any formatting component, because the formatting component is everything from the colon to the end of the escape sequence—including commas followed by an integer.

An alignment component specifies the field width. A negative integer is a left-aligned field, while a nonnegative field width is a right-aligned field. For example, String.Format("{0, 3}", 7) returns space-space-seven, while String.Format("{0, -3}", 7) returns seven-space-space.

Any padding is done with blanks: a three-character string in a five-character field will be padded with two blanks. Wide parameters are **not** clipped: a seven-character string in a five-character field will not be clipped to five characters, and will slide any subsequent fields to the right. When there is no alignment component, the field width is 0—or just as wide as necessary, with no pad characters.

A formatting component starts with a colon; everything between the colon and the closing } character is a format string that is fed to a parameter object's ToString(string, IFormatProvider) overload, if the parameter object supports IFormattable.

Note Any white space before and after an alignment component's comma is ignored, as is any white space before an alignment component's colon—but any white space **after** an alignment component's colon is part of the format string.

When there is no format string (or the parameter object doesn't support IFormattable), String.Format ignores any formatting component and calls each parameter object's ToString() overload, the overload that takes no parameters.

Standard types like numbers and dates define standard and custom formatting strings, and custom types can declare their own formatting strings. For numbers and dates, not specifying a format string is the same as explicitly specifying the :G ("general") format.

There is no guarantee that a custom type's ToString methods will honor locale settings, but the standard types always get elements like thousands separators, national currency symbols, and date-time pictures from an IFormatProvider. Most String.Format overloads give localized results by getting the IFormatProvider from

```
/* System.Threading. */ Thread.CurrentThread.CurrentCulture
```

but there is an overload that allows you to explicitly supply the IFormatProvider and get results localized for another culture. You can specify a customer's culture, or an *invariant* (canonical) culture, which is useful for text files that will be shared by users with different culture settings.

Numeric Formats

How numeric types interpret the optional formatting component

Standard numeric formats consist of a single alphabetic character, the *format specifier*, and an optional *precision specifier*, which is an integer from 0 to 99.[5] A format string like j6, which does fit this template but does not contain a supported format specifier, will throw an exception. Any format string that does not fit this template is a custom numeric format, which I cover (briefly!) after Table 11-1.

Remember that these numeric formats are implemented by the numeric types' ToString methods. Calling ThisFloat.ToString ("R") will return the same string as String.Format("{0:R}", ThisFloat). (The right and left padding of the alignment component, however, comes from String.Format, not the ToString methods.)

---

5. In regex terms, this is two capture groups—the mandatory format specifier is ([a-zA-Z]), and the optional precision specifier is (\d{0,2}). That is, the regex ([a-zA-Z])(\d{0,2}) matches (and rips) a standard numeric format.

Table 11-1 summarizes standard numeric formats, and aims only to show you what's available; when it comes to details, I encourage you to experiment and to read the FCL documentation. The pages for "Standard Numeric Format Strings" and "Custom Numeric Format Strings" are particularly helpful.

Note Most numeric format specifiers are case insensitive: c has the same effect as C. With exponential formats the specifier's case controls the case of the E, and with hexadecimal formats the specifier's case controls the case of the digits A through F.

Table 11-1. *Standard Numeric Formats*

Format	Notes
C—Currency	The number is formatted using the current (or supplied) culture's rules for currency symbol, thousands and decimal separators, &c. An explicit precision specifier overrides the culture's default currency precision.
D—Decimal	Integer only. An explicit precision specifier will cause left padding with 0 characters.
E—Exponential	Scientific notation with six digits after the decimal point, unless you explicitly specify the precision. The exponent is always signed, and contains at least three digits; your choice of E or e controls the case of the E in the output. You can get more precise control with a custom numeric format string.
F—Fixed-point	A floating point number, with a fixed number of digits to the right of the decimal point. The number of digits is specified by the current culture, if you don't explicitly supply a precision specifier.
G—General	This is the default when you don't specify a format—the most compact string representation of the number. The precision specifier has complex effects; see the SDK "Standard Numeric Format Strings" help page.
N—Number	Integer and float point. Thousands separators (i.e., 10,001, not 10001) and fixed-point decimal, as with the F format. Use N0 (that's "n-zero," not "n-oh") to format integers with thousands separators and no decimal point.
P—Percent	The number multiplied by 100, and formatted according to the appropriate culture's percentage conventions.
R—Round-trip	Floating point only. System.Double.Parse will precisely re-create an R-formatted double, and System.Single.Parse will precisely re-create an R-formatted float.
X—Hexadecimal	Integer formatting. The specifier case controls the digit case; the optional precision controls the minimum number of result digits desired, with low values zero-padded on the left.

In the rare cases where the standard numeric formats don't give you the formatting you need, you can "draw" a custom numeric format "picture." For example, :E3 will format 1234.1234 as 1.234E+003. To get the terser 1.234E3, you could use the custom :#.###E0 format.

Custom numeric formatting uses a familiar sort of picture language, with # and 0 place-holders that allow you to control rounding, scaling, left-padding with 0s, and so on. You can specify multiple pictures, separated by semicolons, to format positive and negative numbers differently; you can also special-case 0 formatting.

Most people will have little use for custom numeric formatting, and know enough when they know that it exists. If you do need precise control over numeric output, the SDK "Custom Numeric Format Strings" topic covers it pretty well.

Date Formats

How the DateTime type interprets the optional formatting component

The DateTime object supports standard and custom formatting strings, much like the system numeric types. Standard date formatting strings are single characters: unsupported characters generate exceptions, while longer strings are custom date formats. As with the numeric types, if you don't specify a formatting component, you get the :G format.

Table 11-2 is a brief overview of the standard DateTime formats; for more details, see the SDK "Date and Time Format Strings" section. Note that many DateTime format specifiers are case sensitive, with an uppercase letter specifying a long form and a lowercase letter specifying a short form.

Table 11-2. *Standard DateTime Formats*

Format	Notes
D, d	Date. Uppercase D uses the current culture's **long** date pattern, while lowercase d uses the **short** date pattern.
T, t	Time. Uppercase T uses the current culture's **long** time pattern, while lowercase t uses the **short** time pattern.
F, f	Full. Current culture's long date; space; and either the long time (F format) or the short time (f format).
G, g	General. Current culture's short date; space; and either the long time (G format) or the short time (g format). G is the default format that you get if you don't specify any formatting component.
M, m	Day of the month, but neither year or time. No difference between M and m formats.
Y, y	Month of the year, but neither date nor time. No difference between Y and y formats.
R, r	RFC1123-compatible, OS- and culture-independent date/time format. Note that while the result will say GMT, R formatting does **not** convert local time to GMT; this conversion is your responsibility.
s, u, U	Sortable date/time pattern. These three are **not** equivalent; experiment and read the documentation to find the format most suitable for your applications.

The String.Format function does use a very different pattern language than Delphi's Format function and other printf-like functions. But the new pattern language is easy to learn, and not only is more extensible than the old language but also handles repeated and/or out-of-order use of parameters much better.

Substrings

Another common overload model

The String.Substring methods are similar to Delphi's Copy function—they extract a string from an existing string. There are two overloads. The first,

```
public string Substring(int startIndex);
```

copies from an offset to the end of the string, while the second,

```
public string Substring(int startIndex, int length);
```

copies a specific number of bytes, starting at an offset.

■**Caution** The Substring methods act differently from Delphi's Copy function. If you try to Copy() from an starting offset that's past the end of the string, you'll get an empty string; the Substring methods will throw an exception. Similarly, if you try to Copy() past the end of the string, you'll get everything from the starting character to the end of the string; the Substring methods will throw an exception.

Now, extracting long substrings is always an expensive operation, especially in a loop. Copying thousands of characters from one location to another slows the CPU to memory rates and, as per Chapter 3, repeatedly allocating large heap blocks makes full garbage collections much too common.

The FCL makes it easy to avoid extracting most substrings. Methods that search or replace within a string usually have overloads that search or replace within a substring. These overloads honor what I'll call the *Substring* model, with overloads that take a string and either one or two integers. The one-integer overloads specify a right tail operation, where each scan starts where the last left off. The two-integer overloads specify an interior slice, like all the text between two matching XML tags. Just as with the eponymous Substring method, accessing any character outside the base string generally raises an exception.

The Chapter11\Substrings C# project contains a Substring class that encapsulates a few common uses of the *Substring* model, including especially the Regex methods I cover later in this chapter. Substring instances contain both a reference to a Base string, and the two integers that define a substring: the starting Index[6] and the substring Length. The point is to avoid actually calling String.Substring as much as possible, using instead references to portions of a single base string.

---

6. A substring's Index is the address of the first character, the substring's offset from the start of the base string.

Compare Methods

You can choose to heed or ignore both case and culture

The static String.Compare method is similar to the Delphi AnsiCompare methods. It compares two strings and returns an integer, where a negative value indicates that the first parameter is less than (sorts before) the second parameter, zero indicates that the two parameters are equal, and a positive value indicates that the first parameter is greater than the second parameter. The comparison defaults to case and culture sensitive, but there are overloads that allow you to specify a case- and/or culture-insensitive search (this is, finally, an example of the *Defaults* model).

Compare also has overloads that let you compare substrings. It may not be clear that Compare follows the *Substring* model: since String.Compare only compares equal-length substrings, String.Compare only takes a single length parameter. The case-sensitive substring overload takes a string and then an offset, followed by another string and then an offset, followed by a length:

```
static int String.Compare(String, Int32, String, Int32, Int32 Length)
```

The following method from the Chapter11\Substrings C# project uses this overload (which specifies case sensitivity) to compare a Substring to a string:

```
public int Compare(string CompareTo, bool IgnoreCase)
{
  return String.Compare(Base, Index, CompareTo, 0, Length, IgnoreCase);
}
```

Should this method do any error checking? For example, what if the CompareTo string's Length is less than the Length parameter? My Substring methods generally leave error checking to the FCL routines, which raise exceptions when you try to index out of a substring. There's no reason to replicate those error checks, and every reason not to—a replicated test might be (subtly, one hopes) wrong, or might become so in some future FCL version.

When you want to do a culture-**insensitive** string comparison, without regard for cultural rules that may, e.g., equate e with é or put é before f, you use the String.CompareOrdinal methods, which (like the String.Compare methods) are static methods[7] that compare two strings. The CompareOrdinal methods compare each character (which is usually, but not always, the same as a single Unicode code point) by its *ordinal value*—that is, they compare characters as 16-bit unsigned integers in much the same way as a native code Delphi evaluates expressions like ThisString >= ThatString.

You can compare either whole strings or substrings:

```
static int String.CompareOrdinal (String, String)
static int String.CompareOrdinal (String, Int32, String, Int32, Int32 Length)
```

---

7. In Delphi, you have to call String static methods like Compare as System.String.Compare, not just String.Compare or even &String.Compare.

Finally (though the String class's comparison repertoire is far from exhausted), I should mention that one common thing to ask about a string instance is whether it sorts ahead of, with, or behind some other string instance. The CompareTo instance method does a case- and culture-sensitive, whole-string comparison. CompareTo returns zero if the strings match, a positive number if the string instance is lexically greater than (after) the string parameter, and a negative number if the string instance is lexically less than (before) the string parameter.

Search and Replace

Find and/or replace strings and characters within the instance string

The FCL's equivalent of Delphi's Pos procedure is the String.IndexOf method. The IndexOf methods are instance methods, so ThisString.IndexOf(ThatString) searches for ThatString in ThisString. There are overloads to search in substrings of the instance string. All IndexOf searches are sensitive to both case and culture.

The IndexOf method also has overloads to search for an individual character. If you need to search for any of several characters, the IndexOfAny methods search the instance string (or an instance substring) for the first occurrence of any of the characters in the char[] anyOf parameter.[8] While string search with IndexOf is culture **sensitive**, character search with both IndexOf and IndexOfAny is culture **insensitive**—characters are compared by ordinal value as in the CompareOrdinal methods.

■**Tip** You might use IndexOfAny as part of a search tree that finds the first occurrence of any of a set of strings, but it's much easier to use a Regex (discussed later) for this and other complex searches.

The StartsWith and EndsWith methods are convenience methods. StartsWith(Value) is roughly equivalent to IndexOf(Value) == 0, while EndsWith(Value) is roughly equivalent to IndexOf(Value) == Length - Value.Length. Both StartsWith and EndsWith are case and culture sensitive, and both handle empty strings and other edge conditions properly.

There are also LastIndexOf and LastIndexOfAny methods, which find the last occurrence of a string or character in a string or substring, instead of the first occurrence.

Remember, because strings are immutable, you can't replace characters or substrings within a string. The String.Replace methods are instance methods that return new strings and leave the instance untouched.

```
string Replace(char Target, char Replacement)
string Replace(string Target, string Replacement)
```

---

8. This array is **not** marked with the params keyword, so you're always aware that you are passing an array, in C# as in Delphi.

For example, in Delphi, ThisString.Replace('\', '\\') returns a new string, where every \ in ThisString is replaced with \\. You would need to code ThisString := ThisString.Replace('\', '\\') to actually change ThisString.

The Replace methods always do case- and culture-sensitive matching. The Replace methods are ideally suited for tasks like escaping characters (converting \ to \\ as shown earlier, or using HTML escapes like & or <) and converting template text like %CurrentDirectory% to the actual current directory.

Tip The Regex.Match and Replace methods (later in this chapter) give much more control over both matching and replacing than these String methods, but the Regex methods are slower and more complicated. The Chapter11\Replacement C# project shows that repeated calls to String.Replace are usually faster than a single Regex.Replace with an alternation pattern (like "This|That", which matches "This" or "That").

Split and Join

From delimited strings to string arrays, and back again

The String.Split methods break a string instance into an array of strings. The string is scanned for characters (or, in 2.0, substrings) that match any of the characters or strings in an array parameter. If the array is null (Nil, in Delphi) or has a Length of 0, Split supplies an array of white space characters and splits on (broadly speaking) words. To split ThisString on lines, use the C# ThisString.Split('\n') or the Delphi ThisString.Split([^M]).[9]

Character and substring matching is a matter of bit equality—a case-sensitive and culture-insensitive comparison.

The extracted strings do not contain the break characters (or strings). The first element in the result is the substring to the left of the first delimiter. If the string you Split doesn't contain any of the delimiters, you get back a one-element string array, which contains the Split string. Similarly, if the Split string starts with a delimiter, the first result string will be empty, with a Length of 0.

The last element in the result is the substring to the right of the first delimiter. If the Split string ends with a delimiter, the last result string will be empty, with a Length of 0.

Every other result element is the text between two delimiter elements. An empty string (one with a Length of 0) is the text 'between' a pair of delimiter elements. For example, when you Split on white space, there is an empty string 'within' every CR-LF. Because of these empty strings, there is one result string for each occurrence of any of the delimiter elements, plus one result string that holds the 'remainder,' the text to the right of the last delimiter, if any. (In 2.0, you can optionally suppress the empty strings between delimiters.)

For example, there are five path delimiter characters in the filename @"c:\Program Files\Shazzubt\Read Me.txt": one colon, three backslashes, and one dot. Thus, splitting the string @"c:\Program Files\Shazzubt\Read Me.txt" on the char[] delims = {':', '\\', '.'} gives a

---

9. The overload that takes only a single char[] parameter takes a params array.

six-element string array. The second string has a Length of zero—it is the empty string between the : and the \. The first string is "c" and the second to last string is "Read Me".

If you care about what break character preceded or followed a particular result string, you have to look at the original Split string. To get the break character **before** the *Nth* string, you sum the lengths of all previous result strings, and add *N* - 1. This is the offset of the break character within the Split string. Similarly, the offset of the break character **after** the *Nth* string is the sum of the lengths of the first *N* result strings, plus *N*. (The Chapter11\Split C# project demonstrates the Common\Utilities.cs implementation of both of these methods.)

■**Note** Split is comparatively expensive, and often one doesn't need all the delimited strings. Regex.Matches (see later) is not only more flexible than Split, it can actually be faster when you only need one or two substrings from a long string, because it doesn't have to examine the whole string and because it doesn't have to do a character-by-character copy of each substring. See, for example, the Chapter11\BenchmarkSplitVsRegex C# project.

Split produces an array of strings from a single string. I've already covered two ways to go the other way, to turn an array of strings into a single string:

1. String.Concat concatenates each element in an array of strings (or objects) without any interpolation; the first character of the second string follows immediately after the second character of the first string.

2. String.Format offers great control over both interpolation and selection from the string array.

String.Join is sort of midway between Concat and Format—Join concatenates each element in an array of strings, adding a delimiter string between each element. Both this C# code

```
string MethodName = "System.String.Split";
string[] MethodComponents = MethodName.Split('.');
string MethodName2 = String.Join(".", MethodComponents);
Debug.Assert( ! Object.ReferenceEquals(MethodName, MethodName2)); // different addr
Debug.Assert(MethodName == MethodName2); // same value
```

and its Delphi equivalent (from the Chapter11\InverseFunction Delphi project)

```
var
  MethodName: string = 'System.String.Split';
  MethodComponents: array of string;
  MethodName2: string;
begin
  MethodComponents := MethodName.Split(['.']);
  MethodName2 := System.String.Join('.', MethodComponents);
  Assert(not TObject.ReferenceEquals(MethodName, MethodName2)); // different addr
  Assert(MethodName = MethodName2); // same value
end.
```

Split the string "System.String.Split" on a '.' character, then Join the resulting string array with a "." separator string, getting a new string, "System.String.Split". As these examples may suggest, Join can be a very useful method.

You may have noticed that Join is **almost** an inverse function for Split. Join is not quite a true inverse function for Split because you can Split strings on multiple delimiter characters, and not just a single delimiter.

Miscellaneous Methods

More standard functionality

The String class supports most standard string-handling operations. Table 11-3 briefly summarizes String methods that mirror familiar Delphi System and SysUtils routines.

Table 11-3. *Miscellaneous String Methods*

Method	Delphi Equivalent	Notes
String.Insert	System.Insert	Insert one string into another, at a specific position.
String.Remove	System.Delete	Remove a substring.
String.ToLower	SysUtils.AnsiLowerCase	Lowercase every character. Culture sensitive.
String.ToUpper	SysUtils.AnsiUpperCase	Uppercase every character. Culture sensitive.
String.Trim	SysUtils.Trim	Remove white space from beginning and end; overload lets you remove **any** characters.
String.TrimEnd	SysUtils.TrimRight	Remove white space from end; overload lets you remove **any** characters.
String.TrimStart	SysUtils.TrimLeft	Remove white space from start; overload lets you remove **any** characters.

Always remember that where the Delphi procedure Insert(ThisString, 3, ThatString) modifies ThisString, inserting ThatString before the third character, the equivalent FCL function ThisString.Insert(2, ThatString) returns a new string, and does not affect ThisString in any way: you have to code ThisString = ThisString.Insert(2, ThatString). Also, never forget that the first character in a .NET string is at position 0, not at position 1.

Constructors

The explicit constructors are quite specialized

Most strings are loaded from disk or the network, or created from the myriad permutations of the various string operations on loaded strings and ToString() results and on string literals embedded in code. (The next subsection, "Interning," has details on string literals.) String values **are** instances of the System.String class, though, and there are String class constructors that you may need to call at various times (see, for example, the "File IO" subsection, later in this chapter).

The simplest constructor—String(Char, Int32)—creates a string with a specific number of copies of a single character. You can thus create a string with, say, three spaces, or five tabs, or two zeroes, and so on.

```
new string('\t', 5);          // C# for five tabs
System.String.Create(^T, 5); // Delphi for five tabs
```

More complicated constructors allow you to copy all or part of a character array to a new string. These constructors apply the *Substring* model to the character array: you can copy either the whole array or an interior slice. For example,

```
const
  CharacterArray: array[0..3] of char = 'test';
var
  test, es: string;
begin
  test := System.String.Create(CharacterArray); // 'test'
  es   := System.String.Create(CharacterArray, 1, 2); // 'es'
end.
```

You might use the character array constructor to build a string character by character: you allocate a character array; use character indexing to populate it; then pass the array to the appropriate string constructor. This is not a technique you will have much occasion to use directly, as the StringBuilder class, discussed later, uses exactly these techniques and may well provide all the functionality that you'll ever need.

There are also unsafe versions of the character array constructors, which can copy C-style null-terminated strings (or substrings thereof) to managed System.String values. (The point of the unsafe constructors is interfacing with legacy code. Chapter 10 and Appendix 0 cover unsafe code.) By default, text is assumed to be UTF8, but an optional Encoding parameter allows you to specify that the SByte* parameter points to null-terminated strings in formats from ASCII and UTF7 to UTF8, UTF16, and UTF32.

Interning

Only one copy of each string literal

Two strings are equal if they have the same number of characters and each character matches—which **has to be** true if they both refer to the same String object. Obviously, comparing two references is faster than comparing the lengths and then comparing each character (especially with long strings), so String.Equals(string, string) checks for reference equality first, only comparing lengths and characters if it's comparing two distinct String objects.

All string literals are *interned* to save space and comparison time. Interning means that the strings are stored in an internal hash table (Chapter 12) whose keys and values are both strings. When an assembly is loaded, all its string literals are loaded into memory, as interned strings, and the assembly's string literal table is set to point to the interned strings.[10] If a literal matches an existing interned string, the assembly's string literal table will refer to the existing string; if a literal does not match an existing interned string, the run time creates a new interned string. The CIL ldstr instruction turns a metadata string token—essentially, an index into the assembly's string literal table—into a normal string reference.

The intern table is maintained on a per-process basis. This means that

1. Strings are interned across assembly boundaries. If assembly A contains a string literal <p> and assembly B also contains a string literal <p>, applications that use both assemblies A and B will only use a single copy of the string literal <p>.

2. Strings are also interned across AppDomain boundaries (Chapter 14). This can save space, and makes it cheaper to marshal interned strings from one AppDomain to another: all that needs to be marshaled is the string reference, not the string value.

The String.IsInterned static method allows you to look up a string value in the intern table. String.IsInterned(StringValue) returns null (or Nil, in Delphi) if StringValue is not in the intern table and returns the interned string if StringValue **is** already in the intern table. Note that a non-null return will always Equal the passed StringValue—but will not necessarily ReferenceEqual the passed StringValue.

C# allows you to switch on string values. The generated code uses String.IsInterned to check the string you're switching on against the interned string literals. If IsInterned returns null, the string you're switching on **can't** match any of the string literals in the case clauses. If, however, IsInterned returns a non-null value, the switch code can use a series of beq CIL instructions to simply compare the reference to the interned switch string to each interned string literal.

The String.Intern method lets you add strings to the intern table. Intern takes a string and returns a string; unlike IsInterned, the result is always Equal to the input. If the input string is already interned, Intern returns the interned value; otherwise, it adds the new string to the intern table, and then returns it.

Interning a string can save space and speed up comparisons with a set of standard strings— but it also means that the value will persist until the process terminates. Note that interning a newly created string only makes it immortal by adding it to the intern table; it does not change its garbage collection generation. An immortal interned string will incur garbage collection costs every time it is relocated.

---

10. In 2.0, the [assembly:StringFreezing] attribute allows NGEN-ed applications (Chapter 4) to turn off interning on an assembly-by-assembly basis. String literals in an assembly with frozen strings aren't interned when the assembly is loaded. Rather, the frozen literals are stored in the native code at NGEN time in a format compatible with run-time String objects: instead of turning a token into a reference to a native string, the NGEN-ed code simply loads an address in the NGEN-ed code, and uses that as a string reference.

Tip If you want to save space and comparison time without making strings immortal, you can use your own hash table (see Chapter 12).

String Conversions

Formatting and parsing numbers and dates

As you've already seen, the various overrides and overloads of the Object.ToString method are the FCL equivalent of Delphi's functions like IntToStr and IntToHex. A 'bare' ToString() call gives the default format, which is generally the most compact format. Numbers and dates also support a ToString(FormatString) overload, which allows you to format values as in String.Format.

That is, values are responsible for formatting themselves. Similarly, each built-in value type is responsible for validating and converting a string to an appropriately typed value. For example, the Int32.Parse methods convert strings to 32-bit integers in various ways (or raise an exception), while the Int64.Parse and DateTime.Parse methods do the same, except that they return a 64-bit integer or a DateTime.

The various Parse methods are the most direct way to convert a string containing a formatted value to an actual value type. There are overloads that understand cultural conventions (so you can parse numbers like 123.456,789, even in the US) and that can parse hexadecimal strings.

Alternatively, the higher-level Convert class contains methods that will interconvert a variety of types. For example, it has a ToInt32 method that is overloaded to convert booleans, strings, and various numbers to an Int32. There are also ToBoolean, ToDouble, and ToString overloads that take an Int32. The various Parse methods offer fine-grained control, while the Convert class offers "one-stop shopping" and a consistent interface. Convert excels at tasks like converting floating point values to integer values in a language-independent way, and can handle tasks that the Parse methods don't support, like parsing binary and octal strings or doing base-64 (MIME) conversion of data blocks.

The StringBuilder Class

Concatenation and replacement

.NET strings are immutable—you can read individual characters, but you can't change them. Delphi allows you to write code like ThisString[Index] := UpCase(ThisString[Index]), but this is implemented as two Substring operations and a Concat, and is comparatively expensive.

The efficient way to change several characters is to use the String.ToCharArray method, change the character array, and then pass the changed character array to a string constructor. However, as with building a string character by character, you will seldom write code to do this directly, as the (System.Text) StringBuilder class encapsulates all the necessary logic, in a fairly general way.

A StringBuilder is basically a (private) character array with a Length and a Capacity. The Capacity is the number of characters in the array, while the Length is the number of those characters that have actually been set and that belong in the string. You can create empty string builders with a default Capacity; there are also constructor overloads that allow you to specify an initial string and/or initial Capacity. When you know (even roughly) how big the final string will be, passing the Capacity to the constructor minimizes both character copying and memory management overhead.

You can Append characters or strings to the StringBuilder, and it will copy them, character by character, to the private character array, incrementing the Length and increasing the Capacity as necessary. Append is heavily overloaded, and you can append many standard types directly, without having to either call ToString (e.g., you can Append(ThisInt) and don't have to Append(ThisInt.ToString())) or box common value types. There is also an AppendFormat method, which is the same as Append(String.Format()) but *Smaller* and *Simpler*.

The StringBuilder.ToString method passes the first Length characters to a String constructor, returning a new string. (ToString also has a *Substring* overload, which lets you extract a slice of the StringBuilder.) The ToString method does not affect the character array; you can call ToString, make some changes, and then call ToString again, if necessary. The StringBuilder.Clear method sets the Length to 0, but you can also set the Length directly: decreasing it truncates the string, increasing it pads it with blanks.

You can read and write characters directly, using array indexing. The StringBuilder. Replace methods change all instances of a character or string with another character or string; there are overloads that allow you to Replace within a *Substring* region of the character array. You can also Insert strings within the character array, or Remove substrings.

Note The Insert, Remove, and Replace methods are loosely modeled on their String class equivalents. That is, they return a StringBuilder reference, so code like Builder = Builder.Replace("this", "that") will compile. However, they do modify the StringBuilder instance; they do **not** create new StringBuilder instances. I presume the point of returning a reference is that you can chain code like Builder.Replace("\n", "\\n").Replace("\r", "\\r").

There's surprisingly little overhead involved in creating a StringBuilder and then calling its ToString method. The Chapter11\BenchBuilder C# project shows that to change a single character, it's actually faster to use code like

```
StringBuilder Builder = new StringBuilder(ThisString);
Builder[0] = Char.ToUpper(Builder[0]);
ThisString = Builder.ToString();
```

than the much simpler

```
ThisString = Char.ToUpper(ThisString[0]) + ThisString.Substring(1);
```

The difference isn't great, however, and it's not a bad decision to emphasize clarity over speed in a case like this, reserving the StringBuilder class for code that does extensive surgery on a string.

Regular Expressions

What and how

Regular expressions are much more central to Unix programming than they have been to Windows programming. Under Unix, regular expressions are everywhere, from Perl and grep to shell filename expansions. There's even a POSIX regular expression API so Kylix applications can easily use regular expressions. On Windows, though, many Delphi programmers use regular expressions only to form the occasional complex search/replace string in the code editor—if they use regular expressions at all. There are a few Delphi regular expression libraries, but they're not widely used and there's no standard syntax.

Those days are over. The FCL System.Text.RegularExpressions namespace includes a standard Regex class with a Perl-compatible pattern language[11] and a comprehensive set of search and replace methods.

The next two subsections are a brief introduction to regular expressions, mostly for Delphi programmers who are new to regular expressions. The "Regex Introduction" subsection covers when you would and wouldn't use a regex. "The Regex Engine" gives you just enough background on the regex engine to understand the syntax and to work through mysterious behavior. You may benefit from this background if your regex skills are just a handful of puzzling tips—but most of you with even a little regex experience will probably want to skip ahead to either "Regex Pattern Language," which covers the FCL regex pattern language; or "The Regex Class," which explains how to actually use the FCL Regex class.

Regex Introduction

What a regex does, and when you use a regex

A regular expression (or *regex*) is a description of certain types of text, expressed as a set of algebraic rules. Text that follows the rules is *regular,* while text that does not follow the rules is not regular. When you create and use a new instance of the Regex class, your pattern string gets compiled to a state machine.[12] You can then apply the state machine (your compiled regex) to a bit of text to get all the substrings that match—or you can replace all the matching substrings.

What makes regexs so useful is that the syntax allows you to do much more than just search for keywords. You can do things like find the next < character followed by an identifier;

---

11. The FCL regex pattern language embraces and extends Perl's regex pattern language. Chapter 12's Hashtable and Dictionary<K, V> are similarly more general than Perl's hashes: a Perl hash is reference[string], while an FCL hash is object[object] or K[V]. Between hashes, regexs, and boxing, you can write all sorts of symbolic code—C# and Delphi stuff that feels like LISP.

12. This is related to the Compiled option, which I cover later in this section, but is not the same thing. A Perl-style regex is compiled to a set of tables that a state machine rockets around until it matches or doesn't match. This is the default behavior for .NET regexs, too. A normal Regex instance refers to private tables in normal (collectable) managed data. The state machine in a Compiled .NET Regex doesn't interpret tables. Instead, all its decisions are implemented in custom CIL that gets jitted and run just like any compiler-generated CIL loaded from disk. Jitted code stays in memory until the application domain unloads at (or before—see Chapter 14) process termination. That is, the default is fairly fast, and uses collectable data; the Compiled option **is** faster, but uses non-GC code space.

followed maybe by white space and any number of identifier=value pairs, where a value is either a string of letters or a quoted string; all followed by > or />. And then you can easily extract—or modify—the HTML tag, and all its attributes, and the closing > or />.

A regular expression consists of literal text—which must be matched exactly—mixed freely with various expressions that describe which characters are acceptable at this point in the match. The expressions can be as specific as 'match this character only' or as broad as 'match any character.' You can specify sets of characters to match, and there are various predefined sets for matching alphanumeric characters, white space, and so on. In addition, you can group elements with parentheses, and specify exactly how many times an element should or may appear.

The pattern language is very terse: a+ means "at least one a character" while a* means "any number of a characters, including no (zero) a characters." \d means "any digit" and \d{3} means any three digits,[13] so \d{3}-\d{2}-\d{4} matches US Social Security numbers.

In some ways, regexes are an inverse function for String.Format. Format takes a 'picture' of the output and pours data into it; regexes take a 'picture' of the input and pull data out of it. Neither 'picture' is a model of clarity, but both save significant amounts of your time.

In fact, using regexes can save both programmer time and run time. You wouldn't use a regex where String.IndexOf will do. However, regex compilation does produce an efficient matcher, and as per the earlier "Split and Join" subsection, regexs are competitive with comparatively simple matching jobs like String.Split, especially when you only need the first or last few matches.

But it's complex matches (like finding unquoted attribute values in HTML tags) or even only slightly complicated matches (like finding all identifiers between % characters) where a regex really shines. The latter is % [a-z_] [a-z_0-9]* %, ignoring case and pattern white space. With just a little experience you can see that this is four easy-to-read elements, four simple states: find the literal %; followed by a letter or underscore; followed by any number of letters, digits, or underscores; followed by another literal %.

Imagine writing a method that would do that match efficiently: would it take you fifteen minutes? Would it take less than the 44 lines that the Chapter11\ManualMatch C# project does? Would it work the first time, the way my code did? Would it be easy to read, or would it be a state machine—like the regex compiler builds? Would it be slower than a regex, the way my code is?[14]

---

13. As you can see, regex elements come in different lengths.

14. Yes, I was shocked to find that my hand-built matcher is nearly 50% slower than even the 'interpreted' regex. It turns out that a large chunk of the discrepancy lies in my use of the Char.IsLetter and Char.IsDigit methods, which don't even exactly match the *a to z* rules I use in the regex. (For example, in many countries, é is a letter.) When I replace those calls with substantially bulkier inline code like (ThisChar >= 'a' && ThisChar <= 'z') || (ThisChar >= 'A' && ThisChar <= 'Z'), my manual matcher becomes **almost** as fast as an interpreted regex—but still slower.

I'm sure I could bum a few cycles—for instance, it's possible that String.IndexOf(Char) is faster than my FindFirstLiteral state—but then I'd be spending even more time writing complex code in a perhaps futile attempt to beat the performance I got with fifteen seconds' work writing a one-line regex.

Note You can think of regex patterns as a state machine–specification language. What you get is about as efficient as what you'd write by hand—and the pattern is much easier to write, much easier to read, much easier to debug, and much easier to maintain.

In addition to flexible matching and good performance, regexs support a wide range of operations. You can simply test whether some string contains any substrings that match the regex. You can find the first substring that matches, and extract the whole match or specific portions of it. You can find the next match; you can find the last match; you can get all matches. You can replace all matches with the same string—or you can use the match text to generate a replacement: examples include lowercasing XML tags, or replacing %token% strings by looking up token in a table.

The Regex Engine

How patterns match text

A regular expression is a stream of *elements*. When the regex engine matches a regex against a string, it looks for a text stream that matches each element in turn. If the regex finds a match, the match may be the whole string, or the match may be a substring, or there may even be several substring matches.

The regex engine looks for the first character of the string that matches the first element of the regex. If it finds one, it finds all the characters that match the first element of the regex, then compares the next character of the string with the second element of the regex, and so on. If it makes it to the last element of the regex, it has a match, and the *next match* operation would start just after the last character of this match. If the engine doesn't make it to the last element of the regex, it *backtracks*, looking for the last character that it might have interpreted differently, and giving that a try. (It may help to think of this as a depth-first traversal of the match space.) If the engine backtracks all the way to the first character of the match, it starts all over, looking for the next character that matches the first element of the regex, and so on.

For example, imagine matching the pattern ".*" against the string `There are "two" quotes in "this" string`. There are three elements in the ".*" regex—the literal ", the wild card .*, and the literal ". The literal " can only match a " in the string, so you go into a nice tight loop, looking for the first " in the string. The wild card .* matches 0 or more of any character, so you skip to the end of the string. At the end of the string, you proceed to the next element in the regex, the " literal. There's no match for the " literal at the end of the string, so you backtrack to the last " in the string, and match the `"two" quotes in "this"` substring.

If you were matching against a string like `this string has a "mismatched quote`, you would backtrack all the way to the first ", and conclude that there was no match.

Now, while writing a regex **is** always faster than writing the corresponding matching code by hand, it can be maddening at times, with seemingly fine distinctions that can mean the difference between your regex matching as you expect it to and your regex matching *almost* as you expect it to. That is, mismatching is usually not an all or nothing proposition: just as with a hand-coded string parser, you can write a regex that gets part of the match right and part wrong. Or that matches some of the strings that you want it to, but not all of them. Or that matches some of the strings that you don't want it to. Or all three.

When a regex doesn't work as expected, just take your regex an element at a time. At each step, compare what you **wanted** the engine to do with what you **actually** told the engine to do, and you should be fine. Look especially carefully at *-ed elements, which can cause trouble in two ways. On the one hand, they are *greedy*, and may consume more than you expect. On the other hand, they are optional and they always match. You can get some unexpected results when an optional element matches an empty string between two characters.

Regex Pattern Language

Perl compatible, with Microsoft extensions

Regexs have been around for a long time, and the pattern language has gradually gotten more complex. I try to cover the basic elements (that you really have to understand to use regexs) pretty thoroughly, and pretty much ignore the advanced elements (like *look ahead* and *look behind* assertions) that it's OK to look up as the need arises.

For more information, there's the Microsoft documentation—plus, since the Regex pattern language is a superset of the Perl regex language, standard regexs from the various "regex cookbook" sites should work just fine in your .NET programs. Perl compatibility also means that Google and standard regex books like *Mastering Regular Expressions* can help you with FCL regexs.[15]

▪ **Note** The Chapter11\RegexExplorer project lets you experiment with regexs interactively. You can load a text sample, and build regexs to match it. The explorer shows all the matches in the sample, and updates this visible result set with each change to the regex. This makes it easy to see the effect of various changes, as well as what is right and wrong with each part of the regex. (All of the 'documentation' is in the mouseover tool tips.)

White Space

Makes patterns more legible

When you compile a regular expression, you can specify options that change some of the default behavior. For example, the Singleline and Multiline options affect how your pattern matches strings with new-line (\n or ^J) characters. I'll talk about these in the appropriate places—I bring this up now, because one of the available options controls how white space in the pattern affects a match.

Normally, a white character is a literal character, to be matched like any other. This can make multi-element regexs hard to read, with no visual break between elements. The IgnorePatternWhitespace option allows you to override this default behavior, and include white space in your pattern—adding spaces between elements, or adding line breaks between

---

15. The *Programming Perl* "camel book" is another great source of information about writing and debugging regexs. The famous *Compilers* "dragon book" is particularly strong on explaining how regexs are evaluated. All three are in the bibliography (Appendix 5).

groups of elements. When you want to use this "extended mode" but need to match a space or new-line character, you can use the character escape mechanism (discussed later in this chapter) and match \x20 or \n, or you can just match any whitespace character with \s.

The extended mode is much more legible than the default mode, especially since you can also add comments, which run from a # character to the end of the line. You'll find yourself using the extended mode pretty routinely, and the Chapter11\RegexExplorer project sets it by default. What's more, most of the examples in this chapter do use white space to make them more readable, and you should assume that they need to be compiled with the IgnorePatternWhitespace option.

Pattern Elements

Each element can match one or more characters

Each pattern element may be either a literal character or a command in the regex pattern language. A trivial regex (that consists of nothing but literal characters) does a case-sensitive match, much like TargetString.IndexOf(TrivialRegex) would. The IgnoreCase option makes literals match in a culture-sensitive, case-insensitive way, and the pattern the will match the, The, THE, and so on.

There are three basic types of commands in the pattern language: special characters that don't match as literals but act like keywords, affecting the match in various ways; user-defined character classes, where you list the acceptable characters between square brackets; and various backslash escapes, which either name predefined character classes or act like extra keywords.

The ., ^, and $ characters have special meaning as pattern elements (see Table 11-4). If you want to match ., ^, or $ literally, you have to escape them with a backslash—\., \^, and \$. (There **are** other characters with special meanings—like the backslash itself—that have to be escaped if you want to match literally. I will cover these as they come up.)

Table 11-4. *Regex Pattern Characters*

Character	Matches
.	By default, the . is a wildcard that matches any character except \n (^J). In Singleline mode (i.e., when you specify the Singleline option), the . matches any character **including** \n. I'll show some examples of the . wildcard later in this subsection, under the "Quantifiers" heading.
^	By default, the ^ matches only the empty string to the left of the first character. That is, anywhere matches every string that contains anywhere, anywhere in the string, while ^Start matches only strings that begin with Start. In Multiline mode, the ^ also matches the empty string to the left of every line—that is, between a \n and the first character of the line—and ^Start would also match lines that begin with Start.
$	By default, the $ matches only the empty string to the right of the last character. That is, end$ matches only strings that end with end. In Multiline mode, the $ also matches the empty string to the right of every line—that is, between the last character of the line and a \n, and end$ would also match lines that end with end.
\	All multiletter commands start with \. To match a literal backslash, use \\.

You start a pattern with ^ and end it with $ when you want to match only a whole string, or line, with no nonmatching text before or after the matching text. For example, it's not enough that an integer contain a stream of digits—it must not contain any other characters (except, maybe, leading or trailing white space).

A simple user-defined character class consists of a list of letters between square brackets: b[ai]t will match bat and bit. (Note that it will **not** match bait!) The list of letters can also include an ordinal range of characters by separating a pair of characters with a dash: [0-9] will match any digit. Similarly, using the * ("any number of") quantifier, [a-zA-Z_] [a-zA-Z_0-9]* will match a programming language identifier: a letter or underscore, followed by any number of alphanumeric characters or underscores.

You can also specify that an element match every character **except** the ones you specify by starting the class with a ^ (caret): [^0-9] matches any nondigit. Similarly, [^"] matches every character except a double-quote, and " [^"]* " matches a simple double-quoted string: a " character, followed by any number of nonquote characters, followed by a " character.

If your character class needs to include a ^ character, you can simply not list it first—[$^] matches the $ or ^ characters—or you can use a \^ escape, as you would to match a literal ^. (Where a character like ., \, or ^ has a special meaning, escaping it with a \ turns the character into a literal.) So, a* matches a*, not any number of a characters; both [\^$] and [$^] will match either $ or ^; and [\[\]]will match either [or].[16]

A backslash before characters that **don't** have special meaning is a sort of compound keyword. These may be either a predefined character class that matches any character in the class or a special *assertion* that (like ^ and $) matches an empty string if certain conditions are true. The six character classes in Table 11-5 are all from Perl: note that they **are** case sensitive, with the uppercase versions including all characters **not** in the corresponding lowercase version.

Table 11-5. *Perl-compatible Predefined Character Classes*

Escape	Matches
\w	Word (alphanumeric) characters: letters, digits, and underscores
\W	Nonword characters—any characters that **don't** match \w
\s	White space
\S	Nonwhite space—any character that puts pixels on the background
\d	Digit characters
\D	Nondigit characters

By default, these predefined classes include Unicode characters; in ECMAScript mode, these predefined classes include only 7-bit ASCII characters.

In addition to the predefined character classes in Table 11-5, .NET's regex pattern language also includes \p{name}, which matches any member of the Unicode character group *name*, and \P{name}, which matches any character that's **not** in the named Unicode character group. For example, \p{Lu} matches any uppercase letter, and \P{Ll} matches anything except lowercase letters.

Both the character classes in Table 11-5 and \p{} and \P{} Unicode character group escapes can be used **either** in place of literals (in the same way as ., ^, and $) **or** within square brackets, as part of a character class. Thus, [a-z\d] is the same as [a-z0-9], while \p{Lu} \p{Ll}* matches

---

16. The Regex.Escape method can take any string and turn it into a regex literal, escaping all characters as necessary. See "The Regex.Escape Method," later in this chapter.

any Proper Cased substring, and [\p{Lu}\p{Ll}]+ (the + quantifier means "at least one") matches any sequence of uppercase or lowercase letters.

Tip See the System.Globalization.UnicodeCategory enum for a list of Unicode character groups.

In 2.0, regexs support *character class subtraction*. Character classes can now include a -[*class*] between the 'positive' class and the closing bracket. For example, [a-z - [aeiou]] matches any lowercase consonant. Similarly, [\p{Ll} -[a-z]] matches any lowercase character that's not on an American keyboard, like é.

Table 11-6 contains six escape sequences that act as assertions that match zero-length strings when some conditions are satisfied. When the conditions are **not** satisfied, the assertion does not match, and so (unless you've carelessly made the assertion optional) neither does the regex. For example, \b asserts that there is a \w character on the left or the right, but not on both sides—\b verb matches the first four characters of verbose but not the last four characters of adverb.

Table 11-6. *Two-character Regex Assertions*

Escape	Effect
\A	Matches empty string to the left of the first character in the string. Like ^, except not affected by the Multiline option.
\z	Matches empty string to the right of the last character in the string. Like $, except not affected by the Multiline option.
\Z	Like \z, except will ignore a single trailing \n.
\G	Matches empty string before the first character and after the previous match. That is, there can be no unmatched characters between matches. For example, you only get three matches when you match \G\w+\s+ against Three words but then, no more.—because then, doesn't fit the \w+\s+ pattern, and no doesn't match, even though it does fit the \w+\s+ pattern.
\b	Matches the empty string between a \w character and anything but a \w character. That is, \b matches between \w and \W characters, and also at the start (or end) of the string if the first (or last) character is a \w.
\B	Matches whenever \b does not.

Finally, there are several ways to specify literals that don't appear on the keyboard:

- \a, \f, \n, \r, \t, and \v have the same meanings as in C# literals (Table 5-4), while \e matches the ASCII escape character 1B (#27 or ^[, in Delphi), and (though only within a character class) \b matches the ASCII backspace character 08 (#8 or ^H, in Delphi).

- You can specify (most) ASCII control characters with \c—for example, \cH is ^H and \c^ is ^^, but \c[is **not** ^[.

- You can specify ASCII literals in hexadecimal with \x followed by two hexadecimal digits—for example, \x20 is a space, and \x1B is the ASCII escape character, \e.

- You can specify Unicode literals in hexadecimal with \u followed by four hexadecimal digits—for example, \u00A3 is the British currency symbol, £, and \u20ac is the euro symbol, .

■ **C# Note** Don't be confused by the parallelism between regex escapes like \n and C# character and string escapes. In C#, escapes are processed as string (and character) literals are compiled, and if you use "\\" as a regex pattern, your regex pattern contains a **single** backslash character—which is not a valid regex, and will raise an exception. To match a single backslash, you need to use the regex pattern "\\\\"—or @"\\". Similarly, "\n" is a single new-line character, not the \n escape. To match \n, you need to use "\\n"—or @"\n". In general, C# @"" literals are your best choice for regex patterns, both because you don't have to double backslashes (though you **do** have to double double-quotes) and because they can span multiple lines.

Quantifiers

Each element can have an optional repeat count

By itself, every element matches once. It doesn't matter whether the element is an assertion that matches empty strings, or whether the element is a literal or a wildcard that matches a single character: if the element doesn't match, neither does the regex; while when an element does match, the regex engine tries to match the next element to the next character. However, every pattern element can be followed by an optional *quantifier*, which specifies a minimum and maximum number of times the element can match. When an element can appear at least 0 times, it is optional.

There are single character abbreviations (+, ?, and *) for the three most common quantifiers. The + quantifier means that an element is mandatory, but may repeat: the element may appear one or more times. For example, um+ will match um, umm, ummm, and so on. You can use parentheses to group a series of elements into a compound element: (ha)+ will match ha, haha, hahaha, and so on.[17]

The ? and * quantifiers make an element optional. A ? element may appear 0 or 1 times, while an * element can appear any number of times. For example, Sam(uel)? will match both Sam and Samuel. Similarly, umm* will match um, umm, ummm, and so on.

Both * and + are *greedy* and will match as much as possible. For example, matching ".*" against This "string" has "three" "" quotes will match "string" has "three" "". You can specify *lazy* (nongreedy) repeats with *? and +?. Lazy repeats match as little as possible, and matching ".+?" against This "string" has "three" "" quotes will match "string" and "three", while matching ".*?" against the same string will match "string", "three", and "".

---

17. Because parentheses have meaning grouping elements, but not within character classes, you have to escape them to do a literal match, but you do not have to escape them within a character class— \([^)]+ \) matches a (character followed by at least one character besides a), followed by a) character.

Less-common quantifiers use a {} syntax. {*n*} specifies **exactly** *n* repeats—\d{2} is the same as \d\d, and matches exactly two digits. {*n,*} specifies **at least** *n* repeats—\d{2,} is the same as \d\d+ or \d\d\d* and matches at least two digits. {*n,m*} specifies at least *n* but no more than *m* repeats—\d{1,3} is the same as \d\d?\d?, and matches one, two, or three digits.[18]

You can also specify lazy repeats with the {}? syntax. {*n*}? is supported, but is exactly the same as {*n*}—exactly *n* repeats. {*n,*}? is as few as possible, but at least *n* repeats, while {*n,m*}? is as few as possible, but at least *n* and no more than *m* repeats.

Capture Groups

Substrings within the match

When you match a regex against a string, you get a Match object that contains information about the match. If the Match object's Success property is true, the match succeeded and the Value property is a string containing the substring of the match string that matches the regex.[19] For example, when you match \d{3}-\d{2}-\d{4} against

The Social Security Administration says "Any number beginning with 000 will NEVER be a valid SSN" and so numbers like 000-00-0000 or 000-45-6789 can safely be printed in books or used as dummy data.

you get two valid matches, with a Value of 000-00-0000 and 000-45-6789. (You can either call the Regex.Matches method to get [a class that acts like] an array of Match objects, or you can call the Regex.Match method to get a single Match object, and then call Match.NextMatch while the Match.Success property is true. See "The Regex Class," later in this chapter.)

If you care about fields within each match, the match operation can also divide each match into fields—you don't have to create a regex that describes each field, and then apply each field regex to each match. By default, every matching pair of parentheses creates a *capture group* in addition to providing logical grouping. For example, when you match (\d{3}) - (\d{2}) - (\d{4}) against the preceding SSN text, you still get two matches with Value properties of 000-00-0000 and 000-45-6789, but now each Match object has four Groups.

The first group corresponds to the substring that matched the whole regex— AnyMatch.Value == AnyMatch.Groups[0].Value. Subsequent Groups entries contain any capture groups, so when you match (\d{3}) - (\d{2}) - (\d{4}) against 000-45-6789 you get four groups:

Groups[0].Value	000-45-6789
Groups[1].Value	000
Groups[2].Value	45
Groups[3].Value	6789

---

18. The ?, +, and * quantifiers are equivalent to longer {} quantifiers involving 0 and 1—? is the same as {0,1}, while * is the same as {0,} and + is the same as {1,}. No quantifier at all is the same as {1}.

19. Note that the Match object does not actually contain the substring. Rather, it contains a private reference to the string that was matched, and the Index and Length of the match substring within the base string. Reading the Value property actually calls String.Substring.

This is also true of the Group and Capture objects, discussed later. Match descends from Group, which descends from Capture; both Group and Match inherit the Index, Length, and Value properties from Capture.

In general, group numbers correspond to left parentheses, so when `\. ((\d) (\d))` matches .45, you get

`Groups[0].Value`	`.45`	The regex as a whole
`Groups[1].Value`	`45`	The leftmost parenthesis
`Groups[2].Value`	`4`	The first nested capture group
`Groups[3].Value`	`5`	The second nested capture group

It's not particularly hard to count parentheses in these simple regexs, and thus to know which group will contain which field. However, with longer regexs, it does get easier to make a mistake. More importantly, if you add any parenthesized expressions to a regex, any capture groups to the right of the new expression get renumbered—and this is not uncommon, since parentheses serve both as logical groups (applying a single quantifier to a stream of pattern elements) **and** as capture groups.

Accordingly, you can name a capture group by adding a `?<name>` (or `?'name'`) between the left parenthesis and the first pattern element in the group. Thus,

`\. ((?<first> \d) (?'second' \d))`

matches just like `\. ((\d) (\d))` except that you can read `Groups["first"]` and `Groups["second"]` as synonyms for `Groups[2]` and `Groups[3]`. Using named capture groups is slightly slower than using numbered capture groups, but using named capture groups can be much clearer and more stable than using numbered capture groups.

■**Note** You can access a named capture group by name **or** number.

Creating a capture `Group` object takes time and memory. The `ExplicitCapture` option changes parentheses so that they serve only as logical groupings; only named capture groups will actually capture fields and create capture `Group` objects. Alternatively (since named capture groups can make a regex harder to read), you can use `(?: )` as an explicit *noncapture group*—the parentheses serve only as logical groupings.

For example, matching `\. (?: (\d) (\d))+` against .4567 gives only three groups—.4567, 6, and 7. The noncapture group that encloses the two `(\d)` groups is just a logical grouping that lets the + quantifier apply to the pair of `(\d)` capture groups. This example also illustrates that when a quantifier makes a capture group match repeatedly, the group `Value` is the **last** match. You can read the other match(es) from the group's `Captures` collection:

Group	Value	Captures.Count	Captures[0].Value	Captures[1].Value
`Groups[0]`	`.4567`	1	`.4567`	
`Groups[1]`	6	2	4	6
`Groups[2]`	7	2	5	7

For a more complex and realistic example, this regex

```
#[ExplicitCapture | IgnorePatternWhitespace]20
< (?<Tag> [a-zA-Z_] \w+ )                # the tag
  ( \s+ (?<Attribute> [a-zA-Z_] \w+) = # optional attribute=
        ((" (?<Value> [^"]* ) ")         # a quoted value
        |(?<Value>  [^"\s]+) )           # or, an unquoted value
  )* \s*                                 # trailing white space
>
```

will match an HTML tag, and parse it into the tag name (like div or table or whatever) and an optional collection of attribute=value pairs, where the values may or may not be quoted. When this regex matches, there are always four capture groups. The first group is the tag, from < to >; the second group is the tag name; the third group is the attribute names, if any; and the fourth group is the attribute values, if any.

Note This regex is included in the Chapter11\RegexExplorer project, which makes it easy to examine the results with different HTML tags.

When this regex matches a simple HTML tag like <html>, the first group's Value is <html>; the second group's value is html; while the third and fourth groups do not match (i.e., Success is false). When this regex matches an HTML tag with attributes:

```
<table border=0 width="100%" cellspacing=0 cellpadding=8>
```

the first group's Value is the whole tag; the second group's value is table; and the third and fourth groups each have four captures:

Group	Captures[0]	Captures[1]	Captures[2]	Captures[3]	Value
Groups[2]	border	width	cellspacing	cellpadding	cellpadding
Groups[3]	0	100%	0	8	8

---

20. I use this #[ExplicitCapture | IgnorePatternWhitespace] syntax (with RegexOption member names in square brackets, separated by |) to show the options a particular regex needs both because it seems clear enough, and the Chapter11\RegexExplorer project understands this syntax as a sort of pragma— if there's one and only one such comment, and each name **is** a RegexOption, the Regex Explorer will use the specified options. (This allows the right-click menu to paste pattern **and** options.)

Note that these pragmas are **not** regex syntax—the Regex class ignores everything between a # and the end of the line when it compiles a pattern in the IgnorePatternWhitespace (aka "extended") mode.

Alternation

Match multiple subpatterns

So far, a regex has been a series of pattern elements, each with an optional quantifier. Pattern elements can be grouped with parentheses, to form a compound element that can have its own quantifier, but each is joined by an implicit concatenation operator—each pattern element must match.

The *alternation operator*, | (the C "or" operator), allows a regex to contain two (or more) different ways to match. For example, in the complex HTML parsing regex shown earlier,

```
(("  (?<Value> [^"]* ) ")     # a quoted value
 | (?<Value>  \S+) )          # or, an unquoted value
```

matches either a quoted value **or** an unquoted sequence of at least one non-white-space character.

The alternation operator has lower precedence than the implicit concatenation operator, so this|that is **not** the same as thi [st] hat. That is, this that matches this or that, not thishat or thithat (though it will match the this in thishat and the that in thithat.)

The regex engine will always try to match the left side of the alternation operator before the right side. Thus, when you match that|th([a-z]*)t against that thought, you will get two matches, each with two capture groups:

Match	Groups[0]	Groups[1]
Matches[0]	that	No match!
Matches[1]	thought	ough

Back References

Matching captured text

Sometimes you want to look for a repeat of a captured substring. For example, you might want to match HTML like <h1>text</h1> or text. You can do this with *back references*: \N matches capture group number *N*, and \k<Name> matches the capture group named *Name*.

Thus, <(?<Tag>[a-zA-Z] \w*) [^>]*> matches an HTML tag, saving the tag text in the named capture group, Tag, and ignoring any attributes. The more complex variant

```
#[SingleLine | IgnorePatternWhitespace]
< (?<Tag>[a-zA-Z] \w*) [^>]*  > # the opening HTML tag
(?<Text> .*?)                   # text within the tag
</ \k<Tag> >                    # the matching </ tag
```

matches text from <tag> to </tag>, saving the text between the tags in the named capture group, Text.

The Capture Stack

Matching nested text

The preceding example works pretty well until you try to match nested text like

```
<div class="Outer">
  <div class="Inner">
  </div>
  This text will not be part of the match.
</div>
```

The match will stop at the first `</div>`, skipping everything between that and the end of the outer `<div>`. An inability to match nested text is a traditional, well-known limitation of the regular expression engines in Perl, Linux, and JavaScript. The FCL Regex class includes an extension that **does** allow you to match nested text.

For example, the following regex will match nested parentheses:

```
#[IgnorePatternWhitespace]
\(                         # a literal (

(?:                        # non-capture group
   (?<Stack>  \( )         # on nested (, push empty capture
 | (?<-Stack> \) )         # on nested ), pop empty capture
 | [^()]                   # anything except ( or )
)*                         # any number of chars between parens

(?(Stack)                  # if stack not empty:
   ^                       # then, match beginning of string (ie, fail)
 | \) )                    # else, match literal )
```

Step by key step:

1. The regex scans for a (character, at which point it proceeds to a normal, greedy noncapture group—`\( (?: )*`—which consists of three alternate subexpressions.

2. The first alternative, `(?<Stack>  \( )`, is a normal, named capture that matches a literal (and saves it to the Stack capture. As earlier, .NET's regex implementation saves **all** captures, not just the last one.

3. The second alternative, `(?<-Stack> \) )` uses a new operator to match a literal) and delete the most recent Stack capture. It fails if there isn't a literal), thus preventing a match of an unpaired left parenthesis.

4. The `(?(Stack)` uses another new operator: `(?(Name) a | b)` matches a if the Name capture group has captured any values, and matches b if the Name capture group is empty. Stack is only nonempty if there is an unpaired (, so we fail by matching ^ (the start of the string) and match \) if the stack is empty.

That is, matching nested text relies on using a named capture group as a stack (pushing on a begin string and popping on an end string) and then using ?() to fail if the stack is not empty. The Chapter11\RegexExplorer project also includes a **much** more complex version of this regex, which is a complete HTML tag parser: it captures the Tag and any Attribute and Value strings; it handles nested tags properly; and it captures the Text between the <Tag> and the </Tag>.

Note The regex pattern language includes several useful operators that I don't discuss here, like the four *zero-width positive/negative lookahead/lookbehind assertions*. While these can be confusing, I think I've explained enough that you can pick up these advanced topics on your own. The Regex Explorer's HTML parsing regex uses an example of the (?>) *greedy subexpression* and the Chapter11\Replace project uses lookahead and lookbehind assertions; otherwise, I leave you to experimentation, Google, and the Microsoft documentation.

The Regex Class

The System.Text.RegularExpressions namespace

The three previous subsections have talked about why you should use regexs, how regexs work, and how to write a regex. What I haven't covered is the actual mechanics of using a regex in your C# or Delphi code.

A regex pattern is a sort of program: a description of a text-matching state machine. Like other programs, a pattern has to be compiled before you can use it. By default, when you create a Regex object, the pattern is compiled to a set of tables that define the states the matcher can be in, and the various conditions that can move it from one state to another. Table interpretation is very cheap and efficient, but it is still interpretation; there are two different ways to compile a regex to jittable CIL instead of to tables, which I talk about in the "Regex Options" and "Precompiled Regexs" topics, in this subsection.

Because regex creation and first use is much more expensive than subsequent uses, you generally want to reuse a regex whenever you can. At the same time, it **does** feel wrong to create a static class member (visible to all of an object's methods) just so that a Regex used only in one method can be reused. This is why the most commonly used Regex match and replace overloads come in both static and instance versions. While the instance versions use the regex that you passed to the Regex constructor, the static overloads allow you to pass a regex as a pattern string (and, perhaps, a RegexOptions bitmap). The point of the static overloads is that the system maintains a Regex object cache (keyed by pattern and regex options) that lets it reuse an already compiled regex.

Note The caching strategy changed in 2.0, where only the static overloads use the regex cache. Creating two Regex objects with the same pattern and the same options means the same regex will be compiled twice. In 1.1, explicitly creating a Regex instance was also cached. Presumably the change was made to minimize the size of the cache, and to allow Regex instances to be garbage collected when you're through with them.

While the Regex cache is not a documented part of the Regex class, and may vary from version to version (and may act differently on CE [or Mono] than on Windows), the cache lookup is not particularly expensive, and you should probably use the static methods most of the time. They make your code a bit simpler and easier to read, without adding a tremendous run-time burden. The three times you would want to use the instance overloads instead of the static overloads are

1. When you want to use Regex functionality that doesn't have a static overload. For example, the static overloads only allow you to match a regex against an entire target string, but there are instance overloads that follow the *Substring* model and that allow you to match a regex against the right tail (or an interior slice) of a target string. These are useful in applications like processing the text between HTML tags without calling String.Substring to create a new string. Similarly, the various methods that give you access to the collection of capture group names are only available through Regex instances.

2. When you don't want a Regex object to stick around in the cache, but want it to be garbage collected after it's used. (For example, it may be used only once, or it might only be used twice a day in a program that runs for days or months.) In this case, you would explicitly create a Regex object as a local variable, and let it be automatically scavenged after the last use.

3. When you repeatedly call a method that uses a regex, in a loop where speed is absolutely critical. In this case, you would either create a Regex object as a class member or a local variable, or you would precompile your regexs to a separate assembly.

The Regex constructor has two overloads. The overload that takes just a pattern string compiles the regex using the default options: interpretive matching; . doesn't match \n; ^ and $ match only at the beginning and end of the search string; white space is significant; and so on. To override any of these options, you use the overload that takes a pattern string and a RegexOptions bitmap (see the "Regex Options" topic, later in this chapter, for details).

When you explicitly create a Regex object, you have full control over its lifetime. A regex that will be used frequently can be declared as a static member,

```
private static Regex Explicit =
  new Regex(Pattern, Options); // created when class 1st referenced
```

which is created and compiled when the class is first referenced, and which lasts until the program exits. Once a Regex has been created, calling Regex methods directly through a class member (or a local variable) **is** slightly faster than calling them indirectly through Regex static methods and the Regex cache.

The Match Object

Capture groups and other information about a match operation

The Match object contains the results of a single match operation. If the regex matches the text, the Match.Success property will be true. If the match succeeded, the Index and Length properties specify a substring within the target string; the Value property and the ToString method call String.Substring to return the substring. As always, calling String.Substring is slower than working with Index and Length.

The Match.Groups property is a collection of Groups objects, containing information about each capture group in the regex. You can index Groups by name or number—it's faster to index by number, but it's safer to index by name. Regex.GroupNumberFromName[21] allows you to do the lookup **once**.

Each Group has a Success property, as well as Value, Index, and Length properties, just like the Match object. (In fact, the Match class descends from the Group class.) As per the earlier "Capture Groups" topic, a group's Value is the **last** substring that matched the capture group. The Group.Captures property is a collection of Capture objects, which contains **each** substring—Value, Index, and Length—that matched the capture group. (The Group class descends from the Capture class.) A Capture object does not have a Success property: Capture objects are only found within groups that matched successfully.

The Match.Result method interpolates capture group values into a pattern string using a Perl-compatible language where $0 is replaced by Groups[0].Value, $1 is replaced by Groups[1].Value, and so on. Thus, for a Match M,

```
M.Result("$1.$2") == String.Format("{0}.{1}", M.Groups[1], M.Groups[2])
```

Finally, there is a certain amount of redundancy in this result object hierarchy, which can be confusing to new users. The first group, Groups[0], contains the substring that matched the whole regex, which is also contained in the Match object's Value, Index, and Length properties. In fact, because a Match object is a Group, in a successful Match M, M and M.Groups[0] are the same object.

That is, Object.ReferenceEquals(M, M.Groups[0]), and referring to Groups[0] is just a waste of CPU cycles. This smacks suspiciously of bad design: it seems like someone wanted a Match to have Value and Success properties, so that you didn't have to index into the Groups array, and the easiest way to do this was to make Match inherit from Group, even if few people would say that a "a Match is-a Group." Another consequence of this decision is that a Match has a Captures property, just like every other Group, even though a Match will never have more than one Capture, which is yet another alias for the match itself. (So Object.ReferenceEquals(M, M.Captures[0]). See the Chapter11\MatchResult C# project.)

■**Tip** As a rule of thumb, don't refer to a Match object's Captures property, and don't refer to Groups[0].

---

21. Group objects do **not** have a name property—the mapping from capture group names to capture group numbers is the responsibility of the Regex object. See the GetGroupNames, GetGroupNumbers, GroupNameFromNumber, and GroupNumberFromName methods.

Regex Match Methods

From binary tests to getting every match

There are three different matching methods: IsMatch, Match, and Matches. If all you really care about is whether the regex matched or not, the IsMatch method is a convenient shorthand for calling the Match method and examining the Match object it returns. That is, code like ThisRegex.IsMatch(ThisText) is a bit smaller and easier to read than ThisRegex.Match(ThisText). Success. (Since all you care about is Success and not all the details of the Match, calling IsMatch is also slightly faster than calling Match.)

The simplest Regex.Match overloads will return the **first** match in a target string (if any). When you want to process each match in turn, you can either call Match.NextMatch, which returns the next match in the original target string, or you can use one of the Regex.Match method's *Substring* overloads, which allows you to restrict the search to a portion of the target string.

You can also call Regex.Matches to get a MatchCollection containing all the matches in the target string. The MatchCollection class acts a lot like an array of Match objects, but implements optimizations that defer calling Regex.Match as long as possible. The MatchCollection maintains a private ArrayList (Chapter 12) that contains every Match that you've read from the Items property.[22] If you ask for a Match that's not in the list, the MatchCollection (effectively) calls Match.NextMatch until it has enough Match items, or until a NextMatch operation fails. (Reading the Count property forces the MatchCollection to create every Match.)

That is, calling Matches creates a MatchCollection but doesn't actually do any matching. In particular, this means that it's not especially expensive to break out of a foreach loop that examines Matches—you haven't 'paid for' any matches that you haven't seen.

Regex Replace Methods

Two main overloads, with permutations

There are a lot of Regex.Replace overloads, but there are only two basic kinds, and the plethora of overloads is produced by multiplying these two kinds by static and instance overloads, and then multiplying again by various *Substring* overloads. Both kinds find all regex matches within a target string, and return a new string where each match is replaced with a string based on the match. One kind of Replace method takes a ReplacementPattern string and replaces each Match M with M.Result(ReplacementPattern). The other kind of Replace method passes each Match to a delegate, and replaces the match with the delegate's result.

The Match.Result form is useful for format conversions. For example, with a regex that matches unquoted attribute values within HTML tags and captures the attribute name and value, you can add quotes to every unquoted HTML attribute value in a whole document (see the QuoteHtmlAttributes method in the Chapter11\Replace project). Similarly, with a regex that matches US phone numbers like (555) 555-1212, 555-555-1212, and 555.555.1212 and captures the area code and phone number fields, you can convert all recognized phone numbers to a single canonical form.

---

22. Surprisingly, 2.0 does still use an ArrayList and not a List<Match>.

The delegate form offers maximum flexibility. A regex that matches tokens between percent signs and captures the tokens can look up the captured tokens in a Hashtable or Dictionary<,> (Chapter 12) and return a string from the symbol table. Or, as in this method from the Chapter11\Replace project, you can use the delegate form to substitute the {number} syntax of String.Format for the $number syntax of Match.Result:

```
public static string Replace(string Input, Regex R, string Pattern)
{
    // Create an object[] with an entry for every capture group in R
    object[] Groups = new object[R.GetGroupNumbers().Length];

    // Pass Regex.Replace a C# 2.0 anonymous method
    return R.Replace(Input, delegate(Match M)
    {
        M.Groups.CopyTo(Groups, 0);
        return String.Format(Pattern, Groups);
    } );
}
```

The Regex.Split Method

More flexible than String.Split

The Split method uses regex matches to split a string into an array of strings. The result array contains the text **outside of** the matches, plus any capture groups. That is, the first item in the result is the text to the left of the first match, if any. If there is at least one match, and its Groups.Count is greater than 1, any successful captures are added to the results. And so on, to the last result item, which is the text to the right of the last match, if any.

For example,

```
Regex.Split("Tom, Dick, and Harry", @", \s* (and)? \s*",
    RegexOptions.IgnorePatternWhitespace|RegexOptions.ExplicitCapture);
```

returns a three string array, {"Tom", "Dick", "Harry"}.

If you care about what the delimiters are, you can have the regex capture them. For example,

```
Regex.Split("(555) 555-1212", @"\s* ([().-]) \s*",
    RegexOptions.IgnorePatternWhitespace);
```

returns a seven-string array, {"", "(", "555", ")", "555", "-", "1212"}. Note that the first string is empty, because there is no text to the left of the first regex match.

■**Note** At the risk of being repetitious, Regex.Split is a comparatively expensive operation because of all the Substring calls it entails.

Regex Options

Details on all nine option bits

Creating a Regex (or using one of the static methods) with just a pattern is the equivalent of explicitly specifying RegexOptions.None—you get all the default behavior. To get the optional behaviors, you construct a RegexOptions bitmap by *or*-ing together various RegexOptions values. For example,

```
RegexOptions.IgnorePatternWhitespace | RegexOptions.Compiled
```

I've mentioned some of these options already: this topic contains a quick summary of each option, in alphabetical order.

Compiled

Compile the regex state machine to actual CIL, instead of to a set of tables that define the various match states and the conditions that move the matcher from one state to another. Since the code must be compiled and jitted before first use, setup costs are even greater for the compiled option than for the interpretive default, but a compiled regex does match significantly faster than an interpreted regex.

In general, you should only use the compiled option when you will be using a regex frequently. Because of compiled regexs' greater speed, you may be tempted to use them even in one-shot cases like splitting a MIME multipart email message on the boundary string. While the greater execution speed may indeed pay for the greater setup costs when applied to a multi-megabyte message, a compiled regex (like all other CIL code) cannot be unloaded once it's been jitted. Compiling single-use regexs to CIL thus represents a sort of memory leak that may become significant in a long-running program; the tables for a normal, interpreted regex are reclaimed when (if) the Regex object is reclaimed.

CultureInvariant

When you specify IgnoreCase, case mapping is done using the current thread's CurrentCulture property. If you are matching, say, 7-bit ASCII Internet protocol text, you may not want this behavior. The CultureInvariant option forces case mapping to be done via CultureInfo. InvariantCulture (i.e., English, without any special country rules).

■**Note** This option only matters when you also specify IgnoreCase.

ECMAScript

Restricts standard character classes (like \s and \w) to 7-bit ASCII values.

> **Note** This option can be used **only** with the `IgnoreCase`, `Multiline`, and `Compiled` options—any other combination causes an exception.

ExplicitCapture

'Bare' parentheses are just logical groupings, not capture groups. To specify a capture group, you have to give it a name with (`?<Name> capture pattern`). In general, capture groups are not free, and you should only capture substrings that you actually use. There is usually a tradeoff between the awkwardness of having to name the capture groups and the awkwardness of using (`?: non-capture pattern`) to specify a noncapture group.

IgnoreCase

Literals and character classes are not case sensitive. The case mapping is done in a culture-sensitive way; see the preceding `CultureInvariant` option. This corresponds to the Perl i option (except for the culture sensitivity).

IgnorePatternWhitespace

Ignore white space in patterns, and enable comments between a # and the end of the line. To match white space, use either \s or a more specific escape like \x20, \t, &c; to match a #, use \#. This corresponds exactly to the Perl x ("extended") option; I highly recommend you use it for all but the simplest regexs.

Multiline

Changes ^ to match the start of any line, not just the start of the string, and changes $ to match the end of any line, not just the end of the string. This corresponds exactly to the Perl m option.

> **Note** `Multiline` does not affect `Singleline` in any way and vice versa. `Multiline` controls the behavior of the ^ and $ assertions; `Singleline` controls the behavior of the . wildcard.

None

All the default behaviors, as in Table 11-7. None can also be used as a null value when you are composing a bitmap by *or*-ing in individual option bits:

```
RegexOptions Bitmap = RegexOptions.None;
foreach (RegexOptions Option in SomeCollection) Bitmap |= Option;
```

Table 11-7. *Default Regex Behaviors, and Their RegexOptions Overrides*

Default Behavior	Override
Interpreted match, using tables that can be garbage collected.	`Compiled`
Ignoring case is culture sensitive.	`CultureInvariant`
Standard character classes include non-ASCII characters.	`ECMAScript`
All parentheses are both logical groupings and capture groups.	`ExplicitCapture`
All literals are case sensitive.	`IgnoreCase`
White-space characters are treated as literals, comments are not supported.	`IgnorePatternWhitespace`
^ and $ match the start and end of the string, not the start and end of a line.	`Multiline`
Match left to right.	`RightToLeft`
. matches every character except \n.	`Singleline`

`RightToLeft`

Starts matching the **last** pattern element to the **last** target character, and works backwards. The effect is to reverse the order of the `Matches`. Very useful when you want only the last match (or the last *N* matches) instead of the first match.

`Singleline`

Changes . to match any character, not any character except \n. This corresponds exactly to the Perl s option.

■**Note** `Singleline` does not affect `Multiline` in any way and vice versa. `Singleline` controls the behavior of the . wildcard; `Multiline` controls the behavior of the ^ and $ assertions.

The `Regex.Escape` Method

An easy way to match literal text

There are a number of characters that have special meaning within a regex pattern. If you want to match them literally, you have to escape them, turning, e.g., `Read Me.txt` into `Read\x20Me\.txt`. It's generally easy enough to do this when you're composing a regex by hand, but when you are composing a regex programmatically and want to match some string literally, you need a way to escape every special character in the string. This is what the `Regex.Escape` method does: it replaces every character in a string that has special meaning in regexs with an escape sequence that allows the string to match as a literal.

For example,

```
String.Format("^--{0}$(.*?)^--{0}$", Regex.Escape(BoundaryString))
```

generates a regex pattern that will match one part of a MIME multipart email message. (This regex needs both the Singleline and Multiline modes, so that . matches new-line characters and so that ^ and $ match the start and end of lines.)

Precompiled Regexs

Compile regexs to CIL ahead of time, so they only have to be jitted

In programs that use a large number of Regex static members, compiling all the regexs can add significantly to startup time. When you have a lot of Regex static members, it can make sense to use Regex.CompileToAssembly to place your regexs in a separate assembly. CompileToAssembly takes an array of RegexCompilationInfo objects (each of which specifies a pattern, options, a name, and a namespace) and creates an assembly containing precompiled regexs. As per the Chapter11\RegexAssembly\Consumer C# project, CompileToAssembly creates Regex descendant classes, which you have to create before you can use the regex. However, these regexs are always compiled to CIL (even if you don't specify RegexOptions.Compiled), and the compilation is done at the time the assembly is created, not when the regex is first used. It takes about as long to create a precompiled regex object as to pass a pattern string to the Regex constructor—but first use is much faster.

You're probably most likely to use CompileToAssembly as in the Chapter11\RegexAssembly C# project, to create an assembly that you install with your application. Alternatively, you might use the dynamic assembly-loading techniques in the Chapter11\DemandCreate C# project (and Chapter 14) to create the regex assembly the first time your application runs on a particular machine. Dynamic type creation **is** a bit more expensive than simply calling a constructor from an assembly you have a reference to, but it's still faster than compiling even a simple regex like .+.

Files

The System.IO namespace

As you would probably expect, FCL file IO is thoroughly object oriented. No FindFirst/FindNext, no "handles" or "cookies" or "opaque types." There are methods to probe and manipulate the file system; there are objects that represent directory entries; there are objects that represent open files.

■**Note** Files and sockets are not unified; sockets have their own object model, in the System.Net.Sockets namespace. I don't cover sockets or networking in this book, because I'm not trying to be exhaustive. I'm trying to give just enough detail on just enough classes for you to see the recurring themes in FCL design. Before the end of these FCL chapters, you'll have expectations about how the various models will come into play in each new set of FCL classes that you use, especially when you have used similar code before.

Most of the filename manipulation and directory enumeration code is pretty straightforward, and the only real issue is knowing where in the System.IO namespace to find the code you want. However, reading and writing files is not very like any of Delphi's file models. FCL file IO involves stream reader and stream writer classes that access an open file (file stream) class. Accordingly, the "File System Information" subsection speeds through the simple stuff, while the "File IO" subsection goes into somewhat more detail on reading and writing file streams.

File System Information

Both low-level, filename-oriented classes and higher-level objects

The System.IO namespace provides two types of access to files. The Path, Directory, and File classes are static classes (in 1.1, they're sealed, abstract classes) with static methods. They provide logical grouping, but are only minimally object oriented. The DirectoryInfo and FileInfo classes are regular classes: each instance represents a file or directory, and there are properties to read and write timestamps and the like.

The Path class doesn't have a PathInfo counterpart. While Path has the GetTempFileName method that creates temporary files and the GetTempPath method that returns the name of the temporary directory, most Path members are direct analogs to various "file name utilities" in the Delphi SysUtils unit—they deal with path strings simply as strings that follow certain rules, and not as pointers to file system entries. Table 11-8 lists a few key Path members to give you an idea what sort of things to look in Path for.

Table 11-8. *Selected Path Members*

Path **Member**	SysUtils **Equivalent**	**Purpose**
DirectorySeparatorChar	PathDelim	Either \ or /, depending on OS.
ChangeExtension	ChangeFileExt	Takes a filename string; returns a filename string with a different extension. **Does not rename a file.**
GetDirectoryName	ExtractFileDir	Returns a string containing only the path, with no filename.
GetFileName	ExtractFileName	Returns a string containing only the filename, with no path.
GetFullPath	ExpandFileName	Gets a rooted, absolute filename.

The Directory and DirectoryInfo classes offer roughly parallel functionality, as do the File and FileInfo classes. When you only need to do a single thing with a file or directory, it will generally be faster and easier to use the low-level File and Directory classes. The static methods don't incur the overhead of creating an object that represents the file system entry. However, when you need to do several operations on each file or directory, it will generally be faster and easier to use the higher-level Info classes. Creating an Info object means that path string validation and security checks only have to be done once, and calling instance methods on file objects means that you don't have to keep passing the path string.

The Directory class has static methods like CreateDirectory and SetCurrentDirectory that do exactly what you'd expect. There are also methods to test whether a directory exists, delete directories, and get and set various timestamps. Where the FCL differs from both the VCL and the Win32 API is in enumerating directories. There's no FindFirst/FindNext: the Directory.GetDirectories methods return an array of strings containing the names of subdirectories; the GetFiles methods return an array of strings containing filenames; and the GetFileSystemEntries methods return an array of strings containing both file and directory names.

For example, the following FileNames method from the Chapter11\RecursiveEnumeration project enumerates every filename in a given directory. You can use this C# 2.0 method in a foreach statement like foreach (string FileName in Enumerate.FileNames(Path, Pattern)) that gives you each filename under Path that matches Pattern.

```
public static IEnumerable<string> FileNames(string Path, string Pattern)
{
  string[] Entries = Directory.GetFileSystemEntries(Path, Pattern);
  foreach (string Entry in Entries)
  {
    if (! Directory.Exists(Entry))
      yield return Entry;
    else
      foreach (string Child in FileNames(Entry, Pattern))
        yield return Child;
  }
}
```

This code is pretty straightforward except for the way it has to call Directory.Exists on every filename. We know the filename exists—but we have to use Directory.Exists or File.Exists to tell whether it names a directory or file.

The DirectoryInfo class has a constructor that takes a path name. Much like the Directory class, there are instance methods like Create and Delete and properties like Exists and Parent that do exactly what you'd expect. The enumeration methods return an array of Info objects, instead of an array of strings. As you'd expect, the GetFiles methods return an array of FileInfo objects, while the GetDirectories methods return an array of DirectoryInfo objects. The GetFileSystemInfos methods are confusingly described as returning an "array of strongly typed FileSystemInfo" objects—which **does** only mean that each entry in the FileSystemInfo[] is either a FileInfo or a DirectoryInfo, and you can tell them apart with the is operator or via GetType.

The FileSystemInfo version of the preceding FileNames method is not all that different:

```
public static IEnumerable<FileSystemInfo> Files
  (DirectoryInfo Directory, string Pattern)
{
  FileSystemInfo[] Entries = Directory.GetFileSystemInfos(Pattern);
  foreach (FileSystemInfo Entry in Entries)
  {
    if (Entry is FileInfo)
      yield return Entry;
```

```
    else
      foreach (FileSystemInfo Child in Files((DirectoryInfo)Entry, Pattern))
        yield return Child;
  }
}
```

As you can see, this is much like the string version that uses Directory methods instead of DirectoryInfo methods—except that the file vs. directory test is more straightforward. It's clearer that we are simply distinguishing files from directories with the Entry is FileInfo test[23] than with the Directory.Exists(Entry) test. These two examples capture in miniature the major difference between the Directory and DirectoryInfo classes—operations on Info objects are smaller and clearer, but the string version is three or four times faster than the Info object's version (because we're doing so little with each Info object we create).

There are other, less-important differences between the static and instance classes. For example, when you create a DirectoryInfo or FileInfo object, the constructor calls Path.GetFullPath to convert a partial name, like .\this or ..\that, to an absolute path, rooted at a drive or share name. Thus, if you do foreach (FileSystemInfo File in Enumerate.Files(@"\..", "*")), no File.FullName will have a \.. in it. If you do foreach (string FileName in Enumerate.FileNames(@"\..", "*")), each FileName will have a \.. in it.

File IO

Reading and writing text and binary files

The File class has static methods like Exists and Delete that do exactly what you'd expect. It also has static methods like Open that return a new FileStream object; a FileStream object represents an open file. Similarly, the FileInfo class has an Exists property and a Delete method as well as various Open overloads that all return a new FileStream.

By itself, the FileStream only offers byte-by-byte access to a file. There are blocking and asynchronous methods to read and write individual bytes or byte arrays, but usually you will use a FileStream through a Reader or Writer object. The StreamReader and StreamWriter classes are character-oriented classes that read and write text files; the BinaryReader and BinaryWriter read and write binary streams.

When you create a Reader or Writer object, you pass it either an open FileStream or a file-name and let it create the FileStream for you. When you are done reading and writing the file, you should Close the Reader or Writer object. This closes the underlying FileStream. The Reader and Writer classes implement IDisposable, and call Close in their Dispose method. Thus, creating a Reader and Writer object within the to-be-Dispose()d expression of a uses statement guarantees that the file will be closed at the end of the uses statement.

For example, the following method reads a text file to a string:

---

23. We could also read the Entry.Attributes property, and test whether the Directory bit is set or do Entry.GetType() == typeof(DirectoryInfo)—any speed difference between the three tests is swamped by the overhead of creating FileSystemInfo objects plus the overhead of actual file IO.

```
public static string Read(string FileName)
{
  using (StreamReader Reader = new StreamReader(FileName))
  {
    int StreamLength = (int) Reader.BaseStream.Length;
    char[] Text = new char[StreamLength];
    Reader.Read(Text, 0, StreamLength);
    return new String(Text);
  }
}
```

This Read method creates a StreamReader that opens the FileName file, and reads the Length of the BaseStream, which is the actual open file. It casts this to an int[24] as Stream.Length is a long; creates a char array that will hold all the characters in the file; reads them in with Reader.Read(); and calls the String constructor that turns a character array to a string. This passes over each character twice (reading it to the character array[25] and then into the string), but this can't be helped, as there is no way to create a string and then modify its character array.

The following Delphi function from the Chapter11\ReadText project also reads a text file to a string:

```
function ReadFile(FileName: string): string;
var
  Reader: StreamReader;
begin
  Reader := StreamReader.Create(FileName);
  try
    Result := Reader.ReadToEnd;
  finally
    Reader.Close;
  end;
end;
```

(as, for that matter, does the FCL 2.0 method File.ReadAll), but the C# method illustrates the actual techniques involved, and will generally be faster than StreamReader.ReadToEnd, which creates a StringBuilder and reads the file in a series of chunks.

The StreamReader class also has a ReadLine method that allows you to read a text file a line at a time.

When you create a StreamReader (or a StreamWriter) without an explicit Encoding parameter, it defaults to System.Text.Encoding.UTF8, which is, basically, the standard Latin-1 8-bit character set, with escape sequences for multibyte Unicode characters. The default UTF8 encoding reads standard 8-bit text files and converts each character to 16-bit Unicode characters. You can use an explicit Encoding parameter to read or write UTF7 or 16-bit or 32-bit Unicode files.

For example, the following method writes a string to a 16-bit Unicode file:

---

24. Raising an exception if the stream is too long to fit in a string.

25. Reading is further complicated when the input stream may contain UTF escape sequences.

```
public static void Write16(string FileName, string FileText)
{
  // The second, false parameter to the StreamWriter constructor makes FileText
  // replace any existing text in the file; a true parameter would append, instead.
  using (StreamWriter Writer = new StreamWriter(FileName, false, Encoding.Unicode))
    Writer.Write(FileText);
}
```

The preceding method writes a string to a file, then closes the file. The Write (and the WriteLine which, like Delphi's WriteLn, appends a line break after the Write) method is heavily overloaded, and you can Write numbers, booleans, and objects to the stream. As with String.Concat, these methods are *Simpler* and *Smaller* than peppering your code with calls to ToString. Both Write and WriteLine also have overloads that follow the *Format* model, taking a format string and any number of object parameters, passing them to String.Format, and writing the result to the stream.

StreamReader and StreamWriter are implementations of the abstract TextReader and TextWriter classes. Their 'sibling' classes, StringReader and StringWriter, allow you to use the text stream methods to read and write strings. These classes are useful when the same code needs to write to either a file or a string,[26] but should probably be avoided when you only need to read and write strings. A StringWriter is basically just a wrapper around a StringBuilder and doesn't really offer any extra functionality to make up for the extra cost. Similarly, while a StringReader does allow you to process a string line by line, you can get similar functionality from String.Split, and you can get better performance with substring techniques that don't create a new string for each line.

Binary streams follow the same general pattern as text streams—an IDisposable reader or writer class that gives access to a Stream instance, and closes the stream when you close the reader or writer—except that the BinaryReader and BinaryWriter constructors don't have overloads that take a filename. You always have to explicitly open a stream and pass the Stream object to the reader or writer.

The binary reader and writer classes have methods to read and write the standard CLR primitives (including strings), but there are no methods to write compound types like records or classes. Field alignment and layout within a compound type is entirely up to the jitter, and can vary from CPU to CPU, and from CLR version to CLR version. You have to read and write element by element, in a way that's probably quite familiar: read and write in the same order, and start every file with some sort of format identifier, preferably one containing version information.

■**Note** .NET also includes serialization support (Chapter 14) that makes it very easy to persist data structures, or to pass them from one machine to another. You will generally use raw binary streams only when you need to read or write standard file formats, or when IO speed really matters.

---

26. For example, automating a console application by reading input from a string.

The .NET Console

Standard input and standard output

The System.Console class is used much like Delphi's ReadLn and WriteLn, but is somewhat broader. The Console class has ReadLine and WriteLine (and Read and Write) methods that parallel the preceding TextReader and TextWriter classes and that (by default) read and write standard input and standard output, but it also has methods and properties to control the appearance of the console window, like Title, WindowTop, and ForegroundColor.

The Console class's static In, Out, and Error properties contain TextReader and TextWriter objects that are, by default, mapped to the standard input, output, and error streams. You can substitute any TextReader and TextWriter objects that you like; the OpenStandardX methods will (re)acquire the standard streams.

While in Win32 Delphi, WriteLn from a forms application will raise an exception,[27] on .NET any application can use Console.Write to write to the Console.Out stream (which, again, is usually standard output), even if it doesn't have an open console window. This can be useful for various 'daemon' processes that normally run invisibly but that nonetheless log their progress to an optional trace window. A "windows application" that doesn't create any forms is invisible, but any windows application can use the same Win32 API calls to create a console that Delphi or C# console applications use automatically.

The FCL offers no methods to manually create a console, but you can use the methods in the Shemitz.GuiConsole namespace to create and release a console on demand. See the Chapter11\ConsoleTest C# project for an example.

Key Points

String and file IO offer standard functionality and a complex but consistent interface

- Many FCL methods are heavily overloaded. These overloads tend to follow a few common models whose permutations account for much of this multiplicity.

- The String class contains a lot of functionality that's long been common in various string libraries but that may be new to Delphi programmers.

- If you already know regexs, the FCL regex classes are a joy to use. If you don't already know regexs, they're a wonderful place to start.

- File IO is object oriented, but the organizing principles should be very familiar.

---

27. Unless you've used Win32 calls to create a console.

CHAPTER 12

■■■

Collections

The Array class provides a great deal of standard functionality. Arrays are fixed length and strongly typed, but list classes with a Capacity and a Length can support appending, inserting, and deleting. An ArrayList is a list of object references, and so can hold any data types; a List<T> is a strongly typed list that can only hold T types. Both these lists are indexed by integers; the Hashtable and Dictionary<K, V> can be indexed by any data type. IEnumerable is everywhere in .NET code; this chapter contains details.

All Delphi and C# arrays are instances of the Array class. This means that all arrays can be enumerated, and that all one-dimensional arrays can be sorted, searched, and copied. This chapter has details on array internals, and covers the standard Array properties and methods.

Arrays are fixed length, but the FCL also has especially fine collections classes. Because every reference type is an object and every value type can be boxed into an object, an object can hold any value of any type, without losing type information. This means that a simple resizable array of references much like Delphi's TList can hold any type of data, not just untyped pointers, like a native code TList. The ArrayList class lets you build lists of values, one by one. You can sort the list or search the list, and you can convert the list to a fixed-length, system-level array at any time.

Because every value supports the GetHashCode and Equals methods, the FCL has a Hashtable class that can associate any value with any other value, instead of just associating strings to strings or associating strings to pointers, the way a native code TStrings does. You can use a Hashtable for sparse arrays as well as symbol tables and dictionaries of all sorts.

Of course, the flexibility and power of these late-bound collections isn't free. Storing a value type in an object is a boxing operation, which creates an object containing the value and its type. Getting a typed value back from an object is either a checked cast of one reference type to another or an unboxing operation that checks the boxed type and retrieves the boxed value. Boxing and unboxing and checked casts are fairly cheap, simple operations, but they do make the heterogeneous, object-oriented collection classes a bit slower than typed arrays.

Accordingly, the collection classes have been extensively revised in .NET 2.0 with its support for generic programming. The new System.Collections.Generic namespace largely parallels the System.Collections namespace, with early-bound, open collection classes that allow you to create, say, variable-length lists of integers or sparse arrays of some sort of Measurement objects indexed by DateTime values. These generic collections can enforce type safety at compile time, without your having to write wrapper code by hand. The early-bound generic collections are also faster than their late-bound counterparts, since they don't need to cast values to and from object.

Generics also affect foreach and the IEnumerable interface. IEnumerable.Current is an object that must be (implicitly) cast to the type of the iteration variable, and this implicit cast has the same run-time cost as extracting typed values from a collection of heterogeneous objects. When you use the generic version of IEnumerable, the Current property is assignment compatible with the iteration variable, which eliminates the need for a checked cast or an unboxing operation on every iteration.

Arrays

All arrays are reference types

As per Chapter 2, the System.Array type is an abstract type that you don't explicitly descend from. Rather, you declare arrays using normal Delphi or C# syntax, and the compiler creates the Array descendant for you.[1] Each array is a single heap block, consisting of a normal class instance header (that is, a pointer to the type information tables and a SyncBlockIndex), followed by an array header, which contains the array dimensions, followed by the array data in standard row major order.

In native code Delphis, dynamic arrays are reference types, but static arrays are inlined within a compound type like a record or class. On .NET, **all** arrays are reference types. Each array, no matter its size or base type, takes the same space (a native reference, whether that's 32 or 64 bits) within a compound type.

Arrays have a Length and a Rank property. The Length is the number of elements, and the Rank is the number of dimensions. (Length is the **total** number of elements—a 2-by-3 matrix has a Length of 6.) The GetLength, GetLowerBound, and GetUpperBound instance methods take a dimension (an integer >= 0, and less than the array Rank) and return the dimension's length or bounds. Most arrays are 0-based and one dimensional—but arrays **can** have any number of dimensions, and each dimension can have any integral lower bound.

Array indices are always integers—Delphi's indexing by character (as in an array['a'..'z'] of {type}) or indexing by enum (as in an array[Red..Blue] of {type}) is implemented via CIL that converts a nonintegral index to its ordinal value. As in Delphi, you cannot index arrays by strings or numbers with a fractional part. You can, however, use a Hashtable or a generic Dictionary (see the "Hash Tables" section, later in this chapter) to create a sort of sparse array, indexed by floats or strings or whatever.

---

1. C# and Delphi both support arrays whose length is not known at compile time. (C# doesn't believe that array length is part of a type definition [int[] Integers, not int[10] Integers], and Delphi supports array of *dynamic arrays*.) Both, however, require you to specify the array's base type, and the array's dimensions. When you **don't** know the base type (or the number of dimensions) at compile time, you can use the Array.CreateInstance method directly, to create an array of a specified size and type. You can't do much with an Array instance. You can enumerate it, but you have to use the GetValue and SetValue methods to read and write elements: you can't use normal array syntax.

   You can do a checked cast of an Array to a specific descendant type. int[] I = (int[]) Array. CreateInstance(typeof(int), 10) is a pretty pointless example, since the compiler will do it for you, but you might cast an untyped Array to a known array type in code that can handle two or more different types of array. You would use as to see if this particular Array was one of the known types, then pass a non-null cast result to the appropriate handler.

Copy

Copy elements from one array to another

You can change the elements of an array, but you cannot change the number of elements in an array. To change an array's Length, you have to first create a new array, with a new size, and then copy elements of the old array to the new array. The Array methods Copy and CopyTo will do the copying, for one-dimensional arrays. Copy is a static method that takes two array parameters, while CopyTo is an instance method that always copies the whole array to an offset within a second array that you pass as a parameter.

▓**Delphi Note** In Delphi, array is a keyword, and you have to call static methods as, e.g., &Array.Copy() or System.Array.Copy(), not just Array.Copy(). Somewhat similarly, you have to cast arrays to &Array (or to System.Array) to call Array instance methods.

The static Copy method allows you to copy portions of an array. You can copy either the first *N* elements from one array to another, or (as with the String.Substring method) you can copy a given number of elements from a given offset within the source array to a different offset within the target array.

Both Copy and CopyTo will raise an exception if the target array is too short, or if the base types are not compatible.

While both Copy and CopyTo will copy array elements from one array to another, they will not create a new array. The Array class also implements ICloneable, with its object Clone method, which creates a new array containing copies of each element in the original. Note that because Clone returns a late-bound object, you have to cast it to an array of the right type before you can assign it to an array variable. For example, given string[] Beatles = {"John", "Paul", "George", "Ringo"}, you can compile string[] Monkees = (string[]) Beatles.Clone() but not string[] Monkees = Beatles.Clone().

Finally, in 2.0, there is a Resize<T> method, which is a static method that takes an array of type T as a reference parameter (ref in C#, and var in Delphi) and so can resize the array 'in place'—it creates a new array of a specified size, copying elements and/or filling with default(T) as necessary, and then changes the existing array variable to point to the new array.

Sort

Several ways to sort an array

The Sort method is heavily overloaded. All but one of the Sort methods fall into one of two groups: the IComparable overloads sort types that know how to compare themselves, in ascending order, and the IComparer overloads take a sorting predicate in the form of an instance of an object that implements the IComparer interface. These two basic models are then multiplied by *Subarray* overloads that sort only a portion of an array; by key/item sorting that sorts two arrays based on the values in just one of them; and (in 2.0) by the strongly typed, generic model.

All these permutations are implemented, making for sixteen Sort methods, plus a (new in 2.0) method that takes a delegate that compares a pair of elements.

All the Sort overloads are static methods that take one or two arrays as parameters, and use the QuickSort algorithm[2] to sort the arrays in place. That is, arrays **aren't** immutable and array methods generally don't follow the String model—you say, e.g., Array.Sort(ThisArray), not ThisArray = Array.Sort(ThisArray). Note also that sorting an array does affect all other references to the same array.

The simplest Sort method takes a single array parameter, and sorts the whole array in ascending order. This method relies on each element in the array implementing the IComparable interface. As you can see from the Chapter12\ArraySort C# project, standard types like strings and numbers do implement IComparable, making it very easy to sort arrays of standard types in ascending order. For example, given the array

```
int[] Integers = new int[] { 0, 1, 3, 5, 7, 9, 2, 4, 6, 8 };
```

the method call Array.Sort(Integers) will set Integers to {0, 1, 2, 3, 4, 5, 6, 7, 8, 9}.

If you try to Sort an array of a type like struct Name { public string First, Last; }, you'll get an InvalidOperationException at run time, because the Name structure doesn't implement IComparable. That is, to sort arrays of your own types (using the one-parameter Array.Sort(Array) form) they need to implement the IComparable interface, which has only one member—int CompareTo(object obj). For example, as in the Chapter12\StructSort C# project, the preceding struct Name might implement CompareTo as

```
public int CompareTo(object obj)
{
  // Can't use as - Name is a struct
  if (! (obj is Name))
    throw new ArgumentException("Parameter is not a Name");
  Name Other = (Name) obj;
  int CompareLast = Last.CompareTo(Other.Last);
  if (CompareLast != 0)
    return CompareLast;
  else
      return First.CompareTo(Other.First);
}
```

IComparable.CompareTo methods take an object parameter, so each CompareTo method first has to make sure that the object it is trying to compare itself to is an object that it knows about. (Here, I had to do an is test and then an explicit cast, because you can't use as with boxed structures.) That done, the preceding method uses String.CompareTo to sort by last name, and by first names in the event of a tie.

In 2.0, the generic IComparable<T> allows you to write strongly typed comparisons:

```
public int CompareTo(Name Other)
{
  int CompareLast = Last.CompareTo(Other.Last);
```

---

2. QuickSort is not a *stable sort*. If you resort the output, items that sorted as equivalent might shift positions.

```
  if (CompareLast != 0)
    return CompareLast;
  else
      return First.CompareTo(Other.First);
}
```

As you can see, the comparisons are identical—except that the IComparable<T> version is smaller and faster because it doesn't have to test (and maybe unbox) its parameter to a known type.

Although there is a generic Array.Sort<T> method, you don't have to use the generic method to get the speed benefit of a strongly typed, early-bound IComparable<T> comparison. When sorting an array of a type T that implements IComparable<T>, both Array.Sort and Array.Sort<T> will use the IComparable<T> comparison method. Array.Sort<T> is type safe (it can only sort arrays of T), but there isn't a substantial speed difference between the two Sort methods. Conversely, you can call Array.Sort<T> even if T only implements IComparable, but this does entail a speed hit if T is a value type that needs to be boxed. In fact, the only time you **need** a late-bound IComparable comparison in 2.0 is when you are sorting an array of a type that doesn't implement IComparable<T>—like a heterogeneous object[].

When you need more control over the sort order—perhaps you need to sort in descending order, or to sort on different fields at different times—you use the IComparer overloads. These take a predicate, passed as an instance of a class that implements the IComparer interface.[3]

For example, the following method from the Chapter12\ArraySort project will sort any type in descending order:

```
public int Compare(object x, object y)
{
  IComparable Comparable = x as IComparable;
  if (Comparable != null)
    return - Comparable.CompareTo(y);
  throw new ArgumentException(String.Format("Can't compare {0} and {1}",
    x.GetType(), y.GetType()));
}
```

If x has an IComparable implementation, this method uses that to compare x to y, flipping the sign to force a sort in descending order. Using IComparable like this keeps comparison code in a single place; IComparer implementations generally control **what** gets compared, and whether the sort should be ascending or descending, but generally leave actual comparisons to IComparable.

---

3. If you are writing a method, you may be inclined to add the IComparer interface to the object that contains the method that's calling Sort. Then you would implement the ICompare.Compare method as a peer of the method that's calling Sort, and simply pass this/Self as the IComparer parameter. However, this both limits flexibility and exposes internal functionality to public use. That is, anyone can use the IComparer implementation, if it's the sorting object that can do the comparison. And implementing IComparer on the sorting object causes problems as soon one method wants to Sort with two different IComparer predicates, or two methods want to Sort with different IComparer predicates, etc.

The preferred approach to writing an IComparer interface is to write a private nested class that implements IComparer. You then create a new instance of this nested class, and pass it on to Sort as the IComparer parameter. You can pass the nested class's constructor any state information that the instance will need to do its comparison—it's almost like passing a private method.

Both IComparable and IComparer use late-bound predicates that have to examine and cast their parameters before they can do anything with them. In a class DescendingOrder<T> : IComparer<T> where T : IComparable<T>, the predicate can be much simpler and faster:

```
public int Compare(T x, T y)
{
    return - x.CompareTo(y);
}
```

The predicate doesn't have to check its arguments because the where constraint means that the C# 2.0 compiler will not let you use this predicate on an array of a type that doesn't implement IComparable<T> (Chapter 7). As with the basic IComparable sort, you can pass an IComparer<T> predicate to the late-bound IComparer Sort method:

```
/* any of */ Array.Sort(Integers, new DescendingOrder());
/*   or   */ Array.Sort(Integers, new DescendingOrder<int>());
/*   or   */ Array.Sort<int>(Integers, new DescendingOrder<int>());
```

As with the IComparable sort, there's not a lot of speed difference between Sort and Sort<T>. However, using an early-bound (IComparer<T>) predicate is significantly faster than using a late-bound (IComparer) predicate, especially for value types that have to be boxed and unboxed to be compared.

The four Sort methods I've described so far (IComparable and IComparer multiplied by untyped [1.x] and typed [2.0] versions) are each permuted by two more models. First, all four support a *Subarray* model, much like the *Substring* model, where you sort a portion of an array by specifying the offset of the first element to sort and the number of elements to sort. Do note that the *Subarray* overloads are void methods (procedures, in Delphi) that change their array parameter just like the 'whole array' overloads; the similarity to the *Substring* model does not go so far as to cause them to return a new, partially sorted array.

Second, each of these eight types of Sort methods also supports a key/item model, where two arrays are sorted at once. The arrays do not have to be of the same type or of the same length. For example, as you can see in the Chapter12\ArraySort C# project, you can sort an array of string items by integer keys or vice versa, so long as there are at least as many items as keys. If there are more items than keys, the 'extra' items are not sorted.

Finally, in 2.0 there is a third type of Sort method, which takes a delegate that compares two values of a particular type. This can be particularly convenient when used with an anonymous method. For example, as in the Chapter12\StructSort C# project,

```
Array.Sort<Name>(Names, delegate(Name This, Name That)
{
    int Last = String.Compare(This.Last, That.Last);
    if (Last != 0)
        return -Last;
    else
        return -String.Compare(This.First, That.First);
});
```

Search

Find elements that match a target, and elements that satisfy a custom predicate

In 1.1, there are only two methods that search an array—IndexOf and LastIndexOf. IndexOf searches forward, while LastIndexOf searches backward: both search an array for a target object, returning an array index or a failure code. In 2.0, the index-of methods gain typed overloads, plus there is a suite of new methods that apply a predicate to an array in various ways.

Both IndexOf and LastIndexOf are static methods that take a one-dimensional array and a target object to search for. (As you might expect, both methods have *Substring* overloads that allow you to search the right or left tail of an array, as well as any arbitrary slice.) If IndexOf or LastIndexOf find the target, they return the index of the array element that matched; if they don't find the target, they return the lower bound minus 1 (i.e., ArrayInstance.GetLowerBound(0) - 1). Since both C# and Delphi use 0-based arrays, you will almost always get −1 as an error code, but it is not impossible that you will encounter arrays with a nonzero lower bound, perhaps when working with code written in other languages.

■**Delphi Note**   Delphi does, of course, allow you to **declare** an array indexed by any ordinal subrange (subject to the $2^{31}-1$ element limit) but it **implements** these as 0-based arrays. For example, Delphi implements a var SevenEleven: array[7..11] of integer as a 5-long, 0-based array, automatically emitting CIL to subtract 7 from all your index expressions. Thus, IndexOf will return -1 on search failure— and you need to be sure to add Low(SevenEleven) to a nonnegative result to get a valid array index.

If the array is sorted, you can use the static method Array.BinarySearch to return the index of the match. A binary search requires a sorted array, and may return a false negative when an array that does contain a matching value is anti-sorted in the right way: the array does not contain any sort of tag that says 'not changed since sorted *this* way' that would enable the BinarySearch method to raise an exception when an array was not sorted properly. There are IComparable and IComparer and *Substring* overloads, as well as open BinarySearch methods in 2.0.

That is, in 1.1, BinarySearch is untyped, like both IndexOf and LastIndexOf—each method takes an Array to search in and an object to search for. In 2.0, there are also typed overloads: for example, IndexOf<int> will only search integer arrays for integer targets, without the need to box the target. This is pretty much just a matter of adding strong typing, without any significant performance improvement, but 2.0 also adds a set of typed search methods that apply a custom predicate to array elements.

These new methods use the generic type declaration

```
delegate bool Predicate<T>(T obj);
```

an open delegate declaration (Chapter 8) method that matches any method that takes a single parameter, of generic type T, and returns either true or false. These new array search methods are all static methods that take an array and a delegate, and they fall into three broad groups.

■**Note** The CLS specification does not include generics: no open method (Chapters 2 and 7) is CLS compliant. As always, this does **not** mean that you cannot use open types and open methods in a CLS-compliant assembly; it merely means that you can't expose them to the public without flagging the open member as being [CLSCompliant(false)].

The first group includes two methods that simply return a boolean result. Exists<T> returns true if the array has any element that satisfies the predicate, while TrueForAll<T> returns true if any and all elements satisfy the predicate. Thus, as in the Chapter12\EmptyArrays C# project, Exists returns false on an empty array, while TrueForAll returns true on an empty array.

The second group of array search methods includes a couple of methods that return array indices. FindIndex<T> and FindLastIndex<T> are almost directly analogous to IndexOf and LastIndexOf—they even have the same *Substring* overloads—except that they return the index of the first (last) element that satisfies the predicate instead of the index of an element that matches a target. (Like IndexOf<T> and LastIndexOf<T>, they also **require** that the array use 0-based indexing. This means the failure code [one less than the low bound] is always –1.)

The third and final group of array search methods returns actual array element(s). The Find<T> and FindLast<T> methods return the first (or last) array element that satisfies the predicate—they do **not** have *Substring* overloads. If there is no element that satisfies the predicate, they return default(T)—which is usually 0 or null. The FindAll<T> method returns a T[] containing all the elements that satisfy the predicate. If the source array was empty or there were no elements that satisfy the predicate, FindAll returns an empty array (one whose Length is 0), not null.

■**Tip** Don't forget that C# can often infer that you are calling an open method from the arguments. If you pass Array.Find an int array and a predicate that takes an int and returns a bool, it can tell that you are calling Array.Find<int>. You can code Array.Find(IntArray, IntPredicate), and you don't **have to** code Array.Find<int>(IntArray, IntPredicate).

Miscellaneous

Two methods you'll probably find useful

The static method Array.Reverse does just what it sounds like—swaps the first and last elements, the second and penultimate elements, and so on. Like the Sort methods, it changes an existing array in place (and so affects all other references to the same array). It does not create or return a new array, nor does it take a reference parameter in order to point a variable to a new array.

In 2.0, the static method Array.ConvertAll<Old, New> takes an array of type Old, a delegate that converts an Old to a New, and returns a new array of type New.

Lists

A familiar design, with some new features

Arrays are great, if they never need to change size, or if they only change size very rarely. However, when you need to add items to a collection one by one, and won't know how big your collection is until you're done, continuously resizing an array is an expensive operation. Typically, you would use an array with an auxiliary Count variable—the array length is the current Capacity, while the Count is the number of array elements that actually hold real data. You only have to resize when you want to add an element and the Count already equals the Capacity.

In Delphi, a TList implements this strategy. However, because the D7 TList holds pointers, you have to use blind casts to store integers or class instances in a TList. While you can use wrapper code to minimize the chance that you will miscast a pointer in a list, you do have to write that wrapper code, and you can never totally eliminate the risk that you will miscast a list element. Similarly, you can't store records or doubles or other data that takes more than 32-bits without doing heap allocations and running the risk of failing to free the memory when you're done.

Because a .NET object can hold **any** value and a miscast always raises an exception, the .NET equivalent of a TList—the ArrayList class in the System.Collections namespace—doesn't have any of these problems. You can add any type of data and never misuse it, nor do you have to worry about memory leaks.

However, when you want a homogeneous list of all integers (or all strings, or whatever), you still need to write the strongly typed wrapper code. What's more, even when you have a typed collection that can only hold one type of data, you still have to cast each object in the underlying ArrayList back to the right type before you can use it. This is not particularly expensive, but it's never free—and boxing and unboxing value types does consume memory and thus makes the next garbage collection happen sooner.

Accordingly, in 2.0, the generic List<T> (in the System.Collections.Generic namespace) allows you to create lists of a particular type. This gives you strong typing without having to write wrapper classes by hand, and eliminates the performance hit of casting each item back to the right type before you can use it.

Late-bound Lists

An ArrayList is like an Array that you can Add to

The ArrayList class (in the System.Collections namespace) is a variable-sized list of object values—basically an array with an extra count of the slots actually used. The read-only Count property is the number of items in the list. The Capacity property is the size of the underlying array, the number of items the list can hold before it needs to be resized. The ArrayList class has three constructors: the no-parameter constructor gives you a new ArrayList that doesn't actually refer to a private object array yet; the int constructor creates a private array with a specified Capacity; the ICollection constructor (see this chapter's "Other Collection Interfaces" subsection) copies the collection to the private array, setting Capacity equal to the Count of items in the collection. (The static method ArrayList.Repeat(object, int) is something like the string(char, int) constructor in that it returns a new ArrayList, containing an arbitrary number of copies of its object parameter.)

The most common way to add items to an ArrayList is the Add method, which appends to the end of the list. There is also an AddRange method, which appends each item in an ICollection. Note that all arrays implement ICollection, as does ArrayList itself. You can thus create an ArrayList from an array or another ArrayList. You can also append any array (or ArrayList) to an ArrayList.

The Insert and InsertRange methods insert values at a specific location. Naturally, insertion is more expensive than appending, as it has to shift values to the right.

The Remove method removes items by value, using Object.Equals to test for equality, while the RemoveAt and RemoveRange methods remove items by location. The Clear method deletes all items in the list (sets Count to 0) and the TrimToSize method resizes the internal array, so that Capacity matches Count.[4]

The Item property allows you to read (and, usually, write) items by index. The Item property is the this property (the default array property, in Delphi), which means you can use array syntax to read and write individual items of an ArrayList, as in the following extract from the Chapter12\ArrayLists Delphi project:

```
const
  SevenEleven: array[7..11] of integer = (7, 8, 9, 10, 11);
var
  List: ArrayList;
begin
  List := ArrayList.Create(SevenEleven);
  List[0] := TObject( integer(List[0]) + 1 );
```

Note how this code has to cast read items from object before it can use them, and has to box integers (a value type) before it can write them.[5]

An ArrayList manages a private array so we can grow lists efficiently. It also replicates large chunks of the Array API, with methods like IndexOf, LastIndexOf, Sort, and Reverse that simply call the Array static method on the private object array. The ArrayList does not track its sorted state any more than a simple Array does—an ArrayList doesn't throw an exception when you try to BinarySearch an unsorted list, any more than a raw Array does. (I actually find this somewhat surprising, having grown used to prodigious feats of thoughtfulness and good design all through .NET.)

Further replicating the Array API, an ArrayList has CopyTo methods, which copy the list contents to an existing array. In addition, an ArrayList has ToArray methods, which create new, fixed-size arrays with copies of the list's data. The ToArray() overload creates an object array; the ToArray(Type) overload creates a typed array, casting each element in the list to the specified Type and copying the result to the new, typed array. Note that the typed overload does return a typed array, but that the method returns an Array (the only type compatible with **all** arrays) so you have to cast the result to the right type:

---

4. When Count equals 0, TrimToSize resets Capacity to the default value, not to 0.
5. The Delphi {$AUTOBOX ON} pragma would let you write List[0] := integer(List[0]) + 1 instead of List[0] := TObject(integer(List[0]) + 1), but there would still be a boxing operation involved.

```
ArrayList List = new ArrayList(new object[] { 1, 2, 3 });
int[] IntArray = (int[]) List.ToArray(typeof(int));
```

Note also that the typed overload **does** cast each element of the list to the result type. This means that

```
ArrayList List = new ArrayList(new object[] { 1, "2", 3 });
int[] IntArray = (int[]) List.ToArray(typeof(int));
```

will compile, but it will raise an InvalidCastException when ToArray tries to cast the string "2" to an integer (see the Chapter12\ArrayLists C# project).

An ArrayList can be read-only. You create a read-only ArrayList with the ReadOnly static method, which has overloads that take either an IList (see the "Other Collection Interfaces" subsection, later in this chapter) or an ArrayList. A read-only ArrayList is not actually an instance of the ArrayList class; rather, it is an instance of the ReadOnlyArrayList class (which is an internal class, nested within the ArrayList class) that descends from the ArrayList class and overrides all its methods. A ReadOnlyArrayList does not copy the data in its IList or ArrayList; rather, it is a wrapper for the underlying collection, which delegates all read operations to the underlying collection and raises an exception on all write operations. That is, while you cannot change the collection via the read-only ArrayList, any changes to the underlying collection **will** be reflected in the read-only wrapper.

The SyncRoot property supports threaded operations: you lock[6] the SyncRoot for any statement(s) that need to be atomic. The point of the SyncRoot property is that an ArrayList may actually be just a wrapper around some other collection, and locking the wrapper doesn't lock the underlying collection. In a 'true' ArrayList, the SyncRoot property is a private object; in an ArrayList that wraps another collection, the SyncRoot property actually returns the SyncRoot of the underlying collection.

The Synchronized static method takes an ArrayList and returns an ArrayList wrapper that locks the SyncRoot around every operation. If all you need to do is lock the list while you Sort or while you add or subtract a single item, you should use the Synchronized wrapper. If you need to do multiple operations atomically (like doing something only if the Count is greater than 0), you should lock the SyncRoot. (Chapter 17 has a more thorough discussion of lock targets.)

Early-bound Lists

Type safe without wrappers, and with no need for boxing value types

The generic equivalent of the ArrayList class is the List<T>, in the System.Collections.Generic namespace. This is, basically, an ArrayList that stores the open type T instead of the object type. Thus, the Add method takes a T, not an object; the Item property acts like an array of T instead of an array of object; and the 'bare' ToArray() method call returns an array of T, not a comparatively untyped Array. In addition, the List<T> class also supports all the predicate methods that arrays support in 2.0—Exists, TrueForAll, &c.

Basically, almost everything you can do with an ArrayList you can do with a List<T>, and you don't need to write wrapper classes when you want a list of integers, or a list of strings, or

---

6. Delphi doesn't have a lock statement, even in Delphi 2006. As per Chapter 6, use (System.Threading) Monitor.Enter, a try/finally statement, and Monitor.Exit. Or switch to C#.

a list of some custom type. In this sense, the early-bound List<T> obsoletes the late-bound ArrayList, and VS 2005 adds System.Collections.Generic to a class file's default list of using directives to encourage you to use the new generic collections instead of the original late-bound collections.

In addition to not having to write wrapper classes, you don't have to cast each Item to the appropriate type—the Item property acts like an array of T. This saves some modest amount of CPU time with reference types—no more run-time checking that you are casting each item to the right type—but it really shines with value types. You don't have to box value types to store them in a List<T>, and you don't have to unbox them when you read them from a List<T>. This means that writing and reading a List<int> in the Chapter12\Collections C# project (the "Typed list" benchmark) is about twice as fast as writing and reading the same integers to and from an ArrayList (the "Untyped list" benchmark). Almost all of the speed difference comes from the boxing and unboxing that the ArrayList needs, as you can see from the "Boxed list" benchmark, which writes and reads integers to and from a List<object> and which runs at almost the same speed as the "Untyped list" benchmark.

■**Note** The List<T> class doesn't have a SyncRoot property. It does, however, support ICollection (discussed later), which **does** have a SyncRoot property. Thus, you can cast your List<T> instance to an ICollection reference—ICollection ThisCollection = (ICollection) ThisList—and then lock the SyncRoot on the interface—lock (ThisCollection.SyncRoot) {}.

Hash Tables

Arrays indexed by value

Hash tables, like regexs, may be more novel to Delphi programmers than to most other programmers: the VCL has no hash tables, though the C++ STL does, as do languages like Perl, Python, and Ruby. In general, a hash table is a mapping of *keys* to *values*. The syntax is usually modeled on arrays, so you can say Hash[Key] := Value or Value := Hash[Key]. (As in this example, people with a Perl background will often refer to a hash table as simply *a hash*.) The difference between a hash table and an array is that arrays are indexed by numbers[7] that map directly to positions in a sequential stream of locations, while hash tables are indexed by the value of the key. Some hash table implementations can only use strings as keys; the FCL implementation can use any reference or value type as a key or as a value.

When you store a value in a hash table, a *hash function* reduces the key to an integer, the *hashed key.* The hashed key, modulo the number of buckets, specifies a *bucket.* A bucket contains zero or more key/value pairs. The store operation looks in the bucket for a pair with a (cached) hash value that equals the hashed key. If the hash values match, the store operation compares the actual keys. (Comparing integers is a fast way to avoid doing a slow operation like string comparison. A hash match doesn't mean equality, but a hash mismatch guarantees

---

7. Again, while Pascal does allows you to index by characters and enums, this is implemented via code that turns these indices into numbers.

inequality.) If the keys match, the store operation sets the key/value pair to the new value. If the keys don't match, the store operation goes back to scanning the bucket for a matching hash value. If the scan sails past the end of the bucket, the store operation simply adds a new key/value pair.

When you retrieve a value from a hash, the same hash function is used to reduce the key to an integer, which again determines which bucket to look in. If the appropriate bucket does not contain the key, the hash table has no value for the key.

Obviously, this is more expensive than array indexing. However, it is **much** cheaper than either doing a linear search through a long list of keys or maintaining a key/value list sorted in key order. Hash tables are comparatively expensive for small collections, but (assuming a good hash function, one that doesn't favor certain results over others, and that gives different results for similar keys) hash table cost goes up much slower than collection size.

Hash tables are useful for many common programming tasks. Obviously, they make good symbol tables in compilers, interpreters, and web browsers (you need a symbol table to interpret JavaScript, or CSS style sheets), as well as in any sort of program that maps strings to array indices, or that applies macros or templates. An object in a language like JavaScript, where you create a field simply by assigning a value to it, is basically just a hash table. Somewhat less obviously, hash tables can be used for sparse arrays and sets.[8] Also, a program that often generates the same string expression (perhaps extracting XML tags from various documents) can use a hash table to save memory by replacing the new string with the first copy—see the Chapter12\Canonic C# project.

Late-bound Hashes

The HashTable class can associate any object key with an object value

The (System.Collections) HashTable class associates object keys with object values. This means you can write code like ThisHash[Math.PI] = "π", but it also means that any value you read is an object and has to be cast to the right type before it can be used—(string) ThisHash[Math.PI].

HashTable CONSTRUCTORS

Usually you will create a HashTable using the parameterless constructor that sets a default initial capacity. As with the ArrayList and StringBuilder classes, passing the constructor an initial capacity can avoid some resizing when you know something about the initial population. You can specify the initial capacity as an integer, or you can pass the constructor an IDictionary (such as another HashTable), which both prepopulates the HashTable and sets the initial capacity to the number of key/value pairs in the IDictionary.

There are also constructors that let you specify the *load factor*, which is a number between 0.1 and 1.0 (inclusive) that controls how full the buckets are allowed to get: a smaller number makes for faster lookup at the cost of greater memory consumption. You can only set this when you create the HashTable (there are no properties or methods to change the load factor), but you may never need to.

---

8. When using a Hashtable as a set, you'd usually just associate each key with a null value—you only care whether or not the set Contains(Key). The Chapter12\Sets C# project contains an implementation that uses the generic hash table, Dictionary.

By default, HashTable uses each key's implementation of System.Object.GetHashCode as the hash function and System.Object.Equals as the key comparer. The default implementations of these two functions mean that two different boxed values are equal, if the underlying values and types are equal (e.g., TObject(45) = TObject(3 * 3 * 5). The same is also true of strings: two distinct string objects are equal if they have the same length and same characters. However, with most other classes, two distinct class instances are **not** equal, even when they are of the same type and have identical internal states. As in Chapter 2, you need to override GetHashCode (*xor*-ing the hash of each field is a reasonably effective approach) and Equals to implement value equality for reference types.

Sometimes you want to compare keys using only part of their information. For example, you might want a case-insensitive comparison, or you might only care about the first five characters in a zip code or the first three significant digits of a number. At the same time, coding these features into the key's hash and comparison functions means that you are using this partial comparison every time you compare two different instances of the type. Accordingly, there are HashTable constructors that allow you to specify the hash function and key comparison, as in the Chapter12\Caseless1 project. In 1.1, you specified these independently, as an IHashCodeProvider and an IComparer; in 2.0, these two interfaces are deprecated, and you are urged to use the new IKeyComparer, instead.

Most of the time you'll just read and write the Hashtable through the Item property, which allows you to use array-like syntax to read and write values. Assigning a value to a new key adds the key and value to the hash; assigning a new value to an existing key overwrites the old value. Values can be null, but keys cannot be null. Reading an existing key returns the value, as an object; reading a key that does not exist returns null. (You can use the ContainsKey method, see the paragraph after next, to distinguish between an unset key and a null value.)

The read-only Count property tells you how many key/value pairs the hash contains; the Clear method deletes all keys and values. A Hashtable acts like an ICollection (discussed later) of DictionaryEntry structures: a DictionaryEntry contains a Key and a Value. Thus, the CopyTo method fills an array with DictionaryEntry structures, and the default enumerator returns a DictionaryEntry. That is, when you want both the keys and the values, you use the default enumerator like foreach (DictionaryEntry Entry in ThisHash) {}, while if you want only the keys or the values, you would enumerate the Keys or Values properties like foreach (object Key in ThisHash.Keys) {}.

The Add method adds a key and value pair to the hash if the key is new; however, unlike assigning to the Item property, the Add method will raise an exception if the hash already has a value stored under that key. The Remove method removes a single key/value pair, without raising an exception if the key does not exist. ContainsKey (and its IDictionary synonym, Contains) tests whether the hash already 'knows about' a key. Naturally, ContainsValue tests whether the hash contains a value; this is a much slower search than ContainsKey, as it has to test (potentially) every key/value pair, whereas ContainsKey can use the normal hashing mechanism.

The Hashtable class has essentially the same SyncRoot property and Synchronized method as the ArrayList class: use the Synchronized wrapper so multiple threads can write values without scrambling the internal state, but lock the SyncRoot when you need to do multiple operations atomically.

Early-bound Hashes

Strongly typed dictionaries avoid boxing and wrappers

The generic equivalent of the Hashtable class is the System.Collections.Generic namespace's Dictionary<K, V> class.[9] The Add method takes a K key and a V value instead of two object parameters, and the Item property acts like an array of V, indexed by K values. As with other generic collections, this allows you to create type-safe hashes just by declaring them, and spares the cost of boxing and unboxing value type keys and values.

Hashing does involve more overhead than simple array indexing and, as you can see from the Chapter12\Collections C# project, the speedup going from a Hashtable of integer values indexed by integer keys (the "Untyped int/int hashes" benchmark) to a Dictionary<int, int> (the "Typed int/int hashes" benchmark) isn't **quite** as dramatic as going from an ArrayList to a List<int>. Still, a 1.6× speedup is quite respectable, and the Dictionary largely obsoletes the Hashtable in the same way the List largely obsoletes the ArrayList. Internally, a Dictionary acts much like a Hashtable, and almost all of the speed difference comes from the boxing and unboxing that the Hashtable version does, as you can see from the "Boxed int/int" hashes benchmark, which runs at almost the same speed as the "Untyped int/int" hashes benchmark.

One key difference between the Hashtable and a Dictionary is that a Hashtable returns null when you read an unknown key—which can be ambiguous if you do sometimes store null values—while a Dictionary raises an exception when you read an unknown key. A more minor difference is that the default enumerator returns a KeyValuePair<K, V> instead of a DictionaryEntry: foreach (KeyValuePair<K, V> Entry in ThisDictionary) {}.

The Dictionary supports custom hashing and comparison functions, in much the same way as the Hashtable does, via the IComparer<K> open interface. See, for example, the Chapter12\Caseless2 C# project.

Note In general, the generic collections don't have a SyncRoot property, and when you don't know if you're locking a 'real list' or a list wrapper, you'll need to cast to ICollection as with the List<T>—that is, lock ((Hash as ICollection).SyncRoot) {} or the equivalent.

Stacks and Queues

Just so you know about them

The FCL System.Collections namespace includes Stack and Queue classes, which support stacks and queues of objects. These act much like the TStack and TQueue classes in the Borland Contnrs unit, except that the Queue class is substantially more efficient than the TQueue class.[10]

---

9. I have read that the 2.0 team chose Dictionary<,> over Hashtable<,> because they wanted to be free to use multiple implementations in the future, but that the only current implementation is a Hashtable. Using *Reflector*, Dictionary<,> and Hashtable appear quite similar, though not absolutely identical.

10. The Borland TQueue does an enqueue operation by insertion at position 0, shifting all queued items to the right.

As usual, the Stack and Queue classes store object values and can thus hold any value, but when you Pop the Stack or Dequeue the Queue you need to cast the result to the right type. System.Collections.Generic includes the type-safe Stack<T> and Queue<T> classes that eliminate the need for boxing and casting.

Both are implemented as 'growable arrays,' à la the ArrayList and StringBuilder classes. (That is, whenever an addition would overflow the list, they allocate a new, larger array and copy the existing array's contents into it.) Despite what the documentation says about the Stack class being "implemented as a circular buffer," it actually does a perfectly normal list[top++] to push, and a list[--top] to pop. The Queue class, though, **does** use a circular buffer: it maintains head and tail pointers into its list, and advances them modulo the list size (see Figure 12-1).

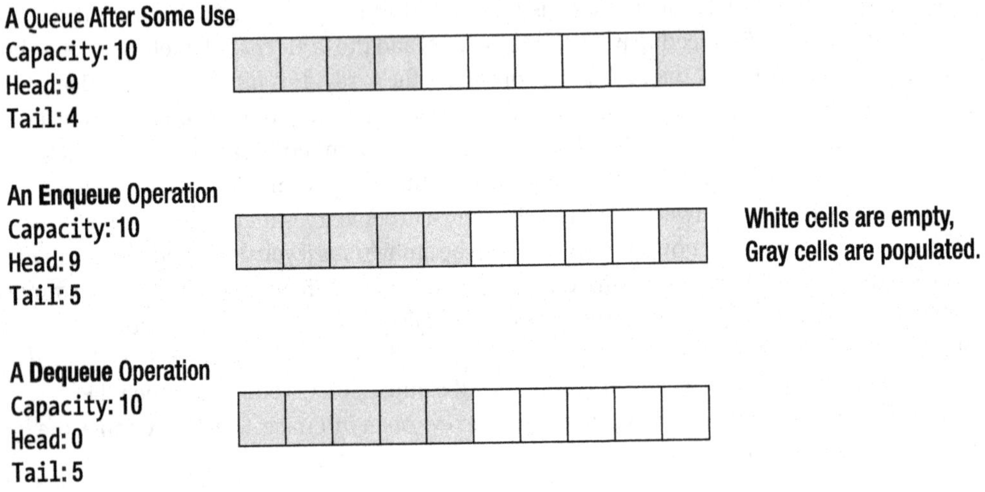

A Queue After Some Use
Capacity: 10
Head: 9
Tail: 4

An Enqueue Operation
Capacity: 10
Head: 9
Tail: 5

White cells are empty,
Gray cells are populated.

A Dequeue Operation
Capacity: 10
Head: 0
Tail: 5

Figure 12-1. *The Queue class's circular buffer*

Enumerations

Implementing and manipulating enumerators, before and after iterators

All .NET collections support enumeration: you can do a C# foreach or Delphi for in on all the types I've covered in this chapter, from Array through Queue<T>,[11] and process the elements one by one. As many programming tasks do involve looping over various collections, the ubiquity of IEnumerable (and the interfaces that descend from it, like ICollection and IList) means that many .NET methods consist of little more than a series of foreach loops. It doesn't matter if these loops are nested inside each other, or strung one after another like beads, or both: cutting down on boilerplate not only makes code more readable, it also destroys the habitat in which the Careless Error flourishes best.

The previous chapters have included more examples of using IEnumerable than of classes that implement it. This section redresses that balance a bit, with a focus on implementing and

---

11. Well, obviously you can't do a Delphi for in on an open type like a Queue<T> because Delphi doesn't yet support generics. But it will, probably in the next release.

manipulating enumerators. C# 2.0 *iterators* make implementing an enumerator much easier, without adding significantly to the enumerator's run-time overhead. I cover enumerator implementation and manipulation both manually (without iterators) and automatically (with iterators) because Delphi doesn't (yet?) have iterators and because iterators are new to C# 1.0 programmers. (Chapter 8 has the details on C# 2.0's iterator syntax.)

Fundamentals

Details on the interaction between IEnumerable, IEnumerator, and IDisposable

To recap Chapter 2, compilers special case some enumerations, but in general foreach and for in call a GetEnumerator method, which returns a (reference or value) object that supports both a Current property and a MoveNext method.[12] MoveNext is a method that takes no parameters and returns a boolean. A foreach wraps a while loop around the MoveNext: while the MoveNext returns true, the foreach loop assigns the Current value to the iteration variable and executes the loop statement(s).

The IEnumerator.Current property is an object, so unless you're doing foreach (object O in SomeCollection) {}, each iteration of the foreach loop includes a cast (which may be an unboxing operation) from object to the type of the iteration variable. In 2.0, the open IEnumerator<T> (that replaces the closed IEnumerator that it inherits from) has a Current property of type T, so the loop does not require a cast operation.

■**Note** When you enumerate an array, the compilers do **not** use the array's IEnumerable interface. Instead, they effectively generate a for loop that steps through the array, using standard array indexing, in the same order as the array's enumerator. This avoids the cost of calling GetEnumerator and running a while (MoveNext) loop, and (in 1.*x*) this avoids the cost of casting the enumerator's Current property to the array's element type on each pass through the loop.

IEnumerator also includes a Reset method, but foreach and for in loops never call Reset— GetEnumerator should always return an object in the reset state, usually by creating a new object that supports IEnumerator. (In 2.0, iterators' implementations of the IEnumerator<T> interface's Reset method throw a NotSupportedException.)

If GetEnumerator returns an object that also supports IDisposable, both foreach and for in will call Dispose at the end of the loop. (You can think of this as automatically wrapping the

---

12. Normally, you pass foreach an object that implements IEnumerable (which consists only of the GetEnumerator method) but, when C# code is calling C# code, it suffices for the object to have a visible GetEnumerator method, even if the object doesn't explicitly implement IEnumerable. Similarly, GetEnumerator normally returns an object that implements IEnumerator, but when C# code is calling C# code, it suffices for the object to support the Current property and the MoveNext method. Delphi 2006 has similar rules for Delphi code calling Delphi code: you can enumerate a Delphi object that doesn't implement IEnumerable but does have a visible GetEnumerator method, and it is OK if GetEnumerator returns an object that supports the Current property and the MoveNext method without explicitly implementing IEnumerator—but the iteration variable has to be a TObject.

while loop in a using statement.) This gives you an opportunity to close any handles, or to return an IEnumerator to an enumerator pool.[13]

Always remember that the IDisposable implementation that matters is on the enumerator object, not the enumerable object—the object that GetEnumerator() returns, not the object that supports GetEnumerator. An IEnumerable or IEnumerable<T> that also implements IDisposable is **not** automatically disposed of: for example,

```
foreach (int I in new Enumerable()) ;
```

will not call Enumerable.Dispose even if the Enumerable class supports IDisposable.

■**C# Note** The IEnumerator object that the C# 2.0 compiler builds to implement an iterator does support IDispose. Additionally, all code in an iterator's execution path gets executed. Code between the last yield return (if any) and a yield break (or the end of the method) will be executed once, after the last enumerated item (see the Chapter12\Disposable C# project).

As always (and Chapter 3), the Dispose pattern is primarily for interfacing to legacy code that needs to avoid resource leaks by explicitly releasing things like OS handles (file, window, GDI, &c) when done, and secondarily for providing a sort of OnDone event. The garbage collector reclaims memory faster than manually freeing memory, and there's no point in writing a Dispose method to clear lists or null out various fields.

Threading

Thread safety and reusing an enumerable

It's usually a mistake to implement both IEnumerable and IEnumerator on the same object.[14] The Chapter12\Wrong C# project makes this mistake:

```
class Wrong : IEnumerable, IEnumerator
{
  public IEnumerator GetEnumerator()
  {
    return this;
  }
```

---

13. If you have an enumerator that's expensive to construct, perhaps because it has to connect to a server, you might want to maintain an enumerator pool (as in the Chapter12\Pooling C# project) so that you can Reset() the enumerator instead of re-creating it.

14. As a special case, it is OK to implement IEnumerable and IEnumerator on a private object that can only be obtained through a thread-safe static method, if that static method can guarantee it will never reissue an instance that is still being enumerated. See, for example, the Chapter12\Pooling C# project.

```
  private int[] Data = new int[] { 1, 2, 3, 4, 5 };
  private int Pointer = -1;
  public object Current
  {
    get { return Data[Pointer]; }
  }
  public bool MoveNext()
  {
    return ++Pointer < Data.Length;
  }
  public void Reset()
  {
    Pointer = -1;
  }
}
```

There are two problems with this code, and neither may be immediately obvious. In fact, `foreach (int Item in new Wrong())` will even work as expected. What **won't** work, though, is

```
Wrong W = new Wrong();
foreach (int Item in W)
  Console.Write(Item);
foreach (int Item in W)
  Console.Write(Item);
```

The preceding code will write 12345, not the 1234512345 that you might have expected. Neither foreach loop calls Reset, so the second foreach loop's while (MoveNext()) never executes the loop body.

If you ran into this problem implementing a class that may be enumerated again and again, like an ArrayList or a Dictionary<>, you might simply change your IEnumerable. GetEnumerator implementation to public IEnumerator GetEnumerator() { Reset(); return this; }. However, while resetting this before returning it does mean that you can enumerate the collection more than once, it doesn't do anything for the second problem—an enumerable that's also an enumerator will get horribly jumbled if one thread calls GetEnumerator while another thread is still enumerating the collection.

GetEnumerator should almost always return a new object. As per Chapter 2, this is often a private, nested class that contains just a reference to the object that actually contains the data, and a pointer into the dataset for MoveNext to advance and for Current to read.

C# Note You don't have to worry about this when you use iterators—the compiler will automatically generate a thread-safe implementation of IEnumerator. Every call to your iterator method executes all the code before, between, and after every yield return, in the thread that is doing the enumeration.

Multiple Enumerators

Collections should implement IEnumerable and may add IEnumerable members

All the FCL collection classes in this chapter can be directly enumerated. That is, you can write a foreach (int I in IntList) just like you can write IntList[Index] or IntList.Add(Value). This means that they implement GetEnumerator by creating a tiny object that pairs a reference to the collection with an index into the collection.

I hesitate to say "all" collections should implement GetEnumerator directly, but I can't imagine why one wouldn't. A collection should only have properties or methods that return an IEnumerable when it needs secondary ways of enumerating itself. For example, the Hashtable and the Dictionary<,> have a primary enumerator that supplies key/value pairs, along with secondary enumerators that supply only Keys or only Values.

In a Hashtable or Dictionary<,>, all three enumerators show different aspects of the same data. You can, of course, create synthetic, or manufactured, enumerations as in the Chapter12\Sorted C# project, which adds a Sorted() method to a List<> descendant:

```
public IEnumerable<T> Sorted(Comparison<T> comparison)
{
    List<T> Copy = new List<T>(this);
    if (comparison == null)
        Copy.Sort();
    else
        Copy.Sort(comparison);
    return Copy;
}
```

Perfectly straightforward code that takes a snapshot by adding each enumeration element to a new list; sorts the snapshot; and returns the snapshot as an IEnumerable<T>. But notice how Sorted only uses this as an IEnumerable<T>: this Sorted method doesn't know anything about its host that's not true of every class in this chapter, which makes it a good candidate for a library class.

The Chapter12\Shemitz.Collections C# project shows an Operator class that can sort, reverse, or shorten IEnumerable<T> enumerations. For example, you use this Sorted method by saying foreach (T Item in Operator.Sorted(Data)) instead of foreach (T Item in Data):

```
public static IEnumerable<T> Sorted<T>(IEnumerable<T> Collection,
  Comparison<T> Comparison)
{
  List<T> Result;
  lock (Collection)
    Result = new List<T>(Collection);
  Result.Sort(Comparison);
  return Result;
}
```

Using this class, or one like it, keeps your code smaller and reduces your exposure to careless errors. Note that both these Sorted operators work by copying the enumeration to a list—

or taking a *snapshot*. Snapshots work, but can go stale and can lead to lots of swapping as datasets pressure or overfill memory.

By contrast, a foreach loop that doesn't make any sort of snapshot doesn't consume much memory. Even in 1.*x*, the IEnumerable abstraction is simple, and easy to add to just about any sort of data provider. It's even easier in 2.0 with iterators, but it's hardly difficult without iterators. Enumerating a large dataset is GC friendly even when the whole dataset will easily fit in memory, and is absolutely essential when the dataset strains or exceeds available memory.

Delegates

Flexible processing of each element in an enumeration

Most foreach loops will use hard-coded logic. However, as always, delegates add flexibility and can save space.

For example, sometimes you need to apply the same logic to several different input streams. You can write a series of foreach loops that passes each element of each stream to the same method, or you can make a series of calls to a method that takes an enumeration parameter and a predicate parameter. Each method call takes a lot less CIL than each foreach loop.

For another example, sometimes you need to process an enumeration either *this* way or *that* way (or, perhaps, some other way). You can write a conditional statement that chooses between different foreach loops, or you can write a conditional statement that sets a delegate, and then apply the delegate to the enumeration. Using a delegate again takes less CIL than multiple foreach loops, and gives you the chance to select a delegate from a collection of installable code.

The Chapter12\Shemitz.Collections C# project sketches these techniques. The Shemitz.Collections.Generic namespace contains generic classes that apply delegates to enumerations in a number of ways:

- Apply.Apply passes each item to a void Action<T> delegate, and returns nothing.

- Apply.Find returns the first item in the enumeration that satisfies a bool Predicate<T> delegate. (Apply.Find returns default(T) on failure, which means it's mostly useful with collections of reference types.)

- Apply.FindAll returns a new enumeration, containing every item that satisfies the Predicate. This new enumeration is a sort of wrapper: the wrapper's MoveNext method always calls the wrapped MoveNext method until the wrapped MoveNext returns false or until the wrapped Current item satisfies the wrapper's Predicate.

- Apply.ConvertAll calls a Converter<In,Out> delegate on each element of the input enumeration, returning a new enumeration of the Converter output type.[15]

---

15. The Converter<InType, OutType> delegate seems backward to me; a prototype modeled on assignment, like Mapper<OutType, InType>, can be read as OutType = Intype. Apply.Map is just like Apply.ConvertAll, except that it takes a Mapper<> delegate, not a Converter<> delegate.

> ■**Note** I leave writing CLS-compliant (CLR 1.*x*–compatible) versions of these methods as an exercise for the reader.

Iterators

Performance is nearly identical to manual enumerators

As you've seen, it's not very hard to implement IEnumerable for simple enumerations. Iterators are clearly **much** simpler for recursive or other complex enumerations, but should you reserve iterators for complex enumerations that aren't easy to implement as two methods and a property? One final thing the Chapter12\Shemitz.Collections C# project shows is that iterators perform about as well as manual enumerators. The benchmarks vary a bit from run to run, but the performance difference between manual enumerators and automatic iterators is always around 5% to 15%. Not nothing, but not all that much, either—and sometimes the iterators are actually faster than the manual enumerator.

> ■**Tip** Use iterators freely in C# 2.0 and above. The same will probably be true in Delphi, if Delphi gains iterator support.

Other Collection Interfaces

Who offers what, and where it matters

There are five collection interfaces worth paying attention to: IEnumerable, ICollection, IList, IDictionary, and (in 2.0) IEnumerable<T>. There are also the open interfaces ICollection<T>, IList<T>, and IDictionary<K, V>, but these are not used quite as heavily as their closed counterparts.

This section has covered IEnumerable and IEnumerable<T> fairly thoroughly. The two are ubiquitous in FCL code: you will always **use** enumerators, and you will often **implement** them. There are two major differences between IEnumerable<T> and IEnumerable: first, the open interface is faster, because a foreach loop on a IEnumerable<T> doesn't have to cast each item, which is especially nice when that cast involves an unboxing operation. Second, while the 1.0 list classes can be initialized with an ICollection, the 2.0 lists can be initialized with an IEnumerable<T>.

This matters, because an ICollection has a (read-only) Count property, unlike both IEnumerable and IEnumerable<T>. When you, say, populate an ArrayList from an ICollection, the ArrayList reads the collection's Count so it can set the new list's Capacity and do a single allocation, and then calls the collection's CopyTo method to populate the new array. Sometimes, though, the Count property is **very** expensive to calculate, and so in 2.0 List<T> can populate itself by adding to the list in a foreach enumeration of the IEnumerable<T>.

This means that occasionally the list has to reallocate its internal array and recopy existing items—but there aren't all **that** many overflows, since each overflow doubles Capacity. An occasional reallocation seems like a low price to pay for being able to populate a list without having to run an expensive enumeration twice (once to get the Count and once to populate the internal array). It also means that you don't need to supply an implementation of the other three ICollection members—CopyTo, SynchRoot, and IsSynchronized—just to be able to copy your enumeration to a list.

This last point is somewhat less than it may seem, because you can easily use a wrapper class (as in the Chapter12\ICollection Delphi project) to convert an IEnumerable to an ICollection. In fact, you are much less likely to implement an IEnumerable or IEnumerable<T> descendant like ICollection<T> or IList than you are to implement an IEnumerable or IEnumerable<T>. You'll almost always use an existing implementation when you need an IEnumerable descendant, and it's less important to learn what a collection interface does than it is to know who offers it.

When you call a method that takes an IList parameter, you'll almost always pass it an array, an ArrayList, or a List<T>. Similarly, when you call a method that takes an IDictionary parameter, you'll almost always pass it a Hashtable or a Dictionary<K, V>. Table 12-1 summarizes the key facts about the collection interfaces.

Table 12-1. *The Five Main Collection Interfaces*

Interface	Implemented By	Notes
IEnumerable	Array, ArrayList, List<T>, Hashtable, Dictionary<K, V>, Stack, Queue, &c	Every FCL collection class supports IEnumerable, and can be enumerated. foreach loops never call the Reset method, so you can generally just raise a NotImplementedException.
ICollection	Array and all of the collection classes discussed in this chapter	Has a Count and can CopyTo an flat array.
IList	Array, ArrayList, List<T>	An ICollection with random access, insertion, and deletion for integral indices.
IDictionary	Hashtable, Dictionary<K, V>	Like an IList with object indices. Can enumerate keys, values, and key/value pairs.
IEnumerable<T>	List<T>, Dictionary<K, V>, Stack<T>, Queue<T>, &c	Every FCL open collection class supports IEnumerable<T>. C#'s yield return iterators return IEnumerable<T>.

The FCL documentation generally obscures interface inheritance, although the 2.0 documentation does do a somewhat better job than the 1.x documentation. For example, while the root "ICollection interface" page shows that ICollection descends from IEnumerable, the "ICollection Members" and "ICollection Methods" pages for the ICollection interface don't include GetEnumerator and they don't mention IEnumerable. This is strange, because class pages do list inherited members. You're almost certain to lose some time doing something like looking all over the hierarchy for an IEnumerable but not remembering that the IList some class supports is an IEnumerable because it is an ICollection, which is an IEnumerable.

Key Points

The FCL includes flexible and capable collection classes that should look rather familiar

- Fixed-length .NET arrays support methods like Sort, Reverse, and CopyTo.

- An ArrayList can hold any data type (although that may involve boxing) and appending is reasonably cheap. Many methods build a list using an ArrayList, then use ToArray to build a fixed-length array.

- The open collection class List<T> is virtually identical to the ArrayList, except that it's type safe, and faster.

- A Hashtable is a flexible data structure that can associate any key with any value, in a reasonably efficient way. The open Dictionary<K,V> is virtually identical to the Hashtable, except that it's type safe, and faster.

- The FCL Stack and Queue classes are a bit faster than their D7 TStack and TQueue equivalents.

- Enumerations are everywhere in .NET code. Using enumerations can save programmer time, object code size, and memory usage.

Reflection

Type information is not discarded in the jitter. At run time, every type and every value is described by a Type *value, which is an instance of the* System.Type *class. There are several different ways to get* Type *values—including "building" them at run time by "emitting" IL code—and you can do a lot with each* Type *value. You can find the ancestry of the described type. You can create an instance of the described type. You can find members of the described type by name, and you can enumerate the members of the described type. You can read, write, and call the members of an instance of the described type. And you can compare* Type *values, to see whether two values are of the exact same type, or if they are assignment compatible.*

This chapter is shorter than you might expect. Reflection has a reputation for being hard to understand—but the truth is that Reflection involves a real minimum of core concepts, a lot of predictability, and plenty of online examples. Once you understand what a Type value is, and all the ways to get and use Type values, you should be able to find the answers to your questions in the help files. And, of course, you can always Google for anything that you can't find in your favorite IDE.

This chapter consists of four sections on basic concepts and standard operations, followed by a lengthy introduction to Reflection.Emit. The first section, "Run-time Type Information," introduces .NET run-time Type information, while the second, "Type Values," covers the most straightforward ways to get Type values. The bulk of the chapter is the third section, "Type Details," which has subsections that enumerate the main things you can do with a Type value. The fourth section, "Assemblies," covers the uses of the System.Reflection.Assembly class: enumerating loaded assemblies; loading assemblies at run time; and getting type information from those assemblies. Finally, the "Emit" section outlines how you can turn streams of CIL instructions into an assembly like any other, and walks through a Delphi example of run-time code generation.

Run-time Type Information

Type values give your code access to metadata

The first chapters of this book talk about how the .NET loader uses *metadata* to lay out method tables at load time, and how the run time uses metadata for type safety and garbage collection. Metadata is also what lets our applications use assemblies that they load at run time. The literal meaning of metadata is data about data. Metadata is represented at run time as a set of instances of the System.Type class, most of which refer to several other Type instances. Each of these Type values describes a CLR type, and every instance of a type points to the same Type value. It's called *Reflection* when your application uses this run time Type representation, because your program is looking at itself (as in a mirror), discovering and accessing resources.

You can use Reflection for the sort of things you might have already done in Delphi with Run Time Type Information (RTTI). For example, you can read a schema, perhaps from a DB or the network, and build a UI with a widget set specified in the schema. Using the classes in the System.Reflection namespace, you can install event handlers on the widgets that you create—even though you didn't know about them at compile time—and you can read and write the properties and fields of these schema-driven widgets.

Metadata is much more extensive than Delphi's RTTI. Delphi's RTTI was grafted onto an existing system in order to support form streaming, so there are large chunks of Delphi that don't use RTTI at all. By stark contrast, on .NET, both type safety and garbage collection absolutely rely on having metadata on each and every type in the system. Hence, Delphi's RTTI is elective, and not the default—while .NET maintains metadata on all data in the system, not just the self-published parts of it.

Since all assemblies include metadata, and all assemblies use the same metadata format, applications can reflect on **all** their code and data. The public face of all the FCL (run-time) classes they use. Every single application class. And the public face of each and every third-party assembly they use.

You can get a System.Type value for every datum in the system, and you can use that to find every property, field, or method. Outside an object's assembly, you can see and touch the public details. Inside an object's assembly, or with special permissions, you can see and touch **all** the details.[1] In or out, you can read and write both properties and fields. (This is great for streaming code, which can discover what it needs to persist.) You can find methods by name or by signature, or both. You can also call the methods that you find.

This chapter goes into less detail than the last two, both because you should be getting a feel for the FCL by now and because the Microsoft documentation is quite clear, once you have the core concepts down. As always, the Sync Contents button is quite useful.

Type **Values**

The run time creates a Type value for every type

A Type value is an instance of the System.Type class. It's an object-oriented representation of metadata. A Type instance has methods and properties that describe the type and that let you retrieve attributes, or find type members by name or prototype. When you find a type member, you get an instance of a MemberInfo descendant class. Given the right MemberInfo instances, you can read and write static properties and fields, and you can call static methods. Add a class instance, and you can read and write instance properties and fields, and you can call instance methods. I discuss MemberInfo in more detail in the next section, "Type Details." This section

---

1. Do note that, by default, code installed on a local drive has *full trust,* and **can** access private members of types in other assemblies. However, this is just the default, and you have no guarantee that your code will actually have permission to Reflect upon private members of types in other assemblies.

focuses on getting and comparing Type values, with some discussion of Type values as instances of the Type class.

Always remember that a Type value is a run-time description of a type, not the compile-time (or jit-time) type itself. You can't use a Type value to declare a variable of the described type. You can't use a Type value in an is test or a cast the way you can use a type name in an is test or a cast. [2] And you can't new a Type value the way you can new a type name, though you can find and call a constructor you like. (ConstructorInfo is one of the specialized MemberInfo descendants.)

The CLR acts like it creates a new Type value every time it jits code for a type it's not yet 'seen' in the current AppDomain.[3] Now, it doesn't really matter if this is the actual behavior, or if the CLR only actually creates a Type value when it's first needed: what's important here is that there are zero or one Type values for every type in your application, but there is never more than one Type value per type, no matter how many instances of the type you create.

I discuss several different ways to get a Type value in this chapter, starting in the next subsection. These values can be directly compared to each other: if the Type references are equal, the types are the same.

The typeof() Operator

Converts a metadata token to a Type reference

In both C# and Delphi, the most straightforward way to get a Type value is to use the typeof() operator:

```
Type TypeofNode = typeof(Node); // C#
var TypeofNode: System.Type = typeof(Node); // Delphi
```

The typeof() operator takes a compile-time type name and returns the run-time Type value that describes the type. You can use the typeof() operator on the name of any type (whether class, struct, enum, interface, or delegate), but you can **only** use the typeof() operator on the name of a type. You cannot use the typeof() operator to get the Type of a local variable, and you cannot use the typeof() operator on a type (or instance) member: that is, while you can say typeof(Foo.Bar) to get the Type of the Bar type in the Foo namespace, you **cannot** say typeof(Foo.Bar) to get the type of the Foo member, Bar.[4]

Because Type values are run-time singletons, the typeof() operator always returns the same Type value for the same compiler symbol. In particular, this is true whether you qualify the compiler symbol or not—in the Chapter13\QualifiedTypes C# project,

---

2. For that matter, typeof(AnyType) is Type is true for every type you can pass to the typeof() operator.
3. The AppDomain class represents an *application domain*. The CLR automatically creates a *default* AppDomain when it loads an application, and the application executes in this default AppDomain. Code cannot be unloaded from an AppDomain, but you **can** explicitly create an AppDomain; load and execute code in the new AppDomain; and unload the AppDomain when you are done. Communication between application domains is comparatively expensive, as it uses the *remoting* mechanisms I discuss in the next chapter.
4. Delphi 2006 offers a limited exception to this rule: you can use typeof() on any value, but this is just an alternative way of calling GetType. That is, it gives you the actual type of the value, which may be a descendant type of the declared type of the variable. Also, using typeof() on an **uninitialized** local variable has unpredictable results!

```
namespace QualifiedTypes
{
  class Program
  {
    static readonly Type ProgramType1 = typeof(Program);
    static readonly Type ProgramType2 = typeof(QualifiedTypes.Program);
  }
}
```

`ProgramType1 == ProgramType2` because both `Program` and `QualifiedTypes.Program` represent the same compile-time type.

Because you pass `typeof()` a compile-time symbol, not a string, you can only use the `typeof()` operator with types that you know at compile time—types in your output assembly, or in an assembly you reference at compile time. That is, you can write expressions like `typeof(ThisClass)` and `typeof(System.Text.StringBuilder)`, but you can't use `typeof()` on types declared in assemblies that you load manually, at run time (see the "Assemblies" section of this chapter).

While you pass `typeof()` a compile-time symbol, not a string, `typeof()` **is** a run-time operation that returns the `Type` singleton corresponding to the type, in somewhat the same way that a (checked) cast is a run-time operation that takes a compile-time symbol and generates a new value of the specified type (if it can). That is, each `typeof()` expression calls run-time library code that turns a 32-bit metadata token into a `Type` instance. For example, in C#, `typeof(Namespace.Program)` generates

```
ldtoken Namespace.Program
call    System.Type::GetTypeFromHandle(System.RuntimeTypeHandle)
```

which pushes the same 32-bit class token that the `castclass` and `isinst` instructions use, and then calls a static method of the `Type` class to return a `Type` instance.

■ **C# Note**   Because `typeof()` is a run-time operation, you can initialize a `readonly` member with a `typeof()` expression, but you cannot initialize a `const` member with a `typeof()` expression. You can code `readonly Type readonlyType = typeof(Type)`, but you **cannot** code `const Type constType = typeof(Type)`.

With generic types, you can take the `typeof()` open types as well as the `typeof()` constructed types. For example, as in the Chapter13\OpenTypes C# project,

```
Type OpenList = typeof(List<>);
Type ClosedList = typeof(List<int>);

Type OpenDictionary = typeof(Dictionary<,>); // note the comma
Type ClosedDictionary = typeof(Dictionary<Type, string>);
```

The ContainsGenericParameters property is true for an open type's Type value. As with an abstract class, you can't create instances of open types, but you **can** examine an open type's members. The Name (see "Type Details," later in this chapter) of a generic type is the name as in code, plus a backtick, `, and the number of parameters: e.g., List`1 and Dictionary`2. (This is an unambiguous name, because you can't overload the open class Example<A, B> with the open class Example<C, D>.)

GetType

A value's actual run-time type

Since the System.Object root class includes a Type GetType() method, you can call GetType() on any .NET value[5] to get the value's actual run-time Type. This might be the typeof() the value's declared type, or it might be the typeof() a descendant type.

For example, if you have a Base class and a Derived class that inherits from Base, and you have a Value of type Base that holds a Derived instance, Value.GetType() == typeof(Derived), just as in Delphi Value.ClassType = Derived.

▨ **Delphi Note** While the .NET method GetType acts like the Delphi method ClassType in terms of returning the actual type of a value, not the declared type, GetType returns a Type value while ClassType returns a meta-class value, an instance of a class that descends from TClass. While Type values can be used in many of the same ways as Delphi's metaclass values, they are not identical. See Chapters 2 and 10 for more details.

For what it's worth, the Type class is an abstract class, and run-time Type values are actually instances of the RuntimeType class. The RuntimeType class doesn't exist at compile time, so you can't get the typeof(RuntimeType), but when you call GetType on any Type value, you get the Type value for the RuntimeType class. (That is, there's no infinite recursion, because the Type of every Type value is the Type whose GetType returns itself.)

---

5. Do note that this works by looking at the class pointer in every heap block. Calling GetType on a value type boxes the value, and then calls GetType on the object that contains the boxed value.

Get Type by Name

You generally have to know which assembly the type is defined in

Occasionally you need to be able to take a string that holds a type name, and match it against the tables of loaded types to get a Type value. While it's obviously possible—compilers do it all the time—it's much more complicated than you might think. Fortunately, you really don't need to look up type names all that often, as there are usually alternate approaches that are superior in various ways.[6] This subsection is particularly short on details because you may never need to know about this.

The Type class supports GetType static overloads that take a type name and return the corresponding Type. Three rules summarize type lookup behavior:

1. Type names must be qualified. For example, Type.GetType("String") returns null, while Type.GetType("System.String") returns typeof(string).

2. Given a qualified name without any assembly information, Type.GetType will only return a Type for types in the current assembly or in mscorlib. Given the name of a type in any other assembly, Type.GetType will return null. For example, Type.GetType("System.Text.RegularExpressions.Regex") returns null.

3. To get the Type of a type in an assembly besides mscorlib or the current assembly, you need to pass Type.GetType a name that contains assembly information in the same comma-delimited format as Type.AssemblyQualifiedName. Alternatively, you can use any assembly information you have to find the type's Assembly, and then you can call Assembly.GetType directly.

Rule three could use a little elaboration. For types in library assemblies loaded from the same directory as the application assembly, you can just add a comma and an assembly name, and look up names like Namespace.Identifier,AssemblyName. For types in assemblies in the GAC (Global Assembly Cache), you need to add Version, Culture, and PublicKeyToken information. For example,

```
"System.Text.RegularExpressions.Regex, System, " +
"Version=2.0.3600.0, Culture=neutral, PublicKeyToken=b77a5c561934e089"
```

This string is parsed, and used to search the list of loaded assemblies. You can find a Type faster by searching the list of loaded assemblies manually, and not formatting information that will be immediately parsed back. Doing a manual search also allows you to use type-matching rules that are a bit less strict than the ones the run-time uses. For example, if you simply wanted the Type of the Regex class, and you don't care whether it's version 1.0, 1.1, 2.0, or whatever, you might use a method like

---

6. For example, deserializing an object graph requires turning a serialized type name into a run-time Type, and thence into a run-time instance that can be populated. However, the FCL serialization code (Chapter 14) is pretty good, and it's unlikely that you'll really need to do manual serialization. Similarly, you **might** design a plug-in interface that required plug-ins to export a PluginMain class, but you'll generally require plug-ins to implement a particular interface, because that's so much safer—no versioning issues, and no name collision issues. I believe, in fact, that the only time I've needed to look up types by name was in script compilation.

```
static Assembly GetAssembly(string Name)
{
    foreach (Assembly A in AppDomain.CurrentDomain.GetAssemblies())
        if (A.GetName().Name == Name)
            return A;
    // else
    return null;
}
```

in an expression like GetAssembly("System").GetType("System.Text.RegularExpressions.Regex") to get typeof(Regex). (The "Assemblies" section discusses the Assembly class, and Appendix 2 discusses assembly loading.)

Type **Details**

Member manipulation and type description

There are two main ways you will use a Type value. The first, finding and manipulating members and attributes, is probably the more common of the two. The second, using the type's meta-data to answer questions about the type as a whole, is a lot lower level and more specialized. I discuss *Member access* first, because it's an easier read that offers immediate gratification. The subsequent subsection on *Type metadata* tries to help you master the large API by grouping the most important properties and methods into functional groups, but speed readers will prob-ably still want to skip the "Type Metadata" subsection until they find they need to know things like whether this object value implements the right interface(s), or what type of data this particular Array instance holds.

Member Access

Access members by name and/or behavior

Member access centers on the MemberInfo class, although the MemberInfo class itself has few members, and most of the action is in the various specialized descendants. While the MemberInfo members I talk about here **are** key members, you will only rarely have to deal with members via MemberInfo references, because in most cases you will get references to specialized MemberInfo descendant classes, like ConstructorInfo, FieldInfo, PropertyInfo, MethodInfo, and Type itself.[7]

Every MemberInfo has a string property, Name, which contains a short, unqualified name like String or MemberInfo. (The FullName is a namespace qualified name, like System.String or System.Reflection.MemberInfo.) Each MemberInfo also has Type properties ReflectedType and DeclaringType, which correspond to the type that contains this member and the type where the member is defined. When DeclaringType does not equal ReflectedType, the member was

---

7. Yes, the Type class really is a specialized MemberInfo. This reflects the fact that a nested type is a member of its parent type, but it is a bit strange that the Type class is part of the System namespace, while the MemberInfo class is part of the System.Reflection namespace. That is, System.Type descends from System.Reflection.MemberInfo. Normally, one would expect classes in the derived namespace to inherit from classes in the base namespace.

inherited from the ancestral class, DeclaringType. As the existence of this Declaring/Reflected type pair may suggest, you will get a different MemberInfo when you look at an inherited member of typeof(DerivedClass) than when you look at the same member in typeof(BaseClass).

The MemberInfo method IsDefined will tell you whether or not the member has a particular custom attribute. The first parameter to IsDefined is the Type of the attribute that you are testing for, while the second parameter is a boolean that specifies whether you want to know about attributes inherited from ancestral types. For example,

```
typeof(string).IsDefined(typeof(NonSerializedAttribute), false)
```

will return false because the string class does not have the [NonSerialized] attribute. Similarly,

```
AnyValue.GetType().IsDefined(typeof(NonSerializedAttribute), true)
```

will return true if AnyValue is of a type (or descended from a type) marked [NonSerialized].

IsDefined is fine in the common case where you only care whether or not a member has a particular attribute. When an attribute has properties that you care about, the MemberInfo method GetCustomAttributes will return an array of attribute instances.[8] You can choose whether to get all attributes for this member (i.e., both inherited and 'local'), or whether to get only attributes defined in the actual ReflectedType. In addition, there's an overload that restricts the results to attributes that inherit from (are assignment compatible with) a particular attribute.

Finally, when you work with MemberInfo instances you will usually know what type of MemberInfo you have, because you got it from a Type method like Type.GetConstructor or Type.GetProperty that always returns specialized MemberInfo instances. When you need to pick through a relatively untyped array of MemberInfo instances, as when working with the Type.GetMember and Type.GetMembers methods, you can use code like is ConstructorInfo or is MethodInfo, or you can examine the MemberInfo.MemberType enum.

Overloads and Permissions

As is so often the case with FCL classes, the Type methods that return instances of MemberInfo types tend to be named and overloaded in very predictable ways. The MemberInfo overloads follow what I call the *Thing* model, which offers both GetThing methods that return a ThingInfo, and GetThings methods—note the trailing s—that return ThingInfo arrays.

The GetMember and GetMembers methods follow the *Thing* model, returning MemberInfo instances and MemberInfo arrays. You'll see this *Thing* model at work in all five of the next topics in this "Member Access" subsection, although the last topic (nested types) does do some violence to the model.

As a general rule, you will use the GetThings array-returning methods in code that needs to discover and stream object state, while you will use the GetThing methods that return a single ThingInfo in code that is looking for members with the right name (case matters!) or signature. You will usually not need to get an array of all members of a particular type and hunt through it; the Type API is generally rich enough to supply you with what you need.

---

8. As per Chapter 8, each call to GetCustomAttributes creates new instances of attribute objects. If there is some reason for your custom attributes to have custom methods, remember that changing the state of an attribute instance only affects that instance. The next call to GetCustomAttributes will return new instances, initialized from invariant metadata.

The *Thing* model is two-dimensional—not only are there GetThing and GetThings methods, but also both have overloads that take an explicit BindingFlags bitmap and overloads that use a default BindingFlags bitmap. The BindingFlags bitmap specifies whether to search static and/or instance members, public and/or private members, and so on.

The examples in the next four topics ("Constructors," "Methods," "Fields," and "Properties") use the overloads that supply a default BindingFlags bitmap, but keep in mind that specifying a BindingFlags bitmap gives you control over the sorts of members you find. For example, you can restrict your search to static members.[9] If you have the right permission, you can find private members by including BindingFlags.NonPublic.

The default BindingFlags exposes public instance and static members. With types defined in the current assembly and an explicit BindingFlags, you can get public and private members, while with the ReflectionPermission.TypeInformation security permission, you can get public and private members of every type in every loaded assembly. If you don't have TypeInformation privileges, the various Get methods will return null when you try to find a private member, as if the member doesn't exist.

That is, Reflection fails gracefully in a low-trust environment—it doesn't raise an exception. If your code will not work without Reflection access to private members of types in other assemblies, you should mark it with the System.Security.Permissions attribute, ReflectionPermission:

```
[assembly: ReflectionPermission(SecurityAction.RequestMinimum,
    TypeInformation = true, MemberAccess = true)]
```

The RequestMinimum means that loading the assembly in an environment where the requested reflection permissions are not available will throw an exception; your code will not load without the right permissions. TypeInformation lets you browse information about the private members of types in other assemblies, while MemberAccess lets you manipulate those members. That is, if you have TypeInformation permission but not MemberAccess permission, you can get MemberInfo values for private members, but you can't use those MemberInfo values to call private methods or to get and set the values of private fields and properties.

Constructors

One of the first things one needs to do with a Type value is to create instances of the type. For example, a system options dialog, where each subsystem can choose to register (at startup time) the typeof() of their UserControl descendants along with the appropriate catalog data. (A UserControl is much like a Delphi TFrame—see Chapter 15.) When/if the dialog is actually created, the dialog creates each page's UserControl the first time it comes to the front.[10]

---

9. One thing to note when you explicitly construct a BindingFlags bitmap is that if you don't include either BindingFlags.Instance or BindingFlags.Static, you will find no members. It's OK to include both.

10. See www.midnightbeach.com/jon/pubs/ModelsViewsAndFrames.html for some older examples of Delphi code that works with TClass values.

Note Chapter 2 introduced the `Activator` class and its `CreateInstance` method, which creates an instance of an object from its `Type`, optionally passing arguments to the constructor. `Activator.CreateInstance` is a wonderfully convenient method, and you will probably use it 99% of the times that you need to create an instance of a `Type`.

However, there **are** places where you shouldn't use `Activator.CreateInstance`. For example, a loop that creates thousands and thousands of instances of the same `Type`. Each `Activator.CreateInstance` call finds the right `ConstructorInfo` and *invokes* it. When you will be repeatedly creating the same sort of object, you want to find the right constructor before you enter the loop. If you are passing arguments, you want to only create an `object` array once. Then the per loop cost is only the comparatively cheap invocation, not the comparatively expensive lookup and setup.

Constructors follow the *Thing* model, with `Type.GetConstructors` returning an array that contains a `ConstructorInfo` for each of the type's constructors. You certainly **can** select from this `ConstructorInfo` array by calling `GetParameters` on each `ConstructorInfo` to get a `ParameterInfo` array, and then matching each `ParameterInfo.ParameterType` against the appropriate parameter type—and don't forget that the right test is whether the `ParameterType` is assignable from the parameter type, and not whether `ParameterType` is equal to the parameter type—but it's much easier to just use `Type.GetConstructor`, which takes an array of Type values, one per parameter, and returns a `ConstructorInfo` instance (or `null`) that matches the prototype information you pass.

There are several `GetConstructor` overloads (plus the `Type.TypeInitializer` property, which returns the static constructor), but the simplest overload, the one that takes an array of Type values, one per parameter—`ConstructorInfo GetConstructor(Type[])`—is the one you'll use the most. You might wonder about the lack of parameter names (if you didn't read Chapter 4), but the CIL in a compiled assembly knows nothing of parameter names: just the parameter's type and its position in the parameter list.

For example, as in the Chapter13\ConstructorInfo C# project, to get a constructor that takes a single string, you'd use

```
Type SimpleType = typeof(Simple);
ConstructorInfo OneString =
   SimpleType.GetConstructor(new Type[] { typeof(string) });
```

to get the constructor, and

```
Simple Explicit = (Simple) OneString.Invoke(new object[] { "Explicit" });
```

to actually invoke the constructor and create an object. To get the parameterless constructor, you'd use

```
ConstructorInfo NoParams = SimpleType.GetConstructor(Type.EmptyTypes);
```

and you'd invoke it as

```
Simple Default = (Simple) NoParams.Invoke(null);
```

I think this code speaks for itself, but there are a few subtleties here that are worth mentioning:

- To get a constructor (or method) with no parameters, you pass a Type array with 0 elements, **not** null. You can explicitly create this as new Type[] {} or new Type[0] (or TypeArray. Create() in Delphi, given type TypeArray = array of System.Type) but you should do as I do here, and use the Type.EmptyTypes static field. This is a bit more self-documenting and is even slightly faster, as the empty array is precreated.

- Conversely, to invoke a constructor (or method) with no parameters, you can pass an empty object array—but you'll usually just pass null. (Passing null/Nil instead of an empty array is what the FCL documentation means by "omitting" parameters when invoking.)

- Even in .NET 2.0, Type is a closed type, not a parameterized open type. ConstructorInfo. Invoke returns an object, not a more specialized type, and you will always have to cast the result to the type that you expect.

Also, a couple of more repetitive points. First, do remember that a typeof() call **is** an actual call: it does not generate a compile-time constant. A method can call typeof() to get the same Type value several times without any really noticeable performance hit, but using a Type local can only help performance—and will reduce the chances of careless maintenance breaking your code. Second, both the GetConstructor and the Invoke calls take array parameters—and neither array parameter is a params parameter. This means that you have to explicitly create the Type and object arrays. This has no impact on performance or object code size—it just makes your source code a bit bigger and a bit harder to read and write.

C# Note   The Chapter13\ReflectionWrappers C# project contains wrappers for ConstructorInfo and MethodInfo that use params array parameters to simplify lookup and invoke code.

Methods

Methods are represented by MethodInfo values, just as constructors are represented by ConstructorInfo values. Both MethodInfo and ConstructorInfo descend from MemberInfo by way of the MethodBase class, and so share the Invoke mechanism and lots of properties that reveal things like whether this is a static method or an instance method, a virtual method or an abstract method, and so on.

Methods, but not constructors, have a ReturnType property that specifies the method's result type. Note that procedures (methods that return void) have a ReturnType equal to typeof(void); the ReturnType will **not** equal null.

As with constructors, you can get all of a type's methods with Type.GetMethods, but you will usually use Type.GetMethod to get a specific MethodInfo. The simplest GetMethod overload takes the method's name, as in the Chapter13\MethodInfo C# project:

```
MethodInfo OneOverload = SimpleType.GetMethod("OneOverload");
```

This single-string overload will return null if there are no methods with the specified name, and it will return a MethodInfo if there is one and only one method with this name. This overload will raise an exception if there is more than one method with this name, and this overload pays no attention to the method's parameters.

Using Invoke is the only way to call a constructor or method via Reflection. Invoke is comparatively slow, as it must check parameter types, and may have to box value type results. There **are** faster ways to call dynamically loaded and dynamically created code: I discuss these in the "Emit" section, later in this chapter.

As with invoking a constructor, when you Invoke a method you will have to cast the object result to the actual result type; invoking a void method (a Pascal procedure) returns null. Besides this possibility of a null result, the only big difference between ConstructorInfo.Invoke and MethodInfo.Invoke is that invoking a MethodInfo requires an instance parameter before the parameters array; as you might imagine, you pass null to invoke a static method.

Since the Simple class's public void OneOverload() is an instance method, the Chapter13\MethodInfo C# project invokes MethodInfo OneOverload as

```
Simple SimpleInstance = new Simple();
OneOverload.Invoke(SimpleInstance, null); // instance method with no parameters
```

The GetMethod method has overloads that take prototype information, just as does the GetConstructor method. While there are complex overloads for special situations, you will almost always use the MethodInfo GetMethod(String, Type[]) overload that takes a method name and an array of parameter types. (As with parameterless constructors, use the standard empty Type array, Type.EmptyTypes, to locate parameterless methods.)

For example, in the Chapter13\MethodInfo project, SimpleType.GetMethod("TwoOverloads", Type.EmptyTypes) finds the public static void TwoOverloads() overload, while SimpleType.GetMethod("TwoOverloads", new Type[] {typeof(string)}) finds the public string TwoOverloads(string S) overload. To call the latter, and use the result, you'd write something like

```
string Result =
  (string) StringFn.Invoke(SimpleInstance, new object[] { "string value" });
```

Fields

As you should expect by now, there are Type.GetFields methods (which return FieldInfo arrays) and Type.GetField methods (which return FieldInfo instances); both have overloads with and without explicit BindingFlags parameters. FieldInfo GetField(string) returns a FieldInfo if it finds a matching public field and null if it doesn't.

The FieldInfo.GetValue method takes an object instance parameter and returns the current field value as an object, which usually has to be cast to the right type before use. The FieldInfo.SetValue method takes two object parameters—an instance and a value—and sets the instance or static field to the right value. (For static fields, the instance parameter is ignored, and can be null.)

There are several FieldInfo properties that reveal field visibility; when and if the field can be written; and the like. The FieldInfo.FieldType property returns the Type of the field—FieldType will never be null or typeof(void).

Properties

The PropertyInfo API is much like the other MemberInfo APIs, though a bit complicated by the need to support indexed properties. The Type.GetProperties method returns an array of PropertyInfo instances, and the Type.GetProperty method returns a PropertyInfo instance or null. The simplest GetProperty overload takes the property name and it works just fine for simple properties and nonoverloaded this properties—which are, after all, the majority of properties.

To get the this property, you have to remember that it's almost always 'really' named Item,[11] so that you can get a nonoverloaded this property with GetProperty("Item"). If the this property is overloaded, GetProperty("Item") will throw an AmbiguousMatchException and you'll need to use the GetProperty(string, Type[]) overload, which takes an array of the indexer types. For example, the Chapter13\Properties C# project gets the PropertyInfo for public string this[string Index] with GetProperty("Item", new Type[] { typeof(string) }).

You get and set property values with the 'same' GetValue and SetValue methods as field values, except that the PropertyInfo GetValue and SetValue methods have an extra object array parameter that holds indexer values: pass null for normal, nonindexed properties.

The PropertyInfo class has fewer metadata properties than most of the other MemberInfo classes. While it does have a PropertyType property, and CanRead and CanWrite properties, the PropertyInfo class does not have the visibility properties that the FieldInfo class does, nor does it have properties that reveal things like whether the property is virtual or static. Since all property access is via get and set methods, you access much of a property's metadata through its get and set methods, using GetSetMethod to get a MethodInfo for the set method and GetGetMethod to get a MethodInfo for the get method; you then access the metadata through the MethodInfo's Is methods. (While it may seem weird to get property info through the get and set methods, this does make the API simpler and more orthogonal—and it kept working, unchanged, when C# 2.0 let property get/set methods have different visibility, as in Chapter 7.)

Nested Types

Applying the *Thing* model to nested types, you might expect Type.GetType to return a nested type's TypeInfo object, and Type.GetTypes to return an array of TypeInfo objects. But nested types are a special case: types can exist outside of a type in way that fields and properties can not. So, even though a Type is a MemberInfo (so that Type.GetMember and Type.GetMembers can return Type instances), the Type class is more important than the other MemberInfo classes, and has a short name in the System namespace instead of a compound name in System.Reflection.

Also, as shown earlier, Type.GetType(string) looks up the type name in the current assembly and/or mscorlib. Accordingly, nested types bend the *Thing* model nearly to the breaking point, and you access nested types with the GetNestedType and GetNestedTypes methods, which return Type instances and Type arrays.

Every Type has a boolean IsNested property that reveals whether the type is nested or not. Nested types' DeclaringType property points to their enclosing type; DeclaringType is null in normal, nonnested types.

---

11. There are rare counterinstances: For example, the string class's indexed property is named Chars.

The CLR treats nested type names a bit differently than C# and Delphi do. Within

```
namespace NestedTypes
{
  class Outer
  {
    public class Inner { }
  }
}
```

you'd refer to typeof(Outer.Inner), or do a new Outer.Inner(). However, the CLR uses + to show nesting, and typeof(Outer.Inner).FullName is NestedTypes.Outer+Inner—**not** NestedTypes.Outer.Inner—and you need to say Type.GetType("NestedTypes.Outer+Inner") in order to get typeof(Outer.Inner).

Open Types

In 2.0, you can get the typeof() of an open type or a closed constructed type (just as you can get the typeof() a normal closed type such as you can create in 1.x), and the Type class has some new properties and methods to handle open types.

The Type.IsGenericType property tells you if a given Type is either an open type or a closed constructed type: for example, IsGenericType is false for typeof(int) but true for both typeof(List<>) and typeof(List<int>). The related Type.IsGenericTypeDefinition is true for open types like typeof(List<>) and false for closed constructed types like typeof(List<int>).

The Type method MakeGenericType is an instance method that takes a params array of Type parameters and returns the Type of a constructed type. Thus, as in the Chapter13\ MakeGenericType C# project:

```
typeof(List<>).MakeGenericType(typeof(int)) == typeof(List<int>)
```

The converse function, Type.GetGenericTypeDefinition, returns the Type of a constructed type's generic template:

```
typeof(List<int>).GetGenericTypeDefinition() == typeof(List<>)
```

Type **Metadata**

Several different types of information

The Type class has a lot of properties and methods that can reveal all sorts of interesting and useful things about the types in your application. Most are pretty straightforward: the biggest problem in using Type metadata is simply that it can be hard to find the members you need in the long alphabetical lists. I've picked out some of the most useful Type members, and grouped them functionally.

Names

The Type.Name property returns the type's name without the namespace. For example, if Type RegexType = typeof(System.Text.RegularExpressions.Regex), then RegexType.Name equals "Regex". The Type.Namespace property returns the type's namespace, without the name. For example, RegexType.Namespace equals "System.Text.RegularExpressions". And the Type.FullName property returns the qualified name—Namespace + "." + Name.[12] For example, RegexType.FullName equals "System.Text.RegularExpressions.Regex".

Nature

While the biggest problem in using the Type class **is** simply that it's a bit overwhelming, there also times when your questions are not answered directly, and you have to synthesize an answer from the available Type members. The type categorization members appear to reflect the underlying metadata, rather than trying to anticipate likely questions.

For example, you may need to know which of the five types of types[13] a particular Type value represents. Or you may need to check whether a parameter is the right type of Type. Some of these tests are easy: Type.IsClass, Type.IsEnum, and Type.IsInterface. But a structure is a value type that is neither a primitive (number, character, or boolean) nor an enum:

```
static bool IsStruct(Type T)
{
  return T.IsValueType && ! T.IsPrimitive && ! T.IsEnum;
}
```

Similarly, there is no direct way to tell if a type is a delegate, but you can check whether it is assignment compatible with System.Delegate, which is the base class for all delegates:

```
static bool IsDelegate(Type T)
{
  return typeof(System.Delegate).IsAssignableFrom(T);
}
```

You can also use Type.IsAssignableFrom (and the narrower Type.IsSubclassOf) to test ancestry at run time.[14] The documentation for Type.IsAssignableFrom can be confusing, but the method is actually pretty straightforward and looks somewhat like assignment. That is, the Type **instance** (on the left) is the type of a possible variable, while the Type **parameter** (on the right) is the type of a possible value. That is, if typeof(A).IsAssignableFrom(typeof(B)), you can assign a value of type B to a variable of type A. Similarly, if typeof(A).IsAssignableFrom(C.GetType()), you can assign the value C to a type A variable.

---

12. Or, more properly, Namespace + Type.Delimiter + Name.

13. Once again: classes, structures (i.e., a C# struct or a Delphi record), enums, interfaces, and delegates. See Chapter 2.

14. Remember that, as in Chapter 2, every Type is assignment compatible with every other Type. You can't declare a type that inherits from Type and is, say, only assignment compatible with the Type of a UserControl descendant.

I hope that these simple examples give the flavor of using the type categorization members. Table 13-1 provides a brief summary of the uses and/or peculiarities of some of the more useful—or confusing—type categorization members.

Table 13-1. *A Few Type Categorization Members*

Name	Notes
IsValueType	Not a reference type: simple, primitive values; enums; and custom value types (i.e., structures).
IsByRef	Passed by reference, which does **not** mean that this is a reference type— IsByRef is true of reference parameters and unsafe pointers.
HasElementType	True for arrays, reference parameters, and unsafe pointers.
IsInstanceOfType	This is the closest you can come to using a Type value with the is operator, although the syntax is backwards: typeof(A).IsInstanceOfType(B) is the same as B is A.

There are also some useful, self-explanatory members, like IsAbstract, ContainsGenericParameters, *and* IsArray.

Arrays

Arrays are a bit peculiar in that array objects don't have any methods or properties that reveals the type of the array elements. Rather, you have to call GetType on the array instance, and then call GetElementType on the array's Type. For example, if int[] Integers = new int[0], then Integers.GetType().GetElementType() equals typeof(int).[15]

Note that while you can call GetElementType on any Type value, it will only return a non-null value when HasElementType is true. Note also that HasElementType is true for pointers and reference parameters, not just array types.

Interfaces

Probably the most common interface-related Reflection task is enumerating the public types in a dynamically loaded assembly (see the "Assemblies" section, later in this chapter) to find types that support a particular interface.

If you are only looking for a single interface, perhaps an IPlugin that your application uses to control its plug-ins, the most obvious way to check whether a type supports an interface is probably to pass Type.GetInterface the interface name: a null result means the interface is not supported, while a non-null result (the Type of the interface) means that the interface **is** supported. However, you can also use Type.IsAssignableFrom, as in typeof(IPlugin).IsAssignableFrom(ExportedType). While using IsAssignableFrom is not quite as obvious or clear as using GetInterface, it doesn't have to do a string lookup and is several times faster than GetInterface (see the Chapter13\ BenchmarkInterfaceReflection C# project).[16]

---

15. In Delphi, you have to cast an array to System.Array or &Array before you can call GetType on it.

16. Also, IsAssignableFrom doesn't suffer from ambiguity the way that GetInterface does. If a type supports both ThisNamespace.IAmbiguous and ThatNamespace.IAmbiguous, calling GetInterface("IAmbiguous") will throw an AmbiguousMatchException. (Calling GetInterface("ThatNamespace.IAmbiguous") is not ambiguous and will not throw an exception.)

In more complicated situations, such as when you are looking for any one of a set of interfaces (but not their common ancestor, if any) you will probably want to enumerate the interfaces that a Type supports, and see if you know what to do with any of them. One way to do this is to call Type.GetInterfaces and examine the Type array that it returns. Another way is to use Type.FindInterfaces, which applies a delegate to each interface Type, and returns an array of the ones that pass your tests.

Finally, while I'm venturing into "I've never needed to use this" territory, Type. GetInterfaceMap returns potentially useful information about how a particular type implements an interface. The InterfaceMapping structure's InterfaceMethods array contains a MethodInfo for every method in the interface; the same position in the TargetMethods array contains a MethodInfo for the object's implementation of the interface method. This allows you to tell things like whether the interface method is implemented in the type that supports the interface, or whether it was inherited from an ancestral type.

Assemblies

Examine and/or load assemblies

The System.Reflection.Assembly class is important in much the same way as the Type class. Static Assembly methods load assemblies into the current application domain, and return an Assembly instance that describes the loaded assembly. An Assembly instance gives you access to the assembly's types and the assembly's resources. There are also static methods that reveal occasionally invaluable bits of information about the call stack, like GetExecutingAssembly, which returns the Assembly that contains the currently executing method, or GetCallingAssembly, which returns the Assembly that contains the method that called the current method. (As in the earlier "Type Values" section, AppDomain.CurrentDomain.GetAssemblies() will return an array of loaded assemblies.)

There are actually several different ways to dynamically load an assembly. Some are quite simple; others are not. I'll mention only the very simplest method—Assembly.LoadFile, which loads a library file into the current application domain—which probably covers 99% of the programs that need to dynamically load code. LoadFile is a static method that takes a filename and (assuming the file is a .NET assembly, and assuming that your code is running with sufficient permissions) loads the assembly, returning an Assembly instance.

Once you've loaded an assembly, you typically enumerate its public types, looking for classes that implement the right interface(s). (Less often, you may look for types with certain attributes.) Most applications that support plug-ins use an architecture like Figure 13-1, where both the application and (all) the plug-in(s) have a compile-time reference to the same Contract library. The Contract library defines both a services interface that the application implements, which contains all the services that the application offers its plug-ins, and a plug-in interface that the plug-ins implement, which contains all the handshaking necessary to load and host a plug-in in your application. (It's not uncommon for applications to support 'basic' and 'advanced' plug-ins, where, e.g., IAdvancedPlugin inherits from IPlugin, nor is it uncommon for a mature application to support several versions of the services or plug-in interfaces, but I'll talk about 'the' services interface and 'the' plug-in interface for simplicity.)[17]

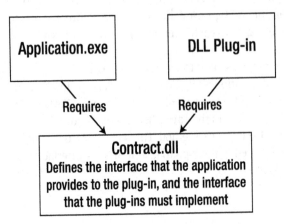

Figure 13-1. *The standard plug-in architecture*

The point of putting the interfaces into a contract library is that this allows both the application and the plug-ins to refer to the same interface, at compile time. When your application uses Activator.CreateInstance to create an instance of a Type that your application got from a loaded plug-in, it saves the instance as that interface, in a location of that interface type. Your application can then make early-bound calls to the plug-in (just as if the interface were implemented within the application itself) and doesn't have to always Invoke a MethodInfo or SetValue a PropertyInfo.

So, when you load an Assembly, you want to find all types that support, say, IPlugin. As per the earlier "Type Details" section, typeof(IPlugin).IsAssignableFrom(ExportedType) is the best way to see if ExportedType supports IPlugin. You can get an assembly's public types with Assembly.GetExportedTypes, which returns an array with the Type of each of the public types in the assembly. Alternatively, if you have TypeInformation permission, you can get all of an assembly's types with Assembly.GetTypes, which returns an array[18] with the Type of every top-level types in the assembly, whether public or not. I hope it's obvious that you should only use Assembly.GetTypes when you **need** access to private or internal types, both because it's more expensive to construct and examine a larger array, and because you do need special permission to see and manipulate nonpublic types.

---

17. The services and plug-in interfaces are typically extremely asymmetrical, with the application offering much more in the way of services than it demands in the way of handshaking. Not only does only one assembly have to implement the services interface while many assemblies must implement the plug-in interface, plug-ins are application extensions, while in many ways the services that the application provides **are** the application.

It can make a lot of sense to split a large services interface up into a set of properties, each of which returns a single-service interface. As with namespaces, this reduces naming conflicts, and makes code that uses the services interface easier to read and write. It also makes it easier to implement the services interface: it can be just a collection of private objects, each of which supports one single-service interface, and which are exposed to the outside world only via the interfaces they support.

18. Note that these methods both return fully populated arrays and not an enumeration-friendly collection like Regex.Matches—even if you abort a foreach on the first term, both GetExportedTypes and GetTypes have already allocated and populated their result array.

One final thing you can do with an `Assembly` instance is to use `Assembly.GetManifestResourceStream` to load resources (bitmaps, text files, and the like) that are stored in a compiled assembly as an `Embedded Resource`. Note that the resource type **must** be `Embedded Resource`—trying to load a resource that's not an `Embedded Resource` is a common cause of `GetManifestResourceStream` failure.

- In Visual Studio, add an embedded resource by right-clicking a project in the Solution Explorer and selecting Add ➤ Existing Item. After adding the item, right-click the new item, select Properties, and change the Build Action from Content to Embedded Resource.

- In BDS, add an embedded resource by right-clicking a project in the Project Manager and selecting Add. It will automatically be added as an Embedded Resource.

C# stores manifest resources in the assembly using a name qualified with the assembly's default namespace—i.e., `DefaultNamespace.Name`—and you need to pass `GetManifestResourceStream` either a string containing the qualified name, or a `Type` defined in the default namespace, which `GetManifestResourceStream` can use to turn `Name` into `DefaultNamespace.Name`. That is, you call `GetManifestResourceStream` as either `MyAssembly.GetManifestResourceStream("MyPlugin.PrettyPicture.png")` or `MyAssembly.GetManifestResourceStream(typeof(MyForm), "PrettyPicture.png")`.

Baking the default namespace into a resource name string is a risky thing to do: while the default namespace may not change very often, when it does change it may not be immediately obvious why, say, all the assembly's images are suddenly blank. Using the overload that takes a `Type` and uses `Type.Namespace` to get the default namespace is a bit safer, but not perfect either, as an assembly may contain several namespaces. The safest—if slowest—way to load resources is to use the `Assembly.GetManifestResourceNames` method, and use the name that `EndsWith` your resource's unqualified name, if there is one and only one. See the Chapter13\ManifestResources C# project for an example.

Delphi stores a resource named `MyPicture.bmp` as `MyPicture.bmp`—no default namespace—and you can load the resource stream with code like

```
Assembly.GetExecutingAssembly.GetManifestResourceStream('MyPicture.bmp')
```

This returns a stream that you can use to create, e.g., a `Bitmap`—see the Chapter13\Delphi.ManifestResources project for an example.

Emit

.NET is script friendly

You can reflect on the code that is statically bound into your application, and you can reflect upon assemblies loaded dynamically, whether from disk or over a network. You can even *emit* CIL code at run time, and bake it into an assembly like any other. You can run code in this new assembly right away, and/or you can cache your new assembly for later.

The methods you create with `System.Reflection.Emit` are just as strongly typed as normal, compiled methods. They can create objects, call methods, and set fields and properties, just like normal, compiled methods.

You can easily pass typed data back and forth between compiled and emitted code.

I cover Emit here because you might want to construct code to test your understanding of how various bits of CIL work. Beyond that, you might need to build a very custom shim to a bit of legacy code. Or you may be interested in automatically generating scripts (tailored to your users' situations and preferences) that are compiled to CIL, which is jitted to native code not all that much different than the native code from your C# or Delphi code. Or you may be interested in implementing "latent typing," where you can do things like treat any object with a Text property as if it implements

```
public interface IText
{
  string Text { get ; set ; }
}
```

Chapter13\Emit is a Delphi project group that contains two projects. The EmitBench project is a template for you to play around with CIL. The CompileTest project is a simple expression parser, which takes a string with a mathematical expression in X, and returns a pointer to a function that implements that expression.[19] Both projects rely on the MidnightBeach.FnEmit unit that lets you create new assemblies containing a single, static method. You can use my code as is, or for a jumpstart to more functional code.

The first thing you need to do is create an AssemblyBuilder object, so you can Emit an assembly.

```
function Emitter.CreateAssemblyBuilder(const Name: string): AssemblyBuilder;
var
  DynamicAssembly: AssemblyName;
begin
  DynamicAssembly := AssemblyName.Create;
  DynamicAssembly.Name    := Name;
  DynamicAssembly.Version := Version.Create;
  Result := AppDomain.CurrentDomain.DefineDynamicAssembly(
      DynamicAssembly, AssemblyBuilderAccess.Run);
end; // Emitter.CreateAssemblyBuilder
```

Before the CreateAssemblyBuilder method asks the current AppDomain to define a dynamic assembly, it creates and populates an AssemblyName object, which contains a Name string and Version information. Here, I just use default Version settings (version 0.0.0.0).

The AssemblyBuilderAccess parameter to the DefineDynamicAssembly method allows you to specify Run, Save, or RunAndSave behavior. If you create the assembly as Save or RunAndSave, you can use the Save method to save it to disk. A saved, emitted assembly can be used by other code just like a normal, compiled assembly can.

---

19. This code is interesting in four ways: 1) It's some of the first code I wrote for this book, having been originally written for the Delphi for .NET Preview compiler that came out before Delphi 8. 2) It includes what I hope is the last recursive descent parser I ever write by hand. 3) The tokenizer uses boxing (Chapter 2) in an interesting way. 4) And it emits CIL instructions that I don't mention in this chapter. If you're interested in this sort of thing, www.midnightbeach.com/ethiopia has some information about the more elaborate script compiler I built for the Midnight Beach content management system.

```
function Emitter.NewTypeBuilder: TypeBuilder;
var
  Assembly:    AssemblyBuilder;
  Module:      ModuleBuilder;
begin
  Assembly := CreateAssemblyBuilder(CommonName);
  Module   := Assembly.DefineDynamicModule(CommonName, True);
  Result   := Module.DefineType(CommonName, TypeAttributes.Public);
end; // Emitter.NewTypeBuilder
```

The AssemblyBuilder class's DefineDynamicModule method creates a new instance of the ModuleBuilder class. The ModuleBuilder class's DefineType method creates a new TypeBuilder instance.

Note In general, an assembly is a collection of *modules*, each of which must have a unique name. A module is simply a PE file—an EXE or a DLL. The simple code in this example generates a single module per assembly, and a single type (class) per module, and a single method per class—but you can have multiple modules per assembly, and multiple types per module, and multiple methods per class.

I use the preceding NewTypeBuilder method in the following code, which takes both a description of a function prototype (i.e., the parameter and result types) and a callback that emits the CIL, and returns a delegate that can be used to call the newly emitted code.

```
type
  Generator = procedure (IL: ILGenerator);
  GenericFn = function(A: array of TObject): TObject of object;

function Emitter.GenerateGenericFn(returnType: System.Type;
  parameterTypes: array of System.Type; Generate: Generator): GenericFn;
var
  NewType:     TypeBuilder;
  Method:      MethodBuilder;
  DynamicType: System.Type;
  Info:        MethodInfo;
begin
  NewType := NewTypeBuilder;
  Method := NewType.DefineMethod(CommonName,
    MethodAttributes.Public or MethodAttributes.Static,
    returnType, parameterTypes );

  Generate(Method.GetILGenerator);
```

```
   DynamicType := NewType.CreateType();
   Info      := DynamicType.GetMethod(CommonName, parameterTypes);
   Result := Invoker.Create(Info).generic;
end; // Emitter.GenerateGenericFn
```

The TypeBuilder class's methods let you declare fields, properties, and methods, both public and private. DefineMethod takes a method name and signature, and creates a new MethodBuilder object that lets you generate CIL for the method.

The returnType parameter specifies the method's result type. For example, to define a function that returns an integer, pass typeof(integer) as the returnType parameter, as in MethodInfo lookup; to define a procedure that returns no result, pass typeof(void) as the returnType parameter. (If you create a void method that returns no result, the GenericFn wrapper will return Nil, just as when you Invoke the MemberInfo for a normal, precompiled void method.)

The parameterTypes parameter is an array of typeof(typeName) values that contains the types of each parameter in the new method (again, as in MethodInfo lookup). For example, [typeof(integer)] defines a method that takes an integer parameter, while [typeof(string), typeof(integer)] defines a method that takes two parameters, a string and an integer. To define a method that takes no parameters, pass System.Type.EmptyTypes as the parameterTypes parameter.

Having created a MethodBuilder, GenerateGenericFn uses the Generate parameter to call back to a procedure that uses ILGenerator.Emit to define the body of the function. I'll walk through a simple Generate routine when I get to the end of the GenerateGenericFn method—for now, I'll just say that the only thing a CIL method **has** to contain is a ret instruction.

The TypeBuilder class's CreateType method 'bakes' the type definition and, if there are no errors, it returns a System.Type for the emitted type. GenerateGenericFn uses GetMethod to find the generated method, and gets a MethodInfo for the method.

While emitting code, you can emit a call to a MethodInfo. This turns into the same CIL as any other call—a 1-byte call opcode followed by a 4-byte method-table token—and jits to the same call through a method table as any other call. In normal, compiled code, you can Invoke() a MethodInfo: that is, you call code in dynamically **generated** assemblies in exactly the same way that you call code in dynamically **loaded** assemblies.

```
function Invoker.generic(A: array of TObject): TObject;
begin
   Assert(Assigned(Info));
   Result := Info.Invoke(Nil, A);
end;
```

As in the earlier "Type Details" section, the first parameter to Invoke is an instance reference, or Nil in the case of a static method. The second parameter to Invoke is an array of TObject values. Each value in the array will be checked to see that it is the same as the type declared in the method's prototype; pass an empty array (Nil) to Invoke a method that takes no formal parameters.

The GenerateGenericFn function returns a standard Delphi procedural type[20] so that you can call the emitted function as if it were a normal, flat function. The Invoker class does go

---

20. Delphi procedural types are implemented as .NET *delegates*. Chapters 2 and 8 have more on delegates.

through MethodInfo.Invoke, and is slower than calls within compiled or emitted code. Invoke is the most general way to call dynamically generated dynamically loaded code, but there are a couple of significantly faster alternatives that you should use when you can:

- If dynamic instance methods implement an interface that your application knows about at compile time, you can make early-bound calls through the interface, rather than using Invoke.

- You can use Delegate.CreateDelegate to turn a MethodInfo that describes a method into a delegate you can call normally.[21] The call to CreateDelegate checks that the parameters and result types are compatible with the MethodInfo, and returns a normal delegate that runs at normal speed. (The Emitter.GenerateRealFn method uses this technique.)

Finally, the EmitCIL routine in Chapter13\Emit\EmitBench.dpr generates a routine that does a little bit more than just return:[22]

```
procedure EmitCIL(IL: ILGenerator);
var
  SystemConsole: System.Type;
  WriteLine:         MethodInfo;
begin
  SystemConsole := typeof(System.Console);
  WriteLine    := SystemConsole.GetMethod('WriteLine',
    [ typeof(string) ]); // get the Console.WriteLine(string) overload

  IL.Emit(OpCodes.Ldstr, 'This string is being printed by emitted code.');
  IL.Emit(OpCodes.Call, WriteLine);

  IL.Emit(OpCodes.Ret);
end; // EmitCIL
```

This method does two different types of things. First, it reflects upon the Console class, and obtains an object describing the appropriate overload of the WriteLine method. Second, it uses this MethodInfo to emit code that will, when called, call Console.WriteLine() to write a string in a console window. When you emit code, you are continually switching mental gears from code generation to run-time operations on types and back.

In detail: I first get the Type of the Console class. The Type object gives me the MethodInfo for the Console.WriteLine(string) method. The ldstr instruction loads a string constant onto the stack; the IL.Emit call locates the string parameter in the dynamic assembly's string constant table

---

21. In 1.x, the Delegate.CreateDelegate overload that takes a MethodInfo can only create a delegate to a **static** method; in 2.0, it can also create delegates to instance methods. All versions of .NET support Delegate.CreateDelegate overloads that can create delegates to static or instance methods, given the Type of the class and the name of the method.

The Delegate.CreateDelegate method is best used with dynamically **generated** code; dynamically **loaded** code should use interfaces, as in the "Assemblies" section of this chapter. Creating an exported object and then casting it to an interface from a Contract library solves the versioning issues (and the possibilities of inadvertent conflict) that are caused by binding to dynamically loaded code by name. Dynamically generated code does not pose these problems.

22. What? You were expecting irony? The EmitCIL method emits two instructions besides ret.

(adding it, if necessary), and generates a string token for it. Finally, the IL.Emit(OpCodes.Call, WriteLine) call generates a call to the Console.WriteLine(string) method. (The ILGenerator. EmitWriteLine method will do all this for you—but calling that wouldn't be quite as interesting as the four steps in the EmitCIL method.)

Key Points

- Reflection gives your programs access to metadata, and lets them act interpretively.

- The Type class is key to this. There are zero or one instances of the Type class for every type your application has used.

- The Type class lets you create and manipulate instances of a type, and it lets you discover the type's capabilities.

- The Assembly class can load dynamic assemblies, and gives you access to the assemblies' types and resources.

- It's easy to interface run-time-loaded or run-time-generated code with your statically linked code.

CHAPTER 14

■■■

Serialization and Remoting

The FCL includes several distinct serialization libraries. These stream and restore objects and object graphs, using both binary and XML formats. The FCL uses serialization for communication between different machines and processes, and for communication between different application domains within a process; you can also use the serialization libraries to persist your application's state and user's preferences.

Historically, persistence has been a labor-intensive process. Whether you save your settings to a file or to the registry, you've had to write code to save and restore each datum that you want to pass from one session to the next. Persistence is much easier in .NET, as the FCL includes two different ways to stream and restore object graphs,[1] using multiple formats. Both approaches to streaming can be used for both persistence and for communicating between machines and between processes—which only makes sense, as persistence is just a special type of (one-way) interprocess communication.

The standard streaming method is field oriented, and uses Reflection (Chapter 13) to save and restore every field (both public and private) of a class or record. You won't be able to use this approach in certain limited-trust environments. The other streaming method will only save and restore a class instance's public state, and does this by generating and compiling C# code that reads and writes every public field and public read-write property. This second approach isn't affected by limited trust per se—you can always stream objects to and from memory—but you will not always have permission to save streams to disk, or to send streams to other processes or other computers.

The field-oriented, Reflection-based method supports binary and SOAP formatting. The binary format is very .NET specific, while you may be able to exchange SOAP-formatted streams with non-.NET systems. Both formats preserve object identity: if you serialize a graph that has multiple references to the same object, each deserialized reference will refer to the same deserialized object.

The code-based XML serialization method saves the public face of an object graph as a single XML entity. You can use XML streaming for communicating with both .NET applications and non-.NET applications. There is considerable control over the XML representation, for when you need to communicate with an existing XML-based application—you can even use SOAP. XML serialization does **not** preserve object identity: if you serialize a graph that has multiple references to the same object, each deserialized reference will refer to a different

---

1. That is, a root object; plus all the objects the root refers to; plus all the objects the referred-to objects refer to; and so on.

deserialized object. Each deserialized reference will have the right value, but each reference will be to a distinct object.

Note The XML streaming classes are a bit fragile, and can be difficult to use. You can also use the XML libraries of Chapter 18 to manually stream and restore structured values without serializing an object hierarchy.

The first two sections of this chapter, "Standard Streaming" and "XML Streaming," cover the two different approaches to streaming. The third section, ".NET Remoting," covers the use of standard, Reflection-based streaming to pass objects between processes on the same or different computers, and to pass objects between application domains within a process.

Standard Streaming

Two easy options

Serializing objects with the binary and SOAP formatting classes is very simple. You mark the object(s) you want to serialize with the Serializable attribute. For example,

```
[Serializable]
public class Node
{
    public string Text;
    public Node Next;
}
```

and

```
type
  [Serializable]
  List = class
  public
    Text: string;
    Next: List;
  end;
```

Note All data in the graph must have the Serializable attribute. (Strings, arrays, and system primitives are all serializable.) Because of inheritance, compilers cannot check this for you: trying to serialize a graph that contains a nonserializable object will throw an exception at run time.

You can serialize instances of class types as well as value types like Delphi records and C# structures. Normally, serialization will save and restore the entire object state—all fields, both public and private. You can keep a field from being serialized by marking it with the NonSerialized attribute—for example,

```
[NonSerialized] int trouble = -1; // I explain why this is "trouble" in a few pps
```

To save one or more objects, create a BinaryFormatter or a SoapFormatter instance.[2] Both support the IFormatter interface, which can Serialize objects to a stream and Deserialize objects from a stream. (Persistence uses file streams, while interprocess communication uses sockets or named pipes.)

For example, the Chapter14\BinarySerialization C# project saves objects as

```
using (Stream Write = new FileStream(Filename, FileMode.Create))
{
    BinaryFormatter Serializer = new BinaryFormatter();
    Serializer.Serialize(Write, One);
    Serializer.Serialize(Write, Two);
}
```

and restores them as

```
using (Stream Read = new FileStream(Filename, FileMode.Open))
{
    BinaryFormatter Serializer = new BinaryFormatter();
    OneA = (Data)Serializer.Deserialize(Read);
    TwoA = (Data)Serializer.Deserialize(Read);
}
```

Note Deserialization returns an object that has to be cast to the proper type.

These printed excerpts show that a single stream can contain more than one serialized object. You can explore the code, and see how preserving object identity allows Reflection-based serialization to handle cyclical object graphs properly: each object will only be serialized once. See, for example, the Chapter14\GraphSerialization Delphi project, which serializes an object with a field that points to a circular list with three elements.

It's important to note that standard deserialization works at a low level that creates an object without calling its constructor.[3] The object table pointer is set correctly, but all data

---

2. The BinaryFormatter class is in the System.Runtime.Serialization.Formatters.Binary namespace, which is contained in the standard mscorlib.dll (MS Core Library) assembly. You will need to add a uses or using clause, but you will not have to add a reference. The SoapFormatter class is in the System.Runtime.Serialization.Formatters.Soap namespace, which is in its own system.runtime.serialization.formatters.soap.dll assembly. You will need to add a uses or using clause **and** you will have to add a reference to the system.runtime.serialization.formatters.soap.dll assembly.

3. See FormatterServices.GetUninitializedObject.

bytes are zeroed out. Since deserialization restores both `public` **and** `private` fields, this only matters if you have `NonSerialized` fields. A nonserialized field like

```
[NonSerialized] int trouble = -1;
```

might still be -1 when you serialize the object, but it will be 0 after you deserialize a copy.

An initialized, nonserialized field may seem rather bizarre—if the value is not essential to the object's state, then why are you bothering to initialize it?—but it might be something like an index into a cache array, with -1 indicating No Cache. You wouldn't want to serialize a cache index, but you would want to reinitialize the index to -1. Other times, you will want to reconstruct a `NonSerialized` field from some other field. One example might be loading a bitmap from a URL.

The simple way to set `NonSerialized` fields to nondefault values is to implement a *deserialization callback*. If a `Serializable` object implements the (`System.Runtime.Serialization`) `IDeserializationCallback` interface, its `OnDeserialization` method will be called when the whole graph has been deserialized. This gives you an opportunity to set `NonSerialized` fields, or to do any other fix-up that may be necessary. Note that the `OnDeserialization` method will be called for each deserialized object that supports the `IDeserializationCallback` interface—not just for the root object. `OnDeserialization` is called in the same order that objects are serialized and deserialized, and the order thus depends on the dynamic contents of lists and the implementation details of the serialization code. It seems safe to assume that `OnDeserialization` will be called for the root object before it is called for any objects the root refers to,[4] but you probably shouldn't write code that makes any other assumptions about the order in which `OnDeserialization` will be called.

In 2.0, there's a more powerful callback mechanism, involving four new attributes in the `System.Runtime.Serialization` namespace. `OnSerializing` marks a method that will be called before an object is serialized, giving you a chance to hide or encrypt data, or perhaps to convert a reference to a nonserializable object to a reference to a serializable surrogate. (The surrogate may be slower but more portable. For example, it may contain the names of environment strings, instead of their current value on this machine.) An `OnSerialized` method will be called after an object is serialized, giving you a chance to undo any changes you made in the `OnSerializing` method. An `OnDeserializing` method is a sort of constructor, called before actual deserialization, which gives you a chance to initialize any `NonSerialized` fields, while an `OnDeserialized` method is called after serialization, giving you a chance to reconstruct various fields from the deserialized state. These new attributes may be applied to private methods, which reduces the chances that you will call them directly, as is possible with an `IDeserializationCallback`.

More importantly, all four of these new serialization callbacks take a `StreamingContext` parameter, which tells you what sort of serialization is involved—you may need to act differently when an object is being persisted than when the object is serialized between machines, which in turn may impose different requirements than serialization between processes on the same machine. The compiler doesn't (currently) check that methods with one of the serialization callback attributes have the proper prototype: you will get an exception at serialization/deserialization time if your callback method doesn't have a single `StreamingContext` parameter.

---

4. See, for example, the Chapter14\DeserializationCallback C# project.

The most complex (and most flexible) way to reset NonSerialized fields is to implement (System.Runtime.Serialization) ISerializable and do *custom serialization*. An object that implements custom serialization not only has the Serializable attribute but also supplies both an ISerializable method that handles serialization and a constructor (with a special signature) that handles deserialization. This not only gives you the same opportunity to do fix-ups at deserialization time that a deserialization callback does, but also gives you full control over the content and order of the serialized stream, which is useful when your need to stream a large field depends on the value(s) of other field(s). Also, because custom deserialization **is** handled by a special constructor, any initialized fields will be set properly, even when they are not serialized.

■**Caution** .NET interfaces can't include constructors, so compilers can't check that you have both methods in place. Deserializing an object that supports ISerializable but that doesn't have the right constructor will throw an exception at run time.

You can freely mix objects that support custom serialization with objects that rely on standard serialization, because objects that implement ISerializable are only responsible for serializing and deserializing their own fields. The FCL supplies methods to save and restore primitive types and objects, and the methods that handle objects take care of deciding whether to use standard or custom serialization.

Both the serialization method and the deserialization constructor receive a SerializationInfo parameter. You call methods of the SerializationInfo object to save and restore field data. As with any other streaming code, you need to be sure to follow a *Queue Law*—deserialize fields in the same order that you serialized them. If you serialize A, then B, then C, be sure to deserialize A, then B, then C—**not** C, then B, then A!

The details of custom serialization are beyond the scope of this book: while deciphering the Microsoft documentation is not exactly trivial, custom serialization is not something you will need to do on a regular basis. For example, I've done a decent amount of serialization at this point, and have never had any need to use custom serialization.

I'd like to conclude this section by pointing out that binary serialization is faster than SOAP:[5] The binary stream is smaller, and there's no need to format and unformat each field, the way there is with an XML dialect like SOAP, which deals in text representations of each datum. Conversely, a SOAP file **can** be read (and modified) in any text editor, and can be exchanged with programs that aren't .NET based, or that don't share the class definitions of the streamed data.

- Use binary streaming by default, as it is smaller and faster. Binary streaming is particularly appropriate where you want a measure of security through obscurity.

- Use SOAP streaming where you want to be easily able to view the persisted data, or where you need to share it with non-.NET programs.

---

5.   See the Chapter14\SerializationBenchmark C# project.

XML Streaming

Flexible and complex

Serialization with the binary and SOAP formatters is quite easy, and you can exercise a lot of control over the serialization and deserialization process, but you don't have a lot of control over the stream format. Also, Reflection-based serialization requires a fair degree of trust from the system it's running on—untrusted code can't use Reflection to discover private fields in types from other assemblies, much less read and write private members.

By contrast, the XmlSerializer class honors a wide variety of attributes that give you a high degree of control over how a particular object tree will be represented. By default, you get a reasonably compact XML that's significantly smaller than the equivalent SoapFormatter stream. You can also plug in an XML type mapping to format your object tree as a SOAP message.

Control over the representation can be invaluable when you need to exchange XML with other systems. A further advantage of the XmlSerializer class is that discovering the public members of a public type requires no special trust, and so XmlSerializer can be used where SoapFormatter cannot.

Against these advantages of control and trustworthiness, you unfortunately have to set the disadvantages that XML serialization is much slower than its Reflection-based peers, and that XML serialization can be much harder to use. It's definitely prone to throwing mysterious exceptions, and it can take a while to get your XML serialization working. Also, XML serialization is early bound in the sense that it can only serialize types that the XmlSerializer constructor 'saw' and generated code for.

You pass the XmlSerializer constructor the root object's Type, and the constructor generates code to read and write every public member. The constructor will also generate code to serialize every type that the root object contains references to, and so on recursively. However, serialization will raise an InvalidOperationException at run time if any member contains a (late-bound) reference to a descendant class that the constructor didn't generate code for.[6]

For example, you might have an Ancestor class and a Descendant class that inherits from the Ancestor class. Naturally, if you have an Ancestor field in a ToBeSerialized object, at run time the field may actually refer to a Descendant instance. However, when XmlSerializer serializes the Ancestor field in a ToBeSerialized instance, it will raise an exception if the field contains a Descendant instead of an ancestor.

You get the same behavior with any late binding. The XmlSerializer documentation (for the constructor that takes (Type, Type[]) parameters) talks about object arrays, but the reality is that XmlSerializer needs to be provided with type information for **any** late-bound types it may encounter. This is true whether the late binding is through an object, an object[], an ancestral class, or a late-bound container class like an ArrayList. There are two different ways you can provide this information.

---

6. It certainly seems like XML serialization **could** write code on demand. My guess is that not doing so is an optimization—XML serialization is strangely slow, even without the overhead of checking an assembly cache every time you move from one type to another.

First, when you lay out an object hierarchy, you can give the root object XmlInclude attributes, one for each descendant. That is, if you have a class like this one from the Chapter14\DynamicSerialization C# project

```
[XmlInclude(typeof(Child)), XmlInclude(typeof(GrandChild))]
public abstract class Ancestor
{ }
```

that has a descendant class Child, which in turn has a descendant class GrandChild, XmlSerializer will know how to serialize Child and GrandChild values of an Ancestor field or property. Obviously, this only helps when you have source for an assembly—you can't add an XmlInclude attribute to System.Object!

Second, when you create the XmlSerializer that will serialize your object, you can pass it an array of Type information for every class that the serializer might run into. For example, the DynamicSerialization project creates an XmlSerializer as

```
new XmlSerializer(typeof(Root), new Type[] { typeof(Descendant) })
```

so that the serializer doesn't raise an exception when it reaches the Root type's

```
public Ancestor LateBoundTrouble = new Descendant();
```

field.

■ **Note** The ban on late-binding goes beyond needing Type information for late-bound members. Because an IDictionary associates a late-bound value with a late-bound key, an XmlSerializer can't serialize types like Hashtable or Dictionary<,> that implement IDictionary. It's not really clear to me why this is—you can serialize a (variable-length) ArrayList if you supply Type information for every object it may hold, so why can't you serialize a Hashtable if you supply Type information for every possible key or value?[7]

Beyond the need to pass Type information to the constructor, the basic interface looks like BinaryFormatter and SoapFormatter, though XmlSerializer doesn't support their IFormatter interface: to save an object, create an XmlSerializer, and tell it to serialize an object to a stream. To restore an object, create an XmlSerializer, and tell it to deserialize an object from a stream.

For example, the Chapter14\XmlSerialization C# project saves an object as

```
using (Stream Write = new FileStream(Filename, FileMode.Create))
{
    XmlSerializer Serializer = new XmlSerializer(typeof(Data));
    Serializer.Serialize(Write, One);
}
```

---

7. Hallvard did some research on this and the answer appears to be partly schedule constraints way back in the 1.0 days, and partly a lack of urgency since then: XML serialization is mostly for use with XSD, and hash tables aren't an XSD type. Hallvard also found a workaround: see the Chapter14\XmlSerializerTest C# project.

and restores it as

```
using (Stream Read = new FileStream(Filename, FileMode.Open))
{
    XmlSerializer Serializer = new XmlSerializer(typeof(Data));
    OneA = (Data)Serializer.Deserialize(Read);
}
```

These examples save to and restore from a Stream, just like the formatting classes do, but this is about the extent of the similarity between XmlSerializer and the formatting classes. I've already talked about the slowness, complexity, and early-bound nature of XML serialization, but there are several other differences from the Reflection-based formatting classes. For example, XmlSerializer has Serialize and Deserialize overloads that take TextWriter and TextReader or XmlWriter and XmlReader parameters. This difference isn't very important, because you will only use these overloads in rather specialized situations, but some of the other differences **are** more significant.

Different Representation

A tree, not a graph

While the SoapFormatter represents a graph as a stream of objects and represents a reference from one object to another as an href link, the XmlSerializer represents a graph as a single, nested XML entity. This means that

1. The XmlSerializer can only store a single object per stream, while Reflection-based serialization can store multiple objects per stream.

2. The XmlSerializer cannot store any object graph that contains a cyclic reference. Attempting to serialize a cyclic graph will raise an exception at run time.

3. The XmlSerializer preserves *object state* but not *object identity.* If you serialize a graph that contains, say, two references to the same array, you will get back a graph that contains two copies of the array.

Different Technology

XML serialization generates code at run time

Other differences between Reflection-based serialization and XML serialization stem from the way that the binary and SOAP formatters use Reflection to read and write all fields, while the XmlSerializer class only uses Reflection to get the set of public fields and read-write properties, then generates and compiles C# code to read and write the public members. XML serialization executes generated code that reads each public member, builds an XML representation, then writes the XML to a stream. XML deserialization builds an XML representation from the stream, then executes generated code that creates one or more new objects and sets each public member. This in turn means

1. The XmlSerializer constructor does a fair amount of work, creating and compiling an assembly in the process's TEMP directory. Assemblies can't be unloaded,[8] so the XmlSerializer class keeps track of all the types it knows how to serialize—the second time you create an XmlSerializer for a particular type is significantly faster than the first (see the Chapter14\SerializationBenchmark C# project).

2. The generated code creates new objects in the normal way. That is, every object you serialize needs a public, parameterless constructor. Since C# structures and Delphi records cannot have parameterless constructors, you can only serialize reference types (i.e., classes but not records) with XmlSerializer. However, because deserialization **does** call a constructor, nonserialized members (both read-only properties and the [XmlIgnore] fields and properties that I cover later) **will** be initialized properly.

3. Because serialization and deserialization executes generated code that reads and writes public members, you can only serialize public classes. The BinaryFormatter and SoapFormatter classes can also serialize private (and internal) classes.

More Attributes

Useful for conforming to XSD schemas

As I mentioned at the start of this section, control over the stream format can be a key reason to use the XmlSerializer. You can control the stream format by using the XML attributes (classes that start with Xml and end with Attribute) in the System.Xml.Serialization namespace. Using these attributes can be pretty complicated, and you only need them when you want your classes to serialize to and from an XML stream that conforms to a particular XML schema.

XML schema, in turn, are only necessary when you need to communicate with a system you don't share code with: the default XML serialization works just fine for persistence, or for communicating with other copies of your program, or for communicating with programs that use the same classes that you do (and, except in low-trust cases, the standard Reflection-based serialization is generally a better choice for this sort of communication). When you have a schema, you can use the Xsd.exe tool to generate class definitions, complete with XML attributes, that will serialize to and from the schema.

I don't want to cover XSD schemas and Xsd.exe both because it would take too much room and because only some .NET programmers will need to deal with them. I'll say only that, for the most part, you should leave the XML attributes to Xsd.exe. If you need to read and write XML in a particular format and you don't have a formal schema, you are probably better off using the XML libraries (Chapter 18) than trying to get XmlSerializer to read and write the format. While it's very convenient to serialize a class straight to XML and to deserialize straight from XML to a class, it can require a lot of fighting with XmlSerializer and the XML attributes to get this to work: it can be easier just to manually write code to copy each datum to and from an XML writer or XML reader, or to and from an XML DOM data tree.

---

8. This is true in general, even if it's not literally true. Unloading assemblies involves application domains, and communication between app domains imposes specific requirements and is comparatively expensive. See the "Application Domains" subsection of this chapter.

Accordingly, I'm only going to talk about one XML attribute besides XmlInclude.[9] Just as applying NonSerialized to a member of a Serializable class tells the standard serialization libraries to skip the NonSerialized member, so applying the XmlIgnore attribute to a class member tells the XmlSerializer to skip that particular member. Note that XML serialization does treat nonserialized members somewhat differently than standard serialization does: because XML serialization calls the parameterless constructor, nonserialized fields **are** initialized after XML deserialization. (Remember, this can be a problem with standard serialization: since the constructor is not called, nonserialized fields are **not** initialized and will always be filled with 0 bytes, even if the C# class definition specifies an initial value.)

SOAP Bubbles

A dead end off of a bad street

Finally, you can force an XmlSerializer to generate SOAP-formatted XML by using an XmlTypeMapping. You create an XmlTypeMapping by creating a SoapReflectionImporter and passing the root Type to the importer's ImportTypeMapping method. You then pass the type mapping to the XmlSerializer instead of the root Type. That is, instead of serializing like

```
using (Stream Write = new FileStream(Filename, FileMode.Create))
{
    XmlSerializer Serializer = new XmlSerializer(typeof(Data));
    Serializer.Serialize(Write, One);
}
```

you serialize like

```
using (Stream Write = new FileStream(Filename, FileMode.Create))
{
    XmlTypeMapping Mapping = new SoapReflectionImporter().
        ImportTypeMapping(typeof(Root));
    XmlSerializer Serializer = new XmlSerializer(Mapping);
    Serializer.Serialize(Write, One);
}
```

and deserialize in the same way.

There is no overload that takes an array of Type or XmlTypeMapping objects to help resolve late-bound types the way there is with the XmlSerializer constructor that takes a root Type. The only way to tell the serializer to prepare for late-bound types is to apply the SoapInclude attribute to an ancestral type, listing all descendant types that the serializer might encounter. This is exactly analogous to the way you use the XmlInclude attribute—but be sure to note that SOAP formatting ignores the XML attributes and standard XML formatting ignores the SOAP attributes. In particular, SOAP formatting ignores the XmlIgnore attribute, and there is a SoapIgnore attribute that you use with SOAP formatting.

---

9. Which I already discussed as an alternative to supplying late-bound types to the XmlSerializer constructor.

▪**Note** SOAP-mapped serialization is even more fragile than standard XML serialization—there are object trees that you can serialize with XmlSerializer that you cannot serialize when you use an XmlTypeMapping. I'd strongly suggest that you not use SOAP-mapped XML serialization unless you need to communicate with another program using SOAP-formatted messages.

.NET Remoting

Proxies use serialization to pass data across boundaries

Serializable is a standard (or *intrinsic*) attribute, one that's a member of the TypeAttributes bitmap that you retrieve with Type.Attributes, not a custom attribute that you retrieve with MemberInfo.GetCustomAttributes or check with MemberInfo.IsDefined. The intrinsic attributes represent features that the CLR needs to check quickly: Serializable is intrinsic because the CLR uses serialization to implement *remoting*.

Remoting is used to pass data across various boundaries: between processes on the same or different computers, and between *application domains* within the same process.[10] Remoting is based on *remotable types*, which are classes that descend from System.MarshalByRefObject. Remoting takes an instance of a remotable type on one side of a boundary, and automatically creates a transparent *proxy* for that instance on the other side of the boundary. When you call a method of a proxy object, any arguments are *marshaled* across the boundary to the base object, and any result is marshaled back. (A few method calls, like GetType, actually happen in the proxy's domain, without any marshaling involved.) Any public fields of the base object are, in effect, translated into properties of the proxy, so that reading or writing a proxy field is also a method call that marshals arguments or results.

Data can only be marshaled if it is either remotable or serializable.[11] Remotable arguments or results are marshaled by creating another proxy, and any member access involves more marshaling. (This is called *marshal by reference*.) Serializable arguments or results are marshaled by serializing the data on one side of the boundary and deserializing on the other. (This is called *marshal by value*.) Serialization creates an independent copy, not a proxy: copied objects have true fields, and method calls operate on the copied state, and so do not require additional marshaling.

---

10. Technically, **all** remoting is communication between a pair of application domains, as all .NET code runs in an AppDomain, but since interprocess remoting looks so different from intraprocess remoting—even though it is using the same infrastructure—I think it's probably clearer to speak of remoting across process boundaries vs. remoting across AppDomain boundaries.

11. Remember: because of polymorphism, compilers cannot check that data is [Serializable]. You can compile code that tries to copy nonserializable code, but you will get an exception when it runs.

Note While it might seem that marshaling via a proxy is inherently less efficient than marshaling via a copy—all member access requires additional marshaling—it really depends on the amount of state data, and how often it is actually accessed. Copying an object with a large amount of state data requires a lot of streaming at copy time. If that state data is then never accessed, you've incurred a lot of copy costs for nothing. Proxying an object with a large amount of state data means that you only stream data when it's actually accessed: members that are not accessed are not streamed.

Interprocess Communication

Uses serialization to make remote calls

Historically, communication between processes and between machines has been a complex affair. However, as in so many other areas, the designers of .NET took all the best ideas, and the result is a subsystem that makes communication between .NET processes almost absurdly easy—while still being quite configurable. Using the defaults, you can get .NET remoting working with just a few lines of code, yet you can easily change the communications channel, add encryption or compression, and control remote object lifetimes. This subsection won't do much more than hint at these details, for two main reasons: full coverage would merit a book of its own,[12] and I'm not really all that far from the Hello, world stage, myself.

To start with, all remoting involves a pair of applications—a client and a server. (The same application can be both client and server, as in peer-to-peer networking or an n-tier application, but these more complex scenarios involve multiple connections, and in each connection, a given application is either a client or a server.) Servers do **not** have to be hosted by a web server like IIS: both client and server can be any sort of .NET application, whether a console app or a Windows service, a GUI app or a ASP web app. This flexibility makes .NET remoting apps easier to install and configure than ASP apps, which can require dedicated support staff to keep the web server running.

The server starts things off by registering a URI (Uniform Resource Identifier) with the remoting system, as in this code from the Chapter14\Chatlet C# project:

```
TcpChannel Channel = new TcpChannel(Port); // private const int Port = 0x1226
ChannelServices.RegisterChannel(Channel);
RemotingConfiguration.RegisterWellKnownServiceType(
    typeof(Remote),
    URI, // private const string URI = "Chatlet.message.object";
    WellKnownObjectMode.Singleton);
```

---

12. Apress, in fact, offers just such a book. See Appendix 5, "Bibliography."

This code associates the Remote type with a protocol, a port, and a request string. The TcpChannel and the HttpChannel use sockets, and can be used for communication between machines; the (new in 2.0) IpcChannel uses named pipes, and is used for communication between processes or app domains, on a single machine. (You can also define your own channel types, though this is not a trivial task. Additionally, channel *message sinks* allow you to build a chain of stream operators on top of an existing channel. You can use message sinks to add encryption and/or compression.)

The TcpChannel uses binary serialization and the low-level TCP protocol, while the HttpChannel uses SOAP serialization and the higher-level HTTP protocol. The IpcChannel uses binary serialization over the standard Windows IPC (Interprocess Communication) system. The TcpChannel is more efficient, while the HttpChannel may be more appropriate for communicating through firewalls; when you don't have to talk to another machine, the socketless IpcChannel is faster than either TcpChannel or HttpChannel.

■**Tip** The TcpChannel class is in the System.Runtime.Remoting.Channels.Tcp namespace, while the HttpChannel class is in the System.Runtime.Remoting.Channels.Http namespace, and the IpcChannel class is in the System.Runtime.Remoting.Channels.Ipc namespace. You'll have to add a reference to the System.Runtime.Remoting.dll to 'see' any of these namespaces.

You can change protocols simply by changing the channel the server creates, and by changing the protocol part of the client-side URI. In production code, you will generally put all this information into the server's XML configuration file, and replace the new Channel/RegisterChannel/ RegisterWellKnownServiceType calls with a call to RemotingConfiguration.Configure: this allows you to change the protocol, port, and/or request string without recompiling your server.

Both the TCP and HTTP protocols require you to specify a port number. IPC doesn't use port numbers, and you specify a pipe name instead of a port number (see the Chapter14\ IpcDemo C# project). The TCP and HTTP channel constructors take a port number as a 32-bit int, but port numbers are actually unsigned 16-bit numbers[13] specified in .NET as an int only for CLS-compliance reasons: you'll get an exception if you specify a port number greater than ushort.MaxValue.

---

13. The Internet Assigned Numbers Authority (www.iana.org) divides ports into three ranges: the "well known" ports, from 0 to 1023, which are reserved for standard services like HTTP and FTP; "registered" ports, from 1024 to 49151, which are used for obscure and/or proprietary services; and "dynamic" ports, from 49152 to 65535, which are used in protocols that listen on one port, then open a connection on a new port. While it doesn't really matter which port number you use during development—so long as it doesn't conflict with an existing service—production port numbers may have to be negotiated with IT departments, which may have policies on which port numbers will be allowed through their firewall. In addition, if your application will be used outside your organization, it may make sense to register the port number with the IANA.

The second parameter to RemotingConfiguration.RegisterWellKnownServiceType specifies the request string that the client will pass to the server. The same server can register multiple types, each associated with its own protocol, port, and request string, but it's generally better to register a single 'factory' class (that can return several different types of objects) than to register a lot of different classes.

The third, (enumerated) parameter to RemotingConfiguration. RegisterWellKnownServiceType specifies the server's object creation policy, which can be either SingleCall or Singleton. The SingleCall policy means that each client connection request will create a new server-side object, while the Singleton policy means that the same server-side object will be used to answer each request.

Note that a Singleton policy does **not** mean that a server-side object will live forever and never be garbage collected! Every server-side object has a *lease* that controls how long it lives. By default, a Singleton object lives for a certain amount of time after each connection request, and every call from a client extends the lease for a somewhat shorter time. This default policy is perfectly adequate when the server-side object doesn't maintain any state; if your server-side objects do need to maintain state between requests, you can override MarshalByRefObject. InitializeLifetimeService and return an ILease implementation that changes the default lease times and/or registers your client(s) as *sponsors*. When a server-side object's lease runs out, the lease manager tries to contact each registered sponsor. If any sponsor responds in time, the lease manager keeps its reference to the object; if no sponsor responds in time, the lease manager forgets about the object, and it will ultimately be garbage collected.

Once the server has registered a URI, it can just sit around and wait for a client to establish a connection and make remote calls. The remoting system takes care of handling each call from a client-side proxy to a server-side object in its own server-side thread; from the server's point of view, calls 'just happen,' and 'all' you have to do is be aware that the same Singleton object may be handling requests in multiple threads simultaneously. (GUI servers do need to take some care that all GUI access happens in the GUI thread. I talk about this a bit more below, and also in Chapter 15.)

■**Note** .NET remoting will not start a server process: a client can only connect to a running server.

On the client side of the Chapter14\Chatlet C# project, the same Load event handler that registers the server-side URI also sets up for a client-initiated connection by populating a combo box with the names of all other machines in the local "Network Neighborhood." Since Chatlet **is** just a simple demo app and the FCL doesn't include a way to enumerate the local network, the code that populates the combo box is a bit quick and dirty: it uses the System. Diagnostics.Process class to capture the output of the Windows net command-line program, using the view switch; uses a Regex to extract the machine names; and checks each against the System.Environment object's MachineName property.[14]

---

14. The Environment object exposes other useful information, like command-line parameters; machine, user, CLR, and OS information; environment variables and key directories; and your app's memory usage.

When the user selects from the drop-down, the Chatlet app uses the machine name to build a URI and uses `Activator.GetObject` to get a proxy to a *Server-Activated Object.* (The client can also new a *Client-Activated Object,* but this involves all sorts of complexities that I won't cover here.) `Activator.GetObject` takes a URI that specifies the protocol, the machine name (or IP address), the port, and the request string. (To talk to a process on the local machine, use the machine name `localhost`—or use IPC, where the URI is simplified to something like `ipc://PortName/Verb`.) The Chatlet project uses this code to connect to a remote machine:

```
string Request = String.Format("tcp://{0}:{1}/{2}", MachineName, Port, URI);
return (Remote) Activator.GetObject(typeof(Remote), Request);
```

For example, when the Chatlet project tries to open a connection to a machine named Entropy, the Request URI is `"tcp://ENTROPY:4646/Chatlet.message.object"`.

`Activator.GetObject` parses the URI and creates a proxy, backed by an `ObjRef`, which is a sort of pointer to the remote object; the proxy uses the `ObjRef` to communicate with the actual server-side object. Note that **creating** the proxy does not actually talk to the server-side object—there is no network traffic until you actually call a proxy method. Thus, you can create a proxy for an object on a nonexistent or unreachable server: you won't get an exception until you actually **use** the proxy.

Proxy calls look and act just like ordinary calls, although they take much longer and can always raise network-related exceptions. The main complexity in the Chapter14\Chatlet project comes from the fact that—as a peer-to-peer networking application—it's simultaneously a server to another instance of itself and a client to that other instance. The detailed comments in the `Remote.cs` and `ChatletForm.cs` files may give you some idea of the care I had to take in writing the code.

A secondary complexity comes from the fact the Chatlet project is a GUI app. I'll talk about GUI thread issues more in Chapter 15, but the basic rule is that one should only touch a `Control`[15] from the thread that created it. The Chatlet project's server-side object, `Remote`, uses both `Control.Invoke` and `Control.BeginInvoke` to run C# 2.0 anonymous methods (i.e., delegates) in the GUI thread. `Invoke` calls a delegate synchronously, not returning until the delegate returns; `BeginInvoke` calls a delegate asynchronously, immediately returning an `IAsyncResult` that you can (optionally) later pass to `Control.EndInvoke` to wait for the delegate to return and/or collect its result.

Finally, for the remoting system to be able to pass types between a client and a server, both the client and the server must share the types that will be communicated. In the normal remoting scenario (see Figure 14-1), where the client and the server are distinct applications, this means that all shared types must be defined in a common assembly, somewhat as in the standard plug-in architecture in Chapter 13. In the special case of a peer-to-peer application, where each partner is a client on one connection and a server on the other, there is no need to put the shared types into a separate assembly: the types that will be serialized or proxied can be included in the application assembly, just like any other type the application uses.

---

15. .NET forms and GUI controls all descend from the `Control` class, just as VCL forms and controls all descend from the `TControl` class.

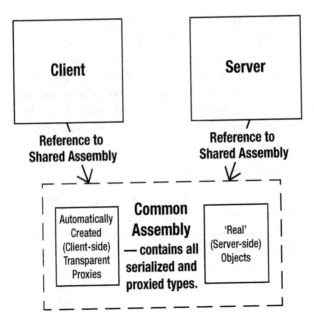

Figure 14-1. *The normal remoting scenario*

Application Domains

Isolated, like a process, but cheaper

I've mentioned a few times that—in general—jitted code is never unloaded: data comes and goes, but code sticks around forever. I've also mentioned that while this is mostly true, it **is** an oversimplification. This subsection covers some of the details.

All code runs in an *application domain*, or AppDomain. The CLR creates a couple of hidden app domains for its own use, and then loads application code into the *default* AppDomain. Any code loaded into the default AppDomain will stay in memory until the process terminates. However, you can explicitly create and unload an AppDomain, and any code you load into the new AppDomain will be unloaded with the AppDomain.

A single process can host several application domains that share threads and the CLR, but that do not share jitted code, types, or values. A type loaded in one AppDomain is not visible in another AppDomain, and you must use remoting to call methods across app domain boundaries. You get the safety of a process boundary without the switching costs, and with lower memory use. This is a feature you may find useful in any sort of "expandable" application:

- You can run multiple .NET applications—either console, GUI, or both—within a single process.

- You can run untrusted code without danger of it accidentally or maliciously tampering with your program's state. (However, unsafe code [Appendix 0] can still cause problems.)

- You can load and unload plug-ins as needed.

Unlike most FCL objects, you don't create a new domain by calling its constructor, and you don't unload a domain by calling Dispose or allowing it to go out of scope.[16] Rather, you create a new domain by calling the static method AppDomain.CreateDomain, passing it a domain name string and various optional security and configuration parameters. To free an AppDomain you've created, you call the static method AppDomain.Unload, passing it the AppDomain that you got from CreateDomain.

Once you've created an AppDomain, there are three different ways to execute code in it: calling a delegate, executing an application, or creating a remoting proxy. These are roughly ordered by both ease of use and degree of communication between domains: calling a delegate is easy, but you can't pass any parameters and you can't get any results; executing an application is slightly harder, and allows you to pass command-line arguments and get back an integer result code; while creating a proxy takes the most work, but allows you to make method calls to and from another domain.

Note None of these three methods creates a new thread. If you call code in a secondary AppDomain from your application's main thread, your application will be blocked until the code returns. You can, however, use the system ThreadPool (or explicitly create a background thread—Chapter 17 covers both) and make your call into your secondary AppDomain from the background thread.

Delegates

The AppDomain instance method DoCallBack executes a delegate (in the instance domain) that takes no parameters and that returns no results. This is the easiest method of executing code in a temporary AppDomain, because you don't have to specify an assembly to load: the DoCallBack method will automatically load the delegate's assembly into the temporary AppDomain.[17] This can be an expensive proposition if, as in the Chapter14\AppDomainDemo C# project's first callback example, the delegate comes from the application assembly. In this case, the whole application assembly—though **not** the assemblies that your application references—will be loaded before your delegate is called.

You can avoid this expense by calling a delegate located in a small shim assembly, as in the AppDomainDemo C# project's second callback example. This loads only the shim assembly; the savings depend on the size of your application's metadata tables.

---

16. My guess is that the unusual syntax somehow reflects the way application domains are used within the CLR itself, but I haven't seen anything from Microsoft saying that this is the case.

17. When you run the AppDomainDemo, you will see that mscorlib appears to have been loaded into the callback's domain as well. This is an illusion, however, as mscorlib is a *domain-neutral* assembly, shared by all app domains in the process. A domain-neutral assembly can never be unloaded; it is automatically loaded into every app domain you create; and the jitted code is shared by all app domains. Any static variables, however, are replicated in each new app domain. This means that static variables in domain-neutral assemblies are more expensive than static variables in normal, *domain-bound* assemblies.

You have very little control over whether an assembly will be loaded domain neutral or domain bound. The choice is made by the Win32 code that loads the CLR so, unless you write your own loader, you simply have to live with the defaults: in stand-alone .NET executables, only mscorlib is loaded domain neutral; in ASP.NET, all strongly named assemblies are loaded domain neutral.

While the delegate cannot return any sort of result, DoCallBack can be a useful way to run some code that has to dynamically load some assemblies to do some disk or network IO—without keeping the dynamic assemblies in memory when you're done.

NAÏVE LOADING

The first time I tried to use an AppDomain, I wrote code like

```
AppDomain Sandbox = AppDomain.CreateDomain("Sandbox");
try
{
  Assembly Suspect = Sandbox.Load(LibraryName);
  // Use the Suspect assembly
}
finally
{
  AppDomain.Unload(Sandbox);
}
```

I thought that anything I did with the Suspect assembly magically executed in the Sandbox domain, and that the Suspect assembly would be unloaded with the Sandbox domain. I was amazed at how easy it was to use an AppDomain! It wasn't until some weeks later that I found that, while the Suspect assembly **was** unloaded with the Sandbox domain, the Sandbox.Load call was also loading the library into the default AppDomain—and unloading a secondary domain has no effect on the default domain.

Judging from various online venues, this seems to be a common mistake. While the AppDomain.Load documentation specifically warns about the dangers of this, the warning can be impossible to understand without some remoting background.

The Assembly class is serializable but not remotable. The Sandbox.Load call does indeed load an assembly into the new AppDomain, but deserializing the returned Assembly also loads the assembly into the original domain. (As per the SDK documentation, this can cause assembly mismatch issues if the two domains have different assembly search paths.) Doing anything like creating instances of types defined in the Suspect assembly only increases the 'pollution' of the original AppDomain if the types from the Suspect refer to any assemblies that aren't already loaded into the original AppDomain.

The main text discusses ways to load code into a new AppDomain without affecting the original AppDomain.

Applications

The AppDomain instance method ExecuteAssembly runs a .NET executable you specify, optionally passing command-line arguments. ExecuteAssembly returns an integer containing the application's result code. In a C# app, the result code is the value that the Main method returns; a Delphi app can set a result code by calling Halt with an explicit result code. (As in the AppDomainDemo's ExecuteDomain example, you'll get 0 from a static void Main C# app, or from a Delphi app that doesn't call Halt with an explicit result code.)

ExecuteAssembly can be a lightweight alternative to spawning a whole process with the System.Diagnostics.Process class—any assembly you execute in a secondary AppDomain runs in your process, using your copy of the CLR, and using (perhaps) a preexisting thread—while still providing the same isolation as a separate process.

■ **Note** You do have to use a process to run a Win32 executable. `ExecuteAssembly` can only run .NET assemblies.

Proxies

Getting a remoting proxy with the `AppDomain` instance method `CreateInstanceAndUnwrap` is the most flexible way to make calls between application domains. The `CreateInstance` family of methods all load the assembly you specify into the instance `AppDomain`; do a `GetType` on that assembly to find a type that you specify by name; create an instance of that type; and return a proxy for that new instance. Thus, in the AppDomainDemo's `Plugin` example,

```
Gateway Proxy = (Gateway)ProxyDomain.Domain.
  CreateInstanceAndUnwrap("Shim", "Shim.Gateway");
```

loads the `Shim` assembly and creates an instance of the `Shim.Gateway` class.

The point of using a shim assembly is that—as with any remoting—you can only proxy types known in both app domains. Using a shim allows you to use the architecture in Figure 14-2 where the shim loads plug-ins into secondary app domains, and interfaces in the shim assembly let you call between app domains much as in the standard (unloadable) plug-in architecture of Chapter 13.

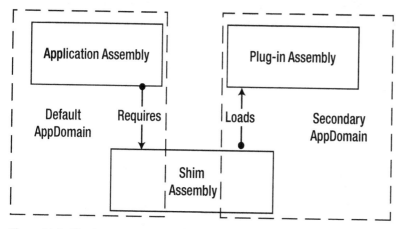

Figure 14-2. *The AppDomain architecture*

For example, the `Gateway` object in the AppDomainDemo's `Shim` assembly supports a method that takes an assembly name; loads the assembly; and returns a proxy for the first type it finds in that assembly that supports its `IMatch` interface:

```
IMatch MatchPluginProxy = Proxy.LoadAndGetIMatchPluginProxy("Plugin.dll");
```

As you might expect, a proxy can only return an interface when the class that supports the interface is itself a proxyable `MarshalByRefObject` descendant. What is 'really' returned is a standard proxy class, and when you call the interface methods, you call proxy methods, which stream arguments and/or results across app domain boundaries in the normal way.

Key Points

- Reflection-based serialization is fast, easy to use, and preserves object identity; it can handle circular references, and will deserialize multiple references to a single object **as** multiple references to a single object.

- Reflection-based serialization supports binary and SOAP formats. The binary format is the best for most purposes, being smaller and faster.

- XML serialization is slower, more limited, and does not preserve object identity. It will deserialize multiple references to a single object as references to distinct objects with the same state.

- You can use either serialization method for persistence, but the Reflection-based `BinaryFormatter` class is generally the best choice for persistence. (`BinaryFormatter` does depend on access to private members of types from other assemblies, and low-trust situations may force you to use the otherwise inferior XML serialization.) You can store multiple object graphs in a single stream with Reflection-based formatting.

- .NET remoting is used both for communication between processes on the same or different machines, and for communication between application domains within a single process. Remoting uses serialization to pass values across boundaries, and to pass arguments and results between remote objects and their local proxies.

CHAPTER 15

■ ■ ■

WinForms Basics

WinForms and Delphi forms are very similar. There's no T in Form, Control, or Component, but all three play the same roles in WinForms as in Delphi. Similarly, a control's Visible, Enabled, and Parent properties act the same in WinForms as in Delphi. There are differences, of course, from eye-catching differences like form loading to significant differences in message handling and event dispatching. There are also plenty of petty little close-but-different annoyances. Overall, though, the similarities strongly outweigh the differences, and Delphi programmers find WinForms easy and familiar.

The .NET GUI classes in the System.Windows.Forms namespace—commonly known as *WinForms*—are a lot like familiar Delphi VCL forms. The WinForms Form class descends from the Control class, which descends from the Component class—just as the VCL TForm class descends from the TControl class, which descends from the TComponent class. Controls have Visible, Enabled, and Parent properties, which work just like their VCL counterparts.

This chapter catalogs the differences, because you need to know when to do familiar things in new ways. This chapter doesn't talk about the core similarities, because you don't want to waste your time reading about what you already know. But, without an architecture to cover, this chapter is just a jumpy collection of topics. It may be easy to lose sight of the essential truth: WinForms and VCL forms are more alike than different, and you will find it easy to apply your Delphi experience.

This chapter is divided into five sections. The first four cover the largest differences: form design and loading, control docking, event dispatch, and threading. Recursively, the last section is a collection of short topics and a table, covering some of the more important of the smaller differences.

This chapter does not contain a comprehensive list of all the differences. There **will** be times when a member that you expect doesn't show up under any variant of the name you expect.

When this happens, the property grid shows a short description of every property and event. This description (and the property grid's category view) can often be enough to find what you are looking for. Sometimes, though, you'll just have to read through alphabetical lists of member names, looking for some other way to describe the missing member. For example, Delphi's form OnCreate event is the form Load event, on WinForms. (Remember, the FCL is similar to Delphi, but it is not a Delphi port.)

■**Delphi Note**   When I say Delphi or VCL forms in this chapter, I mean Win32 Delphi or VCL forms, not VCL for .NET forms. I don't cover VCL for .NET in this book, and do recommend that you use it only for porting code, not for new development. First, there will always be more third-party WinForms components than third-party components for VCL for .NET. Second, there will always be more WinForms experience that you can tap via Google than VCL for .NET experience that you can tap via Google. And third, there will always be more demand for WinForms experience than for VCL for .NET experience.

Form Design and Loading

Different designers and different run-time form creation

There are some eye-catching differences between WinForms and traditional Delphi forms: The designers are different, and run-time form creation is different. WinForms designers place the tool palette and property grid on pinnable windows that compete for screen space[1] with various sorts of editors (code editors, form editors, XML editors, &c) that live in a central tabbed window. By contrast, the traditional Delphi form designer placed the tool palette on a comparatively short, wide strip across the top of the screen; the property grid on a tall, free-floating window maybe three to five words wide; and the form editors in free-floating windows that can overlap (be above or below) the various tool windows.

In both VCL and WinForms, a form is an object with fields that refer to the objects that implement the form's components and visual controls. The difference is that VCL forms are loaded from a stream, while WinForms forms are created by custom code in the form's (IDE-maintained) InitializeComponent method. The VCL form stream lists each component and child control, and each nondefault property value. The WinForms InitializeComponent method explicitly creates each component and child control, and explicitly sets each nondefault property value.

The WinForms designer can be shocking to a Delphi programmer[2]—we're used to overlapping windows, and find it strange to have toolwindows compete for space with edit windows. We're used to free-floating form editors, and find it strange to have form editors in the same tab set as code editors. We're used to a discrete, if cryptic, {$R *.dfm}, and find it strange to see form creation code.

But, after the shock, you start to see reasons.

Pinning and unpinning toolwindows allows your space allocation to change as you need it to. You do need a big screen[3] to have a toolwindow open on the left and on the right, and a

---

1. A pinnable window opens on top of the main window when you click a tab at the side of the screen, and closes up when you move the mouse off of it. You can also click the pin icon to pin the window open, at which point it no longer closes when you move the mouse off. Also, when you pin a window open, it is placed beside (i.e., no longer on top of) the tabbed main window, and the main window resizes.

2. You'll survive the shock. There were a few places in this chapter where I couldn't remember how something was done in Delphi.

3. For what it's worth, I find 1280×1024 to be a practical minimum—1024×768 is a bit cramped.

decent-size code or form editor in the middle. But, if you have that big screen, the pinned tool-windows seem to require a lot less mousing about than do overlapping, resizable windows.

The more you think of overlapping windows as a concession to a small screen, the less you miss free-floating form editors. It's nice and consistent to put form editors into the main, tabbed, window along with hex editors and icon editors. And (what's the opposite of "sour grapes"?) I find it's not that horrible to keep my code under 80 columns, and my dialogs to a minimum size of no more than maybe 500 or 600 wide. Long lines of code are easier to write than to read, and huge forms can really lose the user.

As for form loading, Delphi's form-loading code is certainly smaller per form than WinForms form-creation code, but the price is high: form loading uses a lot of library code, and the smart linker can't remove any unused published methods. Overall, WinForms form-creation code is probably smaller than Delphi's form-loading code in all but the largest programs, and the WinForms approach is certainly faster. VCL form loading is slower because it has to look up each component and property name at run time, while WinForms form creation executes compiled custom code. (Yes, WinForms is faster even the first time you create a form, when you have to jit the custom code. The VCL is looking up strings in reasonably large tables.)

The code that creates forms at run time is created by the form designer at design time, in the same language as the rest of the class: C#, VB, Pascal, and so on. When you add and remove controls and property settings, the form designer changes the InitializeComponent method. When you change your source file, the form designer can find the InitializeComponent method and reinterpret it.

This works on a sort of glorified template basis and, while the form designer can always find the InitializeComponent method in a file that can be compiled, the form designer can't always understand code that it wouldn't write. Obviously enough, you can add or remove extra white space. You can change property settings—in C#, you can even use multiline @ strings. You can change parentage and creation order, by editing and moving the lines that add controls to their Parent.Controls collection. But don't add comments or code.

Caution In Win32 Delphi programming, you're much more likely to read .dfm text than you are to change it by hand. Similarly, while it can be useful to see how the form designer creates and initializes various components and controls, you should be very reluctant to change the auto-generated InitializeComponent code.

In .NET 1.x, both VS and BDS put all the form source in one file—not only the control and component member declarations, but also the InitializeComponent method is in the same source file as your manually created form members. This means that when you search for the places where you refer to a component or a control, you usually end up having to plow through both the declaration and all the places where InitializeComponent sets a control or component property. In addition, the InitializeComponent method can easily run to many hundreds of lines long, which makes it a bit harder to get a quick sense of a form's complexity. Visual Studio 2005 takes advantage of C# 2.0's partial classes to split a form's code into FormName.cs and FormName.Designer.cs. The FormName.cs file contains only your code; the FormName.Designer.cs file contains the component field declarations and the InitializeComponent method. Future Delphis will support partial classes, and so presumably future BDS WinForms designers will also separate (mostly) user-edited code from (mostly) machine-edited code.

Docking

The large difference between Delphi's Align *and WinForms'* Dock

WinForms controls don't have an Align property the way VCL controls do. Instead, WinForms controls have a Dock property, which does pretty much what the VCL Align property does: both allow you to force a control to take all available space along an edge of its container control, and to resize with the container. This is somewhat different than an Anchor property, which allows a control to move and resize with its container, but which does not force the anchored control to fill. For example, in both the Chapter15\Win32_AlignVsAnchor Delphi project and the Chapter15\AlignVsAnchor C# project, no matter how you resize Form1, the TopAlignedPanel is always at position 0, 0, and its Width always matches the form's ClientWidth (ClientSize.Width, in WinForms), while the BottomAnchoredPanel is always at 25 Left, and its Width is always 50 less than the form's ClientWidth / ClientSize.Width.

The WinForms Anchor property acts pretty much exactly like the VCL Anchors property, but the WinForms Dock property does act differently than the VCL Align property in one key way. When the VCL lays out a container control's aligned child controls, it walks the container's Controls array several times, laying out top-aligned controls, then bottom-aligned controls, then left-aligned controls, and so on.

When it lays out, say, top-aligned controls, it walks the Controls array, building an AlignList of top-aligned controls, in Top order. (For each top-aligned control in the container's Controls array, the VCL scans the AlignList to find all controls closer to the container's top, and then inserts the top-aligned control at the appropriate place in the AlignList. It may seem cheaper to simply append each top-aligned control, then sort the AlignList—but the insertion sort probably isn't all that expensive, given that very few containers have even two children aligned the same way, let alone three or more.) The VCL then walks the AlignList, placing the first child on the list at the top of the unallocated rectangle, the second child below that, and so on.

This is complicated, but it makes it very easy to change docking in the form designer—you can just drag controls around to change, say, which right-aligned child is rightmost. This multi-pass implementation also affects the way the VCL allocates space to aligned child controls. Because the VCL lays out top- and bottom-aligned controls before left- and right-aligned controls, top- and bottom-aligned controls always get the full width, and a left- or right-aligned control is always vertically between any top- and bottom-aligned controls. If you want left- and/or right-aligned controls to take the full height, with top- and bottom-aligned controls horizontally between them, you have to use nested panels: you add a fill-aligned panel between the left and right controls, and nest the top- and/or bottom-aligned controls on the fill panel. (See Figure 15-1, or Form2 in the Chapter15\Win32_AlignVsAnchor Delphi project.)

By contrast, the WinForms Dock property has a much simpler implementation: the Controls collection is walked once, in *z-order* (I explain z-order later in this section), and each docked control gets all available space along its edge. That is, if the first docked child in the z-order is top docked, it gets the full width of the container, and keeps its undocked height, if the container is tall enough. The next docked child in the z-order is fit into the remaining space. If that second docked control is right-docked, it gets the full remaining height, and a width up to its undocked width. A third docked child is fit into the remaining space, and so on.

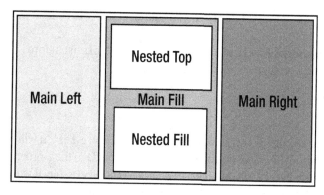

Figure 15-1. *Mixing top- and side-aligned panels takes nesting, under VCL rules.*

This implementation does make form design a bit harder, as you can't turn the leftmost left-aligned child into the rightmost left-aligned child by dragging it, nor by setting Location.X to a large number like 10000. However, without a hierarchy that sets top and bottom over left and right, the FCL leaves form layout to you—it doesn't impose a style. Also, a single pass through the z-order is certainly more efficient than walking the Controls array several times, and it can make for fewer nested panels, which is a further efficiency. For example, using the FCL rules, Figure 15-2 places narrow top- and bottom-aligned panels between full-height left- and right-aligned panels, without any need for a panel to hold nested top- and bottom-aligned panels.

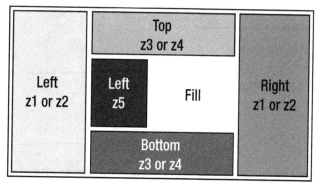

Figure 15-2. *Mixing top- and side-aligned panels takes no nesting, under WinForms rules.*

By default, z-order corresponds to creation order. The first control you drop on a container will be first in the z-order, and gets to carve out space first. The second control you drop on a container will be second in the z-order, and gets to carve out space next. The last control you drop on a container will be last in the z-order, and gets to carve out space last.

If you remember this simple rule, and always carefully plan the sequence in which you add controls to a container, you'll never have any problems with docking. Most of us won't, though, and will occasionally need to edit the z-order.

For some reason, z-order is the **reverse** of the order of controls in the container's Controls collection: the last control added to the container's Controls collection is the first in the z-order, and the first control added to the container's Controls collection is the last in the z-order. (This **might** be some sort of optimization for large forms: the designer only has to find the InitializeComponent method's first reference to a container's Controls collection, not every reference.)

Thus, if you drop two panels on a form, Panel2 will be added to the Controls list before Panel1, as in the Chapter15\z_order C# project:

```
this.Controls.Add(this.Panel2);
this.Controls.Add(this.Panel1);
```

which places Panel1 at the top of the z-order. If you set Panel1.Dock to DockStyle.Left, it will snap to the left edge of the form, taking up the whole height. Panel2 is below Panel1 in the z-order, and so if you Dock it, it grabs space after Panel1. If you set Panel2.Dock to DockStyle.Top, it will snap to the top edge of the form, but its left edge will be flush with Panel1's right edge, not with the left edge of the form (see Figure 15-3).

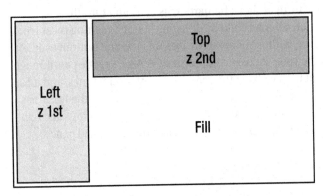

Figure 15-3. *No precedence rules in WinForms docking*

If you manually edit the InitializeComponent method so that Panel1 is at the top of the z-order:

```
this.Controls.Add(this.Panel1);
this.Controls.Add(this.Panel2);
```

you have reversed the z-order, and now the top-docked Panel2 takes the whole form width, and the left-docked Panel1 is fit in under Panel2.

■**Tip** If you are creating a form programmatically, remember to add controls to the Controls collection in reverse order: the last added is first in the z-order, and gets priority in docking. (Setting a control's Parent property is the same as adding it to the parent's Controls collection.)

The WinForms z-order design is a lot simpler than the VCL's multipass design. But the VCL asks a lot less of a form designer than WinForms does. Or something like that because, until recently, if you didn't create your docked controls in just the right order, your options were to either cut and paste controls in the form editor—losing event handlers in the process—or to edit the InitializeComponent source to change the order that you add controls to the container's Controls collection. In VS 2005, the Document Outline window lets you drag and drop controls within containers and between containers. This, or some future BDS equivalent, can probably keep you from needing to edit the `InitializeComponent` method by hand.

Events

All events are inherently multicast

WinForms uses the same basic event model as VCL: Windows messages from the form's controls are mapped to events, typically handled by the form's instance methods. Both the VS Property Grid and the BDS Object Inspector expose control events, and allow you to assign event handlers to them. Both allow you to create a new event handler by double-clicking and/or typing a new method's name, and both allow you to choose from a drop-down list of existing methods with compatible signatures.

The big difference is in event dispatch. VCL calls each event handler through a *method pointer*, a data structure that pairs an instance reference with a pointer to a method's entry point. A method pointer is either `Nil` or pairs a (single) instance reference with a (single) pointer to a method's entry point. Code that fires an event typically looks like

```
if Assigned(EventHandler)  // if the EventHandler is not Nil,
  then EventHandler(Self); // then call the EventHandler
```

and every event has zero or one handlers. If you need to have more than one handler for an event (perhaps because you need to allow various parts of your application to subscribe and unsubscribe to a particular notification as their state changes), you need to manually maintain a list of subscribers, and your event handler needs to manually call each subscriber on the list.

.NET event handlers are delegates with some special rules (Chapters 2, 8, and 10). All delegates (and hence all events) are inherently multicast: any given delegate may have zero, one, or many method pointers on its invocation list. A delegate with no handlers is null, while a delegate with one or more handlers is non-null. The special part of .NET event handlers is that, outside of an event's class, all you can do is subscribe and unsubscribe to the event. Within the event's class, you can treat an event like a normal delegate, writing code like

```
if (EventHandler != null)            // if the EventHandler is not null
  EventHandler(this, EventArgs.Empty); // then call the EventHandler
  // you would typically use a more descriptive EventArgs than EventArgs.Empty!
```

Event Multiplexing

Don't touch `InitializeComponent`

You can have multiple event handlers by adding extra subscribers to an event. However, the .NET form designer supports only zero or one handlers per event, just as with Win32 VCL forms. Modifying `InitializeComponent` to add multiple handlers to an event will break the form designer. How the form designer breaks varies from IDE to IDE and from version to version, but the basic message is, **Don't add multiple event handlers in `InitializeComponent`!**

Do note that this is a design-time limitation, not a run-time limitation.

As in Delphi, so in WinForms: forms are special objects that come into the world configured by the form designer. As in Delphi, you can do things at run time that you can't do at design time. Do all your subscribing and unsubscribing in event handlers. The form Load event is a good place to add event subscribers.

Low-level GUI Access

When WinForms doesn't wrap the functionality you need

In WinForms as in Delphi, controls are object-oriented facades for the flat functions that create and manipulate the various specialized windows that Windows can create—panels, buttons, edit boxes, tree views, and the like. These specialized windows send messages to the form, which the window function handles and dispatches to our event handlers. Our facades control their specialized windows by calling the right flat functions and/or sending messages to their window.

This is much easier and clearer than handling numbered messages with their WParam and LParam parameters, but the control facades don't always expose all the behavior of the underlying window. Some windows send messages that the control doesn't map to events, and some windows respond to messages and flat function calls that the control doesn't wrap.

When we need this extra functionality, we need to handle the extra messages and call the extra functions. For example, in 1.*x*, a tree view click handler may want to send the TVM_HITTEST message to see where on a node the user clicked, because it wants to act differently when the user clicks the node's +/- button than when the user clicks the node's icon or text. (In 2.0, the TreeView class has a HitTest method.)

Calling Win32 functions like SendMessage is a matter of using the (System.Runtime. InteropServices) DllImport attribute to call external functions from DLLs like Win32 and User32, almost like in Delphi. In fact, the Win32 Delphi import units can be a useful guide to generating a DllImport declaration for a Win32 function, if Google doesn't provide a pretested declaration.

Handling extra messages works a bit differently in the VCL than in WinForms. With VCL forms, handling extra messages is a simple matter of adding message wm_Whatever after a method with the right procedure wmWhatever(var Message: TMessage) prototype. With WinForms, you have to override the form object's protected void WndProc(ref Message m) and dispatch on the message's Msg integer.

You **can** do dispatch via a long switch statement as in Windows 1.*x*, but you don't **have** to. For example, the Chapter15\WndProc C# project includes code that defines MessageAttribute and MessageMap classes. The MessageMap class's constructors find void MessageName(ref Message M) methods with a [Message(int)] attribute, and add them to a private Dictionary<int, MessageHandler>. The MessageHandlingForm initializes its MessageMap in its constructor. The form's WndProc then looks up each message in its MessageMap, and calls registered message handlers, almost like in Delphi:

```
protected override void WndProc(ref Message m)
{
    base.WndProc(ref m);
    if (Messages.IsAssigned(m.Msg))
        Messages[m.Msg](ref m);
}
```

You can inherit from the WndProc project's `MessageHandlingForm`, or you can add a `MessageMap` and this `WndProc` to your own forms. The WndProc project's `ClipboardWatcher` form is a `MessageHandlingForm` that uses message handlers and `DllImport` to add itself to the clipboard viewer chain, so it can examine the clipboard contents every time the user puts new data on the clipboard. You can use this to enable a Paste command only when the clipboard contains data in a format that you can currently paste.

Threads

Don't touch other thread's controls

The GUI threading model is very simple. Any thread can create a WinForms control, but only that thread should call the control's methods or set the control's properties. If the default thread created a control in `InitializeComponent`, then only the default thread should touch that control.

There are only two exceptions to this rule. Any thread can ask any control to `CreateGraphics` at any time. This returns a `Graphics` object that lets the thread draw on the control. I cover the `Graphics` object in Chapter 16.

The other exception is that any thread can ask any control to `Invoke` a delegate at any time.[4] The control will run the delegate, in the control's thread, as soon as it is safe to do so. Just as if the delegate had been called normally, the call to `Invoke` doesn't return until the delegate runs to completion in the control's thread: the thread that calls `Invoke` is blocked until the delegate runs.

You don't always want a background thread to wait for its UI update to complete. You may want to go right back to waiting for IO, or to doing calculations. As an alternative to calling `Invoke`, you can call `BeginInvoke`, which asks a control to run a delegate as soon as it can, just as with `Invoke`, but which does not wait for the delegate to return. Instead, `BeginInvoke` returns an `IAsyncResult` that you can either ignore or save to pass to `EndInvoke` later.

You will need to call `EndInvoke` when you want to be sure that one update will be finished before a new one begins. `EndInvoke` will block until the delegate returns, just as `Invoke` does.

There are occasions where you can call `BeginInvoke` without ever calling `EndInvoke`. For example, if a control is only updated every few seconds or every few minutes, you probably don't have to worry about out-of-order updates. Synchronization issues aside, it's perfectly safe to simply ignore the `IAsyncResult` result from `BeginInvoke`.

Note It is safe to ignore the `IAsyncResult` from `Control.BeginInvoke`. It is **not** safe to ignore the `IAsyncResult` from a delegate's `BeginInvoke`. Never confuse the two!

Note also that while it is perfectly safe to ignore the `IAsyncResult` result from `Control.BeginInvoke`, it's not perfectly free: `IAsyncResult` has a `WaitHandle` member (Chapter 17), and `WaitHandle` has a finalizer. If you don't `EndInvoke`, the `WaitHandle` will eventually be finalized.

---

4. See the Microsoft documentation for details on the delegate prototypes you can `Invoke`.

As per Chapter 2, this is a comparatively expensive operation, though it does seem safe to assume that a WaitHandle will never point to lots of other objects that will need to be resurrected.

If you use Control.BeginInvoke to fire-and-forget a lot of operations from non-GUI threads, you can minimize this finalization cost (and reduce OS resource usage) by calling WaitHandle.Close on the IAsyncResult that you get from Control.BeginInvoke—but be sure that the IAsyncResult.IsCompleted property is set (true) before you call Close. Closing the WaitHandle before the asynchronous operation signals completion will cause an exception when the invoked delegate returns.

One way to minimize resource usage without blocking is to append each fire-and-forget IAsyncResult to a synchronized list. A low-priority background thread could scan this list every few seconds, and Close the WaitHandle of any IAsyncResult that IsCompleted.

The Small Stuff

Lots of same-but-different, some new stuff

Each chapter presents its own challenges. Because WinForms and Delphi forms are so architecturally similar, this chapter is just a collection of big and little differences. When the differences get down to a paragraph or three, any sort of smooth transition from one topic to the next would overwhelm the topics. That's why what follows is just a bunch of small topics and a table of tiny topics, covering the more important of the smaller differences.

The Biggest Small Stuff

Roughly sorted by anticipated audience size

ShowModal vs. ShowDialog

In both Delphi and WinForms, you can Show and Hide a modeless form, or you can set the Visible property. The two also handle modal forms identically, though they use slightly different syntax:

- In Delphi, you call ShowModal to show a form as a modal dialog. The call to ShowModal doesn't return until the user closes the dialog, and the result is an integer like mrOK.

- In WinForms, you call ShowDialog to show a form as a modal dialog. The call to ShowDialog doesn't return until the user closes the dialog, and the result is a DialogResult enum.

Where the Delphi wrappers for common dialogs (file open and the like) have an Execute method that returns a Boolean, the WinForms dialog controls use ShowDialog, and return a DialogResult enum.

Layout vs. Resize

WinForms has a Resize event that's much like Delphi's OnResize event: Resize is called when the control or form is resized for any reason. The WinForms Layout event is a bit broader: Layout is called when the control or form is resized, and when the control's `Parent.Controls` collection changes (because a control has been added or removed).

Note Because form loading populates the form, the `Layout` event is called at form load time, which the `Resize` event is not. This makes `Layout` the event to handle if you need to track a container's size.

When adding a set of controls to a container control, or making other large changes, you should call `SuspendLayout`, and call `ResumeLayout` when you're done. (These are much like the VCL `DisableAlign` and `EnableAlign` methods.) `SuspendLayout` increments a counter and `ResumeLayout` decrements the counter: the `Layout` event will not fire while the counter is not zero, no matter how many times the `Controls` or `Bounds` properties change.

Label/Control Linkage

In Delphi, every `TLabel` has a `FocusControl` property. If the `FocusControl` property is set and the label's `Caption` has an & character that defines an Alt+*Char* shortcut, the form gives focus to the `FocusControl` when the user presses Alt+*Char*. (For example, if the `Caption` is `'&Name'`, Alt+N will give focus to the `FocusControl`.)

WinForms labels have no `FocusControl` property. Instead, typing the shortcut specified in their `Text` property passes control to the next control in the `TabIndex` order whose `TabStop` property is `true`.

Caution You are responsible for maintaining `TabIndex` order within each container. The designer does not complain about duplicate `TabIndex` values, nor does it remove gaps.

You can edit the `TabIndex` as in Delphi, by selecting a control and changing its `TabIndex` property in the property grid. This can be a tedious and difficult process; it's hard to see conflicts without cycling through each control in each container. The form designer offers an alternate tab-order editing mode (in VS, View ➤ Tab Order; in BDS, right-click on a form and select Tab Order) that removes the `TabIndex` property from the grid, and displays each component's tab order in a box at the top left (see Figure 15-4). You can then simply click each control in turn, and the tab order will be set properly. The tab edit mode doesn't avoid or resolve conflicts, but it does make it much easier to get the tab order right.

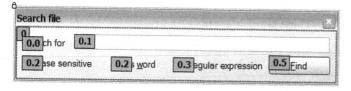

Figure 15-4. *The form designer's tab-order editing mode*

Object Collections, Not String Lists

In Delphi, the TListBox and the TComboBox controls have an Items property that's a TStrings. The equivalent WinForms ListBox and ComboBox controls have an Items property that's an ObjectCollection. You **can** add a string to the Items collection, but you can also add any object at all. What is displayed is the item's ToString() value, but when you read the Items collection, you get the object you put in, which may be arbitrarily complicated. You can use is and as on an object from the Items collection, and you can cast the object to a specialized descendant type, so that you can call methods on it or pass it to some other object's methods.

For example, a ComboBox might have a list of Action objects. Their ToString() overload shows a user-friendly name, and when the user selects an Action object from the drop-down, you call the Action object's Invoke method. Or, when the user drags[5] a Factory object from an Available ListBox to an Active ListBox, you might call the Factory object's Create method and add the result to the Active ListBox.

Polymorphic Controls

Many controls present view(s) of a collection of a particular type of item. For example, each ListView.Item is a ListViewItem, and each TreeView.Node property is a TreeNode. You can generally populate these view controls with specialized items—a ListView of ListViewItem descendants, a TreeView of TreeNode descendants, and so on.

You can use this to add, say, a virtual OnClick method to your abstract CustomTreeNodeBase class, and give each node in a heterogeneous tree the ability to handle a click event in its own way.

Colors

WinForms specifies colors using the (System.Drawing) 32-bit ARGB Color structure. A, or *alpha*, is an 8-bit opacity code, where 255 is a solid color and 0 is transparent. The R, G, and B components are standard 8-bit RGB components. Each Color structure has methods to get its Hue, Saturation, and Brightness values, but there are no methods to create a Color from an HSB triplet, nor are there methods to go from an ARGB Color to a CMYK color or vice versa. (You can, however, convert images to CMYK, and examine the value of each "color channel." See Chapter 16, which also has HSB-to-Color code.)

The Color structure has a great many static properties corresponding to the known (named) colors that you can select at design time, like Color.Turquoise and Color.HotPink. The Color.FromKnownColor method will convert a member of the KnownColor enumeration (like KnownColor.Turquoise) to a Color structure, and Color.FromName will convert a string like Turquoise to Color.Turquoise (returning Color.FromArgb(0, 0, 0, 0) if the name is not in the KnownColor enumeration). Conversely, Color.ToKnownColor will return a KnownColor value, if the Color was created from a KnownColor or a KnownColor name; otherwise, Color.ToKnownColor will return 0, even if the Color's ARGB components precisely match a known color.

The SystemColors class has static Color members that correspond to user-settable colors like ControlText and AppWorkspace. (These are also KnownColors.)

---

5. If you've done drag and drop in Delphi, you can do drag and drop in WinForms. If you haven't already done drag and drop, just experiment—drag and drop is very easy under WinForms. Take care that you always know whether this or sender is the drag target or the drag data and you'll be fine.

Ambient Properties

Delphi has several properties with associated ParentX properties: Color and ParentColor, Font and ParentFont, and so on. When ParentColor is True, a control automatically assumes its Parent control's Color: when the Parent control's Color changes, so does the child control's; if you set the child control's Color, you also set its ParentColor to False.

WinForms has a similar effect with a slightly different interface. A control's Font, Cursor, Color, and BackColor properties are *ambient properties*. If a parented control's ambient property is not set, it will use its Parent control's value. That is, an ambient property like Color acts like a Delphi property with its ParentX property set to true by default.

For example, if a container control (like a Form or a Panel) has a BackColor of Color.Transparent, every control you place on it will have an initial BackColor of Color.Transparent. This is useful when the container has a BackgroundImage (discussed later in this chapter) as in Figure 15-5.

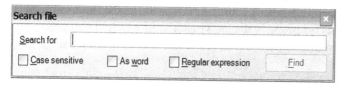

Figure 15-5. *A dialog with transparent controls on a* BackgroundImage

If a control overrides an ambient property, you can make it use the ambient property simply by deleting the override value in the property grid (that is, select all the text and press the Delete key, or simply backspace over it all). This deletes the line in the InitializeComponent method that sets the property, thus causing the control to use its Parent's value for the property. Once set, a property cannot be reverted to using ambient values: in particular, setting a control's property to the control's Parent's value of the property does **not** make the control resume using an ambient property at run time. (For example, see the Chapter15\Ambience C# project.)

Validation

When a control loses focus, its Leave event fires. Also, if its CausesValidation property is true (the default), the Validating and Validated events will fire after the Leave event. The Validating event is an opportunity to check the contents of the control that is losing focus. If the control's contents are invalid in any way, you can display a warning message and perhaps disable the dialog's OK button. You can also set the Cancel property of the Validating event's CancelEventArgs parameter to true, which will return focus to the invalid control. If you **don't** set the Cancel property to true, the Validating event will be followed by the Validated event. (You may not want to prevent the user from leaving an input control with bad data, but the Validating event is an easy place to put validation code.)

The CausesValidation logic is actually somewhat complicated. As best I can make out, it works like this: when a CausesValidation control (a "validating control") loses focus, it's saved in some sort of private LastValidator field. When a validating control gets focus, if it's not the same control as the LastValidator control, the LastValidator is validated. Thus, in the Chapter15\CausesValidation C# project, when control moves from A (a nonvalidating control) to B (a validating control), or from B to A, neither A nor B is validated. When control moves from B to C (also a validating control) or from C to B, the control that is losing focus is validated.

When control moves from B or C to the Cancel button (a nonvalidating control), neither B nor C is validated—but when control moves to the OK button (another validating control), the LastValidator gets validated.

Note In general, you should either set CausesValidation to false for all controls on a form, or leave it true for all but a Cancel button. You can get some strange behavior when the Validating event sets Cancel after a nonvalidating control has the focus. "Canceling" the "loss" of focus means that focus jumps back to the LastValidator.

Tool Tips

WinForms supports tool tips just like Delphi does, but in a slightly weird way: a form has no tool tips until you drop a ToolTip control onto the form. At that point, all the controls on the form will show a ToolTip on toolTip1 property that acts much like the Delphi Hint property. (You can have multiple ToolTip controls on a form, but each control will only show a single hint when the user hovers the mouse.)

Tip To support mouse hover hints, be sure to add a ToolTip control to your forms.

BackgroundImage

All WinForms controls have a BackgroundImage property that allows you to set a (System.Drawing) Image (i.e., either a Bitmap or a Metafile) as the control's background. However, controls that don't support transparency hide the BackgroundImage properties from the property grid[6]— containers and buttons and picture boxes can have a background image, but list views and tree views and text editors can't.

You can use the BackgroundImage property to set a tiled, textured background, or you can use it to set a background gradient. (I cover gradient fills in Chapter 16.) A gradient background has to be sized to the client rectangle, so you'll generally generate a gradient BackgroundImage in the form Layout event, which is called both when the form is created and when the form is resized.

Controls that don't support transparency can't set BackColor to Transparent. Controls that do support transparency **can** set a BackColor to Transparent. Note that, because of ambient properties, when you place a control that supports transparency on a container with a

---

6. The property grid can display any object. By default, it displays all public properties and public events. Various attributes allow you to hide public properties and events, or to control the way they appear in the grid. You can include property grids in your own applications as a convenient alternative to modal property dialogs. The grid is quite customizable (though the API is not simple), and you can control each property's visible and read-only states at run time, as well as translating property names to user-friendly strings and controlling how the property values are displayed and/or edited.

Transparent BackColor, the control will be transparent by default. For example, a Label on a transparent Panel is transparent, unless you explicitly set the BackColor.

The search box (Ctrl+F) in the Chapter15\OwnerDemo C# project uses a customized Panel control that sets a BackgroundImage in the OnLayout method, which fires the Layout event.[7]

Locked

The Locked 'property' is not a member of the Control class or of Control descendants, as you'll find if you try pressing F1 for help on it. But the Locked 'property' appears in the property grid when you select a control, just as if it **were** a normal property.

The Locked property is an artifact of the designer: when a control is locked, it can't be moved. That is, you can never accidentally click and drag a locked control when you just want to see the control in the property grid. You can set Locked to true on a control-by-control basis, or you can lock all controls on a form with Format ➤ Lock Controls menu command (in Visual Studio—in BDS, use Edit ➤ Lock Controls).

Component Scope

In Delphi, a form's controls are published fields. Since published is public (with RTTI), you can write code that reads and writes EditBox4 from outside the form. (Your coworkers may shun you—both for accessing another form's controls directly and for not giving the control a more distinctive name—but the compiler won't stop you.)

In WinForms, control fields default to private, but can be set to protected or internal or whatever by changing their Modifiers property. You should be very suspicious of any "design" that relies on public form controls, but when one form is tightly linked to another (for example, a search/replace dialog), it's not **so** horrible for it to touch an internal control on its partner. For example, a form with a text editor control *might* create a pair of internal, form-level properties, SelectionStart and SelectionLength, that expose the text editor's SelectionStart and SelectionLength properties. But it's sure easier (and smaller, and more efficient) to just make the RTF control internal, as I do in the Chapter15\OwnerDemo C# project.

TopLevel **Forms**

In Delphi, you can place a form on another form by setting its Parent to the containing control, and setting BorderStyle and the bounds and/or Align properties properly. In WinForms, you can place a form on another form by setting its Parent to the containing control, and setting FormBorderStyle and the bounds and/or Dock properties properly—plus you have to set TopLevel to false before setting Parent. If you don't, you'll get an exception.

In Delphi, the TFrame is a sort of lightweight, borderless form, designed precisely for dropping composite controls onto forms. The controls on the TFrame can have event handlers of their own, as can the frame itself: the handlers are typically methods in the frame class. In WinForms, the UserControl class plays almost exactly the same role.

---

7. WinForms controls are like Delphi controls in this way, too. Events are generally fired by protected methods that you can override. When you create a specialized version of a WinForms control, you should add custom behavior to the event firing methods; your customized control shouldn't subscribe to its own events.

A form can host any UserControl in the current assembly or in an assembly that the current assembly references. Every 'available' UserControl with a public, parameterless constructor will appear in the Visual Studio toolbox (or the BDS tool palette) as a composite control that you can drop on a form. A UserControl that you drop on a form is sealed, in the sense that you can't drop controls onto it: when you drop controls onto a UserControl, they go onto the user control's Parent control.

■**Tip** The assembly that contains a UserControl has to be compiled before you can actually drop the UserControl on a form, and you will have to recompile the project before a change in a UserControl class is reflected in design-time changes to any hosted instances.

Owner

The Owner property means something quite different in WinForms than in Delphi. The VCL Owner is responsible for streaming in a component at load time, and freeing a component at dispose time. In WinForms, the Owner property is more a visual property, like Parent. The difference between Owner and Parent is that a parented Control is contained within its parent; if it extends outside the parent's bounds, it's clipped. By contrast, an owned Form floats above its owner and is not clipped: an owned form is minimized and closed when its Owner is minimized or closed. This is useful for search boxes (and various pop-up windows), as in the Chapter15\OwnerDemo C# project.

In much the same way that setting a control's Parent property has the same effect as adding a control to its Parent's Controls array, setting a form's Owner property to an owner form or to null has the same effect as calling the owner's AddOwnedForm and RemoveOwnedForm methods.

VCL-to-FCL Map

Same but different

Just as WinForms' ShowDialog is almost identical to Delphi's ShowModal, there are several common VCL features that are almost identical to WinForms features, but which are located in different classes or have different names under WinForms. Table 15-1 contains the most commonly used features, with their WinForms equivalents. (I cover the differences between Delphi's TCanvas and .NET's Graphics in the next chapter.)

Table 15-1. *FCL Equivalents for Common VCL Constructs*

Delphi Name	.NET Name	Notes
Application.KeyState	Control.ModifierKeys	Useful in event handlers that don't supply the shift states.
Application.ProcessMessages	Application.DoEvents	The Application class also has several useful static properties.
Mouse.CursorPos	Control.MousePosition	**In screen coordinates.** Useful in event handlers that don't supply the mouse position.
TControl.ClientHeight and TControl.ClientWidth	Control.ClientSize.Height and Control.ClientSize.Width	ClientSize is a Size structure with Height and Width members.
TControl.ClientRect	Control.ClientRectangle	The Rectangle structure has many useful members.
TControl.ScreenToClient and TControl.ClientToScreen	Control.PointToClient and Control.PointToScreen	Controls also have RectangleToClient and RectangleToScreen methods.
TForm.BorderStyle	Form.FormBorderStyle	
TFrame	UserControl	Can also use a Form, if you set its TopLevel property to false. Cannot add controls to a UserControl hosted on a form.

Key Points

WinForms and Delphi forms differ in details, but the architecture is similar

- VCL forms are loaded from a stream; WinForms are created by custom code. The WinForms approach is smaller and faster.

- The Dock property is the WinForms version of Delphi's Align property. The Dock property depends on the parent's Controls collection: the last control in the parent's Controls collection is laid out first, and the first control in the parent's Controls collection is laid out last.

- WinForms events can have multiple handlers, but you can't set multiple handlers in the designer.

- Don't touch a control that another thread created.

- There are lots of little differences, but nothing that should be hard to figure out.

CHAPTER 16

■ ■ ■

Graphics

The FCL Graphics class is a lot like the Delphi TCanvas. It hides many of the differences between screens, bitmaps, and printers. You get a drawing surface, and you draw on it with fonts, brushes, pens, and bitmaps. There are differences in the way you get a drawing surface and the way you select drawing tools, but these are pretty minor. The larger differences are in the fancy stuff you can do under GDI+ that you can't do with Delphi's VCL—gradient and bitmapped brushes, transparency and color manipulation, and various coordinate transformations. (The flip side of this is that GDI+ may never be supported in hardware, and does run slower than GDI.)

Familiar, but Not Identical

Two different object-oriented GDI wrapper libraries

You will find the FCL graphics classes to be broadly familiar: object-oriented wrappers for *Graphical Device Interface* (GDI) data structures. For example, Delphi wraps the Windows *Device Context* (DC) in a TCanvas object, and wraps pen, brush, and font handles in TPen, TBrush, and TFont objects. Similarly, the FCL wraps a GDI+ drawing surface in a Graphics object, and wraps GDI+ pens, brushes, and fonts in Pen, Brush, and Font objects.

GDI objects are limited system resources—even on NT-based platforms like XP—and must be closed when you are done with them. In native code Delphi, this means that you have to Free every GDI wrapper that you create. On .NET, the GDI wrappers do have finalizers, so you don't leak resources if you don't dispose of the wrappers when you're done with them—but you **can** run out of resources before finalization frees them up, and finalization is expensive (Chapter 2), so it's best if you clean up after yourself. In Delphi for .NET, this means banging out the same old try {...} finally Free boilerplate, even in a garbage-collected environment. In C#, this means creating your GDI wrappers in a using statement, wherever possible, so that they will be automatically closed when they go out of scope.

Remember that you can create multiple objects of the same type in a using statement, and they will all be automatically disposed of when control leaves the using statement. This can keep you from having to nest using statements, making your code a little smaller and easier to read. For example, the Chapter16\TwoBrushes C# project uses this code in a paint event handler to write a couple of strings to the Graphics passed in the e parameter, which is a PaintEventArgs:

```
using (Brush
  RedBrush = new SolidBrush(Color.Red),
  GradientBrush = new LinearGradientBrush(Gradient, Color.Yellow, Color.Red,
    LinearGradientMode.Vertical))
  {
    e.Graphics.DrawString("Red", DefaultFont, RedBrush, 10, 10);
    e.Graphics.DrawString("Gradient", DefaultFont, GradientBrush, 10, 30);
  }
```

I cover both brushes and DrawString, in the "GDI+ Details" section of this chapter. For now, I'd like you to notice how I had to pass both a Font and Brush to the DrawString method.

There are two very noticeable (though rather minor) differences between Delphi graphics and FCL graphics, and this is an example of the first difference: you pass drawing tools explicitly, instead of selecting them into the drawing surface and using them implicitly.

That is, in Delphi every TCanvas has a Pen property, a Brush property, and a Font property. These represent the current pen, brush, and font: drawing lines uses the current pen; drawing text uses the current font and the current brush. To change tools, you select a new tool into the drawing surface, by changing the canvas's Pen, Brush, or Font property.

The FCL Graphics class does **not** have Pen, Brush, or Font properties. Each drawing primitive takes its drawing tools as explicit parameters. For example, a Pen has properties like Color and Width, and when you draw a line, you specify the end points and the pen to use. The color and width of the line will depend on the pen you pass to the DrawLine method.

FCL graphics takes fewer method calls than Delphi graphics, but each method call takes more parameters. Despite the extra parameters, the GDI+ approach is probably a bit more efficient, overall: in Delphi, code like Canvas.Pen := ThisPen is not a simple assignment, but calls the TPen.Assign method to copy ThisPen's state to Canvas.Pen. That is, changing drawing tools is comparatively expensive under Delphi and GDI, but is basically free on .NET and GDI+.

The second eye-catching difference between Delphi graphics and FCL graphics lies in how you get a drawing surface. Getting a drawing surface is pretty simple in Delphi: both controls and bitmaps have a Canvas property that you can draw on. Getting a drawing surface is a bit more complicated in the FCL:

- Within a paint event handler, a Graphics instance is supplied as the Graphics member of the PaintEventArgs parameter.

- To draw on a (form or) control outside of a paint event handler, you call the control's CreateGraphics method, which returns a new Graphics that lets you draw on the control.

- To draw on a bitmap, you pass the bitmap to the static Graphics.FromImage method,[1] which returns a new Graphics that lets you draw on the bitmap.

A paint event handler should **not** call Dispose on the Graphics instance it's passed. However, when you create a Graphics instance by calling CreateGraphics or Graphics.

---

1. Both Bitmap and Metafile descend from the abstract Image class. Logical though this makes Graphics. FromImage, I seem to have a hard time remembering that 1) you have to call a static method of the Graphics class to draw on a Bitmap (instead of calling the [hypothetical] Bitmap.CreateGraphics instance method) and that 2) the method is FromImage, not FromBitmap. I don't draw on a Bitmap every day, and it seems like every time I do, I spend minutes hunting for the right way to get a Graphics instance.

FromImage, you **should** be sure to Dispose of it when you are done. For example, in the Chapter16\TwoBrushes C# project, the code in the DrawButton's click event is virtually identical to the code in the paint event, except that it explicitly creates (and implicitly disposes of) a Graphics instance:

```
using (Graphics Explicit = this.CreateGraphics())
{
  // ...
}
```

GDI+ Details

Lots of cool new features

Once again, Delphi and the FCL have similar graphics architectures. Both TCanvas and Graphics are object-oriented wrappers that hide the messy details of the Windows drawing API, and turn all the flat calls into properties and methods. Similarly, drawing tools like Delphi's TPen and the FCL's Pen hide the details of the Windows pen API, and turn all the flat calls into method calls and property values.

There **are** differences in the way you get drawing surfaces and select drawing tools, but these are relatively minor. The larger differences between the two graphics libraries come from the fact that the FCL wraps the newer GDI+, while Delphi wraps the original GDI. Supporting GDI+ means that the FCL has support for bitmapped brushes, gradients, and transparency that Delphi does not.

That is, GDI+ offers some of the same drawing tools as bitmap editors like Adobe's *Photoshop* or Jasc's *Paint Shop Pro*. This lets you create at run time the sort of effects that might once have taken predrawn bitmap resources, which both increases flexibility and also cuts assembly size: even a small bitmap is bigger than a page or two of code.

This chapter is not a comprehensive guide to GDI+. The basic concepts **are** familiar, and the documentation is pretty clear—and few business applications ask much more of GDI+ than generating a nice gradient for a BackgroundImage. (Obviously, consumer software gets to look prettier.) Accordingly, I discuss the few surprises (like immutable fonts) and cover the core features, trusting that you'll be able to generalize from there, as needed. For example, I cover transparency and rotations, but I don't cover more recherché details like scaling and translation, or saving and restoring a Graphics state.

Colors

Manipulating color and opacity

As per Chapter 15, every pixel that you draw or fill has a 32-bit ARGB color, where A is eight bits of opacity, or *Alpha*. Except for Color.Transparent, the system colors like Color.Red or Color.LightSeaGreen are all fully opaque. (Their *alpha channel* is 255, or 100%.) Similarly, the standard pens and brushes, the Pens.Black and Brushes.LightBlue (that I cover later in this chapter) are all fully opaque. When you draw an opaque color to a pixel, the pixel's color is set to the color's RGB components.

You can make translucent versions of any opaque color, simply by setting the alpha channel to less than 255. When you draw any color that's not fully opaque, the RGB is blended with the existing RGB according to the alpha level. That is, the RGB component of each pixel is set to the existing RGB component plus alpha/255f times the difference between the new component and the existing component.[2]

For example, an alpha level of 64 (0x40) is roughly one quarter. Drawing an ARGB of 0x40506070 onto an RGB of 0x4080C0 will result in an RGB of

```
0x40 + (0x50 - 0x40) * 64/255f,
0x80 + (0x60 - 0x80) * 64/255f,
0xC0 + (0x70 - 0xC0) * 64/255f
```

or 0x4478AC. (See the Chapter16\AlphaTest Delphi project.)

The Color structure has a set of static FromArgb methods that return a Color given various different sets of parameters. You can create a Color from R, G, and B components; from A, R, G, and B components; from a single integer that specifies the ARGB levels as AARRGGBB; or from an existing Color and a new alpha level. This last overload is particularly useful in generating transparent versions of existing colors: for example, Color.FromArgb(0x7F, Color.White) returns a 50% opaque white Color.

In color circles, RGB and ARGB are considered implementation details, much like the Cyan/Magenta/Yellow/Black (CMYK) that printers use. The color-centric coordinate system of choice is HSB—for *Hue*, *Saturation*, and *Brightness*. HSB is a polar coordinate system, with one rotation coordinate and two displacement coordinates.

- **Hue** is a float that specifies degrees, 0 to 360. Imagine the Newtonian colors red, orange, yellow, green, blue, indigo, and violet arranged around a wheel, so that red is next to both orange and violet. (This doesn't work in grayscale, but see the Chapter16\ColorWheel C# project.) 0 is red, 120 is green, and 240 is blue.

- **Saturation** is a float from 0 to 1. Fully saturated colors are vivid, and can be jarring. Partially saturated colors are muted, or pastel. An unsaturated color is gray. Colors in the distance tend to be less saturated (because of *distance haze*) than the colors of nearby objects.

- **Brightness** is also a float from 0 to 1. 0 is black and 1 is white; low Brightness is a dark color, and high Brightness is washed out.

Changing any of Hue, Saturation, or Brightness gives you a different color, with different RGB values. However, when you hold Hue and Saturation constant and change only Brightness, you get what look like shadowed or highlighted versions of the same color. (See, for example, the "3D spheres" in the "Brushes" subsection, later in this chapter.) Also, gradients from dark to bright versions of the same color gives a different effect than gradients all the way to white, or gradients between different hues. The Chapter16\Gradients C# project will let you experiment with this.

---

2. Strictly speaking, this is a function of the Graphics.CompositingMode. What I have described is the default, SourceOver mode. In SourceCopy mode, each pixel is set to the RGB of the drawn color, scaled by the color's alpha level. (That is, SourceCopy blackens low alpha colors: in HSB terms, this changes both Hue and Saturation—it does **not** reduce Brightness while leaving Hue and Saturation untouched.)

FCL support for HSB is rather limited. While the Color structure has GetHue, GetSaturation, and GetBrightness methods, there is no FromHsb method that can take arbitrary HSB values and make an RGB out of them. Accordingly, my HSB class (in the Common\Shemitz.Drawing C# project) includes some code I found online[3] that turns a HSB triplet into an opaque Color.

The (Shemitz.Drawing) Change class uses the HSB to RGB code to implement SetHue, SetSaturation, and SetBrightness methods, which take a Color, change a component, and return a new Color. You can set Hue to any value (–10 is the same as 350, 420 is the same as 60, and so on), while Saturation and Brightness should be at least 0 and at most 1. For example, Change.SetBrightness(Color.LightSeaGreen, 0.80f) produces a color a little lighter than Color.LightSeaGreen.

Pens

Very like Delphi's, but with more features

In the FCL as in Delphi, a pen outlines and a brush fills. You use a pen to draw lines and curves, rectangles and polygons. The FCL Pen has a Color and a Width property, as well as a DashStyle and an optional DashPattern property. These let you draw solid or patterned lines, and act almost exactly like the Color, Width, and Style properties of the Delphi TPen.

Most of the Graphics class Draw methods (that is, all the Draw methods except DrawString, DrawIcon, and DrawImage) take a Pen parameter and produce (part of) a line drawing. You can draw lines, rectangles, and polygons. You can draw ellipses, pie wedges, and various curves. You can even trace out an arbitrary GraphicsPath. (For example, you can use GraphicsPath with a Pen to draw outline text—see the Chapter16\OutlineText C# project.)

■**Note** None of the Draw methods have overloads that take a Brush; unlike Delphi with its Rectangle, FillRect, and FrameRect methods, with GDI+ you always outline and fill as two separate method calls.

In addition to the same dotted and dashed lines that you can draw with Delphi's TPen, the FCL Pen also offers various features like compound lines, miters, and end caps that will be useful in specialized drawing programs. That is, most of us will have little use for these features, so I won't do anything more than mention that they exist.

The Brush property, though, is useful even in standard business applications. When a Pen has a non-null Brush, the Brush overrides the pen's Color. This doesn't make any visible difference with a solid color brush, but with a bitmapped or gradient brush (next subsection) the pen strokes define a region that the brush fills. Thus, in the Chapter16\OutlineText C# project, the filled and outlined text is filled with a gradient brush that shades from red to yellow, and outlined with a complementary gradient brush that shades from yellow to red (see Figure 16-1).

---

3. www.bobpowell.net/RGBHSB.htm

Figure 16-1. *Outlined and filled text*

The Pen constructors take either a Color or a Brush, and an optional Width. If you use the overloads that don't specify a Width, you get a 1-wide pen. Since most pens are solid color, opaque, and 1-wide, the FCL includes the Pens class,[4] which provides predefined 1-wide pens in all the standard, opaque colors. Thus, Pens.Black is a 1-wide black pen and Pens.Red is a 1-wide red pen.

The standard, predefined pens are immutable, though not quite in the way that strings are. Strings are immutable in the sense that there are no methods that will change the contents of a string. Syntactically, the predefined pens you get from the Pens class are perfectly normal pens, and you can compile code like Pens.Black.Color = Color.White or using (Pen Black = Pens.Black) {}—but both statements will raise an exception at run time. **Don't** change any properties of a standard pen, and **don't** Dispose of a standard pen—use the standard pens as if they were system-supplied constants.

Brushes

A wide range of fill options

Once again, pens outline and brushes fill. You use a brush to draw text and to fill the interior of geometric figures like rectangles and other polygons; circles and ellipses; complex curves and arbitrary graphics paths. (Again, you can also wrap a Pen around a Brush, and use the brushed pen to draw outlines with the brush.) Graphics.DrawString and all of the Graphics.Fill methods take a Brush parameter.

The FCL Brush is significantly more flexible than the Delphi TBrush. The Delphi TBrush only supports 8 types of hatch styles, and doesn't support bitmapped brushes more than 8 pixels wide by 8 pixels high. The FCL Brush supports 53 different hatch styles; bitmaps of any size; and a wide range of gradients. To manage this complexity, Brush is an abstract class, with descendants that include the SolidBrush, the bitmapped TextureBrush, and the LinearGradientBrush.

---

4. The SystemPens class has static properties that give you 1-wide, immutable pens in the various system colors. (System colors are the user-settable color categories like ButtonFace and GrayText.) There is also a SystemBrushes, SystemFonts, and SystemIcons class.

Solid Brushes

The simplest brush is a solid color brush, which you create as new SolidBrush(Color) and which has only a single Color property. With fully opaque colors (i.e., alpha channel at 255, or 100%) a Fill operation sets every pixel it changes to the brush color, as in the earlier "Colors" subsection. With translucent colors (alpha channel less than 255), a Fill operation will combine the brush color with the existing color of every pixel it changes, as in the Chapter16\SolidBrushes Delphi project.[5] (See Figure 16-2—the top-left square is lighter where it is drawn over the white background than where it is drawn over the bottom-right square.)

Figure 16-2. *Drawing and filling with translucent colors combines with existing colors.*

Somewhat as with the Pens class, the Brushes class has properties that return solid color, opaque brushes in all the standard colors. That is, Brushes.Red returns a SolidBrush with Color equal to Color.Red, and Brushes.AliceBlue returns a SolidBrush with Color equal to Color.AliceBlue. However, unlike the standard pens you get from the Pens class, the standard brushes you get from the Brushes class are **not** immutable: changing the Color of a standard brush with code like

```
SolidBrush LightBlue = (SolidBrush)Brushes.LightBlue;
LightBlue.Color = Color.Blue;
```

will change the color of the Brushes.LightBlue brush to Color.Blue, and all subsequent uses of the Brushes.LightBlue brush will be affected. Worse, code like

```
using (SolidBrush LightBlue = (SolidBrush)Brushes.LightBlue)
    LightBlue.Color = Color.Blue;
```

will leave the Brushes.LightBlue brush in an unusable state—any subsequent use will raise an exception. So, even though the implementation of the standard brushes is inconsistent with the implementation of the standard pens, the rule of thumb is the same: **don't** change any properties of a standard brush, and **don't** Dispose of a standard brush—use the standard brushes as if they were system-supplied constants.

---

5. The same is also true of translucent pens and Draw operations—see the Chapter16\TranslucentPen C# project.

Hatched Brushes

The (System.Drawing.Drawing2D) HatchBrush lets you fill a region using a ForegroundColor and a BackgroundColor, in one of 53 different hatch styles (see Figure 16-3, and the Chapter16\ HatchBrushes C# project). This is probably of extremely limited utility for desktop apps in an era when full-color displays are so common, but may still be useful when printing to a mono-chrome printer, or when generating bitmaps for web apps if bandwidth is scarce.

Figure 16-3. *Hatch styles for printing and web graphics*

Bitmapped Brushes

The TextureBrush is a bitmapped brush. You can use any Bitmap, of any size and/or color depth. As the name suggests, this is going to be most useful for filling a region with a repeating texture, but you **can** use it with an arbitrary image, to give the effect of seeing a background image through holes in a mask, as in the Chapter16\TextureBrushes C# project, which draws texture-brushed text on a gradient background, using an old picture of me.

Linear Gradient Brushes

There are two types of gradient brushes in the System.Drawing.Drawing2D namespace— the LinearGradientBrush and the PathGradientBrush. The next subsection discusses path gradient basics and uses the PathGradientBrush to draw spherical highlights, but for the most part path gradients are complex and specialized ... and beyond the scope of this book. The LinearGradientBrush, though, is fairly straightforward, and is an easy way to give your applica-tions an attractive "XP look."

Most of the time, you'll create a LinearGradientBrush with a Rectangle (often a control's ClientRectangle), two Color parameters, and a LinearGradientMode parameter that specifies whether the gradient runs left to right, top to bottom, or along one of the two diagonals. For example, in the Chapter16\SimpleGradient C# project this paint event handler

```
using (Brush Linear = new LinearGradientBrush(ClientRectangle,
   Color.White, Color.Gray, LinearGradientMode.ForwardDiagonal))
      e.Graphics.FillRectangle(Linear, ClientRectangle);
```

fills the client rectangle with a gradient running from white at the top left to gray at the bottom right, as in Figure 16-4. (Of course, it's a bit slow to do this in every paint event, and usually you'll spend memory to save time. That is, you'll create a gradient Bitmap in the layout event and set the BackgroundImage, as in the ColorWheel project and the "Bitmaps" subsection, later in this chapter.)

Figure 16-4. *A simple diagonal gradient*

You can also pass the LinearGradientBrush constructor a custom angle, where 0f has the same effect as LinearGradientMode.Horizontal and 90f has the same effect as LinearGradientMode.Vertical.

While you can get very nice effects with simple, two-color gradients, LinearGradientBrush has several properties and methods that you can experiment with. The most useful of these are the SetSigmaBellShape method and the InterpolationColors property. The SetSigmaBellShape method lets you create a gradient that goes from the start color to the stop color and back to the start color, and lets you control where in the gradient the stop color will appear. (See Figure 16-5 and the Chapter16\SimpleGradient C# project.) The InterpolationColors property lets you create multicolor gradients, with fine-grained control over where in the gradient each color will appear. (See the Chapter16\InterpolationColors C# project.)

Figure 16-5. *A diagonal gradient using the* SetSigmaBellShape *method*

Path Gradient Brushes

A path gradient runs from the outside of an arbitrary graphics path to an arbitrary center point. This can be useful, especially with simple, smooth curves. For example, when you use FillPie to fill a quarter circle with a path gradient centered on the circle's center, you get a rounded border gradient, as in Figure 16-6 and the Chapter16\CornerGradient C# project.

Similarly, when you use FillEllipse to fill a circle with a path gradient that's somewhat displaced from the circle's center, you get something that looks roughly spherical, as in Figure 16-7 and the Chapter16\Highlights C# project.

Figure 16-6. *A rounded-corner gradient*

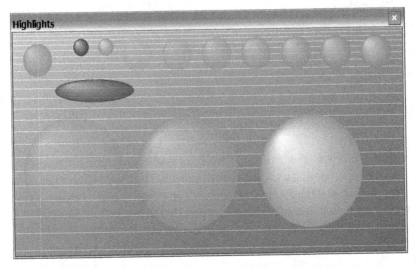

Figure 16-7. *An off-center path gradient creates a spherical highlight.*

GraphicsPath and the PathGradientBrush are not the easiest subjects to master, but they also come up infrequently enough that I feel justified in not really covering them. If you're curious, using the code in the CornerGradient and Highlights projects as a starting point may save you some hours of frustration. (I also talk a little more about the GraphicsPath in the "Paths and Regions" subsection, later in this chapter.)

Fonts and Text

Versatile drawing and immutable fonts

While the syntax differs slightly, the FCL Font is much like the Delphi TFont: it has a font Name that specifies a typeface, as well as Size, Bold, Italic, Underline, and Strikeout properties. You use a Font to draw a string on a Graphics surface, and you can also use a Font to see how many pixels it would take to draw a string on a Graphics surface.

Overall, the biggest surprise is that FCL fonts are immutable: all Font properties are read-only. With a Delphi TFont, you can turn bold or italic on and off by changing the Style property; to do the same in .NET you have to create a new Font. For example, new Font(this.Font, this.Font.Style | FontStyle.Bold) will create a bold version of a nonbold font, and new Font(this.Font, FontStyle.Regular) will create a new font that's neither bold, italic, underline, or strikeout.[6]

Naturally, there are also constructors that will create a Font from a font family Name string, a point Size, and an optional Style. You can also create a Font using the same FontFamily objects that you use to draw text on a GraphicsPath (see the Chapter16\OutlineText C# project). Since a FontFamily is little more than a wrapper for a family Name string, this may not seem incredibly useful—but FontFamily has static FontFamily properties GenericMonospace, GenericSansSerif, and GenericSerif that you can use when you don't really care which font you use, or when the font that you do want is not available on the current machine. (Creating a font that uses a nonexistent typeface does not raise an exception: you get a font with a different Name than you specified.)

The six Graphics.DrawString methods are what you use to actually draw text on a Graphics surface. These six overloads break down into three primary overloads, each of which has an optional StringFormat object that specifies things like word wrap behavior, line spacing, and so on. The three primary overloads in turn break down into two different ways to draw unwrapped text at a particular point, and a way to draw text wrapped within a bounding box.

The location you pass the unwrapped text overloads

```
Graphics.DrawString (String, Font, Brush, Single, Single)
Graphics.DrawString (String, Font, Brush, PointF)
```

is the **top-left** corner of the 'text box.' The Brush is used to draw the text characters in the specified font, and (as in the Chapter16\TextureBrushes C# project) it doesn't have to be a SolidBrush.

The other primary DrawString overload

```
Graphics.DrawString (String, Font, Brush, RectangleF)
```

draws left-aligned text, wrapped within the RectangleF structure that you pass it. You can use the StringFormat overload to get right-aligned or center-aligned text, and to suppress partial lines, but there doesn't seem to be any way to control the line-breaking algorithm: DrawString breaks lines on white space following non–white space. Period. You can't supply a method that will break on hyphens or dots, and you certainly can't use a dictionary to insert a hyphen between syllables.

Do notice that all DrawString overloads take only a single Brush and so (unlike Delphi graphics) DrawString has no concept of background color: DrawString always draws transparently, only changing the pixels where the text and font specify a mark. This means that if you want an opaque (or translucent) background under your string, you have to draw it first, with FillRectangle.

---

6. Font objects do have a finalizer and do support IDisposable, but they present a special problem: because of ambient properties (Chapter 15), many controls will share the same Font instance. Thus, in general you should **not** write code like using (Font ThisFont = this.Font) this.Font = new Font(ThisFont, FontStyle.Bold; that changes a control's font and then disposes of the old font—this is very likely to cause trouble for other controls. Besides, finalizing a simple object like a Font is not incredibly expensive, and because so many controls do share the same Font, removing a single reference is not particularly likely to trigger finalization, anyway.

About the only time you should Dispose of a Font is when you manually create one, in the course of drawing text on a Bitmap, or during a paint event, or whatever.

For example, this excerpt from the Chapter16\RightToLeft C# project

```
Color TranslucentWhite = Color.FromArgb(96, Color.White);
using (Brush TranslucentBrush = new SolidBrush(TranslucentWhite))
  e.Graphics.FillRectangle(TranslucentWhite, Box);
```

puts a translucent white 'layer' over the Box rectangle, which is a particularly useful background when you are drawing text over images.

Note Many of the Graphics methods take either integer or floating point coordinates, but DrawString takes only float (and PointF, and RectangleF) coordinates. The PointF, RectangleF, and SizeF structures are just like their integer counterparts, except that the X and Y (or Top, Bottom, Height, and Width) properties are single-precision floats, instead of 32-bit integers. The Point, Rectangle, and Size structures are assignment compatible with the PointF, RectangleF, and SizeF structures (because there is an implicit conversion operator from the integer to the floating point structures), while the Size, Point, and Rectangle structures have static methods that give you explicit control over the rounding from floating point to integer structures. For example, to get a Point from a PointF, you pass the PointF to either Point.Round, Point.Ceiling, or Point.Truncate.

The three StringFormat overloads allow you to apply various StringFormatFlags options. The two most important of these are DirectionRightToLeft and DirectionVertical. When you use the DirectionRightToLeft flag with unwrapped text

```
using (StringFormat RightToLeft =
  new StringFormat(StringFormatFlags.DirectionRightToLeft))
  SomeGraphics.DrawString(SomeText, SomeFont, SomeBrush, SomePointF, RightToLeft);
```

the only difference is that the point specifies the top **right** corner of the text box. However, when you use the DirectionRightToLeft flag with wrapped text (i.e., pass DrawString a RectangleF instead of a simple point), you get wrapped, right-aligned text[7] (see the Chapter16\RightToLeft C# project).

The StringFormatFlags.DirectionVertical flag draws text rotated 90 degrees clockwise (reading top to bottom, with the baseline on the left) as in Figure 16-8 and the Chapter16\RotatedText C# project. If you want counterclockwise vertical text (reading bottom to top, with the baseline on the right) or any angle besides vertical, you have to use Graphics.RotateTransform to change the Graphics surface's coordinate system.

---

7. Sorry, I have no idea how StringFormatFlags.DirectionRightToLeft interacts with right-to-left languages like Hebrew or Arabic.

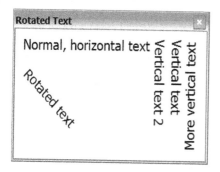

Figure 16-8. *Text rotated with* `StringFormatFlags.DirectionVertical` *and with* `Graphics.RotateTransform`

Coordinate Transforms

All `Graphics` operations are subject to transformation by the `Matrix Transform` property. This is a 3-by-3 floating point matrix that, as per basic linear algebra, efficiently encodes any rotations, translations, and scaling you might want to apply to a set of coordinates. For the benefit of those of us whose linear algebra is long ago and far away, the `Graphics` class provides methods like `RotateTransform`, `TranslateTransform`, and `ScaleTransform` that make it easy to do rotations and to apply limited perspective effects.

■ **Note** I don't cover every sort of `Transform` manipulation. Like so much else in the FCL, once you understand one sort of `Transform` manipulation, you are well on the way to understanding them all. Accordingly, the following discussion of rotated text is meant to serve as a proxy for the whole subject of coordinate transformations. Please remember that the `Graphics.Transform` affects pen and brush and image drawing, not just text drawing.

Overall, drawing rotated text is much easier in .NET than in Delphi: there's no need to create a rotated font or anything like that. Instead, you call `Graphics.RotateTransform` to rotate the coordinate system by any number of degrees clockwise, and then you call `DrawString` in pretty much the normal way. If you need to do any additional drawing, you call `Graphics.ResetTransform` to undo the rotation;[8] you don't need to `ResetTransform` before the end of a paint event, or before `Disposing` of a `Graphics` that you created explicitly.

I use the weasel words "pretty much ... normal" because there **is** one significant issue with drawing rotated text: the rotation applies to the starting point (or bounding box) as well as to the string. That is, while paint event code like

```
e.Graphics.RotateTransform(45);
e.Graphics.DrawString("Naive rotation", Font, Brushes.Black, 10, 10);
```

---

8. If you need to draw several elements, each at a different rotation, rounding error means that you're probably better off doing a `ResetTransform` and applying each rotation to a fresh `Matrix` than doing a `RotateTransform` by the difference between two successive angles.

will draw the string Naive rotation slanting downwards, the top left will **not** be 10 pixels in and 10 pixels down. Instead, it will be rotated off the Graphics surface, as in Figure 16-9 and the Chapter16\NaiveRotation C# project.

Figure 16-9. *Naïve rotation forgets to counter-rotate the starting point.*

To draw rotated text successfully, you have to rotate the starting point as well, perhaps using code like this DrawingTools method from the Common\Shemitz.Drawing C# project:

```
public static PointF RotatePoint(PointF Point, float Angle)
{
    PointF[] PointArray = new PointF[] { Point };
    using (Matrix Rotate = new Matrix())
    {
        Rotate.Rotate(Angle);
        Rotate.TransformPoints(PointArray);
    }
    return PointArray[0];
}
```

The thing to remember is that to rotate text by Angle, you have to rotate the starting point by –Angle. Why? Well, when you actually draw on the rotated Graphics, the starting point you pass in will be rotated by Angle. Counter-rotating the starting point means that the rotations cancel out, and your text appears where you expect it to.

Thus, actual rotated text code might look like this excerpt from the Chapter16\Rotated-Text C# project:

```
e.Graphics.RotateTransform(Rotation);
e.Graphics.DrawString("Rotated text", Tahoma12, Brushes.Black,
    DrawingTools.RotatePoint(25, 50, -Rotation));
```

The only problem with the preceding code is that you have to keep track of the Rotation, and pass a negative Rotation to RotatePoint. In simple code like this, that's no problem; in real code, this can cause maintenance problems. Also, when you're using more complex transforms than a simple rotation, it can get tedious to always create an inverse transform. The more general approach is to use Matrix.Invert to create a matrix that can "untransform" the current Graphics.Transform, so that you can specify a drawing location in untransformed coordinates, like

```
e.Graphics.RotateTransform(Rotation);
e.Graphics.DrawString("Rotated text", Tahoma12, Brushes.Black,
    DrawingTools.Untransform(e.Graphics, 25, 50));
```

without having to manually construct the untransform matrix. For details, see the DrawingTools class in the Common\Shemitz.Drawing C# project.

Measuring Strings

Finally, the Graphics.MeasureString method allows you to find out how much room a given string will take, much like Delphi's TCanvas.TextExtent. This can be used to draw paragraphs containing multiple fonts, to calculate how tall a form has to be to show a particular message, or to decide whether a filename will fit in a given (part of a) form. There are several overloads, including some that take StringFormat parameters: all return a SizeF.

There is no direct counterpart to Delphi's TextWidth and TextHeight: you have to write code like Math.Round(ThisGraphics.MeasureString(ThisString, ThisFont).Width) to get a string's drawn width.

C# Note Remember that casting a float to an int rounds toward 0, so that code like (int) ThisGraphics.MeasureString(ThisString, ThisFont).Width can be low by 1 pixel.

Bitmaps

A wide range of ways to apply and manipulate bitmaps

The FCL Bitmap class can load and save most standard file formats—from BMP and GIF through JPG, TIF, and PNG, at whatever pixel depth you'd like. Getting or setting pixels one by one is painfully slow,[9] but as you draw (all or part of) a bitmap, you can do the same sort of rotation, translation, and scaling with Graphics.Transform that you can with the other draw and fill methods. The various coordinate transformations would certainly be noticeably faster with hardware support, but they're a lot faster than per-pixel access.

You draw a Bitmap on a Graphics surface with the Graphics.DrawImage method. You create a blank Bitmap by passing the constructor the desired bitmap size (and, optionally, the pixel format), and you can draw on a Bitmap by calling Graphics.FromImage, and drawing on the Graphics instance it returns. For example, a form layout event might create a BackgroundImage with code like

```
private void Form1_Layout(object sender, LayoutEventArgs e)
{
  Rectangle Client = ClientRectangle;
  Bitmap BackgroundImage = new Bitmap(Client.Width, Client.Height);
  using (Graphics Background = Graphics.FromImage(BackgroundImage))
  using (Brush Gradient = new LinearGradientBrush(Client,
    Color.White, Color.LightBlue, LinearGradientMode.ForwardDiagonal))
    Background.FillRectangle(Gradient, Client);
  this.BackgroundImage = BackgroundImage;
}
```

---

9. However, if you're willing to resort to unsafe code, you can call Bitmap.LockBits and read/write pixels via C-style pointer code. (This is much like using the VCL's ScanLine property.)

although, in practice, you wouldn't duplicate this code in every layout event, but would push it into a utility method like the (Shemitz.Drawing) Gradient.Rectangle:

```
private void Form1_Layout(object sender, LayoutEventArgs e)
{
  this.BackgroundImage = Gradient.Rectangle(ClientRectangle,
    Color.White, Color.LightBlue);
}
```

Loading and Saving Bitmaps

Hard disks everywhere are chock full of digital image files, and many Bitmap instances are loaded from disk files or other streams. You can open a bitmap file by passing either the filename or an open Stream to the Bitmap constructor—for example, new Bitmap(Filename). The Bitmap constructor understands a wide range of formats, and you don't have to tell it what format a particular file or stream contains.

In particular, support for formats like GIF, JPEG, and PNG is built-in, and (unlike Delphi) you don't have to do anything special to open them. You open a .gif or a .jpeg file just like you open a .bmp file: new Bitmap(@".\This.gif") or new Bitmap(@"..\That.bmp").

Similarly, you can save a file in a specific format simply by using the right extension in the call to Save. For example, the following excerpt from the Chapter16\IcoToPng C# project converts an .ico file to a .png file by loading it into an Icon; drawing the Icon to a new Bitmap; and saving the Bitmap to a file with a .png extension:

```
private static void ProcessIcoFile(string Filename)
{
    using (Icon Original = new Icon(Filename))
    using (Bitmap PngBitmap = new Bitmap(Original.Width, Original.Height))
    {
        using (Graphics Png = Graphics.FromImage(PngBitmap))
            Png.DrawIcon(Original, 0, 0);
        string NewFilename = Path.ChangeExtension(Filename, ".png");
        PngBitmap.Save(NewFilename);
    }
}
```

■ **Note** Simple load/save operations like this will probably cover 99.9% of your needs. See Google for specialized operations like reading and writing TIF tags, or setting JPEG compression.

One thing to keep in mind is that creating a Bitmap from a file keeps the file open for the life of the Bitmap. Similarly, when you create a Bitmap from a stream, that stream must stay open for the life of the Bitmap. This may not matter. However, if it **does** matter that the file or stream is staying open for the life of the Bitmap, you need to make a copy of the Bitmap using code like

```
using (Bitmap FileBitmap = new Bitmap(SelectImageDialog.FileName))
    return new Bitmap(FileBitmap);
```

that closes the temporary FileBitmap (and the file) after creating a copy of FileBitmap that's not linked to the file.

Drawing Bitmaps

Like so many FCL methods, Graphics.DrawImage is heavily overloaded. The simplest overloads draw the whole image at a given location on the Graphics surface. Remember, even the simplest overloads honor both the alpha channel and the Graphics.Transform, so DrawImage can draw transparent images and DrawImage can draw rotated or scaled images.

Every Graphics and every Image has a horizontal and vertical resolution, measured in pixels per inch. When you draw an Image on a Graphics using a basic overload like

```
SomeGraphics.DrawImage(ThisBitmap, ThatPoint);
```

you are drawing a full-size image of ThisBitmap, with the top left at ThatPoint. But, full size is measured in linear inches, not pixels. Drawing an Image on a surface with a different resolution will resize the Image. (This means that a printed bitmap is roughly the same size as its on-screen version.) For example, when you draw a high-resolution bitmap (many pixels per inch) on a lower-resolution surface (fewer pixels per inch), DrawImage will discard pixels. Conversely, when you draw a bitmap on a higher-resolution surface (more pixels per inch), DrawImage will interpolate pixels.

Tip Using a DrawImage overload that allows you to specify the image size (like the overloads that take a Rectangle, or that take a width and height in addition to the top-left point) gives you full control over any scaling.

More complex DrawImage overloads allow you to apply an ImageAttributes object to the Bitmap draw. You can do an awful lot of interesting things with an ImageAttributes. The SetOutputChannel method lets you do *color separations*—draw an RGB color image to a set of four grayscale images that represent the Cyan/Magenta/Yellow/Black (CMYK) level for each pixel. The SetRemapTable method lets you register a list of colors to draw as, say, Color. Transparent, or you can use the SetColorKey method to set a range of colors as transparent. Beyond this sort of special-purpose manipulation, you can use SetColorMatrix to specify a 5-by-5 ColorMatrix that can remap every pixel's ARGB value as it's drawn.

Just as the 4-by-4 Graphics.Transform matrix can simultaneously rotate a drawing, shrink it, and move it along the line towards a vanishing point, so does the 5-by-5 ColorMatrix have a wide variety of uses. You can set the alpha levels of every pixel, to draw a Bitmap translucently. You can create a grayscale version of a photograph, or you can adjust contrast, brightness, and saturation.

The ColorMatrix doesn't come with handy methods that set it to what you want, the way the Graphics.Transform coordinate Matrix does, so you do need to know a bit more linear algebra to use the ColorMatrix effectively than you do to use the coordinate Matrix. A 5-by-5 ColorMatrix specifies four equations in four variables (the current value of each pixel's *red, green, blue,* and *alpha* channel) of the form A*Red + B*Green + C*Blue + D*Alpha. The constants, A through D, are read from the columns of the ColorMatrix: in order, the columns specify the equation for the new value of the pixel's Red, Green, Blue, and Alpha components. (That is, the Red equation is in column 0, and the Alpha equation is in column 3.)

The rows are interpreted similarly. That is, each equation's Red factor is in row 0, and each equation's Alpha factor is in row 3. So, if you think of a `ColorMatrix` as containing the constants A through Y,

A	F	K	P	U
B	G	L	Q	V
C	H	M	R	W
D	I	N	S	X
E	J	O	T	Y

each pixel's new Red level will be A*Red + B*Green + C*Blue + D*Alpha, its new Blue level will be F*Red + G*Green + H*Blue + I*Alpha, its new Green level will be K*Red + L*Green + M*Blue + N*Alpha, and its new alpha level will be P*Red + Q*Green + R*Blue + S*Alpha.

Creating a new `ColorMatrix()` gives you an *identity matrix*, which has ones on the AGMSY diagonal and zeroes everywhere else. Thus, it draws every pixel unchanged—new Red equals old Red, new Green equals old Green, and so on. Similarly, a matrix like

1	0	0	0	0
0	1	0	0	0
0	0	1	0	0
0	0	0	¼	0
0	0	0	0	1

(that is, an identity matrix with ¼ in the Alpha equation's alpha row) will multiply every pixel's Alpha by one quarter, drawing any opaque pixels at 25% opacity, and drawing any translucent pixels even less opaquely. The (`Shemitz.Drawing`) `DrawingTools.Alpha` method will return a matrix like this, that affects only the Alpha component of each pixel.

For a somewhat more complex example, the standard grayscale formula sets each pixel's Red, Green, and Blue components to 0.30*Red + 0.59*Green + 0.11*Blue. Thus,

0.30	0.30	0.30	0.00	0.00
0.59	0.59	0.59	0.00	0.00
0.11	0.11	0.11	0.00	0.00
0.00	0.00	0.00	1.00	0.00
0.00	0.00	0.00	0.00	1.00

will draw an image in grayscale. The Chapter16\Saturation C# project's `SaturationForm.Recolor` method "morphs" this grayscale `ColorMatrix` with the identity matrix, thus allowing you to specify any degree of graying: 0 is full grayscale, and 1 is full natural color. Interestingly, when you supply values larger than 1, you get "over color"—the classic saturation effect.

Paths and Regions

Tracing, filling, and hit detection in compound shapes

A GraphicsPath represents a set of shapes that can be traced or filled. The Chapter16\
OutlineText C# project used the tracing ability to draw outlined text. You can also use a
GraphicsPath to fill a compound shape that can't be drawn in a single Graphics operation,
as in Figure 16-10 and the Chapter16\CompoundShape C# project.

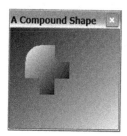

Figure 16-10. *A compound shape can be filled in a single operation when you use a GraphicsPath.*

The GraphicsPath supports most of the drawing operations that the Graphics surface does:
strings, lines, polygons, ellipses, and pie wedges. You may have to experiment with the FillMode
to get the various primitives to combine the way you want them. Note that 'drawing' on a
GraphicsPath only generates a description of a shape, and you have to use Graphics.DrawPath
or Graphics.FillPath to transfer the description to an actual Graphics drawing surface.

In addition to outlining text and filling compound shapes, you can use a GraphicsPath to
support hit testing like "Is the mouse over my hyperlink?" You do this by creating a Region from
the path—new Region(SomePath)—and calling the region's IsVisible method. IsVisible can
tell you whether a single point is in the region, or whether any points in a rectangle are in the
region. Uses include nonrectangular forms and nonrectangular buttons, as well as graphical
editors, like a music editor, a CAD program, or a forms designer.

The Region class supports logical operations like Intersection and Union, Exclude and Xor.
These let you calculate things like the visible parts of a partially obscured shape, which can be
useful in hit testing if you only care about **some** of the shapes on the screen, and/or don't want
to maintain your regions in z-order.

For example, the Chapter16\HitTesting C# project draws an ellipse over a rectangle, with
part of the ellipse outside of the rectangle (see Figure 16-11). The project maintains regions
that correspond to both the ellipse and the rectangle, and uses them to update a label on the
bottom of the screen as you move the mouse over the form. The project uses RectangleRegion.
Exclude(EllipsePath) to remove the ellipse from the RectangleRegion, so that hit testing
code like

```
if (RectangleRegion.IsVisible(e.X, e.Y))
    MouseStatus = "Mouse is over rectangle";
else if (EllipseRegion.IsVisible(e.X, e.Y))
    MouseStatus = "Mouse is over ellipse";
else MouseStatus = "Mouse is over background";
```

works even though the rectangle is 'under' the ellipse.

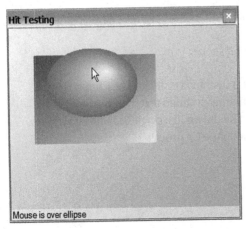

Figure 16-11. *The HitTesting project uses regions to classify the mouse position.*

Printing

A clean and simple API

.NET printing is based on the PrintDocument component. (You can place a PrintDocument on a form as a nonvisual component, or you can create one as necessary.) A PrintDocument has a PrintPage event that allows you to specify page settings; draw to a supplied Graphics (much like a Paint event); and specify whether there are any more pages. The PrintDialog component has a Document property that allows the printer setup dialog to set a PrintDocument to the user's choice of printers and settings. The PrintPreviewDialog has a Document property so that generating a print preview uses exactly the same code that actual printing does—no need to mess around with metafiles and the like.[10]

A new PrintDocument() will print to the default printer, with the default settings. The normal way to change this is via the printer setup dialog, PrintDialog. If a printer setup dialog's ShowDialog() == DialogResult.OK, the linked Document.PrinterSettings property has been set to the user's choice of printer and printer settings. You can also just set the PrinterSettings. PrinterName property directly, and the PrinterSettings will change to reflect the selected printer's capabilities and defaults. You can get a list of all valid printer names from the PrinterSettings.InstalledPrinters static property.

If a PrintDocument's PrinterSettings.IsValid property is true, the PrintDocument is set to an actual printer, and you can call its Print method to start printing. A PrintDocument has several different events, but the key event is the PrintPage event, which supplies you with a Graphics to draw on. The default unit of measure for a printer Graphics is hundredths of an inch, not pixels, but you can change this with the PageUnit property. (Each page can use a different printer resolution and/or PageUnit, if necessary.) To print a multipage document, each PrintPage handler (except the last) must set the PrintPageEventArgs parameter's HasMorePages property to true.

---

10. See the Chapter16\PrintTest C# program for a simple demo.

When you use a PrintPreviewDialog, calling ShowDialog will call Print on the linked PrintDocument. Drawing to the supplied Graphics in the PrintPage event simply draws to the screen; the Graphics takes care of all the scaling details. If the user clicks the dialog's print button, the PrintDocument will fire all the PrintPage events again—but the Graphics will go to the actual printer, this time.

In most cases, you don't have to worry about printer resolution or printer capabilities; you can let the printer driver handle details like scaling and/or mapping color to halftones. You do generally need to know how big a piece of paper you're printing on, though: the PrintPage event's PrintPageEventArgs parameter has a PageSettings property that specifies the Height and Width of the PaperSize in hundredths of an inch.

Key Points

A familiar architecture, with lots of new features

- Colors are 24 bits of RGB, plus 8 bits of opacity (the "alpha channel").

- Pens outline, as in Delphi. Pens can draw dotted and/or compound lines; pens can be created from brushes, and can thus draw complex color patterns.

- Brushes fill, as in Delphi. Brushes can be solid, hatched, bitmapped, or gradients.

- Drawing text is much like in Delphi. Drawing rotated text is straightforward.

- It's easy to simply draw a bitmap. There are numerous options that can involve fairly complex transformations.

- Paths and regions support operations on compound shapes.

- The PrintDocument component is the key to printing.

Threads and Synchronization

*It's easy to write multithreaded code—what's hard is to write **reliable** multithreaded code. (Threading primitives are not hard to understand, and the .NET implementations are particularly good, but it's all too easy to write code that fails randomly and so is hard to debug.) The Thread class executes a delegate in a new thread, and the ThreadPool can execute delegates without creating a new thread every time. The Monitor class provides efficient locking and simple signaling, and there are object wrappers for the OS synchronization functions that can do what Monitor cannot.*

Thread Basics

Threads present unique challenges

Writing multithreaded applications is never easy. The concepts are not particularly difficult, and the System.Threading implementations of the various primitives are especially easy to master, but few (if any) other areas of programming offer so many opportunities to get it **almost** right.

For example, Reflection offers a large and complex API (Chapter 13) and Reflection requires you to pay careful attention to the distinctions between types and values, and between Type values and compile-time types. It's easy to make a mistake, but your mistakes mean your code doesn't compile, or maybe it raises an exception at run time, or it delivers an obviously wrong result. Whatever the details, your mistakes are generally pretty obvious. Similarly, code generation is hard because it involves a constant switching of mental gears from operating on compile-time symbols to outputting tangible code that implements your abstractions. Here too, making mistakes is easy, but catching them is not incredibly hard: you can build test suites to verify that you are generating the right code in every situation.

Mistakes with thread synchronization, however, can be incredibly hard to catch. It's easy to write code that works properly almost all the time, but a moment's inattention can create a *race condition* that will occasionally cause errors or hang the system. Such code may easily pass your initial tests, and not fail until you ship ... or at least not before many weeks have passed and you've layered thousands of lines of code on top of the bug.[1]

If you've already mastered the required disciplines, you'll find .NET threading quite easy. Skip on ahead to the ".NET Threads" section, which starts a brief overview of the threading primitives and should be all that you'll need to make sense of the Microsoft documentation. If you're new to threading, the rest of this "Thread Basics" section may be helpful.

Threads and Processes

A thread is a lightweight process that shares memory with its parent process

Threads are special processes that allow an application to do more than one thing at once. On a single processor machine, this is always done through traditional timesharing. Each process gets a tiny slice of CPU time, and the CPU switches attention many times a second, creating the usually effective illusion that the machine is doing several things at once. By contrast, a multiprocessor machine (hyperthreaded and/or multicore and/or multichip) can quite literally execute instructions from two or more different threads or processes, in the same clock cycle.[2] This can make for a much more responsive server or workstation—and it can also help reveal any bugs in your synchronization code.

The difference between a thread and a "normal" process is simple: threads share their parent's address space, while normal processes do not. That is, if you have two copies of the same program running as normal, separate processes, each has separate global variables and a separate heap. One process can't read or write the global variables or the objects of the other process, unless they've explicitly requested shared memory from the operating system. The FCL does not include any shared memory support: if you need to use shared memory in a .NET app, you'd have to use P/Invoke to call the operating system's shared memory API, and you'd probably have to use unsafe code (Appendix 0) to manipulate the shared memory. Remoting (Chapter 14) is the managed alternative to shared memory.

But both of those copies could be running multiple threads, and each thread is part of its parent's process. Each thread in the process can read or write any of its parent's public data

---

1. *Unit testing* (Appendix 1) can be useful, here: when you add a test to a test suite, you don't test once and move on; you keep rerunning the test every time you run the test suite. The primary point of this is that it can help find changes that broke previously working code—but when a test "occasionally" fails, you probably have an undetected race condition that needs addressing.

   Unfortunately, unit testing is no panacea. It's not easy to write a test that can realistically simulate the behavior of a system with multiple asynchronous requests. Even if you do write good tests, a test suite run once (or even dozens of times) a day is not as likely to trigger a race condition as code in the field with thousands of simultaneous users, using your code in ways you didn't anticipate. And finally, while unit testing is great for "engine" code, it isn't so useful with GUI code and, in particular, can't really help much with the interactions between GUI and background threads.

   Multiprocessor machines are very good at revealing flaws in your threading code. Maybe even to the point where it's irresponsible not to develop and test your threading software on a multiprocessor machine. Sooner or later, multiprocessing will be in all workstations and in all servers.

2. Of course, when there are more active threads than processors, even multiprocessor machines will do traditional timesharing.

structures, and it can execute any of its parent's public code. Similarly, any thread can read and write any public data structures created by any other thread in the process.

Each thread has its own stack and register image, so that each thread can execute totally different code, and so that each thread's local variables are totally independent of every other thread's local variables. (While each stack lives in the process's address space and shares the same garbage collector, setting a local variable in ThisThread has no effect on the 'same' local variable in ThatThread, even if both threads **are** running the same method at the same time.)

Each thread can be assigned a different priority, so that a process can assign a lower priority to a long-running computation than to a short handshake over a socket.

Even on single-processor machines, threads can be executed in a thoroughly interleaved way—the processor can switch from one thread to another in the middle of a C# or Delphi statement. Thus, you have to exercise great care when reading and writing shared data structures both to avoid reading a partially updated structure and also to prevent competing transactions from corrupting a structure.

Synchronization

Preventing race conditions

Multithreaded programs have synchronization issues that single-threaded programs do not. You don't want two threads to try to change a value at once; you want them to take turns. You don't want a consumer to start eating until the producer has finished cooking—and you don't want the consumer to take any processor cycles while it's waiting.

At the kernel level, both these examples are applications of *semaphores*, special flag variables that can be set *atomically*, and that can be waited on cheaply. Atomically means that raising or lowering the flag is an indivisible, uninterruptible operation: the result can't be distorted by two processes trying to do it at once.

At the application level, it's more convenient to think in terms of *critical sections* and *events*. A critical section (also known as a *mutex*, which is short for Mutual Exclusion) allows one and only one thread to pass at a time. If two or more threads need to read and write a shared value, they would use a critical section to be sure that only one is doing so at any one time. When one thread has the critical section locked, any other thread that tries to lock the critical section is suspended until the first thread unlocks the critical section.

An event lets a thread wait—without consuming CPU cycles—until it has something to do. A producer/consumer pair might use a critical section around queue operations to be sure that they don't scramble the data structure—and would use an event to let the consumer wait until the queue's not empty. The consumer starts life waiting to be fed. When the producer adds to the queue, it "signals" the event, which wakes up the consumer. In turn, every time the consumer finds the queue empty, it goes back to sleep by "waiting" on the event.

Critical Sections

Critical sections are more commonly used than events. It's hard, in fact, to overstate their importance. The operating system can switch control from one thread to another between just about any pair of machine language instructions. The important thing, here, is that the OS does not know—or care—about statement boundaries in your source code. Control can switch from one thread to another within the middle of even a simple statement like ThisInt += 1 just as easily as it can switch between statements. In fact, given that each statement compiles to IL that jits to several machine language instructions, the OS is actually considerably more likely to switch within a single statement than it is to switch between statements. The OS saves the registers and the stack, so that the thread picks up where it left off—but the global environment may have changed around it.

This can lead to a race condition, where the result of the interaction between threads can depend on the exact order that each thread executes instructions. The race can come out differently every time it's run, which makes for a "Mandelbug" that can be hard to track down. Consider what can happen if two threads try to execute that ThisInt += 1 statement simultaneously, as in Table 17-1. Assume that ThisInt is originally 0. The first thread reads ThisInt, and adds 1. But, before it can write it back, the second thread also reads ThisInt, adds 1, and writes it back. ThisInt is now 1. When the first thread gets control back and writes ThisInt, it will also write 1.

Table 17-1. *A Race Condition*

Time	Thread 1	Thread 2
1	Read ThisInt (is 0)	
2	Add 1	
3		Read ThisInt (is 0)
4		Add 1
5		Write ThisInt (is 1)
6	Write ThisInt (is 1)	

Clearly, ThisInt should be 2 at this point, and yet it's 1. The results get wronger and wronger the more threads you imagine to be racing. If you object that this is all so hypothetical, that the threads have to be aligned Just So for this to be an issue, remember that code that works 99.99% of the time will still average one failure a day if you have a thousand users, each of whom executes that particular part of the code ten times a day. That is, race conditions can easily slip past testing, only to bite you hard when the application is released.

The answer is to be vigilant, and to protect shared variables with a critical section. You don't have to protect **every** shared variable—if, for example, you've safely ensured that ThisThread is beavering away on one row of a matrix while ThatThread is working on a different row, you don't need to protect matrix access—but you do need to protect every variable that two threads might try to change at the same time, and you do need to protect every data structure that shouldn't be read during a multipart update.

The name "critical section" is actually a bit of a misnomer. It does sort of suggest that what you're protecting is a section of code; that it only applies when two different threads might be executing the same code at the same time. What you are actually protecting is a section of your program's state: you use the same critical section to guard against simultaneous updates to a variable from anywhere in your code.

Further, you can protect more than one variable at a time. For example, an ArrayList consists of several related variables, including the length, the capacity, and the actual array. If multiple threads Add a value without using a critical section, you can end up with one of the transactions being overwritten, somewhat as in Table 17-1—or worse. If, however, you use the lock state-ment[3] to keep all access to the list within a critical section, code like

```
lock (PrivateList) // You should usually lock private or protected fields
  PrivateList.Add(SomeValue);
```

and

```
lock (PrivateList)
  if (PrivateList.Count > 0)
  {
    // do something with the first element
  }
```

can manipulate the list atomically: other threads can see the list before and after the locked operations, but not during them. If ThisThread tries to lock PrivateList while ThatThread has it locked, it is *blocked* until ThatThread releases the lock. That is, ThisThread waits, consuming no CPU cycles, until the lock has been released. At that point, ThisThread is given the lock, and starts running again.

It is quite easy to use critical sections in .NET. You can lock **any** reference type, and you don't have to first create a special object like TCriticalSection. Locking and unlocking is not free, though: use critical sections where you need them—and don't use them where you don't need them. Unnecessary locking will just slow down your application. More importantly, holding a lock will block any thread that tries to acquire it. Lock as little code as possible; release the lock as quickly as possible.

Pay attention, too, to the scope of what you lock. You open yourself to deadlock (next topic) every time you lock a public reference. It's safer for a class to offer atomic methods than to have the user lock the instance and then call Add or whatever. A self-synchronized class should lock on a private reference, not a public reference like this. For example, a synchronized stack like

```
class LockedStack<T>
{
  private Stack<T> Data = new Stack<T>();

  public void Push(T Datum)
  {
    lock (Data)
      Data.Push(Datum);
  }

  public T Pop()
  {
    lock (Data)
      return Data.Pop();
  }
}
```

---

3. Delphi doesn't have a lock statement, even in Delphi 2006, so Delphi programmers have to use explicit try/finally blocks and the Enter and Exit methods of the System.Threading.Monitor class. See the "Synchronization" section of this chapter.

locks the private Data, not the public this. (This is a simplified excerpt from the Chapter17\
LockedStack C# project.)

Deadlock

Any time you lock more than one resource at a time, you open yourself up to the possibility of
deadlock. Deadlock happens whenever one thread has locked a resource that another thread is
trying to lock, and is waiting on a resource that the second thread has locked—while the
second thread is waiting on the resource that the first thread has locked, as in Table 17-2.

Table 17-2. *Deadlock*

Time	Thread 1 Status	Thread 1 Action	A Locked By	B Locked By	Thread 2 Status	Thread 2 Action
1	Running	Lock A			Running	Lock B
2	Running	Lock B	Thread 1	Thread 2	Running	Lock A
3	Blocked		Thread 1	Thread 2	Blocked	

As you can see, both threads are blocked, and will never be unblocked. The application as
a whole may not be hung, but whatever these threads were doing will never be finished. The
problem is that they tried to lock the resources that they need in a different order. Had they
both locked A and then locked B, as in Table 17-3, there could have been no deadlock.

Table 17-3. *No Deadlock*

Time	Thread 1 Status	Thread 1 Action	A Locked By	B Locked By	Thread 2 Status	Thread 2 Action
1	Running	Lock A	--		Running	Lock A
2	Running	Lock B	Thread 1		Blocked	
3	Running	(Transaction)	Thread 1	Thread 1	Blocked	
4	Running	Unlock B	Thread 1	Thread 1	Blocked	
5	Running	Unlock A	Thread 1		Blocked	
6	Running	(Whatever)	Thread 2		Running	Lock B
7	Running	(Whatever)	Thread 2	Thread 2	Running	(transaction)
8	Running	(Whatever)	Thread 2	Thread 2	Running	Unlock B
9	Running	(Whatever)	Thread 2		Running	Unlock A
10	Running	(Whatever)			Running	(Whatever)

So, it's not hard to avoid deadlock—within a single application, or a single subsystem. Just be sure that you always lock A and then lock B, and that you never lock B and then lock A. However, if you are writing utility code that will be used by programmers in other organizations—especially if they won't have access to the source code—discipline and code reviews are not enough. If you lock public values, even the best documentation in the world won't keep someone from locking them in the 'wrong' order.

As earlier, offering atomic methods can be the best protection against deadlock. A 'need' to lock a public data structure (so that you can do some sort of compound operation) should be taken as an indication that your design is wrong. You may need to move the public data structure into a new class that locks its private member before doing the compound operation, or you may need to add some atomic methods to the structure you were considering locking. For example, you may want to atomically pop a stack—iff it's not empty—and apply a delegate to the result. The Chapter17\LockedStack C# project does this as

```csharp
public void ConditionalPop(Handler<T> Handle)
{
    T Top = null;
    lock (Data)
        if (Data.Count > 0)
            Top = Data.Pop();
    // unlock as soon as possible; DON'T call the Handler in the lock!
    if (Top != null)
        Handle(Top);
}
```

.NET Threads

.NET threads execute delegates

Delphi's TThread class is a little strange: you use it by defining a class that inherits from TThread and overrides the Execute method. When you create an instance of your thread class, it runs its Execute method in a new thread. This is bad because it tends to violate encapsulation. Typically we want our threads to act with and on the program's existing objects—our forms and our data models. Putting the thread code into a separate thread object means that that thread object has to know an awful lot about other objects. Often, too, the other objects have to create special fields just for sharing data with the thread, so that thread creation can involve a lot of code. This is tedious. It's also a bad, dangerous coding practice for all the reasons that encapsulation is a good, safe coding practice: making thread objects heavily dependent on other objects' internals creates opportunities for any small change in ThisObject to break the thread running on ThatObject, and creates the possibility of unrelated code breaking the 'contract.'[4]

The FCL (System.Threading) Thread class does not have this problem: you pass a delegate to the Thread constructor. You can then set various Thread instance properties, like Priority, before (or after) calling the Start method. When you call the Start instance method, the new

---

4. www.midnightbeach.com/jon/pubs/MsgWaits/MsgWaits.html

Thread instance runs your delegate in a new thread, and the thread terminates when the delegate returns.[5] In the common case where your threads run delegates to methods of existing object instances, the .NET approach is easy and maintains encapsulation. At the same time, the .NET approach does not prevent you from creating a new object that contains some thread-local state information, and then creating a thread that runs a delegate to a method of your new thread-state instance.

For example, in .NET 2.0, you can create a thread that will run either a ThreadStart delegate or a ParameterizedThreadStart delegate. A ThreadStart delegate is a void method that takes no parameters (delegate void ThreadStart(), or type ThreadStart = procedure of object) while a ParameterizedThreadStart delegate is a void method that takes a single object parameter. The ParameterizedThreadStart delegate is new in 2.0, and in 1.*x* you can only use the constructor that takes a ThreadStart. To pass information to a ThreadStart thread, you simply create an object that contains the information, and create a thread that runs a ThreadStart delegate to a method of this parameter object, as in Listing 17-1 (and the Chapter17\ThreadParameters C# project).

Listing 17-1. *Passing a Parameter to a ThreadStart Delegate*

```
public abstract class GetFile
{
    /// <summary>
    /// Create a state packet that contains a thread parameter
    /// </summary>
    /// <param name="FilenameOrUrl">Filename or URL,
    /// to pass to the ThreadStart delegate</param>
    public GetFile(string FilenameOrUrl)
    {
        this.FilenameOrUrl = FilenameOrUrl;
        IoThread = new Thread(new ThreadStart(IoRoutine));
        IoThread.Start();
    }

    protected string FilenameOrUrl; // The delegate can 'see' this string
    protected string Result;        // The delegate sets this string
    protected Thread IoThread;      // The delegate runs in this thread

    protected abstract void IoRoutine();
```

---

5. If the delegate is a multicast delegate that contains more than one instance/method pointer pair, the thread will execute **all** the methods, one after the other, just as if you invoked the delegate in the ordinary way.

```
/// <summary>
/// Wait for the IoRoutine method to return; return the Result string
/// </summary>
public string Join()
{
  IoThread.Join();
  return Result;
}
}
```

As you can see from Listing 17-1, the Thread class supports standard Join functionality—if ThisThread calls ThatThread.Join(), then ThisThread is blocked until ThatThread terminates. You might use code like that in Listing 17-1 when downloading a file (or reading it from disk) is just one of the things that you need to do before you can perform some particular operation. You'd initiate the IO and continue with the other setup in your original thread, only calling Join when all the other setup is completed and you can't proceed without the file contents.

Now, you may be thinking that Listing 17-1 is a lot of code just to do some asynchronous IO, especially since it doesn't do any actual IO but just calls an abstract method that does all the real work. Why not create a delegate of the type delegate string Download (string Url), and call it asynchronously? Code like

```
Download DownloadDelegate = new Download(GetWebPage);
IAsyncResult AsynchResult =
  DownloadDelegate.BeginInvoke("http://www.midnightbeach.com", null, null);
// Do the other setup
string WebPage = DownloadDelegate.EndInvoke(AsynchResult));
```

is a lot simpler than Listing 17-1. However, using threads explicitly gives you more control. For example:

- You can set a thread's Priority.

- A thread delegate can be multicast while an asynchronously invoked delegate must be single-cast.

- You can specify whether your thread should keep the parent process from terminating, or whether app shutdown should terminate your thread.

- You can Interrupt a blocked thread, if necessary.

- You can spawn several threads, do some other setup, and then block until they **all** finish.

Not every application needs any of these (or other) Thread features. Many algorithms don't have **any** parts that can run asynchronously, and many algorithms that do have parts that can run asynchronously will only have a single step that involves, say, an IO wait: invoking a delegate asynchronously will often be a perfectly adequate way of minimizing total run time by doing some work while waiting for IO. However, if your needs do go beyond simple asynchronous execution, then you should keep reading this chapter. (Also, the "Thread Pool" section of this chapter talks a bit about how asynchronous delegates are implemented.)

Thread Priority

Long-running threads can be nice and request a low priority

Every Thread has a Priority property. You can read and write Priority at any time: in particular, you can change a thread's Priority while the thread is running, not just before you call Start. Priority is an enumerated value with only five settings: Lowest, BelowNormal, Normal, AboveNormal, and Highest. While scheduling strategies differ from OS to OS, smooth multitasking relies on the general principle that most tasks spend most of their time in a blocked state, waiting for input.

A long, compute-bound task running at normal priority can make the whole system sluggish. (Imagine the effect of even a millisecond pause between every mouse message!) A long calculation for a desktop app should generally run at BelowNormal priority, while Lowest priority is appropriate for something like a grid-computing app[6] that should only run when the system is idle.

Use AboveNormal and Highest priorities rarely and with great caution, as they will keep most other threads from running. You might use high priority for a thread that's doing a multi-step network handshake, where each step involves relatively modest amounts of computation: a high priority will ensure rapid response each time the thread is unblocked, while quickly reentering the blocked state will prevent the high-priority thread from impacting overall system responsiveness.

Foreground and Background Threads

Foreground threads keep a process alive

.NET threads are divided into foreground and background threads. This has nothing to do with thread scheduling: while a workstation OS may give higher priority to the application with the UI focus than it gives to other applications, foreground threads do not execute before background threads. Rather, the difference between foreground and background threads is that a process will stay alive as long as it contains at least one active running foreground thread, while a process will terminate when its last foreground thread terminates, no matter how many background threads are still running.

When the last foreground thread terminates, any background threads are terminated by calling their Thread.Abort instance method. Aborting a thread immediately raises an exception in that thread. This normally allows threads to clean themselves up gracefully, by unwinding any finally blocks on the stack. However, it's not impossible for an Abort to occur within a finally block, which may have consequences like leaving files unflushed. (I cover some of the other consequences of aborting threads, later in this chapter.)

By default, threads that you explicitly create are foreground threads—their IsBackground property is false. As with thread Priority, you can change IsBackground at any time, not just before calling Start. The only time the IsBackground property really matters is when a foreground thread terminates: if any and all remaining threads are background threads, the process aborts them and then the process shuts down.

---

6. Like SETI@Home—http://setiathome.ssl.berkeley.edu.

Threads that you get from the ThreadPool (discussed later) are always background threads, and should always be returned in that condition.

Thread-local Storage

Ways for each thread to have its own variables

One of the reasons to use a thread, as opposed to a process, is that it has access to its parent process's address space. It can 'see' any public static variables and—if the thread delegate points to an instance method—the thread delegate can access any instance members in a perfectly ordinary way. An object created in one thread can be accessed by any other thread that can 'see' the object. Still, there are times when a thread needs its own copy of a variable, separate from any other thread's copy of that variable. There are four different ways to do this.

First, and most obviously, any local variables that the thread creates live on the thread's stack, and can't be seen by any other thread[7] unless you store a reference in a shared data structure. This is generally the most efficient way to create a private variable, but of course local variables are local to the method (or block) that declares them, and can't be seen by other methods unless they're explicitly passed as parameters.

The second way to create a per-thread variable is to simply declare it as a member of the class that supplies the thread delegate. The thread delegate has a this/Self reference just like any other object method, and can read and write instance members in exactly the same way as can any other object method. The only caveat with this approach is that these **are** perfectly normal instance methods: any thread with a reference to the thread delegate's instance can read and write its instance members, subject to the normal public/private rules.

The other two approaches create global variables that are unique to each thread. Thread static fields are strongly typed fields, declared at compile time, while *data slots* are dynamically typed object fields, created at run time.

Marking any static field with the [ThreadStatic] attribute means that each thread gets its own copy of that field. Much as with a native code Delphi threadvar, thread static fields are somewhat slower than normal static fields, because each reference jits to a call to a method that returns the address of this thread's copy of the field. (In fact, Delphi for .NET implements a threadvar as a [ThreadStatic] field of the same unit class that holds global variables and flat procedures.) In C#, you can initialize a thread static field, but this is generally a mistake: thread static initialization is done in the same compiler-generated part of the static constructor as any other static initialization. This means that the first thread to refer to the class will get an initialized thread static, while all other threads will get a zero-filled default value. It's generally best to just leave a thread static uninitialized, and to explicitly set it in each thread that uses it. Delphi will not let you initialize a threadvar at all.

---

7. Well, not by any user thread, at any rate. Each thread's stack lives in the same address space as the rest of the process's data, and the garbage collector does includes all thread locals in the set of roots that it scans for references to live data.

■**Note** Thread static fields can be `public` or `private`, `internal` or `protected`, just like any other static field. They do not have to be `public`.

The fourth and final approach to thread-local storage involves the Thread class's data slots. The static methods `Thread.SetData` and `Thread.GetData` take a `LocalDataStoreSlot` 'cookie' and set or get an `object` value. While the `LocalDataStoreSlot` cookie can be shared across threads, each thread has its own set of slots: ThisThread will not get the data that ThatThread set, even when it uses the same `LocalDataStoreSlot`. If a thread tries to GetData a slot that it has not yet set, GetData will return `null`.

Data slots can be named or anonymous. `Thread.AllocateDataSlot` creates an anonymous data slot, returning a `LocalDataStoreSlot` that each thread can use to store its own data. `Thread.GetNamedDataSlot(string)` will return a `LocalDataStoreSlot` that's associated with the name you pass, creating it if necessary.[8] While data slots are per thread resources, the symbol table is a process global, so that calling GetNamedDataSlot(ThisName) will always return the same `LocalDataStoreSlot`, no matter which thread you call it from. (See the Chapter17\ DataSlots C# project.)

Aborting and Interrupting Threads

It's safer to `Interrupt` than to `Abort`

In unmanaged code, aborting a thread is a very dangerous thing to do. If you simply stop a thread when the user hits Cancel, you don't really know what the thread was doing. Open files or graphics handles will never be closed, which is a resource leak that could destabilize the system. Worse, any resource the thread had locked will never be released: any thread waiting for that resource (and any thread that subsequently tries to lock that resource) would simply hang.

When you first look at the `Thread.Abort` method, it may look like aborting threads is safe in a managed code environment. When ThisThread calls ThatThread.Abort(), the CLR raises a `ThreadAbortException` within ThatThread, which (usually) causes the thread to unwind its stack gracefully, executing all cleanup code in `finally` blocks, and eventually exiting the thread delegate and so terminating the thread.

Why "usually"? Well, as the Microsoft documentation points out, it's not impossible that a `finally` block will take a long time to complete—nor is it impossible that a `finally` block may contain an infinite loop. While this is obviously true, it's not particularly helpful, as the average competent programmer rarely, if ever, writes an infinite loop, and is not incredibly likely to write a very long running `finally` block. In fact, I'd go so far as to call the Microsoft comments about "an unbounded amount of computation" counterproductive: by making it look like this is the worst that can happen, they hide the true dangers of Abort.

You might be tempted to think—as I did, at first—that the only real issue is to make sure that your thread code always properly uses `finally` blocks to free locks and resources. That is, always use the C# lock and using statements—or the equivalent nested try/finally blocks, in Delphi—and never tell yourself that code like

---

8. There's also a low-level `AllocateNamedDataSlot`/`FreeNamedDataSlot` API—see the SDK documentation.

```
Monitor.Enter(CounterLock);
unchecked { I++; }
Monitor.Exit (CounterLock);
```

will never raise an exception so that you can forgo a try/finally block for "performance reasons." After all, the system might raise a ThreadAbortException at any time.

But the problem goes much deeper than that. The system might raise a ThreadAbortException **at any time**. That means that it might raise a ThreadAbortException within Monitor.Enter after the thread has actually acquired a lock and before Monitor.Enter returns and the thread enters the try part of the lock statement. Or, the system might raise a ThreadAbortException within a finally block, before your thread has unlocked a datum or freed a handle.

In other words, it's not safe to use Thread.Abort to cancel an operation within a program that's going to keep running. It **is** safe to use Thread.Abort to close running threads as part of a program shutdown process, because the OS will close any open resources when the process terminates—but I think it's probably better to just set all threads' IsBackground property to true, and let the system abort your threads for you. While calling Abort is somewhat shorter and more self-documenting than setting IsBackground to true, I think there's a benefit to following a simple rule: don't call Thread.Abort.

So, how **do** you cancel a threaded operation when the user presses the Cancel button, or closes the window that the thread is drawing in?

The Thread.Interrupt instance method is significantly safer than Thread.Abort. Calling Interrupt raises an exception in a blocked thread, or raises an exception when the thread next blocks. In a properly written thread—one that never blocks within a finally block—an unhandled exception within a wait operation will fall through all of any and every finally block, and thus cleanly release any locks or other resources.

Of course, if a thread never blocks, Interrupt doesn't do much good. In this case, your best policy is to do pretty much what you would do in unmanaged code: have the thread delegate periodically check a volatile bool Stop field every so often (at the top of a loop, perhaps), so that you can abort the thread simply by setting Stop to true. Thus, code like

```
ThisThread.Interrupt(); // raise an exception in a blocked thread
ThisThreadDelegateObject.Stop = true; // set the volatile flag
```

uses Interrupt to forcibly terminate the thread, if possible, and a volatile field to have the thread terminate itself, if the thread polls the Stop variable before the thread next blocks.

■ **Note** I cover volatile variables in "The .NET 'Memory Model'" subsection, later in this chapter.

There may be times when you want to Interrupt a thread and have it catch the ThreadInterruptedException, but you wouldn't generally do this to time out of a wait. All the synchronization primitives that I describe in this chapter support waits that can time out.

Synchronization

Coordinating access to shared resources

For in-process locking and update signaling, you will usually use the (System.Threading) Monitor class. The Monitor class is very efficient, as it is 100% CLR code that does not make any operating system calls.

Even so, a lock and block can be a lot of overhead for a simple Instances++, and so the Interlocked class allows you to do a few very simple operations, atomically but without explicit locking. For more complex synchronization scenarios, including interprocess synchronization, you will use the various (System.Threading) WaitHandle classes that wrap OS synchronization primitives.

Multiprocessor machines present special synchronization challenges, but the CLR handles most of them for us. Despite the fact that each processor on a multiprocessor machine may have its own cache, the standard locking operations are usually enough to assure that all threads see the same values. In general, you only need to use *volatile variables* and *memory barriers* when you want to avoid locking (because you don't want threads to block any more than is absolutely necessary to keep operations atomic).

Managed Locking

Fast and efficient, and covers most of your needs

Like strings, arrays, and delegates, the (System.Threading) Monitor class is a special class with deep roots in the CLR. You can lock **any** reference type with Delphi code like

```
Monitor.Enter(PrivateReference);
try
  // locked code
finally
  Monitor.Exit(PrivateReference);
end;
```

or the equivalent C# lock (PrivateReference) {/*locked code*/}[9] because the header of every object on the heap contains a "synch block index" in addition to a method table pointer. (As per previous chapters, the method table pointer is a lot like Delphi's VMT. It points to CLR-maintained tables that specify type information like the run-time size and field layout, method entry points, class attributes, and so on.) The synch block index is an integer offset into a table of "synch blocks." A –1 means the object is unlocked; any other value is an index into a table of synch blocks.

---

9. As per Chapter 6, the C# lock statement does a Monitor.Enter; try {} finally {Monitor.Exit}.

> **Note** Value types do not have a synch block index and cannot be locked. Boxed value types do have a synch block index and can be locked, but each boxing operation creates a new reference type. You can **compile** code like `lock ((object) SomeInt) SomeInt++` ... but each thread will lock a different object, and `SomeInt` will not be protected at all. Locking a value type usually involves creating a private `object` field 'next to' the value type, and locking that with code like `lock (SomeIntLock) SomeInt++`.

Objects that have their synch block index set (i.e., not –1) are not necessarily locked. Each synch block refers to both the thread that owns the lock and also to two queues: the *ready queue* contains any threads that are waiting to obtain the lock when the current owner releases it, and the *waiting queue* contains any threads that are waiting for a signal from the lock owner. (I'll get to `Monitor.Wait` in a few paragraphs.) A locked instance will always point to a synch block; an unlocked instance will point to a synch block as long as there are threads in the waiting queue.

Locking

When you use `Monitor.Enter` or `Monitor.TryEnter`[10] to lock an unlocked instance, the CLR will make sure that the synch block index points to a synch block. If there are waiting threads, the instance will already have a synch block; if not, the CLR will either reuse an existing synch block or will create a new synch block. In either case, once the synch block index is set, the CLR will set the instance's synch block to point to the current thread, thus locking the object. When you try to lock an instance that's already locked, `Enter` will add the current thread to the ready queue, and will then block the current thread until it obtains the lock. When the lock owner calls `Monitor.Exit`, the first thread in the ready queue will get the lock and be unblocked.

> **Caution** Letting you lock your actual data makes for smaller, clearer code than if you had to always explicitly create critical section objects. However, any time you lock `public` members of a class, you run the risk of deadlock. You may lock A then B, and someone else may lock B then A. As a general rule, you should never lock a `public` member of any class, and you should think long and hard before locking an `internal` member. You can, perhaps, use careful documentation and code review to safely break this rule in assemblies that will only be used internally; code that will be used by third parties should only lock `private` or `protected` members.

---

10. `Monitor.TryEnter` will return `true` if it was able to lock the instance you pass it, and `false` if it couldn't lock it. There are overloads that always return immediately, and overloads that will wait for a specified amount of time before giving up. Using `TryEnter` means that your code can't deadlock, but it's not easy to write code that does anything more than raise an exception when it can't get a lock. Carefully written code never deadlocks and never holds a lock open for more than a very few statements: `TryEnter` is rarely necessary in production code. (Timeouts on event waits are a different story.)

As an alternative to manual locking, you can lock whole methods by applying the

`[System.Runtime.CompilerServices.MethodImpl(MethodImplOptions.Synchronized)]`

attribute to the method. This may aid clarity a bit by cutting down the nesting level within the method, but it's generally disparaged for two rather good reasons:

1. The lock is obtained before entering the body of the method, and is not released until the method returns. Using explicit locking gives you finer-grained locking—you only keep the lock open as long as you absolutely need to. While this isn't really an issue with simple methods that add or remove an element from some sort of data structure, these are also not usually the sort of complexly structured methods where cutting one level of indenting can have any real effect on clarity.

2. Synchronized methods are still using the `Monitor` mechanism, but it's no longer obvious which object is being locked. (Static methods lock the object's `Type`; instance methods lock `this`/`Self`, the object's instance.) This can lead to locking failure or even deadlock. A hidden lock can lead to lock failure if you 1) forget that synchronized static methods do not lock the same data structure as synchronized instance methods, if you 2) access the same static data structures while explicitly locking something besides the class type, or if you 3) access the same data structures from the synchronized methods of a different class. A hidden lock can lead to deadlock, both because you are now locking a data structure that may be publicly visible, and also because somebody maintaining your code may not be aware what a synchronized method is actually locking.

Waiting

The `Monitor` class supports basic event notification through the `Wait`, `Pulse`, and `PulseAll` methods. The thread that currently owns the lock on an object can call `Monitor.Wait` to release the lock and enter the waiting queue. Waiting threads block until some subsequent lock owner both calls `Monitor.Pulse` or `Monitor.PulseAll` **and** releases the lock by passing out of a lock statement or explicitly calling `Monitor.Exit`. When the lock owner does a `Pulse`, one thread is moved from the waiting queue to the ready queue; when the lock owner does a `PulseAll`, all threads in the waiting queue are moved to the ready queue.[11] Each time a lock owner releases the lock, the first thread in the ready queue will get the lock.

---

11. There are `Wait` overloads that let you specify a maximum time to wait for a `Pulse`. It's easy to misinterpret the SDK documentation and think that timeouts establish a priority mechanism, that `Pulse` will wake threads with `Wait` timeouts before `Pulse` will wake threads with no `Wait` timeout, but this is not the case. Threads receive a `Pulse` and are moved to the ready queue in the order they were added to the waiting queue. All the SDK means by "bypassing ... threads ahead of it in the wait queue" is that a thread is removed from the wait queue when it times out, even if there are threads ahead of it in the waiting queue.

Do note that `Wait` **always** returns with an open lock, even if it times out: the boolean result tells you only whether or not you now have the lock because you were pulsed or because you timed out. You must always `Exit` the lock after a `Wait`. Also, because you will not get the lock and return from a `Wait` until any threads ahead of you in the ready queue have obtained and released a lock, a `Wait` that specifies a timeout may actually take considerably longer to return than the maximum `Wait` time that you specify.

That is, you always pulse within a lock

```
lock (Data)
{
  Monitor.Pulse(Data);
}
```

and no waiting thread will unblock and reacquire the lock until you exit the lock by (implicitly or explicitly) calling Monitor.Exit. Similarly, you always wait within a lock

```
lock (Data)
{
  Monitor.Wait(Data); // release the lock and enter the waiting queue
  // Data is locked when Wait returns
}
```

because you return from the Monitor.Wait call with a lock, and you need to (implicitly or explicitly) call Monitor.Exit, just as if you'd never been blocked.

The basic Enter/Exit locking mechanism allows you to turn a sequence of operations into an atomic transaction—e.g., if you increment a Count property and add an element to an array, no other thread (that uses the same lock) can see your data structure in an inconsistent state, and no other thread can perform another transaction on the same data structure at the same time. The Wait/Pulse mechanism allows you to extend that so that one or more "consumer" threads can be notified whenever a "producer" adds data to the shared data structure.

For example, you may have to do a set of computations that can be easily split into a hard first part and an easy second part. On a multiprocessor machine, you could create several producer threads to do the hard parts. Each producer thread adds its results to a queue and pulses the queue, waking the first of the smaller number of consumer threads that was waiting on the queue and that can now do its postprocessing.

■**Note** While Wait and Pulse are similar to Win32 event waits in many ways, a Pulse will **only** wake a waiting thread. If no thread is waiting, a Pulse will **not** set a flag so that the next Wait gets the last Pulse; the Pulse will just be 'wasted.' The next thread that calls Monitor.Wait will block until the next Pulse (if any). If your producer thread(s) may get ahead of your consumer thread(s), you may need to use one of the WaitHandle descendants that I cover in the "Wait Handles" subsection, later in this chapter.

The .NET "Memory Model"

Hides the details of memory synchronization

In native code on a single-processor machine, careful use of the various synchronization primitives is all that you need to build reliable multithreaded applications. However, multiprocessor systems can present special challenges, because each processor may have its own cache.[12] If ThisThread

---

12. Hyperthreaded processors share cache, as do some (not all) multicore machines.

has SomeVariable in its cache and then ThatThread changes SomeVariable, you want ThisThread to see the updated value—yet by default ThisThread will see the cached value, not the current value.

This is complicated, especially as there are differences between processors in a processor family (think of the differences just within the Pentium family) and there are differences between multicore and multichip machines ... and you usually can't control what sort of hardware your customers install your applications on.

To simplify this, .NET uses a *memory model*. Much as CIL is a sort of abstracted machine language that doesn't correspond directly to any preexisting machine language, so the memory model is a sort of abstracted architecture that ignores most of the complications in real architectures. The key abstraction is that despite all the differences between board-level and chip-level caches and between single-processor and multiprocessor caches, each ultimately accesses the main, shared, system memory, and "all" that cache does is change when those accesses happen. For example, when a processor gets a value from cache instead of actual memory, you can say that the cache moved the read back in time; the actual read happened some time before the instruction executed.

This is pretty simple, and it may at first seem like talking about a memory model is as pompous as calling program behavior "semantics." The point of the memory model is that when the definitions of the threading primitives talk about when reads and writes happen, they're talking in terms of the nice, simple memory model, and abstracting away the actual messiness of all the different hardware that the memory model might be implemented on. Saying that ThisThread reads a variable after ThatThread writes the variable is not talking about statement ordering—it's **promising** that ThisThread will read what ThatThread wrote.

For example, when the .NET specs say that "Acquiring a lock ... shall implicitly perform a volatile read operation," (ECMA 335, section 11.6.5) this is actually setting us up for something rather significant. A *volatile read* is a read that is guaranteed to return the current value in main memory. (A volatile write is guaranteed to go to main memory.) When you lock a datum, the CLR guarantees that your next read will give the current global values, not whatever outdated value may happen to be in the current thread's processor's cache. You don't have to worry about flushing or updating the caches; the CLR takes care of all that.

The memory model comes in when section 11.6.7 goes on to say that "A volatile read has 'acquire semantics' meaning that the read is guaranteed to occur prior to any references to memory that occur after the read instruction in the CIL instruction sequence." Again, this is not just making bland statements about instruction ordering; it's actually making a rather strong promise. Memory reads that follow a lock in the instruction sequence also follow a lock in the memory model. The lock constitutes a sort of *memory barrier*, and the CLR guarantees that instructions that follow the barrier will see valid, current data.

Similarly, when section 11.6.5 says "releasing a lock ... shall implicitly perform a volatile write operation" and section 11.6.7 adds that "A volatile write has 'release semantics' meaning that the write is guaranteed to happen after any memory references prior to the write instruction in the CIL instruction sequence," it means that releasing a lock guarantees that any memory writes the thread did before releasing the lock will be visible to all processors, regardless of cache and CPU architecture.

This means that using the lock statement (or manually using the Monitor class) works on multiprocessor systems just as it does on single processor systems. A properly locked transaction is atomic and immediately visible: not only will a thread that waits on a lock not be able to see a partially completed transaction, it will always see the transaction outcome, even when the transaction was processed by a different CPU.

Note Another consequence of the memory model is that there is comparatively little need for explicit volatile reads or writes.

The CIL includes the volatile instruction prefix, which guarantees that a memory access comes from or goes to main memory. You can control exactly when you do volatile read or writes by using the Thread.VolatileRead and VolatileWrite methods, or you can declare fields to be volatile.[13] In general, you only need to use volatile reads or writes when you are trying to avoid locking. For example, as earlier, you would make a thread abort boolean volatile: the thread would periodically do a simple if test (that does a volatile read) to see if it should stop what it's doing, and any thread that needs to stop the thread would simply set the volatile thread abort field to true.

Similarly, you only need to use Thread.MemoryBarrier when you don't want to lock and you also don't want to use a volatile variable. A MemoryBarrier after some updates guarantees that the updates will be visible in main memory; a MemoryBarrier before some reads guarantees that you get current data. Thread.MemoryBarrier is not often needed: I mention it mostly so that you will not run into it and think you should be using it everywhere.

Interlocked Access

Atomic operations without explicit locking

The Interlocked class offers .NET static method wrappers for the Windows "Interlocked Variable Access" functions like InterlockedIncrement and InterlockedExchangeAdd. The methods of the Interlocked class allow you to do simple operations like ThisInt++ or ThisInt += ThatInt in an atomic fashion (so that no other thread or process sees a partially updated variable) without having to write code like

```
lock (TransactionLock) // can't lock value types - see "Managed Locking," earlier
  ThisInt += ThatInt;
```

or

```
Monitor.Enter(TransactionLock);
try
  ThisInt := ThisInt + 1;
finally
  Monitor.Exit(TransactionLock);
end;
```

Instead, calling Interlocked.Add(ref ThisInt, ThatInt) will add ThatInt to ThisInt, returning the old value of ThisInt, in an atomic fashion. Specifically, two simultaneous calls to

---

13. One pitfall of the VolatileRead and VolatileWrite methods is that you might forget to read or write a variable through the VolatileRead and VolatileWrite methods—that you might use a 'raw' access in one or more places. Occasional raw access may be a deliberate optimization, but it's more likely to be an accident that creates an intermittent, unpredictable error that will be hard to track down. The C# volatile keyword tells the compiler to make **all** references to the variable volatile.

Interlocked.Add will always yield the right result: unlike the example in the earlier "Thread Basics" section, it is not possible for both calls to work with the same original value. If ThisInt is originally 42, two simultaneous calls to Interlocked.Add(ref ThisInt, 2) will always leave ThisInt set to 46—never 44.

In addition to Add, Increment, and Decrement operations on 32-bit and 64-bit integers, the Interlocked class supports Exchange and CompareExchange operations on integers, floats, objects, and generic types (i.e., Exchange<T>(ref T, T) and CompareExchange<T>(ref T, T, T)). The Exchange methods set the first (reference) parameter to the value of the second parameter, and return the original value of the first parameter. The CompareExchange methods do the same—if and only if the original value of the first (reference) parameter equals that of a third "comparand" parameter. That is, CompareExchange does the atomic equivalent of

```
if Target = Comparand then
begin
  Result := Target;
  Target := NewValue.
end;
```

Note The Interlocked class has been greatly expanded in 2.0. Some of the functionality I describe here is not available in 1.1.

On 32-bit systems, the 64-bit (long) integer type is a double-precision type. This means that all reads and writes require a pair of instructions, and it is always possible that a thread switch between the first and second instruction could give you a scrambled value. In 2.0, the Interlocked class's expanded 64-bit support allows you to do all reads and writes through the Interlocked class—e.g., long Local64 = Interlocked.Read(ref Variable64) and Interlocked.Exchange(ref Variable64, Local64)—so that you can write double-precision code without having to use explicit locking.

Never forget that (somewhat as with volatile variables) Interlocked only protects you if all access to a variable is through Interlocked.

Wait Handles

More sophisticated locking, at a noticeably higher cost

The Monitor class will cover maybe 90% of your synchronization needs. Because using the Monitor class involves neither operating system calls nor finalizers, you should always make the Monitor class your default synchronization solution, only turning to WaitHandle descendants when you need to do cross-process (or cross-AppDomain) synchronization, or when the Wait/Pulse mechanism can't solve your signaling needs.

The abstract WaitHandle class is a wrapper for operating system synchronization primitives. Its Mutex, AutoResetEvent, ManualResetEvent, and Semaphore descendants support different types of functionality, but all wrap OS handles: use WaitHandle objects within a using block where you can, and call Close where you can't automatically call IDispose.Dispose. (As with the GDI+

objects of Chapter 16, not closing a WaitHandle doesn't have such immediately noticeable consequences as not closing a file or other stream, but avoiding finalization does help keep your app [and other apps on the same machine] running smoothly.)

All WaitHandle descendants support the WaitOne instance method, which waits for their handle to be signaled. Mutexes signal when they acquire a lock; events signal when some other thread explicitly sets them; and semaphores signal when there is 'room' for your thread to enter.

Additionally, the static methods WaitHandle.WaitAll and WaitHandle.WaitAny allow you to specify an array of WaitHandle descendants and to block until all (or any) of the handles are signaled. WaitAny is useful when you can do something sensible as each piece of a whole transaction comes in, like a browser resizing a web page's grid as it gets new pieces of the page.

WaitAny is also useful when it is desirable to have one thread respond to any of several different signals, as opposed to having a single thread per signal: WaitAny returns an integer index that tells you which handle was signaled. (You can also use the system ThreadPool in this latter sort of situation—see the "Wait Callbacks" subsection, later in this chapter.)

WaitAll could be useful when you are working with unreliable agents, like network queries that may time out or otherwise fail. It would let you wait for a certain amount of time for all your agents to report. If they haven't all reported after a decent interval, you might try to go with what you've got, or you might try to fire off 'redundant' queries in the hope that these will get load-balanced onto a free server and actually return before their predecessors.

There's probably not much point to using WaitAll with reliable agents, though. For example, if you fire off multiple delegates to read files and return strings, you can pretty safely assume that all the delegates will return, and simply call EndInvoke on each, at the point where you first need its result.

Caution You can pass different types of wait handles in the same call to WaitAll or WaitAny, but you should have a **very** good reason to pass WaitAll a heterogeneous array containing mutexes, as you can end up holding a lock for a very long time if, say, server overload means that an IO thread takes "forever" to signal an event. There are good reasons to use WaitAll and WaitAny with events, but there are few good reasons to use WaitAll and WaitAny with mutexes.

Mutexes

Mutex is short for "mutual exclusion," and in synchronization theory is used pretty much interchangeably with "critical section." The Win32 API, however, uses critical sections for in-process locking and mutexes for interprocess locking. The FCL pretty much preserves this distinction: WaitHandle descendants include the (System.Threading) Mutex class but no CriticalSection class. While you **can** use the Mutex for in-process locking, you'd better have some incredibly compelling need to use WaitHandle.WaitAll or WaitHandle.WaitAny—as per the Chapter17\MutexTimer C# project, using the Monitor class is about two orders of magnitude faster than using a Mutex—and transactions that create and close a Mutex are another factor of five slower.

The Mutex constructor allows you to specify the name of a mutex that can be shared across processes, creating one if necessary. In 2.0, the Mutex.OpenExisting static method will return a new Mutex instance that wraps the existing OS mutex, or will raise an exception if the OS mutex doesn't already exist.

To acquire (lock) a `Mutex`, call the `WaitOne` method, inherited from the `WaitHandle` class. Presumably this remarkably unspecific name hasn't been supplemented with a more mnemonic method like `Acquire` or `Open` because Microsoft wanted to remind you that the call may not return immediately, that `WaitOne` will block until you have acquired the lock, and also to remind you that you can pass the `Mutex` to `WaitHandle.WaitAll` or `WaitHandle.WaitAny`. Or perhaps it's just an unthinking reflection of the Windows API.

In any case, you acquire a `Mutex` by waiting for it, and you release (unlock) a `Mutex` by calling the `ReleaseMutex` instance method.

Events

An event is either set (signaled) or reset (not signaled). A thread that waits on a signaled event passes right on through, without blocking. Conversely, a thread that waits on an unsignaled event will block until some other thread sets the event to the signaled state. Events may either reset automatically, after a single thread has passed through, or they may require manual reset. An auto reset event will only let one thread through at a time: each thread that passes through resets the signal, so that any threads that wait (or are waiting) on the event block (or stay blocked) until you set the signal again. Conversely, setting a manual reset event will unblock all threads that may be waiting for the event, and subsequent waits will not block until you call the `Reset` method to reset the event to the unsignaled state.

In 1.x, there are two types of event wait classes that descend directly from `WaitHandle`: the (`System.Threading`) `AutoResetEvent` and the `ManualResetEvent`. Both classes are still supported in 2.0, but they now descend from the new (`System.Threading`) `EventWaitHandle` class, which descends directly from `WaitHandle`. `EventWaitHandle` is **not** an abstract class: you can create an `EventWaitHandle` as either a manual reset event or as an auto-reset event, by passing the appropriate `EventResetMode` enum to the `EventWaitHandle` constructor.

Neither `AutoResetEvent` nor `ManualResetEvent` can be used across processes—you have to use the `EventWaitHandle`. As with mutexes, the `EventWaitHandle` can be anonymous, and used entirely within a process, but you will usually use the overloads that take a name and that can be accessed from other processes. The `EventWaitHandle` constructor has overloads that can either wrap an existing named OS event or can create and wrap a new named OS event. Also as with mutexes, the `OpenExisting` static method returns an `EventWaitHandle` wrapper for an existing OS named event and raises an exception if the named event doesn't already exist.

Semaphores

The `Semaphore` class, which is new in 2.0, limits the number of threads that may pass through at any one time.[14] For example, in a parallelized application that has a number of threads running the same code on different data, each thread might have a section that does a lot of computation and an IO-bound section that communicates results and gets the next workpiece. As in Figure 17-1, you could set up a semaphore with a capacity one less than the number of processors on the machine, so that each thread in the computation phase gets a processor to itself, while the threads in the handshaking phase share the remaining processor.

---

14. The `Semaphore` class is just a wrapper for Win32 functionality, and you can get the same effects in 1.1 by P/Invoking Win32 functions like `CreateSemaphore`.

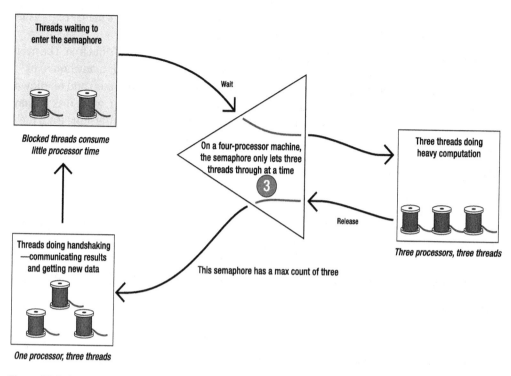

Figure 17-1. *Using a Semaphore to limit the number of compute-intensive threads*

You create a Semaphore by passing it a capacity integer, which initializes an internal counter. You can create an anonymous Semaphore that can only be used in-process, or a named Semaphore that can be shared across processes. Creating a named semaphore that already exists will attach to the existing semaphore, ignoring the capacity information you passed; you can also call OpenExisting to either attach to an existing semaphore or raise an exception.

When you wait on a Semaphore whose counter is 0, your thread will block until some other thread calls Release to increment the counter. Conversely, waiting on a Semaphore whose counter is greater than 0 decrements the counter and lets your thread through without blocking.

Thread Pool

Use the ThreadPool for short, simple tasks

As you've seen, it's easy to start a new thread. You just pass a delegate to the Thread constructor and call Start on the new Thread instance. With C# 2.0 anonymous methods, you don't even need to define a special method to run in the thread—you can just say

```
string Source;
Thread ReadMe = new Thread(delegate()
{
  using (StreamReader Reader = new StreamReader(@"..\..\Program.cs"))
    Source = Reader.ReadToEnd();
} );
ReadMe.Start();
```

to launch a thread that (in a Visual Studio environment) reads the process's main Program file to the Source string.

However, while creating a Thread is cheaper than creating a process, it's not free. The overhead is pretty insignificant when a thread will consume several seconds (or many hours) of CPU cycles. But, with a thread routine as short and simple as this, thread setup and teardown may take nearly as many CPU cycles as the thread routine itself. (Remember, while disk IO may take milliseconds, the overwhelming majority of that is spent waiting for interrupts from the disk controller.)

Worker Threads

What the system uses to run asynchronous delegates

This is why the FCL supplies a ThreadPool that can run a delegate in a background thread (creating a new thread, if necessary) and then cache the thread for later reuse.

For example, the preceding simple thread could be recoded, using the ThreadPool, as

```
string Source;
ThreadPool.QueueUserWorkItem(delegate
{
  using (StreamReader Reader = new StreamReader(@"..\..\Program.cs"))
    Source = Reader.ReadToEnd();
} );
```

A WaitCallback delegate is a delegate to a method that takes a single object parameter and returns nothing—delegate void WaitCallback (object state). The QueueUserWorkItem static method takes a WaitCallback delegate and executes it. The delegate executes right away, if a thread is available or the pool size is within the configurable limits, while if the ThreadPool **is** empty, the delegate will wait until a thread is returned to the pool. (The ThreadPool has static methods to get and set the size of the pool.) Reusing a thread is cheaper than explicitly creating a new Thread, and using ThreadPool is also a bit smaller, as you don't have to call Start.

Of course, reusing threads imposes its own tradeoffs. For example, when you explicitly create a single-use thread, you can set properties like Priority and IsBackground without the trouble of saving and restoring the original values. After all, the thread will go away when your delegate returns. With a ThreadPool thread, while you can still set the various Thread properties (via Thread.CurrentThread), you should save and restore the original values, because otherwise your settings will affect subsequent users of the pooled thread.[15] While the overhead of saving and restoring Thread properties doesn't compare to the cost of creating a Thread, it does add size and complexity to your thread routine.

More importantly, you can't fire off an asynchronous agent, do some other work, and then Join the agent's thread to use the agent's output—you have to use *wait handles*. Of course, that's exactly what the system does when you execute a delegate asynchronously, and it's precisely this *worker thread* pool that the system uses to run delegates asynchronously.

In fact, with simple agents, or methods that will run in a thread but that ultimately return a result, your best solution remains running a delegate asynchronously with BeginInvoke/EndInvoke.

---

15. Various bits of run-time library code share the ThreadPool with application code.

That is, if you can use asynchronous delegates, then you should use asynchronous delegates. Only manually queue user work items if you really need to.

If you will be repeatedly running the same method in a thread (some sort of IO routine, or perhaps a ray-tracing method), you should explicitly create a `Thread`, and try to reuse the same wait handles for the life of the thread.

Note The `ThreadPool` supports a limited number of worker threads. `ThreadPool` worker threads are for short operations, and any long-running threads should be explicitly created threads. The `ThreadPool` is designed to avoid the overhead of thread creation for short operations, not to host lengthy calculations.

Wait Callbacks

Reducing the number of blocked threads

Many tasks that take significant clock time actually take comparatively little CPU time, because they spend most of their time blocked, waiting for an OS wait handle. They may be waiting for network activity, file IO, a timer, or whatever. As an alternative to creating a thread that spends a lot of time blocked, waiting for one event or another, you can use `ThreadPool.RegisterWaitForSingleObject` to register an OS wait handle and a `WaitOrTimerCallback` delegate that gets called when the handle is signaled. The `ThreadPool` uses OS functions that block a single thread until any of several wait handles is signaled. This thread determines which wait handle was signaled, then calls the associated delegate in a worker thread.

This not only avoids thread creation overhead, but also reduces the number of blocked threads. For example, it may be easier, clearer, and safer to implement a network protocol as a thread that blocks at each step of the protocol—but it may be more efficient to implement the protocol as a web of delegates called as each handle is signaled, most of which fire off some response and then register another delegate and another wait. (The safest way to create such a web is probably to compile some sort of blocking script.)

Each wait can timeout or the wait can be infinite; the `WaitOrTimerCallback` delegate takes a parameter that tells the delegate whether it is being called because the handle was signaled or because the wait timed out.

Registering a wait with the `ThreadPool` is perhaps most appropriate where the event will keep being signaled, and you want to do the same thing each time. (You may be monitoring some sort of news feed, for example, or trading messages with another process on the same system.) Each call to `ThreadPool.RegisterWaitForSingleObject` includes an `executeOnlyOnce` parameter; when the Only Once parameter is `false`, the `ThreadPool` will keep waiting for the registered event until you call `Unregister` on the `RegisteredWaitHandle` you get from `RegisterWaitForSingleObject`.

GUI Issues

A very brief recap

Chapter 15 discussed the principles of multithreaded GUI programming. Just to reiterate, for those of you who are dipping in a chapter at a time: the key rule is that you should only touch a form or control from the thread that created it. There are only two exceptions: First, any thread can call CreateGraphics on another thread's forms or controls, and can then do arbitrarily complex operations on that Graphics. Second, any thread can ask another thread's forms or controls to Invoke a delegate (or use the lower-level BeginInvoke/EndInvoke pair) at any time; the control will run the delegate (in its own thread) when it is safe. While you must EndInvoke every IAsynchResult that you get when you invoke delegates asynchronously, it **is** safe to ignore the IAsynchResult that you get when you ask a control to BeginInvoke a delegate for you.

Key Points

.NET has great thread primitives, but threading is still a lot harder than it looks

- Threads allow a program to do several things 'at once.' A thread shares memory with other threads in its process.

- Locking critical sections is the key to ensuring that simultaneous access to data structures doesn't result in scrambled data structures or meaningless results.

- The .NET Thread class is a simple class that runs a delegate in its own thread.

- The Monitor class and the C# lock statement cover most of your synchronization needs.

- The .NET "memory model" allows you to ignore the details of how caching hardware works.

- The various WaitHandle classes are harder to use and more expensive than the Monitor class, but they let you address more complex synchronization issues.

XML

XML is increasingly used for all sorts of data and configuration files, as well as its 'traditional' role in passing data between systems. The FCL includes a rich set of XML classes that make it easy to read, write, and manipulate XML. The XmlWriter and XmlReader are fast, low-level classes that write and read a single datum at a time. The XML DOM is slower and consumes a lot of memory, but is very easy to use. XSLT can transform an XML document: to another XML document; to HTML; or to pretty much any other format, from simple formats like CSV to complex formats like PDF.

While the XML classes aren't anywhere near as fundamental as the other classes I've covered in these FCL chapters, they are simply too well done and too useful not to cover. This chapter pretty much treats XML as a text file format that you need to read and write—I recommend *XML in a Nutshell* (see Appendix 5, the bibliography) for coverage of XML schemas and Document Type Definitions (DTDs) and the like.

This chapter is divided into four sections. The first two are a quick overview of the XmlWriter and XmlReader classes. These classes are well documented and easy to learn, so I don't do much more than cover the basics and refer you to sample projects in the Chapter18 directory.

The third section is an even quicker introduction to the XML DOM (Document Object Model). The DOM classes are probably even more accessible than the XmlWriter and XmlReader classes: I cover the DOM mostly so that you understand the differences between the DOM and the lower-level XmlWriter and XmlReader classes, and know how to choose between them.

The first three sections focus on the mechanics of using the FCL classes, because I think it's safe to assume that you already have some familiarity with XML. On the other hand, XSLT (Extensible Stylesheet Language Transformations) is probably new to most Delphi programmers, so the fourth section is a longish XSLT tutorial. It doesn't try to be comprehensive: It only tries to take you to the point where an online table of XSL elements and XPath functions is all you need to write your own XSLT code.

XML Writer

The standard way to output XML

If you're like me, the first time you are asked to write an XML file, you'll write some classes that write XML entities to a TextWriter (Chapter 11) and that implement IDisposable, so that you can write code like

```
using (MyXmlElement Element = new MyXmlElement("Entry")
{
  // Populate the entry
}
```

that automatically writes </Entry> tags for you. It's not very hard, and the nested using clauses map nicely to the XML document's nested elements. However, it does take some time to write and debug that code, and whoever inherits your code will have to master your XML classes. Given that Microsoft has supplied two perfectly good libraries to write XML, the only reason to use a 'raw' TextWriter to write XML is that … you don't know about the supplied classes. If this book does nothing more than spare you three hours of writing your own classes to output XML, then it's worth every penny you paid for it.

The (System.Xml) XmlWriter class is an abstract class, and in 1.*x*, you have to explicitly create an XmlTextWriter with a particular encoding, and then call WriteStartDocument to write the XML header. For example, the Chapter18\WriteXml1_1 Delphi project does this as

```
var
  XML: XmlWriter;
begin
  XML := XmlTextWriter.Create('test.xml', Encoding.UTF8);
  try
    XmlTextWriter(XML).Formatting := Formatting.Indented;
    XML.WriteStartDocument;
    XML.WriteStartElement('Entry'); // the top-level element
  finally
    XML.Close;
  end;
end.
```

which produces a file containing an XML header and a single, *empty*[1] top-level element:

```
<?xml version="1.0" encoding="utf-8"?>
<Entry />
```

Setting the XmlTextWriter.Formatting property to Formatting.Indented makes the XmlWriter put each element on its own line, and also indent nested elements. The default is to just run everything together on a single line, which saves disk space and/or bandwidth but is much harder to read or edit—especially if your favorite editor truncates (or splits) long lines.

The XmlWriter has been extensively reworked in 2.0. Although it's still an abstract class, you should create a descendant instance by calling the new XmlWriter.Create static method and optionally passing it an XmlWriterSettings instance, instead of explicitly creating an instance of an XmlWriter descendant and then optionally setting its properties. You can still explicitly create an XmlWriter descendant, but this limits you to the 1.1 feature set: calling XmlWriter. Create lets you take advantage of features that were added in 2.0.

XmlWriter.Create implicitly calls WriteStartDocument, so the C# 2.0 equivalent of the preceding Delphi code is

---

1. Most XML elements come in pairs, like <tag attribute="value"></tag>, with any attributes in the start tag and any child elements between the tags. An empty element is a tag like <tag/> that ends with a /> and has neither child elements nor a </tag> end tag.

```
XmlWriterSettings Settings = new XmlWriterSettings();
Settings.Indent = true;
```

```
using (XmlWriter XML = XmlWriter.Create(XmlFilename, Settings))
  XML.WriteStartElement("Entry"); // the top-level element
```

As you can see, the XmlWriter class implements IDisposable, so your C# code doesn't have to explicitly call the Close method. XmlWriter.Close automatically closes "elements or attributes left open" so you don't need to manually call WriteEndElement before calling either Close or Dispose. Calling WriteStartElement without calling WriteEndElement creates nested elements; calling WriteStartElement after a call to WriteEndElement creates sibling (same parent) elements.

The WriteStartElement method 'opens' an XML element. For example, Writer.WriteStartElement("Entry") writes <Entry to the XML stream. An XML element can have zero or more *attributes*, and zero or more *child elements* (that is, it can have both or neither, or only one or the other). If a call to WriteStartElement is followed by one or more calls to WriteAttributeString, the element will have attributes. Calling WriteStartElement with an open element will generate a child element; calling WriteEndElement without writing any child elements will generate an empty element.

For example, as per the earlier example, code like

```
XML.WriteStartElement("Inventory");
XML.WriteEndElement();
```

will write the empty element <Inventory/>,[2] while

```
XML.WriteStartElement("Author");
  XML.WriteAttributeString("Name", "Jon Shemitz");
XML.WriteEndElement();
```

will write the empty element <Author Name="Jon Shemitz"/>, and

```
XML.WriteStartElement("Inventory");
  XML.WriteStartElement("Book");
    XML.WriteAttributeString("Title",
      "Kylix: The Professional Developer's Guide and Reference");
    XML.WriteAttributeString("Name", "Jon Shemitz");
  XML.WriteEndElement();

  XML.WriteStartElement("Book");
    XML.WriteAttributeString("Title", ".NET 2.0 for Delphi Programmers");
    XML.WriteAttributeString("Name", "Jon Shemitz");
  XML.WriteEndElement();
XML.WriteEndElement();
```

---

2. You may be troubled by the lack of a try/finally block in this code! You probably only need a finally block to protect the Close/Dispose call—odds are that any exception while writing an element will leave you with invalid XML, anyway. Nonetheless, while I've omitted the try/finally blocks in this section's printed code snippets (to save paper, and to make the logic a bit clearer by cutting out "background noise"), I do use them in real code, like the samples that accompany this chapter.

will write an Inventory element with two Book child elements:

```
<Inventory>
  <Book Title="Kylix: The Professional Developer's Guide and Reference"
  Author="Jon Shemitz"/>
  <Book Title=".NET 2.0 for Delphi Programmers" Author="Jon Shemitz"/>
</Inventory>
```

A well-formed XML document has one and only one top-level element. However, that element may have any number of attributes and any number of child elements. Each child element may also have any number of attributes and any number of child elements, and so on, recursively: XML elements may be as deeply nested as you like.

For example, the Chapter18\WriteDirectoryFile Visual Studio solution[3] reads the structure of the Chapter18 sample directory, and writes it to the Chapter18\Contents.xml file—projects in the other sections of this chapter read this file (and won't work without it). The top-level <Entries> element contains a single <Entry> element that corresponds to the Chapter18 directory; this directory entry has an <Entry> element for every file system element (i.e., file or directory) in the Chapter18 directory, and so on recursively. Files and empty directories are empty elements, while populated directories have child elements. Listing 18-1 is a heavily pruned version of the Contents.xml file, just to make the structure clear for subsequent sections.

Listing 18-1. *A Heavily Pruned* Contents.xml *File*

```
<?xml version="1.0" encoding="utf-8"?>
<Entries>
  <Entry Name="Chapter18" Attributes="Directory">
    <Entry Name="FileSystemEntries" Attributes="Directory">
      <Entry Name="bin" Attributes="Directory">
        <Entry Name="Debug" Attributes="Directory">
          <Entry Name="FileSystemEntries.dll" Attributes="Archive" Bytes="20480" />
          <Entry Name="FileSystemEntries.pdb" Attributes="Archive" Bytes="28160" />
        </Entry>
      </Entry>
    </Entry>
    <Entry Name="Contents.xml" Attributes="Archive" Bytes="27547" />
  </Entry>
</Entries>
```

---

3. This solution includes a FileSystemEntries class library plus a trivial program that reads a directory and writes it to XML. The Chapter18\ReadDirectoryFile solution includes the same FileSystemEntries project.

XML Reader

Fast, read-only access to XML data

Using the XmlReader class is a bit more complicated than using the XmlWriter class, especially in 1.*x*. Using the XmlWriter is a matter of writing a start element; writing any attributes or child elements; and then writing an end element. The XmlWriter class takes care of details like indenting, and it keeps track of whether the current element has any child elements or not, so that when you write an end element the XmlWriter knows whether it should just write /> to close an empty element, or whether it needs to write a </tag> to close a <tag> </tag> pair. By contrast, while 2.0 adds some high-level functions that simplify things a bit, the XmlReader basically works one *node* at a time. A node is an XML lexical component—white space, start elements, attributes, end elements, and so on—and you have to handle a stream of node states.

In general, you read an XML file by skipping to the first child of the top-level element. You read that element (and any child elements), and then you skip over any white space to either the next element or the top-level node's close tag. The most basic method, XmlReader.Read, steps through the XML stream a node at a time, setting the XmlReader properties to reflect the current node. For example, when the NodeType property is XmlNodeType.Element, the Name property contains the element's name. Similarly, when the NodeType property is XmlNodeType.Attribute, the Name property contains the attribute's name, and the Value property contains the attribute's value.

As with the XmlWriter, XmlReader is an abstract class. In 1.*x*, you have to manually create an instance of a descendant, like the XmlTextReader; in 2.0, you should use XmlReader.Create. For example, the Chapter18\ReadDirectoryFile project reads the Contents.xml file as

```
using (XmlReader Xml = XmlReader.Create(XmlFilename))
  return (DirectoryEntry)FileSystemEntry.ReadElement(Xml);
```

Most XML files contain several different types of elements. In this case, you would call XmlReader.Read until you get to the **second** node with an NodeType of XmlNodeType.Element, and then do some sort of dispatch on the element name. The Chapter18\ReadDirectoryFile project does 'know' that all (child) elements will be <Entry> elements, so the ReadElement method calls NextElement(Xml, "Entry") to skip straight to the first <Entry> element:

```
protected static void NextElement(XmlReader Xml, String Name)
{
  while (Xml.NodeType != XmlNodeType.Element || Xml.Name != Name)
    Xml.Read();
}
```

Each XML element can contain any number of attributes, in any order. There are three different ways to read attributes. The fastest way is to call MoveToFirstAttribute to position the current node on the first attribute (if any) and to then read attributes while MoveToNextAttribute returns true. A somewhat slower alternative is to use MoveToAttribute to index attributes from 0 to AttributeCount - 1. Both of these approaches read attributes in node order—the order that the attributes appear in the XML. The slowest (if easiest) approach is to pass MoveToAttribute a string containing the attribute name: MoveToAttribute will change the current node and return true if it found an attribute with the right name; it will return false (and not change the current node) if the current element does not have an attribute with the right name.

The Chapter18\ReadDirectoryFile project uses move first/move next, and reads attribute name/value pairs to a Dictionary<K,V> (Chapter 12) so that the attribute order doesn't matter:

```
private static Dictionary<string, string> GetAttributes(XmlReader Xml)
{
  Dictionary<string, string> Result = new Dictionary<string, string>();
  if (Xml.MoveToFirstAttribute())
    do
      Result[Xml.Name] = Xml.Value;
    while (Xml.MoveToNextAttribute());
  return Result;
}
```

The ReadDirectoryFile project then reads values from the Dictionary without having to worry about the order of the attributes in the XML file. This lets the code be as simple as code that uses MoveToAttribute to index by name, without incurring the expense of moving the current node "read pointer" back and forth. Alternatively, you might write code that sets attribute fields and properties in the order that you read it from the XML stream. One way to do this is to switch on the attribute name; another is create an object when you see a start element node, and then use Reflection (Chapter 13) to set properties and fields, based on attribute names.

Whatever order you read attributes in, you have to deal with the fact that attribute values are always strings, or formatted values. The Chapter18\ReadDirectoryFile project's ReadElement method uses DateTime.Parse, Enum.Parse, and Int64.Parse to convert formatted values to typed, binary values. If you use Reflection, each MemberInfo will have a FieldType or PropertyType property, and you can use code like

```
ThisFieldInfo.SetValue(ThisInstance,
  Convert.ChangeType(AttributeValue,
  ThisFieldInfo.FieldType));
```

or

```
ThisPropertyInfo.SetValue(ThisInstance,
  Convert.ChangeType(AttributeValue,
  ThisPropertyInfo.FieldType), null);
```

to set a field or property on ThisInstance to the (typed version of) AttributeValue.

Note There's nothing to stop you from writing arbitrarily complicated ToString routines, and writing the results as an attribute value, or as element text. Of course, then you have to write correspondingly complicated Parse routines! While regexs (Chapter 11) can make this pretty easy, it's probably a good idea to restrict your attributes and/or element text to formatted numbers and formatted dates (that you can Parse with the standard FCL routines) or to literal strings, especially if you will be sharing your XML with other programs. A complicated Parse routine may have bugs or be out of date ... plus, the whole point of XML is making the data's structure explicit. Adding structure within a string makes it harder to share the XML with other apps.

Syntactically, an XML element that contains text and/or child elements extends from the start <tag> to the close </tag>. While each child element shares the same syntax and may also enclose text and/or child elements, each <tag>/</tag> pair is a single element, however much may lay between the start and end nodes. Typically, your XML reading code will reflect this: an element-reading method will read the whole element (probably returning an object that contains a collection of subelement objects) and leaving the current node on the last node of the current element.

An element-reading method must first read any attribute values, then it can process any text and/or child elements. While XML syntax places no constraints on the amount or type of element content, most XML domains have their own semantics that imposes rules that your code needs to enforce: some element types should always be empty; other element types will contain only text, not child elements; others will only contain a particular type of child element; while some may contain any of several different types of child element.

For example, the FileSystemEntry.ReadElement method in the Chapter18\ReadDirectory-File project reads the attributes that every FileEntry has, and uses the Attributes attribute to tell whether this XML Entry represents a FileEntry or a DirectoryEntry: the Attributes attribute contains a (System.IO) FileAttributes, and (as in Chapter 11) a directory has the FileAttributes.Directory bit set, while a file does not. If the XML Entry represents a file, or is an empty element that represents a directory, the ReadElement method simply passes the attributes to the appropriate constructor, and returns the new object. However, if the XML Entry represents a directory that contains files or subdirectories, the XML Entry will have child elements, and the ReadElement method passes the XmlReader to a DirectoryEntry constructor that reads the child elements.

This constructor simply advances the current node from the last attribute to the first child with NextElement(Xml, "Entry"), and then recursively adds directory entries to its Contents collection until the current node is the current directory's ending </Entry>:

```
while (Xml.NodeType == XmlNodeType.Element && Xml.Name == "Entry")
    Contents.Add(FileSystemEntry.ReadElement(Xml));
```

In effect, XmlReader code like the Chapter18\ReadDirectoryFile project contains a simple recursive descent parser that uses the XmlReader as a tokenizer. Recursive descent parsers can be quite complex, but most XML files have rather simple semantics, so you should be OK if you

- Always know which Next States each element-reading method needs to handle.

- Establish conventions for how to handle unexpected elements.

- Take care that every element-reading method leaves the current node in the same place when it exits. Every method should leave the current node on the last node of its element **or** on the first node of the next element—don't mix the two.

Note Thinking of reading XML as recursive descent parsing naturally makes me wonder if there are any tools that can take a description of the XML file (perhaps in XSD) and create a parser for us, so that we don't have to do anything except parse attribute value strings, and store attribute values and child elements in the right fields. Xsd.exe and the XmlSerializer class (Chapter 14) are close, but these base the class structure on the XSD schema: a parser generator would write the code to read the XML, without making assumptions about the classes that you're pouring the data into. There don't seem to be any such tools as of January 2006 ... but I might have been searching for the wrong keywords.

The XML DOM

Less custom code, but slower and takes more memory

Using the XmlReader and XmlWriter requires you to know something about the structure of the XML document that you're reading and writing. By contrast, the XmlDocument class can load **any** XML document into memory, building a tree structure of W3C-approved entities like XmlElement and XmlAttribute—you don't have to build a recursive descent parser to read an XML file.

This can save you hours (or perhaps even days) of coding time,[4] but the tradeoff is that the XmlDocument tree is a late-bound, string-oriented representation of the XML document structure. Instead of a tree of, say, FileSystemEntry objects, you have a tree of XmlElement objects. Instead of each tree node having domain-specific fields and properties and methods, XmlElement instances have a collection of XmlAttribute objects, which represent an XML attribute as a Name string and a Value string.

An XmlElement that contains an Entry element from the Chapter18\Contents.xml file takes a lot more memory than the equivalent FileSystemEntry instance. It's also a lot slower to access: instead of reading, say, the Attributes field, you have to call GetAttribute("Attributes") and parse the returned string. That is, XML DOM nodes are big and slow. Plus, while you can use an XmlReader to extract just the information that you need from an XML stream, calling XmlDocument.Load loads the whole tree into memory.

So, while using the XML DOM is so easy that I'm not even going to outline it, it's really only appropriate for generic XML code (like the Visual Studio XML editor) that must display and/or edit any arbitrary XML, or for small, infrequently used utilities, where speed and memory consumption are a lot less important than development time. In production code, where speed or memory consumption do matter, you really should invest the time it takes to use the fast, low-level XmlReader and XmlWriter.

---

4. For example, the Chapter18\DomTree C# project can read the Chapter18\Contents.xml file and populate a TreeView in 23 lines of fairly sparse code.

XSLT

Converts XML to just about any imaginable format

Over the last few years, XML has pretty much become the de facto standard default file format—the file format you have to justify **not** using—for everything from app-specific configuration files to transaction logs and data collection. Part of this is probably just a desire to seem up to date, but there are also some honest technical reasons driving the migration: XML is an open standard, and there are good XML libraries on just about every platform.

XSL (Extensible Stylesheet Language) and XSLT (XSL Transformations) are just another good reason to use XML. XSLT is an open standard that lets you write a description of an XML transformation and apply it to an XML document. You can transform XML from one schema to another. You can turn an XML document into a browser-friendly HTML report. You can even use XSLT to convert XML documents to legacy formats like CSV or tab-delimited files.

XSL is worth learning because it can save you serious amounts of time. The first time I used it, I produced some reports in two-and-a-half days that would have taken me probably ten days if I had to handwrite the code to read the XML data files and extract the bits I wanted—and those two-and-a-half days included learning XSL. I bring this up because XSL has two things that can make it seem pretty daunting:

First, it's a descriptive language, not an imperative language. You don't write code that reads *this* and writes *that*—you write templates that are applied when the XSLT processors sees a particular type of XML element.

Second, XSL is written in XML, and is unbelievably verbose and hard to read. Every XSL *stylesheet* is a single XML element, with nested elements that declare templates. For example, Listing 18-2 shows a very simple XSL stylesheet, from the Chapter18\XSLT C# project:

Listing 18-2. *A Simple XSL Stylesheet*

```
<?xml version="1.0"?>
<xsl:stylesheet version="1.0" xmlns:xsl="http://www.w3.org/1999/XSL/Transform">
    <xsl:template match="Entries">Matched the top-level element.</xsl:template>
</xsl:stylesheet>
```

When you apply the stylesheet in Listing 18-2 to the Chapter18\Contents.xml file (Listing 18-1), the template matches the top-level element, and the output is the single line

```
Matched the top-level element.
```

■**Note** I'm not going to cover the details of how the FCL classes apply XSL to XML streams. See the method Xsl.ApplyXslt in the Common\Shemitz.Utility C# project for details—or just use it directly. There are overloads that transform from an input stream to an output stream, and there are overloads that transform from an input file to an output file. (I also include a 1.1 version as well as the default 2.0 version.)

On top of the verbosity and illegibility, each stylesheet **must** have version="1.0" and xmlns:xsl="http://www.w3.org/1999/XSL/Transform" attributes, or the XSLT transformation will fail. But don't despair, it's not as bad as it looks. The Xsl class in the Common\ Shemitz.Utility C# project contains methods that generate many XSL elements (and it's not hard to add the ones it doesn't supply, on an as-needed basis). These methods follow a simple overload model: each method has an overload that takes a string containing the element's contents, and an overload that takes a params object[] that's concatenated to generate the contents string. This makes it easy to build stylesheets and templates as a stream of elements, without getting lost in the nested tags. The Xsl class is particularly useful in a report generator, or any other scenario where you need to generate XSL at run time.

Thus, the Chapter18\XSLT C# project actually generates Listing 18-2 as

```
Xsl.Stylesheet(
  Xsl.Template("Entries", "Matched the top-level element.")
)
```

which is much easier to read and write than the 'raw XSL,' and is also much less error prone than always writing out all the boilerplate. The XSL examples in this section will all use the Xsl class methods instead of raw XSL, except when I'm talking about a single XSL element.

While an XSL template can actually match arbitrarily complicated *XPath expressions*,[5] a simple string will match an XML element name. If we change Listing 18-2 to match an Entry element, and not the top-level Entries element,

```
Xsl.Stylesheet( Xsl.Template("Entry", "Matched an <Entry/> element.") )
```

we get the single line

```
Matched an <Entry /> element.
```

There are a few things to notice here. First, because the top-level Entries element has only a single Entry child element (<Entry Name="Chapter18"></Entry>), the template matched only once. If the top-level Entries element had two Entry child elements, the template would have matched both elements—but you have to explicitly tell the XSLT processor to apply the template to nested elements. (I'll get to that in a bit.)

Second, remember that the second parameter to Xsl.Template is actually the body of an xsl:template XML element. At some point in the chain, the empty element <Entry/> (with no space) got turned into <Entry /> (with a space before the />). Anything in the template body that looks like an XML tag is subject to similar munging.

Third, it's really critical that you remember that the second parameter to Xsl.Template is actually the body of an xsl:template XML element. **All text in a template body must be valid XML!** Invalid XML will throw an XslLoadException (in 2.0—in 1.1, you get an XmlException).

---

5. This section is more an introduction than a reference. I cover some XPath expressions later in this section, but I don't try to be comprehensive. Depending on how much auxiliary documentation you loaded when you installed your .NET IDE, you may have XPath and XSL Element documentation in the integrated help viewer. If you don't, there are plenty of online reference sites.

XSL:TEXT

All text in a template body must be valid XML, and it would be invalid if you wanted the preceding `SecondXsl` to read `"Matched an <Entry> element."` instead of `"Matched an <Entry/> element."` because `<Entry>` would be a start element without a matching `</Entry>` end element.

You might try `Xsl.Template("Entry", "Matched an &lt;Entry&gt; element.")` or `Xsl.Template("Entry", "Matched an %3CEntry%3E element.")`, but then you'd get

```
Matched an &lt;Entry&gt; element.
```

or

```
Matched an %3CEntry%3E element.
```

as output, which isn't what you want, even if it does make sense. (The point of the `&lt;` or `%3C` escapes is that they are **not** XML markup—they get passed on to a browser, which translates them.)

You have to use the `<xsl:text>` element to get output like `Matched an <Entry> element`. The `<xsl:text>` element outputs its contents, and lets you put whitespace and other XML special characters into your output, without having them interpreted as XML. By default, the `<xsl:text>` element will escape characters like `<` and `&` to `&lt;` and `&amp;`—the optional `disable-output-escaping` attribute allows you to override this behavior. Thus, to get output like `Matched an <Entry> element`, you have to use a template like

```
Xsl.Template("Entry",
  "Matched an ",
  Xsl.Text("&lt;", true), "Entry", Xsl.Text("&gt;", true),
  " element\n")
```

Note how you have to pass the `Xsl.Text` method `"&lt;"` and `"&gt;"`, instead of `"<"` and `">"`—otherwise, you'd actually be coding something like

```
<xsl:text disable-output-escaping="yes">></xsl:text>
```

which would throw an illegal XML exception. The XSLT processor unescapes the content of an `xsl:text` element and emits it literally, subject only to the `disable-output-escaping` attribute.

The final thing to notice with stylesheets like

```
Xsl.Stylesheet( Xsl.Template("Entry", "Matched an <Entry/> element.") )
```

is that they don't **really** produce a single line of output: they actually produce three lines, with a blank line above and below the `Matched an ... element.` text (see Figure 18-1). Because they do not contain a template that matches the top-level element, the XSLT processor applies an implicit template, which outputs the top-level element's contents (which is just white space in `Contents.xml`) and matches the child element(s) against the available templates.

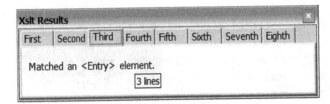

Figure 18-1. *The third XSL stylesheet produces **three** lines of output.*

To suppress these blank lines, we must supply a template that matches the top-level element. The fourth stylesheet in the Chapter18\XSLT project

```
Xsl.Stylesheet(
  Xsl.Template("Entries", ""),
  Xsl.Template("Entry", "Matched an ", Xsl.Text("&lt;", true), "Entry",
    Xsl.Text("&gt;", true), " element.")
  )
```

isn't quite right—it results in no output at all! The Entries template matches the top-level element, and the XSLT evaluates its (empty) content.

This is where the xsl:apply-templates element comes in. The xsl:apply-templates element allows us to tell the XSLT processor to apply templates to a particular *node set*. If the xsl:apply-templates element doesn't have the optional select attribute, the node set includes all child nodes of the current node—usually attributes and child elements. If the select attribute is a name like Entry, the node set includes all Entry child elements. If the select attribute is a name like @Name, the node set includes the current element's Name attribute.

Almost every XSL stylesheet contains a template that matches the top-level element, and tells the XSLT processor how to process the top-level children. For example, the fifth stylesheet in the Chapter18\XSLT project

```
Xsl.Stylesheet(
  Xsl.Template("Entries", Xsl.ApplyTemplates("Entry")),
  Xsl.Template("Entry",
    "Matched an ", Xsl.Text("&lt;", true),, "Entry", Xsl.Text("&gt;", true),,
    " element.")
)
```

does produce a single Matched an <Entry> element. line: the Entries template outputs no text, but tells the XSLT processor to match the Entry template against the child element(s) of the top-level Entries element.

A bit more usefully, the sixth stylesheet in the Chapter18\XSLT project outputs each Entry element's Name on a separate line:

```
Xsl.Stylesheet(
  Xsl.Template("Entries", Xsl.ApplyTemplates("Entry")),
  Xsl.Template("Entry",
    Xsl.ApplyTemplates("@Name"), Xsl.Text("\n"), Xsl.ApplyTemplates("Entry"))
  )
```

The Entry template contains three XSL elements. The first, Xsl.ApplyTemplates("@Name"), applies the default template rule to the current Entry element's Name attribute. The default attribute rule simply outputs the attribute value, so Xsl.ApplyTemplates("@Name") outputs the value of the Name attribute.[6] The second element, Xsl.Text("\n"), outputs a new line string. (If the "\n" string were not escaped with the xsl:text element, the XSLT processor would ignore it as white space between elements.) The third element, Xsl.ApplyTemplates("Entry"), tells the XSLT processor to match the available templates against any Entry child elements of the current element.

Of course, to be really useful, a directory listing needs to do more than just list the names of each file and directory. At a minimum, you want some sort of indenting that can show the parent-child relationships and you probably want to see the last access time, as in Figure 18-2. The seventh stylesheet in the Chapter18\XSLT project does this, while introducing a few new XSL elements:

```
Xsl.Stylesheet(
  Xsl.Template("Entries",
    Xsl.ApplyTemplates("Entry",
      Xsl.WithParam("Indent", true, "'''")
    )),
  Xsl.Template("Entry", Xsl.Param("Indent")),
    Xsl.ValueOf("$Indent"), Xsl.ValueOf("@Name"),
    Xsl.Text(" "), Xsl.ValueOf("@LastWriteTime"),
    Xsl.Text("\n"),
    Xsl.ApplyTemplates("Entry",
      Xsl.Sort("@Name"),
      Xsl.WithParam("Indent", true, "concat($Indent, '  ')")
    ))
)
```

This stylesheet includes the same two Entry and Entries templates as in previous stylesheets, but they've each gotten a bit more complicated. As with Chapter 11's regexs, the best way to read this is one element at a time.

Once again, the top-level Entry template is telling the XSLT processor to apply templates to its Entry child elements. What's new here is that I'm using the XSLT parameter-passing mechanism.

This is a rather loosely bound mechanism. Any template can include an xsl:param element that declares a named parameter, and an optional default value. For example, if a template includes the Xsl.Param("Parameter") element (<xsl:param name="Parameter"/>), it can then output Xsl.ValueOf("$Parameter"), or it can pass $Parameter in XPath functions like Number() or Concat(). If a named parameter has no default value, it defaults to an empty string—"" or ''.[7]

---

6. You may not be entirely comfortable invoking the default rules. Will the guy who inherits your code know what code like <xsl:apply-templates select="@Name"/> does? The <xsl:value-of select="NodeSet"/> element explicitly outputs the value of the selected NodeSet. For example, in the sixth stylesheet, Xsl.ValueOf("@Name") has the same effect as Xsl.ApplyTemplates("@Name")— it outputs the value of the Name attribute.

7. As in JavaScript, XSL string literals can use single- and double-quoted strings interchangeably, which is a great convenience when you're including an XSL string literal in a C# string literal—"Concat('this', 'that')" is a lot clearer than "Concat(\"this\", \"that\")".

Every xsl:apply-template element can be an empty element, or it can include xsl:with-param and xsl:sort child elements. (I'll get to xsl:sort in a couple of paragraphs.) What an xsl:with-param child element does is to override the default value for any parameters in any templates that its parent invokes. Thus, the Entries template specifies that the Indent parameter will be '' in any Entry element that's a child of the Entries top-level element. (Since '' is the default value, the Entries template doesn't really need to specify Xsl.WithParam("Indent", true, "''"). However, it can't hurt, and only makes the code clearer.)

The Entry template declares that it has an Indent parameter with Xsl.Param("Indent")—this is quite analogous to a 'real' method declaring its parameters in its prototype. (The Xsl.Param("Indent") element does not include a default value.) The Entry template then outputs the value of Indent, followed by the Name attribute—Xsl.ValueOf("$Indent"), Xsl.ValueOf("@Name"). The Entry template then outputs the last write time and a new line, and tells the XSLT processor to apply templates to any Entry child elements.

The xsl:apply-templates element in the Entry template is a bit more complicated than the xsl:apply-templates element in the Entries template. First of all, it has an Xsl.Sort("@Name") child element that tells the XSLT processor to sort any child elements by the value of their Name attribute. The xsl:sort element has options that allow you to specify sort order, and whether the field you're sorting on is alphabetic or numeric.

Second, the xsl:apply-templates element passes a nonempty value to the Indent parameter—<xsl:with-param name="Indent" select="concat($Indent, ' ')">—or Indent + " ". That is, the value of Indent that each Entry template sees depends on how deeply nested the current Entry element is.

The seventh stylesheet takes this demo about as far as it makes sense to go—the demo form places the XSLT output on a (System.Windows.Forms) Label so that I can show the bounding box by setting the label's background color, but a Label doesn't support tabs (or any other form of columnar output), and as you can see in Figure 18-2, the "report" is already getting pretty busy and hard to read. Still, it would be nice to show file sizes, and this gives me an opportunity to demonstrate xsl:call-template and xsl:if in the eighth stylesheet.

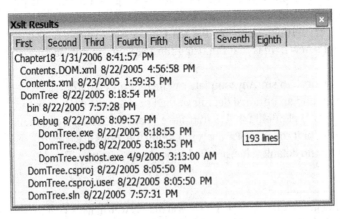

Figure 18-2. *The seventh stylesheet shows the directory structure.*

```
Xsl.Stylesheet(
  Xsl.Template("Entries",
    Xsl.ApplyTemplates("Entry",
      Xsl.WithParam("Indent", true, "'''")
    )),
  Xsl.Template("Entry", Xsl.Param("Indent"),
    Xsl.ValueOf("$Indent"), Xsl.ValueOf("@Name"),
    Xsl.CallTemplate("Filesize",
      Xsl.WithParam("Bytes", false, Xsl.ValueOf("@Bytes"))),
    Xsl.Text(" "), Xsl.ValueOf("@LastWriteTime"),
    Xsl.Text("\n"),
    Xsl.ApplyTemplates("Entry",
      Xsl.Sort("@Name"),
      Xsl.WithParam("Indent", true, "concat($Indent, '  ')")
    )),
  Xsl.NamedTemplate("Filesize", Xsl.Param("Bytes"),
    Xsl.If(" $Bytes != '' ",
      Xsl.Text(" "), Xsl.ValueOf("$Bytes"), " bytes")
  ))
)
```

The big difference between this eighth stylesheet and the seventh stylesheet is the new
Filesize named template, and the line that calls the Filesize template:

```
Xsl.CallTemplate("Filesize", Xsl.WithParam("Bytes", false, Xsl.ValueOf("@Bytes")))
```

CallTemplate can only call a named template. (A named template is an xsl:template with a
name attribute instead of a match attribute.) Unlike xsl:apply-templates, which specifies a set
of nodes to match against all templates, xsl:call-template specifies a single template, which
is applied to the **current node**, with optional parameters. It is almost exactly like making a
method call in C# or Delphi, except that the only 'instance' you can 'pass' is the this/Self node.

Notice also how the Xsl.WithParam child element has a second (Select) parameter of
false:

```
Xsl.WithParam("Bytes", false, Xsl.ValueOf("@Bytes"))
```

When the Select parameter is true, the xsl:with-param element is an empty element, with
the passed value specified in the select attribute; when the Select parameter is false, the
xsl:with-param element's child elements are a template that is evaluated and passed as the
value of the named parameter. When you are setting a parameter to an XPath expression (like
'' or concat($Indent, ' ')), you can use the empty element form; when you are setting a
parameter to an XSL expression (like <xsl:value-of select="$Bytes"/> in the Filesize named
template), you have to use the container form, because an attribute value (the select=) can't
contain XML elements.

The Filesize named template takes a Bytes parameter, with no default, and uses <xsl:if test=" $Bytes != '' "> to check whether or not the Bytes parameter is empty. If the Entry doesn't have a Bytes attribute, Xsl.ValueOf("@Bytes") will pass an empty string. If the test returns true, the Filesize template evaluates and returns all the child elements of the xsl:if element: a literal space, the value of the Bytes attribute, and a bytes literal. If the test returns false, the Filesize template doesn't output anything. There is no else element—to do anything more than a simple if/then, you need to use the xml:choose element (which is beyond the scope of this tutorial, but which shouldn't pose any problems to anybody who's followed this far).

Note This last section has been a bit of a departure from the style of the rest of the book—more a walk-through than an explanation. I think it's a better introduction than I had to work with, and hopefully it's enough for you to get started with XSLT and to make sense of the other XSL elements.

Key Points

- Use System.XML to read and write XML. Don't use raw file IO to write XML.

- The XmlWriter class is particularly easy to use. XmlReader is harder to master, but lets you write a reasonably efficient parser.

- The XML DOM is easy to use, but it's also slow and it consumes lots of memory.

- XSLT can translate an XML stream into just about any format.

- This is the last chapter of the FCL part of this book. By now, you should have a pretty good feel for how the FCL works, and should be able to master new namespaces on your own.

PART 4

■ ■ ■

Appendixes

All the appendixes put together come to only about as many pages as a short chapter. The chapters try to maintain some sort of narrative arc, but the appendixes are reference material—the sort of stuff you want the fastest access to.

The first appendix covers unsafe C#, including pointer arithmetic, and is thus named Appendix 0. Appendix 1 pairs a handy NUnit quick reference with a prolog that introduces unit testing in general and NUnit in particular. Appendix 2 is a quick overview of assembly loading rules. Appendix 3 is a brief introduction to application configuration files. Appendix 4 is a short glossary, and Appendix 5 is a shorter bibliography.

APPENDIX O

███

Unsafe C# Code

Safe code is adequate almost all the time. Probably more than even 99.99% of the time. But you do occasionally have to work with legacy code that stacks variable-length buffers one after the other—and that does require pointer arithmetic. Or maybe you can triple a transaction speed by coding a bottleneck routine in unsafe code, with raw pointer arithmetic. Unsafe C# gives you C-like * and & operators; a fixed statement that pins an area of local memory; and a stackalloc keyword that creates local typed arrays.

Unsafe code is managed code that lets you do pointer arithmetic. Unsafe code has some safety rules that do cut out certain classes of mistakes, but unsafe code will still let you get all sorts of things wrong. Unsafe code adds uncertainty to your system and removes some of the advantages of managed code.

In safe code, you work with references, not pointers. References are restricted pointers—references are pointers that you can't do pointer arithmetic with. References point to managed memory, and may change at any time, as the memory they refer to is relocated by garbage collection.

In unsafe code, you work with real pointers, and you can do pointer arithmetic like `*(ThisRecord++)` to advance a pointer and dereference the new value, much like in C. Pointers point to memory that won't be relocated, either because it is managed memory that has been *pinned down*, or because it is allocated from a pool that the memory manager won't relocate.

Tip The more you fear unsafe code, the better your code will be. Add unsafe code in very small pieces. Test each piece very thoroughly. Look for erratic behavior in code that worked before you started using the new unsafe code. Lazy coworkers may use the presence of unsafe code in the system to avoid debugging their own code, blaming any undesirable behavior on the unsafe code.

Unsafe Code

As a safety measure, C# makes you double-declare unsafe code. That is, you can only declare pointer variables or use pointer operators in unsafe code blocks, and only assemblies compiled with the /unsafe switch can have unsafe code blocks.

The /unsafe switch merely allows you to have unsafe code; it doesn't in itself make code unsafe. That is, even when you throw the /unsafe switch (either through an IDE dialog, or through the eponymous /unsafe command-line compiler switch), a normal class like class Foo {} is still a normal, *safe class*. You can't have pointer fields in a safe class, and by default all methods in a safe class are *safe methods*. Safe methods can't have pointer parameters or pointer results, and can only create pointer local variables or use pointer operators within an explicitly unsafe {} *unsafe block.*

In /unsafe mode, you can declare a whole class as an *unsafe class* by adding the unsafe modifier before the class keyword. A class like

```
unsafe class UnsafeClass
{
  private char* cp = null;
}
```

can have pointer fields, like the char pointer field, cp, and any UnsafeClass methods are *unsafe methods* that can have unsafe parameters or return unsafe results. The main block of an unsafe method is an unsafe block—an unsafe method can create pointer-local variables and use pointer operators, even outside of an explicit unsafe {} unsafe block.

You can also have unsafe structures—unsafe struct Foo {}—that can have unsafe fields and whose methods are all unsafe.

Safe classes and safe structs (safe objects) can have unsafe methods. An explicitly unsafe method has the unsafe modifier before the method's return type:

```
private unsafe void Foo() { }
```

The unsafe modifier makes its method an unsafe method, even in a safe object. You don't need to use the unsafe modifier in an unsafe object, because all methods in an unsafe object are unsafe methods—but it can never hurt to be explicit.

Similarly, if a bit repetitiously, all blocks in an unsafe method are *unsafe blocks* that can create local pointer variables and can use pointer operators. However, any block can be explicitly made unsafe, by using the unsafe modifier. For example, you can both execute a conditional statement in an unsafe block

```
unsafe { if (Test) {} }
```

and execute an unsafe statement within a conditional statement

```
if (Test) unsafe {}
```

Do note that you can only use unsafe blocks within a method's main block—you can have an unsafe method like unsafe void Foo() {}, but you can't have a safe method with an unsafe main block, like void Foo() unsafe {}.

Unsafe Operators

Within unsafe code, you can use the four pointer and address operators. The * and & operators are as complex as the -> and [] operators, and C pointer syntax cannot be enumerated in a single paragraph.

A * operator to the **right** of a value type, like int* or Rectangle*, is a pointer type—a pointer to an int and a pointer to a Rectangle. A * operator to the **left** of a pointer value, like *ThisInt or *(++ThisRectangle) is a pointer dereference. A pointer dereference in an expression is a read operation, and a pointer dereference to the left of an assignment operator is a write operation.

An & operator to the left of an address expression, as in &PinnedArray[0] or &PinnedArray[Count-1], returns the address of the variable. For example,

```
int* IntPtr1 = &ThisInt;
Rectangle* AsRectangle1 = &RectangleArray[3]; // the 4th Rectangle in the array
```

declares and initializes two pointers.

void* is an untyped pointer, like Delphi's pointer. You can't dereference a void* value until you cast it to a more specific type. That is, you can assign one void* value to another, or compare a void* value to null, but you can't treat it as an actual pointer to an address.

You can't have a pointer to a reference type. The star can't appear to the right of a reference type. (The first statement is a bit broader.) You can't have a Graphics* G, or a string* S, and you can't have an int[]* A.

Banning pointers to reference types keeps errors in unsafe code from cascading into safe code. Unsafe code can damage managed data structures, but only directly, within unsafe code. Unsafe code can't store up trouble for the garbage collector by not initializing a reference field, and thus 'creating' a new managed instance at some random location, nor can unsafe code damage safe code by actively setting a reference field to a bad value.

You can only have pointers to value types—structures like Point and Rectangle, and system primitives like float and char and bool. The ban on pointers to references extends to structure fields: you can only have a pointer to structures that have no reference fields. For example, given struct Safe { int X, Y; } and struct Unsafe { string A, B, C; } from the Appendix0\ StructPointer project, you can have a Safe* but **not** an Unsafe*.

■**2.0 Note** You can't have normal .NET arrays in structures that you will use in unsafe code because arrays are a reference type. (Array data is contiguous, but an actual array field is a pointer to an array object on the managed heap.) In C# 2.0, the fixed keyword lets an unsafe structure declare an array of primitive types within the structure. An unsafe struct ShortCString { public fixed char Buffer[257] } is a structure with a single 257-character field named Buffer, much like a native code Delphi's type ShortCString = record Buffer: array[0..256] of char; end. Structures with fixed fields can only be used in unsafe code.

You may not have pointers to methods, but you can have pointers to structs that have instance methods, like struct Method { public int Fn(int N) { return N; } }. Given a Method* M, you'd *dereference* M and call Fn as either (*M).Fn(1) or M->Fn(2)—I cover dereferencing with * and -> in the next few paragraphs.

The * operator to the left of a pointer value dereferences the pointer—it does a typed read or a typed write of the address the pointer contains. For example, if you have

```
int This = 10;
int That = 16;
int* IntPointer = &This;
```

`*IntPointer = That` has the same effect as saying `This = That`. If you set `IntPointer = &That`, then `*IntPointer = 47` has the same effect as saying `That = 47`.

Pointer arithmetic is by element size, not by bytes: `*(++Ptr)` steps `Ptr` and dereferences the next element, whether that is a single byte, or a multibyte number or character, or a multibyte struct. `*(FloatPtr+11) += 1` increments the twelfth `float` in an array (or, at least, the eleventh `float` ahead of the current `FloatPtr`).

▪**Caution** Pointer arithmetic is not range checked. It is fast, but it **is** unsafe. Errors in unsafe code can affect safe code in unpredictable ways.

There are two other ways of dereferencing pointers besides the `*` operator. When you have a pointer to a structure, you can access individual fields with the `->` operator. When you have a pointer to an array, you can use `[ ]` array notation to access table elements by index.

The `->` operator is the simpler of these two operators. C# operator precedence means that `*p.X` is read as `*(p.X)`. If `p` points to a struct, you need `(*p).X` to access the X field. The `->` operator is useful here: it dereferences structure members, and accessing a field like `p->X` and calling a method like `p->Set(10, 40)` is often clearer than `(*p).X` or `(*p).Set(10, 40)`.

The array operator is really equally simple, but it's tied in with larger issues of allocation and pinning. As in C, an array index expression to the right of a pointer is the same as dereferencing the pointer plus the array index expression: `FloatPtr[11] += 1` increments the twelfth array element, just like `*(FloatPtr+11) += 1` does. Similarly, `StructPtr[7].Count = 0` resets the eighth structure's `Count` property, as does `*(StructPtr + 7).Count = 0`.

Allocating Local Arrays

An unsafe block can use the `stackalloc` keyword to create a local array, on the stack. The syntax is a bit like creating a new array, except that a `stackalloc` array can't have an initializer. That is, you can say `int* buffer = stackalloc int[32]` or `char* characters = stackalloc char[Count]`, but you **cannot** say `int* table = stackalloc int[2] {1, 2}`. Also, you can only use `stackalloc` to allocate types that you can have pointers to: you cannot `stackalloc` a `struct S { string s; }` because it contains a string.

▪**Note** C# locals are block scoped, and the compiler may use the same stack space for two locals that are never in scope together—but allocated stack space is not freed until the method returns. Also note that a thread's stack has a maximum size, set when the `Thread` is created. The default stack size is ample for most needs—but a large `stackalloc` buffer should be a few kilobytes, not hundreds of kilobytes.

A local array is invisible to the garbage collector. Allocating a local array with stackalloc will never trigger a garbage collection, and a garbage collection will neither relocate a local array nor scan it for roots (since it can't contain any reference types).

For example, this pointless method from the Appendix0\UnsafeStack project

```csharp
public static unsafe int Answer()
{
  int* Stack = stackalloc int[32];
  int* Top = Stack;

  *(Top++) = 42;     // push
  return *(--Top);   // pop
}
```

creates a fixed-size buffer on the stack and uses C-style pointer math to do some cryptic operations that return 42. The Answer method can also be written using array notation as

```csharp
public static unsafe int OtherAnswer()
{
  int* Stack = stackalloc int[32];
  int Top = 0;

  Stack[Top++]  = 42;  // push
  return Stack[--Top]; // pop
}
```

Caution Using the array indexing operators with unsafe pointers is unchecked pointer arithmetic in exactly the same way as explicit code like *(ThisInt+1). In the preceding examples, Stack[33] or *(Stack-666) can do damage that may only show as mysterious behavior at some future time.

Pinning Managed Data

Before unsafe code can read or write managed data, you have to lock the managed data, or *pin* it down, so that the garbage collector won't move it while you're working with it.[1] The C# fixed statement pins data down within C# code. The fixed statement abstracts many different ways to pin data. This section of the appendix primarily covers pinning with the fixed statement; the Delphi chapter has manual pinning details.

A pointer you initialize in a fixed block will be pinned down until it goes out of scope at the end of the fixed block. A fixed block is like a using block in that it opens a resource and binds it to a variable, and implicitly generates a finally block that closes the resource when done.

---

1. Pinning is fairly cheap. If there is no GC before the instance is unpinned, you're simply setting and resetting a property. Fitting data around pinned data means extra work for a GC's relocation phase, but that control overhead is tiny next to the costs of shifting byte streams from one address to another.

A using statement's finally block calls Dispose; a fixed statement's finally block unpins the managed instance.

With one big exception, which I cover in the next paragraph, you can only fix pointers to system types like characters and numbers. Getting a fixed pointer to a field of a class instance pins the whole instance. For example, fixed (char* P = & Instance.Field) {} will pin the whole Instance and set P to the address of the Field character.

You can also pin the special reference types, strings and arrays. That is, an expression like fixed (char* Tail = & Source[Index]) {} pins the whole Source string and sets Tail, a C-style string pointer, so that it points to a null-terminated substring of Source. The simpler expression fixed (char* CString = ManagedString) {} locks ManagedString and sets CString to point to &ManagedString[0], the first Unicode character in ManagedString. Similarly, you can lock an array and get a pointer to an element—fixed (int* SecondRow = &Square[1, 0]) {}—or you can say fixed (int* SecondRow = Square) {} to pin the Square array, and get a pointer to the first element.

You can pin strings and do character-by-character examination without range checking, but you should never change a string value. String immutability goes beyond the fact that there are no public methods to change a string once it has been created: there are undocumented (and subject to change) bits in the header that control the way strings are compared and the like. Do not change a string with a pointer in an unsafe block—use unsafe code to populate a char array, and create a new managed string instance from this array. For example, here's a method from the Appendix0\LowerCase project:

```
public unsafe static string Lowercase(string S)
{
  fixed (char* Character = S)
  {
    char* Buffer = stackalloc char[S.Length + 1];
      // leave room for the null, now that you're programming in C!
    char* Output = Buffer;
    char* Input = Character;
    while (*Input != 0x00)
    {
      char ThisChar = *(Input++);
      *(Output++) = Char.ToLower(ThisChar);
    }
    *Output = (char) 0x00; // terminate the cstring

    return new string(Buffer); // unsafe, cstring to managed-string constructor
  }
}
```

Like the using block, you can declare many variables of the same type within a single fixed statement. To do mixed types, you need nested fixed statements.

Variables you declare in a fixed block are special in that you cannot change them. You can make copies of a fixed pointer, and ++ or -- a copy to your heart's content—but you can't change a fixed value, which will be unpinned at the end of the block. They are initialized readonly variables.

Other Ways to Pin

The fixed statement is definitely the simplest way to pin data in a C# program, but you may occasionally need to lock memory manually. Manual pinning takes a lot more code than automatic pinning with the fixed statement, because you have to explicitly write a finally block to manually unlock every instance that you manually lock.

Most of the manual pinning methods use the value type, IntPtr. On 32-bit platforms, an IntPtr is a struct that's both an int and a pointer: you can cast an IntPtr to an int and can cast an int to an IntPtr; you can cast an IntPtr to a pointer and can cast a pointer to an IntPtr. The IntPtr is actually defined to be the size of a native pointer: on 64-bit platforms, you can cast an IntPtr to a long, not to an int. The IntrPtr.Size property returns the actual runtime size, in bytes.

The GCHandle.Alloc static method pins down a reference type, and returns a new GCHandle. The AddrOfPinnedObject instance method returns an IntPtr that points to the first byte of the instance. When you work with GCHandle instances, you must be sure to unpin memory when you're done, by calling the GCHandle.Free instance method.

The Appendix0\UnsafeSaturation C# project is an example of using unsafe code to process a bitmap pixel by pixel. It uses LockBits to obtain an IntPtr to the first pixel; casts the IntPtr to a uint*; and then does pointer arithmetic to read each pixel from the source bitmap, process it, and then write the pixel to the result bitmap. Feel free to examine the code and/or modify it and use it in your own code (as with all the other sample code in the book) but do note that while I could undoubtedly "bum" a few cycles from the key Program.Copy method, the sample transform—applying a saturation formula to each pixel—runs about half the speed of the ImageAttributes/ColorMatrix version from Chapter 16!

Key Points

K&R (standard C) pointer operators, with new keywords and rules

- Think twice before using unsafe code. Then think again.

- You can only have unsafe code in unsafe blocks.

- You can only have unsafe blocks if you compile in a special /unsafe mode.

- * and &, -> and [ ] work much as in K&R C.

- You cannot have pointers to reference types, or to structures containing reference types.

- You can pin instances of reference types. Pinning tells the GC to not move the instance.

■ ■ ■

NUnit

With unit testing, you test an assembly's public members: the assembly's API. Unit testing allows you to both track down bugs in new code and be sure that later changes haven't brought back old bugs. NUnit is a unit-testing framework (based loosely on Kent Beck and Erich Gamma's JUnit) that provides a simple set of attributes and assertions that make it easy to write tests that create objects and manipulate their public members. If you've used DUnit, you'll find NUnit familiar.

Unit Testing

Unit testing checks that a unit's public interface (its API) behaves as it should. "Unit" is a carefully ambiguous term that means something like "part" and something like "piece," something like "component" and something like "module": a "unit" of code can be anything from a single static method to a whole compiled module. An individual unit test is a method that makes assertions about the behavior of some (or all) public members of the unit you're testing. An NUnit test suite is a library assembly that contains one or more such test methods, along with optional setup and teardown methods. You normally run this assembly from a GUI app, but an automated build process (or whatever) can also run unit tests from a console app.

Delphi Note In Delphi, a unit is a single source file, with optional include files. Compiled modules like executables and libraries are typically made up of many Delphi source units. The "unit" in unit testing doesn't have anything to do with Delphi source units!

Unit testing has two main points. First, you can test code as you write it, to be sure that your code works as expected—**before** you or your coworkers layer any code on top of it. Fixing a fresh bug is always easier than fixing an old bug, because you still understand the code and don't have to spend time figuring out what you meant to do. Also, writing a few tests as you write the code takes a lot less time than tracking down just which method call isn't doing quite what it should be doing.

Second, you never throw tests away. (If you change an API, don't discard any old tests that suddenly break—make them compile and run.) When you add a new feature or when you change the way you implement a method, you can instantly tell if new code has broken old code. The more tests you write, the faster you can make changes: a bigger test suite is more likely to catch a mistake than a small test suite. The more frequently you run tests, the more obvious it is which change caused the test to fail: when I'm making big changes, I may recompile after each incremental step, and run my unit tests every time I compile an assembly without any syntax errors.

You don't have to write test suites before you start to code, and a unit test does not have to be 100% comprehensive to be useful. *Test first* does make sense when you have an Architect designing an API down to the parameter list of each method of every class. Turning a specification into a set of tests lets you certify that the code monkeys did their job. But test first isn't very practical in the much more typical case where a team of programmers is bootstrapping a system, with APIs that evolve as the spec shifts and functionality is added.

Test all may seem to make more sense than test first—when a change passes thorough tests of every public member of every public class, you can be pretty confident that the change hasn't broken any working code. But a thorough test is a lot of work: every possible combination of default and nondefault parameters; all the edge values of each parameter; setting properties in every possible order; and so on. That is, in most cases, test all is just as undesirable as test first: it takes significant effort to thoroughly test every public member, and much of that effort is wasted. In fact, a 90-10 rule probably does apply, with roughly 90% of the benefit coming from maybe 10% of the possible tests.

Never forget that you can get real value from just an assertion or two about the behavior of some tricky code. When the code passes the tests—or when you have modified the tests so that they indeed test what you meant them to—you may be done with the code, or you may have some more bugs to track down. The key is that you never throw tests away. A bigger, more comprehensive test suite **is** more valuable than a small, narrowly focused test suite—but any tests are more valuable than no tests at all.

What to Test

Some things are easier to test than others. GUI events triggered by programmatic changes to GUI controls are a common cause of GUI errors, as are incorrect assumptions about the order that events are fired in. Unit testing can't really help much with either: unit tests are all code, without any user input. While it's easy to test your utility code, it's quite difficult to test your user interface.

The standard advice here is to maintain a separation between an "engine" and a "skin." The engine is a set of classes that does all your data manipulation, while the skin is a set of form classes that contain the event handlers that call engine methods (as well as any GUI state variables that you may need). Since the engine does not depend on user input, it **can** be tested via code-only unit tests. Additionally, since the GUI contains only high-level engine calls, it's comparatively easy to change your GUI when it turns out that users don't find it as intuitive as you do.

Obviously, this is good advice. Equally obviously, it's easier said than done, as the RAD tools that make it so easy to throw together a prototype also make it easy to simply pour all the logic into your event handlers. Less obviously, perhaps, while separating engine from skin does make it easier to modify the skin, it doesn't necessarily leave you with all that much in the way of an engine to test. Most of the complexity in the typical "departmental" application is not in the engine but in the skin: there needs to be multiple ways to do the same thing; *this* feature is only available in *that* state; and so on. You can test that the engine implements your "business rules" properly, but that was already the easiest part to get right.

So, while the engine/skin idea is a useful architectural pattern, you'll often find that unit testing isn't particularly helpful in an UI-intensive app. However, unit testing is invaluable when you're writing utility code, whether this is complex, app-specific engine modules or library code that will be used in multiple applications. Any code that does no UI, whose behavior is completely defined by its parameters and/or the environment, is a candidate for unit testing. Obviously enough, the more complex the code, the more you will benefit from testing it.

As earlier, you can start by testing only the hard parts, the parts that take your full attention. When you've verified that the key functionality works, testing edge conditions will often catch careless errors: does it work with, say, an empty file? How about a read-only or missing file? Does it work as well with zero or one elements as with many elements? And so on.

Using NUnit

Tip You can download NUnit from `http://www.nunit.org`. You need to use NUnit version 2.2.3 (or later) to test 2.0 assemblies. Version 2.2.6 works with the 2.0 run time "as is": with earlier versions, you may need to uncomment the `<startup>` section of the `nunit-gui.exe.config` file to force the test harness to use the 2.0 run time.

An NUnit test assembly is an assembly containing NUnit tests, which are individual methods of [`TestFixture`] classes. The NUnit test harness loads the test assembly in an app domain; uses Reflection to find the tests; and shows the test structure in a standard `TreeView` control (see Figure A1-1).

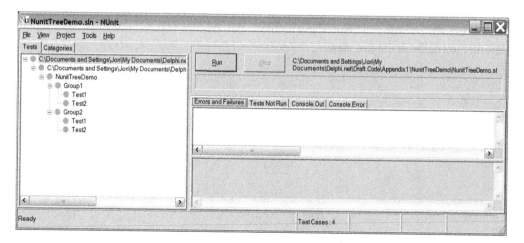

Figure A1-1. *The Appendix1\NunitTreeDemo project in the NUnit GUI*

The test harness can load an assembly directly, but it can also load either a Visual Studio project or solution file. When you load a project or solution file, the GUI tree view shows the project or solution file as the root node, with the assembly as its only child; when you load an assembly directly, the tree view shows the assembly as the root node.

Each test assembly can contain multiple namespaces, just like any other assembly. The tree view shows the assembly's namespaces as children of the assembly node. Each namespace can contain multiple *test fixtures*, which are classes that contain test methods along with optional setup and teardown methods. The tree view shows each namespace's test fixtures as children of the namespace node, and shows each test fixture's tests as leaf nodes under their test fixture's node.

By default, the tree view's root node will be selected, and clicking the Run button will run all tests. However, if you select a child node, clicking Run will only run the tests under that node. This can be useful in a large test suite, where running all tests might take a while.

A test fixture is simply a class with three key features: a [TestFixture] attribute; public visibility; and a public, parameterless constructor. If you omit any of these three key features, the test harness will simply skip the class and any test methods it may contain. (Remember, C# will automatically generate a public, parameterless constructor if you don't define any constructors. In most cases, all you have to do to write a test fixture is to define a public class with the [TestFixture] attribute.) Test fixtures can have any name; the NUnit GUI will show the class name in the tree view.

Test fixtures contain zero or more tests, which are methods with **four** key features: a [Test] attribute; public visibility; no parameters; and no result. That is, either

```
[Test] public void CSharpTest() {}
```

or

```
public [Test] procedure DelphiTest;
// With, of course, the method body defined in the implementation section!
```

As with test fixtures, omitting any of these key features is not an error: omitting the [Test] attribute or using the wrong visibility or the wrong signature means the test harness will skip over the test method, neither showing it in the GUI's tree view nor running it when you run its test fixture. Also as with test fixtures, test methods can have any name: the NUnit GUI will show the method name in the tree view.

A test method that returns normally is a successful test. A test that raises an exception (either on its own, or by failing an NUnit assertion) is an unsuccessful test.[1] The test harness traps any exceptions and reports them as failed tests, then proceeds to run any remaining tests. Selecting a failed test's node in the GUI's tree view will show the details of the test, including a stack trace that shows the test's location in the test source.

An NUnit assertion is simply a call to one of the static methods of the (NUnit.Framework) Assert class. As with the standard (System.Diagnostics) Debug.Assert method, you can simply assert that a given expression is true, and supply an optional message that's displayed only when the assertion fails. There are also a host of specialized methods, like AreEqual, AreSame, and IsNull (see the upcoming "Quick Reference" section) that are a bit clearer and easier to use than always having to write a boolean expression.

Do note that test methods are perfectly ordinary instance methods of their [TestFixture] classes. In particular, you can factor any common code into private methods that are neither displayed nor run as tests, and you can load test data into instance fields. You should **not** use the public, parameterless constructor to initialize any instance fields, as you have no control over when (or how often) the test harness will run your test fixture's constructor. Instead, you should use the [TestFixtureSetUp] and [TestFixtureTearDown] attributes to designate a public instance method (with no parameters and no results—i.e., just the same as a test method) as the test fixture's optional setup and teardown methods. Whether you run all the test fixture's tests or just a single test, the setup method (if defined) is run once per test run, before any of the test fixture's tests are run, while the teardown method (if defined) is run once per test run, after any of the test fixture's tests have run.

Tip An NUnit test assembly must be compiled with a reference to the nunit.framework DLL so that it can use the attributes and assertions in the NUnit.Framework namespace. While you **can** test nonpublic code by compiling your tests into your production assembly (and the test harness can load either library or executable assemblies), this does mean that you have to use conditional compilation to keep your production assembly from requiring the nunit.framework DLL to be installed (and at the same location as on your system) in order to run. Usually, you will keep your tests in a separate assembly from your deliverables, and will only test public members.

---

1. As a special case, you can use the ExpectedException attribute to specify that a particular test method should raise a specific exception. See Table A1-2 in the "Quick Reference" section.

Quick Reference

This section consists of three tables. Table A1-1 describes the class attributes that mark a class as a test fixture and that control test execution. Table A1-2 describes the method attributes that make a method into a test and control its behavior; there are also method attributes to declare setup and teardown methods. Table A1-3 describes the NUnit assertions that you use within a test method.

Table A1-1. *Class (Test Fixture) Attributes*

Attribute	Usage
TestFixture	Marks a public class as a test fixture. Any [Test] methods will be ignored, unless they are contained in a public class marked with the [TestFixture] attribute.
Ignore	The test fixture will be ignored, which means that none of the tests it contains will be run. This is useful when you **know** that some lengthy tests are currently failing—the fixture will still be compiled, and you will be reminded of the skipped tests at run time.
Explicit	Like [Ignore], except that you can run the test fixture by explicitly selecting it.

Table A1-2. *Method Attributes*

Attribute	Usage
Test	Marks a public method that takes no parameters and returns no result as a test method.
ExpectedException	Specifies that the test method must raise a particular exception to succeed: the test fails if it returns normally or if it raises any other exception. Takes a Type parameter, like [ExpectedException(typeof(ArgumentException))].
TestFixtureSetup	Marks a public method that takes no parameters and returns no result as a setup method that is run (once per test run) before any of the fixture's tests are run.
TestFixtureTeardown	Marks a public method that takes no parameters and returns no result as a teardown method that is run (once per test run) after any of the fixture's tests have run.
Ignore	The test will be ignored, which means that it will be specially flagged, but not run.
Explicit	Like [Ignore], except that you can run the test by explicitly selecting it.

Table A1-3. *NUnit Assertions*

Assertion	Usage
AreEqual	Tests that the second value equals (using **value** equality—Object.Equals) the first, target, value. Overloaded for strings, objects, and various types of numeric values.
AreSame	Tests that the second value equals (using **reference** equality—Object.ReferenceEquals) the first, target, value. Both values are objects.
IsTrue/IsFalse	Close analogs to Debug.Assert—asserts that the first parameter is true (or false).
IsNull/IsNotNull	More distant analogs to Debug.Assert—asserts that the first parameter is null (or non-null).
Ignore	Somewhat like the [Ignore] attribute, in that the test is shown as ignored (yellow) instead of successful (green) or failed (red). However, Assert.Ignore only takes effect when executed. That is, you can use this to conditionally ignore a test—perhaps because the setup method couldn't load a data file, or because some other test has already failed.

All NUnit assertions have overloads that allow you to specify a message string as the optional last parameter— as with standard assertions, the message is only displayed if the test fails.

APPENDIX 2

■ ■ ■

Assembly Loading and Signing

The first thing that happens when you run a .NET executable is that a bit of native stub code initializes the CLR, which loads all the assemblies your application refers to, and all the assemblies that they refer to, and so on. Only after the CLR has located all the assemblies that it needs will it JIT and run your `Main` method (Chapter 1).

Assembly loading is a complicated process that has been designed to allow multiple versions of the same assembly to coexist on a single machine. An assembly's full name consists of four parts:

1. The *short name*, which is the filename without path or extension. For example, `mscorlib` or `system`.

2. A culture. Code assemblies are usually *culture neutral*—typically, only *satellite assemblies* (which contain localized forms and strings) are culture specific.

3. A `Version`, which consists of four integers—major, minor, build, and revision. If you use a *strongly named* assembly (discussed later in this appendix), your code will usually run with the same version of the assembly that you compiled it with, eliminating any version mismatch issues. (The application's configuration file can *redirect* the loader to use an alternate version.) If the assembly is **not** strongly named, the loader will ignore the version information.

4. When an assembly is strongly named, its full name includes a *public key token*, a 64-bit hash of the public portion of the key used to sign the assembly.

The *Fusion* subsystem uses four parts of the assembly name so that it can always load the right version of an assembly. The Fusion loader looks for assemblies in a definite order:

1. If an assembly refers to a strongly named assembly, the reference will include the public key token and the assembly version. Fusion will first look for a strongly named assembly in the Global Assembly Cache (GAC), which is a special directory on every system that has the .NET run time installed.[1]

2. Fusion will then check the application's configuration file (Appendix 3) for redirection information. Strongly named assemblies can be redirected to another version, or to a local folder, or to a URL. An assembly that is **not** strongly named can be redirected to a directory under the *application directory*, which is the directory that contains the executable assembly.

3. Fusion next looks for the assembly in the *application directory*, which is the directory that contains the application executable.

4. Failing that, Fusion will look for a subdirectory of the application directory that matches the assembly's short name. For example, it will look for `MyLibrary.dll` in the `MyLibrary` directory under the application directory.

If Fusion can't find the assemblies it needs in any of these places, it will throw an exception.

■**Note** Fusion does **not** use the PATH environment variable to find assemblies.

Strong Naming

There are basically three reasons why you might want to give an assembly a strong name. First, only strongly named assemblies can be placed in the GAC. While in most cases it does make sense to keep assemblies private, component vendors might want to install their component assemblies to the GAC simply so that every project that uses one of their components isn't forced to make a copy of the component assemblies.

Second, as earlier, the Fusion loader will only pay attention to the assembly version when the assembly has a strong name. By default, Fusion will load the exact version of a strongly named assembly that you compiled against: newer or older versions will not be used, unless you use an `assemblyBinding` element in the `runtime` section of the application's configuration file. (I outline the structure of the XML configuration file in Appendix 3.)

■**Note** As a special case, when the run-time version that you built your application with is not installed on the target machine, the CLR will use the latest version of the run time that is installed. For example, apps built with VS.2002 (.NET 1.0) will run on a machine that only has 2.0 installed, as will apps built with VS.2003 or Delphi 2006 (.NET 1.1). You can override this default with `supportedRuntime` elements in the `startup` section of the configuration file.

---

1. On Windows machines, the GAC is the `Assembly` subdirectory of the directory named by the `windir` environment variable—i.e., it's usually either `C:\Windows\Assembly` or `C:\WinNT\Assembly`.

The third reason to strong name an assembly is that it provides a measure of tamper protection. A strongly named assembly's manifest contains a cryptographic hash of the assembly's contents. This hash is recomputed at load time, and the assembly will not load if the two hashes do not match. While it is not **impossible** to change the assembly's contents without changing the hash, it is rather extremely unlikely: you can be reasonably confident that a strongly named assembly hasn't been changed since it was signed by the publisher.

Most libraries are distributed as part of an application, and live in the application directory. Versioning isn't a big deal, if each version of the application has its own directory and hence its own set of private libraries. The only reason to sign such private libraries is tamper protection, which may or may not seem important to you.

If you do need to strong name your assemblies, you have two basic options. Both involve a key file that you produce with the `sn.exe` utility that comes with the .NET SDK. The simplest option is to use the `AssemblyKeyFile` attribute to specify a key file at compile time. This guarantees that every build is strongly signed, but it does require that every development machine can read the key file. Alternatively, you can use the assembly linker, `al.exe`, to sign an existing library assembly. This option is more secure, as the key file only needs to be on the build machine—it can even be kept on removable storage, like a USB key, which is kept in a locked safe until it's necessary to sign assemblies before distribution.

APPENDIX 3

■ ■ ■

Configuration Files

An application configuration file is an XML file in the application directory, with the same name as the application, with `.config` appended. For example, the configuration file for `MyApp.exe` would be `MyApp.exe.config`. The file should have a standard `<?xml version="1.0" encoding="utf-8" ?>` XML header and a `configuration` root element.

Tip In Visual Studio, using the Add New Item dialog to add an "Application configuration file" adds an `App.config` source file with a minimal XML structure. When you compile your application, this file is copied to the output directory and named appropriately.

The configuration file is entirely optional—all .NET applications will run just fine without a configuration file. You only need a configuration file to override various defaults or to specify optional application settings. For example, the `startup` section can specify which run-time version(s) your application supports, and the `runtime` section can specify version policy for signed assemblies (see the SDK documentation for details).

Similarly, the optional `appSettings` section can contain named strings that you can retrieve at run time. You can use this to provide 'hidden' configuration that most users will never touch, like logging options for system administrators or web service URLs. In 1.*x*, you can retrieve `appSettings` strings via `ConfigurationSettings.AppSettings`; in 2.0, this is obsolete, and you should use `ConfigurationManager.AppSettings`. Both return a `NameValueCollection`, a class that acts like an array of strings, indexed by strings.

For example, a configuration file like

```xml
<?xml version="1.0" encoding="utf-8" ?>
<configuration>
  <appSettings>
    <add key="Foo" value="Bar"/>
  </appSettings>
</configuration>
```

defines an appSettings string named Foo. In C# 1.*x*, you could read this as

```csharp
string FooSetting = ConfigurationSettings.AppSettings["Foo"]; // read app settings
if (FooSetting == null) // no "Foo" key?
  FooSetting = "Default"; // then use default value
```

In C# 2.0, you could read this as

```csharp
string FooSetting = ConfigurationManager.AppSettings["Foo"] // read app settings
  ?? "Default"; // Default value, if no "Foo" key
```

■ ■ ■

Glossary

&c

An alternate form of *etc.*, which is an abbreviation for the Latin phrase *et cetera,* or "and so on." & was originally a *ligature* for *et.*

application domain

A process-like boundary, within a process. Application domains share a process, its threads, the CLR machinery, and any *domain-neutral* assemblies, but they do not share jitted code, types, or values from *domain-bound* assemblies. All communication between app domains involves *remoting*. App domains can be unloaded, taking their domain-bound assemblies with them (see Chapter 14).

assembly

A standard PE (Portable Executable) file—a DLL or an EXE—that contains *CIL* and *metadata*. An assembly can actually consist of multiple modules, linked by a manifest that contains the metadata, but **most** assemblies are a single file.

CIL

Common Intermediate Language. The high-level, object-oriented assembler that is output by compilers for high-level language (like C# and Delphi); that is stored in .NET *assemblies*; and that is *JIT* compiled at run time (see Chapter 4).

class method

In Delphi, a method whose Self parameter is the class of the type (or instance) used to call the method. (Note that .NET static methods do not get an 'invisible' Self parameter—be sure to use *static methods,* not class methods, in code that may be called from other languages.)

CLR

Common Language Runtime. The .NET run-time code, written mostly in C++, that handles *garbage collection, JIT compilation,* and the *CTS.*

CLS

Common Language Specification. A subset of the *CTS* that all *first-class languages* can understand.

Code Insight

Borland's umbrella term for tool tips about identifiers, parameter descriptions, code completion, &c. Much like Microsoft's *IntelliSense*.

CTS

Common Type System; the .NET object model. Because the CTS is part of the *CLR*, all *assemblies* can share data structures, even when they're written in different languages.

domain bound

Domain-bound code is tied to an AppDomain in the normal way, and is unloaded with the AppDomain. In stand-alone .NET executables, every assembly except mscorlib is domain bound; in ASP.NET, *strong-named* assemblies are loaded *domain neutral*, not domain bound.

domain neutral

Domain-neutral code is loaded as part of the process. It is not tied to the AppDomain that loads it, and cannot be unloaded. In stand-alone .NET executables, only mscorlib is loaded domain neutral; in ASP.NET, all *strong-named* assemblies are loaded domain neutral.

early bound

Matching method names to object code at compile time—compare with *late bound*.

element

In XML (and HTML), a <tag> that may contain attributes, like <tag this="that">. An element is either a normal element, which is part of a <tag></tag> pair and can enclose text or child elements, or an *empty element* like <tag/>.

empty element

An XML element that contains no text or child elements, and that has no stop tag—a single <tag/>, as opposed to a <tag></tag> pair.

first-class language

A language that can create and extend class types and that can understand all *CLS* constructs.

garbage collection

Automatic heap management. User is not responsible for manually freeing memory: the system does this automatically (see Chapter 3).

hyperthreading

Modern processors use pipelining to try to keep the processor busy: they may be reading the operands for one instruction, while adding two numbers for the previous instruction. Because the processor must act as if it is only executing one instruction at a time, in the order that the instructions are encountered, the pipeline usually has spare capacity. Hyperthreading allows a single processor to act like multiple virtual processors, executing instructions from multiple threads at the same time. This makes better use of the processor resources—but from a programmer's point of view, the key fact is that hyperthreading means that a single chip really can execute more than one instruction at a time.

iff

If and only if.

infix

Standard algebraic notation, where you say A + B. See *postfix* and *prefix*.

instance

On .NET, a member of a class instance: a regular member, as opposed to a *static member*. An *instance method* is a 'regular,' early-bound method, as opposed to a *virtual method* or a *static method*.

IntelliSense

Microsoft's umbrella term for tool tips about identifiers, parameter descriptions, code completion, &c. Much like Borland's *Code Insight*.

JIT

Just In Time compilation. Your source code is compiled to *CIL*, which is compiled to native object code on a procedure-by-procedure basis before the code is first run (see Chapter 4).

late bound

Finding out what code to run at run time, by table lookup. Often used to describe *virtual* method dispatch—compare with *early bound*. On .NET, usually reserved for information obtained by *Reflection*.

ligature

In traditional typesetting, a special character that combines two or more characters into one, reducing the intercharacter spacing, or perhaps slightly changing the characters' shapes. Common ligatures include *ff*, *ffi*, and &.

managed code

Type-safe code with automatic memory management. (Managed code may include unsafe code, but always subject to permissions and various rules that minimize the possible damage.) See Chapter 1.

metadata

Comprehensive information about every member of every type. Like Delphi's RTTI, except that it's not restricted to published members.

MSIL

Microsoft Intermediate Language. An old name for *CIL* that still crops up in older web pages and at some points in the Microsoft documentation.

postfix

An algebraic notation where you say AB+ instead of A+B. Very easy for a computer to interpret, and eliminates any need for parentheses to change the order of execution.

Power Law

A common relationship where a few elements account for most of the activity.

prefix

An algebraic notation where you say +AB instead of A+B. Method calls like Foo.Method(A, B, C) are also examples of prefix notation. Like *postfix*, prefix never needs parentheses to change the order of execution, the way that *infix* does.

Queue Law

A basic principle of serialization—deserialize in the same order that you serialized. FIFO, not LIFO.

race condition

Any situation where the result depends upon the relative timing of two or more events. Any code that (unintentionally) gives different results on a multiprocessor machine than on a single-processor machine has race conditions. A race condition is always a bug.

Reflection

Reading and manipulating *metadata* at run time to discover and access resources (see Chapter 13).

remoting

.NET remoting is a general-purpose technology that can be used for communication between computers (RPC, or remote procedure calls); for communication between processes (IPC, or interprocess communication); and for communication between application domains within a process (see Chapter 14).

safe code

Code that always follows type-safety rules—no unchecked casts, and no pointer arithmetic. Most .NET code is safe code.

static

On .NET, a member of a class, not of an instance. You do not need to create an instance to access static members. Static members have the same access options as instance members. That is, a static member might be `public` and visible to all code in the application; it might be `private` and visible only to methods of its class; or anywhere in between.

static field

A global variable, created when the class containing it is first referenced.

static method

A method that does not get an 'invisible' `this`/`Self` parameter the way that a 'normal,' instance method does. (Note that .NET static methods differ from Delphi *class methods* in that they don't get a `Self` reference parameter.)

static property

A property of the class as a whole—a property with static `get`/`set` methods.

strong name

A cryptographic signature attached to an assembly (see Appendix 2).

unsafe code

Code that can break type-safety rules, doing unchecked casts and indulging in pointer arithmetic. Most unsafe code is used to interface with unmanaged legacy code.

verification

Checking code to be sure it doesn't break any type-safety rules.

virtual

Virtual methods are *polymorphic*: the actual method to call is determined by table lookup, at run time. On .NET, *virtual methods* are contrasted with *instance methods* and *static methods*.

XML doc

The special `///` comments that allow you to write structured comments about types and methods. In C#, the `/doc` compiler switch allows you to generate an XML file that you can distribute with your class libraries, so that your XML doc is available to users as pop-up tips on every identifier. The `/doc` compiler switch also checks both that your XML doc is well formed and that you have documented every public member of every public class. Delphi can also generate an XML file that drives tool tips, but doesn't automatically build templates for you (the way Visual Studio does), nor does it syntax check your XML doc comments.

■ ■ ■

Bibliography

Advanced .NET Remoting, Second Edition

Rammer and Szpuszta. Apress, 2005. ISBN: 1-59059-417-7.
More depth and detail than Chapter 14, though it does contain an awful lot of printed source.

Applied .NET Framework Programming

Richter. Microsoft Press, 2002. ISBN: 0-7356-1422-9.
Poorly named but well-written: an excellent introduction to the CLR. However, between Part 1 and your Delphi background, you may find there's not much new in it.

CIL Programming

Under the Hood of .NET

Bock. Apress, 2002. ISBN: 1-59059-041-4.
Not the most essential book, but it does have more detail than Chapters 4 or 13, and includes a great (1.x) opcode quick-ref on the inside front cover and facing page.

Compilers

Principles, Techniques, and Tools

Aho, Sethi, and Ullman. Addison Wesley, 1986. ISBN: 0-201-10088-6.
Commonly known as the Dragon Book. *Among other things, a good source of insight into how regular expressions are evaluated.*

Design Patterns

Elements of Reusable Object-Oriented Software

Gamma, Helm, Johnson, Vlissides. Addison Wesley, 1995. ISBN: 0-201-63361-2.
One of those books that's absolutely indispensable less because of the content than because of the way it's referred to so religiously by so many people. It starts with the hard-to-contest assertion that a common vocabulary makes it possible to talk about designs in an unambiguous way, then proceeds to a pompous and poorly written catalog of patterns that mixes truly common patterns with quite esoteric patterns. (The inside cover and facing page contain a quick reference to their named patterns, which can be very useful when someone starts talking about the Foo pattern.)

Essential .NET, Volume 1

The Common Language Runtime

Box and Sells. Addison Wesley, 2003. ISBN: 0-201-73411-7.
Covers much of the same ground as Applied .NET Framework Programming—*even though* Essential .NET *includes different details, few people will find that they really need both. What I've read is very fast moving—this is a book to be studied, not browsed—but I can't really vouch for the overall quality, as I got my copy relatively late in the game and so have only read selected topics, on an as-needed basis. It does seem fair to say, though, that they mean "essential" in the sense of "fundamental," not "necessary"—an awful lot of the material seems more "nice to know" than "need to know."*

Mastering Regular Expressions, Second Edition

Friedl. O'Reilly, 2002. ISBN: 0-596-00289-0.
The standard guide to using and writing regular expressions.

Rare Earth

Why Complex Life Is Uncommon in the Universe

Ward and Brownlee. Springer, 2000. ISBN: 0-387-98701-0.
Not a programming book—just one of the most interesting books I've read in years. Multicellular life required such a series of fortunate coincidences that algae may be common while technological species are rare.

Programming Perl, Third Edition

Wall, Christiansen, and Orwant. O'Reilly, 2000. ISBN: 0-596-00027-8.
The "Camel Book"—at least in the second edition, which is the edition that I have—is a charming, if dense, introduction to a language that's very different from C# or Delphi. It also includes more material on regular expressions than Chapter 11 does. If you don't already know Perl, get a copy of Programming Perl *and learn it; you can download the ActiveState compiler for free, and getting a different perspective on common problems will make you a better programmer.*

Refactoring

Improving the Design of Existing Code

Fowler et al. Addison Wesley, 1999. ISBN: 0-201-48567-2.
A somewhat mixed book: The first part is a great introduction to refactoring and unit tests, but then it (like Design Patterns*) tails off into a rather bloated and useless catalog of refactorings.*

The C# Programming Language

Hejlsberg, Wiltamuth, and Golde. Addison Wesley, 2003. ISBN: 0-321-15491-6.
The print version of the online reference (which doesn't come with 2.0, anyway). I find it easier to stick multiple bookmarks in the book and flip back and forth than to do the same thing with the HTML pages. There **are** *modest differences between C# 2.0 syntax as shipped and as described in this book ...*

The Red Ape

Orangutans and Human Origins

Schwartz. Westview Press, 2005. ISBN: 0-8133-4064-0.
Also not a programming book—but a serious paleontologist's argument that orangutans are actually our closest evolutionary cousins, not chimpanzees. The morphology says yes; the molecules seem to say no. Schwartz makes a good case for the molecules being wrong.

XML in a Nutshell, Third Edition

Harold and Means. O'Reilly, 2004. ISBN: 0-596-00764-7.
A great, succinct introduction to XML for anyone who still thinks of XML as just an over-hyped text file format. Also has decent coverage of technologies like XSLT.

Index

Find it faster at http://superindex.apress.com

Find it faster at http://superindex.apress.com

You Need the Companion eBook

Your purchase of this book entitles you to buy the companion PDF-version eBook for only $10. Take the weightless companion with you anywhere.

We believe this Apress title will prove so indispensable that you'll want to carry it with you everywhere, which is why we are offering the companion eBook (in PDF format) for $10 to customers who purchase this book now. Convenient and fully searchable, the PDF version of any content-rich, page-heavy Apress book makes a valuable addition to your programming library. You can easily find and copy code—or perform examples by quickly toggling between instructions and the application. Even simultaneously tackling a donut, diet soda, and complex code becomes simplified with hands-free eBooks!

Once you purchase your book, getting the $10 companion eBook is simple:

❶ Visit **www.apress.com/promo/tendollars/**.

❷ Complete a basic registration form to receive a randomly generated question about this title.

❸ Answer the question correctly in 60 seconds, and you will receive a promotional code to redeem for the $10.00 eBook.

2560 Ninth Street • Suite 219 • Berkeley, CA 94710

eBookshop

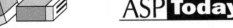

THE EXPERT'S VOICE™

Printed in the United States
By Bookmasters